VENN DIAGRAMS FOR CATEGORICAL STATEMENTS

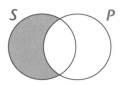

All *S* are *P*

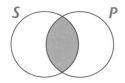

No *S* are *P*

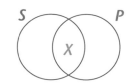

Some *S* are *P*

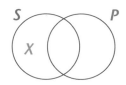

Some *S* are not *P*

TRUTH TABLES FOR LOGICAL OPERATORS

Conjunction	Negation	Disjunction	Conditional	Biconditional
P · Q	~ P	P v Q	P ⊃ Q	P ≡ Q
T *(T)* T	*(F)* T	T *(T)* T	T *(T)* T	T *(T)* T
T *(F)* F	*(T)* F	T *(T)* F	T *(F)* F	T *(F)* F
F *(F)* T		F *(T)* T	F *(T)* T	F *(F)* T
F *(F)* F		F *(F)* F	F *(T)* F	F *(T)* F

VALID INFERENCE FORMS

MODUS PONENS

p ⊃ *q*

p

q

MODUS TOLLENS

p ⊃ *q*

~ *q*

~ *p*

INVALID INFERENCE FORMS —FORMAL FALLACIES

Fallacy of Affirming the Consequent

p ⊃ *q*

q

p

Fallacy of Denying the Antecedent

p ⊃ *q*

~ *p*

~ *q*

pw = KF 92PL3X

Praise for LOGIC by Stan Baronett

"I would describe this book as the most student-friendly and instructor-friendly logic text that I have found."

Stewart Clem, Oklahoma State University

"I really liked Baronett's approach to logic. It seems very 'modern' and 'hip' yet instructive. This is a book that I think my students would really relate to with regard to tone, style and level of instruction."

Emily Kulbacki, Pierce College

"It has some of the best writing of any introductory logic book I have encountered."

Bernard Jackson, Washington and Lee University

"A long-awaited fresh approach to teaching Logic."

Courtney Hammond, Cuyamaca College

"I think that this book is pedagogically excellent. Baronett's examples are much more likely to engage the interest of the student than are examples in most elementary logic texts. He also has numerous touches of humor in the exercises, and this will keep both student and teacher engaged."

Val Dusek, University of New Hampshire

"This book is a good read for a logic text. It offers an exceptional focus on the relationship of logic and truth and sustains a similar focus throughout the chapters. Organization definitely serves this central story, which is engagingly told with clear narration and the aid of very helpful diagrams. Amid myriad introductory logic books, this one actually looks to do the subject a new and fresh turn."

Ron Jackson, Clayton State University

"The text is user-friendly. It is very methodical and addresses a major difficulty students have in introductory logic courses, namely, their difficulty in building upon what they have previously learned in the course."

David O'Connor, Seton Hall University

"Baronett's clear prose and careful examples recommend this text. Students should be able to extract a lot of meaning from the text and instructors should be able to facilitate their learning without losing time in class on remedial issues."

Gerald Mozur, Lewis & Clark Community College

"Baronett's Logic covers traditional subject matter in an uncluttered, innovative, way.... his approach will be successful because he addresses the difficulties students tend to have learning this subject—in the order in which they experience them."

Jayne Tristan, University of North Carolina at Charlotte

ANNOTATED INSTRUCTOR'S EDITION

LOGIC

○— STAN BARONETT —○

University of Nevada, Las Vegas

PEARSON

Prentice
Hall

Upper Saddle River, New Jersey 07458

President: Yolanda de Rooy
Editor-in-Chief: Sarah Touborg
Senior Editor: Dave Repetto
Editorial Assistant: Carla Worner
Editorial Assistant: Christina DeCesare
Director of Marketing: Brandy Dawson
Marketing Manager: Sasha Anderson-Smith
Director of Development: Rochelle Diogenes
Developmental Editor: Deena Cloud
Senior Managing Editor: Mary Rottino
Production Editor: GEX Publishing Services
Production Liaison: Joe Scordato
Media Project Manager: Brian Hyland
Senior Operations Supervisor: Brian Mackey

Operations Specialist: Cathleen Petersen
Senior Art Director: John Christiana
Interior and Cover Design: Kathy Mrozek
Cover Illustration/Photo: Getty Images/Tim Flash
Illustrator (Interior): GEX Publishing Services
Director, Image Resource Center: Melinda Patelli
Manager, Rights and Permissions: Zina Arabia
Manager, Visual Research: Beth Brenzel
Manager, Cover Visual Research & Permissions: Karen Sanatar
Image Permission Coordinator: Richard Rodrigues
Composition/Full-Service Management: GEX Publishing Services
Printer/Binder: The Courier Companies
Cover Printer: Phoenix Color Corp.

Credits and acknowledgments borrowed from other sources, with permission, in this textbook appear on page xiv.

Pearson Education LTD.
Pearson Education Singapore, Pte. Ltd
Pearson Education, Canada, Ltd
Pearson Education—Japan

Pearson Education Australia PTY, Limited
Pearson Education North Asia Ltd
Pearson Educacion de Mexico, S.A. de C.V.
Pearson Education Malaysia, Pte. Ltd

10 9 8 7 6 5 4 3 2 1

Student:
ISBN-13: 978-0-13-193312-5 (paper)
ISBN-10: 0-13-193312-4 (paper)
ISBN-13: 978-0-13-602636-5 (case)
ISBN-10: 0-13-602636-2 (case)

Annotated Instructor's Edition:
ISBN-13: 978-0-13-615249-1
ISBN-10: 0-13-615249-X

For Carly,
our parents,
and Shane

{ Brief Contents }

1   LOGIC AND TRUTH   2

2   INFERENCES: ASSESSMENT, RECOGNITION, AND RECONSTRUCTION   42

3   CATEGORICAL STATEMENTS AND INFERENCES   84

4   TRUTH-FUNCTIONAL STATEMENTS   112

5   TRUTH TABLES AND PROOFS   152

6   NATURAL DEDUCTION   194

7   THE LOGIC OF QUANTIFIERS   248

8   LOGIC AND LANGUAGE   276

9   APPLIED INDUCTIVE ANALYSIS   320

APPENDIX 1   Mapping Premises and Conclusions   374

APPENDIX 2   The Square of Opposition and Standard-Form Categorical Syllogisms   381

ANSWERS TO SELECTED EXERCISES   201

GLOSSARY   456

INDEX   465

{ Contents }

PREFACE   xvi

1 LOGIC AND TRUTH   2

1.1 Truth Content and Logical Component   4

1.2 Logic and Relationships   4
Exercise Set 1.2   8

1.3 Truth Content Errors, Logical Component Errors, and the Analysis of Inferences   11
Exercise Set 1.3   17

1.4 Reasoning, Judgment, and Deductive Analysis   20
BIOGRAPHY: The Women Who Programmed ENIAC   23
Equivocation   23
Exercise Set 1.4   24

1.5 Deductive and Inductive Inferences   28
Deductive Inferences   29
Inductive Inferences   30

1.6 Uncertainty and Inductive Analysis   31
BIOGRAPHY: Blaise Pascal   32
Exercise Set 1.6   37

Summary 39 • Key Terms 40 • Logic Challenge: The Problem of the Hats   40

2 INFERENCES: ASSESSMENT, RECOGNITION, AND RECONSTRUCTION   42

2.1 The Role of New Evidence   43
Exercise Set 2.1   46

2.2 Inference Analysis and Evaluation   47
Exercise Set 2.2   51

2.3 Logical Structure   55
More on Equivocation and Stipulations   60
Logical Loop   61
Logical Possibilities   62
Adding New Premises   67
Exercise Set 2.3   67

2.4 Expanding Skills   70
Recognizing and Reconstructing Inferences   71
BIOGRAPHY: Augusta Ada Byron   72
Exercise Set 2.4A   73
Explanations   76
Exercise Set 2.4B   77
Missing Information   78
Exercise Set 2.4C   81

Summary 82 • Key Terms 82 • Logic Challenge: A Classic Problem   83

3 CATEGORICAL STATEMENTS AND INFERENCES   84

3.1 Categorical Statements   85
BIOGRAPHY: Aristotle   86
Translating Ordinary Sentences into Categorical Statements   87
BIOGRAPHY: John Venn   88
Diagramming Categorical Statements: Venn Diagrams   89
Exercise Set 3.1   94

3.2 Categorical Syllogisms   97
Exercise Set 3.2   106

Summary 110 • Key Terms 110 • Logic Challenge: A Group Problem   111

4 TRUTH-FUNCTIONAL STATEMENTS 112

4.1 Logical Operators 113
Conjunction 114
Negation 115
Disjunction 116
Exercise Set 4.1A 118
Translations and Common Terms 119
Exercise Set 4.1B 120
BIOGRAPHY: The Stoics 122

4.2 Conditional Statements 122
Understanding and Diagramming
  Conditional Statements 123
BIOGRAPHY: Leonhard Euler 123
"If" and "Only if" 126
Exercise Set 4.2 127

4.3 Rules for Symbolic Notation 130
Well-Formed Formulas 130
Exercise Set 4.3A 131
The Main Logical Operator 132
Exercise Set 4.3B 133
Translations and the Main Operator 134
Exercise Set 4.3C 135

4.4 Truth Tables for Complex Truth-Functional Statements 136

4.5 Contingent and Noncontingent Statements 138
Tautology 138
Self-Contradiction 139
Exercise Set 4.5A 140
Material Equivalence 141
Exercise Set 4.5B 142

4.6 Logical Equivalence 144
Exercise Set 4.6 146

4.7 Contradictory, Consistent, and Inconsistent Statements 147
Exercise Set 4.7 149

Summary 150 • Key Terms 150 • Logic Challenge:
A Tricky Problem 151

5 TRUTH TABLES AND PROOFS 152

5.1 Truth Tables and Inferences 153
BIOGRAPHY: Charles S. Peirce 156
A Note on Technical Validity 156
Exercise Set 5.1A 156
Conditional Inferences 159
Analyzing Complex Inferences 163
Exercise Set 5.1B 164

5.2 Indirect Truth Tables 168
Thinking through a Proof 168
An Indirect Truth Table 170
Exercise Set 5.2 177

5.3 Sufficient and Necessary Conditions 182
Sufficient Conditions 182
Necessary Conditions 185
Analyzing Conditional Inferences 188
Exercise Set 5.3 191

Summary 192 • Key Terms 192 • Logic Challenge:
A Guilty Problem 193

6 NATURAL DEDUCTION 194

6.1 Proving Validity Using Natural Deduction 195
BIOGRAPHY: Gerhard Gentzen 196

6.2 Rules of Inference—Part One 197
1. Addition (Add) 197
2. Conjunction (Conj) 198
3. Modus Ponens (MP) 199
4. Modus Tollens (MT) 201

6.3 Justification—Applying the Rules of Inference 202
Exercise Set 6.3 202

6.4 Rules of Inference—Part Two 205
5. Disjunctive Syllogism (DS) 206
6. Hypothetical Syllogism (HS) 206
7. Constructive Dilemma (CD) 207
8. Simplification (Simp) 208
Exercise Set 6.4 210

6.5 Tactics and Strategy Using the Rules of Inference 212
Using Natural Deduction 212
Working through Proofs 212
Exercise Set 6.5 214

6.6 Substitution Sets—Group One 215
9. Association (Assoc) 216
10. Double Negation (DN) 217
11. Commutation (Comm) 218
12. De Morgan (DeM) 219
   BIOGRAPHY: Augustus De Morgan 221
13. Distribution (Dist) 221
Exercise Set 6.6 223

6.7 Substitution Sets—Group Two 224
14. Transposition (Trans) 224
15. Material Implication (MI) 225
16. Exportation (Exp) 226
17. Material Equivalence (ME) 227
18. Tautology (Taut) 228
Expanding the Proof Procedure 229
Exercise Set 6.7 231

6.8 Conditional Proof (CP) 236
Exercise Set 6.8 240

6.9 Indirect Proof (IP)—*Reductio ad Absurdum* 242
Exercise Set 6.9 244

Summary 246 • Key Terms 246 • Logic Challenge: A Standing Problem 247

7 THE LOGIC OF QUANTIFIERS 248

7.1 Prelude to the Logic of Quantifiers 249
   BIOGRAPHY: George Boole 251
Exercise Set 7.1 253

7.2 Integrating Categorical and Truth-Functional Statements 254
   BIOGRAPHY: Gottlob Frege 256
Exercise Set 7.2 257

7.3 Quantification 257

7.4 Statement Functions and Categorical Statements 259

Normal-form Formulas 261
Bound and Free Variables 261
Complex Statements 262
Exercise Set 7.4 262

7.5 Quantification and Proofs of Validity 264
Universal Instantiation 264
Universal Generalization 264
Existential Instantiation 265
Existential Generalization 265
Conditional Proof and Indirect Proof Using Quantifiers 266
Exercise Set 7.5 267

7.6 Quantification and Proofs of Invalidity 270
Exercise Set 7.6 273

Summary 274 • Key Terms 275 • Logic Challenge: An Arrangement Problem 275

8 LOGIC AND LANGUAGE 276

8.1 Definitions 277
Lexical Definitions 278
Stipulative Definitions 278
Precising Definitions 279
Operational Definitions 279
Functional and Ostensive Definitions 280
Exercise Set 8.1 281

8.2 Informal Fallacies 283
Fallacies of Ambiguity 283
Exercise Set 8.2A 289
Fallacies of Unwarranted Assumption 291
Exercise Set 8.2B 298
Fallacies of Relevance 300
Exercise Set 8.2C 305

8.3 Rhetorical Language 308
Rhetorical Questions 308
Rhetorical Conditionals 309
Rhetorical Disjunctions 311
Exercise Set 8.3 314
   BIOGRAPHY: Arthur Schopenhauer 315

Summary 316 • Key Terms 318 • Logic Challenge: A Clever Problem 319

9 APPLIED INDUCTIVE ANALYSIS 320

9.1 Analogical Reasoning 321
Structure of Analogical Inferences 322
Exercise Set 9.1A 325
Analyzing Analogical Inferences 327
Exercise Set 9.1B 329
Strategies of Evaluation 331
   BIOGRAPHY: David Hume 333
Exercise Set 9.1C 336

9.2 Statistical Reasoning and Probability Theory 338
Analyzing Statistical Inferences 338
Samples and Populations 341
Exercise Set 9.2A 342
A Priori Theory of Probability 345
Relative Frequency Theory of
   Probability 346
Subjectivist Theory of Probability 347
Probability Calculus 348
Exercise Set 9.2B 352
True Odds in Games of Chance 353
Bayesian Theory 354
Exercise Set 9.2C 356

9.3 Scientific and Causal Reasoning 356
Theoretical and Experimental Science 356
Cause-Effect Analysis 357
Hypotheses, Experiments, and
   Predictions 360
Exercise Set 9.3 363

9.4 A Medical Mystery 365
Exercise Set 9.4 368

Summary 369 • Key Terms 371 • Logic Challenge:
A Perplexing Paradox 372

APPENDIX 1 Mapping Premises and Conclusions 374

Exercise Set A1 377

Summary 380 • Key Terms 380

APPENDIX 2 The Square of Opposition and Standard-Form Categorical Syllogisms 381

A2.1 Categorical Statements 382
Exercise Set A2.1 383

A2.2 Quantity, Quality, and Distribution 383
Exercise Set A2.2 386

A2.3 The Aristotelian Square of Opposition 386
Exercise Set A2.3 391

A2.4 Immediate Inferences—Conversion, Obversion, and Contraposition 394
Conversion 394
Obversion 396
Contraposition 397
Exercise Set A2.4 399

A2.5 The Problem of Existential Import and Its Consequences 402

A2.6 The Boolean Square of Opposition 404

A2.7 Conversion, Obversion, and Contraposition Revisited 407
Exercise Set A2.7 409

A2.8 Standard-Form Categorical Syllogisms 411
   BIOGRAPHY: Christine Ladd-Franklin 412

A2.9 Diagramming Categorical Syllogisms 413
Exercise Set A2.9 417

A2.10 Mood and Figure in Categorical Syllogisms 420
Exercise Set A2.10 422

A2.11 Rules and Fallacies Associated with Standard-Form Categorical Syllogisms 423

Rule 1: A negative premise cannot have an affirmative conclusion.   423

Rule 2: A negative conclusion cannot have all affirmative premises.   424

Rule 3: An inference cannot have two negative premises.   425

Rule 4: Two universal premises cannot have a particular conclusion.   425

Rule 5: Any term that is distributed in the conclusion must be distributed in the premises.   426

Rule 6: The middle term must be distributed in at least one premise.   427

Exercise Set A2.11   428

Summary 432 • Key Terms 434

ANSWERS TO SELECTED EXERCISES   435

GLOSSARY   456

INDEX   465

{ Quick References }

1.1 • Summary of Deductive and Inductive Inferences 35

2.1 • The Four Possible Combinations of Truth Values for an Inference with One Premise and a Conclusion 63

2.2 • The Eight Possible Combinations of Truth Values for an Inference with Two Premises and a Conclusion 64

2.3 • Conclusion Indicators 72

2.4 • Premise Indicators 73

3.1 • The Four Categorical Statements 87

3.2 • Translating Ordinary Sentences into Categorical Statements 89

3.3 • Venn Diagrams Are Used to Illustrate the Four Kinds of Categorical Statements 93

4.1 • Logical Operators and Their Symbols 114

4.2 • Rules and Truth Tables for Logical Operators 117

4.3 • Translation of Logical Operator Symbols 119

4.4 • Summary of the Rules of Grammar (Syntax) for Logic Symbols 131

4.5 • Truth Tables for Conditionals and Biconditionals (Material Equivalence) 141

5.1 • The General Logical Structure of *Modus Ponens* 159

5.2 • The General Logical Structure of the Fallacy of Affirming the Consequent 161

5.3 • The General Logical Structure of *Modus Tollens* 162

5.4 • The General Logical Structure of the Fallacy of Denying the Antecedent 163

5.5 • Truth and Falsity of Conjunctions, Disjunctions, Negation, and Conditional Statements 176

6.1 • Rules of Inference 1–8 209

6.2 • Strategies and Tactics for Using Natural Deduction 213

6.3 • The 10 Substitution Sets 229

7.1 • Boolean Translations of the Four Categorical Statements 250

7.2 • Use of Symbols in Singular Statements 256

7.3 • Quantifier Substitution Sets *(QSS)* 261

7.4 • Summary of the Rules of Inference for Quantifiers 266

7.5 • The Three-Step Method for Proving the Invalidity of an Inference Using Quantifiers 271

8.1 • Types of Definitions 281

8.2 • Fallacies of Ambiguity 289

8.3 • Fallacies of Unwarranted Assumption 297

8.4 • Fallacies of Relevance 304

8.5 • Fallacies of False Dichotomy 313

9.1 • Criteria for Analyzing Analogical Inferences 328

9.2 • Strategies for Evaluation of Analogical Inferences 335

9.3 • The Five Criteria for Analyzing Causality 358

9.4 • Requirements for a Fair Test of a Causal Hypothesis 360

A2.1 • Quantity, Quality, and Distribution Applied to *A*, *E*, *I*, and *O* 385

A2.2 • Structure of Standard-Form Categorical Syllogisms 411

A2.3 • Rules and Associated Fallacies for Categorical Syllogisms 428

Credits

Dear Reader,

When some people hear the word "logic" they immediately think of a completely abstract subject with no connection to the real world. To logic instructors this is surprising, since they know that logical thinking is used every day. If a lamp goes out most people, without hesitation, quickly replace the bulb. When you drive through an intersection under a green light, you infer that the stopped cross traffic is seeing a red light. If you watch a mystery program you actively use the clues to figure out who did it. These simple everyday situations involve the use of basic logical principles and skills, without which we would not know what to do in even the simplest situations.

The challenge of any introduction to logic textbook is to bring logic down to earth, to reveal its connection to immediate problems of life, to reinforce and improve the basic skills of reasoning we all rely on in daily life. The goal of this book is to show you that learning logic can be challenging, but not threatening; instructive, but not intimidating; educational, yet entertaining; humorous, yet relevant. It is my hope that this text helps you to understand the fundamentals of logic and to sharpen the logical thinking you already employ everyday.

Stan Baronett

Life Takes Logic

Logic offers students a comprehensive yet accessible introduction to the fundamentals of logical thinking. In addition to clear and detailed coverage of logic theory, author Stan Baronett emphasizes real-world applications of the principles of logic. Because of this dual focus—on how to think logically as well as how to apply logic in everyday situations—*Logic* shows students how life takes logic.

1.1 TRUTH CONTENT AND LOGICAL COMPONENT

Our initial concern in the study of logic is with two important ways in which we evaluate the information we receive in our conscious interaction with the world. First is the **truth content**—*Is the information true or false?* Second is the **logical component**—*If the information is true, then what follows?* For example, if someone enters a room and appears to be soaking wet, we might conclude that it is raining outside. This very natural and nearly instantaneous thought is actually the result of two processes. The first is the evaluation of the visual information—the person "appears to be wet." The second process, although complex, happens so quickly that it can escape notice. Its complexity lies in the remarkable process of extending a piece of information beyond its boundaries. From "a wet person" we conclude that "it is raining." From one piece of information we have developed, or *inferred*, a consequence. The complexity is realized only when we become aware of the process. We are then confronted with the further process of *evaluating* and *justifying* our inference. If we remark to someone that it is raining outside, we might be asked to explain why we think so. Only then do we become conscious of the need to analyze and justify our conclusion. Pointing to the wet person might help to justify our conclusion, but further analysis raises the possibility that we were wrong, that it is not

Author Stan Baronett employs a ***clear and accessible writing style*** in which he addresses the reader as if in a one-on-one discussion. Throughout the text, Baronett anticipates, asks, and answers the questions that typically arise during discussion of each topic—leading readers to a deeper understanding of the material.

LOGIC

STAN BARONETT

BARONETT

LOGIC

An Innovative Visual Presentation

Logic explains the principles of logic through an innovative visual presentation. Diagrams and illustrations throughout the text help students visualize concepts. The text's engaging visual design helps student comprehension and sparks interest in the material—helping bring logic to life for today's students.

Truth-Functional Statements

overview

4.1 LOGICAL OPERATORS
4.2 CONDITIONAL STATEMENTS
4.3 RULES FOR SYMBOLIC NOTATION
4.4 TRUTH TABLES FOR COMPLEX TRUTH-FUNCTIONAL STATEMENTS

4.5 CONTINGENT AND NONCONTINGENT STATEMENTS
4.6 LOGICAL EQUIVALENCE
4.7 CONTRADICTORY, CONSISTENT, AND INCONSISTENT STATEMENTS

In Chapter 3 we saw that in categorical statement structures, the variables are replaced by class terms, which cannot, by themselves, be true or false. In this chapter we will learn about another important kind of statement structure, called truth-functional statements, in which variables are replaced by statements, which are either true or false. Understanding the logical commitments of truth-functional statements facilitates the uniform and consistent determination of complex inferences as either valid or invalid. As we have seen, the logical structure of statements and inferences is what determines validity and invalidity. Therefore, the ability to translate ordinary language into symbols aids in the construction of a system of analysis of the logical structure of inferences.

4.1 LOGICAL OPERATORS

The statement, "Green apples are sour *and* unripe bananas cause belly-aches," is an example of a complex **truth-functional statement**. It consists of two distinct simple statements, (1) "Green apples are sour," (2) "unripe bananas cause bellyaches." Each of the simple statements has a **truth value**, either true or false. The word "and" is called a **logical operator**, or *logical connective*. Logical operators have no truth value (they are neither true nor false). They only reveal the logical commitments of each type of statement.

chapter 4

Engaging chapter openers draw students into each chapter and demonstrate how logic is used in everyday life.

A Clear Framework

Logic offers students a clear framework for learning the fundamentals of logic. Each chapter features a number of learning tools designed to help students master the material, as well as resources that enable students to review as they read.

Each chapter of the text features *Exercise Sets* that are directly relevant to the material at hand, providing students with opportunities to apply the skills they've learned.

EXERCISE SET 4.1A

Exercises 1–10 Choose the correct answer.

1. If the statement structure "X · Y" is true, which of the following would you know to be correct?

    (a) X must be true.
    (b) X must be false.
    (c) X could be true or false.

    Answer: (a) X must be true. The only way for a conjunction to be true is if all the conjuncts are true.

2. If the statement structure "X · Y" is false, which of the following would you know to be correct?

    (a) X must be true.
    (b) X must be false.
    (c) X could be true or

Translations and Common Terms

When we translate sentences from English into the symbolic notation of truth-functional operators we must try our best to capture the logical intent. Quick Reference 4.3 contains a list of common terms that may occur in English sentences and, for the most part, can be translated by using one of the logical operators discussed so far.

Quick References provide summaries of topics, concepts, and processes in a reader-friendly format.

Quick Reference 4.3 • Translation of Logical Operator Symbols

Symbol	Logical Function	Meaning
·	Conjunction	*and, but, while, however, also, moreover, although, yet, whereas*
~	Negation	*not, it is not the case that, it is false that, it is not true that*
∨	Disjunction	*or, either ... or, unless, otherwise*

Conjunction, negation, and disjunction symbols can be used for translating many common English sentences into symbolic notation.

Main Logical Operator

P Q || ~ (P · Q) ∨ Q
1. T T	(F) T (T) T (T) T
2. T F	(T) T (F) F (T) F
3. F T	(T) F (F) T (T) T
4. F F	(T) F (F) F (T) F

The text's *Truth Tables* include complete step-by-step explanations and visual cues that enable students to analyze and create their own truth tables.

BIOGRAPHY   THE WOMEN WHO PROGRAMMED ENIAC

The first electronic digital computer was named ENIAC (Electronic Numerical Integrator and Computer). It was developed during World War II in order to quickly compute and compile a set of "firing tables" that could be used to calculate the speed and trajectory of field artillery. Six women, Frances Bilas, Betty Jean Jennings, Ruth Lictermann, Kathleen McNulty, Elizabeth Snyder, and Marlyn Wescoff, were hired to do the programming of the computer. Their task was to get the computer to mathematically model all possible ballistics trajectories, which required solving complex differential equations. The team had to create their own programming manuals because none existed.

It soon became apparent that the programming could not be done without physically reconfiguring the huge computer in order to match the program with the machine. Using today's language, they had to create software and hardware at the same time. This meant that they had to work with the engineering specifications and diagrams of the machinery in order to design the first programs. They had to physically arrange the computer's complex set of wires, circuits, cable connections, and vacuum tubes to coordinate the physical sequencing with the differential equation sequencing. This intricate programming combined a complete knowledge of the physical state of the computer with sophisticated knowledge of *logical thinking*. In fact, as Betty Jennings remarked, it was "a physicalization of *if-then* statements."

Mathematicians, quickly sought out help solve long-sta complex it would ta out a computer.

The text features *biographies* of important logicians that shed light on the people whose work informs the text.

Strategy boxes offer students tips on how to approach challenging material.

Strategy

Analyzing inferences from the bottom up is a useful strategy for avoiding logical loops. This approach involves making the conclusion false and then trying to get all the premises true at the same time.

The text's *end of chapter material* includes a bulleted summary of the major concepts discussed in the chapter, as well as *Logic Challenges* that encourage students to apply what they've learned to more complex problems.

---

82 ○ CHAPTER 2 • Inferences: Assessment, Recognition, and Reconstruction

SUMMARY

- In determining the logical structure of an inference, the first step is to substitute symbols for the terms used in the inference. The next step is to determine whether the inference is valid or invalid, which can be done by creating a logical picture that visually displays the logical relationship. Because only the logical component of the inference is under consideration, the truth content of the statements is irrelevant.
- Inferences can be analyzed from the bottom up, which involves making the conclusion false and then trying to make all the premises true.
- Validity guarantees that no matter what is substituted for the symbols in the logical structure of an inference, there will never be a substitution instance with true premises and a false conclusion.
- Two skills are fundamental to the reasoning process: (1) You must be able to analyze inferences by understanding the logical commitments in the individual statements that make up the inference, as well as the inference as a complete network. (2) You must be able to evaluate inferences by assessing the strengths and weaknesses of inference through both logical and truth content analysis.
- Because in real life inferences are rarely found in neat packages, you must be able to recognize and correctly identify inferences, even incomplete ones. Complementing the skill of inference recognition is the ability to reconstruct inferences by displaying the correct relationship between the premises and conclusion.
- When necessary, you must be able to reconstruct an inference by providing any missing premises and/or conclusion. An inference with missing premises or conclusion is called an enthymeme. Inferences can be reconstructed deductively or inductively. One way to decide this is to complete the evaluation by analyzing the truth content. The reconstructed inference that gives the benefit of the doubt to the person presenting the inference is the preferred one; this is called the principle of charity.
- New information (premises) can seriously affect the strength of inductive inferences because these inferences have built-in uncertainty. Additional premises ... from weak to strong, or vice versa. Since deduc... ... cannot change

---

LOGIC CHALLENGE: A CLASSIC PROBLEM

To begin this problem we must do some groundwork. For games of chance, we will define a "winning strategy" as one where employing the strategy ensures that you will win the game more than 50 percent of the time. A "losing strategy" is one where the strategy ensures that you will lose the game more than 50 percent of the time. Not all games allow for winning or losing strategies. For example, if we repeatedly toss a coin and you have to guess whether it will come up heads or tails, there is no winning or losing strategy (provided we stipulate that it is a "fair" game). However, suppose a game requires you to guess the color of a marble that is to be picked from a jar. You are told that there are ten marbles in the jar—six red marbles and four blue ones (again stipulating a "fair" game). In this case, there would be a winning strategy (pick red *every* time) and a losing strategy (pick blue *every* time).

Now we can begin our problem. You are picked from an audience and are given the chance to win a prize (the prize of your dreams). You are shown three doors and are told that behind one of the doors is the prize, while behind the other two doors is nothing. You can choose any of the three doors. (We stipulate that this is a fair game and the prize is always randomly assigned to one of the doors before you make your choice.) If all the doors were opened the prize is one in three, or 1/3; and the chances of the probability of your winning the prize, is 2/3. If you were allowed to play this game an infinite your not winning the prize, is 2/3. If you were allowed to play this game an infinite number of times, your odds of winning would never change. No matter what strategy you employ (for example, picking the same door each time), you can never raise the probability of your winning nor increase your probability of losing.

But our game is not going to be so simple. Instead of opening all the doors immediately after you make your choice, the game show host, who knows where the prize is located, puts a little twist in the game. The host says, "Before we open your door, let's see what's behind one of the doors that you did *not* pick." (The door is opened and nothing is behind it.) The host continues, "I am feeling generous today. I'm willing to let you change your mind. You can give up the door you originally picked and switch to the remaining door, or you can stick with your original pick. As soon as you make your final decision the game is over, and we will open both doors. Make your final choice."

If you were allowed to play this game over and over, what should you do? There are three possible answers for you to consider:

... doors; this is a winning strategy as defined above.
... ...a winning strategy as

Resources for the Student and Instructor

Save Time. Improve Results.

MyLogicLab is an easy-to-use online learning management system that allows instructors to assess student progress and adapt course material to meet the specific needs of the class. Based on the results of an online self-assessment test, all students are provided with a customized study plan, including a variety of tools to help them fully master the material. *MyLogicLab* reports the self-assessment results to the instructor, as individual student grades as well as an aggregate report of class progress. Based on these reports, the instructor can adapt course material to suit the needs of individual students or the class as a whole. For more information, visit www.mylogiclab.com and click *Prentice Hall*.

For students: © 2008, access code, 978-0-13-235723-4

An *Annotated Instructor's Edition* of the text includes the majority of answers to the problems in the student version of the text, as well as cross-references to detailed explanations included in the Instructor's Manual.

© 2008, paper, 600 pages, 978-0-13-615249-1

An *Instructor's Manual* written by the author includes explanations for every exercise set and a complete Test Item File.

© 2008, paper, 200 pages, 978-0-13-193696-6

8. deductive analysis: valid
inductive analysis: strong

9. deductive analysis:
invalid/unsound
inductive analysis: weak/
not cogent

10. deductive analysis:
invalid/unsound
inductive analysis: weak/
not cogent

11. deductive analysis:
invalid/unsound

8. Every fire needs oxygen.
   There is no oxygen in that room.
   There is no fire in that room.

9. Carly tossed a coin ten times and in each case it came up heads.
   I have a feeling that it is a trick coin.
   The next toss will be heads.

10. Carly tossed a coin ten times and in each case it came up heads.
    The law of averages says that this cannot go on indefinitely.
    The next toss will be tails.

*11. No element with an atomic weight less than 46 is a metal.
    Z is an element with an atomic weight of 79.

Additional Resources

- Test Gen
  © 2008, online supplement
- PowerPoint® Set
  © 2008, online supplement
- WebCT—MyLogicLab
  © 2008, online supplement
- Blackboard—MyLogicLab
  © 2008, online supplement

Your Course, Your Way

Logic is available in several formats, allowing you to select the option that best suits your course. Choose a paperback or casebound edition of the text, or opt for online delivery with the CourseSmart eBook edition. For even more flexibility, you can create a Pearson Custom Publishing edition of *Logic*, including your own course notes and original content. Pearson custom editions are available in either value-priced black and white or groundbreaking full color. Visit **www.pearsoncustom.com** to begin building your ideal text.

Suggestions for customizing this textbook for different courses:

Introduction to Logic	Critical Thinking
Chapter 1	Chapter 1
Chapter 2	Chapter 2
Chapter 3 (or Appendix 2)	Chapter 3
Chapter 4	Chapter 4
Chapter 5	Chapter 5
Chapter 6	Chapter 8
Chapter 7 (Optional)	Chapter 9
Chapter 8 (Optional)	Appendix 1 (Optional)
Chapter 9 (Optional)	

Developing *Logic*

Logic is the result of an extensive development process involving the contributions of numerous instructors and students. Every round of reviews produced fantastic suggestions and new ideas. The remarkable dedication and concern of the reviewers and accuracy checkers showed how truly interested they were in helping create a logic textbook that works in the classroom. Many thanks to the following reviewers and class testers:

Reviewers

Robert Arp, *Florida State University*
Robert Barnard, *University of Mississippi*
Michael Beaty, *Baylor University*
Peter Bezanson, *Mesa Community College*
Kevin J. Browne, *University of Louisville*
John Casey, *Northern Illinois University*
Stewart Clem, *Oklahoma State University*
Darian De Bolt, *University of Central Oklahoma*
Valentine Dusek, *University of New Hampshire*
S.L. Dwyer, *Georgia State University*
William Ferraiolo, *San Joaquin Delta College*
Janet Grouchy, *Louisiana State University A&M*
Courtney Hammond, *Cuyamaca College*
Liam Harte, *Westfield State College*
Willis D. Heusser, *Cypress College*
Bernard Jackson, *Washington and Lee University*
Ronald L. Jackson, *Clayton State University*
Sandra Johanson, *Green River Community College*
Mark Johnson, *Pierce College*
Emily Kulbacki, *Pierce College*
Lory Lemke, *University of Minnesota—Morris*
Armen T. Marsoobian, *Southern Connecticut State University*
Gerald Mozur, *Lewis and Clark Community College*
Wm. Gregory Murrell, *Central New Mexico Community College*
Paul Newberry, *California State University—Bakersfield*
David O'Connor, *Seton Hall University*
Alex Orenstein, *University of New York Graduate Center*

Rohit Parikh, *City University of New York Graduate Center*
Laurence F. Peck, *Georgia Perimeter College*
Timothy Quandt, *Fullerton College*
Robert Redmond, *Virginia Commonwealth University*
Gregory Rich, *Fayetteville State University*
Michael Russo, *George Washington University*
Robert Shanab, *University of Nevada—Las Vegas*
Kenneth Stern, *University at Albany*
John Stopple, *Mesa Community College*
Mark Thomas, *Blinn College*
Jayne Tristan, *University of North Carolina—Charlotte*
Patricia Turrisi, *University of North Carolina—Wilmington*
Mia Wood, *Pierce College*
Yiwei Zheng, *St. Cloud State University*

Class Testers

Willis D. Heusser, *Cypress College*
Emily Kulbacki, *Pierce College*
Mia Long, *Pierce College*
Gerald Mozur, *Lewis and Clark Community College*
Gregory Rich, *Fayetteville State University*
Michael Russo, *George Washington University*
Jayne Tristan, *University of North Carolina—Charlotte*
Patricia Turrisi, *University of North Carolina—Wilmington*

Acknowledgments

There are many people to thank at Pearson Prentice Hall. Ross Miller saw the need for a new kind of logic textbook and enthusiastically brought this project on board. The torch was passed to Mical Moser who successfully assumed Ross' duties. Carla Worner has been involved with the manuscript since the beginning. Carla coordinated the many rounds of reviews and kept the ever-expanding list of reviewers and me on track over the entire length of the creation of this textbook. Sarah Touborg's astute decisions helped all stages of development and kept everyone focused on the final goal. Rochelle Diogenes had the daunting task of guiding development. Kathy Mrozek created the playful cover design and the interesting chapter opener images. Sasha Anderson-Smith devised a wonderful marketing campaign—one that captured the best intentions of this textbook. Joe Scordato's unlimited patience and ability kept everyone on track during the production process. Deena Cloud, my developmental editor, worked with me on every sentence in the textbook. Deena's questions, comments, and discussions forced me to rethink and rewrite material, always searching for clarity.

Special Thanks

Many teachers, colleagues, and friends' voices echo through these pages. Among the most influential were Alberto Coffa, Noretta Koertge, Jerzy Kolodziej, Joia Lewis Turner, Husain Sarkar, and John Winnie. Robert Shanab was kind enough to read most of the manuscript. In fact, the section on Rhetorical Language was motivated, and evolved, through a series of discussions with Professor Shanab. My sixteen years of teaching logic courses for the Philosophy department at the University of Nevada, Las Vegas allowed me the opportunity to develop many of the ideas in this book. Ron Wilburn, Ian Dove, and Paul Schollmeier contributed by providing stimulating discussions of many topics in the teaching of logic. The combined experience and knowledge of these people regarding logic and critical thinking helped to clarify many of the techniques developed in this book.

{ About the Author }

I was born on the South Side of Pittsburgh, Pennsylvania, and grew up in the shadows of steel mills. Early on, I was introduced to the ideas of chance and uncertainty through games, way before I understood anything about the nature of probabilities. When I was old enough to gamble, horse racing and poker allowed me to try out betting systems that were meant to reduce uncertainty. It's fair to say I'm still trying. That kind of experience was in sharp contrast to what I encountered in high school, where my teachers in math and geometry showed me how certainty could be reached through reason alone. In college, I discovered that logic was a subject that explored fundamental questions of both certainty and uncertainty. For over twenty-five years, I have tried to impart my fascination with these issues to the students in my logic courses. Along the way, some of my friends pointed out that my winding up in Las Vegas nearly twenty years ago was, to their minds, a near certainty.

LOGIC

Logic and Truth

{ overview }

1.1 TRUTH CONTENT AND LOGICAL COMPONENT

1.2 LOGIC AND RELATIONSHIPS

1.3 TRUTH CONTENT ERRORS, LOGICAL COMPONENT ERRORS, AND THE ANALYSIS OF INFERENCES

1.4 REASONING, JUDGMENT, AND DEDUCTIVE ANALYSIS

1.5 DEDUCTIVE AND INDUCTIVE INFERENCES

1.6 UNCERTAINTY AND INDUCTIVE ANALYSIS

We live in the Information Age. Cable television stations provide local and world news 24 hours a day. The Internet provides access to millions of books, articles, and thousands of newspapers from around the world. Personal Web sites, Web logs (blogs), and chat rooms contain instant commentary about events around the world. We often find that, along with information, various claims are presented. For example, suppose we read the following:

> Some film studios and independent movie directors are releasing their films on DVD rather than placing them in theaters. Soon you will be able to view first-run movie releases in your home for a fraction of the cost of going to a theater, buying, or renting a movie. In fact, ticket sales for U.S. theaters have been steadily declining for the past ten years. Therefore, we can expect movie theaters to become obsolete.

This passage contains an **inference**. An inference, or argument, is a network of **statements** (sentences that are either true or false). The first three sentences of the passage are **premises**; they contain information that is intended to provide good reasons to believe the **conclusion**, the claim that movie theaters will become obsolete. In this passage there are two things to consider: Is the information that is given true? If the information is true, does it offer good reasons to accept the conclusion? These questions offer a glimpse of the role of logic, which is the study of reasoning. Logical analysis reveals the extent of the correctness of the reasoning found in inferences. Logic

chapter 1

Inference: A set of statements whereby the premises are offered as support for a conclusion.

Statement: A sentence that is either true or false.

Premise: A statement (or set of statements) offered as support for a conclusion.

Conclusion: The end point of an inference; the statement that is meant to follow from premises.

Truth content: The actual truth or falsity of a statement and the methods of its determination.

Logical component: The logical relationship between premises and a conclusion.

provides the skills needed to identify other peoples' inferences, putting you in a position to offer coherent and precise analysis of those inferences. Learning logical skills enables you to subject your own inferences to that same analysis, thereby anticipating challenges and criticisms. This book introduces the tools of logical analysis and presents practical applications of logic.

1.1 TRUTH CONTENT AND LOGICAL COMPONENT

Our initial concern in the study of logic is with two important ways in which we evaluate the information we receive in our conscious interaction with the world. First is the **truth content**—*Is the information true or false?* Second is the **logical component**—*If the information is true, then what follows?* For example, if someone enters a room and appears to be soaking wet, we might conclude that it is raining outside. This very natural and nearly instantaneous thought is actually the result of two processes. The first is the evaluation of the visual information—the person "appears to be wet." The second process, although complex, happens so quickly that it can escape notice. Its complexity lies in the remarkable process of extending a piece of information beyond its boundaries. From "a wet person" we conclude that "it is raining." From one piece of information we have developed, or *inferred*, a consequence. The complexity is realized only when we become aware of the process. We are then confronted with the further process of *evaluating* and *justifying* our inference. If we remark to someone that it is raining outside, we might be asked to explain why we think so. Only then do we become conscious of the need to analyze and justify our conclusion. Pointing to the wet person might help to justify our conclusion, but further analysis raises the possibility that we were wrong, that it is not raining. There are certainly other reasons for people being wet—they could have been hit by water balloons, they could have splashed water on themselves because they were hot, they could have run through lawn sprinklers, or the wetness could be from excessive sweating, etc. In fact, as explanations for the wetness begin to pile up, the less confident we may become that it is really raining. This example illustrates that we must consider our interaction with the world in two different ways: (1) Is the information we have received accurate, correct, or true? (2) If it is true, then what can we infer from it; what conclusions follow?

1.2 LOGIC AND RELATIONSHIPS

Evaluating the truth content and logical component of an inference is a complex process, so it is quite easy to make mistakes. There are two potential sources of error—*incorrect truth content* and *incorrect logical component*. Although not likely, it is nevertheless possible that in our previous example we could have been wrong about the person actually being wet (remember, we said that the person "appeared" to be wet). If so, this would be an instance of incorrect truth content. On the other hand, our inference might be faulty, it might not be raining. If so, this would be an instance of incorrect logical component. (It is also possible that we were wrong in both ways—incorrect truth content *and* incorrect logical component.) The first source of error, incorrect truth content, is the most familiar. Much of our formal education is devoted to the truth content of information. However, the second source of error, incorrect logical component, is more difficult to recognize because it is about the *relationship* between statements, and not the statements themselves. To fully understand this it is necessary to look at examples that will clarify the distinctions we are making. Suppose you were given these two pieces of information:

1. Vincent van Gogh was born sometime in the 1800s.
2. Marie Curie was born sometime in the 1800s.

First, we can investigate the truth of the statements. Notice that the truth or falsity of each statement is independent of the other—that is, they may both be true, they may both be false, or one may be true and the other false. We could easily find evidence concerning the truth or falsity of each statement (consulting an encyclopedia, a history of science book, searching the Internet, etc.). The result of this line of analysis would be our knowledge of the truth content; we would have determined the actual truth or falsity of each statement. However, prior to investigating the truth content we might consider the two statements as potential premises. Our focus then would be on what could be inferred from the pair—*What follows from them if they are true?* This line of analysis takes us into the area of logical component, which focuses on the relationship between the pair of statements above, and a new statement, a conclusion, which we could derive from the pair. The following is one possible conclusion:

3. Vincent van Gogh was born before Marie Curie.

Our attention is now focused on different questions, such as, "*What if* the first two statements are true?" "How is the truth or falsity of the first two statements related to the truth or falsity of the third statement?" "Do the first two statements support the third statement?" "Do the first two statements provide good reasons for accepting the third statement?" These considerations are radically different from our concerns with the truth content of the first two statements. Since we are now concentrating on the relationship between the three statements, our analysis has a completely different form. An analogy might help you to grasp this point. When we talk about the relationship between two people, we might consider whether it is "good," "strong," "supportive," "shaky," "very weak," etc. This is similar to what we are now doing. If we display the statements in a different way, we can see this more clearly.

Example 1.1

{R}
  1. Vincent van Gogh was born sometime in the 1800s.
  2. Marie Curie was born sometime in the 1800s.
  3. Vincent van Gogh was born before Marie Curie.

This way of displaying the information reveals that the first two statements are meant to be premises while the statement under the line is the conclusion of an inference. We want to analyze the **logical relationship** {R} between the premises and the conclusion. Specifically, we want to see whether the premises, *if both are true*, guarantee anything about the conclusion. If we accept the information in the first premise as true, then we would be informed that Vincent van Gogh was born

Logical relationship: The logical connection between premises and conclusions.

somewhere between the years 1800 and 1899. If we accept the information in the second premise as true, then we would be informed that Marie Curie was also born somewhere between the years1800 and 1899. At this point, it is important to separate the truth content of the conclusion from the logical consideration of whether or not it follows from the premises, which is a relationship question. This is crucial because we are not always in a position to assess the truth content of statements. However, we can draw a time line to represent the 1800s.

Since we have not determined the truth content of these premises, it is at least logically possible to place van Gogh's and Curie's birth dates on this line such that the conclusion is true.

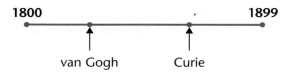

Of course, it is also logically possible to place van Gogh's and Curie's birth dates on this line such that the conclusion is false.

Analysis of Example 1.1 has revealed that even if the information in the premises is true, it is nevertheless logically possible for the conclusion to be either true or false. This example shows that we can determine the logical relationship between statements *without knowing the actual truth or falsity of the statements involved.*
    Now let's consider a slightly different pair of statements.

1. Marie Curie was born sometime in the 1800s.
2. Nelson Mandela was born sometime in the 1900s.

We are now interested in the relationship that exists between this pair of statements and a new statement, one that we could derive as a consequence of this pair. One candidate would be this statement:

3. Marie Curie was born before Nelson Mandela.

This provides us with a new example for logical analysis.

Example 1.2

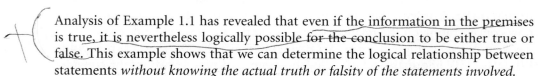

{R}:
1. Marie Curie was born sometime in the 1800s.
2. Nelson Mandela was born sometime in the 1900s.
3. Marie Curie was born before Nelson Mandela.

As before, for purposes of logical analysis we start by accepting the premises as true. If so, the information given is this: Premise 1—Marie Curie was born somewhere between 1800 and 1899. Premise 2—Nelson Mandela was born somewhere between 1900 and 1999. We can again draw a time line to help us with our analysis.

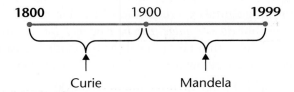

Marie Curie's birth date can be placed anywhere between 1800 and 1899, and Nelson Mandela's birth date can be placed anywhere between 1900 and 1999. Now, if the information in the premises is true, then the relationship {R} between these three statements is such that the conclusion in Example 1.2 must be true, too. Remember that this is a logical analysis only—we are not claiming that any of the statements are really true. Rather, we are considering only the logical component contained in the inference (*what if* the premises are true). Our analysis has revealed something completely different from Example 1.1. Specifically, Example 1.2 shows that it is possible for a relationship in an inference to exist whereby the premises, if true, *guarantee* the conclusion to be true. Logical analysis is thus completely different from truth content analysis, which considers only *what is* the case (whether the statements are true or false).

One final example will be considered here.

Example 1.3

{R}
1. Marie Curie was born sometime in the 1800s.
2. Nelson Mandela was born sometime in the 1900s.
3. Nelson Mandela was born before Marie Curie.

As before, for purposes of logical analysis we start by accepting the premises as true. If so, the information given is the same as before: Premise 1—Marie Curie was born somewhere between 1800 and 1899. Premise 2—Nelson Mandela was born somewhere between 1900 and 1999. If the premises are accepted as true, then the relationship {R} between these three statements is such that *the conclusion must be false.*

The discussion so far has revealed that, as far as the relationship question is concerned, the results can differ. In Example 1.1, the relationship was such that even if the premises were both true, the conclusion *could be either true or false.* In Example 1.3, the relationship was such that if the premises were both true, the conclusion *had to be false.* Most importantly, in Example 1.2, the relationship was such that if the premises were both true, the conclusion was *guaranteed to be true.*

Mastering logical analysis requires the active separation of the two types of information evaluation we have been considering. Since our minds naturally process information in the two ways we have been discussing, it is often confusing when we first try to consciously keep the two distinct. First, is the information I am receiving accurate, correct, or true? Second, if it is true, then what can I infer from it—that is, what conclusions follow? In fact, for most people the first type of evaluation (the truth content) takes priority. If you are not aware of the difference between truth content and logical component, then confusion arises. We can illustrate this by performing a little experiment in which you read a statement, understand what it means, but *do not judge it to be true or false*. Try to understand the meaning of the statement without deciding its actual truth or falsity. The statement will refer to the book you are now reading. Here is the statement:

The book you are now reading weighs 2000 pounds.

Most people, if not all, upon finishing the statement immediately know it to be false. Their "deciding" it was false happened so fast they could not stop it. This shows that one part of our mind is constantly analyzing information for truth and falsity. This is important for our discussion precisely because we must recognize that our minds are constantly working on two different levels, and we must learn to keep those levels separate. In order to evaluate the relationship (the logical component) that exists *between* statements we must disregard the truth content. We must temporarily ignore the actual truth/falsity results—not because they are unimportant, but simply because we are doing something entirely different.

It is possible to get a clear understanding of how the two functions differ by considering how we process other kinds of information. The sense of sight and the sense of smell are two distinct functions. We don't expect our eyes to detect the fragrance of a flower, or our noses to tell us what color the flower is. In fact, people sometimes close their eyes when smelling something in order to give their sense of smell the highest priority. We quite often close our eyes when we want to concentrate on hearing something. Similarly, when we are concentrating on the logical component, we must learn to "close" our truth content faculty for a while.

EXERCISE SET 1.2 ○○○

Strategy

The exercises are specifically designed to reinforce your understanding of the previous section, so do as many of them as you can. Also, the exercises generally range in difficulty from simple to complex, so make sure that you don't limit yourself to the simple ones.

To analyze the *relationships* in the following inferences, (1) Imagine that all the premises are true. (2) Determine whether the conclusion in each inference is then (a) true, (b) false, or (c) either true or false. (3) Explain your results. *(A complete answer to the first exercise in each exercise set is given to provide a model for you to follow. Solutions and explanations for the starred exercises are provided at the back of the book.)*

1. Book A has more than 200 pages.
   Book B has more than 500 pages.
   Book B has more pages than book A.

Answer: (c) either true or false.

We must make sure that whatever number of pages we imagine the books to have the two premises must turn out to be *true*. With this in mind, let Book A have 250 pages and Book B have 525 pages. The conclusion becomes true. But suppose Book A has 600 pages. This is possible because the first premise only claims that Book A has more than 200 pages and 600 is more than 200. The first premise would therefore be true. Now if Book B has 525 pages, the second premise would be true. However, the conclusion now becomes *false*.

2. Book A has more than 200 pages.
   Book B has more than 500 pages.
   Book A has more pages than book B. (c) either true or false

Exercises 2–30: For answers and explanations, see pages 2–5 of Instructor's Manual.

3. Book A has fewer than 200 pages.
   Book B has more than 500 pages.
   Book B has more pages than book A. (a) true

4. Book A has fewer than 200 pages.
   Book B has more than 500 pages.
   Book A has more pages than book B. (b) false

5. S.K. was born before 1989.
   W.R. was born before 1959.
   W.R. was born before S.K. (c) either true or false

*6. S.K. was born before 1989.
   W.R. was born before 1959.
   S.K. was born before W.R. (c) either true or false

7. S.K. was born in 1989 in a month that begins with the letter J.
   W.R. was born in 1989 in a month that begins with the letter F.
   W.R. was born before S.K. (c) either true or false

8. S.K. was born in 1989 in a month that begins with the letter J.
   W.R. was born in 1989 in a month that begins with the letter F.
   S.K. was born before W.R. (c) either true or false

9. S.K. was born in 1989 in a month that begins with the letter M.
   W.R. was born in 1989 in a month that begins with the letter F.
   S.K. was born before W.R. (b) false

10. S.K. was born in 1989 in a month that begins with the letter M.
    W.R. was born in 1989 in a month that begins with the letter F.
    W.R. was born before S.K. (a) true

*11. H.L. spent 1/2 of his yearly income on his car.
    J.G. spent 1/3 of her yearly income on her car.
    H.L.'s income is $50,000/year.
    J.G.'s income is $75,000/year.
    J.G. spent more money on her car than H.L. (b) false

12. H.L. spent 1/2 of his yearly income on his car.

    J.G. spent 1/3 of her yearly income on her car.

    H.L's income is $100,000/year.

    <u>J.G.'s income is $210,000/year.</u>

    J.G. spent more money on her car than H.L. (a) true

13. H.L. spent 1/2 of his yearly income on his car.

    J.G. spent 1/3 of her yearly income on her car.

    H.L's income is $50,000/year.

    <u>J.G.'s income is $75,000/year.</u>

    H.L. spent more money on his car than J.G. (b) false

14. Every jellybean in that jar is either red, or green, or yellow.

    <u>The last jellybean I took from that jar was not red.</u>

    The last jellybean I took from that jar was green. (c) either true or false

15. Every jellybean in that jar is either red, or green, or yellow.

    The last jellybean I took from that jar was not red.

    <u>The last jellybean I took from that jar was not yellow.</u>

    The last jellybean I took from that jar was green. (a) true

*16. Every voter registered as Independent voted for Candidate R in the last election.

    <u>D.W. and S.W. are both registered as "Independent" and they voted in the last election.</u>

    D.W. and S.W. both voted for Candidate R in the last election. (a) true

17. Every voter registered as Independent voted for Candidate R in the last election.

    <u>D.W. and S.W. are both registered as "Independent" and they voted in the last election.</u>

    D.W. and S.W. did not vote for Candidate R in the last election. (b) false

18. Not every steel-belted radial tire is defective.

    <u>I have four steel-belted radial tires on my car.</u>

    None of my tires are defective. (c) either true or false

19. Not every steel-belted radial tire is defective.

    <u>I have four steel-belted radial tires on my car.</u>

    All of my tires are defective. (c) either true or false

20. Not every steel-belted radial tire is defective.

    <u>I have four steel-belted radial tires on my car.</u>

    Some of my tires are defective. (c) either true or false

*21. Ron has more than $10 in his wallet.

    <u>Dave has more than $50 in his wallet.</u>

    Dave has more money in his wallet than Ron. (c) either true or false

22. Ron has more than $10 in his wallet.

    <u>Dave has more than $50 in his wallet.</u>

    Ron has more money in his wallet than Dave. (c) either true or false

23. Paul is younger than 25.

    <u>Mary is younger than 30.</u>

    Paul is younger than Mary. (c) either true or false

24. Paul is younger than 25.

    <u>Mary is younger than 30.</u>

    Mary is younger than Paul. (c) either true or false

25. Chris was born in November 1979.

    <u>Marianne was born in 1979 in a month that begins with a vowel.</u>

    Chris was born before Marianne. (b) false

*26. Chris was born in November 1979.

    <u>Marianne was born in 1979 in a month that begins with a vowel.</u>

    Marianne was born before Chris. (a) true

    April / August

27. The next exam will have us analyze a poem, a short story, or a novel.

    <u>It will not be a poem.</u>

    It will be a short story. (c) either true or false

28. The next exam will have us analyze a poem, a short story, or a novel.

    <u>It will not be a poem.</u>

    It will be a short story or a novel. (a) true

*29. The next exam will have us analyze a poem, a short story, or a novel.

    It will not be a poem.

    <u>It will not be a short story.</u>

    It will be a novel. (a) true

30. The next exam will have us analyze a poem, a short story, or a novel.

    <u>It will not be a poem.</u>

    It will not be a short story. (c) either true or false *possibly either*

1.3 TRUTH CONTENT ERRORS, LOGICAL COMPONENT ERRORS, AND THE ANALYSIS OF INFERENCES

The examples and analyses presented thus far have deliberately avoided the question of the truth content of the statements. This was done to illustrate the difference between true/false determinations and logical decisions. It was also noted that there are two major sources of error—incorrect truth content and incorrect logical component. A **truth content error (TE)** is one in which the information given

Truth content error (TE):
When the information given is determined to be false.

Logical component error (LE): When the premises of an inference, even if true, logically allow the conclusion to be false.

is false. A **logical component error (LE)** is one in which the beginning information, *even if true*, logically allows the final statement, or conclusion, to be false. Again, notice the radical difference between these two processes—truth content considerations take one piece of information at a time, while logical considerations look at the relationship between statements. Now let's apply what we have learned to the analysis of a series of inferences.

The examples in this section contain statements that you might already know to be true or false. However, we are going to proceed as if we did not know the truth content, because the first part of our analysis is to look exclusively for logical errors (*LE*'s). In order to avoid any confusion in dealing with these inferences we will stipulate some rules of procedure. Some of the examples used in the text contain "relative" terms, such as "left," "right," "east," and "west." For example, if two people are facing each other with an object between them, then a spot on the object may be to the "left" of one of the people but to the "right" of the other person. In addition, we stipulate, for normal reference purposes, that New York City is to the east of Los Angeles. Some wise reader might point out that if you go *west* from Los Angeles, you will eventually get to New York City. Thus, we stipulate for reference purposes that when measuring the distance between two objects, we will always use the *shortest* possible path.

Example 1.4

1. Venus is closer to the Sun than Mars.
2. Mars is closer to the Sun than Earth.
3. Venus is closer to the Sun than Earth.

To begin our analysis we need to consider only one question: *What if* the premises are true? To help us visualize the logical component we can draw a picture of what the information is telling us. Premise 1 claims that the distance from Venus to the Sun is shorter than the distance from Mars to the Sun. Since at this point we are not considering the truth of this claim, we are free to draw any picture as long as it depicts the situation mentioned in Premise 1 *as if it were true*. In the figures below, *V* = "Venus," *M* = "Mars," and *S* = "Sun." A visual inspection of this illustration confirms that we have depicted *V*, *M*, and *S* in a way that ensures Premise 1 is true.

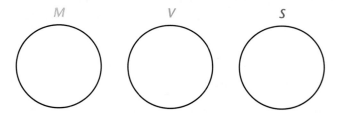

Of course there are many other possible pictures, and you are free to draw *V*, *M*, and *S* in any way you like, *but your picture must clearly depict Premise 1 as being true*.

Next, Premise 2 states that *M* is closer than *E* is to *S*. We simply add this new piece of information to the illustration. In fact, all we have to do now is figure out where to place the *E* in relation to the three circles already drawn in order to depict Premise 2 as being true:

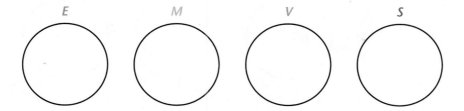

At this point, we have illustrated all the information given in the premises as if it were true and all we have left to consider is how this relates to the conclusion. We must acknowledge that if the information in the premises is true, then the conclusion must also be true. This is actually a much more powerful claim than it might first appear. What we are claiming is that there is no way to draw the information given in the premises (depicting them as if they were both true) such that the conclusion will ever turn out to be false. Therefore, as our logical analysis has shown, Example 1.4 does not contain a logical error (no *LE*). It sometimes helps to test this claim, because by doing so you will see that there is a unique relationship between the premises and the conclusion. If you have any doubt that what we are claiming is correct, try to draw a picture in which the premises are depicted as true and the conclusion false.

The same type of analysis can be applied to the next inference.

Example 1.5

1. Earth is closer to the Sun than Mars.
2. Venus is closer to the Sun than Mars.
3. Earth is closer to the Sun than Venus.

We first draw the information given in the premises by considering what might occur if the information were true (remember to combine the information in the premises to create one picture). The following illustration shows one possibility. It reveals that it is possible for the conclusion to be true as well.

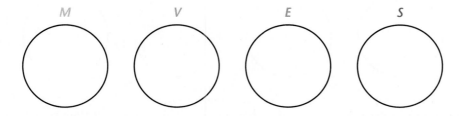

However, at this point we would not be justified in claiming that there is no *LE* because a closer look shows that the premises can be drawn in a different manner.

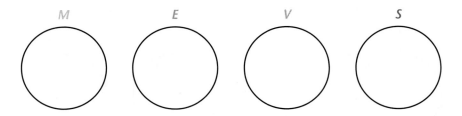

This figure reveals another logical possibility—the conclusion might be false even if the premises are true. It is important to check that we have not cheated or made a simple mistake by drawing either Premise 1 or Premise 2 as if it were false. Close inspection verifies that we have indeed drawn the premises as if they were true. Therefore, as clearly illustrated above, the relationship in this inference is such that *even if the premises are true, they cannot guarantee that the conclusion will be true as well.* Thus, we have revealed a logical error (*LE*) in Example 1.5.

At this point it can be helpful to return to Example 1.4 to verify, once again, that we have not overlooked the possibility that a similar logical error exists there. You should take the time to try to apply the reasoning used in analyzing Example 1.5 to the thinking we did for Example 1.4 in order to completely accept and understand that no comparable error exists there.

In Example 1.6, the truth of the premises cannot guarantee the truth of the conclusion, which can be either true or false:

Example 1.6

1. Earth is closer to the Sun than Mars.
2. Venus is closer to the Sun than Mars.
3. Venus is closer to the Sun than Earth.

We can start by drawing the information given in the premises, as if it were true. Following is one possible arrangement.

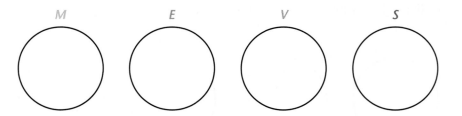

This figure shows that it is possible that the conclusion is true if the premises are true. Further analysis reveals another logical possibility.

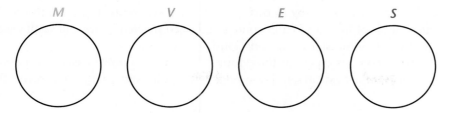

This figure clearly shows the possibility that even if the premises are true, the conclusion might be false. Therefore, we have shown that *the relationship in this inference cannot guarantee the truth of the conclusion.* So, Example 1.6 contains a *LE*.

In Example 1.7, the final inference in this series, the truth of the premises does guarantee the truth of the conclusion.

Example 1.7

1. Venus is closer to the Sun than Earth.
2. Earth is closer to the Sun than Mars.
3. Venus is closer to the Sun than Mars.

One possible way to draw the information contained in the premises is shown below.

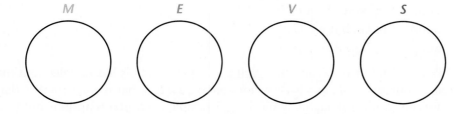

This illustration shows that it is possible for the conclusion to be true if the premises are true. However, what we need to know and verify is whether there is any picture that shows the conclusion to be false when the premises are true. Try as we might, we are forced to admit that this is not possible. Anytime we draw the premises as if they were true, the conclusion is true as well. Thus, there is no *LE* in Example 1.7. It is important to try different pictures to convince yourself of this result. The various attempts will exercise your imagination and logical abilities.

Here is what our logical analysis has revealed:

Example 1.4: No *LE*
Example 1.5: *LE*
Example 1.6: *LE*
Example 1.7: No *LE*

Everything we have done so far has been an analysis of the logical component involved in inferences. We have purposely suspended any consideration of the truth content concerning these four inferences in order to show that the logical component must be analyzed on its own merits, by its own rules. Of course, eventually we want to combine the analysis of logic and truth content into a complete picture, but until we are ready to do that, we must learn to consciously separate them.

The truth content aspect of these four inferences can now be easily discussed. When we access the best current knowledge of the solar system, the facts reveal this picture:

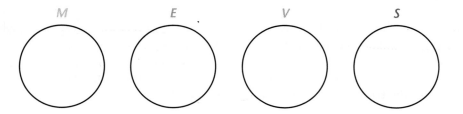

Using this picture, we can analyze the above inferences for truth content errors (*TE*).

Example 1.4: Premise 2 is factually false, so this inference has a *TE*.
Example 1.5: The conclusion is factually false, so this inference has a *TE*.
Example 1.6: No *TE*.
Example 1.7: No *TE*.

We can now combine the results of logical and truth content analysis:

Example 1.4: No *LE*, but there is a *TE*.
Example 1.5: Both *LE* and *TE*.
Example 1.6: *LE*, but no *TE*.
Example 1.7: No *LE* and no *TE*.

Example 1.6 illustrates an important point. Our analysis has revealed that the inference contains a *LE*, but it does not contain a *TE*. What is important is that while we can admit that, factually speaking, Example 1.6 contains nothing but true sentences, nevertheless, the logic is flawed. Even though the conclusion happens to be, in fact, true, it does not logically follow from the premises. This means that it was possible that even though we found out that the premises were true, we might have just as easily found out that the conclusion was false. As a result, the relationship did not guarantee the truth of the conclusion; *the fact that it turned out to be true does not save the logical relationship.*

This discussion can be best understood by comparing Example 1.6 with Example 1.7. Our analysis of Example 1.7 revealed that no *LE* and no *TE* exist. These two inferences have one thing in common; neither contains a *TE*. As far as the truth content aspect is concerned, they are identical. However, the inferences produce radically different relationships. The weakness in Example 1.6 was clearly revealed when we drew the pictures showing the logical possibilities. Logical analysis showed us that Example 1.6 could not guarantee the truth of the conclusion, even if the premises were both true. This is in sharp contrast with Example 1.7, which, upon analysis, revealed the impossibility of ever getting the conclusion false while maintaining the truth of the premises. Thus, while Example 1.6 gets high marks for truth content, it gets low marks as far as logical component is concerned. This illustrates why it is so important to remember that when evaluating inferences, we must always distinguish truth content from logical judgments. Inferences work on two levels, and we must ensure that our assessments correctly and precisely refer to the appropriate level.

EXERCISE SET 1.3

At the beginning of each set of exercises we will stipulate the "rules of game," which will allow a uniform point of reference for analysis. The relationship in each inference is to be analyzed in the following way: Step 1. It is stipulated that all the premises are to be accepted as true. Step 2. Determine whether the conclusion in each inference is, logically speaking, (a) true, (b) false, or (c) either true or false. Explain your results by drawing pictures to illustrate your logical process. Keep in mind that we are not judging these inferences for their truth content, but only analyzing the logical component, the relationship between the statements.

For Exercises 1–10 we stipulate the following reference guide:

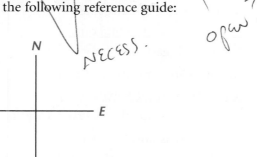

1. Kuala Lumpur is north of the Equator.
   Singapore is north of the Equator.
   Kuala Lumpur is north of Singapore.

Answer: (c) either true or false.

The following picture makes the premises, and the conclusion true.

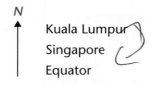

The next picture makes the premises true, but the conclusion false.

Exercises 2–20: For answers and explanations, see pages 5–10 of Instructor's Manual.

2. Kuala Lumpur is north of Singapore.
   <u>Singapore is north of the Equator.</u>
   Kuala Lumpur is north of the Equator. (a) true

3. Chicago is east of Boston.
   <u>Pittsburgh is east of Chicago.</u>
   Boston is east of Pittsburgh. (b) false

4. Detroit is west of Cleveland.
   <u>Detroit is west of Cincinnati.</u>
   Cleveland is west of Cincinnati. (c) either true or false

5. Seattle is west of Reno.
   <u>Seattle is west of Los Angeles.</u>
   Reno is west of Los Angeles. (c) either true or false

*6. St Louis is east of Louisville.
   <u>Columbus is east of St. Louis.</u>
   Louisville is east of Columbus. (b) false

7. Atlantic City is north of Miami.
   <u>Miami is north of Mexico City.</u>
   Atlantic City is north of Mexico City. (a) true

8. Kansas City is north of Dallas.
   <u>Oklahoma City is north of Dallas.</u>
   Kansas City is north of Oklahoma City. (c) either true or false

9. Seattle is south of Reno.
   <u>Seattle is south of Los Angeles.</u>
   Reno is south of Los Angeles. (c) either true or false

10. Seattle is east of Reno.
   <u>Seattle is east of Los Angeles.</u>
   Reno is east of Los Angeles. (c) either true or false

For Exercises 11–15 we stipulate that "closer to" refers to the text definition—measured along the shortest possible path.

11. Jay is closer than Sam is to the TV.
   <u>Sam is closer than Sandy is to the TV.</u>
   Jay is closer than Sandy is to the TV.

Answer: (a) true.

This picture makes the premises, and the conclusion, true.

                    Sandy   Sam   Jay   TV

It is impossible for the premises to be true and the conclusion to be false, at the same time.

12. Jay is closer than Sam is to the TV.
    <u>Sam is closer than Sandy is to the TV.</u>
    Sandy is closer than Jay is to the TV. (b) false

13. Jay is closer than Sam is to the TV.
    Jay is closer than Bill is to the TV.
    <u>Bill is closer than Sandy is to the TV.</u>
    Sam is closer than Sandy is to the TV. (c) either true or false

14. Jay is closer than Sam is to the TV.
    Bill is closer than Sam is to the TV.
    <u>Bill is closer than Sandy is to the TV.</u>
    Jay is closer than Sandy is to the TV. (c) either true or false

15. Jay is closer than Sam is to the TV.
    Sam is closer than Bill is to the TV.
    <u>Bill is closer than Sandy is to the TV.</u>
    Jay is closer than Sandy is to the TV. (a) true

For Exercises 16–20 we stipulate that "larger than" refers to the *number* of people living in that place, not to the *size* of the people in those countries.

*16. Indonesia's population is larger than Malaysia's.
    Malaysia's population is larger than Hong Kong's.
    <u>Hong Kong's population is larger than Singapore's.</u>
    Indonesia's population is larger than Singapore's. (a) true

17. Indonesia's population is larger than Malaysia's.
    Hong Kong's population is larger than Malaysia's.
    <u>Singapore's population is larger than Malaysia's.</u>
    Indonesia's population is larger than Singapore's. (c) either true or false

18. Indonesia's population is larger than Malaysia's.
    Hong Kong's population is larger than Malaysia's.
    <u>Malaysia's population is larger than Singapore's.</u>
    Indonesia's population is larger than Singapore's. (a) true

*19. Indonesia's population is larger than Malaysia's.
    Hong Kong's population is larger than Malaysia's.
    <u>Malaysia's population is larger than Singapore's.</u>
    Singapore's population is larger than Hong Kong's. (b) false

20. Indonesia's population is larger than Malaysia's.
    Malaysia's population is larger than Hong Kong's.
    <u>Singapore's population is larger than Hong Kong's.</u>
    Malaysia's population is larger than Singapore's. (c) either true or false

Exercises 21–23 *Advanced Analysis:* This next example illustrates the value of logical thinking. This is an actual sign that appeared on the refrigerator door in a teacher's lounge.

> Think twice before you open this door!
>
> 1. Do you have something to place inside?
>
> 2. Do you own something you would like to retrieve from inside?
>
> If your answer to either of the above is "NO" then...
>
> DO NOT OPEN THIS DOOR!!

21. Your answer to #1 would be Yes, but you would have to answer No to #2, so you are not allowed to open the door.

22. Your answer to #2 would be Yes, but you would have to answer No to #1, so you are not allowed to open the door.

23. Even if your answer to #1 is Yes, no one could have placed anything inside, because before you can put in anything for the first time you must answer No to #2.

21. What if you wanted to place something inside the refrigerator, *but you do not already have something in there?* According to the sign, are you allowed to open the door?

22. What if you wanted to retrieve something from inside the refrigerator, *but you do not now have something to place inside?* According to the sign, are you allowed to open the door?

23. Answering *both* questions truthfully, is it ever possible for anyone to open the door?

1.4 REASONING, JUDGMENT, AND DEDUCTIVE ANALYSIS

When asked the probability of a coin coming up "heads" on the next toss, most people would likely answer that it has a probability of 50 percent, or a 50-50 chance. But notice that this answer is actually the conclusion of an inference—it is not made in isolation. Information was assumed in order to get the answer. Only by consciously making the missing information *explicit* are we able to reveal that the answer was in fact the result of assumed premises. The claim that the next toss of a coin will be "heads" has 50-50 chance, is actually the conclusion of a complex inference. In Example 1.8, five premises would be sufficient:

Example 1.8

Premises

{R}

1. We are using a two-sided coin.
2. One side is designated "heads" and the other side "tails."
3. It is a "fair" coin (not weighted unequally).
4. It is a "fair" toss (no cheating involved).
5. If the coin lands on its edge, it will not count as a toss.

Conclusion: 6. The next toss of the coin has a 50 percent probability of coming up "heads."

This inference allows us to verify that the conclusion logically follows (must be true) *if all the premises are true.* Our confidence in the conclusion relies completely on the assumption that the premises are true. Disregarding the truth content allows us to determine logically that the conclusion follows with certainty from the premises. In addition, we must acknowledge that *if* any of the premises are false, then the conclusion *might be false* as well. Do not be confused by this. Our logical analysis of Example 1.8 has correctly determined that if the premises are all true, then the conclusion must be true, too. However, this logical result cannot tell us what the truth contents of the statements are because the logical component and the truth content of an inference require different kinds of analysis. Nevertheless, our analysis confirms that the conclusion in Example 1.8 follows logically from the given premises. The premises, if true, guarantee that the conclusion will be true. The inference, therefore, has no logical errors.

Every inference that we have examined thus far has been judged by asking this question: Is the relationship between the premises and the conclusion such that the conclusion is guaranteed to be true if the premises are true? The type of logical analysis concerned with determining whether the conclusion follows from the premises with certainty is called **deductive analysis.** In terms of deductive analysis, an acceptable inference is one is which the truth of the premises *guarantees* the truth of the conclusion. Although the requirement might seem extreme (there must not be any logical errors), there are good reasons for such a strict requirement. The major reason is something that we have been talking about all along, namely, the *guarantee of truth* throughout our reasoning process.

Probability Assessment

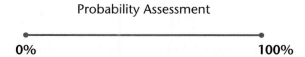

0%   100%

The probability that the conclusion is true if all the premises are true

We sometimes create inferences with the intent of not only starting our reasoning process with true statements (premises), but also with the goal of deriving only true statements as consequences (conclusions). What deductive analysis teaches us is that at least one kind of certainty is achievable—**logical certainty**. In fact, we have already encountered logical certainty in Examples 1.4 and 1.7. The conclusions of both those inferences have a probability of 100 percent of being true if the premises are true. Any inference that meets the deductive criteria is called a **valid inference**. Since Examples 1.4 and 1.7 both contain premises that, if true, guarantee their conclusions to be true, they contain no logical errors; thus they are both valid inferences.

Valid

0%   100%

Example 1.4 (see the following)

Example 1.7 (see the following)

Deductive analysis: Analysis of an inference with the specific goal of determining the logical question of validity or invalidity.

Logical certainty: The kind of certainty achieved by a valid inference.

Valid inference: An inference in which it is impossible for the conclusion to be false if the premises are true.

Invalid inference: An inference in which it is possible for the conclusion to be false even if the premises are true.

Example 1.4

1. Venus is closer to the Sun than Mars.
2. <u>Mars is closer to the Sun than Earth.</u>
3. Venus is closer to the Sun than Earth.

Example 1.7

1. Venus is closer to the Sun than Earth.
2. <u>Earth is closer to the Sun than Mars.</u>
3. Venus is closer to the Sun than Mars.

The requirement for logical certainty allows us to further stipulate that *if* the relationship in an inference is such that ~~the conclusion has~~ anything less than a 100 percent chance of being true (provided the premises are true), then the inference is **invalid**. An inference is thus invalid if it fails to guarantee that its conclusion is true (it contains a logical error). Since Example 1.5 and Example 1.6 both contain logical errors (*LE's*)—neither of the inferences can guarantee that its conclusion is true—they are both invalid. Although we know that these two examples are invalid, it is not possible to give them a definite location on the assessment chart because we cannot calculate a precise probability for the respective conclusions. However, the results can be displayed as shown below.

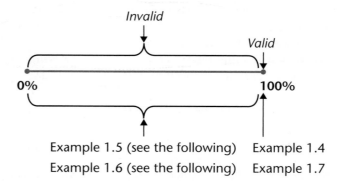

Example 1.5 (see the following)   Example 1.4
Example 1.6 (see the following)   Example 1.7

Example 1.5

1. Earth is closer to the Sun than Mars.
2. <u>Venus is closer to the Sun than Mars.</u>
3. Earth is closer to the Sun than Venus.

Example 1.6

1. Earth is closer to the Sun than Mars.
2. <u>Venus is closer to the Sun than Mars.</u>
3. Venus is closer to the Sun than Earth

Since we have stipulated that premises and conclusions are statements, it is appropriate to refer to them as either true or false. However, since an inference is not a statement but a *network of statements,* it would be incorrect to label an inference as true or false. When we judge an inference to be valid or invalid, we are referring to the relationship between the premises and the conclusion. Because the relationship is not another statement, it would be incorrect to label it as true or false. As stated ~~earlier, the relationship may be~~ strong, weak, supportive, etc. If the premises are true and the relationship guarantees that the conclusion must also be true, then this is the maximum support a relationship can achieve, and the inference is valid.

BIOGRAPHY THE WOMEN WHO PROGRAMMED ENIAC

The first electronic digital computer was named ENIAC (Electronic Numerical Integrator and Computer). It was developed during World War II in order to quickly compute and compile a set of "firing tables" that could be used to calculate the speed and trajectory of field artillery. Six women, Frances Bilas, Betty Jean Jennings, Ruth Lictermann, Kathleen McNulty, Elizabeth Snyder, and Marlyn Wescoff, were hired to do the programming of the computer. Their task was to get the computer to mathematically model all possible ballistics trajectories, which required solving complex differential equations. The team had to create their own programming manuals because none existed.

It soon became apparent that the programming could not be done without physically reconfiguring the huge computer in order to match the program with the machine. Using today's language, they had to create software and hardware at the same time. This meant that they had to work with the engineering specifications and diagrams of the machinery in order to design the first programs. They had to physically arrange the computer's complex set of wires, circuits, cable connections, and vacuum tubes to coordinate the physical sequencing with the differential equation sequencing. This intricate programming combined a complete knowledge of the physical state of the computer with sophisticated knowledge of *logical thinking*. In fact, as Betty Jennings remarked, it was "a physicalization of *if-then* statements."

Mathematicians, physicists, and other scientists quickly sought out the ENIAC programmers to help solve long-standing problems that were so complex it would take many lifetimes to solve without a computer.

Equivocation

At this point we can deal with another possible confusion or mistake and how to avoid it. Consider the inference in Example 1.9:

Example 1.9

Joe is older than Chris.
<u>Chris is older than Dana.</u>
Joe is older than Dana.

One way to analyze the inference above would be to draw a diagram wherein we make both premises true.

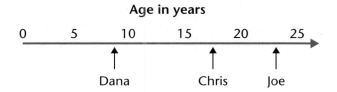

Age in years

Equivocation: The intentional or unintentional use of different meanings or references for words or phrases in an inference.

Of course, there are many other pictures we can draw. However, it is not possible to draw a picture where both premises are true and, at the same time, where the conclusion is false. (You should verify this for yourself.) This means that the conclusion has a 100 percent chance of being true if the premises are true, and the inference is, therefore, valid. But suppose someone draws the following picture:

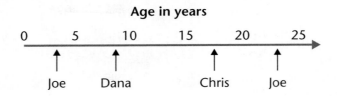

Age in years

We are then told that this picture proves the inference is invalid because the "Joe" referred to in the first premise is not the same "Joe" as referred to in the conclusion. In other words, what if the "Joe" in the first premise is in fact older than Chris (first premise true), and what if Chris is in fact older than Dana (second premise true). Now if the "Joe" referred to in the conclusion is a different person from that referred to in the premise, then it is possible that the conclusion is false, that this new "Joe" is in fact younger than Dana; therefore, the inference is invalid.

The mistake here is one that is easily revealed and just as easily corrected. We stipulate that whenever an object is referred to, or a name is used, the *identical object* be referred to throughout the inference. We can see in the figure above that "Joe" refers to two different people so it violates our stipulation. This mistake, called **equivocation,** involves a change of reference or a change in the meaning of a word.

EXERCISE SET 1.4 ○○○

Exercises 1–8 You can now use the criteria for deductive analysis to determine whether the following inferences are valid or invalid. Imagine there is a game where someone is going to pick one marble out of a box. For uniform analysis we will stipulate the following rules: 1. The person who picks the marble cannot see into the box of marbles. 2. It is a "fair" game. These two rules will be assumed for each analysis, and the conclusion of each inference will be judged in relation to the accepted stipulations plus the specific information given in the premises. Treat each inference independently of the others.

1. All of the marbles in the box are blue.

   The next marble picked will be blue.

Answer: Valid

If every marble in the box is blue and it is a "fair" game (as stipulated), then it would be impossible to pick any color other than blue. *If* the premise is true, then the conclusion is guaranteed to be true (it is impossible to be false).

2. <u>All of the marbles in the box are blue.</u>
   The next marble picked will be red.   Invalid

3. <u>Some of the marbles in the box are not blue.</u>
   The next marble picked will be blue.   Invalid

4. <u>All of the marbles in the box are not blue.</u>
   The next marble picked will be red.   Invalid

5. There are 100 marbles in the box.
   99 of the marbles in the box are blue.
   <u>1 of the marbles in the box is red.</u>
   The next marble picked will be blue.   Invalid

*6. There are 100 marbles in the box.
   99 of the marbles in the box are blue.
   <u>1 of the marbles in the box is red.</u>
   The next marble picked will be red.   Invalid

7. There are 100 marbles in the box.
   99 of the marbles in the box are blue.
   <u>1 of the marbles in the box is red.</u>
   The probability that the next marble picked will be blue is 99 percent (99/100).   Valid

8. There are 100 marbles in the box.
   99 of the marbles in the box are blue.
   <u>1 of the marbles in the box is red.</u>
   The probability that the next marble picked will be red is 1 percent (1/100).   Valid

Exercises 2–31: For answers and explanations, see pages 10–13 of Instructor's Manual.

Exercises 9–25 Determine whether the following inferences are valid or invalid.

9. Anything that can communicate, learn, and solve problems is conscious.
   My computer can communicate.
   My computer can learn.
   <u>My computer can solve problems.</u>
   My computer is conscious.   Valid

10. Anything that can communicate, learn, and solve problems is conscious.
    Chimpanzees can communicate.
    Chimpanzees can learn.
    <u>Chimpanzees can solve problems.</u>
    Chimpanzees are conscious.   Valid

*11. The defendant's fingerprints were found at the scene of the crime.

Blood from the victim was found on the defendant's clothes.

Two eyewitnesses have placed the defendant at the scene just prior to the murder.

The defendant committed the murder. Invalid

12. The defendant's fingerprints were found at the scene of the crime.

Blood from the victim was found on the defendant's clothes.

Two eyewitnesses have placed the defendant at the scene just prior to the murder.

The defendant did not commit the murder. Invalid

13. The defendant's fingerprints were found at the scene of the crime.

Blood from the victim was found on the defendant's clothes.

Two eyewitnesses have placed the defendant at the scene just prior to the murder.

If (a) a defendant's fingerprints are found at the scene of the crime, and (b) blood from the victim is found on the defendant's clothes, and (c) at least two eyewitnesses place the defendant at the scene just prior to the murder, then that defendant committed the murder.

The defendant committed the murder. Valid

14. The defendant's fingerprints were found at the scene of the crime.

Blood from the victim was found on the defendant's clothes.

Two eyewitnesses have placed the defendant at the scene just prior to the murder.

If (a) a defendant's fingerprints are found at the scene of the crime, and (b) blood from the victim is found on the defendant's clothes, and (c) at least two eyewitnesses place the defendant at the scene just prior to the murder, then that defendant committed the murder.

The defendant did not commit the murder. Invalid

15. Every murder is a felony, but not every felony is a murder.

F.C. committed a murder.

F.C. committed a felony. Valid

*16. Every murder is a felony, but not every felony is a murder.

F.C. committed a felony.

F.C. committed a murder. Invalid

17. No registered Democrat voted for Candidate B in the last presidential election.

S.T. is a registered Democrat who voted in the last presidential election.

S.T. did not vote for Candidate B in the last presidential election. Valid

18. No registered Democrat voted for Candidate B in the last presidential election.

S.T. is a registered Republican who voted in the last presidential election.

S.T. voted for Candidate B in the last presidential election. Invalid

19 Some registered Democrats voted for Candidate B in the last presidential election.
   <u>S.T. is a registered Democrat who voted in the last presidential election.</u>
   S.T. voted for Candidate B in the last presidential election. Invalid

20. Every time a Republican is President there is a recession.
   <u>A Republican is President.</u>
   There is a recession. Valid

*21. Every time a Democrat is President there is a recession.
   <u>A Democrat is President.</u>
   There is a recession. Valid

22. Anyone who is a citizen has the right to freedom of speech and freedom of religion.
   <u>K.P. is a citizen.</u>
   K.P. has the right to freedom of speech and freedom of religion. Valid

23. Anyone who is a citizen has the right to freedom of speech and freedom of religion.
   <u>K.P. is a not a citizen.</u>
   K.P. does not have the right to freedom of speech and freedom of religion. Invalid

not only citizens have those rights

24. In order to graduate from T.S. University a student must have at least 124 credits.
   <u>T.R. is a student at T.S. University and has only 123 credits.</u>
   T.R. cannot graduate from T.S. University. Valid

25. Students will be expelled from T.S. University for cheating on exams or plagiarism.
   <u>T.R. is a student at T.S. University and has plagiarized.</u>
   T.R. will be expelled from T.S. University. Valid

Exercises 26–31 Imagine there is a game where someone is going to reach into a jar and grab a coin. We stipulate the following rules: 1. The person picking the coin cannot see which kind of coin he is grabbing. 2. It is a "fair" game. Treat each inference independently of the others. You can use the criteria for deductive analysis to determine whether the following inferences are therefore valid or invalid.

26. There are 1000 coins in the jar.
   999 of the coins in the jar are the state quarter Delaware.
   <u>1 of the coins in the jar is the state quarter Pennsylvania.</u>
   The next coin picked will be the state quarter Delaware.

Answer: Invalid

If all the premises are true and if it is a "fair" game (as stipulated), then the conclusion has a .999 probability of being true; that is, premises true and conclusion true. However, it is logically possible that the coin picked will be the state quarter Pennsylvania (this has a .001 probability); thus, it is possible for the premises to be true and conclusion false.

27. There are 1000 coins in the jar.

    999 of the coins in the jar are the state quarter Delaware.

    1 of the coins in the jar is the state quarter Pennsylvania.

    The next coin picked will be the state quarter Pennsylvania. Invalid

28. All of the coins in the jar are the state quarter Delaware.

    The next coin picked will be the state quarter Delaware. Valid

29. None of the coins in the jar are the state quarter Delaware.

    The next coin picked will be the state quarter Delaware. Invalid

*30. Some of the coins in the jar are not the state quarter Pennsylvania.

    The next coin picked will be the state quarter Pennsylvania. Invalid

31. All of the coins in the jar are not the state quarter Pennsylvania.

    The next coin picked will be the state quarter Delaware. Invalid

1.5 DEDUCTIVE AND INDUCTIVE INFERENCES

Traditionally, inferences are classified as *deductive* or *inductive*. A **deductive inference** is one in which it is asserted that the conclusion is guaranteed to be true if the premises are true. An **inductive inference** is one in which it is asserted that the conclusion has a high probability of being true if the premises are true. There are three ways to help identify inferences as either deductive or inductive. First, we can look for key words or phrases. For example, the phrases, "It follows with certainty…", and "This proves beyond a doubt…" clearly identify the inference as deductive. On the other hand, the phrases, "It is probably the case…", or "It is highly likely that…" identify the inference as inductive. However, when we encounter inferences in everyday life, these or other specific indicators may not be apparent. A second way to determine whether an inference is deductive or inductive is by judging the intent of the inference. We can ask this question: "Is the conclusion intended to follow with certainty or with high probability?" This method works best when we are familiar enough with the person making the inference to be fairly sure of the intent. The third way to distinguish the two kinds of inferences is to identify their *logical form, or structure*. Deductive analysis reveals that validity and invalidity are functions of the form of inferences. The clearest examples of deductive inferences are found in geometry and mathematics. The goal of these disciplines is the creation of valid inferences, where the conclusions follow with certainty.

Here are two inferences to consider:

Deductive inference:
An inference in which it is asserted that the conclusion is guaranteed to be true if the premises are true.

Inductive inference:
An inference in which it is asserted that the conclusion has a high probability of being true if the premises are true.

(A) All vegetables contain vitamin C.
     Spinach is a vegetable.
     Spinach contains vitamin C.

(B) Most vegetables contain vitamin C.
     Spinach is a vegetable.
     Spinach contains vitamin C.

For inference (A), if the premises are true, the conclusion must be true, so it can be classified as deductive. For inference (B), if the premises are true, the conclusion has a high probability of being true, but it is not certain. Therefore, inference (B) is best classified as inductive.

These considerations will be explored more fully in subsequent chapters, where we will learn specific techniques on how to recognize and reconstruct inferences to reveal the logical relationship. Your ability to classify an inference as deductive or inductive will grow as you are introduced to, and have the opportunity to analyze, many different inferences.

Deductive Inferences

Up to this point we have examined one way of analyzing inferences; we have specified how to evaluate an inference based on deductive analysis criteria. These criteria are extremely rigid in that they allow for only two possible outcomes. Every deductive inference must be either valid or invalid. Moreover, there is only one way for an inference to be valid. The premises must stand in relationship to the conclusion such that the conclusion is guaranteed to be true if the premises are true. In addition, *deductive analysis does not allow any judgment to be made between invalid inferences*. In this sense, all invalid inferences are lumped together. Why does deductive analysis give such polarized results? Isn't an inference that gives its conclusion a 50 percent chance of being true better than one that gives its conclusion only a 20 percent chance of being true? Earlier we mentioned that one of our intellectual goals was to achieve certainty, a quest that can be pursued by deductive analysis.

The use of deductive analysis prompted thinkers to develop systems of thought that reached certainty, systems that would not lead to false conclusions. This system of analysis led to great achievements in geometry, mathematics, and logic. Euclid's geometry is constructed on a simple plan: Start out with principles that are "clear and distinct" (which is defined as being "obviously true to every rational person"), and then derive only truths from those principles. These clear and distinct first principles are called axioms. The axioms cannot be proven to be true, but they are the basis for all subsequent proofs. This is why learning geometry is a matter of first recognizing the truth of the axioms and then *deducing* what follows from those axioms with logical certainty. Geometry and mathematics are highly abstract fields. At their highest level, they consist of symbol manipulation that is devoid of any truth content.

The search for certainty reached unprecedented heights in the seventeenth century in the work of Isaac Newton. Gravity and the motion of matter, two of the fundamental aspects of the physical universe, were explained by Newton's "laws," which were mathematical equations that enabled scientists to deduce consequences of specific physical systems. For two hundred years, the work of Newton was thought to be the correct picture of the entire physical universe. It was believed by many that the laws allowed us to achieve certainty in understanding the

Sound inference:
An inference that (1) is valid (based on the analysis of the logical component), and (2) has all true premises (based on the analysis of the truth content).

Unsound inference:
An inference that (1) is invalid (based on the analysis of the logical component), and/or (2) has at least one false premise (based on the analysis of the truth content).

Inductive analysis: The type of analysis that makes it possible to investigate the strengths and weaknesses of certain inferences, such as analogical, statistical, and causal inferences.

workings of all physical aspects concerning objects in motion. Newton's theoretical system is really an extended discussion of the axiomatic laws that precisely define fundamental aspects of particles in motion and of the consequences that can be derived by rigorously applying the techniques of deduction.

The goal of certainty was achieved by following two simple rules: (1) Start with clear and distinct truths. (2) Create inferences that are deductively valid. This ensures that our deductions are certain.

We might ask, "Is deductive analysis completely immune to truth content analysis?" In the determination of validity, the answer is "yes." But our ultimate goal is to unite the best logical component with the best possible truth content. When logical analysis shows an inference is valid, and when truth content analysis of the premises shows that they are true, then the inference is said to be **sound**. If the inference is invalid or if at least one of the premises is false, then the inference is said to be **unsound**. Applying these distinctions to earlier results will illustrate their use.

Example 1.4: No *LE*. However, a *TE* exists.   *Unsound inference*
Example 1.5: Both *LE* and *TE* exist.   *Unsound inference*
Example 1.6: *LE*. However, no *TE* exists.   *Unsound inference*
Example 1.7: No *LE* and no *TE* exist.   *Sound inference*

Inductive Inferences

There are many times when certainty cannot be achieved, nor should it be expected. Therefore, we need another analysis system to help us to deal with invalid inferences, the kind of inferences we come in contact with on a daily basis, the kind that force us to wrestle with a very difficult opponent—*uncertainty*. Uncertainty can exist in both the logical and the truth content aspects of inferences. Every inference must eventually be evaluated for both logic and truth content. For many real-life inferences, the most difficult aspects are in determining the truth content of the premises and the level of uncertainty.

Some inferences are created such that the conclusion follows with less than a 100 percent chance of being true. These inductive inferences do not attempt to achieve certainty, so they are judged differently from deductive inferences. In a nutshell, **inductive analysis** allows us to analyze an invalid inference, in part, by asking two questions: (1) What is the probability that the conclusion is true (can we calculate it)? (2) What evidence is there that the premises are true? Inductive analysis is, in a sense, more flexible than deductive analysis because it makes it possible to explain why one invalid inference is "better" than another invalid inference, something deductive analysis does not allow. Inductive analysis provides us with the logical skills necessary to compare two invalid inferences by determining which of the two conclusions has the higher probability of being true. Inductive analysis permits us to investigate the strengths and weaknesses of special kinds of inferences, such as *analogical inferences, statistical inferences*, and *causal inferences*, which are three types of inductive inferences.

Analogical inferences are based on the idea that when two things share some relevant characteristics, they probably share other characteristics as well. Here is an example of an analogical inference:

> I previously owned two Toyota station wagons. They both got good gas mileage, both needed few repairs, and both had a high resale value. I just bought a new Toyota station wagon, so it will get good gas mileage, need few repairs, and have a high resale value.

Statistical inferences are inferences based on our ability to generalize. When we observe a pattern, we can create an inference that uses statistical regularity. The following is an example of a statistical inference:

> A survey of 1000 university students in the U.S. revealed that 80 percent of the sample said that they expect to make more money in their lives than their parents. Therefore, the vast majority of all university students expect to make more money in their lives than their parents.

Causal inferences are inferences based on knowledge of either causes or effects. For example, a team of medical scientists may conduct experiments to determine if a new drug (the potential cause) will have a desired effect on a particular disease. On the other hand, a forensic expert might do a series of tests to determine the cause of a person's death. Causal reasoning can even be found in everyday occurrences. For example, someone might say the following:

> The lamp in my room does not work. I changed the light bulb, making sure I replaced it with one that worked, but it still did not work. I moved the lamp to another room just in case the wall outlet was defective, but the lamp still did not work. So, it must be the wiring in the lamp that is defective.

These kinds of applied inductive reasoning give up certainty (because they result in invalid inferences) and replace it with probability (degrees of uncertainty). Chapter 9 provides detailed analysis of these three types of inductive inferences.

1.6 UNCERTAINTY AND INDUCTIVE ANALYSIS

It is easy to figure out that if you flip a coin, the chances are one in two, or 50 percent, of it landing heads up. This is a simple example of one aspect of **probability theory**, which deals with the determination of the chance that an event will occur.

The modern foundations of probability theory were developed in the seventeenth century. Two French mathematicians, Blaise Pascal and Pierre de Fermat, began thinking about specific problems with gambling, trying to calculate the correct odds for various games, such as dice. The foundations of statistics were also being worked out during this time. Probability and statistics were applied to many fields, and we can trace the course of their development alongside that of modern science. In fact, science in the twentieth century was dominated by theoretical systems whose fundamental aspects are based on probabilities. For example, the basic

Analogical inference:
An inference based on the idea that two things that share some relevant characteristics probably share other characteristics as well.

Statistical inference:
An inference based on an ability to generalize. An observed pattern can be used to create an inference that uses statistical regularity.

Causal inference:
An inference based on knowledge of either causes or effects.

Probability theory:
The theoretical frameworks that make it possible to calculate the chance that events will occur.

theoretical framework of quantum physics is based on what has been called "the uncertainty principle." This principle states that subatomic particles have no definite position and motion. Other examples are seen in the modern idea of cause and effect. Risk factors are determined by statistical models based on past experience that enable scientists to predict the chance of contracting a certain disease.

The ideas of chance and probability have been intertwined ever since the foundations of modern probability theory were worked out in the 1650s. We take it for granted today that our basic notions of chance have a solid foundation. In fact, people today have a fundamentally different conception of probability than those living before 1650. For example, most adults not only accept that a coin toss has a 50-50 chance of coming up heads, but moreover, the calculation is trivial. It is not difficult to find statistical information linking smoking cigarettes to lung cancer, coal-mining to "black lung" disease (caused by inhaling coal dust over many years), and sewing factories to "white lung" disease (caused by inhaling cloth fibers over many years). In addition, decisions are often based on conjectures regarding the pluses and minuses of a future outcome. For example, someone might argue that the New York Jets have a 70 percent chance of making the NEL playoffs this year. This kind of calculation is based on such information as the teams' past performance, players drafted, players lost in trades and through free agency, strength of schedule, and many other factual issues deemed relevant to winning football games.

BIOGRAPHY   BLAISE PASCAL

A profound thinker in science, mathematics, and philosophy, Pascal (1623–1662) achieved much in his short life. In science, Pascal became convinced that a vacuum exists, an idea not generally accepted at the time. In mathematics, Pascal did crucial work on many topics, including conic sections and arithmetical triangles (called *Pascal triangles*). In addition, through a series of correspondences with Pierre Fermat, Pascal helped develop the modern theory of *a priori* probability. The foundations of probability were built on the solutions to two related questions: (1) How often can we expect two sixes to appear when we throw a pair of dice? (2) What odds should someone give that will ensure a minimum profit in dice games?

Pascal's most famous and widely read work is the *Pensées*, a recounting of his personal thoughts on human suffering and religious beliefs. In this book, Pascal managed to use his insights into probability theory and gambling as a basis for religious belief. He derived a betting proposition that has come to be known as "Pascal's wager": If God exists and you believe, then you win everything. If God exists and you don't believe, then you lose everything. By applying probabilistic reasoning to the all-too-human question of God's existence, Pascal is able to conclude that part of the human predicament is that we are "*compelled to gamble.*"

For over two thousand years, deduction and the quest for certainty dominated Western thinking. Inductive logic, with its reliance on probability and the understanding of the strengths and weaknesses of certain kinds of inferences, evolved along with modern science and provided the means for dealing with uncertainty. This meant that techniques had to be worked out for evaluating invalid inferences and dealing with uncertainty. The ever-changing results of science made it essential to compare inferences that do not achieve certainty, to help us decide which is "better," and to provide strong reasons for those decisions.

Inductive analysis, like deductive analysis, is based on evaluating inferences by assessing probabilities. However, unlike deductive analysis where our choices are *valid, invalid, sound,* and *unsound,* inductive analysis gives numerous designations that we can assign to inferences. We can classify inferences anywhere from the *strongest* to the *weakest,* from a probability of 99 percent to 0 percent. In addition, we can compare and judge two or more invalid inferences *relative to each other* by claiming that one is "stronger than" or "weaker than" another. We can also use qualitative terms, such as "very strong," "very weak," or "moderately" strong or weak. Although there are many designations we can assign to inductive inferences, we will define the three most common types: *strong, moderate,* and *weak.*

Strong inference: An inference for which logical analysis verifies that the premises, if true, provide evidence that the conclusion has a high probability of being true.

Moderate inference: An inference for which logical analysis verifies that the premises, if true, provide evidence that the conclusion has a good chance of being true.

Weak inference: An inference for which logical analysis verifies that the premises, if true, provide very little or no evidence that the conclusion is true.

When truth content analysis is added to the overall discussion of inductive analysis, we expand our classification of inferences. Combining logical and truth content analysis gives us two new designations: *cogent,* and *not cogent.*

Cogent: An inference is cogent if: (1) it is strong or moderate (based on the analysis of the logical component), and (2) the premises are all true (based on the analysis of the truth content).

Not cogent: An inference is not cogent if: (1) it is weak (based on the analysis of the logical component) and/or (2) it has at least one false premise (based on the analysis of the truth content).

Inductive analysis gives us the tools to investigate the value of an inference on many levels, and it enables us to rationally justify our evaluations based on good reasons. Although we often have to deal with uncertainty, our logical assessments will not be merely subjective. Typically, the reasons behind our assessments will include our understanding of the best knowledge available at the time of the judgment. As an example, consider the two inferences in Examples 1.10 and 1.11.

Strong inference: An inference for which logical analysis verifies that the premises, if true, provide evidence that the conclusion has a high probability of being true.

Moderate inference: An inference for which logical analysis verifies that the premises, if true, provide evidence that the conclusion has a good chance of being true.

Weak inference: An inference for which logical analysis verifies that the premises, if true, provide very little or no evidence that the conclusion is true.

Cogent: A cogent inference must (1) be strong or moderate (based on the analysis of the logical component), and (2) have all true premises (based on the analysis of the truth content).

Not cogent: An inference is not cogent if (1) it is weak (based on the analysis of the logical component) and/or (2) it has at least one false premise (based on the analysis of the truth content).

Example 1.10

Today the sun came up
Yesterday the sun came up.
Throughout recorded history the sun has come up.
Tomorrow the sun will come up.

Example 1.11

Today the sun came up.

Yesterday the sun came up.

Throughout recorded history the sun has come up.

Tomorrow the sun will not come up.

Deductive analysis of these inferences shows that they are both invalid. The conclusion in Example 1.10 has a high probability of being true; nevertheless, it is logically possible that the conclusion could be false, therefore, the inference is invalid. However, inductive analysis allows us to say that the inference in Example 1.10 is far superior to that in Example 1.11, because the probability that the conclusion in Example 1.11 is true is very small. Remember also that since both inferences are invalid, there is some chance that the conclusion in the superior inference could turn out false while the conclusion in the inference with the far smaller probability could turn out true. This is why people carrying signs proclaiming that the world will end tomorrow stand some chance of being correct (and if they carry the sign long enough, they will be correct).

Someone might object that it would be unfair to evaluate these inferences using deductive analysis because they are not deductive inferences, they are inductive inferences. This objection is correct, but at this point in the learning process we want to illustrate how deductive analysis differs from inductive analysis. These examples allow us to place deductive and inductive analysis side-by-side to see the similarities and differences. Deduction and induction both use the logical and truth content aspects, but their goals are different. For deduction, the foremost question is the certainty of the logic in the inference; for induction, the foremost question is the assessment of the degree of uncertainty in the inference. Quick Reference 1.1 and Figure 1.1 summarize what we have learned about deductive and inductive inferences.

For learning purposes, all the early examples in this chapter were analyzed as if they were deductive inferences. In real life, you will often have to decide the best, or most appropriate designation of an inference. If it appears that the inference is deductive, then you can determine whether it is valid or invalid. If it appears that the inference is inductive, then you will have to assess the level of uncertainty involved. (Later on, we will see direct applications of inductive analysis in a variety of settings.)

It is often useful to apply deductive analysis first because we often misjudge the strength of inferences. Some inferences can deceive us and appear to be valid, so deductive analysis can clarify the issue. Recognizing that an inference is invalid has the added benefit of getting us to accept the possibility that the conclusion can be false even if the premises are true. This can prompt us to think of how damaging these possibilities are, which can lead us to a more accurate assessment of the strength of the inference.

Quick Reference 1.1 • Summary of Deductive and Inductive Inferences

Deductive inference: When it is asserted (prior to analysis) that the premises, if true, guarantee the truth of the conclusion.

- **Valid inference:** An inference for which it is impossible for the conclusion to be false if the premises are true.
- **Invalid inference:** An inference for which the conclusion can be false even if the premises are true.
- **Sound inference:** An inference is sound when both of the following requirements are met: (1) The inference is valid, based on the analysis of the logical component. (2) All the premises are true, based on the analysis of the truth content.
- **Unsound inference:** An inference is unsound if either or both of the following conditions hold: (1) The inference has been determined to be invalid, based on the analysis of the logical component. (2) The inference has at least one false premise, based on the analysis of the truth content.

Inductive inference: When it is asserted (prior to analysis) that the premises, if true, do not guarantee the truth of the conclusion, but instead provide good reasons why the conclusion is likely to be true.

- **Strong inference:** An inference for which the premises, if true, provide evidence that the conclusion has a high probability of being true.
- **Moderate inference:** An inference for which the premises, if true, provide evidence that the conclusion has a good chance of being true.
- **Weak inference:** An inference for which the premises, if true, provide very little evidence (or none) that the conclusion is true.
- **Cogent inference:** An inference is cogent when both of the following requirements are met: (1) The inference is strong or moderate, based on the analysis of the logical component. (2) All the premises are true, based on the analysis of the truth content.
- **Not Cogent:** An inference is not cogent if either or both of the following conditions hold: (1) The inference is weak, based on the analysis of the logical component. (2) The inference has at least one false premise, based on the analysis of the truth content.

> Deductive inferences are valid or invalid, sound or unsound. Inductive inferences range from strong to weak, and are cogent or not cogent.

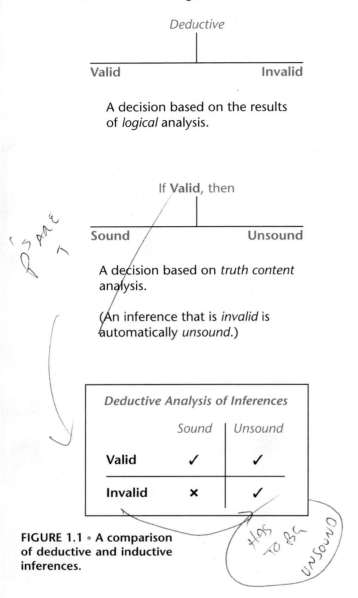

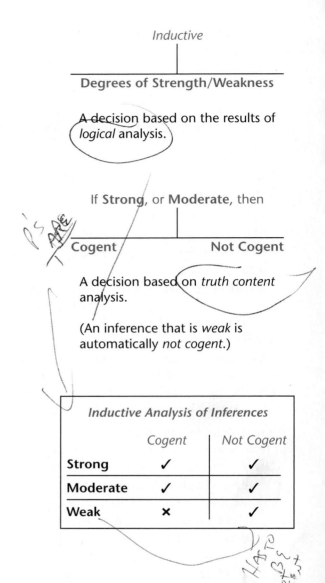

FIGURE 1.1 • A comparison of deductive and inductive inferences.

The classification of inferences into either deductive or inductive is not meant to be exhaustive of all possible inference constructions. Rather, it is meant to be a first approach to learning logic. As an analogy, we often introduce children to the vehicles they commonly see on roadways by first classifying them as either cars or trucks. This is useful because it is not necessary for the beginner to try to distinguish too many subtle distinctions. Later on, after more experience, we can classify vehicles into further groups, such as, passenger cars, compact cars, sports cars, SUV's, minivans, panel trucks, dump trucks, tractor-trailers, mopeds, motorcycles, and Hummers.

A good knowledge of both deductive and inductive analysis will provide you with the skills necessary to evaluate and construct inferences with an eye toward certainty or the acknowledgment of uncertainty.

EXERCISE SET 1.6

The following exercises are intended to apply the different skills used in deductive and inductive analysis. First, use deductive analysis to determine if each inference is *valid* or *invalid*. Second, use inductive analysis to determine if it is *strong*, *moderate*, or *weak*. Finally, discuss whether it is possible to determine if each inference is *sound* or *unsound* (deductive analysis), and *cogent* or *not cogent* (inductive analysis).

1. Every insect has eight legs.

   What's crawling on me has eight legs.

   What's crawling on me is an insect.

Answer:

Deductive Analysis: *Invalid—Unsound*

The first premise tells us something definite about every insect (they all have eight legs), but leaves open the larger class of eight-legged objects. The second premise tells us that something eight-legged is crawling on the person. If the premises are both true, then it might be an insect, or it might not be an insect (the conclusion can be true or false). Since the inference is invalid, it cannot be sound.

Inductive analysis: Even if every insect has eight legs, we can assume there may be eight-legged things that are not insects. The probability of the conclusion being true is, therefore, very small and the inference is weak. This alone makes the inference not cogent. (Additionally, since the first premise is a factually false statement—insects have six legs—the inference is not cogent from this aspect as well.)

2. Every insect has eight legs.

   What's crawling on me does not have eight legs.

   What's crawling on me is not an insect.

3. On the test that Al took the range of "A" scores was 90–100.

   Al got a 98 on the test.

   Al got an "A" on the test.

4. On the test that Al took the range of "A" scores was 90–100.

   Al got an "A" on the test.

   Al got a 98 on the test.

5. On the test that Al took the range of "A" scores was 90–100.

   Al did not get a 98 on the test.

   Al did not get an "A" on the test.

*6. On the test that Al took the range of "A" scores was 90–100.

   Al did not get an "A" on the test.

   Al did not get a 98 on the test.

7. Every fire needs oxygen.

   There is oxygen in that room.

   There is a fire in that room.

Exercises 2–20: For answers and explanations, see pages 14–17 of Instructor's Manual.

2. deductive analysis: valid/unsound

inductive analysis: strong/not cogent

3. deductive analysis: valid

inductive analysis: strong

4. deductive analysis: invalid/unsound

inductive analysis: weak/not cogent

5. deductive analysis: invalid/unsound

inductive analysis: weak/not cogent

6. deductive analysis: valid

inductive analysis: strong

7. deductive analysis: invalid/unsound

inductive analysis: weak/not cogent

8. deductive analysis: valid
inductive analysis: strong

9. deductive analysis:
invalid/unsound
inductive analysis: weak/
not cogent

10. deductive analysis:
invalid/unsound
inductive analysis: weak/
not cogent

11. deductive analysis:
invalid/unsound
inductive analysis: cannot
determine

12. deductive analysis:
invalid/unsound
inductive analysis: weak/
not cogent

13. deductive analysis:
invalid/unsound
inductive analysis: cannot
determine

14. deductive analysis: valid
inductive analysis: strong

15. deductive analysis: valid
inductive analysis: strong

16. deductive analysis:
invalid/unsound
inductive analysis: cannot
determine

17. deductive analysis:
invalid/unsound
inductive analysis: weak/
not cogent

18. deductive analysis: valid
inductive analysis: strong

8. Every fire needs oxygen.
    There is no oxygen in that room.
    There is no fire in that room.

9. Carly tossed a coin ten times and in each case it came up heads.
    I have a feeling that it is a trick coin.
    The next toss will be heads.

10. Carly tossed a coin ten times and in each case it came up heads.
    The law of averages says that this cannot go on indefinitely.
    The next toss will be tails.

*11. No element with an atomic weight less than 46 is a metal.
    Z is an element with an atomic weight of 79.
    Z is a metal.

12. No element with an atomic weight less than 46 is a metal.
    Z is an element with an atomic weight of 32.
    Z is a metal.

13. No element with an atomic weight less than 46 is a metal.
    Z is an element with an atomic weight of 79.
    Z is not a metal.

14. No element with an atomic weight less than 46 is a metal.
    Z is an element with an atomic weight of 32.
    Z is not a metal.

15. Antibiotics have no effect on viruses.
    You have a disease that is caused by a virus.
    You are taking the antibiotic Q.
    The antibiotic you are taking will have no effect on your disease.

*16. Some antibiotics are effective for treating certain bacterial infections.
    You have a bacterial infection.
    You are taking the antibiotic Q.
    The antibiotic you are taking will be effective in treating your bacterial infection.

17. Anyone over 21 years of age can legally play the slot machines in Las Vegas.
    Joyce can legally play the slot machines in Las Vegas.
    Joyce is 33 years old.

18. Anyone over 21 years of age can legally play the slot machines in Las Vegas.
    Joyce is 33 years old.
    Joyce can legally play the slot machines in Las Vegas.

*19. Every orange has seeds.

I am eating a fruit that does not have seeds.

What I am eating is not an orange.

20. Every orange has seeds.

I am eating a fruit with seeds.

What I am eating is an orange.

19. deductive analysis: valid/unsound

inductive analysis: strong/ not cogent

20. deductive analysis: invalid/unsound

inductive analysis: weak/ not cogent

SUMMARY

- It is important to distinguish the truth or falsity of statements from the logical question of what follows from those statements. Concentrating on the logical component of an inference allows us to see how deductive analysis focuses on logical certainty, while inductive analysis deals with uncertainty.

- A truth content error (TE) is one in which the information given is false. A logical component error (LE) is one in which the premises, even if true, logically allow the conclusion to be false.

- A valid inference is one in which the relationship between the premises and the conclusion guarantees that if you start with true premises, you will never get a false conclusion (no LE). An invalid inference occurs when a LE exists.

- The inferences in this text can be classified as deductive or inductive. Since deductive inferences are judged by the criteria of certainty, all deductive inferences are either valid or invalid. However, there are many times when certainty cannot be achieved, nor should it be expected. Since inductive inferences deal with uncertainty, we can classify inductive inferences as strong, moderate, weak, etc., depending on the probability of the conclusion being true if the premises are true.

- Both logical and truth content concerns dictate that our ultimate goal is to achieve the best reasoning possible. For deduction, if an inference has true premises (the truth content) and it is valid, then it is called sound. For induction, if an inference has true premises (the truth content) and it is strong or moderate, then it is called cogent.

- A good knowledge of both deductive and inductive logic provides the skills necessary to evaluate and construct inferences with an eye toward certainty or the acknowledgment of uncertainty. These skills serve dual purposes. First, the skills enable us to show the logical structure of someone else's inference, putting us in a position to offer coherent and precise criticism of those inferences. Second, they enable us to subject our own inferences to that same analysis, thereby anticipating challenges and criticisms.

KEY TERMS

inference   3
statement   3
premise   3
conclusion   3
truth content   4
logical component   4
logical relationship   5
truth content error
   (*TE*)   11
logical component error
   (*LE*)   12

deductive analysis   21
logical certainty   21
valid inference   21
invalid inference   22
equivocation   24
deductive inference   28
inductive inference   28
sound inference   30
unsound inference   30
inductive analysis   30

analogical inference   31
statistical inference   31
causal inference   31
probability theory   31
strong inference   33
moderate inference   33
weak inference   33
cogent   33
not cogent   33

LOGIC CHALLENGE: THE PROBLEM OF THE HATS

We can use what we have learned to help solve logical problems. The *Problem of the Hats* is a good challenge. The answer is not easily discovered; it requires "seeing" a key move. Once you are given the facts of the case, be aware of how you attack the problem, how you take it apart, what you place emphasis on, avenues of pursuit, plausible conjectures, etc. This will provide you with immediate clues as to how scientists, philosophers, mathematicians, detectives, logicians, physicians, etc. solve problems and test explanations.

The problem is this: A teacher comes to class with a box and shows the contents of the box to the students. It contains three white hats, two red hats, and nothing else. There happen to be only three students in this class and the teacher tells them that he is going to blindfold each one of them and then place one of the five hats on each of their heads. The remaining two hats will then be placed back in the box so no one can see them when the blindfolds are removed. The teacher then tells the students that if anyone can tell what color hat they have on their heads, then the teacher will give them an "A." However, the students are not allowed to guess the color of their hats, they must be able to *prove* they have that color hat. The teacher removes the blindfold from the first student who is now able to see the color of the hats on the other two students' heads, but he cannot see his own hat. The first student looks carefully at the other two hats, thinks for a while, and says he does not know the color of his hat. (The student does *not* say aloud the color of the hats he sees on the other two students' heads.)

The teacher then removes the blindfold from the second student who looks at the other two students' hats, thinks for a while, and says he does not know the color of his hat either. (As before, this student does *not* say aloud the color of the hats he sees on the other two students' heads.) Just as the teacher is about to remove the blindfold from the third student, the third student says that she knows exactly the color of the hat on her head, and she doesn't even need to see the hats of the other two students to know this.

The information given regarding this problem is to be considered accurate. No information is being held back, no tricks are being played, and no word-games are used. All the information necessary to solve the problem is contained in the description of the problem.

There are three possibilities for you to consider. Which of the three is correct?

1. She cannot possibly know what color hat she has on her head.

2. She has a red hat and can prove it.

3. She has a white hat and can prove it.

Logic Challenge: See pages 17–18 of Instructor's Manual

Inferences: Assessment, Recognition, and Reconstruction

{ overview }

2.1 THE ROLE OF NEW EVIDENCE

2.2 INFERENCE ANALYSIS AND
    EVALUATION

2.3 LOGICAL STRUCTURE

2.4 EXPANDING SKILLS

In Chapter 1, we concentrated on analyzing and evaluating inferences by looking at the relationship between the premises and the conclusion. We will now expand our discussion and begin considering the role of "new evidence" and how it relates to our judgment of inferences.

2.1 THE ROLE OF NEW EVIDENCE

Imagine a case in which we have the following information:

1. An opaque jar contains exactly 100 marbles.
2. There are 99 blue marbles in the jar.
3. There is 1 red marble in the jar.
4. This is a "fair" game.

Next, we are told that someone is going to reach in and pick one marble, and we are to guess what color it will be. Two people make guesses: one chooses blue, the other red. We now have two separate inferences to evaluate.

Inference #1

1. An opaque jar contains exactly 100 marbles.
2. There are 99 blue marbles in the jar.
3. There is 1 red marble in the jar.
4. This is a "fair" game.
   The marble picked will be blue.

chapter

Inference #2

1. An opaque jar contains exactly 100 marbles.
2. There are 99 blue marbles in the jar.
3. There is 1 red marble in the jar.
4. This is a "fair" game.
   The marble picked will be red.

To exercise our skills, we will analyze these inferences *as if they were deductive*. At this point, you should be able to recognize that both inferences are invalid, because the probability that the conclusion is true is less than 100 percent, if the premises are true. Even though the conclusion in Inference #1 has a of 99 percent probability of being correct if the premises are true, the conclusion is not certain to be true; therefore, Inference #1 is invalid.

On the other hand, and again to exercise our skills, we can analyze these inferences *as if they were inductive*. Doing so allows us to say that Inference #1 is far superior to Inference #2 (and yet both inferences have the same premises). Moreover, we can say that Inference #1 is extremely strong on its own merits.

Now suppose we are shown the actual marble picked and it is blue. Does this mean that Inference #1 now becomes valid? The answer is "No." The truth content results can never affect the discussion of validity, which is a judgment based on the *what if* question alone. Deductive analysis tells us that since it is possible to pick red, the conclusion is not certain, thus Inference #1 is invalid.

What happens if the marble picked is red? Does this affect the inductive analysis? Does Inference #2 become superior to Inference #1? Again, the answer is "No," because we calculated the probability of the conclusion in each case based on premises 1–4 being accepted as true, and the actual results do not affect this— Inference #1 would still be, inductively speaking, stronger than Inference #2. However, at this point new evidence can be a factor in both our understanding and appreciation of the complexity of real-life situations and the role of uncertainty. We saw that picking a red marble (or a blue one) would not affect either our deductive evaluations or our probability calculations, which were done on the assumption that the premises were true. Now suppose that the red marble is returned to the jar, the jar is shaken, and the second pick yields another red marble. The probability of this happening is $1/100 \times 1/100 = 1/10,000$, which is large, but not impossible. In fact, in a very long series of picks, we would eventually expect this to happen. However, suppose that the next five picks all turn up red (each time we return the red marble and shake the jar). The probability is now 1/100 multiplied by itself seven times (that is, the original two picks plus five more, all turning up red). We must not overlook how we are calculating this. We are still under the assumption that premises 1–4 are all true. This is how we are coming up with the probabilities. However, at some point the new evidence (the actual results) might cause us to question the truth of the premises. We might begin to question the proportion of red to blue marbles. We might even doubt that there are any blue ones at all, or if there are one hundred marbles. It could even be that this is a scam; the person picking the marble palms a red one and never really puts it back. In other words, we might start doubting the truth of any or all of the premises. Notice that these possibilities are generated from the new evidence, because we are trying to explain why we are getting these unexpected results.

We can build on this example. Let's restate premises 1–4.

1. An opaque jar contains exactly 100 marbles.
2. There are 99 blue marbles in the jar.
3. There is 1 red marble in the jar.
4. This is a "fair" game.

We can derive a different conclusion and get this inference:

Inference #3

1. An opaque jar contains exactly 100 marbles.
2. There are 99 blue marbles in the jar.
3. There is 1 red marble in the jar.
4. This is a "fair" game.
   The probability that the marble picked will be blue is 99 percent.

Deductive analysis shows that this inference is valid, because if the premises are true, then this particular conclusion is true as well. In fact, this conclusion does not really say anything different from premises 1–4. This is a valid inference because the conclusion does not go beyond what is already in the premises.

Does the new evidence we have gathered (the repeating picking of the red marble) affect the conclusion in Inference #3? What if we decide that one of the original premises is false? Does this change the inference from valid to invalid? No, it does not. Understanding why this is the case reaches the heart of deduction. Since validity/invalidity is merely a question of the logical component (a question of What if the premises are true), any discussion of the actual truth/falsity (what is) of the premises is irrelevant. Validity concerns itself with one question only: "If the premises are true, can the conclusion ever be false?" As far as Inference #3 is concerned, the answer is "No." Although the conclusion in Inference #1 is a statement similar to the conclusion in Inference #3 ("The marble picked will be blue" versus "The marble picked has a probability of 99 percent of being blue"), nevertheless, it is different enough to ensure that Inference #1 is invalid while Inference #3 is valid. Now if the new evidence is such that we seriously doubt the truth of at least one of the premises, then Inference #3 might eventually be considered valid, but not sound, provided we have decided that at least one of the premises is false (the truth content).

This discussion of the actual truth or falsity of a premise and the results of new evidence can have a very serious impact on the results of the inductive analysis of an inference. Additional evidence that, if true, can either support or weaken the conclusion should be considered as part of the complete inductive analysis process. New evidence added as premises can change the strength or weakness of the inference, as well as influence our judgment of the inference as being either cogent or not cogent.

EXERCISE SET 2.1   ○○○

The inference below is, deductively speaking, invalid. However, we can also analyze the inference inductively. In order to apply inductive analysis to the inference you will be given additional information, and you will have to decide whether the new information strengthens or weakens the inference. Evaluate each new piece of information independently of the others.

<u>Your car won't start.</u>
Your battery is dead.

1. The headlights don't work.

Answer: Strengthens the inference
    Headlights draw their power from the battery; therefore, this new evidence strengthens the inference.

Exercises 2–20: For answers
and explanations,
see pages 26–27 of
Instructor's Manual.

2. The headlights do work.

2. Weakens the inference

3. Strengthens the inference

3. The battery is five years old.

4. Weakens the inference

4. The battery is three months old.

5. Weakens the inference

5. The horn works.

6. Strengthens the inference

*6. The horn does not work.

7. Weakens the inference

7. The positive terminal clamp is loose.

8. Strengthens the inference

8. The terminal clamps are tight.

9. Strengthens the inference

9. When you jump-start the car, it starts right up.

10. Weakens the inference

10. When you jump-start the car, it does not start right up.

Apply the same inductive analysis to the next inference. Evaluate the additional information to decide if that particular piece of information strengthens or weakens the inference. Treat each new piece of information independently of the others.

<u>The lamp in your room does not work.</u>
The light bulb is defective.

11. The ceiling light works.

Answer: Strengthens the inference
    If the ceiling light works, then there is electricity available in the room.

12. Strengthens the inference

12. The lamp is plugged into the wall socket correctly.

13. Strengthens the inference

13. Your radio is working and it is connected to the same outlet as the lamp.

14. Weakens the inference

14. The ceiling light does not work.

15. Weakens the inference

15. The lamp is not plugged into the wall socket correctly.

16. Weakens the inference

*16. Your radio is not working and it is connected to the same outlet as the lamp.

17. Strengthens the inference

17. You replace the light bulb and the lamp now works.

18. Weakens the inference

18. You replace the light bulb and the lamp does not work.

*19. Every other electrical fixture in the room works. Strengthens the inference

 20. No electrical fixture in the room works. Weakens the inference

2.2 INFERENCE ANALYSIS AND EVALUATION

In deductive analysis, we use the logical component to determine whether the inference is valid or invalid. Using truth content analysis enables us to judge those inferences as sound or unsound. On the other hand, the classification of inductive inferences as strong, moderate, or weak relies heavily on *qualitative* measurement.

We do not generally quantify the range of probability values that would sharply separate and define a strong, moderate, or weak inference. Nevertheless, this does not mean that there is no objective way to classify inductive inferences. There is general agreement that an inference should be classified as *strong* when the conclusion has at least a 90 percent chance of being true. An inference should be classified as *weak* when the conclusion has a 50 percent or less chance of being true. An inference should be classified as *moderate* when the conclusion has a greater than 50 percent chance of being true, but it is less than 90 percent. These designations are not meant to create sharp boundaries, especially when in most real-life cases we will not be able to precisely calculate the probability of the conclusion. For deductive analysis there is, of course, a sharp boundary: any inference with less than 100 percent chance of the conclusion being true is invalid. Inductive analysis tries to assess uncertainty, a difficult concept to quantify.

It does seem reasonable to expect that any classification decision must be backed up with good reasons. In fact, the qualitative nature of inductive classification allows us to make added distinctions, such as *very strong, very weak,* or *moderately strong.* In addition, a good inductive analysis allows us to assert that one inference is stronger or weaker than another. We can also classify more than two inferences by asserting that one is the strongest, another is the weakest, etc. The following diagram illustrates the different classifications available for both deductive and inductive inferences.

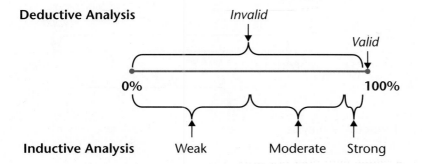

Let's look at another extended example of how to analyze and evaluate a series of inferences using the idea of "new evidence." In the following thought experiment, suppose that you and a friend are in a room where information is going to be relayed to you—information whose truth content you cannot confirm. Nevertheless, you are told to accept it as true (the information might be coming by phone or a loudspeaker). Your friend's task is to *infer consequences* of this information, while your task is to *evaluate* those inferences. The information coming in tells you that someone has thrown a die (one of a pair of identical dice) and your friend has to guess what number came up. Your friend writes down all the incoming relevant information:

Example 2.1

1. One, and only one, die has been tossed.
2. The die was tossed only once.
3. The die has six sides numbered 1, 2, 3, 4, 5, 6.
4. It is a "fair" die and a "fair" toss.

Since there is nothing so far to distinguish one possibility from another, your friend takes a wild guess that the number that came up on the die is "5." Your job is to assess the inference created by this guess.

1. One, and only one, die has been tossed.
2. The die was tossed only once.
3. The die has six sides numbered 1, 2, 3, 4, 5, 6.
4. It is a "fair" die and a "fair" toss.
   Conclusion: The number that came up is "5."

Sentences 1–4 are the premises used by your friend to support the conclusion that the die landed with the number "5" showing. Since there are six possible results, you can easily calculate the probability of your friend's guess (the conclusion) being true as 1/6 (approximately 17 percent), based on the premises given and accepted as true. You can then draw a diagram that uses an X to designate where this inference belongs.

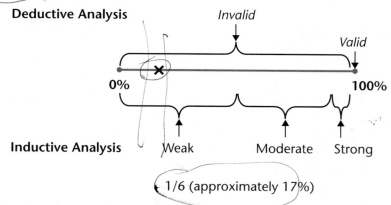

The X designates the probability of the conclusion being true, if the premises are true. With deductive analysis, X falls within the range of invalid inferences; with inductive analysis, X falls within the range of weak inferences. Since your friend was merely guessing the outcome of the die toss, it seems appropriate that we should classify the inference using the inductive assessment. Even though we assert that the inference is weak, we acknowledge that your friend's guess (the conclusion) might be true; it just has a low probability of being correct in relation to the premises.

Next, you are told that the number that came up is not odd. This becomes premise #5. Your friend now chooses the number "4."

1. One, and only one, die has been tossed.
2. The die was tossed only once.
3. The die has six sides numbered 1, 2, 3, 4, 5, 6.
4. It is a "fair" die and a "fair" toss.
5. The number that came up is not odd.
   Conclusion: The number that came up is "4."

Based on the new information given in premise #5, together with the information already given in premises 1–4, you now calculate that there are only three possible outcomes (2, 4, 6—the even numbers). Thus, the logical analysis of the new inference designates the probability of the conclusion being correct (if premises 1–5 are true) as 1/3 (33 percent).

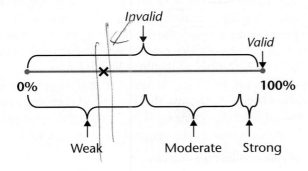

1/3 (33%)

Although the premises of this inference provide a higher probability that the conclusion is true than that given by the inference with only four premises (1/3, or 33 percent, is greater than 1/6, or 17 percent), this, too, is a weak inference. Based on deductive analysis, both inferences are invalid; however, deductive analysis has no provision for claiming that one invalid inference is better than another (or less invalid). On the other hand, the qualitative nature of inductive analysis allows us to assert that the second inference is stronger than the first, although they are both weak.

Now suppose that you are told that the number on the die is not "4." This information becomes premise #6. Your friend now guesses that the number is "2."

1. One, and only one, die has been tossed.
2. The die was tossed only once.
3. The die has six sides numbered 1, 2, 3, 4, 5, 6.
4. It is a "fair" die and a "fair" toss.
5. The number that came up is not odd.
6. The number is not "4."
   Conclusion: The number that came up is "2."

The logical analysis of this new inference is the following: If premises 1–6 are true, then there are only two possible outcomes—"2" and "6" (all the other numbers have been eliminated). This logical assessment is displayed in the following figure:

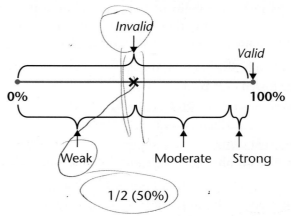

Again, with deductive analysis, we evaluate this inference as invalid. Although this inference has given the conclusion the highest probability so far (1/2, or 50 percent), even using inductive analysis, we would be hard pressed to classify it as anything but weak. If the conclusion has only a 50–50 chance of being true, then we seem to be justified in asserting that the premises do not place the conclusion in the moderate range (which is somewhat greater than 50 percent). However, inductive analysis allows us to assert that this inference is the best or strongest of the three inferences we have considered so far.

Finally, suppose you are told that the number that came up is larger than "3." This new information becomes premise #7. Your friend then announces, with some confidence, that the number that came up is "6." You then reconstruct the new inference by adding the new premise to the original six to get the following:

1. One, and only one, die has been tossed.
2. The die was tossed only once.
3. The die has six sides numbered 1, 2, 3, 4, 5, 6.
4. It is a "fair" die and a "fair" toss.
5. The number that came up is not odd.
6. The number is not "4."
7. The number is larger than "3."
   Conclusion: The number that came up is "6."

If premises 1–7 are true, the conclusion has a probability of 100 percent, the inference is valid, and it is logically certain that the conclusion cannot possibly be false.

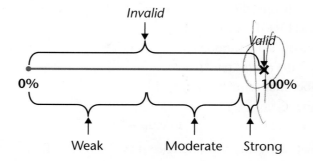

An inductive assessment of this inference is not as appropriate as it was when we were dealing with invalid inferences. Of course, logically speaking, this inference is superior to all the others because it is valid and they were all invalid. Since this is a purely imaginary example, we cannot inquire into the truth content of the premises to decide if this inference is sound or unsound. However, we have clearly and accurately assessed the logical component involved in all the inferences.

EXERCISE SET 2.2

Exercises 1–15 Calculate the probability of the following statements based on the information given. The statements are guesses about where a certain person lives (which house number). Additional information will be given which will require you to recalculate the probability of the guesses. The information given for each case constitutes the premises, and the guesses are the conclusions. In each case, determine whether the inference is weak, moderate, or strong. However, if the conclusion is guaranteed to be true, based on the premises, then it can be classified as valid. Provide explanations for your answers.

AVENUES

	A	B	C	D
76th	1	2	3	4
77th	5	6	7	8
78th	9	10	11	12
79th	13	14	15	16

STREETS

N
W ——+—— E
S

Based only on the information in the picture above, what is the probability of each of these three guesses?

1. The person lives in house #2.

Answer: 1/16, Weak. (Since there are 16 possible houses where the person could live, and no house has yet been ruled out, then each house has the same probability.)

2. The person lives in house #5. 1/16, Weak

3. The person lives in house #14. 1/16, Weak

Exercises 2–45: For answers and explanations, see pages 27–29 of Instructor's Manual.

Suppose you are given this additional information: The person lives north of 78th Street. If this is true, then what is the probability of each of the three guesses?

4. The person lives in house #2. 1/8, Weak

5. The person lives in house #5. 1/8, Weak

*6. The person lives in house #14. 0, Weak

Suppose you are given this additional information: The person lives west of Avenue C. If this is true, then what is the probability of each of the three guesses?

7. The person lives in house #2. 1/4, Weak

8. The person lives in house #5. 1/4, Weak

9. The person lives in house #14. 0, Weak

Suppose you were now given this additional information: The person lives in an odd-numbered house. If this is true, then what is the probability of each of the three guesses?

10. The person lives in house #2. 0, Weak

*11. The person lives in house #5. 1/2, Weak

12. The person lives in house #14. 0, Weak

Suppose you were now given this additional information: The person lives in a house number greater than 2. If this is true, then what is the probability of each of the three guesses?

13. The person lives in house #2. 0, Weak

14. The person lives in house #5. 100%, Vaild

15. The person lives in house #14. 0, Weak

Exercises 16–24 Calculate the probability of the following statements based on the information given. The statements are guesses about where a certain student is studying (which classroom number). Additional information will be given that will require you to recalculate the probability of the guesses. The information given for each case constitutes the premises, and the guesses are the conclusions. In each case, determine whether the inference is weak, moderate, or strong. However, if the conclusion is guaranteed to be true, based on the premises, then it can be classified as valid. Provide explanations for your answers.

CLASSROOMS

| 201 | 202 | 203 | 204 |

Based only on the information in the picture above, what is the probability of each of these three guesses?

16. The student is studying in classroom # 201.

Answer: 1/4, or 25%, Weak. (Since no room has been eliminated, all the rooms have the same probability.)

17. The student is studying in classroom # 202. 1/4, Weak

18. The student is studying in classroom # 203. 1/4, Weak

Suppose you were now given this additional information: The student is not studying in an even-numbered classroom.

19. The student is studying in classroom # 201. 1/2, Weak

20. The student is studying in classroom # 202. 0, Weak

*21. The student is studying in classroom # 203. 1/2, Weak

Suppose you were now given this additional information: The student is not studying in a classroom numbered higher than 202.

22. The student is studying in classroom # 201. 100%, Vaild

23. The student is studying in classroom # 202. 0, Weak

24. The student is studying in classroom # 203. 0, Weak

Exercises 25–45 While it is sometimes possible to calculate the precise probability of a conclusion being true, this is not always the case; it depends upon the information given in the premises. We can, however, always determine if an inference is valid or invalid, because that is an all-or-nothing determination. For the following inferences, if you can, calculate the probability of the conclusion being true, and determine whether the inference is valid or invalid, and if it is strong, moderate, or weak.

25. George was born in a month whose first letter is J.
    George was born in July. 1/3, Invalid, Weak

*26. George was born in a month whose first letter is J.
    George was born in a month that has 31 days.
    George was born in July. 0, Invalid, Weak

27. George was born in a month whose first letter is J.
    George was born in a month that has 31 days.
    George was born in June. 1/2, Invalid, Weak

28. George was born in a month whose first letter is J.
    George was born in a month that has only 30 days.
    George was born in June. 100%, Valid

29. A district attorney says the following:
    There are only three people who could have committed the murder: Joe, Sue, or Mike.
    Mike is the only one who doesn't have an alibi.
    Mike committed the murder. 1/3, Invalid, Weak

30. A district attorney says the following:
    There are only three people who could have committed the murder: Joe, Sue, or Mike.
    Mike is the only one who doesn't have an alibi.
    Any one of the three suspects who doesn't have an alibi is guilty of the murder.
    Mike committed the murder. 100%, Valid

*31. A defense attorney says the following:

There is no credible physical evidence to link my client to the murder.

My client did not commit the murder. Invalid, Weak

32. A defense attorney says the following:

There is no credible physical evidence to link my client to the murder.

Whenever there is no credible physical evidence to link a suspect to a murder, then that suspect did not commit the murder.

My client did not commit the murder. 100%, Valid

33. Capital punishment is the killing of a human being.

All killing of human beings is wrong.

Capital punishment is wrong. 100%, Valid

34. Capital punishment is the killing of a human being.

Not all killing of human beings is wrong.

Capital punishment is not wrong. Invalid, Weak

35. Euthanasia is a morally justified act.

Any morally justified act is not wrong.

Euthanasia is not wrong. 100%, Valid

*36. Abortion is the killing of an embryo or fetus.

An embryo or fetus is an innocent human being.

Any killing of an innocent human being is murder.

Abortion is murder. 100%, Valid

37. Abortion is the killing of an embryo or fetus.

An embryo or fetus is not an innocent human being.

Any killing of something that is not an innocent human being is not murder.

Abortion is not murder. 100%, Valid

38. If you smoke two packs of cigarettes a day, then you have a 75% chance of getting lung cancer.

G.H. smokes two packs of cigarettes a day.

G.H. will get lung cancer. 75%, Invalid, Moderate

39. If you smoke two packs of cigarettes a day, then you have a 75% chance of getting lung cancer.

G.H. smokes two packs of cigarettes a day.

G.H. will not get lung cancer. 25%, Invalid, Weak

40. Everyone who learned to play a musical instrument does well on math tests.

Walter learned to play the drums.

Walter does well on math tests. 100%, Valid

*41. Linda was born in a month whose first letter is A.

Linda was born in August. 50%, Invalid, Weak

42. Linda was born in a month whose first letter is A.
    <u>Linda was born in a month that has 31 days.</u>
    Linda was born in April. 0, Invalid, Weak

43. Linda was born in a month whose first letter is A.
    <u>Linda was born in a month that has 31 days.</u>
    Linda was born in August. 100%, Valid

*44. Going 55 mph in a 25 mph speed zone is speeding.
    <u>Not all speeding is a violation of the law.</u>
    Going 55 mph in a 25 mph speed zone is not a violation of the law. Invalid

45. Going 55 mph in a 25 mph speed zone is speeding.
    <u>Not all speeding is a violation of the law.</u>
    Going 55 mph in a 25 mph speed zone is a violation of the law. Invalid

2.3 LOGICAL STRUCTURE

An understanding of the logical structure of inferences can help you to recognize their logical commitments (what is being claimed) and to evaluate the support for those claims. The **logical structure** is the underlying logical relationship, and inferences can be analyzed by diagramming their logical structure. We have already used diagrams to analyze some inferences. In this section, the discussion will be expanded to illustrate the value and power of "visualizing" the logic of an inference.

Let's consider the inference in Example 2.2.

Example 2.2

Abdul is taller than Bette.
<u>Chris is taller than Bette.</u>
Abdul is taller than Chris.

The first step in uncovering the underlying logical structure of this inference is to substitute symbols for the names used in the inference. One assumption most people make when they read this inference is that "Abdul," "Bette," and "Chris" refer to humans. But notice that nothing in the inference states that they are humans. All we are told by the first sentence is that some *object* named "Abdul" is taller than some other *object* named "Bette." For all we know the names might refer to cats, plants, or even imaginary objects. Furthermore, because we are now interested only in the logical component of the inference, the truth content of the statements is irrelevant. One great advantage of symbolizing the inference is that it effectively defuses the truth content concern, thereby allowing us to concentrate entirely on the logical questions at hand. We will substitute the following symbols in the inference: A = "Abdul," B = "Bette," and C = "Chris."

Logical structure: The underlying logical relationship of an inference.

Example 2.3

Premise 1: A is taller than B
Premise 2: C is taller than B
Conclusion: A is taller than C

The use of symbols to replace names reveals the logical structure of the inference because it eliminates any specific reference to the named objects. In addition, the use of letters as variables allows us to replace the variables with any names of objects to test multiple substitution instances for the inference structure. Therefore, it allows us to concentrate on the relationship between the premises and the conclusion, because any specific content has been removed. Specifically, we want to know whether it is possible for the premises to be true and the conclusion false; in other words, is the inference valid or invalid? This can be answered by creating a *logical picture* that visually displays the logical relationship. If we start by making the premises true (working from the top down), we could get the following picture.

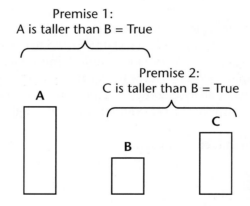

Premise 1:
A is taller than B = True

Premise 2:
C is taller than B = True

The next step is to interpret the diagram to determine the truth value of the conclusion.

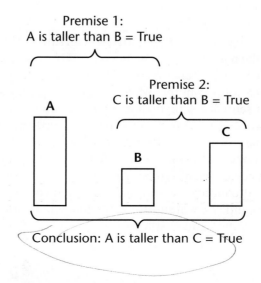

Premise 1:
A is taller than B = True

Premise 2:
C is taller than B = True

Conclusion: A is taller than C = True

This diagram reveals the possibility of true premises leading to a true conclusion. However, before we make any final decisions regarding the question of validity, we need to know if there is any possibility that true premises can lead to a false conclusion at the same time in one picture.

> **Logical loop:** A situation in which we miss alternatives because our minds are locked into one path of analysis.

At this point it will help to change strategy so that we do not get caught in a **logical loop**, a situation in which a problem is attacked from the same angle each time. Repeating the same approach to a problem may cause us to miss other possibilities. For the current example we can reverse course and analyze the inference from the bottom up, meaning we will temporarily ignore the premises and concentrate on the conclusion. It is important to recall that we want to find out if there is a case in which the conclusion is false while all the premises are true. For our current example, we must consider what the conclusion is asserting—that

Strategy

Analyzing inferences from the bottom up is a useful strategy for avoiding logical loops. This approach involves making the conclusion false and then trying to get all the premises true at the same time.

"A is taller than C." Since we want to draw a picture that will make this assertion false, we are left with two possibilities—we can make C taller than A or we can make C and A the same height. Suppose we make C taller than A.

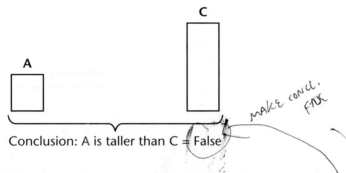

make concl. fals

Conclusion: A is taller than C = False

This logical picture effectively shows that it is possible to make the conclusion false. The next step in testing for validity is to see if we can make both premises true at the same time. Notice that the only missing part of our drawing is the B rectangle. We stipulate that each letter A, B, and C can be drawn only once per picture, which means that we can draw only one rectangle depicting B; however, we are free to make the B rectangle as tall or short as we like. Look again at the two premises. The two claims being made are that "A is taller than B" *and* "C is taller than B." We have to put B in a position relative to A and C such that the claims of both premises turn out to be true at the same time. If we can do this, we have shown that the inference is invalid, because we started by making the conclusion false.

Premise 1:
A is taller than B = True

Premise 2:
C is taller than B = True

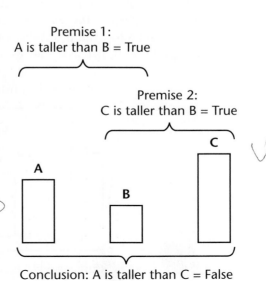

Conclusion: A is taller than C = False

This logical picture clearly illustrates the possibility that true premises can lead to a false conclusion. We have used the pictures to represent the logical structure in Example 2.3 to show that it is invalid. Therefore, we have also shown that the original inference in Example 2.2 is invalid as well (because it rests on an invalid structure).

Let's analyze another inference (Example 2.4):

Example 2.4

A is taller than B
B is taller than C
A is taller than C

This is similar to the logical structure in the inference in Example 2.3. In fact, the first premise and the conclusion are identical. As before, we are going to try to see if the truth of the premises guarantees the truth of the conclusion.

We can begin our analysis by working from the top down.

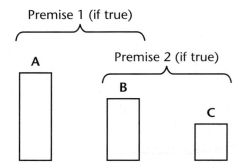

This picture is drawn from the information given by assuming both premises are true. Next, we interpret the picture by considering the case for the conclusion. Does the picture allow the possibility of a false conclusion? Well, in this picture with both premises drawn as if they were true, the conclusion is true, too.

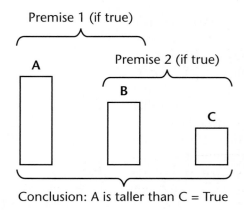

Conclusion: A is taller than C = True

However, before we declare this to be a valid inference we must be sure that it is impossible to draw a picture in which the premises are depicted as true and the conclusion false. Once again, we will analyze the inference from the bottom up, meaning that we will temporarily ignore the premises and concentrate on the conclusion. The conclusion of this inference is identical to that in Example 2.3, so we already know how to draw the conclusion as if it were false.

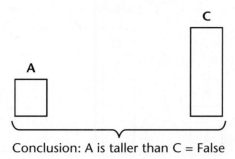

Conclusion: A is taller than C = False

Once again, this logical picture effectively shows that it is possible to have a false conclusion. Now, our next step in testing for validity is to see if both premises can be true at the same time. The only missing part of our drawing is the B rectangle, and we are free to make the B rectangle as tall or short as we like. Look again at the following two premises: The two claims being made are that "A is taller than B" and "B is taller than C." Can you draw B so that A will be taller than B (Premise 1 will be true) and at the same time B will be taller than C (Premise 2 will be true)? You can do one or the other, but not both. For example, we can draw the B rectangle as shown below.

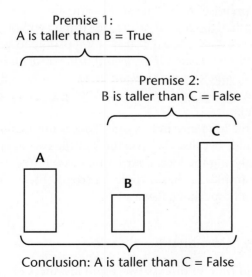

Conclusion: A is taller than C = False

We can see that with Premise 1 true, it is possible to have a false conclusion, but in this case, Premise 2 is also false. In order to prove that an inference is invalid, both premises must be true while at the same time the conclusion is false. This picture did not accomplish this task.

Suppose we try one more picture. This time let's draw B as shown below

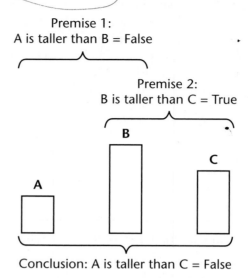

Premise 1:
A is taller than B = False

Premise 2:
B is taller than C = True

Conclusion: A is taller than C = False

We now can see that ensuring that Premise 2 is true results in Premise 1 being false. There is no picture we can draw in which both premises are true at the same time and the conclusion is false. Therefore, we have shown that if both premises are true at the same time, then the conclusion must be true as well—in other words, this is a valid inference. Make sure you try enough sizes of the B rectangle to convince yourself of this result. Also try using the second choice mentioned earlier; that is, to make the conclusion false, you can draw C as being the identical height of A. Once you have drawn this relationship, you should be able to verify that it is impossible for both premises to be true at the same time.

We have proven that the logical structure (using symbols) in Example 2.4 is indeed valid because we have shown that it is impossible to get a combination of true premises and false conclusion. *If the logical structure of an inference is valid, any substitution instance of that structure is valid as well*. If you replace the variables in Example 2.4 with any names, such as Abdul, Bette, etc., every specific substitution inference will be valid.

The reason that the inference in Example 2.3 was invalid while the inference in Example 2.4 was valid is because the structures of the two inferences are different. By revealing and analyzing the logical structure of each inference, we proved that the inference in Example 2.3 has a logical error (*LE*), while the inference in Example 2.4 is, logically speaking, flawless.

More on Equivocation and Stipulations

This would be a good time to discuss two more instances of equivocation, a type of mistake, or fallacy, introduced in Chapter 1. Example 2.4 dealt with the phrase "*is taller than.*" If we substitute the names of people for the symbols, "Abdul" for *A*, "Bette" for *B*, and "Chris" for *C*, then someone might try to upset our analysis of this inference by using photographs taken at different times. In one photo, Abdul, who is a now a full-grown adult, is clearly taller than Bette, making Premise 1 true.

In a different photo, Bette is clearly taller than Chris, making Premise 2 true. However, a third photo was taken when Abdul was young and short, and in this photo, Chris is taller than Abdul, making the conclusion false and the inference invalid.

To avoid this type of equivocation we need to stipulate that both the premises and the conclusion are to be analyzed using the same time frame, so we are referring to Abdul, Bette, and Chris (or A, B, and C) at one point in time. Now, for Example 2.4, if the premises are true, then the conclusion must be true, because we are stipulating that the identical time frame must be used throughout the inference.

Other instances of equivocation occur because many words have multiple meanings. Someone can use this to try to confuse us, as shown in these two inferences:

Tom is in a deep depression.
A deep depression is a hole in the ground.
Tom is in a hole in the ground.

Paul is feeling blue today.
Blue is a color.
Paul is feeling a color today.

To avoid these mistakes we stipulate that the meanings of all terms remain constant throughout the inference. This will eliminate the kinds of situations that occur in the above two inferences, and stop anyone from upsetting our analysis by changing the meanings of terms in our inferences.

Logical Loop

Earlier we mentioned falling into a logical loop. This happens when we fail to see alternative paths because our minds are locked into one way of analysis. We have all experienced the phenomenon of being in the dark when trying to solve a problem and then all at once the "light bulb" goes on and we instantly see the answer. The following puzzle illustrates how this happens.

Imagine that you are given a cake (with no icing) and a knife and are told to cut the cake into two equal pieces with one slice of the knife. However, (1) you must always cut the cake in straight lines, (2) you cannot stop a cut halfway through the cake and resume it at another place, and (3) you cannot touch the cake in any other way. This is easily accomplished as follows:

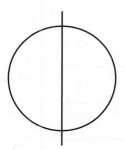

Once you have successfully cut the cake into two equal pieces, you are asked to cut the cake into four equal pieces with one more slice. You should be able to do this quite easily:

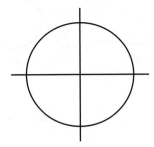

At this point the puzzle gets interesting. You are now asked to cut the cake into eight equal parts with just one more slice. Remember the rules: you must cut the cake in straight lines, you cannot start a cut in one place and resume it somewhere else, and you cannot touch the cake in any other way. Can you do it? Do you think it is impossible?

The solution will now be given. However, you should not read it until you have struggled with the problem for a while in order to experience fully the logical loop phenomenon. Here is the answer: The puzzle, as stated, has set your mind thinking in one direction by imagining the cake as a two-dimensional object, as depicted in the two pictures above. That being the case, it becomes difficult for most people to "see" the problem in any other manner. In other words, looking down on the cake makes it appear that it is impossible to cut the cake in eight equal pieces with one slice. But the cake is a three-dimensional object. It can be cut in half through its middle, leaving four pieces on top and four on the bottom, all equal to each other.

Logical Possibilities

Learning what logical thinking is all about is like learning a new language. You are being introduced to new terms, new ways of talking, and new ways of thinking. We are starting to build a logical vocabulary that allows us to talk coherently about some important ideas. One way we are building this vocabulary is by defining a small set of statements and then using them in simple inferences, allowing us to probe deeper into the concepts of validity and invalidity. This means that we have to define all circumstances in which they can be true and all circumstances in which they can be false. This process will be considerably expanded in the remainder of this chapter and in the next.

Our knowledge of logical structure will allow us to expand our understanding of validity. Validity guarantees that no matter what you substitute for the symbols in the logical structure of an inference, you can never get a substitution instance with true premises and a false conclusion. We make this claim because we have discovered that the structure of the inference is what establishes validity. If we are dealing with an inference that has only one premise and a conclusion, we can reconstruct all the combinations that are possible regarding the truth and falsity of the statements involved. Remember that when we are dealing with the inference's structure, the symbols have no truth content. (We can, however, imagine many possibilities if we substitute words for symbols.) It has already been stipulated that every statement can be either true (T) or false (F); therefore, if we consider an inference with two statements (one premise and one conclusion), we get four (4) possible combinations. Two statements, each of which can be taken in two different ways (true or false), give us $2 \times 2 = 4$ (Quick Reference 2.1).

Quick Reference 2.1 • The Four Possible Combinations of Truth Values for an Inference with One Premise and a Conclusion

	1.	2.	3.	4.
Premise	T	T	F	F
Conclusion	T	F	T	F

> There are four different combinations of truth values for an inference with one premise and a conclusion.

If you can show that it is possible for the premise to be true and the conclusion false (Column 2), then the inference has been proved invalid. If you can show that it is impossible for the premise to be true and the conclusion false, then the inference has been proved valid.

A valid inference guarantees that if the premise(s) are true, the conclusion cannot be false. Therefore, no matter what we substitute for the symbols revealed in the logical structure of a valid inference we will never have a false conclusion with true premises. Thus, validity eliminates one of the four possible combinations above. From what we have just said, it also follows that an invalid inference does not eliminate any of the four possibilities, because an invalid inference allows for the possibility of true premises and a false conclusion. Although a valid inference structure does not tell you what you will get when you substitute words for the symbols, it does tell you what you will *not* get, namely, an instance of Column 2.

We can expand this principle. If we are dealing with an inference that has two premises and a conclusion, there are eight possible combinations. Three statements, each of which can be taken in two different ways (true or false), give us $2 \times 2 \times 2 = 8$ (Quick Reference 2.2). If you can show that it is possible for the two premises to be true and the conclusion false (Column 2), then the inference is invalid. If you can show that it is impossible for the two premises to be true and the conclusion false, then the inference is valid. Therefore, a valid inference with two premises and a conclusion eliminates only one of the eight possibilities shown in Quick Reference 2.2. On the other hand, an invalid inference with two premises and a conclusion does not eliminate any of the eight possibilities, because an invalid inference allows for the possibility of true premises and a false conclusion. In Example 2.5 parts A and B we will use the same inferences as were used in Examples 1.4 and 1.5 (from Chapter 1) to show these results.

There are eight different combinations of truth values for an inference with two premises and a conclusion.

> **Quick Reference 2.2** • **The Eight Possible Combinations of Truth Values for an Inference with Two Premises and a Conclusion**
>
> | | 1. | 2. | 3. | 4. | 5. | 6. | 7. | 8. |
> |---|---|---|---|---|---|---|---|---|
> | *Premise 1* | T | T | T | T | F | F | F | F |
> | *Premise 2* | T | T | F | F | T | T | F | F |
> | *Conclusion* | T | F | T | F | T | F | T | F |

Example 2.5

A

Venus is closer to the Sun than Mars.
Mars is closer to the Sun than Earth.
Venus is closer to the Sun than Earth.

B

Earth is closer to the Sun than Mars.
Venus is closer to the Sun than Mars.
Earth is closer to the Sun than Venus.

Our analysis showed that the inference in part A was valid while that in part B was invalid. Following are the logical structures of these inferences.

A—Structure

V is closer to *S* than *M*
M is closer to *S* than *E*
V is closer to *S* than *E*

B—Structure

E is closer to *S* than *M*
V is closer to *S* than *M*
E is closer to *S* than *V*

Because the symbols *E, M, V,* and *S* do not stand for anything specific, they are *variables* for which we can substitute any planets, cities, countries, people, etc., that we wish. Sticking with planets will allow us to refer to the factual aspect (the truth content) of the statements referring to our solar system. The correct order of the planets in relation to the Sun is shown below.

Sun—Mercury Venus Earth Mars Jupiter Saturn Uranus Neptune Pluto

Since we have claimed that the inference in Example 2.5B is invalid, we should be able to show that Column 2 in Quick Reference 2.2 can be realized. In fact, the original statements in Example 2.5B already reveal this. Referring to the correct order of the planets we see that both premises are true, while the conclusion is false. Of course, we can also show a substitution instance of the logical structure in Example 2.5B, whereby we get an instance of Column 1. If this time we let *E* = "Jupiter," *M* = "Pluto," *S* = "Sun," and *V* = "Neptune," then we get the inference in Example 2.6.

Example 2.6

Jupiter is closer to the Sun than Pluto.
<u>Neptune is closer to the Sun than Pluto.</u>
Jupiter is closer to the Sun than Neptune.

Checking these statements confirms that we have created an instance of Column 1 from Quick Reference 2.2. Since we know that an invalid inference does not eliminate any of the eight possibilities, we readily admit that a Column 1 instance is possible. However, for deductive analysis purposes, we do not want inferences that sometimes have true conclusions and true premises (Column 1)—we want inferences that never have true premises and a false conclusion (Column 2). The fact that Column 2 is possible (as we have shown) proves that the inference in Example 2.5B—*Structure* is invalid.

If Example 2.5A—*Structure* is valid, then we should not be able to get any substitution instances of a Column 2. Validity means the elimination of only one out of eight possibilities (true premises with false conclusion). To confirm that this is correct you should use the information on the correct order of the planets to try to substitute some combinations for the variables in Example 2.5A—*Structure* to prove to yourself that you can never get a Column 2 substitution.

We can use the information in the illustration of the correct order of the planets for another discussion of some earlier inferences (Chapter 1).

Example 2.7

A

Venus is closer to the Sun than Mars.
<u>Mars is closer to the Sun than Earth.</u>
Venus is closer to the Sun than Earth.

B

Earth is closer to the Sun than Mars.
<u>Venus is closer to the Sun than Mars.</u>
Earth is closer to the Sun than Venus.

C

Earth is closer to the Sun than Mars.
<u>Venus is closer to the Sun than Mars.</u>
Venus is closer to the Sun than Earth.

D

Venus is closer to the Sun than Earth.
<u>Earth is closer to the Sun than Mars.</u>
Venus is closer to the Sun than Mars.

Truth content analysis reveals the following:

Example 2.7A: Premise 2 is false, so this inference has a truth content error (*TE*).
Example 2.7B: The conclusion 3 is false, so this inference has a *TE*.
Example 2.7C: No *TE*.
Example 2.7D: No *TE*.

Logical analysis has previously revealed this:

Example 2.7A: Valid; no logical errors (no *LE*).

Example 2.7B: Invalid; has a *LE*.

Example 2.7C: Invalid; has a *LE*.

Example 2.7D: Valid; no *LE*.

Looking closely, we can see that Examples 2.7A and 2.7D have the same logical structure:

W is closer to *Z* than *X*

<u>*X* is closer to *Z* than *Y*</u>

W is closer to *Z* than *Y*

If we combine our two analyses, we get this:

Example 2.7A: *TE* (premise #2); no *LE*.

Example 2.7D: No *TE*; no *LE*.

Since Examples 2.7A and 2.7D are both valid, only Column 2 in Quick Reference 2.2 has been ruled out as being impossible. The other seven columns can be realized, depending on the substitution instances. Our combined analyses for Examples 2.7B and 2.7C are this:

Example 2.7B: *TE* (conclusion); *LE*.

Example 2.7C: No *TE*; *LE*.

The most interesting inference for our consideration is in Example 2.7C. Notice that our analyses revealed two things: (1) the inference has a logical error (*LE*); (2) the inference does not have any truth content errors (no *TE*). What is important is that although Example 2.7C contains nothing but true statements, the logic is flawed. *Even though the conclusion is true, it does not logically follow from the premises.* This means that it is possible that even though the premises are both true, the conclusion can be false. The fact that the conclusion turned out to be true does not save the logical relationship.

This discussion of logical relationships can be best understood by comparing Example 2.7C with Example 2.7D. Example 2.7C had (1) a *LE*, and (2) no *TE*. Example 2.7D had (1) no *LE*, and (2) no *TE*. These two inferences have one thing in common—neither contains a *TE*. However, they produce radically different relationships. The flaw in Example 2.7C was clearly exposed when we drew the pictures showing the logical possibilities. Our logical analysis revealed that the premises, even if true, could not guarantee the truth of the conclusion. This is in sharp contrast with Example 2.7D, which, upon analysis, revealed the impossibility of ever getting the conclusion false, while maintaining the truth of the premises. Thus, while Example 2.7C gets high marks for truth content, it gets low marks as far as the logical component is concerned.

The results of our analysis of the inferences above show why it is so important to remember that when we evaluate inferences, we must always distinguish truth content from logical judgments. Inferences work on two levels, and we must ensure that our assessments refer to the appropriate level. It is therefore possible that, before analysis, any inference might turn out to have any combination of high/low marks on the truth content level and high/low marks on the logical level.

We can apply our understanding of the deductive concepts *valid*, *invalid*, and *sound* to what we have done. Thus, although the inference in Example 2.7A is, indeed, valid, it is not sound because premise #2 is false. The inferences of Examples 2.7B and 2.7C are not sound because they are both invalid. However, the inference of Example 2.7D, is both valid and sound.

Adding New Premises

We can sometimes add a premise to turn an invalid inference into a valid one.

Frank committed a murder.
Frank committed a felony.

This inference is invalid because it is missing a premise, which if added, would make it valid.

Frank committed a murder.
Every murder is a felony.
Frank committed a felony.

We can add a premise to make an inference valid but we must make sure that the new premise does not prevent the inference from being sound. If we add a premise that is false, it might make the inference valid but at the price of making it unsound. For example,

Frank committed a felony.
Frank committed a murder.

This is an invalid inference. It can be made valid by adding a new premise.

Frank committed a felony.
Every felony is a murder.
Frank committed a murder.

This is now a valid inference, but the new premise is false (not every felony is a murder; selling illegal drugs is a felony). So we must be careful to add premises that not only logically support the conclusion, but that must also be true.

EXERCISE SET 2.3

Refer to the following diagram for Exercises 1–6.

Los Angeles   Denver   St. Louis   Chicago   New York City   Boston

(1) Show whether the inference structures are valid or invalid. (2) If an inference is invalid, then substitute cities from the above chart for the variables to get true premises and a false conclusion (Column 2 in Quick Reference 2.2). Next, see how many other columns in Quick Reference 2.2 you can get by substituting cities for the symbols. (3) If an inference is valid, then see how many columns in Quick Reference 2.2 you can get by substituting cities for the symbols. In addition, show why it is impossible to substitute cities to get true premises and a false conclusion for the valid inferences.

1. X is east of Y
   Z is east of Y
   X is east of Z

Answer: Invalid. Here is one possible picture.

$$\longrightarrow E$$

Y   X   Z

There are many possible substitutions that will give factually true premises and a false conclusion. Here is one: Let X = "Chicago," Y = "St. Louis," and Z = "Boston."

Exercises 2–20: For answers and explanations, see pages 29–35 of Instructor's Manual.

2. X is east of Y
   Y is east of Z
   X is east of Z Valid

3. X is east of Y
   Z is west of Y
   X is east of Z Valid

4. X is east of Y
   Y is west of Z
   X is east of Z Invalid

*5. X is west of Y
   Z is east of Y
   X is west of Z Valid

6. X is west of Y
   Z is west of Y
   X is west of Z Invalid

Exercises 7–20 (1) Reveal the logical structure of the inference, and (2) show whether it is valid or invalid.

7. John is older than Mike.
   John is older than Sue.
   Sue is older than Jane.
   Mike is older than Jane.

Answer: Invalid

Let W = "John," X = "Mike," Y = "Sue," and Z = "Jane." The logical form of the inference is:

> W is older than X
> W is older than Y
> <u>Y is older than Z</u>
> X is older than Z

This picture shows that the inference is *invalid:*

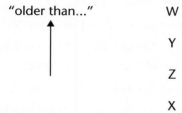

8. New York City has a larger population than Chicago.
   Chicago has a larger population than Pittsburgh.
   <u>Pittsburgh has a larger population than Los Angeles.</u>
   New York City has a larger population than Los Angeles.   Valid

9. New York City has a larger population than Paris.
   Chicago has a larger population than Paris.
   <u>Los Angeles has a larger population than Paris.</u>
   New York City has a larger population than Los Angeles.   Invalid

10. Bill Gates has more money than the author of this book.
    <u>The Sultan of Brunei has more money than the author of this book.</u>
    Bill Gates has more money than the Sultan of Brunei.   Invalid

*11. Sophie has a higher GPA than Nick.
    <u>Louis has a higher GPA than Nick.</u>
    Louis has a higher GPA than Sophie.   Invalid

12. Sophie has a higher GPA than Nick.
    <u>Nick has a higher GPA than Louis.</u>
    Sophie has a higher GPA than Louis.   Valid

13. Khalid has a higher GPA than Rahman.
    <u>Rahman has a *lower* GPA than Aziz.</u>
    Khalid has a *lower* GPA than Aziz.   Invalid

14. Khalid has a higher GPA than Rahman.
    <u>Rahman has a *lower* GPA than Aziz.</u>
    Khalid has a higher GPA than Aziz.   Invalid

15. Sue has more work experience than Lou.
    <u>Sue has more work experience than Tim.</u>
    Lou has more work experience than Tim. Invalid

*16. Sue has more work experience than Lou.
    <u>Lou has more work experience than Tim.</u>
    Sue has more work experience than Tim. Valid

17. Sue has more work experience than Lou.
    <u>Lou has more work experience than Tim.</u>
    Tim has more work experience than Sue. Invalid

18. My hybrid car gets better gas mileage than your SUV.
    <u>My hybrid car gets better gas mileage than his truck.</u>
    Your SUV gets better gas mileage than his truck. Invalid

19. My hybrid car gets better gas mileage than your SUV.
    My hybrid car gets better gas mileage than his truck.
    <u>Her moped gets better gas mileage than your SUV.</u>
    Her moped gets better gas mileage than my hybrid car. Invalid

20. My hybrid car gets better gas mileage than your SUV.
    My hybrid car gets better gas mileage than his truck.
    <u>Her moped gets better gas mileage than your SUV.</u>
    My hybrid car gets better gas mileage than her moped. Invalid

2.4 EXPANDING SKILLS

Studying logic enables us to master many important skills. It helps us to recognize and correctly identify inferences, whether in written or oral form. It provides the tools to analyze inferences by determining the logical commitments in the individual statements that make up the inference. **Logical commitments** are the necessary requirements for a statement to be true. Since statements are either true or false, there is a logical component in addition to the truth content. For example, the statement "She is going to a movie tonight *and* so is he," differs logically from the statement "She is going to a movie tonight *or* he is." The logical commitment of the first statement requires that both people go to the movie in order for the statement to be true. If either one or both of the people do not go, then the statement is false. The logical commitment of the second statement only requires that one person goes to the movie in order for the statement to be true. The second statement is false only if both people do not go to the movie.

We have analyzed and evaluated many inferences that were "given," that is, the premises and conclusions were presented whole. But in real life, inferences are rarely found in nice neat packages. We often have to dig them out, like prospectors searching for nuggets of gold. In addition, we often encounter incomplete inferences, so we must be able to recognize inferences even if they are not completely

Logical commitment:
The necessary requirements for a statement to be true.

spelled out. Since you already know a lot about how inferences work and how they are structured, you can draw on this background to help you in this new task. Complementing the skill of inference recognition is the ability to reconstruct inferences by displaying the correct relationship between the premises and conclusion. When necessary, we must also be able to reconstruct the inference by providing any missing premises and/or conclusions.

Recognizing and Reconstructing Inferences

An inference offers reasons (premises) in support of a conclusion. However, not all groups of sentences are inferences. A series of sentences that express beliefs or opinions, by themselves, do not constitute an inference. For example, suppose someone says the following:

> I think that the government is doing nothing about the unemployment situation. It makes me angry to see some CEOs of large corporations getting huge bonuses, while at the same time the corporation is laying off workers.

The sentences certainly let us know how the person feels about issues. Also, the sentences may be true or false with respect to the person's opinions. However, none of the sentences seem to offer any support (premises) for a conclusion. In addition, none of the sentences seem to be a conclusion. There is no assertion that one sentence follows from the others. Of course, it sometimes happens that opinions are meant as premises. For example, suppose someone says the following:

> I don't like movies that rely on computer-generated graphics to take the place of intelligent dialogue, interesting characters, and an intricate plot. After watching the ads on TV, I have the feeling that the new movie, *Bad Blood and Good Vibes*, is not very good. Therefore, I predict that it will not win any Academy Awards.

Although the first two sentences express opinions and feelings, they are, nevertheless, offered as reasons in support of the last sentence, which is the conclusion.

Many newspaper articles are good sources of information. They often are written specifically to answer the five key points of reporting, *Who, What, Where, When,* and *Why*. A well-written article will provide the details to the key points, but it is not necessary for the article to conclude anything. Often the reporter is merely trying to convey information that is not intended to provide evidence or reasons in support of some further claim. On the other hand, the editorial page of newspapers is a good source of inferences. Editorials generally provide extensive information (premises) that are meant to support a position strongly held by the editor. Also, the editorial page often contains letters-to-the-editor. Although these pieces are often highly emotional responses to social problems, some of them do contain inferences.

When people write or speak, it is not always clear that they are trying to conclude something. Written material can be quite difficult to analyze because we are generally not in a position to question the author for clarification. Although we cannot always be certain that what we think is the conclusion and the reasons to support it are, in fact, what the author had intended, we can, and should, attempt to provide justification for our interpretation. (If we are speaking with someone, at

Ada Byron (1815–1852) was the daughter of the poet Lord Byron. Her parents separated when Ada was only a month old, so she never got to know her father. When she was eighteen she met Charles Babbage, the inventor of the "Analytical Engine," an elaborate calculating machine. Ada Byron worked with Babbage for the next ten years trying to solve the complex problems associated with what we now call "computer programming," specifically, how to get a machine to do complex mathematical calculations and analysis. A major problem for Babbage was to get a machine to calculate Bernoulli numbers, which are sequences of rational numbers that are important in mathematical analysis and number theory. Ada Byron's work on this difficult problem culminated in her explanation of how the analytical engine could calculate Bernoulli numbers. What she created was an algorithm, a series of steps that achieve a final result. Her detailed plan regarding this problem is considered to be the first computer program ever developed.

Ada Byron envisioned machines that could do far more than just calculate numbers. She wrote of a general use machine that could "compose elaborate and scientific pieces of music of any degree of complexity or extent." In the late 1970s, the U.S. Department of Defense began work on a programming language capable of integrating many complex embedded computer applications. The successful program was given the name *Ada*, in recognition of Ada Byron's achievements.

least we can always stop the conversation and ask for clarification.) However, when we believe that we share a language and have similar sets of background knowledge, we can recognize the occurrence of inferences by calling on those shared properties. Since every inference must have a conclusion, it sometimes helps if we try to identify it first. Our common language provides a useful set of terms that nearly all of us call on when we wish to conclude something. For example, it is commonplace to use the word "therefore" to indicate the main point we are trying to make. Quick Reference 2.3 contains a list of **conclusion indicator words** or phrases you can use for help in recognizing the conclusion of an inference.

Quick Reference 2.3 • Conclusion Indicators

Therefore	Consequently	It proves that
Thus	In conclusion	Suggests that
So	It follows that	Implies that
Hence	We can infer that	We can conclude that

> Conclusion indicators include such words as "therefore" and "thus."

Here are examples showing the occurrence of some of these conclusion indicators.

> **Conclusion indicator words:** Words or phrases that indicate the probable existence of a conclusion.

1. Salaries are up. Unemployment is down. People are happy. *Therefore*, reelect me.
2. Salaries are down. Unemployment is up. People are not happy. *Consequently*, we must throw the governor out of office.

3. The book was boring. The movie based on the book was boring. The author of both the book and the screenplay is Horst Patoot. *It follows that* he is a lousy writer.

Although conclusion indicators can help us to identify the occurrence of inferences, they are not always available. In such cases, we must decide what the author's final point is. The following is an example of an inference without a conclusion indicator.

> We should boycott that company. They have been found guilty of producing widgets that they knew were faulty and that caused numerous injuries.

If you are not sure which sentence is the conclusion, you can simply place the word "Therefore" in front of each of them to see which works best. In this case, the second sentence seems to be the reason being offered for why we should boycott the company. In other words, *because* the company has been found guilty, *therefore*, we should boycott it.

This analysis leads us directly to the recognition of premises. A conclusion is meant to follow from a premise or premises. Analysis of the example above revealed the use of a premise indicator word. The word "because" was added to separate the premise from the conclusion. The word "because" can be a good indication that a reason, or premise, is forthcoming. Quick Reference 2.4 is a list of **premise indicator words** or phrases to which you can refer for help in recognizing an inference.

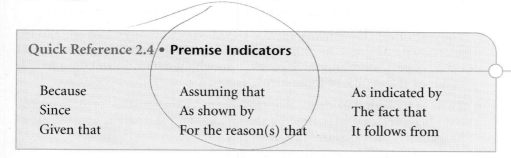

Quick Reference 2.4 • Premise Indicators		
Because	Assuming that	As indicated by
Since	As shown by	The fact that
Given that	For the reason(s) that	It follows from

Premise indicators include such words as "because" and "since."

When premise and conclusion indicator words are present, they can help us to identify the parts of an inference. When such words are not present, there are two other strategies we can use. To help locate the conclusion, try placing the word "Therefore" in front of the sentences. To help locate the premise(s), try placing the word "Because" in front of sentences.

EXERCISE SET 2.4A

Exercises 1–10 The exercises have been invented specifically to reinforce your logical analysis skills. They are not taken from outside sources; instead, they are fictional creations that reflect the kinds of information you might come across in newspapers, magazines, and journals. Determine whether or not the following passages contain inferences. Explain your answers.

Premise indicator words: Words or phrases that indicate the probable existence of a premise.

1. Our company has paid the highest dividends of any Fortune 500 company for the last five consecutive years. In addition, we have not had one labor dispute. Our stock is up 25% in the last quarter.

Answer: Not an inference

The three statements are not connected by any inferential structure. They can be used to support some other claim, but together they simply form a set of statements with no apparent premise or conclusion.

Exercises 2–11: For answers and explanations, see pages 35–36 of Instructor's Manual.

2. Our cars have the highest resale value on the market. Customer loyalty is at an all-time high. I can give you a good deal on a new car today. You should really buy one of our cars. Inference

3. I hate the new music played today. You can't even find a station on either AM or FM that plays decent music anymore. The movies are no better. They are just high-priced commercials for ridiculous products, designed to dupe the unsuspecting, unintelligent, unthinking, unenlightened consumers. Not an inference

4. We are going to have a recession. For 100 years, anytime the stock market has lost at least 20% of its value from its highest point in any fiscal year, there has been a recession. The current stock market has lost 22% of its value during the last fiscal year. Inference

5. It follows from the fact that she doesn't eat pork, chicken, beef, mutton, veal, venison, turkey, or fish, that she must be a vegetarian. Inference

*6. It seems like everyone I know has a computer or cell phone. The electronics industry is making better and better products every year. Not an inference

7. The cost of electronic items, such as televisions, computers, and cell phones, goes down every year. In addition, the quality of the electronic products goes up every year. More and more people throughout the world will soon be able to afford at least one of those items. Inference

8. There is biological evidence that the genetic characteristics for nonviolence have been selected over time by the species, and the height and weight of humans has increased over the centuries. Not an inference

9. She won the lottery, so she will quit her job soon. Inference

10. Income tax revenues help pay for many important social programs, and without that money some of the programs would have to be eliminated. If this happens, many adults and children will suffer needlessly. That is why everyone, individuals and corporations, should not cheat on their income taxes. Inference

Exercises 11–25 Pick out the premises and conclusions of the following inferences.

11. Exercise helps strengthen your cardiovascular system. It also lowers your cholesterol and increases the blood flow to the brain, enabling you to think longer. Thus, there is no reason for you not to start exercising regularly.

Answer:

Premises: (a) Exercise helps strengthen your cardiovascular system.

           (b) It (exercise) also lowers your cholesterol.

           (c) It (exercise) increases the blood flow to the brain, enabling you to think longer.

Conclusion: There is no reason for you not to start exercising regularly.

The indicator word, "Thus," helps identify the conclusion. The other statements are offered in support of this claim.

12. If you start a strenuous exercise regimen before you know if your body is ready, you can cause serious damage. Therefore, you should always have a physical checkup before you start a rigid exercise program.

Exercises 12–25: For answers and explanations, see pages 36–38 of Instructor's Manual.

13. Since television commercials help pay the cost of programming, and because I can always turn off the sound of the commercials, go to the bathroom, or get something to eat or drink, it follows that commercials are not such a bad thing.

14. Since television commercials disrupt the flow of programs, and given that any disruption impedes the continuity of a show, we can safely say that commercials are a bad thing.

15. We should never take our friends for granted. True friends are there when we need them. They suffer with us when we fail, and they are happy when we succeed.

*16. It is said that, "absence makes the heart grow fonder." So, my teachers should really love me, since I have been absent for the last two weeks.

17. "I think, therefore I am." Rene Descartes, *Meditations*

18. I believe that humans will evolve into androids. This follows from the fact that we will eventually be able to replace all organic body parts with artificial parts, and we will be able to live virtually forever by simply replacing the parts when they wear out or become defective.

19. Gary Kasparov has the highest ranking of any chess grand master in history. He was recently beaten in a chess tournament by a computer program. So, the computer program should be given the highest ranking in history.

20. It is true that $1 + 4 = 5$, and it is also true that $2 + 3 = 5$. Thus, we can conclude with certainty that $(1 + 4) = (2 + 3)$.

*21. The digital camera on sale today at Cameras Galore has 5.0 megapixels and costs $200. The digital camera on sale at Camera Warehouse has 4.0 megapixels and it costs $150. You said that you did not want to spend over $175 for a camera, so you should buy the one at Camera Warehouse.

22. You should buy the digital camera at Cameras Galore. After all, you did say that you wanted the most megapixels you can get for up to $200. The digital camera on sale today at Cameras Galore has 5.0 megapixels and costs $200. But the digital camera on sale at Camera Warehouse has only 4.0 megapixels and it costs $150.

23. The world will end on August 6, 2045. I know this because my Guru said it would, and so far, everything he predicted has happened exactly as he said it would.

*24. Fast food products contain high levels of cholesterol. They also contain high levels of sodium, fat, and trans fatty acids. These things are bad for your health. I am going to stop eating in fast food places.

25. You should eat more vegetables. They contain low levels of cholesterol. They also contain low levels of sodium, fat, and trans fatty acids. High levels of those things are bad for your health.

Explanations

Although we can generally rely on premise indicators to help recognize inferences, there are exceptions. The word "because" is often placed in front of an explanation, which provides reasons for why or how an event occurred. A simple example can reveal the difference between an inference and an explanation. Imagine that during an exam a student's cell phone starts ringing. After class, one of the students says the following to the cell phone owner:

> *Because* you failed to turn off your cell phone before entering the classroom, the loud ringing startled and disturbed the rest of the class when we were trying to concentrate on the exam. So I think it is safe to say that your behavior shows that you are self-centered, inconsiderate, and rude.

The speaker concludes that certain "character flaws" have been revealed by the facts of the case. In this setting, the word "because" is used to indicate that evidence is being offered in support of a conclusion; so we have an inference in the above passage.

Now suppose that the student whose cell phone started ringing responds as follows:

> I forgot to turn off my cell phone *because* I was almost in a car accident on my way to take the exam this morning, and I was completely distracted thinking about what happened.

In this setting, the word "because" is used to indicate that an *explanation* is being offered. This speaker does not dispute the fact that the cell phone went off during the exam, he is attempting to explain why it happened.

Let's consider another example. Suppose your car does not start. A friend might say, "Your car doesn't start *because* you have a dead battery." If you think the word "because" is acting as a premise indicator ("you have a dead battery"), then the conclusion would be, "Your car doesn't start." The problem with treating this example as an inference is that the alleged conclusion is not in doubt; it has already been established as true. We generally construct inferences in order to provide good reasons (premises) to support a statement (the conclusion) *whose truth is in question*. But in this example you do not need any reasons to believe that your car doesn't start—you already know that. Therefore, explanations do not function directly as premises in an inference, if they explain an already accepted fact.

Strategy

In analyzing inferences, always determine whether "because" is being used as part of an explanation or as part of a premise of an inference.

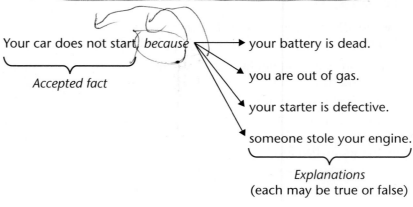

However, explanations can be used to construct inferences—the goal being to *test* the explanation (to see if it is correct). This is accomplished by doing an *experiment* in order to get a *prediction.* For example, if we propose to turn on the headlights (the experiment), then the person who offered the explanation ("your battery is dead") should predict that the headlights will not work (headlights draw power from the battery). We now have the makings of an inference. It would look like this:

> The car does not start. (*Accepted fact*)
> The battery is dead. (*Explanation*)
> Turn on the switch for the headlights. (*Experiment*)
> The headlights will not come on. (*Prediction*)

If the headlights come on normally, then the prediction (the conclusion) is false. This would tell us that the explanation is probably false. However, if the headlights do not come on, then the prediction (the conclusion) is true. This would tell us that the explanation is probably true. (The topic of explanations is further developed in Chapter 9, Applied Inductive Analysis.)

EXERCISE SET 2.4B ○○○

Decide whether each of the following passages is an inference or an explanation.

1. He did not come to work today. He must have found a better job.

Answer: Explanation

It is a fact that he did not come to work today; so an explanation is being offered.

2. For the last 10 years the best picture Oscar has gone to a drama. A comedy has no chance of winning the Oscar for best picture this year. Inference

3. Many Democrats have won midterm elections this year, even beating out strong incumbents. It must be because voters are disappointed with the way the Republicans are running the government. Explanation

4. The Republicans won the race for the White House and both houses of Congress, because they are in touch with what the majority of Americans think, feel, and believe. Explanation

5. An Independent candidate will never win the Presidency of the United States. This is because the two-party system of Democrats and Republicans is too powerful to ever let a third party get any wide base of support among the American voting public. Inference

*6. Computers will soon be in every home because the cost of buying one goes down dramatically every year. Inference

7. There has been an overall decrease in violence among humans worldwide throughout recorded history. Biologically speaking, this is because the genetic characteristics for nonviolence have been selected over time by the species. Explanation

8. Since there is biological evidence that the genetic characteristics for nonviolence have been selected over time by the species, we should see an overall decrease in violence among humans worldwide in the coming centuries. Inference

Exercises 2–10: For answers and explanations, see pages 38–39 of Instructor's Manual.

9. She just inherited one million dollars from a rich relative, so she will quit her job soon. *Inference*

10. She quit her job today because she inherited one million dollars from a rich relative. *Explanation*

Missing Information

It is not unusual to find inferences that appear to be missing some important information. Some people purposely leave out information because they assume we will fill in the missing parts. For example, someone might say the following:

> The novel I just bought is by Judy Prince, so I'm sure I'm going to like it.

If the speaker is someone you know quite well, then the assumption is that you will supply the missing premise by doing the following:

> The novel I just bought is by Judy Prince. *I liked every novel of hers that I have read so far*, so I'm sure I'm going to like it.

Inferences with missing premises, missing conclusions, or both, are called **enthymemes.** This term derives its meaning from the two roots, "*en*" meaning "in," and "*thymos*" which refers to the "mind." It means, literally, "to keep *in the mind*." The missing information is implied. Enthymemes are context-driven. Our recognition and subsequent reconstruction of the inference depends on the setting in which the information appears. However, sometimes we are expected to supply missing information with which we are not necessarily familiar. For example, suppose someone says this:

> I have a Toyota, so I don't have to spend much on maintenance.

The assumption is that we will supply something like the following:

> I have a Toyota; *Toyotas require very little maintenance,* so I don't have to spend much on maintenance.

Advertisements sometimes are effective because they are really enthymemes with missing conclusions. A billboard ad once had the following message:

> Banks lend money. We're a bank.

The advertisers were clever enough to know that most people would easily fill in the conclusion: "We lend money." Some slick television ads say very little, but they imply a lot. The visual nature is created in order for you to mindlessly fill in the missing conclusion: "If I buy this product, I will live the kind of life depicted on the screen." (Of course, nobody falls for this.)

We might encounter an enthymeme where the missing information must be filled in by adding a premise and a conclusion. Suppose a professional boxer is asked if he will win his upcoming fight. Displaying an air of confidence, he replies:

> The only way I can lose is if I die.

Enthymeme: Inferences with missing premises, missing conclusions, or both.

The boxer expects us to fill in the missing information in the following manner:

> The only way I can lose is if I die.
> I don't intend to die. *(Missing premise)*
> I will win. *(Missing conclusion)*

What we choose to supply as a missing premise or conclusion can affect the subsequent evaluation of the inference. For example, suppose someone says the following:

> My horse is fast, because she is a thoroughbred.

We might fill in the missing information in the following two ways:

1. My horse is fast, because she is a thoroughbred, and *all thoroughbreds are fast.*
2. My horse is fast, because she is a thoroughbred, and *most thoroughbreds are fast.*

The first reconstruction makes the inference appear to be *deductive*, and as such, if the premises are true, we can evaluate it as being valid. On the other hand, the second reconstruction seems to make the inference inductive. For present purposes we can stipulate that "most" means "at least 70 percent." In this case, the premises, if true, appears to make the conclusion likely to be true, so this inference might be classified as moderately strong. (Stipulations regarding the term "most" and some consequences of those stipulations are discussed in more detail in Chapter 9.) Which reconstruction is correct? One way to decide this is to complete the evaluation by analyzing the truth content. In the first reconstruction (the deductive inference), the added premise, "all thoroughbreds are fast," is false if even one thoroughbred is not fast. It would not be difficult to find at least one slow thoroughbred. If so, the inference would still be valid, but it would be unsound.

For the second reconstruction (the inductive inference), the added premise, "most thoroughbreds are fast," is probably true. If the other premise is true (if the horse in question is in fact a thoroughbred), then the inference is cogent. Given both analyses, we should choose the reconstructed inference that gives the benefit of the doubt to the person presenting the inference. This is sometimes referred to as the **principle of charity**. In this case, reconstructing the inference as inductive gives it the best possible interpretation.

Let's analyze the following inference:

> Bill Gateway is rich; it follows that he cheats on his taxes.

We can fill in the missing premise in these two ways:

1. Bill Gateway is rich, and *since all rich people cheat on their taxes*, it follows that he cheats on his taxes.
2. Bill Gateway is rich, and *since most rich people cheat on their taxes*, it follows that he cheats on his taxes.

Let's do a logical analysis first. The first reconstruction makes the inference deductive, and if the premises are true, it is valid. The second reconstruction makes the inference inductive, and if the premises are true, it is a moderately strong inference. Now let's do a truth content analysis. In the first reconstruction the added premise, "all rich people

Principle of charity: When we have to choose between different reconstructions of another person's inference, we should choose the reconstructed inference that gives the benefit of the doubt to the person presenting the inference.

Strategy

Supplying alternative missing premises allows us to assess someone else's inference fairly. This strategy can help us determine whether the inference is invalid or weak.

cheat on their taxes," is false if even one rich person does not cheat on his or her taxes. It seems likely that at least one rich person has successfully gone through an exhaustive tax audit. Thus, the inference is valid, but unsound.

For the second reconstruction (the inductive inference), the truth content of the added premise, "most rich people cheat on their taxes," is not so obvious. Whether you see this as probable might depend, in part, on your socioeconomic status. While most people probably have strong feelings regarding the truth or falsity of this added premise, what is needed is objective evidence to decide the issue. If the Internal Revenue Service (IRS) published a report stating that 70 percent of all *rich* people who have been audited have been found to cheat on their taxes, then this could be used as objective evidence to show the premise is true. If so, the inference is cogent. (The word "rich" was italicized because we would have to define, for purposes of analysis, what amount of income constitutes someone being rich.) However, if the IRS published a report stating that only 15 percent of all *rich* people who have been audited have been found to cheat on their taxes, then this could be used as objective evidence to show the premise is false. If so, we would classify the inference as not cogent, because a premise is false.

There is another interesting point to consider regarding inductive inferences. Since they have a built-in uncertainty, it turns out that new information (premises) can seriously affect their strength. Additional premises can cause inductive inference to go from weak to strong, or vice versa. Consider the following inference:

> I just drank a bottle of Sunrise Spring Mineral Water. Since it has been shown that most bottled water is safe, I can conclude, with some confidence, that the water was safe.

If the premises are true, then this is a moderately strong inference. However, suppose we pick up the newspaper and read an article reporting the following:

> Happy Sunshine Manufacturing Corporation has announced that it is recalling all of its Sunrise Spring Mineral Water due to a suspected contamination occurring in one of its bottling facilities. Anyone having purchased this product is advised to return it to the store of purchase for a full refund.

When added as additional premises this new information makes the original conclusion unlikely to be true, thus its addition makes the inference weak.

New information can affect a deductive inference, but only in one direction. As we saw in the early example where someone was guessing what number came up on a die, the new information made the conclusion more and more likely to be true (although the inferences were still invalid). However, enough information eventually became available to ensure that the final inference was valid. Nevertheless, the opposite result cannot happen. Since valid deductive inferences provide logical certainty, additional information can never affect that *logical* determination. *New premises cannot change a valid inference into an invalid one.*

EXERCISE SET 2.4C

For each of the following enthymemes, supply either the missing premises or the missing conclusion. First, try to make the inference valid. Second, try to make the inference strong. Explain your answers.

1. I am talking to a human; therefore, I am talking to a mammal.

Answer:

Missing Premise: All humans are mammals.

This will make the inference *valid*. In addition, since the *truth content* of the added premise is *true*, if the first premise is true, then it will be a *sound* inference.

Missing Premise: The vast majority of humans are mammals.

This will make the inference *strong*. However, since we saw above that we can create a *sound* inference, this would *not* be the best reconstruction.

2. I am talking to a mammal; therefore, I am talking to a human.

3. Shane owns a Honda, so it must be a motorcycle.

4. Shane owns a motorcycle, so it must be a Honda.

5. I have a headache. I just took two aspirins. Aspirins relieve headaches.

*6. The office laser printer can print 20 pages a minute in black and white or 10 pages a minute in color. It took one minute to print John's 10-page report on the office laser printer.

7. Vincent just had a big lasagna dinner, so I know he is very happy now.

8. Since Vincent just had a big lasagna dinner, it follows that he will soon be looking for the antacid tablets.

9. Jake has a viral infection. He decided to take some penicillin pills he had sitting in the medicine cabinet. But he doesn't realize that penicillin has no effect on viruses.

10. Jake has a bacterial infection. He decided to take some penicillin pills he had sitting in the medicine cabinet. Penicillin can be effective when treating bacteria.

*11. Hal must be an honest person, because he is an educated person.

12. There are 10 marbles in the jar, 9 red and 1 blue. I picked, at random, one of the marbles from the jar.

13. Susanna is a safe driver, so her insurance rates are low.

14. Walter has an expensive camera, therefore he takes perfect pictures.

15. Shane is a well-prepared and diligent student. Teachers respect students who are well-prepared and diligent.

Exercises 2–15: For answers and explanations, see pages 39–41 of Instructor's Manual.

SUMMARY

- In determining the logical structure of an inference, the first step is to substitute symbols for the terms used in the inference. The next step is to determine whether the inference is valid or invalid, which can be done by creating a logical picture that visually displays the logical relationship. Because only the logical component of the inference is under consideration, the truth content of the statements is irrelevant.

- Inferences can be analyzed from the bottom up, which involves making the conclusion false and then trying to make all the premises true.

- Validity guarantees that no matter what is substituted for the symbols in the logical structure of an inference, there will never be a substitution instance with true premises and a false conclusion.

- Two skills are fundamental to the reasoning process: (1) You must be able to analyze inferences by understanding the logical commitments in the individual statements that make up the inference, as well as the inference as a complete network. (2) You must be able to evaluate inferences by assessing the strengths and weaknesses of inference through both logical and truth content analysis.

- Because in real life inferences are rarely found in neat packages, you must be able to recognize and correctly identify inferences, even incomplete ones. Complementing the skill of inference recognition is the ability to reconstruct inferences by displaying the correct relationship between the premises and conclusion.

- When necessary, you must be able to reconstruct an inference by providing any missing premises and/or conclusion. An inference with missing premises or conclusion is called an enthymeme. Inferences can be reconstructed deductively or inductively. One way to decide this is to complete the evaluation by analyzing the truth content. The reconstructed inference that gives the benefit of the doubt to the person presenting the inference is the preferred one; this is called the principle of charity.

- New information (premises) can seriously affect the strength of inductive inferences because these inferences have built-in uncertainty. Additional premises can cause the inference to go from weak to strong, or vice versa. Since deductively valid inferences provide logical certainty, new information cannot change a valid inference into an invalid one. However, it is possible for new information to change an invalid inference into a valid one.

KEY TERMS

logical structure 55	conclusion indicator words 72	enthymeme 78
logical loop 57		principle of charity 79
logical commitment 70	premise indicator words 73	

LOGIC CHALLENGE: A CLASSIC PROBLEM

To begin this problem we must do some groundwork. For games of chance, we will define a "winning strategy" as one where employing the strategy ensures that you will win the game more than 50 percent of the time. A "losing strategy" is one where the strategy ensures that you will lose the game more than 50 percent of the time. Not all games allow for winning or losing strategies. For example, if we repeatedly toss a coin and you have to guess whether it will come up heads or tails, there is no winning or losing strategy (provided we stipulate that it is a "fair" game). However, suppose a game requires you to guess the color of a marble that is to be picked from a jar. You are told that there are ten marbles in the jar—six red marbles and four blue ones (again stipulating a "fair" game). In this case, there would be a winning strategy (pick red *every* time) and a losing strategy (pick blue *every* time).

Now we can begin our problem. You are picked from an audience and are given the chance to win a prize (the prize of your dreams). You are shown three doors and are told that behind one of the doors is the prize, while behind the other two doors is nothing. You can choose any of the three doors. (We stipulate that this is a fair game and the prize is always randomly assigned to one of the doors before you make your choice.) If all the doors were opened at this time, then we know that the probability of your winning the prize is one in three, or 1/3; and the chances of your not winning the prize, is 2/3. If you were allowed to play this game an infinite number of times, your odds of winning would never change. No matter what strategy you employ (for example, picking the same door each time), you can never raise the probability of your winning nor increase your probability of losing.

But our game is not going to be so simple. Instead of opening all the doors immediately after you make your choice, the game show host, who knows where the prize is located, puts a little twist in the game. The host says, "Before we open your door, let's see what's behind one of the doors that you did *not* pick." (The door is opened and nothing is behind it.) The host continues, "I am feeling generous today. I'm willing to let you change your mind. You can give up the door you originally picked and switch to the remaining door, or you can stick with your original pick. As soon as you make your final decision the game is over, and we will open both doors. Make your final choice."

If you were allowed to play this game over and over, what should you do? There are three possible answers for you to consider:

1. You should switch doors; this is a winning strategy as defined above.
2. You should stick with your original pick; this is a winning strategy as defined above.
3. It doesn't matter whether you switch or stick with your original choice; the probability is now 50–50.

Which of the three possible answers is correct? Why? You should give up your door and switch to the remaining door; this is a winning strategy. (See explanation on pages 41–42 in Instructor's Manual.)

Categorical Statements and Inferences

An important part of the logical analysis of inferences involves clarifying the possible conditions under which the individual statements that make up the inference can be true or false. To prove an inference is valid or invalid you must understand the logical commitments of the individual statements involved and you must be able to analyze the logical relationship between the premises and the conclusion of the inference. The foundation of our discussion in this chapter is the logic of categorical statements.

3.1 CATEGORICAL STATEMENTS

A **categorical statement** asserts a specific relationship between classes of objects. A **class** is defined as a group of objects having some recognizable common characteristics. Classes can also be referred to as *categories* or *sets*. We will use *S* for the class designated by the **subject term** of a categorical statement and *P* for the class designated by the **predicate term**. Every categorical statement either *affirms* that the subject term is related partially or completely to the predicate term or *denies* that the subject term is related partially or completely to the predicate term. In other words, we can say any of the following regarding S and P:

All *S* are *P*   No *S* are *P*   Some *S* are *P*   Some *S* are not *P*

The first categorical statement, "All *S* are *P*," is called a **universal affirmative statement**, because it claims that *all* members of the subject term are members of the predicate term. These claims are either true or false, but they can be decided only when the *S* and *P* are replaced by actual class terms, e.g., "All *trees* are *deciduous*." We can see in this example the assertion that every tree (the class designated by the subject term) is deciduous (the class designated by the predicate term). Since we know that there is at least one class of trees that is not deciduous (pine trees, etc.), the truth content of this particular instance of a universal affirmative statement is false.

chapter

Categorical statement:
A statement that uses sets, categories, or groups of objects (real or imaginary) to replace the variables in one of four specific forms—"All *S* are *P*," "No *S* are *P*," "Some *S* are *P*," "Some *S* are not *P*."

Class: A group, set, or collection of objects that have a common characteristic attributed to each member.

Subject term: The class designated by the first term in a categorical statement.

Predicate term: The class designated by the second term in a categorical statement.

Universal affirmative statement: The statement form "All *S* are *P*," which asserts that all members of the subject term are members of the predicate term.

Universal negative statement: The statement form "No *S* are *P*," which asserts that no members of the subject term are members of the predicate term.

Particular affirmative statement: The statement form "Some *S* are *P*," which asserts that some (at least one) members of the subject term are members of the predicate term.

Particular negative statement: The statement form "Some *S* are not *P*," which asserts that some (at least one) members of the subject term are not members of the predicate term.

BIOGRAPHY ⟩ ARISTOTLE

Aristotle (384 BC–322 BC) is often considered to be the originator of the study of logic. His ideas dominated Western thought for two thousand years, and his writings influenced every aspect of European culture: metaphysics, ethics, politics, aesthetics, and epistemology. So dominant were Aristotle's ideas that all subsequent scientific and logical thinking had to be reconciled with his work.

Aristotle's system of logic is based on relationships of terms. Categorical statements, such as "All humans are mortal," contain a subject term ("humans") and a predicate term ("mortal"). This is an example of a universal affirmative statement. It makes the assertion that the entire class of humans is included in the class of mortal beings. Aristotle wanted logic and science to complement each other, so it is not surprising that his logic was developed, in no small part, to solidify scientific reasoning. Aristotle's science relied on the idea of classification. Scientific knowledge is gained by the ability to classify a group of objects as a subclass of a class that is already well understood. This scientific disposition meant that Aristotle understood that at least some universal statements assume that the class of objects being referred to has members that actually exist. This requires that the truth content of certain statements be investigated in order to analyze some inferences. However, modern logical ideas have stressed the separation of the truth content and the logical component of inferences.

If we substitute "trees" and "deciduous" for the subject and predicate terms of the three remaining categorical statements, we get the following results: "No trees are deciduous," "Some trees are deciduous," and "Some trees are not deciduous." The first of these, "No trees are deciduous," is called a **universal negative statement** because it claims that *no* members of the subject term are members of the predicate term. This statement claims there is not even one member of *S* that is a member of *P*. However, since some trees are deciduous, the truth content of this statement is false.

The next example, "Some trees are deciduous," is called a **particular affirmative statement** because it claims that *some* members of the subject term are members of the predicate term. In other words, this statement claims that at least one member of *S* is a member of *P*. Our background knowledge of trees tells us that this statement is true.

The next example, "Some trees are not deciduous," is called a **particular negative statement** because it claims that *some* members of the subject term are *not* members of the predicate term. In other words, this statement claims that at least one member of *S* is *not* a member of *P*. Reference to our background knowledge of trees tells us this statement is true, too.

When a categorical statement refers to objects, such as "pine trees," the reference to the truth content of the statement seems natural. But consider this statement: "All unicorns are one-horned creatures." How do we interpret the truth content of this statement? On the one hand, we might say that the statement is true *by definition* (the term "unicorn" is defined as "a one-horned creature"). On the other hand, we might say the statement is false because no unicorns exist. This raises an important question regarding the interpretation of universal categorical statements. A statement is said to have **existential import** if it asserts the existence of objects. Given this, should it be assumed that *every* universal statement has existential import? If the answer is "yes," then the statement, "All unicorns are one-horned creatures" is false, since no unicorns exist. If the answer is "no," then the statement, "All unicorns are one-horned creatures" is true by definition, even though no unicorns exist.

It is obvious, then, that some universal categorical statements clearly have existential import ("All trees are deciduous") while others do not ("All unicorns are one-horned creatures"). However, if we have to decide in each instance whether an individual universal categorical statement has existential import, then we would be doing truth content analysis instead of logical analysis. Thus, a statement having the structure "All *S* are *P*" is understood as asserting that "*If* something is an *S*, then it is also a *P*." A statement having the structure "No *S* are *P*" is understood as asserting that "*If* something is an *S*, then it is not a *P*." This interpretation sets aside the truth content question concerning the existence of the objects referred to by the statement. Since the phrase "*If* something is an *S*," does not imply the existence of members of the class *S*, this interpretation can be used to diagram the logical commitment of the statement. Diagramming categorical statements will be discussed after the next section.

Existential import:
In a statement, the assertion of the existence of objects of some kind.

Quick Reference 3.1 • The Four Categorical Statements

All *S* are *P*	*Universal affirmative*
No *S* are *P*	*Universal negative*
Some *S* are *P*	*Particular affirmative*
Some *S* are not *P*	*Particular negative*

The four kinds of categorical statements include two universal statements and two particular statements.

Translating Ordinary Sentences into Categorical Statements

In Chapter 2 we saw that missing information required us to reconstruct inferences based on our understanding of the context in which the information was presented. Similarly, many sentences in ordinary language do not mirror the structure of the four types of categorical statements. These cases require us to reconstruct and translate the sentences into the structures we have been using. The translations are helpful because they clarify the meaning and reveal the logical commitments of the statements.

Ordinary language contains an unlimited number of possible sentences, so we will explore only a few of the most common occurrences. For example, the ordinary sentence "All sharks hunt" can easily be translated as the universal affirmative categorical statement "All sharks are hunters." The ordinary sentence "No sharks hunt" gets translated as the universal negative categorical statement "No sharks are

BIOGRAPHY   JOHN VENN

Although many people extended the ideas of Boolean algebra, perhaps the most useful of these extensions was brought to fruition by John Venn (1834-1923), in the creation of what has been come to be known as Venn diagrams. These diagrams differ from the use of Euler circles in a few important ways. If we want to analyze categorical syllogisms using Venn's system, we always start by drawing three overlapping circles of identical size. Each circle is then designated as representing one of the three terms in the syllogism: the subject term of the conclusion, the predicate term of the conclusion, or the middle term, the term that occurs only in the premises. When used in logical analysis, the distinct areas are then annotated to display all the possible class inclusion and exclusion assertions of the three categorical statements making up the categorical syllogism. Shading an area indicates emptiness and is used for universal categorical statements. The presence of an "X" indicates that a class is not empty and is used for particular categorical statements. These annotations are used for both affirmative and negative assertions.

The uniformity of Venn diagrams offers a perfectly mechanical method for determining the validity or invalidity of any categorical syllogism. In addition, Venn diagrams are often used in mathematical analysis to represent the union and intersections of sets.

hunters." Similarly, the sentence "Some people bowl" can be translated as the particular affirmative categorical statement "Some people are bowlers," and "Some people don't bowl" can be translated as the particular negative categorical statement "Some people are not bowlers."

Translating some ordinary language sentences requires an interpretation of the normal reference of the classes mentioned. For example, the sentence "A dolphin is a mammal" is best translated as the universal affirmative statement "All dolphins are mammals," since we normally refer to the entire class of dolphins when we classify them as mammals. For the same reason we would translate the sentence "A dolphin is not a fish" as the universal negative statement "No dolphins are fish." On the other hand, the sentence "A dolphin lives at the local aquarium" would be translated into the particular affirmative statement "Some dolphins live at the local aquarium," since the sentence surely is not referring to all dolphins. (The use of "some" is appropriate in this translation because its use in categorical statements means "at least one.")

The sentence "Every computer is a complex machine" refers to all computers, so it gets translated as the universal affirmative statement "All computers are complex machines." The same translation holds for the sentence "Any computer is a complex machine." However, the sentence "Not every computer is expensive" should get translated as the particular negative statement "Some computers are not expensive," because it is unlikely that the sentence is claiming that no computers are expensive. On the other hand, the sentence "Not any computer is expensive" should be translated as the universal negative statement "No computers are expensive," because it refers to the entire class of computers.

Quick Reference 3.2 • Translating Ordinary Sentences into Categorical Statements

Ordinary sentence	Translation
All sharks hunt.	All sharks are hunters.
No sharks hunt.	No sharks are hunters.
Some people bowl.	Some people are bowlers.
Some people don't bowl.	Some people are not bowlers.
A dolphin is a mammal.	All dolphins are mammals.
A dolphin is not a fish.	No dolphins are fish.
A dolphin lives at the local aquarium.	Some dolphins live at the local aquarium.
Every computer is a complex machine.	All computers are complex machines.
Any computer is a complex machine.	All computers are complex machines.
Not every computer is expensive.	Some computers are not expensive.
Not any computer is expensive.	No computers are expensive.

An ordinary sentence can be translated into one of the four categorical statements after reconstruction.

Diagramming Categorical Statements: Venn Diagrams

In diagramming categorical statements we use Venn diagrams. A **Venn diagram** consists of overlapping circles that designate classes, along with specific annotations attached to the circles. Since categorical statements contain two classes, we draw two intersecting circles and then annotate the drawing depending on the claim made by that statement. The basic structure of a Venn diagram for a categorical statement is shown below.

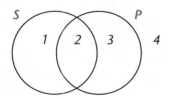

Area #1 designates those members of S that are *not* members of P. Area #2 designates those members of S that are members of P. Area #3 designates those members of P that are *not* members of S. Finally, in area # 4 there are *no* members of either S or P.

All S are P Our diagrams need to capture the logical commitments asserted by the categorical statements. In the statement "All S are P," the word "All" attaches

Venn diagram: A diagram that uses overlapping circles to represent categorical statements and to illustrate the validity or invalidity of a categorical inference.

itself directly to the *S* and *not* to the *P*. The statement is asserting something defi-nite about *S* (that every member of this class is a member of *P*), but it leaves open the question of the extent of the *P* domain.

All S are P

With this in mind, we can produce the Venn diagram for this statement.

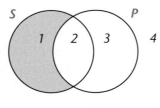

All S are P

Since Area #1 designates those members of *S* that are *not* members of *P*, the dia-gram must illustrate that this area is empty, that it contains no members of *S*. In order to show that an area is empty it is shaded. Therefore, the diagram illustrates what the statement asserts: *If* any object is a member of *S*, then it is a member of *P*. This diagram can be used to illustrate the logical commitment of any universal affirmative categorical statement.

The Venn diagram above provides the mechanism needed to do simple infer-ence analysis. To prove validity/invalidity we need only to consult the diagrams of the statements involved in an inference. For example,

All *S* are *P*
All *P* are *S*

If we assume the premise is true, then we can use our Venn diagram to represent it. The diagram will then reveal whether the premise does or does not logically sup-port the conclusion. The completed diagram will reveal whether the conclusion must be true (in which case we will have proven the inference is valid) or it will reveal the possibility of a false conclusion (in which case we will have proven the inference is invalid). This visual method of analysis enables us to *see* the logic of inferences. So, for the inference above, we can ask the following question: Is it pos-sible for the premise to be true and the conclusion false? Using the above diagram for the premise "All *S* are *P*" gives us the answer.

Premise: All *S* are *P* = *True*
Conclusion: All *P* are *S* = *False*

This one picture is all we need to prove that the inference is invalid. All we had to show was the possibility of a true premise and a false conclusion, and this we have done.

No S are P Our diagram of this statement needs to capture the logical commit-ments asserted by the statement. The assertion is that no member of the class S is a member of the class P. This is captured by the following Venn diagram.

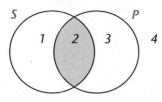

No S are P

Since Area #2 designates those members of S that are members of P, the diagram must illustrate that this area is empty, so it is shaded. This diagram can be used to illustrate the logical commitment of any universal negative categorical statement.

Once again, a simple inference can be constructed and analyzed using this statement structure.

No S are P
No P are S

Is it possible to make the premise true and the conclusion false? It turns out that it is not possible. The diagram shows the only way for the premise to be true.

Premise: No S are P = *True*

Conclusion: No P are S = *True*

As the diagram illustrates, if we make the premise true, we automatically make the conclusion true as well. Since it is impossible to make the premise of this inference true and the conclusion false at the same time, we have proven that this is a valid inference.

Some S are P We stipulate that "some" means *at least one,* so what the statement claims is that at least one member of S is a member of P. Unlike universal state-ments, particular categorical statements are always understood to have existential import. Therefore, the statement "Some S are P" is actually asserting that there exists at least one S and that it is a P. If it is claimed that there exists at least one member of a class of objects, then an **X** is placed inside the circle.

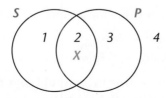

Some S are P

Since Area #2 designates those members of *S* that are members of *P*, the diagram illustrates that this area has at least one member. This diagram can be used to illustrate the logical commitment of any particular affirmative categorical statement.

We can now analyze a simple inference for validity using this statement structure.

> Some *S* are *P*
> Some *P* are *S*

The diagram shows the only way for the premise to be true.

> **Premise:** Some *S* are *P* = *True*
> **Conclusion:** Some *P* are *S* = *True*

As the diagram illustrates, if we make the premise true, we automatically make the conclusion true as well. Since it is impossible to make the premise of this inference true and the conclusion false at the same time, we have proven that this is a valid inference.

Some *S* are not *P* This statement structure is making a claim about the class of *S*—that there exists at least one member of *S* and it is not a member of *P*. As we saw earlier, if it is claimed that there is at least one member of a class of objects, then an **X** is placed inside the circle.

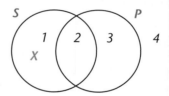

Some *S* are not *P*

Since Area #1 designates those members of *S* that are *not* members of *P*, the diagram must illustrate that this area has at least one member. This diagram can be used to illustrate the logical commitment of any particular negative categorical statement.

We can now analyze a simple inference for validity using this statement structure.

> Some *S* are not *P*
> Some *P* are not *S*

The diagram shows the only way for the premise to be true.

> **Premise:** Some *S* are not *P* = *True*
> **Conclusion:** Some *P* are not *S* = *False*

In order for the conclusion to be true there would have to be an **X** in Area #3 in the *P* circle. However, the information in the premise does not allow us to place an **X** there. Since we have clearly shown the possibility of a true premise and a false conclusion, we have proven that the inference is invalid.

Let's work through a simple, but interesting inference.

<u>All *S* are *P*</u>
Some *S* are *P*

As before, we can use the Venn diagram for a universal affirmative statement to diagram the information in the premise.

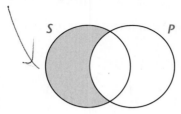

Premise: All *S* are *P* = *True*
Conclusion: Some *S* are *P* = *False*
The inference is invalid.

This illustrates the importance of understanding existential import. Universal statements are interpreted as not making any existence claims. This is why the diagrams for "All *S* are *P*," and "No *S* are *P*," use only shading of areas. The diagrams for these statements do not contain any **X's** to indicate that an object actually exists in a given area. However, particular statements are always understood to assert existence (that's why an **X** is used to illustrate that at least one of the objects actually exists). So, even it is true that "All unicorns are one-horned creatures," (by definition), it is false that "Some unicorns are one-horned creatures," because this asserts that at least one unicorn actually exists. In the diagram above, for the conclusion to be true there would have to be an **X** in the area where *S* and *P* overlap. But there is no **X** because a universal premise does not allow us to place an **X** anywhere, only a particular statement does. By claiming that this is an invalid inference, we are merely asserting the *possibility* of a true premise and a false conclusion, which is revealed by the Venn diagram.

Quick Reference 3.3 shows the Venn diagrams for categorical statements.

Quick Reference 3.3 • Venn Diagrams Are Used to Illustrate the Four Kinds of Categorical Statements

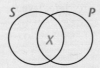
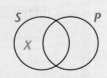

| All *S* are *P* | No *S* are *P* | Some *S* are *P* | Some *S* are not *P* |

Venn diagrams are used to illustrate the four kinds of categorical statements.

EXERCISE SET 3.1   ○○○

Exercises 1–20 Translate the following sentences into categorical statement structures by stipulating what **S** and **P** will stand for in each case. Then draw Venn diagrams to represent the logic of each statement.

   1. Some snowmen are permanent lawn fixtures.

Answer: S = "snowmen," P = "permanent lawn fixtures"

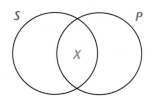

Exercises 2–67: For answers
and explanations,
see pages 50–66 of
Instructor's Manual.

2. No S are P

3. Some S are P

4. All S are P

5. All S are P

6. Some S are not P

7. No S are P

8. All S are P

9. All S are P

10. Some S are P

11. Some S are not P

12. No S are P

13. All S are P

14. Some S are P

15. All S are P

16. Some S are not P

17. Some S are P

18. No S are P

19. All S are P

20. Some S are P

   2. No leeches are lawyers.

   3. Some television newscasters are good actors.

   4. All donuts are lean cuisine.

   5. All psychics are frauds.

 *6. Some children are not following in their parents' footsteps.

   7. No volcanoes are currently active geologic structures.

   8. All ducks are daffy creatures.

   9. All teachers are miserable wretches.

  10. Some poems are beautifully written works of literature.

*11. Some viruses are not lethal to humans.

  12. No Nobel laureates are Olympic champions.

  13. All sea creatures are bivalves.

  14. Some rock stars are good parents.

  15. All condiments are free.

*16. Some exotic vegetables are not edible.

  17. Some scientific research is fraudulent.

  18. No television commercials are worthy of our attention.

*19. All finely tuned instruments are soothing to the ear.

  20. Some floppy disks are defective.

Exercises 21–35 Translate the following ordinary sentences into categorical statements.

21. An apple is in the refrigerator.

Answer: Some apples are in the refrigerator.

Although the sentence is referring to a particular apple, the use of "some" is appropriate in this translation because it has been stipulated that it means "at least one."

22. Any medical doctor is well-educated.

23. No insects sing.

24. A flower is a plant.

25. All happy people dance.

*26. Some bears hibernate.

27. Some cars don't pollute.

28. A mango is not a vegetable.

29. Not every dog is friendly.

30. Every office worker is under pressure to perform.

*31. A tsunami is dangerous.

32. Some people don't jaywalk.

33. Not any final exam in calculus is easy.

34. Every opera is easy to understand.

35. Not every novel is a satire.

22. All medical doctors are well-educated.

23. No insects are singers.

24. All flowers are plants.

25. All happy people are dancers.

26. Some bears are hibernators.

27. Some cars are not polluters.

28. No mangoes are vegetables.

29. Some dogs are not friendly.

30. All office workers are under pressure to perform.

31. All tsunamis are dangerous.

32. Some people are not jaywalkers.

33. No final exams in calculus are easy.

34. All operas are easy to understand.

35. Some novels are not satires.

Exercises 36–67 Draw Venn diagrams to prove whether each inference is valid or invalid.

36. <u>All *S* are *P*</u>
    All *P* are *S*

Answer:

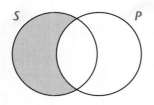

All *S* are *P*

Premise: All *S* are *P* = *True*
Conclusion: All *P* are *S* = *False*
The inference is invalid.

37. Valid

All S are P

38. Invalid

All S are P

39. Invalid

All S are P

40. Invalid

All S are P

41. Invalid

All S are P

42. Invalid

All S are P

43. Invalid

All S are P

37. <u>All S are P</u>
All S are P

38. <u>All S are P</u>
No S are P

39. <u>All S are P</u>
No P are S

40. <u>All S are P</u>   *INVALID*
Some S are P

*41. <u>All S are P</u>
Some P are S

42. <u>All S are P</u>
Some S are not P

43. <u>All S are P</u>
Some P are not S

44. <u>No S are P</u>
All S are P

45. <u>No S are P</u>
All P are S

*46. <u>No S are P</u>
No P are S

47. <u>No S are P</u>
No S are P

48. <u>No S are P</u>
Some S are P

49. <u>No S are P</u>
Some P are S

50. <u>No S are P</u>
Some S are not P

*51. <u>No S are P</u>
Some P are not S

52. <u>Some S are P</u>
All S are P

53. <u>Some S are P</u>
All P are S

54. <u>Some S are P</u>
No S are P

EXISTENTIAL import P. 93

44. Invalid

No S are P

45. Invalid

No S are P

46. Valid

No S are P

47. Valid

No S are P

48. Invalid

No S are P

49. Invalid

No S are P

50. Invalid

No S are P

INVALID

51. Invalid

No S are P

52. Invalid

X

Some S are P

53. Invalid

X

Some S are P

54. Invalid

X

Some S are P

55. <u>Some S are P</u>
    No P are S

*56. <u>Some S are P</u>
    Some P are S

57. <u>Some S are P</u>
    Some S are P

58. <u>Some S are P</u>
    Some S are not P

59. <u>Some S are P</u>
    Some P are not S

60. <u>Some S are not P</u>
    All S are P

*61. <u>Some S are not P</u>
    All P are S

62. <u>Some S are not P</u>
    No S are P

63. <u>Some S are not P</u>
    No P are S

64. <u>Some S are not P</u>
    Some S are P

65. <u>Some S are not P</u>
    Some P are S

*66. <u>Some S are not P</u>
    Some S are not P

67. <u>Some S are not P</u>
    Some P are not S

55. Invalid

Some S are P

56. Valid

Some S are P

57. Valid
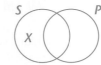
Some S are P

58. Invalid

Some S are P

59. Invalid

Some S are P

60. Invalid

Some S are not P

61. Invalid

Some S are not P

62. Invalid

Some S are not P

63. Invalid
Some S are not P

64. Invalid
Some S are not P

65. Invalid
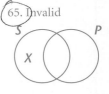
Some S are not P

66. Valid
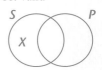
Some S are not P

67. Invalid

Some S are not P

3.2 CATEGORICAL SYLLOGISMS

In this section the discussion of categorical statements will be expanded to include the analysis of categorical syllogisms. A **syllogism** is any inference that has exactly two premises and a conclusion. A **categorical syllogism** is an inference constructed entirely of categorical statements. If we assume that the premises of an inference are true, then we can use a Venn diagram to represent a premise and then add a second premise to our drawing. The completed diagram will reveal whether the conclusion must be true, in which case we will have proven the inference is valid,

Syllogism: Any inference that has exactly two premises and one conclusion

Categorical syllogism: An inference constructed entirely of categorical statements.

or it will reveal the possibility of a false conclusion, in which case we will have proven the inference is invalid. This visual method of analysis using Venn diagrams enables us to *see* the logic of inferences.

Using pictures to reveal validity and invalidity is helpful because it gives us something to visualize. To further illustrate the logical questions we are asking it will be helpful to show just how confusing and misleading the truth content of an inference can be when we are doing a logical inference analysis. For example, consider the inference in Example 3.1A.

Example 3.1A

Truth Content
All squares are triangles = *False* (F)
All triangles are rectangles = *False* (F)
All squares are rectangles = *True* (T)

The truth content of these statements has been displayed in order to help illustrate the point that this information cannot help us decide whether the inference is valid or invalid because the logical question is completely different. The logical analysis begins by recognizing that every categorical syllogism contains exactly three terms, each of which is used two times. The two terms in the conclusion are referred to as the *subject(S)* and *predicate (P)* terms of the inference, while the term that occurs only in the premises is called the *middle (M)* term. Given this, we can reveal the structure of the inference by letting S = "squares," P = "rectangles," and M = "triangles."

Example 3.1B

Structure
All *S* are *M*
All *M* are *P*
All *S* are *P*

Since categorical syllogisms have three terms, we have to add a circle to our basic Venn diagram. The diagram below is the model for the logical analysis of categorical syllogisms.

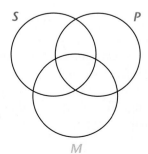

In this Venn diagram, **S** stands for the subject term of the conclusion, **P** for the predicate term of the conclusion, and **M** for the middle term, which is found only in the premises. Since the logical concern is with validity, we must see what happens when we make both premises true. We can now complete a Venn diagram with the appropriate annotation. We start by drawing the information given in the first premise as if it were true. It asserts that any area of the *S* circle outside the *M* is empty, so we shade in the correct areas.

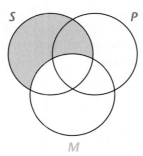

The next step is to annotate the diagram by drawing the information in the second premise. It asserts that any area of the *M* circle outside the *P* is empty, so, once again, we shade in the correct areas.

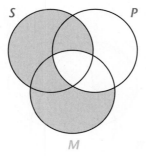

The diagram is complete when it contains the information given in the two premises. To decide whether the inference is valid or invalid, we check to see if the conclusion must be true. In our example, the conclusion asserts that the class *S* is completely contained in the class *P*. The Venn diagram verifies this, so the inference is valid.

Let's analyze an inference that is similar to that in Example 3.1A.

Example 3.2A

Truth Content

All squares are triangles = *False* (F)
All rectangles are triangles = *False* (F)
All squares are rectangles = *True* (T)

The truth content of this inference matches the inference in Example 3.1A; that is, both have false premises and a true conclusion. If validity depended on this, we might conclude that since the first inference was valid, then this one must be valid, too. We can reveal the structure of the inference by letting S = "squares," P = "rectangles," and M = "triangles."

Example 3.2B

Structure

All S are M
All P are M
All S are P

Once again, we start by drawing the information given in the first premise, as if it were true. It asserts that any area of the S circle outside the M is empty, so we shade in the correct areas.

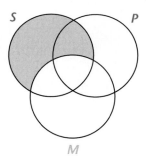

The next step is to annotate the diagram by drawing the information in the second premise. It asserts that any area of the P circle outside the M is empty, so, once again, we shade in the correct areas.

The diagram is complete when it contains the information given in the two premises. To decide whether the inference is valid or invalid, we check to see if the conclusion must be true. The conclusion asserts that the class S is completely contained in the class P, but the Venn diagram clearly shows that the conclusion is false. Therefore, we have proven that this is an invalid inference.

Once we have shown that an inference is invalid, we know that it is logically possible to substitute something for the symbols and get true premises and a false conclusion. Consider the following substitutions for the symbols in Example 3.2B, *Structure*: Let S = "men," P = "women," and M = "human beings."

Example 3.3

Truth Content
All men are human beings = *True* (T)
<u>All women are human beings</u> = *True* (T)
All men are women = *False* (F)

This example illustrates that *since invalid inferences allow for the possibility of true premises and a false conclusion, they cannot guarantee that truth will be preserved throughout the infer*ence.

To show that we have not cheated, we can substitute the same words for the symbols in Example 3.1B, *Structure* (which proved to be a valid inference). Once again, let S = "men," P = "women," and M = "human beings."

Example 3.4

Truth Content
All men are human beings = *True* (T)
<u>All human beings are women</u> = *False* (F)
All men are women = *False* (F)

Remember what validity guarantees—*if the premises are true, the conclusion cannot be false.*

Let's analyze another inference to get more practice.

Example 3.5A

All persons who drive GEOs are persons with well-adjusted egos.
No persons who desire to be ultra rich are persons with well-adjusted egos.
No persons who drive GEOs are persons who desire to be ultra rich.

If we let S = "persons who drive GEOs," P = "persons who desire to be ultra-rich," and M = "persons with well-adjusted egos," we get the following inference structure:

Example 3.5B

Structure
All S are M
No P are M
No S are P

We can start our analysis by making both premises true, as shown below.

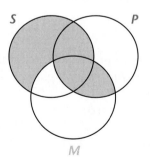

Premise 1: All S are M = *True*
Premise 2: No P are M = *True*

The completed Venn diagram confirms that if the premises are true, then the conclusion, "No S are P," is true. Therefore, we have proven that the inference is valid.

We will work through the analysis of two more inferences to get familiar with using the statements "Some S are P" and "Some S are not P." This time we will start with the inference structure.

Example 3.6

All *S* are *M*
Some *M* are *P*
Some *S* are *P*

We are going to do one premise at a time because the analysis of this inference will reveal the need for a new technique to diagram particular categorical statements. We start by drawing the information given in the first premise, as if it were true.

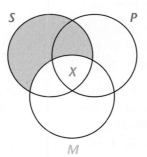

The next step is to annotate the diagram by drawing the information in the second premise. This is a particular statement and it asserts that there exists at least one *M* that is a *P*. So we must place an **X** somewhere in the areas where *M* and *P* overlap. Let's consider three possibilities, which are labeled (a)–(c).

(a)

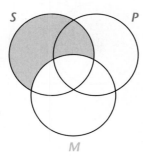

(b)

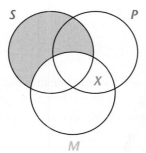

In illustrations (a) and (b) the **X** represents an object that is an **M** and a **P**, as required by the statement "Some *M* are *P*." However, in (a), the **X** asserts that the object is also an **S**, while in (b) the **X** asserts that the object is *not* an **S**. Although both of these diagrams represent logical possibilities if the second premise is true, the objects referred to by the **X's** in the two diagrams are not the same. In fact, both diagrams "say too much." The information in the second premise does not permit us to choose one of these possibilities over the other. We solve this problem by diagramming the second premise as shown in illustration (c).

(c)

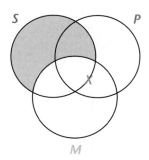

The reason for the placement of the **X** in (c) is that there cannot be more than one **X** representing the assertion for any one particular statement. So, in (c) the **X** is placed on the line separating the two possible areas where the object might exist. This location of **X** informs us that it can be located either in the area depicted in (a) or (b); however, it cannot be in both areas at the same time. The final illustration (c) reveals the following possibility:

> **Premise 1:** All S are M = *True*
> **Premise 2:** Some M are P = *True*
> **Conclusion:** Some S are P = *False*

Since it is possible that the **X** referred to in premise 2 exists only in the area depicted in (b), the logical analysis reveals the possibility of true premises and a false conclusion. Therefore, the inference is invalid.

Example 3.7 presents the final inference analysis for this section.

Example 3.7

> Some *P* are not *M*
> All *S* are *M*
> Some *S* are not *P*

We are going to do one premise at a time because the analysis of this inference will reveal a new strategy for diagramming particular categorical statements. We can start by drawing the information given in the first premise "Some *P* are not *M*," as if it were true.

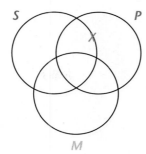

The next step is to annotate the diagram by drawing the information in the second premise "All *S* are *M*".

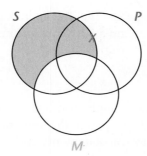

Since one of the possible areas for the placement of *X* has now been eliminated, the *X* must be moved to the only remaining possibility.

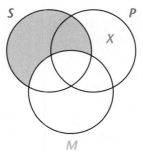

In order to avoid having to change the placement of the *X* in the diagram, we could have started the analysis by drawing the second premise. So, whenever an inference has a particular and a universal premise, the strategy to employ is to always diagram the universal premise first. This will often eliminate the need to change the location of the *X* within the Venn diagram.

The final analysis of the inference can now be completed.

Strategy

For an inference that has both a universal premise and a particular premise, always diagram the universal premise first.

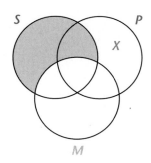

Premise 1: Some *P* are not *M* = *True*
Premise 2: All *S* are *M* = *True*
Conclusion: Some *S* are not *P* = *False*

The completed Venn diagram proves that the inference is invalid, because it reveals the possibility of true premises and a false conclusion.

EXERCISE SET 3.2

Exercises 1–20 (1) Substitute symbols to reveal the logical structure of the categorical inferences, and then (2) prove that the inferences are either valid or invalid. Use your knowledge of categorical statements and Venn diagrams to help create your proofs.

1. All cartoon characters are fictional creations.
   <u>Some fictional creations are believable objects.</u>
   Some cartoon characters are believable objects.

Answer: Invalid

Let *S* = "cartoon characters," *P* = "believable objects," and *M* = "fictional creations." The structure of the inference is:

All *S* are *M*
<u>Some *M* are *P*</u>
Some *S* are *P*

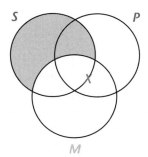

Exercises 2–30: For answers and explanations, see pages 67–76 of Instructor's Manual.

2. No movie stars are Pulitzer Prize winners.
   <u>No Pulitzer Prize winners are illiterate.</u>
   No movie stars are illiterate. Invalid

3. Some Nobel Prize winners are screenwriters.
   <u>Some screenwriters are millionaires.</u>
   Some Nobel Prize winners are millionaires. Invalid

4. All teachers are gurus.
   <u>All gurus are in touch with their Buddha nature.</u>
   All teachers are in touch with their Buddha nature. Valid

5. Some auto mechanics are trustworthy people.
   <u>Some auto mechanics are happy people.</u>
   Some trustworthy people are happy people. Invalid

*6. Some CEO's are not honest people.
   <u>Some honest people are not people interested in maximizing profits.</u>
   Some CEO's are not people interested in maximizing profits. Invalid

7. Some humans are featherless bipeds.
   <u>Some featherless bipeds are shaved chickens.</u>
   Some humans are shaved chickens. Invalid

8. All computers are helpful inventions.
   <u>All helpful inventions are expensive items.</u>
   All computers are expensive items. Valid

9. Some movies are things known to make people sick.
   <u>Some things known to make people sick are toxic to humans.</u>
   Some movies are toxic to humans. Invalid

10. No government agencies are perfectly efficient organizations.
    <u>All perfectly efficient organizations are fictional.</u>
    No government agencies are fictional. Invalid

*11. All dogs are four-legged creatures.
    <u>All dogs are canines.</u>
    All four-legged creatures are canines. Invalid

12. No dogs are four-legged creatures.
    <u>No dogs are canines.</u>
    No four-legged creatures are canines. Invalid

13. Some dogs are four-legged creatures.
    <u>Some dogs are canines.</u>
    Some four-legged creatures are canines. Invalid

14. Some dogs are not four-legged creatures.
    Some dogs are not canines.
    Some four-legged creatures are not canines. Invalid

15. All drummers are physically dexterous.
    All drummers are musically inclined people.
    All musically inclined people are physically dexterous. Invalid

*16. All drummers are physically dexterous.
    All drummers are musically inclined people.
    Some musically inclined people are physically dexterous. Invalid

17. Some drummers are physically dexterous.
    Some drummers are musically inclined people.
    Some musically inclined people are physically dexterous. Invalid

18. Some drummers are not physically dexterous.
    Some drummers are musically inclined people.
    Some musically inclined people are not physically dexterous. Invalid

*19. Some movies are comedies.
    Some movies are tragedies.
    Some comedies are tragedies. Invalid

20. Some movies are not comedies.
    Some movies are not tragedies.
    Some comedies are not tragedies. Invalid

Exercises 21–30 Use Venn diagrams to prove that the inferences are either valid or invalid.

21. No *S* are *M*
    No *M* are *P*
    No *S* are *P*

Answer: Invalid

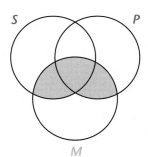

22. Some *M* are *S*
    Some *M* are *P*
    Some *S* are *P*

23. Some *M* are not *S*
    Some *M* are not *P*
    Some *S* are not *P*

24. All *S* are *M*
    Some *M* are *P*
    Some *S* are *P*

25. All *M* are *S*
    Some *M* are *P*
    Some *S* are *P*

*26. No *M* are *S*
    Some *M* are *P*
    Some *S* are *P*

27. Some *M* are *S*
    Some *M* are not *P*
    Some *S* are not *P*

28. No *S* are *M*
    All *M* are *P*
    Some *S* are not *P*

29. No *S* are *M*
    All *M* are *P*
    Some *S* are *P*

30. No *S* are *M*
    All *P* are *M*
    Some *S* are not *P*

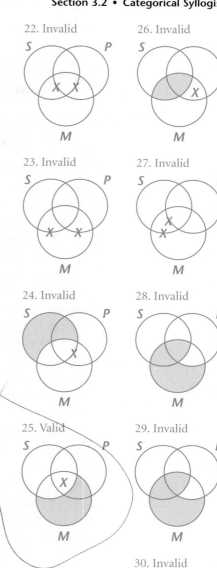

SUMMARY

- A class is a group of objects having some recognizable common characteristic.
- The class designated by the subject term of a categorical statement is shown with an S, and the class designated by the predicate term is shown with a P.
- Every categorical statement either affirms that the subject term is related partially or completely to the predicate term or denies that the subject term is related partially or completely to the predicate term.
- There are four types of categorical statements: *All S are P, No S are P, Some S are P,* and *Some S are not P.*
- The first two categorical statements are called universal because they assert something about every member of the subject term. The third and fourth categorical statements are called particular because they assert a relationship between some (at least one) member of the subject term and the predicate term.
- A statement has existential import if it asserts the existence of objects. To avoid having to decide in each instance whether a universal categorical statement has existential import, universal statements are diagrammed without asserting that the objects referred to actually exist. However, every particular categorical statement is understood to assert the existence of certain objects.
- Venn diagrams consist of overlapping circles along with specific annotations attached to those circles. The circles represent classes. The completed diagrams represent the logical commitments of the categorical statements making up an inference.
- A syllogism is any inference that has exactly two premises and a conclusion.
- A categorical syllogism is an inference constructed entirely of categorical statements.
- If the premises of an inference are assumed to be true, then we can visually represent a premise and then add a second premise to the drawing. The completed diagram reveals whether the conclusion must be true (in which case the inference is proven valid) or whether there is a possibility of a false conclusion (in which case the inference is proven invalid). This visual method of analysis enables us to see the logic of inferences.

KEY TERMS

categorical
   statement   85
class   85
subject term   85
predicate term   85

universal affirmative
   statement   85
universal negative
   statement   86
particular affirmative
   statement   86

particular negative
   statement   86
existential import   87
Venn diagram   89
syllogism   97
categorical syllogism   97

LOGIC CHALLENGE: A GROUP PROBLEM

The Masons are a somewhat secretive group with various subdivisions. Based on the following information, draw a Venn diagram using four interlocking circles that correctly captures the relationship between the four groups mentioned.

1. Every member of the Scottish Rite must be a Mason.
2. Every member of the York Rite must be a Mason.
3. It is possible to be a member of both the Scottish and the York Rites. *[handwritten: ? AT LEAST ONE ?]*
4. Every Shriner must be a member of the Scottish Rite, the York Rite, or both.
5. Mason's do not have to be members of the Shriners, or the Scottish Rite, or the York Rite.

(See page 76 of Instructor's Manual for explanation)

Logic Puzzle:

Masons   Scottish

York   Shriners

{ overview }

4.1 LOGICAL OPERATORS

4.2 CONDITIONAL STATEMENTS

4.3 RULES FOR SYMBOLIC
    NOTATION

4.4 TRUTH TABLES FOR COMPLEX
    TRUTH-FUNCTIONAL
    STATEMENTS

4.5 CONTINGENT AND
    NONCONTINGENT
    STATEMENTS

4.6 LOGICAL EQUIVALENCE

4.7 CONTRADICTORY,
    CONSISTENT, AND
    INCONSISTENT STATEMENTS

In Chapter 3 we saw that in categorical statement structures, the variables are replaced by class terms, which cannot, by themselves, be true or false. In this chapter we will learn about another important kind of statement structure, called truth-functional statements, in which variables are replaced by statements, which are either true or false. Understanding the logical commitments of truth-functional statements facilitates the uniform and consistent determination of complex inferences as either valid or invalid. As we have seen, the logical structure of statements and inferences is what determines validity and invalidity. Therefore, the ability to translate ordinary language into symbols aids in the construction of a system of analysis of the logical structure of inferences.

4.1 LOGICAL OPERATORS

The statement, "Green apples are sour *and* unripe bananas cause bellyaches," is an example of a complex **truth-functional statement**. It consists of two distinct simple statements, (1) "Green apples are sour," (2) "unripe bananas cause bellyaches." Each of the simple statements has a **truth value**, either true or false. The word "and" is called a **logical operator**, or *logical connective*. Logical operators have no truth value (they are neither true nor false). They only reveal the logical commitments of each type of statement.

chapter

The truth value of a complex statement is determined by looking at the individual simple statements, together with the logical operator. The truth-functional logical operators that will be introduced in the first part of this chapter are "and," "not," "or," and "if...then..." We will begin by introducing symbols for the logical operators, which are shown in Quick Reference 4.1:

Quick Reference 4.1 • Logical Operators and Their Symbols

Symbol	Name Used	Meaning	Logical Function
·	Dot	and	Conjunction
~	Tilde	not	Negation
v	Wedge	or	Disjunction
⊃	Horseshoe	if...then...	Conditional

> Logical operators include conjunction, negation, disjunction, and conditional.

Conjunction

The statement "Today is Monday *and* it is raining outside" is a complex statement called a *conjunction*. A **conjunction** is made up of two distinct simple statements, or conjuncts: (1) "Today is Monday," (2) "It is raining outside," plus the logical operator "*and.*" We determine the truth value of the complex statement by looking at the truth values of the individual conjuncts, together with the logical operator. If it is true that today is Monday *and* that it is raining outside, then we say that the complex statement has the truth value "true."

Truth-functional statement: A complex statement whose truth value is determined by an analysis of the individual components (the simple statements) together with the logical operator(s).

Truth value: Statements have one of two possible truth values—true or false.

Logical operator: A term such as *and, or,* or *not,* which performs a specific logical function that determines the logical possibilities of truth and falsity for a complex statement.

Conjunction: Two or more statements connected by the logical operator "and." The individual statements are called conjuncts.

Truth table: The listing of all possible combinations of the truth values of a statement.

Example 4.1

Today is Monday and it is raining outside. = *True*

If True   *and*   **True**

If we let P = "Today is Monday" and Q = "it is raining outside," the symbolic translation of the statement becomes "P · Q." The logical operator "and" is a logically strong word requiring both conjuncts to be true at the same time for the complex statement to be true. If one conjunct is false, then the complex statement is false, because when we use "and," we are claiming that all conjuncts are true. A simple rule for conjunction holds for all cases: *for any complex statement containing "and" as the logical operator to be true, all the conjuncts must be true.*

We can construct a **truth table**, which is a table that lists all the possible truth values of each simple statement, in order to determine the truth value of a complex statement. Consider the statement structure "P · Q." Since there are two variables (P, Q), each of which can be either true or false, we get four possible combinations (2 truth values for each variable means that there are $2 \times 2 = 4$ possible combinations of truth values). Table 4.1 shows the truth table for conjunction.

Table 4.1 Truth Table for Conjunction

$$P \cdot Q$$

T *(T)* T
T *(F)* F
F *(F)* T
F *(F)* F

Notice that there are parentheses around the truth values placed under the conjunction to indicate that this is the result of the application of a logical operator. The "·" symbol for conjunction has no truth value itself. The column containing the red *(T)* and *(F)'s* thus represents all the possible truth values of the complex statement structure "P · Q." The truth table displays what we recognized earlier, namely, that the only way for a conjunction to be true is if all the conjuncts are true.

Negation

Another very useful logical term is "not." The function of "not" is referred to as **negation**, and it changes (negates) the truth value of the statement that follows it. For example, if the statement "Today is Monday" is true, then the negation of that statement, "Today is not Monday" would be false. Written in symbols it would look like this: If P = "Today is Monday," its negation would be ~ P = "Today is not Monday." (Notice that for logical notation the "not" is moved from its normal position in the English sentence.) On the other hand, if the statement "Today is Monday" is false, then its negation would be true. Negation is somewhat like a minus sign in arithmetic—it changes the value of what you started with. Consider this statement:

Succotash does contain corn and lima beans.

The negation of this statement is formed by adding "not" in the correct place:

Succotash does *not* contain corn and lima beans.

Whatever the truth value of the original statement, the second one has the opposite truth value. If we want to form the negation of the second statement, we can either write the original one or reapply the rule and get:

Succotash does *not not* contain corn and lima beans.

The negation of this statement is either the previous one or:

Succotash does *not not not* contain corn and lima beans.

The only time negation is problematic is when the statement is very complex. For example, "Today is not Monday or this book is green and there is not both black and not blue lettering on the pages but this is not ...." Having to form the negation of this entire statement by applying the appropriate "nots" in the right places would be both time-consuming and tricky. Luckily, there is a simple procedure that avoids this confusion: All you need to do is to place *in front of the complex statement* the phrase "It is not the case that..." and you have automatically negated whatever follows this phrase.

Negation: The operation of logically changing the truth value of a statement to its opposite truth value.

Since negation simply changes the truth value of the statement that follows it, the truth table for negation is easy to construct (Table 4.2).

Table 4.2 Truth Table for Negation

~	P
(F) T	
(T) F	

The reason that the truth values T and F are directly under the P is that P stands for a statement that can be either true or false, whereas the ~ (not) is neither true nor false—*it changes the value of the statement that follows it*. Therefore, if P is true, then its negation is false, which is what the truth table indicates.

Disjunction

The next type of truth-functional statement we will look at has "or" as the logical operator and is called **disjunction**. The truth value of a complex disjunctive statement is determined by analyzing its component parts, called disjuncts, as shown in Example 4.2A.

Example 4.2A

The book you are reading is green or the moon is made of green cheese. = *True*

$$\textbf{\textit{If} True} \qquad or \qquad \textbf{\textit{If} True}$$

If we let P = "The book you are reading is green" and Q = "the moon is made of green cheese," the symbolic translation of the statement becomes "P ∨ Q." With disjunction, for a statement to be true it is sufficient for either one of the disjuncts to be true, because when we use disjunction, we are not claiming that both statements are true, just that one or the other is true. It is perfectly acceptable for both disjuncts to be true, but it is just not necessary. (Contrast this with conjunction where it is necessary for all the conjuncts to be true in order for the complex statement to be true.) Therefore, *the only way for a complex disjunctive statement to be false is for all the disjuncts to be false at the same time*. Since a disjunction is true if either one or both of the disjuncts is true, it follows that a disjunct can be false only if none of the disjuncts is true.

When we consider the truth content of a statement, we can encounter two kinds of disjunctions—*inclusive* and *exclusive*. With **inclusive disjunctions** it is possible for both (all) disjuncts to be true at the same time. With **exclusive disjunctions** both disjuncts cannot be true at the same time—the truth of one *excludes* the truth of the other. Example 4.2A is an example of inclusive "or" where both disjuncts can be true (even though in that example they are obviously not both true). Example 4.2B reveals another instance of inclusive "or" where both disjuncts are, in fact, true.

Disjunction: Two or more statements connected by the logical operator "or." The individual statements are called disjuncts.

Inclusive disjunction: A type of disjunctive statement where it is possible for both disjuncts to be true at the same time.

Exclusive disjunction: A type of disjunctive statement where both the disjuncts cannot be true at the same time.

Example 4.2B

Carson City is the capital of Nevada or Albany is the capital of New York. = *True*   *Incl.*

        If **True**   *or*   *If* **True**

Example 4.2C shows an exclusive "or," where if one disjunct is true, the other must be false.   *Exclu.*

Example 4.2C

Today is Monday or today is Wednesday.

In Example 4.2C, you can see that both disjuncts cannot be true at the same time (although both could be false)—the truth of one excludes the truth of the other. Normally the context reveals which kind of disjunction we are dealing with, if it is not obvious from the statement alone (this would usually be a truth content concern). Since an exclusive disjunction is claiming "P v Q" *(but not both)* we can, if necessary, translate this as "(P v Q) · ~ (P · Q)." For logical analysis, however, we will assume that inclusive "or" is being used.

We can use this information to construct a truth table that lists all the possible combinations of truth values for disjunction (Table 4.3).

Table 4.3 Truth Table for Disjunction

P v Q

T *(T)* T
T *(T)* F
F *(T)* T
F *(F)* F

The truth table shows that the only way for a statement using disjunction to be false is for both disjuncts to be false.

Quick Reference 4.2 summarizes the rules and truth tables for logical operators.

Quick Reference 4.2 • Rules and Truth Tables for Logical Operators

Rule for Conjunction
For any complex statement containing "and" as the logical operator to be true, all the conjuncts must be true.

Rule for Negation
The word "not" changes, or *negates*, the truth value of whatever statement follows it.

Rule for Disjunction
The only way for a complex statement containing "or" as the logical operator to be *false* is if all the disjuncts are false.

Each logical operator has its own set of rules.

The truth tables for logical operators show all possible truth values.

Quick Reference 4.2 continued

Truth Tables for Conjunction, Negation, and Disjunction

P · Q	~ P	P ∨ Q
T *(T)* T	*(F)* T	T *(T)* T
T *(F)* F	*(T)* F	T *(T)* F
F *(F)* T		F *(T)* T
F *(F)* F		F *(F)* F

EXERCISE SET 4.1A   ○○○

Exercises 1–10 Choose the correct answer.

1. If the statement structure "X · Y" is true, which of the following would you know to be correct?

    (a) X must be true.

    (b) X must be false.

    (c) X could be true or false.

Answer: (a) X must be true. The only way for a conjunction to be true is if all the conjuncts are true.

Exercises 2–10: For answers and explanations, see page 90 of Instructor's Manual.

2. If the statement structure "X · Y" is false, which of the following would you know to be correct?

    (a) X must be true.

    (b) X must be false.

    (c) X could be true or false. 2. (c) X could be true or false.

3. If the statement structure "X ∨ Y" is true, which of the following would you know to be correct?

    (a) X must be true.

    (b) X must be false.

    (c) X could be true or false. 3. (c) X could be true or false.

4. If the statement structure "X ∨ Y" is false, which of the following would you know to be correct?

    (a) X must be true.

    (b) X must be false. 4. (b) X must be false.

    (c) X could be true or false.

5. If the statement structure "~ X" is false, then what must X be?

    (a) X must be true. 5. (a) X must be true.

    (b) X must be false.

    (c) X could be true or false.

*6. If the statement structure "~ X" is true, then what must X be?

   (a) X must be true.
   (b) X must be false. 6. (b) X must be false.
   (c) X could be true or false.

7. If the statement structure "X ∨ Y" is true, but X is false, then what must Y be?

   (a) Y must be true. 7. (a) Y must be true.
   (b) Y must be false.
   (c) Y could be true or false.

8. If the statement structure "X ∨ Y" is false, is it possible for one of the disjuncts to be true?

   (a) Yes
   (b) No 8. (b) No

9. If the statement structure "X ∨ Y" is true, is it possible for one of the disjuncts to be false?

   (a) Yes 9. (a) Yes
   (b) No

10. If the statement structure "X · Y" is false, is it possible for both conjuncts to be false?

   (a) Yes 10. (a) Yes
   (b) No

Translations and Common Terms

When we translate sentences from English into the symbolic notation of truth-functional operators we must try our best to capture the logical intent. Quick Reference 4.3 contains a list of common terms that may occur in English sentences and, for the most part, can be translated by using one of the logical operators discussed so far.

Quick Reference 4.3 • Translation of Logical Operator Symbols

Symbol	Logical Function	Meaning
·	Conjunction	*and, but, while, however, also, moreover, although, yet, whereas*
~	Negation	*not, it is not the case that, it is false that, it is not true that*
∨	Disjunction	*or, either ... or, unless, otherwise*

Conjunction, negation, and disjunction symbols can be used for translating many common English sentences into symbolic notation.

We can use Quick Reference 4.3 to help translate the following English sentences.

English Sentence	Symbolic Translation
Bill is cold and Mary is late.	B · M
Today is Monday or today is Tuesday.	M v T
He is not a U.S. Senator.	~ S
Today is Monday unless today is Tuesday.	M v T
My car is old, but it is still reliable.	O · R
It is not the case that Halley's Comet will return in 2008.	~ H

EXERCISE SET 4.1B   ○○○

Exercises 1–16 Translate the following statements symbolically using the correct logical operator. Try to capture as closely as possible the logical structure of each statement. For example, the statement "Barbara is going to lose her football bet, and Johnny will get a night at the ballet" can be translated as "B · J" (if we let B = "Barbara is going to lose her football bet," and J = "Johnny will get a night at the ballet").

1. Either it will rain tomorrow or it will be sunny.

Answer: Let R = "it will rain tomorrow," and S = "it will be sunny."

    R v S

2. The food in that restaurant stinks, and the portions are too small.

3. Your ice is not cold.

4. My car does not look great, but it gets great gas mileage.

*5. My test score was high or I am mistaken.

6. Either candy or tobacco is bad for your teeth.

7. Toothpaste is good for your teeth, but tobacco is not.

8. Driving too fast is hazardous to your health; also driving without buckling up.

9. Lava lamps are distracting while music in the background is soothing.

*10. You must get a passing grade on the next exam, otherwise you will fail.

11. It is not true that *Titanic* is the highest grossing film of all time.

12. Your paper was turned in late; however I am willing to grant you an extension.

13. Unless you stop eating too much pepperoni, you will develop a stomach ulcer.

*14. It is false that Grover Cleveland was the greatest U.S. President.

15. She is happy with her box of candy; however, she would have preferred a new car.

16. *Citizen Kane* did not win the Academy Award for best picture, but it is still the greatest movie ever made.

Exercises 2–26: For answers and explanations, see pages 90–92 of Instructor's Manual.

2. F · P

3. ~ I

4. ~ C · M

5. T v M

6. C v T

7. T · ~ B

8. F · B

9. L · M

10. P v F

11. ~ T

12. L · E

13. S v U

14. ~ G

15. H · C

16. ~ C · G

Exercises 17–26 You are given a statement and a set of truth values. (1) Translate the statement symbolically using the correct logical operator. (2) Use the truth tables for the logical operators to determine whether the statement is true or false.

"Either my stock portfolio is strong or I am losing money."
Let X = "my stock portfolio is strong," and Y = "I am losing money."
Let X = True, Y = False.

17. Symbolic translation:

18. Truth value:

Answer:

17. Symbolic translation: X ∨ Y

18. Truth value: True. A disjunction is true if at least one disjunct is true.

"Either my stock portfolio is strong or I am losing money."
Let X = "my stock portfolio is strong," and Y = "I am losing money."
Let X = False, Y = False.

19. Symbolic translation: 19. X ∨ Y

20. Truth value: 20. False

"My room could use a good cleaning, but I am too lazy to do anything about it."
Let X = "My room could use a good cleaning," and Y = "I am too lazy to do any-thing about it."
Let X = True, Y = False.

21. Symbolic translation: 21. X · Y

22. Truth value: 22. False

"My room could use a good cleaning, but I am too lazy to do anything about it."
Let X = "My room could use a good cleaning," and Y = "I am too lazy to do any-thing about it."
Let X = True, Y = True.

23. Symbolic translation: 23. X · Y

24. Truth value: 24. True

"My father is wise and he is honest."
Let X = "My father is wise," and Y = "he is honest."
Let X = False, Y = False.

25. Symbolic translation: 25. X · Y

26. Truth value: 26. False

BIOGRAPHY : THE STOICS

Stoic thought actually has two founders, Zeno of Citium (340 BC–265 BC) and Chrysippus of Soli (280 BC–209 BC). Most of the writings of the Stoics have not survived. We know of their ideas through the fragments that we can piece together, which unfortunately give us only an incomplete picture. We know about Chrysippus and his logical work mostly through other writers who attest to his great reputation as a logician. The Stoics did the first substantial work on what today are called truth-functional statements. One of the Stoics' basic assertions is that every statement is either true or false. Although they did not create truth tables, nevertheless they worked out the possible true-false combinations for conjunction, disjunction, negation, and conditional statements. Although Stoic logic was not initially as influential as Aristotle's logical system, nevertheless, modern developments and applications of truth-functional ideas are recognized as essential to our understanding of the role of logic.

The Stoics emphasized the importance of basic principles of logic. In other words, they were interested in discovering general rules that could be applied to specific kinds of inferences. For example, one of their ideas was that we could understand validity through the use of a conditional statement. What this idea means is that the conjunction of the premises becomes the antecedent and the conclusion the consequent of a conditional statement. If the conditional statement is true, then the inference is valid.

4.2 CONDITIONAL STATEMENTS

The truth-functional statement, "If you wash the car, then I'll give you ten dollars," is an example of a **conditional statement**. It can be translated symbolically using the horseshoe as "P ⊃ Q," which is read as "If P, then Q." A conditional statement is analyzed by the possible configurations of its parts. The first part, which follows the "if," is a statement, and it is called the **antecedent**. The second part, which follows the "then," is also a statement, and it is called the **consequent**. Antecedents and consequents can consist of either simple or complex statements. The key component of a conditional statement is the word "if," which always signifies a conditional statement. It does not matter where in the sentence the "if" occurs; the important thing to recognize is that the "if" *always precedes the antecedent*. Therefore, whatever phrase follows "if" must be placed first in reconstructing the given sentence, in order to match the logical "If P, then Q" structure.

The following example is a conditional statement that needs no rewriting:

If you wash the car, *then* you can go to the movies.

Conditional statement: A complex statement having the form "If P, then Q," where the variables P, Q get replaced by statements.

Antecedent: The statement that follows the "if" in a conditional statement.

Consequent: The statement that follows the "then" in a conditional statement.

If P stands for the simple statement "you wash the car" and Q stands for the simple statement "you can go to the movies" then the logical structure of the complex statement is "P ⊃ Q." However, sometimes the word "then" is missing. For example, in the statement, "*If* you wash the car, you can go to the movies," the word "then" is implied. We can reconstruct the statement structure by simply adding the missing word: "*If* you wash the car, *then* you can go to the movies." (This sentence and similar statements are examples of the fact that conditional statements are commonly used when an incentive is offered for the performance of a task.)

The next example needs to be restructured to place it into the normal "P ⊃ Q" structure.

> You can go to the movies, *if* you wash the car.

We first locate the key word "if." Next, we let P = "you wash the car" and let Q = "you can go to the movies." Rewriting the sentence, we once again get "*If* you wash the car, *then* you can go to the movies."

A common mistake is to think that a conditional statement is an inference. This is not the case because a conditional statement does not assert that either the antecedent or the consequent is true. A conditional statement does assert that *if* the antecedent is true, *then* so is the consequent. It is true that we talk about inferences by asking the question, "if the premises are true, then is it possible for the conclusion to be false?" However, we ask this after we recognize that certain statements (premises) are meant to support other statements (conclusions). Although a conditional statement by itself is not an inference, it can be used as part of an inference.

Understanding and Diagramming Conditional Statements

The logical commitments of conditional statements are often puzzling when they are first encountered. Consider what the conditional statement structure "P ⊃ Q" asserts. The "*if*" connects directly to the P and says something definite, that it is always to be found with Q. The statement is asserting that whenever P is realized, Q will be realized as well. However, since the "if" connects only to the P, the statement does not specify the range of Q possibilities, only those of P. The conditional claim is asserting that every instance of P will be accompanied by an instance of Q, but it is not asserting that every instance of Q will be accompanied by an instance of P. This is because the "if" refers only to the P, the antecedent.

BIOGRAPHY   LEONHARD EULER

Leonhard Euler (1707–1783), who wrote over 800 mathematical treatises, is the most prolific mathematician in history. Euler's abilities and memory were so remarkable that he was still able to offer original contributions to nearly every area of mathematics even after he went blind. His application of special diagrams (today referred to as Euler diagrams) to the understanding of Aristotelian syllogisms advanced the use of geometrical figures as analogues of logical relations. Aristotelian syllogisms deal with class inclusion and exclusion—two ideas that can be captured visually. By providing the first steps leading ultimately to a rigorous proof procedure, Euler diagrams offer an alternative to Venn diagrams and can be used as a foundation to logical analysis.

Although they are perfectly suited for mathematical and logical reasoning, the flexibility of Euler's diagram system allows for many diverse applications. Euler-type diagrams allow for original and intuitive visual displays of many kinds of relationship problems. A modified version of Euler diagrams is used in this chapter in the explanation of the truth table for conditional statements.

Euler gave the name "Latin squares" to matrices filled with symbols that never appear twice in the same row or column. A special version of those squares is a popular pastime today—it is called Sudoku.

Since a conditional statement makes a definite assertion about the antecedent, the only way for a conditional statement to be false is if the antecedent is true and the consequent is false. The idea can be captured like this:

$$P \supset Q$$
$$\downarrow \qquad \downarrow$$

T ----- F = F

This means that any other combination of truth values will result in the conditional statement being true. A completed truth table will show these results (Table 4.4).

Table 4.4 Truth Table for Conditional Statements

$$P \supset Q$$

T *(T)* T
T *(F)* F
F *(T)* T
F *(T)* F

The difficulty in understanding why we get these results is partly because they go against common sense, especially the last two rows. We might ask why, if the antecedent is false, should the statement be true—especially as it does not seem to matter what the truth value of the consequent is in those cases. In order to make some sense of these results we will try to visualize the logical commitments of conditional statements.

We stipulate that a check mark placed within a box indicates that the statement depicted by that box is true. For example, let P stand for the statement, "Today is Monday."

The check mark inside the box indicates that the statement represented by P is true.

We can also use a check mark to indicate when a statement is false. We do this by placing the check mark outside the box. Once again, let P stand for the statement, "Today is Monday."

Strategy

Diagrams are very helpful in analyzing the logical commitments of conditional statements.

The check mark outside the box indicates that the statement represented by P is false. We stipulate that there can be *only one check mark per diagram,* because the check mark is used to indicate the truth value of the entire statement (simple or complex).

Since a conditional statement asserts that every instance of the antecedent will be accompanied by an instance of the consequent, we can capture visually the logical commitment as shown in Figure 4.1.

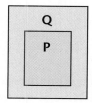

FIGURE 4.1 • A visual representation of the logical commitment of "P ⊃ Q".

This figure shows one way to represent the logical relationship that is asserted by a conditional statement. No matter where you place a check mark in the P box (if P is true), the check mark will automatically be within the Q box as well, thus ensuring that Q is true. The picture therefore shows that *whenever (if)* we are in P, then Q is realized as well, and this seems to be just what the statement is logically asserting.

The next step for us, and the most important, is to see whether this picture can make sense of the truth table for conditional statements (Table 4.4). Can this picture illustrate the first line of the truth table? Can the picture show P as true and Q as true at the same time? If the picture is annotated as shown in Figure 4.2, we see that this can be done.

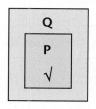

FIGURE 4.2 • Illustration of "P ⊃ Q" with P and Q both true.

The check mark in P indicates the possibility that P is true and Q is true at the same time. Therefore, our new picture verifies the first line of the truth table.

Can the second line in Table 4.4 be realized in our picture? The check mark must be placed so that P is true, but at the same time Q must be false. An inspection of Figure 4.1 reveals that there is no place to position the check mark so that P is true and Q is false, and this is just what the truth table says.

The third line in Table 4.4 indicates true as the result. Can we make sense of this in our picture? We have to place the check mark in a position where P is false, but where Q is true, and we can in fact do this (Figure 4.3).

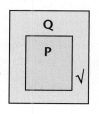

FIGURE 4.3 • Illustration of "P ⊃ Q" with P = false and Q = true.

So the visual representation of the third line reveals that the truth table result does correctly capture the logical relationship.

The last line in Table 4.4 can be drawn as shown in Figure 4.4.

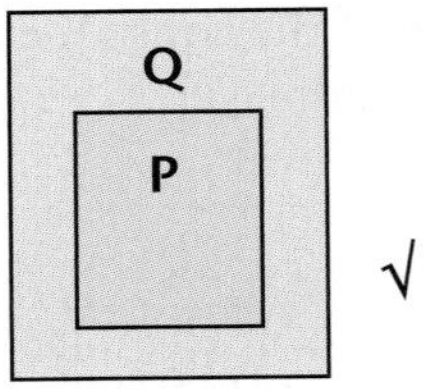

FIGURE 4.4 • Illustration of "P ⊃ Q" with P and Q both false.

We see that it is possible to be in a position where P is false and Q is false at the same time. This shows that the last line of the truth table does correctly interpret the logical relationship that is asserted in a conditional statement. The visual representation has enabled us to make logical sense of a counterintuitive result.

The word "if" is a good indicator word, one that immediately reveals the existence of a conditional statement. But there are other words that have the same logical commitments. Once we learn what they are we can then reconstruct and rewrite those statements into conditional statements having the "P ⊃ Q" structure. For example, consider the logical intent of the statement structure, "Whenever P, then Q." At first glance you might not realize that the logical commitments are identical to the normal conditional statement structure "P ⊃ Q" but on closer inspection you should be able to see that they are the same. In fact, for logical purposes, the word "whenever" specifies the same domain of possibilities as "if." The following sentence structures are also logically equivalent to "if" (Table 4.5):

Table 4.5 Equivalent Sentence Structures for Conditional Statements

Every time P, then Q.	*Given that* P, then Q.
Each time P, then Q.	*Provided that* P, then Q.
All cases where P, then Q.	*In any case where* P, then Q.
Any time P, then Q.	*Supposing that* P, then Q.
In the event of P, then Q.	*On any occurrence of* P, then Q.
On condition that P, then Q.	*For every instance of* P, then Q.

Each of these statement structures can be translated as "P ⊃ Q." This means that once you learn to recognize and understand conditional statements, you will be in a position to analyze conditional inferences, which contain conditional statements.

"If" and "Only if"

If: Designates the antecedent of a conditional statement.

Only if: Designates the consequent of a conditional statement.

We must distinguish the logical use of "if," from "**only if**." We already stipulated that "if" points to the antecedent. We now stipulate that "only if" points to the consequent.

> **Table 4.6 Using *If* and *Only if* in Conditional Statements**
>
> | | |
> |---|---|
> | *If* P, then Q | P is the *antecedent.* |
> | P, *if* Q | Q is the *antecedent* |
> | P, *only if* Q | P is the *antecedent* |
> | *Only if* P, Q | Q is the *antecedent* |

The following statements illustrate the many different uses of "if" and "only if."

1. *If* you manage to win the lottery, then you will be contacted by relatives you never knew existed. (What follows the *if* is the *antecedent.*)

2. *Only if* you manage to win the lottery, you will be contacted by relatives you never knew existed. (What follows the *only if* is the *consequent.*)

3. You will be contacted by relatives you never knew existed, *if* you manage to win the lottery. (What follows the *if* is the *antecedent.*)

4. You will be contacted by relatives you never knew existed, *only if* you manage to win the lottery. (What follows the *only if* is the *consequent.*)

In (1) and (3) "you manage to win the lottery" is the antecedent. However, in (2) and (4) "you manage to win the lottery" is the consequent. Therefore, the assertions (and the meanings) of these statements are different. As always, we must separate the truth content aspect of these assertions from their logical component.

EXERCISE SET 4.2

Exercises 1–6 Choose the correct answer.

1. If the statement structure "X ⊃ Y" is true, which of the following would you know to be correct?

    (a) X must be true.

    (b) X must be false.

    (c) X could be true or false.

Answer: (c) X could be true or false. A conditional can be true if both the antecedent and consequent are true, or if both the antecedent and consequent are false.

2. If the statement structure "X ⊃ Y" is false, which of the following would you know to be correct?

    (a) X must be true. 2. (a) X must be true.

    (b) X must be false.

    (c) X could be true or false.

Exercises 2–30: For answers and explanations, see page 92 of Instructor's Manual.

3. If the statement structure "X ⊃ Y" is true, which of the following would you know to be correct?

   (a) Y must be true.
   (b) Y must be false.
   (c) Y could be true or false. 3. (c) Y could be true or false.

4. If the statement structure "X ⊃ Y" is false, which of the following would you know to be correct?

   (a) Y must be true.
   (b) Y must be false. 4. (b) Y must be false.
   (c) Y could be true or false.

5. If the statement structure "X ⊃ Y" is false, then is it possible that X is false?

   (a) Yes
   (b) No 5. (b) No

6. If the statement structure "X ⊃ Y" is true, then is it possible that Y is false?

   (a) Yes 6. (a) Yes
   (b) No

Exercises 7–30 You are given a statement and a set of truth values. (1) Translate the statement symbolically using the correct logical operator. (2) Use the truth tables for the logical operators to determine whether the statement is true or false.

"If my stock portfolio is weak, then I am losing money."
Let X = "my stock portfolio is weak," and Y = "I am losing money."
Let X = True, Y = False.

7. Symbolic translation:

8. Truth value:

Answer:

7. Symbolic translation: X ⊃ Y

8. Truth value: False. A conditional is false if the antecedent is true and the consequent false.

"My stock portfolio is weak, only if I am losing money."
Let X = "my stock portfolio is weak," and Y = "I am losing money."
Let X = True, Y = False.

9. Symbolic translation: 9. X ⊃ Y

10. Truth value: 10. False

"Only if my room could use a good cleaning, I am too lazy to do anything about it."
Let X = "My room could use a good cleaning," and Y = "I am too lazy to do anything about it."
Let X = True, Y = False.

11. Symbolic translation: 11. Y ⊃ X

12. Truth value: 12. True

"My room could use a good cleaning, if I am too lazy to do anything about it."

Let X = "My room could use a good cleaning," and Y = "I am too lazy to do anything about it."

Let X = True, Y = True.

13. Symbolic translation: 13. Y ⊃ X

14. Truth value: 14. True

"If my father is wise, then he is honest."

Let X = "My father is wise," and Y = "he is honest."

Let X = False, Y = False.

15. Symbolic translation: 15. X ⊃ Y

16. Truth value: 16. True

"My father is wise, only if he is honest."

Let X = "My father is wise," and Y = "he is honest."

Let X = False, Y = False.

*17. Symbolic translation: 17. X ⊃ Y

*18. Truth value: 18. True

"My car is fast, if it has a turbocharger."

Let X = "My car is fast," and Y = "it has a turbocharger."

Let X = False, Y = False.

19. Symbolic translation: 19. Y ⊃ X

20. Truth value: 20. True

"Only if my car is fast, it has a turbocharger."

Let X = "My car is fast," and Y = "it has a turbocharger."

Let X = False, Y = False.

21. Symbolic translation: 21. Y ⊃ X

22. Truth value: 22. True

"If you feel great, then you look great."

Let X = "you feel great," and Y = "you look great."

Let X = True, Y = False.

23. Symbolic translation: 23. X ⊃ Y

24. Truth value: 24. False

"You passed the exam, only if you got at least a C."

Let X = "You passed the exam," and Y = "you got at least a C."

Let X = False, Y = True.

25. Symbolic translation: 25. X ⊃ Y

26. Truth value: 26. True

"If driving too fast is hazardous to your health, then so is driving without buckling up."

Let X = "driving too fast is hazardous to your health," and Y = "so is driving without buckling up."

Let X = False, Y = False.

*27. Symbolic translation: 27. X ⊃ Y

*28. Truth value: 28. True

"Only if your paper was turned in late, I will deduct a letter grade."

Let X = "I will deduct a letter grade," and Y = "your paper was turned in late."

Let X = True, Y = True.

29. Symbolic translation: 29. X ⊃ Y

30. Truth value: 30. True

4.3 RULES FOR SYMBOLIC NOTATION

In the translation of complex truth-functional statements, we must make sure to use the logical operator symbols correctly. Just as there are rules of grammar in English, there are grammatical (syntactical) rules for symbolic notation as well. We immediately recognize that the English sentence, "Carly is an excellent costume designer and a gifted pattern-maker," is grammatically correct. We also know that a different arrangement of the same words may violate rules of grammar. For example, "And excellent costume designer is an Carly gifted pattern-maker a."

Well-Formed Formulas

There are a few simple rules for statements using symbolic notation that ensure that they are grammatically correct. Such statements are also called **well-formed formulas**, or *WFFs*.

> **Rule 1:** The ·, ∨, and ⊃ must always go between two statements (simple or complex). Thus, "P · Q," "P ∨ Q," and "P ⊃ Q" are all grammatically correct. However, "· P," "P ·," "PQ ∨," and " ⊃ P" are all grammatically incorrect because they violate Rule 1.
>
> **Rule 2:** The symbol for negation, ~, must always go in front of the statement it is meant to negate.
>
> **Rule 3:** The symbol for negation, ~, cannot, by itself, go between two statements.

Well-formed formula (*WFF*): Truth-functional statements that have been translated symbolically and are syntactically (grammatically) correct.

For example, the statement structures "~ P," "~ P ∨ Q," "~ (P ∨ Q)," and "P · ~ Q," are all *WFFs*. However, the arrangement "P ~ Q" is not a *WFF* because it violates Rule 3. Some additional complex *WFFs* are "~ P ∨ (Q · R)," "~ (P ∨ Q) · R," and "~ P ∨ ~ (~ Q · ~ R)." In each of these cases, the use of negation has not violated any of the rules.

Main logical operator: The logical symbol that determines the statement's final truth value determination.

> **Rule 4:** Parentheses are required in order to eliminate ambiguity and to distinguish the main logical operator in a complex statement. The **main logical operator** is the logical symbol that determines the statement's final truth value.

The main operator in a complex truth-functional statement is one of the operators that goes between statements, or it is the negation operator. The following three examples show how the parentheses are used:

1. The statement structures "P v (Q · R)" and "(P v Q) · R" are both grammatically correct, both are *WFFs*.
2. The arrangement "P v Q (· R)" is grammatically *incorrect*. The " · " has nothing to the left of it except the parenthesis (the *dot* is not between two statements).
3. The arrangement "(P v Q · R)" is also grammatically incorrect: the parentheses must separate the two logical operators. This is necessary because we need to indicate which one is the main operator. There are two ways to place the parentheses:

$$(P \lor Q) \cdot R \qquad\qquad P \lor (Q \cdot R)$$

In the first instance the " · " is the main operator, while in the second the "v" is the main operator. These are *not* logically equivalent statements. (The tools for proving this are introduced later in this chapter.) Therefore, it is crucial to use parentheses to create *WFFs* that capture the correct use of the logical operators involved in complex truth-functional statements.

We can expand Rule 4 to include the use of *brackets*. For example, the arrangement "[(P v Q) ⊃ (R · S)] v (T · W)" is a *WFF*, but "[(P v Q) ⊃ (R · S) v] (T · W)" is not a *WFF*. Quick Reference 4.4 summarizes the correct use of symbols for logical operators.

Quick Reference 4.4 • Summary of the Rules of Grammar (Syntax) for Logic Symbols

Rule 1. The ·, v, and ⊃ must always go between two statements (simple or complex).

Rule 2. The symbol for negation, ~, must always go in front of the statement it is meant to negate.

Rule 3. The symbol for negation, ~, by itself, cannot go between two statements.

Rule 4. Parentheses are required in order to eliminate ambiguity and to distinguish the main logical operator in a complex statement.

The placement of the symbols for logical operators must follow the four rules of grammar.

EXERCISE SET 4.3A

For each of the following arrangements of logical operator symbols determine whether they are *WFFs*. If any are not *WFFs*, point out the mistake and the rule that is violated (some examples may contain more than one mistake).

1. P v ~ Q

Answer: P v ~ Q This is a *WFF*.

2. R ~ v T   2. This is not a *WFF*. **Rule 1** and **Rule 2**.

3. K   3. This is a *WFF*.

Exercises 2–15: For answers and explanations, see page 93 of Instructor's Manual.

4. K · (P ~ Q)   4. This is not a *WFF*. **Rule 3.**

5. L ⊃ ~ P   5. This is a *WFF.*

*6. L ⊃ ~ (P ∨ ⊃ Q)   6. This is not a *WFF*. **Rule 1.**

7. M(⊃ P ⊃ Q)   7. This is not a *WFF*. **Rule 1** and **Rule 4.**

8. (P ∨ Q ⊃ R)   8. This is not a *WFF*. **Rule 4.**

9. [(P Q] ∨ ~ R   9. This is not a *WFF*. **Rule 1.**

10. ~ P (∨ ~ R) · ~ S   10. This is not a *WFF*. **Rule 1** and **Rule 4.**

*11. P · ∨ Q   11. This is not a *WFF*. **Rule 1.**

12. R ∨ T ~   12. This is not a *WFF*. **Rule 2.**

13. PQ   13. This is not a *WFF*. **Rule 1.**

14. K · (P ∨ ~ Q)   14. This is a *WFF.*

15. L ~ P   15. This is not a *WFF*. **Rule 3.**

The Main Logical Operator

As we saw earlier, the statement structures "P ∨ (Q · R)" and "(P ∨ Q) · R" are both grammatically correct; nevertheless they are not identical statements. In addition, we asserted that "P ∨ Q · R" is not a *WFF.* The rationale behind Rule 4 is to eliminate the ambiguity in "P ∨ Q · R." Let's suppose that we are discussing the possibility that three people, Paul, Quincy, and Rita, are going to a party. Let P = "Paul will go to the party," Q = "Quincy will go to the party," and R = "Rita will go to the party." The operators "∨" and "·" in "P ∨ Q · R" are *each* supposed to connect two statements (simple or complex), but without parentheses the Q gets dragged in two directions at once, so that we do not know whether to connect the Q to the P or to the R. However, in both the statement structures "P ∨ (Q · R)" and "(P ∨ Q) · R" the ambiguity has been eliminated by the correct application of parentheses. Additionally, the parentheses help to explain why these are not identical statements. The first statement, "P ∨ (Q · R)," asserts, "*Either* Paul will go to the party *or both* Quincy *and* Rita will go to the party." In this case the main logical operator is the "∨" because the parentheses enclosed the Q and R and separated them from the P. On the other hand, the second statement, "(P ∨ Q) · R," asserts, "*Either* Paul *or* Quincy will go to the party *and* Rita will go to the party." In this case the main logical operator is the "·" because the parentheses enclosed the P and Q and separated them from the R.

When negation is the main operator, we get a different display of symbols. In those cases the negation sign completely governs the complex statement. For example, "~ K," "~ (P ∨ Q)," and "~ [(K · ~ L) ⊃ (~ P ∨ Q)]" all have the *leftmost* negation symbol as the main operator. Let's compare the statement "~ P ∨ Q" with the statement "~ (P ∨ Q)." Using our substitutions from earlier examples, the first statement asserts that "*either* Paul will not go to the party *or* Quincy will go to the party." This is different from the second statement where the negation is the main logical operator. Since the negation governs everything inside the parentheses, it asserts that "*neither* Paul *nor* Quincy will go to the party."

EXERCISE SET 4.3B   ○○○

Exercises 1–25 Identify the main logical operator in each of the following *WFFs*.

1. ~ Q ∨ P

Answer: ~ Q Ⓥ P

2. R · (~ T ∨ K)   2. RⓈ(~ T ∨ K)

3. ~ K   3.⊝K

4. (P · ~ Q) ∨ K   4. (P · ~ Q)ⓋK

5. L ⊃ ~ P   5. LⓄ~ P

*6. (L ⊃ ~ P) ⊃ Q   6. (L ⊃ ~ P)Ⓞ Q

7. (M ∨ P) ⊃ (Q ∨ R)   7. (M ∨ P)Ⓞ (Q ∨ R)

8. [P ∨ (Q ⊃ R)] · (~ R ∨ S)   8. [P ∨ (Q ⊃ R)]Ⓢ(~ R ∨ S)

9. (P · Q) ∨ ~ R   9. (P · Q)Ⓥ~ R

10. ~ [(P ∨ ~ R) · ~ S]   10.⊝[(P ∨ ~ R) · ~ S]

*11. (~ Q ∨ P) ⊃ R   11. (~ Q ∨ P)Ⓞ R

12. [R · (~ T ∨ K)] ∨ S   12. [R · (~ T ∨ K)ⓋS

13. ~ K ⊃ ~ P   13. ~ KⓄ ~ P

14. (P · ~ Q) ∨ (K ⊃ R)   14. (P · ~ Q)Ⓥ(K ⊃ R)

15. (L ⊃ ~ P) · ~ R   15. (L ⊃ ~ P)Ⓢ~ R

*16. [(L ⊃ ~ P) ⊃ Q] ⊃ ~ S   16. [(L ⊃ ~ P) ⊃ Q] Ⓞ ~ S

17. [(M ∨ P) ⊃ (Q ∨ R)] ∨ (S · ~ P)   17. [(M ∨ P) ⊃ (Q ∨ R)]Ⓥ(S · ~ P)

18. [P ∨ (Q ⊃ R)] ⊃ ~ (~ R ∨ S)   18. [P ∨ (Q ⊃ R)] Ⓞ ~ (~ R ∨ S)

19. (P · Q) ∨ (~ R ∨ S)   19. (P · Q)Ⓥ(~ R ∨ S)

20. ~ [(P ⊃ ~ R) ⊃ (~ S ∨ Q)]   20.⊝[(P ⊃ ~ R) ⊃ (~ S ∨ Q)]

*21. ~ Q · P   21. ~ QⓈP

22. (R · Q) ∨ (~ T ∨ K)   22. (R · Q)Ⓥ(~ T ∨ K)

23. P   23. P

24. (P · ~ Q) · K   24. (P · ~ Q)ⓈK

25. L ⊃ (~ P ⊃ Q)   25. LⓄ (~ P ⊃ Q)

Exercises 2–25: For answers and explanations, see pages 93–94 of Instructor's Manual.

Exercises 26–35 If P is true, Q is false, R is true, and S is false, determine the truth value of the following statement structures.

26. P · Q

Answer: P · Q *False*

Explanation: If *any* part of a conjunction is false, then the conjunction is false.

27. R · ~ S   27. True

Exercises 27–45: For answers and explanations, see pages 94–95 of Instructor's Manual.

28. S v ~ Q 28. True

29. (Q v R) • S 29. False

30. P v (S v R) 30. True

*31. ~ P v (~ S v ~ R) 31. True

32. ~ (Q • R) • ~ (S • P) 32. True

33. (R • ~ S) • P 33. True

34. [P v (Q • R)] v ~ S 34. True

35. ~ [P v (Q v R)] v ~ (S v P) 35. False

Exercises 36–45 If P is true, Q is false, R is true, and S is false, determine the truth value of the following statement structures.

36. P ⊃ Q

Answer: False

Explanation: If the antecedent is true and the consequent is false, then the conditional statement is false.

37. (R • ~ S) ⊃ Q 37. False

38. S v (~ Q ⊃ R) 38. True

39. (Q ⊃ R) • S 39. False

40. [P v (S v R)] ⊃ ~ Q 40. True

*41. ~ P ⊃ (~ S v ~ R) 41. True

42. ~ (Q • R) ⊃ ~ (S • P) 42. True

43. (R • ~ S) ⊃ P 43. True

44. [P v (Q • R)] ⊃ ~ S 44. True

45. ~ [P v (Q v R)] ⊃ ~ (S v P) 45. True

Translations and the Main Operator

As mentioned earlier, whenever we translate sentences from English using the symbolic notation of truth-functional operators we must try our best to capture the logical intent. Translating complex sentences from English sometimes requires the correct placement of parentheses. For example, the sentence, "Either Tracy or Becky owns a DVD player, but Sophie owns one for sure," can be translated as "(T v B) • S." The parentheses clearly separate the assertion regarding Tracy and Becky from the assertion regarding Sophie. Once we recognize that the main operator in this sentence is the conjunction and not the disjunction, then the parentheses must be correctly placed to ensure that the " • " is the main operator.

The sentence, "Both Toyota and Honda are Japanese owned companies," can be translated without using parentheses, as "T • H." However, the sentence, "Not both Toyota and Honda are Japanese owned companies," requires the use of parentheses. As in the earlier sentence, the claims regarding Toyota and Honda are clearly joined by the conjunction "and." However, notice that the placement of the "not" is intended to *deny the conjunction*. In other words, since the negation is the main operator in this sentence, we must place parentheses around the conjunction. The result is the translation, "~ (T · H)." If this is confusing, consider the case in which my neighbor claims that both my cat and my dog have fleas. This assertion can be translated as "C · D." I can negate my neighbor's claim by asserting, "It is not the case that both my cat and my dog have fleas." Here I am merely claiming that *at least one* of the conjuncts is false. When I negate the conjunction, I am *not* required to assert that both the conjuncts are false. My statement then gets translated as, "~ (C · D)."

The sentence, "Neither Ford nor Chevrolet is a Japanese-owned company," also requires the correct placement of parentheses. One strategy to get started is to recognize that if we eliminate the "n" from "*neither ... nor*" we get "*either ... or*." The "n's" act as a negation device in this sentence. The intent of the sentence is the assertion that "*It is not the case* that either Ford or Chevrolet is a Japanese-owned company." Since the main operator is the negation, there must be parentheses around the disjunction. Under this interpretation the translation would be "~ (F ∨ C)." Since the only way that a disjunction can be false is if both disjuncts are false, the negation sign has to govern the entire disjunction to achieve that goal.

The uses of "not both ...." and "neither ... nor" are discussed again later in the chapter.

EXERCISE SET 4.3C ○○○

Translate the following statements into symbolic notation. Try to capture as closely as possible the logical structure of each statement.

1. It is not the case that Shane and Carly are hungry.

Answer: Let S = "Shane is hungry," and C = "Carly is hungry."

~ (S · C)

The phrase, "Shane and Carly are hungry," contains two distinct statements: "Shane is hungry," and "Carly is hungry." These are conjoined into, "Shane and Carly are hungry," which is best translated as a conjunction. The phrase, "It is not the case that," negates the conjunction; thus, the negation sign is placed outside the parentheses.

Exercises 2–20: For answers and explanations, see pages 95–97 of Instructor's Manual.

2. I am not mistaken and my test score was high, and I am happy about the result.

3. He neither attended a remedial driver's education course, nor did he lose his license.

4. Not both Mike and Jane wear braces on their teeth.

5. If you can save $100 a month, then if you can afford the insurance, then you can buy a motorcycle.

*6. If you exercise for 20 minutes a day and you cut out 1000 calories a day, then you will be in top physical condition in 6 months.

7. It is not the case that if you stop studying, then you will both pass the course and keep your scholarship.

2. (~ M · T) · H *or* ~ M · (T · H)

3. ~ (R ∨ L)

4. ~ (M · J)

5. S ⊃ (A ⊃ B)

6. (E · C) ⊃ T

7. ~ [S ⊃ (P · K)]

8. M ⊃ (A ∨ P)

    8. We will reinstitute a military draft, only if either we are attacked on our soil or too few people sign up voluntarily.

9. ~ (W ∨ S) ⊃ (~ J ∨ F)

    9. If neither Walter nor Sandy can drive to Pittsburgh next weekend, then Jessica will not come home, unless Jennifer is able to arrive on time.

10. ~ (F ∨ R)

    10. It is not the case that his business is fair or reputable.

11. (~ C • ~ O) ⊃ E

   *11. If we are not careful and we don't change the oil often enough, then the engine will be ruined.

12. ~ C ∨ (W ⊃ M)

    12. Either he is not allowed to go to the concert or if he finishes work on time, then he can meet us at the coffee shop.

13. (D ⊃ B) ∨ F

    13. If your disc player breaks, then I will get you a new one for your birthday, or you can see about getting it fixed.

14. ~ C • [L ⊃ (P ∨ A)]

    14. He did not admit to taking the camera, but if he is lying, then either he pawned it for the money or he has it in his apartment.

15. P • (K ∨ S)

    15. Her painting is valuable, and either she can keep it, or sell it for a lot of money.

16. S ⊃ [C ⊃ (F • B)]

   *16. If soccer is the world's most popular sport, then if it catches on in the United States, then football and basketball will lose fans.

17. ~ (S ⊃ T) • ~ (T ⊃ S)

    17. It is not the case that if you eat a lot of salads, then you will get a lot of vitamins, and it is not the case that if you take a lot of vitamins then you will eat a lot of salads.

18. (A • C) ∨ M

    18. She is athletic and creative, unless I am mistaken.

19. (J • B) ⊃ (M • L)

    19. Johnny and Barbara will visit Las Vegas, only if Mary Lynn and Lee Ann can get a seat on the same flight.

20. J • ~ (D ∨ E)

    20. Joyce has visited Hawaii, but neither Judy nor Eddie has been there.

4.4 TRUTH TABLES FOR COMPLEX TRUTH-FUNCTIONAL STATEMENTS

Truth tables for complex statements and for inferences must have a uniform method for displaying work and results. We start with a statement containing two variables, P and Q: "~ (P • Q) ∨ Q." Recall that since there are two variables, each of which can be either true or false, we get 4 possible combinations. (Three variables, each of which can be true or false, generate $2 \times 2 \times 2 = 8$ combinations; four variables generate $2 \times 2 \times 2 \times 2 = 16$ combinations). The 4 combinations that can be developed with two variables are written down the left side of the table below. The variables and the statement are shown across the top of the table.

P Q	~ (P • Q) ∨ Q
1. T T	
2. T F	
3. F T	
4. F F	

An easy way to ensure that you have all and only the correct combinations is to begin with the leftmost column (in this case with P) and divide the number of lines in half. Since we have a truth table with four lines, the first two lines under the P will contain T and the last two lines will contain F. The next column, Q, will then alternate one T and one F.

A general rule to follow for the construction of all the possible truth value combinations in a truth table is this: The leftmost column has the first half of the lines designated as T and the second half as F. The next column to the right then cuts this in half, again alternating T's and F's. This continues until the final column has one T and one F alternating with each other.

After all possible truth values have been written, the next step is to plug in the truth values to the statement variables correspon- ding to each of the four combinations.

Order of operations:
The step-by-step method of generating a complete truth table by correctly identifying the order of handling the logical operators within a complex statement.

Strategy

Follow the order described in the text to assure that all possible truth values are listed in a truth table.

P Q	~ (P · Q) v Q
1. T T	T T T
2. T F	T F F
3. F T	F T T
4. F F	F F F

At this point the main operator and the *order of operations* are identified. The main operator in this example is "v." The **order of operations** is the step-by-step method of generating a complete truth table by correctly identifying the order of handling the logical operators within the statement. Since the main logical operator controls the final determination of the statement's truth value, it will be the last step. In addition, the negation symbol cannot be applied until the truth value of what- ever is contained within the parentheses is known. Therefore, the correct order of operations for this example is ·, ~, v. The next step is to apply the information con- tained within the parentheses to get a truth value for the operation of conjunction.

P Q	~ (P · Q) v Q
T T	T *(T)* T T
T F	T *(F)* F F
F T	F *(F)* T T
F F	F *(F)* F F

The parentheses around the truth value placed under the conjunction indicate that this is the result of the application of a logical operator. We must remember that the conjunction symbol, ·, has no truth value itself. The *(T)* and *(F)* thus represent all the possible truth values of the complex statement "P · Q." The next step is to apply the negation operator.

P Q	~ (P · Q) v Q
1. T T	*(F)* T *(T)* T T
2. T F	*(T)* T *(F)* F F
3. F T	*(T)* F *(F)* T T
4. F F	*(T)* F *(F)* F F

As the arrow indicates, the negation is applied to the truth value of the conjunction of P and Q. The final step connects the truth values of each side of the main logical operator, which in this case is the disjunction (∨).

Main Logical Operator

P Q	~ (P · Q) ∨ Q
1. T T	*(F)* T *(T)* T *(T)* T
2. T F	*(T)* T *(F)* F *(T)* F
3. F T	*(T)* F *(F)* T *(T)* T
4. F F	*(T)* F *(F)* F *(T)* F

The double arrow indicates which columns must be combined to get the correct result. The red truth values under the main logical operator indicate the final truth table column for this statement. We have thus constructed a truth table that reveals all the possible logical results of this complex statement. If this statement was part of an inference (either a premise or a conclusion), then the results of the truth table could be combined with other information in order to decide the question of validity.

4.5 CONTINGENT AND NONCONTINGENT STATEMENTS

Most of the examples we have looked at so far are **contingent statements**, statements that are possibly true or possibly false. A truth table for a contingent statement has both true and false results in the main operator's column. A simple example is the statement structure "P or Q."

P Q	P ∨ Q
T T	T *(T)* T
T F	T *(T)* F
F T	F *(T)* T
F F	F *(F)* F

The truth values for this statement depend on, or are *contingent* on, the truth values of the component parts. All truth tables for contingent statements contain both true and false results in the main operator column. (In order to determine the truth content of contingent statements we must investigate the world.) However, there are some statements that are *noncontingent*. In a **noncontingent statement**, the truth values in the main operator column do not depend on the truth values of the component parts. We will look at two kinds of noncontingent statements: *tautologies* and *self-contradictions*.

Tautology

Consider the following statement: "Horses are carnivorous *or* horses are not carnivorous." Since this is a disjunction, we know that if one of the disjuncts is true, then the entire statement is true. Therefore, *if* the first disjunct is true, the second disjunct must be false because it is the negation of the first part. The entire statement then

Contingent statement: A statement whose truth or falsity is not based on its logical form but is dependent on other factors; it is therefore possible for the statement to be either true or false.

Noncontingent statement: A statement whose truth or falsity is based on its logical form, not on truth content.

gets the truth value *true*. The only other possibility is that the first disjunct is false, which then makes the second disjunct, the negation, true, and thus the entire complex statement will again be true. Since there are no other possibilities, we have shown that it is impossible for the statement to be false; it must be true. This complex statement does not require us to investigate the truth content of its parts. The result is achieved without investigating the world; our decision is based on the logical possibilities. More specifically, we can see that the statement must be true because of its structure. The way the sentence is built around the logical operator "or," ($\vee$), guarantees that the statement will be true regardless of any empirical information regarding horses. If we examine the structure more closely, we see it as "P or not P." We can construct a truth table to analyze the possible outcomes.

P		P	$\vee$	$\sim$	P
T		T	*(T)*	*(F)*	T
F		F	*(T)*	*(T)*	F

The truth table clearly shows that no matter what you substitute for P you will always get a true statement. This type of statement is called a **tautology**, and it shows a very interesting fact of language and logic. It points out how important the structure of a statement can be when discussing truth. We must acknowledge that truth is sometimes a function of structure rather than facts or content.

Tautologies are not very useful statements in everyday conversation. For instance, suppose you ask your friend whether she will meet you for dinner tonight and she responds, "Either I will be there or I will not." Her answer is indeed true; in fact, we now know that it is logically impossible for it to be false. However, has she given you any information? Did you learn anything from her response that you did not already know? Tautologies, although necessarily true, are not helpful conveyors of information; they are "empty truths." This is one reason why scientific hypotheses cannot be tautologies—they would offer no real information about the world, and they would teach us nothing. A scientific hypothesis that turned out to be a tautology would be obviously true, but trivial. Scientific hypotheses must be either true or false because only then will we actually learn something about the way the world is.

Self-Contradiction

Another type of noncontingent statement can be found in the following example: "The number 2 is an even number *and* it is not an even number." This statement, which cannot possibly be true, is a **self-contradiction**. We can see this by applying what we have learned about the use of "and." *If* "the number 2 is an even number" is true, then its negation, the second part, must be false, and since we are dealing with a conjunction, the whole statement is therefore false. The only other possibility is that the first part is false, which automatically makes the second part true. However, the whole statement would still be false. There just is no way to get the statement to be true. The structure of the statement reveals where the problem lies:

P		P	$\cdot$	$\sim$	P
T		T	*(F)*	*(F)*	T
F		F	*(F)*	*(T)*	F

Tautology: A statement that by its logical form is necessarily true.

Self-Contradiction: A statement that by its logical form is necessarily false.

This illustrates the importance of avoiding self-contradictions when we speak or write. If we contradict ourselves, we are saying something that cannot possibly be true, and the structure of the statement decides this. Self-contradictions are similar to tautologies in that we do not have to investigate the world to determine the statement's truth or falsity—the result is a logical one.

EXERCISE SET 4.5A ○○○

Create truth tables to identify the following statements as contingent statements, tautologies, or self-contradictions.

1. $P \vee (Q \cdot \sim Q)$

Answer: Contingent. The truth table reveals that both truth values, true and false, are possible.

P Q	P $\vee$ (Q $\cdot$ $\sim$ Q)
1. T T	T *(T)* T *(F)* *(F)* T
2. T F	T *(T)* F *(F)* *(T)* F
3. F T	F *(F)* T *(F)* *(F)* T
4. F F	F *(F)* F *(F)* *(T)* F

Exercises 2–20: For answers and explanations, see pages 98–102 of Instructor's Manual.

2. $P \cdot (Q \vee \sim Q)$ 2. Contingent

3. $P \vee P$ 3. Contingent

4. $P \cdot P$ 4. Contingent

5. $(P \vee \sim P) \vee Q$ 5. Tautology

*6. $(P \vee \sim P) \cdot Q$ 6. Contingent

7. $(R \cdot \sim R) \vee S$ 7. Contingent

8. $(R \cdot \sim R) \cdot S$ 8. Self-contradiction

9. $\sim (R \cdot \sim R) \vee \sim (S \vee \sim S)$ 9. Tautology

10. $\sim (R \vee \sim R) \cdot \sim (S \cdot \sim S)$ 10. Self-contradiction

*11. $P \supset (Q \cdot \sim Q)$ 11. Contingent

12. $P \cdot (Q \supset \sim Q)$ 12. Contingent

13. $P \supset P$ 13. Tautology

14. $\sim P \supset \sim P$ 14. Tautology

15. $(P \vee \sim P) \supset P$ 15. Contingent

*16. $(P \cdot \sim P) \supset P$ 16. Tautology

17. $(R \cdot \sim R) \supset (S \vee \sim S)$ 17. Tautology

18. $(R \vee \sim R) \supset (S \vee \sim S)$ 18. Tautology

19. $\sim (R \cdot \sim R) \supset \sim (S \cdot \sim S)$ 19. Tautology

20. $\sim (R \vee \sim R) \supset \sim (S \vee \sim S)$ 20. Tautology

Material Equivalence

Consider the following complex statement:

> If you eat your vegetables, then you get ice cream, and you get ice cream only if you eat your vegetables.

If we let P = "you eat your vegetables," and Q = "you get ice cream," then the translation of these statements using logical notation gives us this: $(P \supset Q) \cdot (Q \supset P)$. This pairing of statements creates an interesting truth table:

	P Q	$(P \supset Q) \cdot (Q \supset P)$
1.	T T	T *(T)* T *(T)* T *(T)* T
2.	T F	T *(F)* F *(F)* F *(T)* T
3.	F T	F *(T)* T *(F)* T *(F)* F
4.	F F	F *(T)* F *(T)* F *(T)* F

The truth table reveals that the conjunction is true in two cases (line #1 and line #4): when P and Q are either both true or both false. This result allows us to introduce a new logical operator called **material equivalence**, or *biconditional*, which has the symbol "≡" (Table 4.7). It is called a biconditional because it is the conjunction of two conditionals. The logical symbol "≡" is used to simplify the relationship revealed by the truth table above.

Table 4.7 Material Equivalence, or Biconditional

Symbol	Name Used	Meaning	Logical Function
≡	triple bar	if and only if	biconditional

The complex conjunction "$(P \supset Q) \cdot (Q \supset P)$" can now be simplified to "$P \equiv Q$." Quick Reference 4.5 shows a truth table for the conditional, "$P \supset Q$," and a truth table for the biconditional, "$P \equiv Q$."

Quick Reference 4.5 • Truth Tables for Conditionals and Biconditionals (Material Equivalence)

Conditional	Biconditional (material equivalence)
P ⊃ Q	**P ≡ Q**
T *(T)* T	T *(T)* T
T *(F)* F	T *(F)* F
F *(T)* T	F *(F)* T
F *(T)* F	F *(T)* F

We are now in position to generalize the many uses of the word "if." The following examples illustrate the variety of statements that can be formed. If F = "you got an A on the final project" and C = "you will get an A for the course," the examples are translated into symbolic notation as follows:

1. *If* you got an A on the final project, then you will get an A for the course. F ⊃ C
2. *Only if* you got an A on the final project, you will get an A for the course. C ⊃ F
3. You will get an A for the course, *if* you get an A on the final project. F ⊃ C
4. You will get an A for the course, *only if* you get an A on the final project. C ⊃ F
5. *If* you got an A for the course, then you got an A on the final project. C ⊃ F
6. *Only if* you got an A for the course, you got an A on the final project. F ⊃ C
7. You will get an A for the course, *if and only if,* you got an A on the final project. C ≡ F

The specific examples can be generalized to get the results in Table 4.8.

Table 4.8 Translating "If"

If P, then Q	P ⊃ Q
Only if P, Q	Q ⊃ P
Q, *if* P	P ⊃ Q
Q, *only if* P	Q ⊃ P
If Q, then P	Q ⊃ P
Only if Q, P	P ⊃ Q
Q, *if and only if,* P	Q ≡ P

EXERCISE SET 4.5B   ○○○

You are given a statement and a set of truth values. (1) Translate the statement symbolically using the correct logical operators. Try to capture the logical structure as closely as possible. (2) Determine whether the statement is true or false.

"If it rains tomorrow, then I will not have to water my plants."

Let P = "it rains tomorrow," and Q = "I will have to water my plants."

Let P = true, Q = false.

1. Logical structure:

2. Truth value:

Answer:

1. Logical structure: P ⊃ ~ Q

The main operator is the conditional. In addition, we should display the negation sign in order to capture all the truth-functional operators at work.

2. Truth value: True

If P = T, and Q = F, then ~ Q = T. So, both the antecedent and consequent are true.

Exercises 2–20: For answers and explanations, see pages 102–103 of Instructor's Manual.

"If the dinner and service are excellent, then I will leave a big tip."

Let P = "the dinner is excellent," Q = "the service is excellent," and R = "I will leave a big tip."

Let P = true, Q = false, and R = true.

3. Logical structure: 3. $(P \cdot Q) \supset R$

4. Truth value: 4. True

"My feet smell, and my nose runs."

Let P = "My feet smell," and Q = "my nose runs."

Let P = true, Q = true.

5. Logical structure: 5. $P \cdot Q$

*6. Truth value: 6. True

"If his car is red or green, then he owes me money and interest."

Let P = "his car is red," and Q = "his car is green," R = "he owes me money," and S = "he owes me interest."

Let P = true, Q = false, R = true, and S = false.

7. Logical structure: 7. $(P \lor Q) \supset (R \cdot S)$

8. Truth value: 8. False

"Shane is a good artist and a good mathematician, if and only if, he is a good person."

Let P = "Shane is a good artist," and Q = "Shane is a good mathematician," and R = "he is a good person."

Let P = true, Q = true, and R = true.

9. Logical structure: 9. $(P \cdot Q) \equiv R$

10. Truth value: 10. True

"If Carly agrees to do a job, then she will make sure it is done right."

Let P = "Carly agrees to do a job," and Q = "she will make sure it is done right."

Let P = false, Q = false.

*11. Logical structure: 11. $P \supset Q$

12. Truth value: 12. True

"If I am not mistaken and my test score was high, then I will be happy."

Let P = "I am mistaken," Q = "my test score was high," and R = "I will be happy."

Let P = true, Q = false, and R = false.

13. Logical structure: 13. $(\sim P \cdot Q) \supset R$

14. Truth value: 14. True

"There are not too many circus acts in Las Vegas."

Let P = "There are too many circus acts in Las Vegas."

Let P = true.

15. Logical structure: 15. ~ P

*16. Truth value: 16. False

"Pizza contains all the basic food groups, if and only if, you get it with anchovies."

Let P = "Pizza contains all the basic food groups," and Q = "you get it with anchovies."

Let P = true, Q = false.

17. Logical structure: 17. P ≡ Q

18. Truth value: 18. False

"Watching circus acts is hazardous to your health, and so is falling into deep holes."

Let P = "Watching circus acts is hazardous to your health," and Q = "so is falling into deep holes (hazardous to your health)."

Let P = true, Q = false.

19. Logical structure: 19. P · Q

20. Truth value: 20. False

4.6 LOGICAL EQUIVALENCE

It is possible for two truth-functional statements to appear different but to have identical truth tables. When this occurs, we have **logically equivalent statements**. In order to compare two statements, we must ensure that identical truth values are plugged in on each line of the respective truth tables. Once they are completed, we compare the truth tables by looking at the result for each statement structure (the main operator). Suppose the statement structures are (1) "P ⊃ Q" and (2) "P v Q." Side-by-side truth tables are needed to compare the two statement structures.

P Q	P ⊃ Q	P v Q
1. T T		
2. T F		
3. F T		
4. F F		

As before, we plug in the appropriate truth values and apply the logical operators.

P Q	P ⊃ Q	P v Q
1. T T	T *(T)* T	T *(T)* T
2. T F	T *(F)* F	T *(T)* F
3. F T	F *(T)* T	F *(T)* T
4. F F	F *(T)* F	F *(F)* F

Logically equivalent statements: Truth-functional statements that have identical truth tables.

Comparing the final results for the two statements reveals that lines #2 and #4 are different. Therefore, these are not logically equivalent statements.

We will now use truth tables to compare two other statement structures in the same way: (1) "~ (T · H)" and (2) "~ T v ~ H."

TH	~ (T · H)	~ T v ~ H
1. T T		
2. T F		
3. F T		
4. F F		

As before, we plug in the appropriate truth values and apply the logical operators.

TH	~ (T · H)	~ T v ~ H
1. T T	*(F)* T *(T)* T	*(F)* T *(F)(F)* T
2. T F	*(T)* T *(F)* F	*(F)* T *(T)(T)* F
3. F T	*(T)* F *(F)* T	*(T)* F *(T)(F)* T
4. F F	*(T)* F *(F)* F	*(T)* F *(T)(T)* F

The results for the two statements are identical; therefore, these are logically equivalent statements.

We encountered the statement structure "~ (T · H)" at the end of Section 4.3 in the discussion of how to translate the sentence, "Not both Toyota and Honda are Japanese owned companies." The sentence was translated as "~ (T · H)," because we recognized that the "not" was intended to deny the conjunction. Now, according to the truth table above, the two statement structures, "~ (T · H)" and "~ T v ~ H" are logically equivalent. The truth table reveals what our earlier discussion mentioned—the statement is asserting that at least one of the conjuncts is false. So the negation of a conjunction does not assert that both conjuncts are false (of course, they both might be false). However, it does assert that at least one of the conjuncts is false.

Also, at the end of Section 4.3 we looked at the translation of the English sentence, "Neither Ford nor Chevrolet is a Japanese-owned company." We decided that this could be translated as "~ (F v C)." Part of the reasoning behind this was that the only way that a disjunction can be false is if both disjuncts are false. Therefore, a denial of a disjunction is the same as the assertion that both disjuncts are false at the same time. This means that the two statement structures, "~ (F v ~ C)" and "~ F · ~ C" should be logically equivalent. We can decide this by creating the appropriate truth tables.

FC	~ (F v C)	~ F · ~ C
1. T T	*(F)* T *(T)* T	*(F)* T *(F)(F)* T
2. T F	*(F)* T *(T)* F	*(F)* T *(F)(T)* F
3. F T	*(F)* F *(T)* T	*(T)* F *(F)(F)* T
4. F F	*(T)* F *(F)* F	*(T)* F *(T)(T)* F

Comparing the results for the two statements shows that they are identical and therefore, logically equivalent.

EXERCISE SET 4.6 ○○○

Use truth tables to determine whether any of the pairs of statement structures are logically equivalent.

1. [P ∨ (Q ∨ R)]   [(P ∨ Q) ∨ R]

Answer: Logically equivalent. Both truth tables have identical results for the main operator in every line.

P Q R	[P ∨ (Q ∨ R)]	[(P ∨ Q) ∨ R]
1. T T T	T *(T)* T *(T)* T	T *(T)* T *(T)* T
2. T T F	T *(T)* T *(T)* F	T *(T)* T *(T)* F
3. T F T	T *(T)* F *(T)* T	T *(T)* F *(T)* T
4. T F F	T *(T)* F *(F)* F	T *(T)* F *(T)* F
5. F T T	F *(T)* T *(T)* T	F *(T)* T *(T)* T
6. F T F	F *(T)* T *(T)* F	F *(T)* T *(T)* F
7. F F T	F *(T)* F *(T)* T	F *(F)* F *(T)* T
8. F F F	F *(F)* F *(F)* F	F *(F)* F *(F)* F

Exercises 2–25: For answers and explanations, see pages 104–111 of Instructor's Manual.

2. [P · (Q · R)]   [(P · Q) · R] 2. Logically equivalent

3. (P ∨ Q)   (Q ∨ P) 3. Logically equivalent

4. (P · Q)   (Q · P) 4. Logically equivalent

5. ~ (P · Q)   (~ P ∨ ~ Q) 5. Logically equivalent

*6. ~ (P ∨ Q)   (~ P · ~ Q) 6. Logically equivalent

7. [P · (Q ∨ R)]   [(P · Q) ∨ (P · R)] 7. Logically equivalent

8. [P ∨ (Q · R)]   [(P ∨ Q) · (P ∨ R)] 8. Logically equivalent

9. P   ~~ P 9. Logically equivalent

10. [(P · Q) ⊃ R]   [P ⊃ (Q ⊃ R)] 10. Logically equivalent

*11. (P ≡ Q)   [(P ⊃ Q) · (Q ⊃ P)] 11. Logically equivalent

12. (P ≡ Q)   [(P · Q) ∨ (~ P · ~ Q)] 12. Logically equivalent

13. (P ⊃ Q)   (~ P ∨ Q) 13. Logically equivalent

14. P   (P ∨ P) 14. Logically equivalent

15. P   (P · P) 15. Logically equivalent

*16. (P ⊃ Q)   (~ Q ⊃ ~ P) 16. Logically equivalent

17. ~ (P · Q)   (~ P · ~ Q) 17. Not Logically equivalent

18. ~ (P v Q)   (~ P v ~ Q)   18. Not Logically equivalent

19. [(P · Q) ⊃ R]   [P v (Q ⊃ R)]   19. Not Logically equivalent

20. [(P · Q) ⊃ R]   [P ⊃ (Q · R)]   20. Not logically equivalent

*21. (P ≡ Q)   [(P ⊃ Q) v (Q ⊃ P)]   21. Not logically equivalent

22. (P ≡ Q)   [(P · Q) · (~ P · ~ Q)]   22. Not logically equivalent

23. (P ⊃ Q)   (~ P · Q)   23. Not logically equivalent

24. (P ⊃ Q)   (Q ⊃ P)   24. Not logically equivalent

25. (P ⊃ Q)   (~ Q v P)   25. Not logically equivalent

4.7 CONTRADICTORY, CONSISTENT, AND INCONSISTENT STATEMENTS

Logically equivalent statements have identical truth tables. In contrast, two statements that have opposite truth values on every line of their respective truth tables are **contradictory statements.** Consider this simple pair of statements: (1) "Lincoln was the 16th President." and (2) "Lincoln was not the 16th President." Translating this pair of statements into logical notation we get: (1) "L," and (2) "~ L." Comparing the simple truth tables gives this analysis:

	L		L	~ L
1.	T		T	(F) T
2.	F		F	(T) F

The final results reveal that the two statements have opposite truth values on every line of their respective truth tables, thus they are contradictory statements.

Are the two statements "Today is not Monday or tomorrow is Tuesday" and "Today is Monday and tomorrow is not Tuesday" contradictory? To solve this problem the sentences must be translated into symbolic notation. The first can be translated as, "~ M v T," while the second can be translated as "M · ~ T." We can now complete the truth table analysis.

	M T		~ M v T	M · ~ T
1.	T T		(F) T (T) T	T (F) (F) T
2.	T F		(F) T (F) F	T (T) (T) F
3.	F T		(T) F (T) T	F (F) (F) T
4.	F F		(T) F (T) F	F (F) (T) F

The results reveal that the two statements have opposite truth values on every line of their respective truth tables; therefore, they are indeed contradictory statements.

Contradictory statements:
Two statements that have opposite truth values on every line of their respective truth tables.

Consistent statements:
For truth-functional statements, if there is at least one line on their respective truth tables where the truth values are both true.

Inconsistent statements:
For truth-functional statements, if there is not even one line on their respective truth tables where the truth values are both true. For two statements to be inconsistent it must be impossible for both statements to be true at the same time.

For a pair of **consistent statements**, there is at least one line on their respective truth tables where the truth values are both true. In other words, for two statements to be consistent, it must be possible for both statements to be true at the same time. For example, suppose that someone claims that "Robert is over 30 years of age," while another person claims that "Robert is over 40 years of age." According to the definition, are these two statements consistent? Is it possible that both statements are true at the same time? *If* Robert is 42 years old, then both statements would be true; so, it is possible. Therefore they are consistent. However, the pair of statements, (1) "Robert is over 30 years of age" and (2) "Robert is not over 30 years of age," is not consistent because they are, in fact, contradictory.

Here is another pair of statement structures for analysis of the possibility of consistency: (1) "R ∨ B" and (2) "R ∨ ~ B." A completed truth table reveals the following:

R B	R ∨ B	R ∨ ~ B
1. T T	T *(T)* T	T *(T)(F)* T
2. T F	T *(T)* F	T *(T)(T)* F
3. F T	F *(T)* T	F *(F)(F)* T
4. F F	F *(F)* F	F *(T)(T)* F

The truth table comparison reveals that both line #1 and line #2 contain the truth value *true*. Since statements are consistent if there is at least one line on their respective truth tables, where the truth values are both true, then the two statements are consistent.

Finally, for a pair of **inconsistent statements**, there is not even one line on their respective truth tables where the truth values are both true. In other words, for two statements to be inconsistent it must be impossible for both statements to be true at the same time. For example, suppose that someone claims that "Robert is over 30 years of age," while another person claims that "Robert is under 20 years of age." According to the definition, are these two statements inconsistent? Is it possible that both statements are true at the same time? *If* Robert is 42 years old, then the first statement would be true, while the second would be false. On the other hand, if Robert is 19 years old, then the second statement would be true, while the first would be false. Is this a pair of contradictory statements? They would be contradictory only if they always have opposite truth values. But *what if* Robert is 25 years old? In that case both statements would be false, so they cannot be contradictory. They are, in fact, inconsistent.

Here is another pair of statements for analysis: (1) "My car ran out of gas and I do not have any money," and (2) "My car ran out of gas, if and only if, I have money." Translating them into symbolic notation we get: (1) "C · ~ M," and (2) "C ≡ M." A completed truth table analysis reveals the following:

C M	C · ~ M	C ≡ M
1. T T	T *(F)(F)* T	T *(T)* T
2. T F	T *(T)(T)* F	T *(F)* F
3. F T	F *(F)(F)* T	F *(F)* T
4. F F	F *(F)(T)* F	F *(T)* F

Since there is no line where the truth values are both true, this is a set of inconsistent statements. In addition, because both statements are false on line #3, they are not contradictory.

EXERCISE SET 4.7

Use truth tables to determine whether the following sets of statement structures are contradictory, consistent, or inconsistent.

1.

A B	A ∨ B	~ A ∨ B
1. T T	T *(T)* T	*(F)* T *(T)* T
2. T F	T *(T)* F	*(F)* T *(F)* F
3. F T	F *(T)* T	*(T)* F *(T)* T
4. F F	F *(F)* F	*(T)* F *(T)* F

Answer: Consistent

Explanation: The truth table comparison reveals that line #1 and line #3 contain the truth value true. Since statements are consistent if there is at least one line on their respective truth tables, where the truth values are both true, then the two statements are consistent.

2. ~ A · B   ~ B ∨ A   2. Contradictory

3. M · ~ M   M   3. Inconsistent

4. P ⊃ Q   P · ~ Q   4. Contradictory

5. T ≡ U   T · U   5. Consistent

*6. P ∨ Q   ~ (P ∨ Q)   6. Contradictory

7. (Q ⊃ ~ R) · S   S ≡ (Q · R)   7. Inconsistent

8. Q ∨ P   ~ Q ⊃ ~ P   8. Consistent

9. C · D   ~ C ∨ ~ D   9. Contradictory

10. Q ⊃ P   Q · P   10. Consistent

*11. A ∨ B   ~ A ∨ ~ B   11. Consistent

12. ~ A · B   ~ B · A   12. Inconsistent

13. M ∨ ~ M   M   13. Consistent

14. P ⊃ Q   Q ⊃ P   14. Consistent

15. T ≡ U   T ∨ U   15. Consistent

*16. P ∨ Q   ~ (P · Q)   16. Consistent

17. (Q ⊃ ~ R) ⊃ S   S ≡ (Q · R)   17. Consistent

18. Q ∨ P   ~ Q · ~ P   18. Contradictory

Exercises 2–20: For answers and explanations, see pages 112–118 of Instructor's Manual.

19. C · D   ~ C ⊃ ~ D 19. Consistent

20. Q ⊃ P   Q ∨ P 20. Consistent

SUMMARY

- Conjunction, negation, disjunction, conditional, and material equivalence are truth-functional operators.
- A conditional statement does not assert that either the antecedent or the consequent is true. A conditional statement does assert that if the antecedent is true, then so is the consequent.
- Rules ensure grammatically correct statements, also known as well-formed formulas (*WFFs*).
- The main operator in a complex truth-functional statement is one of the operators that goes between statements, or it is the negation operator.
- The order of operations is the step-by-step method of generating a complete truth table. Since the main operator controls the final determination of the statement's truth value, it is the last step.
- A contingent statement is possibly true or possibly false.
- A tautology is a noncontingent statement that is true because of its logical structure.
- A self-contradiction is a noncontingent statement that is always false.
- Two truth-functional statements that appear different but have identical truth tables are logically equivalent.
- Two truth-functional statements that have opposite truth values on every line of their respective truth tables are contradictory.
- Statements are consistent if there is at least one line on their respective truth tables where the truth values are both true.
- Statements are inconsistent if there is not even one line on their respective truth tables where the truth values are both true.

KEY TERMS

truth-functional statement   113
truth value   113
logical operator   113
conjunction   114
truth table   114
negation   115
disjunction   116
inclusive disjunction   116
exclusive disjunction   116
conditional statement   122
antecedent   122

consequent   122
if   126
only if   126
well-formed formulas   130
main logical operator   130
order of operations   137
contingent statement   138
noncontingent statement   138

tautology   139
self-contradiction   139
material equivalence   141
logically equivalent statements   144
contradictory statements   147
consistent statement   148
inconsistent statements   148

LOGIC CHALLENGE: A TRICKY PROBLEM

There is a large group of cards that you have not seen. You are told (and we stipulate that this is true) that each card has a number on one of its sides and a letter on the other side. No card has numbers on both sides and no card has letters on both sides. You are not told how many cards there are, but you are told that the same number might occur on many different cards, and the same letter might also occur on many different cards.

Someone who has been allowed to inspect the cards makes a claim. "I have looked at all the cards and I have discovered a pattern: *If there is a vowel on one side of the card, then there is an even number on the other side.*" The *italicized* statement could be true or false.

You will be shown four cards. You will only see one side of each card. If you see a letter, then you know there must be a number on the other side. If you see a number, then you know there must be a letter on the other side. Your task is to turn over *only* the cards that have the *possibility* to make the person's italicized statement *false*. The four cards are displayed below.

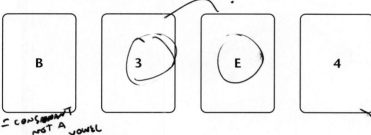

Which cards (if any) should you turn over?

Answer: Turn over only the "3" and "E" cards. See page 119 of Instructor's Manual for explanation.

Truth Tables and Proofs

August

M	T	W	T	F	S	S
		1	2	3	4	5
6	7	8	9	10	11	12
13	14	15	16	17	18	19
20	21	22	23	24	25	26
27	28	29	30	31		

{ overview }

5.1 TRUTH TABLES AND
     INFERENCES

5.2 INDIRECT TRUTH TABLES

5.3 SUFFICIENT AND NECESSARY
     CONDITIONS

Chapter 4 presented the fundamentals of building and using truth tables for analysis of complex truth-functional statements. In this chapter, truth tables will be constructed to determine the validity or invalidity of truth-functional inferences.

5.1 TRUTH TABLES AND INFERENCES

We are ready to apply our knowledge of truth tables to the analysis of inferences. Consider the following inference:

$$\sim (P \cdot Q)$$
$$\underline{P \qquad\qquad}$$
$$Q$$

The first step is to display the inference in a way that will allow us to build on what we already learned. Recall from Chapter 4 that since there are two variables, each of which can be either true or false, we get four possible combinations.

	1st Premise	2nd Premise	Conclusion
P Q	~ (P · Q)	P	Q
1. T T			
2. T F			
3. F T			
4. F F			

We are displaying the information in order to allow a uniform, methodical application of our knowledge of truth tables to the complete analysis of inferences. We start by plugging in the appropriate truth values for each of our four lines.

chapter

	1st Premise	2nd Premise	Conclusion
P Q	~ (P · Q)	P	Q
1. T T	T T	T	T
2. T F	T F	T	F
3. F T	F T	F	T
4. F F	F F	F	F

The next step is to complete the work for the first premise. (1) Apply the truth values for P and Q to get the results for conjunction (the operator at work within the parentheses), and then (2) apply the negation sign to the results for conjunction.

	1st Premise	2nd Premise	Conclusion
P Q	~ (P · Q)	P	Q
1. T T	(F) T (T) T	T	T
2. T F	(T) T (F) F	T	F
3. F T	(T) F (F) T	F	T
4. F F	(T) F (F) F	F	F

The final truth value of each statement appears in red type, and is either directly under a simple statement or under the main operator of a complex statement. As always, the question of validity hinges on the possibility or impossibility of getting true premises and a false conclusion. Since the truth table has revealed all possible cases, we are perfectly situated to decide the question. We need to look at each line of the truth table to see if it contains all the premises true and the conclusion false. Line #2 does indeed reveal an instance of true premises and a false conclusion, which proves that the inference is invalid.

Let's do a more complex inference:

$$P \lor {\sim} Q$$

$$\underline{{\sim} (P \lor S)}$$

$${\sim} S$$

Since this inference contains three variables, P, Q, S, we will have to construct a truth table with eight lines (two truth values for each variable give us $2 \times 2 \times 2 = 8$ possible combinations).

	1st Premise	2nd Premise	Conclusion
P Q S	P ∨ ~ Q	~ (P ∨ S)	~ S
1. T T T			
2. T T F			
3. T F T			
4. T F F			
5. F T T			
6. F T F			
7. F F T			
8. F F F			

Notice that we have followed the general method for constructing the possible truth value combinations.

1. Since the truth table has eight lines, we start by dividing the left-most column in half giving us four T's and four F's.
2. The next column divides this proportion in half giving us two T's followed by two F's alternating until the column is completed.
3. The next column divides by half once again, giving us one T and one F alternating until the column is complete.

We are now in the position to plug in the truth values for each variable corresponding to the appropriate lines.

		1st Premise	2nd Premise	Conclusion
P Q S		P v ~ Q	~ (P v S)	~ S
1. T T T		T T	T T	T
2. T T F		T T	T F	F
3. T F T		T F	T T	T
4. T F F		T F	T F	F
5. F T T		F T	F T	T
6. F T F		F T	F F	F
7. F F T		F F	F T	T
8. F F F		F F	F F	F

Strategy

In constructing a truth table it is best to follow the three steps for getting all possible combinations of truth values for the variables of the inference.

Notice that we have merely applied the appropriate truth values to the designated variables; we have not dealt with any operators yet. We must build the truth table in a methodical way. Skipping steps or combining steps can cause mistakes. Once all the initial truth values are in place we can proceed to the operators.

		1st Premise	2nd Premise	Conclusion
P Q S		P v ~ Q	~ (P v S)	~ S
1. T T T		T *(T)* *(F)* T	*(F)* T *(T)* T	*(F)* T
2. T T F		T *(T)* *(F)* T	*(F)* T *(T)* F	*(T)* F
3. T F T		T *(T)* *(T)* F	*(F)* T *(T)* T	*(F)* T
4. T F F		T *(T)* *(T)* F	*(F)* T *(T)* F	*(T)* F
5. F T T		F *(F)* *(F)* T	*(F)* F *(T)* T	*(F)* T
6. F T F		F *(F)* *(F)* T	*(T)* F *(F)* F	*(T)* F
7. F F T		F *(T)* *(T)* F	*(F)* F *(T)* T	*(F)* T
8. F F F		F *(T)* *(T)* F	*(T)* F *(F)* F	*(T)* F

The truth table is now complete. The validity or invalidity of the inference rests on the results of the eight lines; specifically, whether any line displays true premises and a false conclusion. We do not find a line where both premises are true at the same time until we reach line #8. Inspecting this line reveals that under these circumstances (premises all true) the conclusion is true, as well. Since we have exhausted

BIOGRAPHY : CHARLES S. PEIRCE

According to Charles S. Peirce (1839–1914), the specific goal of mathematics is the creation of inferences having conclusions that follow by necessity, while the general goal of logic is the investigation of any and all kinds of inferences. Peirce created many novel logical notations and did outstanding work in both logic and mathematics. He is recognized as being the greatest American philosopher-mathematician. He founded pragmatism, the application of scientific methods and results to philosophical problems. Peirce believed that deduction and induction were not sufficient to complete logic. He coined the term "abduction" to refer to the nearly all-encompassing activity of generating hypotheses in order to explain facts and to deduce predictions.

Peirce helped pave the way to the universal acceptance of truth tables as a way to reveal the logic behind truth-functional operators. Nevertheless, it took the work of others, most notably the philosopher Ludwig Wittgenstein (1889–1951), to solidify the acceptance and importance of truth tables. Ultimately, this system became the perfect tool for helping create computer languages. The system of truth values (true and false) is one of the foundations of all computer languages and hardware applications.

Technically valid inference: An inference that has a tautology as its conclusion is technically valid because it is impossible for the conclusion to be false. An inference that has a self-contradiction as one of its premises is technically valid because it is impossible for all the premises to be true.

all the possibilities, and since it is impossible to find a line that has true premises coupled with a false conclusion, we have, therefore, proved that the inference is valid. The truth table method provides a mechanical procedure for effectively proving whether an inference using truth-functional operators is valid or invalid.

A Note on Technical Validity

If the conclusion of an inference is a tautology, then it will be impossible to ever get all the premises true and the conclusion false, *because the conclusion is logically true.* This is an example of a **technically valid inference**. Although valid, this kind of inference comes at a high cost since the conclusion is trivial, an empty truth that conveys no real information about the world and illuminates nothing.

Another type of technically valid inference is created by making one of the premises a self-contradiction. In this case it will be impossible to ever get all the premises true and the conclusion false, *because the premise with the self-contradiction is logically false.* However, if we contradict ourselves in the premises, then we are saying something that cannot possibly be true, and the cost of constructing such an inference would be to have created an inference that cannot be *sound*.

EXERCISE SET 5.1A   ○○○

Exercises 1–15 Use your knowledge of conjunction, disjunction, and negation to create truth tables to determine whether the following inferences are valid or invalid.

1. R v S
   R

Answer:

	R S	R ∨ S	R
		Premise	**Conclusion**
1.	T T	T *(T)* T	T
2.	T F	T *(T)* F	T
3.	F T	F *(T)* T	F
4.	F F	F *(F)* F	F

Explanation: The inference is invalid, because line #3 reveals an instance where the premise is true and the conclusion is false.

2. <u>R · S</u>
   R Valid

3. <u>~ P ∨ ~ S</u>
   <u>P   </u>
   S Invalid

4. <u>R ∨ ~ S</u>
   S Invalid

5. <u>~ R ∨ ~ S</u>
   ~ R Invalid

*6. <u>~ R · ~ S</u>
   ~ S Valid

7. ~ (~ R ∨ ~ S)
   <u>S   </u>
   R Valid

8. ~ (~ R · ~ S)
   <u>~ S   </u>
   ~ R Invalid

9. ~ (R ∨ S)
   <u>~ R   </u>
   ~ S Valid

10. ~ (R · S)
    <u>~ R   </u>
    ~ S Invalid

*11. <u>P ∨ (Q ∨ S)</u>
    P Invalid

12. (P · Q) ∨ R
    <u>~ Q   </u>
    R Valid

Exercises 2–22: For answers and explanations, see pages 130–138 of Instructor's Manual.

13. S v (Q v R)

   ~ Q

   ~ R

   S Valid

14. (S v Q) v R

   Q

   R

   ~ S Invalid

15. ~ (~ S v Q) · (P v R)

   ~ Q

   ~ P

   ~ R

   ~ S Valid

Exercises 16–22 Begin by translating the following inferences into the symbolic notation discussed thus far. Then use your knowledge of conjunction, disjunction, and negation to create truth tables to determine whether the inferences are valid or invalid.

16. Either January or February was the coldest month this year. January was clearly not the coldest month. Therefore, it had to be February.

Answer: Let J = "January was the coldest month this year," and B = "February was the coldest month this year."

		1ˢᵗ Premise	**2ⁿᵈ Premise**	**Conclusion**
	J B	J v B	~ J	B
1.	T T	T *(T)* T	*(F)* T	T
2.	T F	T *(T)* F	*(F)* T	F
3.	F T	F *(T)* T	*(T)* F	T
4.	F F	F *(F)* F	*(T)* F	F

Explanation: The inference is valid, because there is no line where the premises are true and the conclusion is false.

17. Either June or July was the hottest month this year. The almanac says that July was the hottest, so it cannot be June. Invalid

18. Either Eddie or Walter is the tallest member of the family. Walter is the tallest, so Eddie is not the tallest. Invalid

19. It is not the case that June and September have 31 days. June does not have 31 days; therefore, September does not have 31 days. Invalid

20. Unless we stop interfering in other countries' internal affairs we will find ourselves with more enemies than we can handle. The president assures us that we will stop interfering in other countries' internal affairs. So it is safe to conclude that we will not find ourselves with more enemies than we can handle. Invalid

*21. It is not the case that both Jim and Mary Lynn are hog farmers. Mary Lynn is not a hog farmer, so Jim cannot be one. Invalid

22. It is not the case that either Lee Ann or Johnny is old enough to collect Social Security benefits. Since Lee Ann does not collect Social Security benefits, we can conclude that Johnny does not. Valid

Conditional inference: An inference that has a conditional statement as one of its premises.

Modus ponens: The method of affirming the antecedent.

Conditional Inferences

We can use our knowledge of conditional statements in the analysis of conditional inferences. A **conditional inference** has a conditional statement as one of its premises, as shown in Example 5.1.

Example 5.1

If you got a 98 on the exam, then you got an A.
<u>You got a 98 on the exam.</u>
You got an A.

Modus Ponens The inference structure in Example 5.1 and in Quick Reference 5.1 is called *modus ponens*. (*Modus*, means "method" and *ponens*, means "affirming." In this particular case, it stands for the "method of affirming the antecedent.")

Revealing the logical structure of the inference will help our analysis. If P = "you got a 98 on the exam," and Q = "you got an A," then we get the following structure:

$$P \supset Q$$

$$\underline{P}$$

$$Q$$

Here is a completed truth table for the inference:

	1st Premise	2nd Premise	Conclusion
P Q	P ⊃ Q	P	Q
1. T T	T *(T)* T	T	T
2. T F	T *(F)* F	T	F
3. F T	F *(T)* T	F	T
4. F F	F *(T)* F	F	F

The truth table shows that the inference is valid, because there is no line with true premises and a false conclusion.

Quick Reference 5.1 • The General Logical Structure of *Modus Ponens*

$$p \supset q$$

$$\underline{p}$$

$$q$$

Any inference with the logical structure of *modus ponens* is valid.

Naming certain inference structures allows us to use the results of logical analysis to make general claims. We can assert that any inference whose structure is identical to *modus ponens* is valid. To see the value of this consider the inference in Example 5.2:

Example 5.2

If your car starts, then you have gasoline.
<u>Your car starts.</u>
You have gasoline.

If we let P = "your car starts," and let Q = "you have gasoline," then we get the following logical structure:

$$P \supset Q$$
$$\underline{P \qquad}$$
$$Q$$

The logical structure of this inference is identical to that of *modus ponens*; thus, we can assert that the inference is valid. This result shows the power of reducing an inference to its logical structure. We can see how two inferences offering different truth content information—one about test scores and letter grades, the other about cars and gasoline—can have identical logical structures. In addition, this means that you can take any statements, place them into a valid inference structure, and the result will always be a valid inference. *The logical structure of the inference determines validity, not the truth or falsity of the premises and the conclusion.*

Fallacy of Affirming the Consequent In Example 5.3 we will analyze another conditional inference to get more experience with the techniques we have learned.

Example 5.3

If your car starts, then you have gasoline.
<u>You have gasoline.</u>
Your car starts.

If we let P = "your car starts," and Q = "you have gasoline," then we get the following logical structure:

$$P \supset Q$$
$$\underline{Q \qquad}$$
$$P$$

Here is a completed truth table for the inference:

Fallacy of affirming the consequent: A fallacy with a form that resembles *modus ponens*.

	1st Premise	2nd Premise	Conclusion
P Q	P ⊃ Q	Q	P
1. T T	T *(T)* T	T	T
2. T F	T *(F)* F	F	T
3. F T	F *(T)* T	T	F
4. F F	F *(T)* F	F	F

As indicated by the box, line #3 shows that for this inference it is possible to get both premises true and the conclusion false at the same time. Since the logical structure has been proven to be invalid, and Example 5.3 is a particular instance of this structure, it is therefore invalid as well.

The inference structure in Example 5.3 and Quick Reference 5.2 has been given a name also; it is called the **fallacy of affirming the consequent**.

Quick Reference 5.2 • The General Logical Structure of the Fallacy of Affirming the Consequent

$$p \supset q$$

$$\underline{q\qquad}$$

$$p$$

Any inference with the logical structure of the fallacy of affirming the consequent is invalid.

The result of our logical analysis allows us to make another general claim. We can assert that any inference whose structure is identical with the fallacy of affirming the consequent is invalid.

Modus Tollens In Example 5.4 we will see how negation functions in a conditional inference.

Example 5.4

If your car starts, then you have gasoline.
<u>You do not have gasoline.</u>
Your car does not start.

If we let P = "your car starts," and Q = "you have gasoline," then the structure of the inference is revealed:

$$P \supset Q$$

$$\underline{\sim Q\qquad}$$

$$\sim P$$

Modus tollens: The method of denying the consequent.

Here is a completed truth table for the inference:

		1st Premise	2nd Premise	Conclusion
P Q		P ⊃ Q	~ Q	~ P
1. T T		T *(T)* T	*(F)* T	*(F)* T
2. T F		T *(F)* F	*(T)* F	*(F)* T
3. F T		F *(T)* T	*(F)* T	*(T)* F
4. F F		F *(T)* F	*(T)* F	*(T)* F

The truth table shows that the inference is valid, because there is no line with true premises and a false conclusion. The name of the valid inference structure in Example 5.4 is **modus tollens**. (*Modus* means "method" and *tollens* means "denying." In this particular case it stands for "the method of denying the consequent.") Quick Reference 5.3 shows the general structure of *modus tollens*.

Quick Reference 5.3 • The General Logical Structure of *Modus Tollens*

Any inference with the logical structure of *modus tollens* is valid.

$$p \supset q$$
$$\underline{\sim q}$$
$$\sim p$$

We can now make another general claim: any inference whose structure is identical to *modus tollens* is valid.

Fallacy of Denying the Antecedent The inference in Example 5.5 appears to be similar to the one we have just analyzed, but as we shall see, different results are obtained.

Example 5.5

If your car starts, then you have gasoline.
<u>Your car does not start.</u>
You do not have gasoline.

If we let P = "your car starts," and Q = "you have gasoline," then the structure of the inference is revealed:

$$P \supset Q$$
$$\underline{\sim P}$$
$$\sim Q$$

Here is a completed truth table for the inference:

	1st Premise	2nd Premise	Conclusion
P Q	P ⊃ Q	~ P	~ Q
1. T T	T *(T)* T	*(F)* T	*(F)* T
2. T F	T *(F)* F	*(F)* T	*(T)* F
3. F T	F *(T)* T	*(T)* F	*(F)* T
4. F F	F *(T)* F	*(T)* F	*(T)* F

As indicated by the box, line #3 shows that for this inference it is possible to get both premises true and the conclusion false at the same time. Since the logical structure has been proven invalid, and Example 5.5 is a particular instance of this structure, it is therefore invalid as well.

The inference structure in Example 5.5 and in Quick Reference 5.4 has also been given a name; it is called the **fallacy of denying the antecedent.**

> **Fallacy of denying the antecedent:** A fallacy with a form that resembles *modus tollens.*

Quick Reference 5.4 • The General Logical Structure of the Fallacy of Denying the Antecedent

$$p \supset q$$

$$\underline{\sim p}$$

$$\sim q$$

> Any inference with the logical structure of the fallacy of denying the antecedent is invalid.

The result of our logical analysis allows us to make another general claim. We can assert that any inference whose structure is identical with the fallacy of denying the antecedent is invalid.

The valid inference structures *modus ponens* and *modus tollens,* and the invalid inference structures of the fallacy of affirming the consequent and the fallacy of denying the antecedent are further developed in Chapter 6, which introduces more formal proof procedure methods. However, the results derived in this section will have a more immediate application, as they will help us explore *sufficient and necessary conditions,* the subjects of Section 5.3.

Analyzing Complex Inferences

We will now use truth tables to analyze a more complex inference. This inference has three premises and a conclusion. The proof procedure is the same no matter how many premises or variables there are.

$$(P \supset Q) \vee R$$

$$R \cdot \sim S$$

$$\underline{\sim P}$$

$$\sim Q$$

Since there are four variables in the inference, we will have to construct a truth table with 16 lines (four variables, each having two possibilities, true or false, gives us $2 \times 2 \times 2 \times 2 = 16$). The steps to truth table proofs are realized in the following truth table: (1) use the general rule for calculating the number of lines needed in the truth table, (2) plug in the truth values associated with each line directly to the statement variables, (3) apply the logical operators at the appropriate time, and (4) determine if any line has true premises and a false conclusion.

	P Q R S	1st Premise $(P \supset Q) \vee R$	2nd Premise $R \cdot \sim S$	3rd Premise $\sim P$	Conclusion $\sim Q$
1.	T T T T	T(T)T(T)T	T (F)(F)T	(F)T	(F)T
2.	T T T F	T(T)T(T)T	T(T)(T)F	(F)T	(F)T
3.	T T F T	T(T)T(T)F	F (F)(F)T	(F)T	(F)T
4.	T T F F	T(T)T(T)F	F (F)(T)F	(F)T	(F)T
5.	T F T T	T(F) F(T)T	T (F)(F)T	(F)T	(T)F
6.	T F T F	T(F) F(T)T	T(T)(T)F	(F)T	(T)F
7.	T F F T	T(F) F(F)F	F (F)(F)T	(F)T	(T)F
8.	T F F F	T(F) F(F)F	F (F)(T)F	(F)T	(T)F
9.	F T T T	F(T)T(T)T	T (F)(F)T	(T)F	(F)T
10.	F T T F	F(T)T(T)T	T(T)(T)F	(T)F	(F)T
11.	F T F T	F(T)T(T)F	F (F)(F)T	(T)F	(F)T
12.	F T F F	F(T)T(T)F	F (F)(T)F	(T)F	(F)T
13.	F F T T	F(T)F(T)T	T (F)(F)T	(T)F	(T)F
14.	F F T F	F(T)F(T)T	T (T)(T)F	(T)F	(T)F
15.	F F F T	F(T)F(T)F	F (F)(F)T	(T)F	(T)F
16.	F F F F	F(T)F(T)F	F (F)(T)F	(T)F	(T)F

The completed truth table now reveals that line #10 has all true premises and a false conclusion, which proves that the inference is invalid.

EXERCISE SET 5.1B   ○○○

Exercises 1–21 Use your knowledge of truth-functional statements to create truth tables to determine whether the following inferences are valid or invalid.

1. $\underline{R \supset S}$
   R

Answer: Invalid. Either line #3 or line #4 is sufficient to prove the inference is invalid.

	Premise	Conclusion
R S	R ⊃ S	R
1. T T	T *(T)* T	T
2. T F	T *(F)* F	T
3. F T	F *(T)* T	F
4. F F	F *(T)* F	F

2. <u>P</u>

   P ∨ Q Valid

3. P

  <u>Q</u>

  P · Q Valid

4. P ⊃ Q

  <u>P</u>

  Q Valid

5. P ⊃ Q

  <u>~ Q</u>

  ~ P Valid

*6. P ∨ Q

  <u>~ P</u>

  Q Valid

7. P ⊃ Q

  <u>Q ⊃ R</u>

  P ⊃ R Valid

8. (P ⊃ Q) · (R ⊃ S)

  <u>P ∨ R</u>

  Q ∨ S Valid

9. <u>P · Q</u>

  P Valid

10. <u>(R · S) ⊃ S</u>

  S Invalid

*11. P ⊃ (~ P ∨ ~ S)

  <u>~ P</u>

  ~ S Invalid

12. ~ (R ⊃ S)

  <u>~ R</u>

  ~ S Valid

Exercises 2–36: For answers and explanations, see pages 139–154 of Instructor's Manual.

13. ~ (R · S)
    ~ R ⊃ P
    ~ S Invalid

14. (P v Q) ⊃ S
    P Invalid

15. (P · Q) v (R ⊃ P)
    ~ Q v ~ R
    R Invalid

*16. [S v (Q v R)] ⊃ Q
    ~ Q
    ~ R
    S Invalid

17. [(S · Q) · R] ⊃ Q
    Q
    R
    ~ S Invalid

18. ~ (~ S v Q) ⊃ (P v R)
    ~ Q
    ~ P
    ~ R
    ~ S Valid

19. P ⊃ Q
    Q ⊃ P
    P v Q Invalid

20. (P · Q) v R
    ~ Q
    R Valid

21. P ⊃ (Q v ~ R)
    Q ⊃ ~ R
    P ⊃ ~ R Valid

Exercises 22–36 For each of the following inferences you are to reveal the logical structure, and then prove it valid or invalid.

22. If the prosecuting attorney's claims are correct, then the defendant is guilty.
    The defendant is guilty.
    The prosecuting attorney's claims are correct.

Answer: Invalid

If we let P = "the prosecuting attorney's claims are correct," and Q = "the defendant is guilty," then the form of the inference is revealed:

P ⊃ Q

Q

P

Here is a completed truth table for the inference:

	1st Premise	2nd Premise	Conclusion
P Q	P ⊃ Q	Q	P
1. T T	T (T) T	T	T
2. T F	T (F) F	F	T
3. F T	F (T) T	T	F
4. F F	F (T) F	F	F

As indicated by the box, line #3 shows that for this inference it is possible to get both premises true and the conclusion false at the same time, therefore this is an invalid inference. (It is also an instance of the fallacy of affirming the consequent.)

23. If the prosecuting attorney's claims are correct, then the defendant is guilty.
    The defendant is not guilty.
    The prosecuting attorney's claims are correct. Invalid

24. If the prosecuting attorney's claims are correct, then the defendant is guilty.
    The defendant is not guilty.
    The prosecuting attorney's claims are not correct. Valid

25. If the prosecuting attorney's claims are correct, then the defendant is guilty.
    The defendant is guilty.
    The prosecuting attorney's claims are not correct. Invalid

*26. If UFOs exist, then there is life on other planets.
    UFOs do not exist.
    There is not life on other planets. Invalid

27. If UFOs exist, then there is life on other planets.
    UFOs do not exist.
    There is life on other planets. Invalid

28. If I am the president of the United States, then I live in the White House.
    I am not the president of the United States.
    I do not live in the White House. Invalid

29. If I live in the White House, then I am the president of the United States.
    I am not the president of the United States.
    I do not live in the White House. Valid

30. If you take 1000mg of Vitamin C every day, then you will not get a cold.
    <u>You get a cold.</u>
    You did not take 1000mg of Vitamin C every day. Valid

*31. If you take 1000mg of Vitamin C every day, then you will not get a cold.
    <u>You did not get a cold.</u>
    You did take 1000mg of Vitamin C every day. Invalid

32. If X is an even number, then X is divisible by 2.
    <u>X is not divisible by 2.</u>
    X is not an even number. Valid

33. If X is not an even number, then X is not divisible by 2.
    <u>X is divisible by 2.</u>
    X is an even number. Valid

34. If Joyce went south on I-15 from Las Vegas, then Joyce got to Los Angeles.
    <u>Joyce did not go south on I-15 from Las Vegas.</u>
    Joyce did not get to Los Angeles. Invalid

35. If you do not finish the job by Friday, then you do not get the bonus.
    <u>You finished the job by Friday.</u>
    You get the bonus. Invalid

*36. If you finish the job by Friday, then you get the bonus.
    <u>You did not finish the job by Friday.</u>
    You do not get the bonus. Invalid

5.2 INDIRECT TRUTH TABLES

A good understanding of the truth tables for the logical operators gives us the ability to analyze inferences in a way that is shorter than creating full-fledged truth tables. However, before we tackle this new method we must learn to think our way through a proof.

Thinking through a Proof

In thinking through a proof, we will rely on our grasp of the logical possibilities associated with the logical operators. We will start with the following inference.

Stocks will go up in value or we will have a recession.
<u>We will not have a recession.</u>
Stocks will go up in value.

If we let P = "Stocks will go up in value," and Q = "we will have a recession," then the inference can be symbolized very easily like this:

P v Q

~ Q

P

If we make the premises true, then what does this tell us? If the first premise "P v Q" = *True*, then what can we say about P and Q separately? If the statement is true, then we know that since we are dealing with a disjunction, *at least one* of the disjuncts must be true; however, we do not know which one, so we will start with both P and Q true:

[T] [T]

P v Q = *True*

Now if the second statement, ~ Q, is true, then what does it tell us? It tells us that the negation of Q is *true*, so Q itself must be *false* (if Q = *False*, then ~ Q = *True*).

[T] [T̸] [F]

P v Q = *True*

~ Q [F] = *True*

From this, we now know that the Q in the first statement can be eliminated as a possibility for being true. Why is this? The first statement does not say that Q *is* true; from the truth of the first statement we know only that Q might be true. But now the second premise, if it is true, tells us for sure that Q is false. The only way to make the second premise true is to make Q itself false. Remember that we wanted to make all the premises true and to see what happens to the conclusion. When we initially encountered the first premise and assumed it was true, we did not know whether P was true or Q was true or both were true. The second premise, if true, showed that Q had to be false. Therefore, going back to the first premise we now know that in order to get both premises true, P must be true. If P must be true in order to get both premises true, then the P in the conclusion must be true, too. This is a perfectly valid inference since the structure does not allow for true premises and a false conclusion. Thus, the original inference concerning "stocks" is valid. In fact, once we know that a particular structure is valid, we know that any instance of that structure will be valid as well. No matter what statements are substituted for P and Q, they will never create an inference that will have true premises and a false conclusion. You might want to try some substitutions just to convince yourself (but don't spend too much time trying to do the impossible).

We can get the same result using the bottom-up technique. This analysis starts by making the conclusion false and then attempting to make all the premises true. Since the conclusion is just P, we must assign it the truth value *false* in order to get the conclusion *false*. Having done this, we must now assign the truth value *false* to every other occurrence of P throughout the inference. Since the first premise is "P v Q," and since we know that P has the truth value *false*, the only way to get the first premise *true* is for Q to be *true*. Having established the only possible value for

Indirect truth table: A truth table for which truth values are assigned specifically to reveal the possibility of true premises and a false conclusion.

Q (if our goal is to make the first premise *true*) requires that all other occurrences of Q get the same truth value. The second premise is ~ Q, and since Q has been assigned the truth value true, ~ Q will be false. Therefore, we have shown that if the conclusion is false, then the premises cannot all be true at the same time.

An Indirect Truth Table

Now that we have thought our way through a proof using the logical operators, we are in position to fully develop a short-cut method of proof. An **indirect truth table** assigns truth values to the statements of an inference in order to quickly reveal the possibility of true premises and a false conclusion. We will use our knowledge of the truth tables to analyze an inference using a technique in which truth values are applied directly to the statements comprising the inferences (Example 5.6).

> ### Example 5.6
>
> $$\sim (P \cdot Q)$$
> $$\underline{P}$$
> $$Q$$

We start by displaying the inference as if we were doing a normal truth table proof. For example,

	1st Premise	2nd Premise	Conclusion
P Q ‖	~ (P · Q)	P	Q

Since an indirect truth table looks for the shortest way to decide the possibility of true premises and false conclusion, it makes sense to assign truth values to those variables that allow us to "lock in" one truth value. In this example, since the conclusion is Q we can start by assigning Q the truth value *F*. Once we do this, we must replace every occurrence of Q with the same assigned truth value.

	1st Premise	2nd Premise	Conclusion
P Q ‖	~ (P · Q)	P	Q
F ‖	F		F

The next step is to try to get all the premises true at the same time. A good strategy is to work on the simplest premises first. Since the second premise is just P, we know that the truth value of P must be *true* to get this premise true, so we add that information to our truth table, making sure that every instance of P gets the same truth value.

	1st Premise	2nd Premise	Conclusion
P Q ‖	~ (P · Q)	P	Q
T F ‖	T F	T	F

Since all truth values have been assigned, we can complete the truth table.

1st Premise	2nd Premise	Conclusion
P Q || ~ (P · Q)	P	Q
T F || (T) T (F) F	T	F

We have constructed a truth table that reveals the possibility of true premises and a false conclusion, thus, we have proven that the inference is invalid.

In this example, since the second premise was P we could have started by assigning P the truth value *T*, because our goal is to determine if the premises can all be true and the conclusion false. Once we do this, we must replace every occurrence of P with the same assigned truth value.

1st Premise	2nd Premise	Conclusion
P Q || ~ (P · Q)	P	Q
T || T	T	

The next step would have been to recognize that the conclusion is easily made false if we assign the truth value *F* to Q. This would have created the complete assignment of truth values for the individual variables.

1st Premise	2nd Premise	Conclusion
P Q || ~ (P · Q)	P	Q
T F || T F	T	F

Once again, since all truth values have been assigned, we can complete the truth table.

1st Premise	2nd Premise	Conclusion
P Q || ~ (P · Q)	P	Q
T F || (T) T (F) F	T	F

We have again constructed a truth table that reveals the possibility of true premises and a false conclusion, thus we have proven that the inference is invalid. These two analyses have revealed a good strategy for constructing indirect truth tables. Start by assigning truth values to the simple statement variables, ones that contain no logical operators.

Analysis of Example 5.7 will reveal more aspects of the indirect truth table method.

Strategy

When constructing an indirect truth table, start by assigning truth values to the statement variables that contain no logical operators.

Example 5.7

~ (P ∨ Q)

P _____

Q

Since neither the second premise nor the conclusion contains a logical operator, we can choose either one to start our indirect truth table. In this case, we have assigned Q the truth value false. Of course, we must remember to replace every occurrence of Q with the same assigned truth value.

	1st Premise	2nd Premise	Conclusion
P Q	~ (P ∨ Q)	P	Q
F	F		F

The next step is to try to get all the premises true at the same time. The second premise is just P so we know that we must assign it the truth value true, again making sure that every instance of P gets the same truth value.

	1st Premise	2nd Premise	Conclusion
P Q	~ (P ∨ Q)	P	Q
T F	T F	T	F

Since all truth values have been assigned, we can complete the truth table.

	1st Premise	2nd Premise	Conclusion
P Q	~ (P ∨ Q)	P	Q
T F	(F) T (T) F	T	F

Our assignment of truth values has revealed the impossibility of getting all the premises true and the conclusion false at the same time. We know this because there was only one way to make the conclusion false and the second premise true. Those specific truth value assignments made the first premise turn out to be false. The inference is valid since there is no possible assignment of truth values that will make all the premises true and the conclusion false at the same time.

What happens if we get to a point in the assignment of truth values where we have a choice to make? Analysis of the inference in Example 5.8 explains the procedure.

Example 5.8

$$\sim P \cdot R$$

$$\underline{P \vee \sim Q}$$

$$Q$$

	1st Premise	2nd Premise	Conclusion
P Q R	~ P · R	P ∨ ~ Q	Q
F		(T) F	F

Once again, we have started the indirect truth table by making the conclusion false, so Q is assigned the truth value false. Replacing all instances of Q with the same truth value gives the second premise one disjunct that is true (Q = F, so ~ Q = T). Thus, as far as the second premise is concerned, no matter what truth value is assigned to P, this premise will turn out to be true. However, for the first premise, it does matter what truth value is assigned to P. If P is true, then the second premise will be true but the first premise will become false. This occurs because the conjunct ~ P in the first premise is false with this assignment of truth values, as revealed below.

	1st Premise	2nd Premise	Conclusion
P Q R	~ P · R	P ∨ ~ Q	Q
T F	(F) T (F)	T (T)(T)F	F

At this point, no matter what we assign to R, the first premise will be false. However, the indirect method is used to reveal *any* possibility of true premises and false conclusion. We must therefore consider the other choice available for P. Assigning the truth value false to P does not affect the truth value of the second premise; it remains true because the disjunct ~ Q is true.

	1st Premise	2nd Premise	Conclusion
P Q R	~ P · R	P ∨ ~ Q	Q
F F	(T) F	F (T)(T)F	F

The truth value of R is now crucial for our analysis. It is possible to make the first premise true by assigning R the truth value true.

	1st Premise	2nd Premise	Conclusion
P Q R	~ P · R	P ∨ ~ Q	Q
F F T	(T) F (T) T	F (T)(T)F	F

This completed indirect truth table reveals the possibility of true premises and a false conclusion. Therefore, we have proven the inference is invalid.

Let's look at another example (Example 5.9).

Example 5.9

If Jennifer is at least 21 years of age, then Jennifer can gamble in Las Vegas.
<u>Jennifer is at least 21 years of age.</u>
Jennifer can gamble in Las Vegas.

If we let P = "Jennifer is at least 21 years of age," and Q = "Jennifer can gamble in Las Vegas," then the structure of the inference is revealed.

$$P \supset Q$$
$$\underline{P}$$
$$Q$$

Once again we have the choice of starting with the second premise or the conclusion. If we start with the conclusion, the truth value of Q must be false. The other occurrences of Q must also be given the truth value false. After step one, the inference will look like this:

P Q	1st Premise P ⊃ Q	2nd Premise P	Conclusion Q
F	F		F

The next step is to try and make all the premises true at the same time. Since the second premise is simply P, the truth value of this must be true in order for the second premise to turn out true. We must also place that same value in all occurrences of P throughout the inference.

P Q	1st Premise P ⊃ Q	2nd Premise P	Conclusion Q
T F	T F	T	F

We are now in position to determine the truth value of the first premise. Since the values for P and Q have already been determined, these truth values are now checked against the truth table for conditional statements. This particular combination (antecedent true, consequent false) makes the first premise false. We can add this result to complete the indirect proof.

P Q	1st Premise P ⊃ Q	2nd Premise P	Conclusion Q
T F	T *(F)* F	T	F

We have proven that it is impossible to get all the premises true and the conclusion false at the same time. This is a valid inference. Since the conclusion had only one variable, Q, in order to get the conclusion false we were forced to make Q false—there were no other options. The same kind of reasoning holds for the second premise. Once this was done, the first premise was decided for us, it had to be false. Thus, we see that it is impossible to make the conclusion false and the premises true at the same time. (You might have recognized that this inference has the form of *modus ponens*.)

Now you can see why we call this type of proof procedure *indirect truth table*. We start out by trying to get the combination of false conclusion and all true premises at the same time. If our analysis shows that it is impossible to get that combination, then we have indirectly proven that the inference is valid. However, if we can get the combination of true premises and a false conclusion, then we have directly proven that it is invalid, because any instance of true premises and false conclusion proves the invalidity of an inference. So the *indirect* label pertains only to the determination of a valid inference because it will have been determined by showing the impossibility of invalidity.

Example 5.10 is another analysis using the indirect proof method.

Example 5.10

$$P \supset Q$$

$$\underline{Q \qquad}$$

$$P$$

Once again we have the choice of starting with the second premise or with the conclusion. If we start with the conclusion, the truth value of P must be *false* (there is no other choice).

P Q	1st Premise P ⊃ Q	2nd Premise Q	Conclusion P
F	F		F

The next step is to make the second premise true. To do this Q must be true (again, there is no other choice). Locking in this truth value we get this:

P Q	1st Premise P ⊃ Q	2nd Premise Q	Conclusion P
F T	F T	T	F

Since there are no other ways to get the conclusion false and the second premise true, we have locked in the values for the first premise. Checking Table 4.4 (page 124), the truth table for conditional statements, tells us that the first premise is true, so the following is our final result:

P Q	1st Premise P ⊃ Q	2nd Premise Q	Conclusion P
F T	F *(T)* T	T	F

Our completed indirect truth table reveals the possibility of getting true premises and a false conclusion, so we have proven that the inference is invalid. (You might have recognized that this inference has the form of the fallacy of affirming the consequent.)

If you can remember the conditions under which conjunctions, disjunctions, negation, and conditional statements are true and false, then you can apply the indirect truth table method quickly and easily. In fact, this is simpler than you might think. You do not need to memorize the truth tables. You merely have to remember four key items (Quick Reference 5.5).

Rules for determining the truth and falsity of logical operators are used in applying the indirect truth table method.

Quick Reference 5.5 • **Truth and Falsity of Conjunctions, Disjunctions, Negation, and Conditional Statements**

1. A conjunction is false if at least one of its conjuncts is false, otherwise it is true.
2. A disjunction is false if all of the disjuncts are false, otherwise it is true.
3. A negation changes the original truth value.
4. A conditional statement is false if the antecedent is true and the consequent is false, otherwise it is true.

We will now analyze one more complex inference (Example 5.11).

Example 5.11

If Jessica is not a citizen and not over 18 years of age and not registered, then Jessica cannot vote.
Jessica is a citizen.
Jessica is over 18 years of age.
<u>Jessica is registered.</u>
Jessica can vote.

If we let P = "Jessica is a citizen," Q = "Jessica is over 18 years of age," R = "Jessica is registered," and S = "Jessica can vote," then the inference structure can be revealed:

$$[\sim P \cdot (\sim Q \cdot \sim R)] \supset \sim S$$

P

Q

<u>R</u>

S

We can display this using the indirect truth table system.

	1st Prem	**2nd**	**3rd**	**4th**	**Conc**
P Q R S ‖	[~ P · (~ Q · ~ R)] ⊃ ~ S	P	Q	R	S

There are several choices as to where to start. If we start with the conclusion, then we must assign the truth value false to S. We then make sure that every other S in the inference is given the same truth value.

P Q R S	[~ P · (~ Q · ~ R)] ⊃ ~ S	P	Q	R	S
	1st Prem	**2nd**	**3rd**	**4th**	**Conc**
F	(T) F				F

Since the second, third, and fourth premises are all simple statements, we need to give the variables P, Q, and R the truth value true in order to get those premises true. We must also give any other instances of those variables the same truth value.

P Q R S	[~ P · (~ Q · ~ R)] ⊃ ~ S	P	Q	R	S
	1st Prem	**2nd**	**3rd**	**4th**	**Conc**
T T T F	(F) T (F) T (F) T (T) F	T	T	T	F

We made sure that we correctly applied all the occurrences of negation (~) in the first premise by taking the truth value of the variables and negating them. The only remaining step is to decide the truth value of the complex antecedent. Since a conjunction is false if even one of the conjuncts is false, the antecedent in this case is false. Now since the first premise has a false antecedent and a true consequent it is, therefore, true.

P Q R S	[~ P · (~ Q · ~ R)] ⊃ ~ S	P	Q	R	S
	1st Prem	**2nd**	**3rd**	**4th**	**Conc**
T T T F	(F) T (F)(F) T (F)(F) T (T)(T) F	T	T	T	F

The completed indirect truth table reveals the possibility of true premises and a false conclusion, thus we have proven that the inference is invalid. Complex inferences should not cause any difficulty if you analyze the inferences in a methodical, step-by-step manner. Do not try to do more than one substitution of a variable at a time, and remember to apply negation correctly when needed.

EXERCISE SET 5.2

Exercises 1–15 This set of exercises will allow you to practice using truth tables with the method of indirect proof. Prove whether each inference is valid or invalid.

1. (R · Q) v S
   R
   ~ Q
   ~ S

Answer:

R Q S	(R · Q) v S	R	~ Q	~ S
	1st Prem	**2nd Prem**	**3rd Prem**	**Conc**
T F T	T (F) F (T) T	T	(T) F	(F) T

The completed indirect truth table reveals the possibility of true premises and a false conclusion, thus, we have proven that the inference is invalid.

Exercises 2–35: For answers
and explanations,
see pages 154–165 of
Instructor's Manual.

2. (R v Q) · S
   Q
   ~ R
   _____
   S Valid

3. (R · Q) v S
   R
   ~ Q
   _____
   S · R Valid

4. (P · Q) v (R · S)
   Q
   S
   R
   _____
   P Invalid

5. [P v (Q v S)] ⊃ R
   ~ P
   ~ Q
   ~ S
   _____
   ~ R Invalid

*6. (P v Q) · (~ S · Q)
   ~ S
   ~ Q
   _____
   ~ P Valid

7. (~ S v ~ Q) ⊃ ~ R
   S
   Q
   _____
   R Invalid

8. R ⊃ (Q · ~ S)
   S
   ~ Q
   _____
   ~ R Valid

9. ~ (P v Q) v ~ (R · S)
   P · Q
   R   Valid
   _____

10. (P · Q) v ~ R
    ~ P
    ~ Q
    _____
    R Invalid

*11. (R ∨ S) ⊃ (P · Q)

~ S

~ Q

~ R Valid

12. (R · Q) ∨ S

R

Q

S · R Invalid

13. (R ∨ Q) ⊃ ~ S

Q ∨ S

R Invalid

14. (R ∨ S) ⊃ (P · Q)

~ S ∨ ~ Q

~ R Invalid

15. [P ∨ (Q ∨ S)] ⊃ ~ R

~ Q ∨ S

~ R Invalid

Exercises 16–35 In this set of exercises, you must first translate the inferences from English to their structures before proving them valid or invalid using the indirect proof method.

16. If either Barbara or Johnny goes to the party, then Lee Ann will not have to pick up Mary Lynn.

Barbara is not going to the party.

Lee Ann has to pick up Mary Lynn.

Johnny is not going to the party.

Answer: If we let B = "Barbara goes to the party," J = "Johnny goes to the party," and L = "Lee Ann has to pick up Mary Lynn," then the structure of the inference is this:

(B ∨ J) ⊃ ~ L

~ B

L

~ J

			1st Prem	2nd Prem	3rd Prem	Conc
B	J	L	(B ∨ J) ⊃ ~ L	~ B	L	~ J
F	T	T	F *(T)* T *(F)* *(F)* T	*(T)* F	T	*(F)* T

Since there is no other way to get the third premise true except to make L true, the consequent of the first premise will have to be false. To get the conclusion false, J has to be true, making the antecedent of the first premise true. So, there is no way to get the first premise true with these assignments. Since it is impossible to get all the premises true and the conclusion false at the same time, we have proven that the inference is valid.

17. Either you take a Breathalyzer test or you get arrested for DUI.

    <u>You did not take the Breathalyzer test.</u>

    You get arrested for DUI. Valid

18. If animals feel pain or learn from experience, then animals are conscious.

    Animals do not feel pain.

    <u>Animals do not learn from experience.</u>

    Animals are not conscious. Invalid

19. If animals feel pain or learn from experience, then animals are conscious.

    Animals do not feel pain.

    <u>Animals do not learn from experience.</u>

    Animals are conscious. Invalid

20. If animals are not conscious or do not feel pain, then they do not have any rights.

    Animals do not have any rights.

    <u>Animals do not feel pain.</u>

    Animals are not conscious. Invalid

*21. If animals are not conscious or do not feel pain, then they do not have any rights.

    Animals are conscious.

    <u>Animals do feel pain.</u>

    Animals have rights. Invalid

22. Either you are right or you are wrong.

    <u>You are not right.</u>

    You are wrong. Valid

23. If either Bill or Gus or Kate committed the crime, then Mike did not do it and Tina did not do it.

    Bill did not commit the crime.

    Gus did not commit the crime

    <u>Kate did not commit the crime</u>

    Mike did it. Invalid

24. If either Elvis or The Beatles sold the most records of all time, then I did not win the contest.

    <u>The Beatles did not sell the most records of all time.</u>

    I won the contest. Invalid

25. If I save one dollar a day, then I will not be rich in ten years.
    If I save two dollars a day, then I will not be rich in ten years.
    If I save three dollars a day, then I will not be rich in ten years.
    I will not save one dollar a day.
    I will not save two dollars a day.
    <u>I will not save three dollars a day.</u>
    I will not be rich in ten years. Invalid

*26. If X is an even number, then X is divisible by 2.
    <u>X is not divisible by 2.</u>
    X is not an even number. Valid

27. If X is not an even number, then X is not divisible by 2.
    <u>X is divisible by 2.</u>
    X is an even number. Valid

28. If Joyce went south on I-15 from Las Vegas, then Joyce got to Los Angeles.
    <u>Joyce did not go south on I-15 from Las Vegas.</u>
    Joyce did not get to Los Angeles. Invalid

29. If you do not finish the job by Friday, then you do not get the bonus.
    <u>You finish the job by Friday.</u>
    You get the bonus. Invalid

30. If you finish the job by Friday, then you get the bonus.
    <u>You do not finish the job by Friday.</u>
    You do not get the bonus. Invalid

*31. Eddie can vote if, and only if, he is registered.
    <u>Eddie is registered.</u>
    Eddie can vote. Valid

32. Eddie can vote if, and only if, he is registered.
    <u>Eddie can vote.</u>
    Eddie is registered. Valid

33. Eddie can vote if, and only if, he is registered.
    <u>Eddie is not registered.</u>
    Eddie cannot vote. Valid

34. Eddie can vote if, and only if, he is registered.
    <u>Eddie cannot vote.</u>
    Eddie is not registered. Valid

35. Ron can think if, and only if, he is conscious.
    <u>Ron is conscious.</u>
    Ron can think. Valid

5.3 SUFFICIENT AND NECESSARY CONDITIONS

Conditional statements are particularly useful in understanding *sufficient* and *necessary conditions*. Recognizing the logic behind these two very important conditions will allow us to bridge the gap between the logical component and the truth content. It will also provide additional information illustrating the intersection of conditional statements and everyday issues. Understanding the commitments behind sufficient and necessary conditions requires us to build on what we have learned about conditional statements.

Sufficient Conditions

A **sufficient condition** is one where, *if* the antecedent is ever true, then the consequent will be true as well. In other words, X being true is enough for Y to be true. Consider Example 5.12, which is a statement we used earlier.

Example 5.12

If <u>your car starts,</u> then <u>you have gasoline.</u>

The *if* sets up a condition that can be understood by analyzing both the logical component and the truth content. We start with the logical analysis. One way to picture the logical commitment of a sufficient condition is shown in Figure 5.1. If X = "your car starts" and Y = "you have gasoline," then we get this diagram:

_If_ X then Y

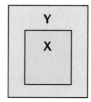

FIGURE 5.1 • **The logical commitment of a sufficient condition.**

We can see why this picture visually captures the logical commitment involved in a sufficient condition. In the picture, if X is ever realized (if we are in X) then Y will be realized. However, remember that this picture reveals only the logical component of a sufficient condition—it does not tell us what the truth content of any particular conditional statement will be.

When we first encounter a conditional statement, we must treat the relationship as a "potential" sufficient condition. Therefore, the diagram above shows the logical relationship in a potential sufficient condition. The eventual truth content analysis will determine whether we truly have an actual sufficient condition.

Look again at Example 5.12 and ask yourself what you would know about the consequent if the antecedent were true. If you get in your car, turn the key, and the car starts, then you should be able to determine that, under this condition, the consequent must be true too—you must have gasoline. When the proposed relationship is correct (the truth content), we say that the antecedent is a *sufficient condition* for the consequent. Another way of saying that something is a sufficient condition is to think of the phrase "is enough for." When X is a sufficient condition for Y, then X's happening *is enough for* Y to be the case as well. In the above example, knowing that your car starts is enough for you to know that you must have at least some gasoline. In this situation, the truth of X *guarantees* the truth of Y. (A bright reader will argue that this is not so if it is an electric or solar-powered car. For our purposes, then, it is hereby stipulated that your car is an everyday regular gasoline-powered car. This eliminates the counterexamples and makes our work a little easier.)

Now let's change the order of the components of our original statement and see what we get (Example 5.13).

Example 5.13

If <u>you have gasoline,</u> then <u>your car starts.</u>

What happens if we now make this new antecedent true? Suppose that it is true that you have gasoline—does that mean that your car will start? Your car might start, but then again it might not. You might have a dead battery, a bad starter, or any number of problems that prevent the car from starting, in which case all the gasoline in the world will not help your car to start. Therefore, having gasoline is *not sufficient* (is not enough) to guarantee that your car will start. Notice the difference between these two analyses. In the first example, the statement "your car starts," if true, guaranteed that you must have gasoline. However, in the second example, the statement "you have gasoline," even if true, cannot guarantee that your car starts. We can now combine our logical and truth content analyses into a diagram.

<u>If your car starts,</u> then <u>you have gasoline.</u>

T ─────────────────► T

(a)   *A sufficient condition*

The diagram displays what is required of a sufficient condition—the antecedent, if true, guarantees the consequent will be true. This illustrates how we can display the logic and truth content analyses of a sufficient condition. However, as our analysis above showed, we do not get the same result with the following statement.

<u>If you have gasoline,</u> then <u>your car starts.</u>

T ─────────────────► T/F?

(b)   *Not a sufficient condition*

The diagram of this statement does not display a sufficient condition—the antecedent, even if true, does not guarantee the consequent will be true.

Let's analyze another set of statements and see what we get. Consider the statement in Example 5.14.

Example 5.14

If you got a 98 on the exam, then you got an A.

We need to know the scale being used before we can begin to analyze the relationship; therefore, let's stipulate that the range of grades is: 90–100 = A; 80–89 = B; 70–79 = C, etc. In the above example then, if it is true that you got a 98, then the consequent could not possibly be false. Therefore, getting a 98 is sufficient to guarantee that you get an A (provided that you didn't cheat and get caught).

Now if we reverse the order, we get this statement:

If you got an A, then you got a 98 on the exam.

Suppose it is true that you got an A on the exam—does this fact guarantee that you got a 98? If the only information you have is the fact that you got an A, could you be certain that you got a 98? Since the range for an A is 90–100, you might have received a 98, but then again, you might have received a 92, or 96, or even a 100. So knowing you got an A is *not sufficient* information for you to know you got a 98. The following figures display the logic of these results.

<u>If you got a 98 on the exam,</u> then <u>you got an A.</u>

A sufficient condition

If the only information available were that you got a 98 on the exam, then you would be able to say, with logical certainty, that you got an A.

However, look at the next figure.

<u>If you got an A,</u> then <u>you got a 98 on the exam.</u>

Not a sufficient condition

In this figure the requirements for a sufficient condition have not been met. If the only information available were that you got an A, then you would not be able to say with any certainty that you got a 98.

When analyzing a conditional statement for a sufficient condition, all you need to do is ask yourself this question: "*If* the antecedent is true, is the consequent guaranteed to be true?" If your answer is yes, then you have a sufficient condition.

Necessary Conditions

Necessary condition:
A condition that must
be met before another event
can occur.

The concept of a **necessary condition** means that one thing is essential, mandatory, or required, in order for another thing to be realized. For example, the statement structure "X *only if* Y" claims that X cannot occur unless Y does. Some actual examples of necessary conditions are these:

1. The presence of oxygen is a necessary condition for a fire to occur.
2. The availability of water is a necessary condition for human existence.

The logical commitment of a necessary condition is illustrated in Figure 5.2.

X *only if* Y

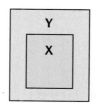

FIGURE 5.2 • The logical commitment of a necessary condition.

We can see that the relationship between X and Y is such that X can never occur without Y. Thus, Y is a necessary condition for X. In the picture, you can be in the X box *only if* you are in the Y box.

If this picture looks familiar, it is because we encountered it earlier in Figure 5.1 in Example 5.12. It is the same picture used to capture the logical commitment of a sufficient condition. How can the same picture capture the logical component of both necessary and sufficient conditions? Part of the answer is revealed when we look closely at the picture. Since the X is within the Y, this ensures that the logic of a sufficient condition has been met, because if X is realized, then Y will be, too. In addition, the same picture ensures that the logic of a necessary condition has been met because X cannot occur without Y.

So now we must learn to analyze a conditional statement for potential necessary conditions. A true necessary condition will exist in the statement structure "X only if Y" only if X can never occur in the absence of Y. But what happens if Y is false? Consider the statement in Example 5.15.

Example 5.15

Your car starts *only if* you have gasoline.

Let X = "Your car starts," and Y = "you have gasoline." Now if Y is *false*, what would that tell you, if anything, about X? Upon reflection, we realize that if Y is false, then you do not have gasoline. Therefore, X cannot possibly be true. Since having gasoline is a necessary condition for your car to start, your car will not start without it. However, as we saw in diagram (b) in Example 5.13, gasoline is, by itself, not sufficient for your car to start. Similarly, we know that water is a necessary condition for human life; we cannot live without it for very long. On the other hand, water, however necessary, is not sufficient for us to live—we need food, oxygen, etc. Thus, we can display a necessary condition relationship as shown below:

Your car starts *only if* you have gasoline.

F ◄————————————————— F

A necessary condition

This diagram displays what is required of a necessary condition—the Y, if false, guarantees that the X will be false. This illustrates how we can display the logical component and truth content analyses of a necessary condition.

Now consider the statement in Example 5.16.

Example 5.16

You got a 98 on the exam *only if* you got an A.

If it is *false* that you got an A (you either received a B, C, D, or F), then it is not possible that you got a 98. If you know for certain that you did not get an A, then you also know for certain that you did not get a 98. The logic is displayed as follows:

You got a 98 on the exam *only if* you got an A.

F ◄————————————————— F

(a) *A necessary condition*

Now let's reverse the order of our statements.

You got an A *only if* you got a 98 on the exam.

T/F? ◄————————————————— F

(b) *Not a necessary condition*

The above figure (b) shows an example where the requirements for a necessary condition have not been met. This means that if you did not get a 98 you still could have received an A because it is *not necessary* that you get a 98 to get an A. Scores of 91, 93, 99, etc. would get you an A as well.

To analyze for a necessary condition all you have to do is to make the statement following the "only if" false and see what that does to the other statement. For the statement structure "X only if Y," if the falsity of the Y guarantees the falsity of the X, then you are dealing with a necessary condition.

There are other relationships that we can find in conditional statements and "only if" statements (Example 5.17).

Example 5.17

(A) If today is Friday, then tomorrow is Saturday.
(B) Today is Friday only if tomorrow is Saturday.

This reveals a different kind of relationship. If we analyze for sufficient and necessary conditions we get the following results:

If today is Friday, then tomorrow is Saturday.

T ———————————————→ T

A sufficient condition has been met.

Today is Friday only if tomorrow is Saturday.

F ←——————————————— F

A necessary condition has been met.

Reversing the order in these statements, as we did in the earlier examples, reveals something new.

If tomorrow is Saturday, then today is Friday.

T ———————————————→ T

A sufficient condition has been met.

Tomorrow is Saturday only if today is Friday.

F ←——————————————— F

A necessary condition has been met.

The relationships in these two statements are different from what we have seen. Each part of the statement is both sufficient and necessary for the other. A little reflection will reveal how this result comes about. The days of the week follow each other in a standard, accepted pattern. Therefore, if today is Friday, then of course tomorrow must be Saturday. In addition, if tomorrow is not Saturday, then today cannot possibly be Friday. (We must also stipulate that we are referring in these cases to one place and not to different places of the world, which have different time zones.)

Now consider the statements in Example 5.18.

Example 5.18

    (A) If today is Friday, then I am 6 feet tall.
    (B) Today is Friday only if I am 6 feet tall.

Let X = "today is Friday," and Y = "I am 6 feet tall." In statement (A), what do we find if we make X true? Since the consequent could be either true or false, the antecedent is not a sufficient condition. In statement (B) what do we find if we make the Y false? Nothing certain can be said about the X in this case, thus this is not a necessary condition. These results are not surprising if we look at the relationship between X and Y in these examples. There is no connection between the two that would make the truth or falsity of one dependent on the other. This result holds if we reverse the order as well. Thus it is possible to find statements that have the logical structure of potential sufficient or necessary conditions, but analysis reveals that neither part is sufficient or necessary for the other part. Therefore, such statements must be analyzed on an individual basis because, as we have seen, we might get a sufficient condition, or a necessary condition, or both, or neither. Since any one of these relationships may occur, you must be able to ask the correct logical and truth content questions in order to arrive at the correct analysis.

Analyzing Conditional Inferences

We are now in a much stronger position to create and analyze conditional inferences. All the work we have done so far can be combined to reveal interesting and useful illustrations of the complexity of these inferences, and at the same time, the possibility of a complete and satisfying understanding of the logical and truth content commitments at play.

Parents often use conditional statements to get children to perform certain tasks. An incentive is created to entice a particular behavior (similar situations can also be seen in the work place.) For example, a parent might say, "If you eat your vegetables, then you will get ice cream." Now suppose the child does not eat the vegetables. The parent will probably feel justified in denying the child the ice cream. This conditional statement is placed in the form of an inference in Example 5.19.

Example 5.19

If you eat your vegetables, then you get ice cream.
<u>You did not eat your vegetables.</u>
You do not get ice cream.

You might be surprised to know that this happens to be an invalid inference. To prove this we can use a simple picture illustrating the logical commitments of the statements involved. If we let V = "you eat your vegetables," and I = "you get ice cream," then the structure of the inference is revealed.

$$V \supset I$$

$$\underline{\sim V}$$

$$\sim I$$

Since this is an instance of the fallacy of denying the antecedent (see Quick Reference 5.4, page 163), we know that the conclusion does not necessarily follow from the premises, thus this is an invalid inference.

So, logically speaking, the children can get the ice cream even if they do not eat the vegetables. The reason for this interesting result is that a sufficient condition has been asserted for getting the ice cream, namely, eating the vegetables. The first premise sets the sufficient condition. However, since it is an invalid inference, the conclusion could be false. In other words, it is *not necessary* to eat the vegetables to get the ice cream.

Seeing this result might cause smart parents to change their statements. They might have intended to make it necessary to eat the vegetables to get the ice cream. This can be accomplished by saying, "You will get the ice cream *only if* you eat your vegetables." (Another way of saying the same thing is this: "If you do not eat your vegetables, then you do not get ice cream.") Now suppose the child does not eat the vegetables. The parent will probably feel justified in denying the child the ice cream. This conditional statement is placed in the form of an inference in Example 5.20.

Example 5.20

You get ice cream *only if* you eat your vegetables.
You did not eat your vegetables.
You do not get ice cream.

Once again, if we let I = "you get ice cream" and V = "you eat your vegetables," then the structure of the inference is revealed:

$$I \supset V$$

$$\underline{\sim V}$$

$$\sim I$$

Since this is an instance of *modus tollens* (see Quick Reference 5.3, page 162) parents will be relieved to know that this is a valid inference. Since a necessary condition has been established, the children cannot get to the ice cream unless they go through the vegetables.

However, a new problem has occurred. Imagine that the child actually eats the vegetables. In that case, the parent would, logically speaking, be justified in not giving the ice cream. By setting up a necessary condition, the parent is stating that it is impossible to get the ice cream without eating the vegetables. However, even if the vegetables are eaten, this does not logically guarantee that the ice cream will be received. This follows because a sufficient condition has not been established. Therefore, to ensure that parents and children are protected requires setting up both sufficient and necessary conditions at the same time. Thus, the parent should say, "*If, and only if,* you eat the vegetables, then you will get ice cream." Another way of capturing this is by saying, "You will get ice cream, *if, and only if,* you eat the vegetables." The "if" sets up a potential sufficient condition, while the "only if" sets up a potential necessary condition. This is an example of a biconditional, which we can translate into "I ≡ V." We can bring to bear our knowledge of truth tables and indirect proof to formalize and strengthen our understanding of this example. Suppose the child eats the vegetables. The structure of the inference is revealed below:

$$I \equiv V$$
$$\underline{V}$$
$$I$$

The following indirect truth table proves that this inference is valid:

	1st Premise	2nd Premise	Conclusion
I V ||	I ≡ V	V	I
F T ||	F *(F)* T	T	F

Now suppose the child does not eat the vegetables. The structure of the inference follows:

$$I \equiv V$$
$$\underline{\sim V}$$
$$\sim I$$

The indirect truth table proves that this inference is valid.

	1st Premise	2nd Premise	Conclusion
I V ||	I ≡ V	~ V	~ I
T F ||	T *(F)* F	*(T)* F	*(F)* T

Analyzing sufficient and necessary conditions requires us to bridge logic with truth content. The logical component spells out the requirements that must be met in order for a conditional statement to be true—it tells us the correct questions to ask to determine the logical possibilities. The truth content part relies on our knowledge of the world to determine if we have a true case of sufficient or necessary conditions.

EXERCISE SET 5.3

Exercises 1–16 Use your logical understanding and truth content knowledge to determine whether an actual *sufficient condition* exists in the following statements.

1. If Ed is a bachelor, then Ed is an adult male.

Answer: Sufficient condition

A bachelor is defined as being an unmarried adult male. Given this, if the antecedent is true (if Ed is a bachelor), then the consequent will be true as well (Ed is an adult male).

2. If Ed is an adult male, then Ed is a bachelor.

3. If there is oxygen in the room, then there is a fire in the room.

4. If there is a fire in the room, then there is oxygen in the room.

5. If this is the month of June, then this month has exactly 30 days.

*6. If this month has exactly 30 days, then this is the month of June.

7. If I live in the White House, then I am the president of the United States.

8. If I am the president of the United States, then I live in the White House.

9. If I have exactly 100 pennies, then I have at least the equivalent of one dollar.

10. If I have at least the equivalent of one dollar, then I have exactly 100 pennies.

*11. If I am over 21 years of age, then I am over 10 years of age.

12. If I am over 10 years of age, then I am over 21 years of age.

13. If I am eating a banana, then I am eating a fruit.

14. If I am eating a fruit, then I am eating a banana.

15. If I hurt a human, then I hurt a mammal.

16. If I hurt a mammal, then I hurt a human.

Exerices 17–32 Use your logical understanding and truth content knowledge to determine whether an actual *necessary condition* exists in the following statements.

*17. Ed is a bachelor only if Ed is an adult male.

18. Ed is an adult male only if Ed is a bachelor.

19. There is oxygen in the room only if there is a fire in the room.

20. There is a fire in the room only if there is oxygen in the room.

*21. This is the month of June only if this month has exactly 30 days.

22. This month has exactly 30 days only if this is the month of June.

23. I live in the White House only if I am the president of the United States.

24. I am the president of the United States only if I live in the White House.

25. I have exactly 100 pennies only if I have at least the equivalent of one dollar.

Exercises 2–32: For answers and explanations, see pages 165–167 of Instructor's Manual.

2. Not a sufficient condition

3. Not a sufficient condition

4. Sufficient condition

5. Sufficient condition

6. Not a sufficient condition

7. Not a sufficient condition

8. Sufficient condition.

9. Sufficient condition

10. Not a sufficient condition

11. Sufficient condition

12. Not a sufficient condition

13. Sufficient condition

14. Not a sufficient condition

15. Sufficient condition

16. Not a sufficient condition

17. Necessary condition

18. Not a necessary condition

19. Not a necessary condition

20. Necessary condition

21. Necessary condition

22. Not a necessary condition

23. Not a necessary condition

24. Necessary condition

25. Necessary condition

26. Not a necessary condition

27. Necessary condition

28. Not a necessary condition

29. Necessary condition

30. Not a necessary condition

31. Necessary condition

32. Not a necessary condition

*26. I have at least the equivalent of one dollar only if I have exactly 100 pennies.

27. I am over 21 years of age only if I am over 10 years of age.

28. I am over 10 years of age only if I am over 21 years of age.

29. I am eating a banana only if I am eating a fruit.

30. I am eating a fruit only if I am eating a banana.

*31. I hurt a human only if I hurt a mammal.

32. I hurt a mammal only if I hurt a human.

SUMMARY

- Truth tables for conjunction, disjunction, negation, and conditional statements are used to analyze complex inferences.
- If the completed truth table reveals the possibility of true premises and a false conclusion, then it proves that the inference is invalid.
- In a truth table, the invalidity of an inference can be indicated by drawing a box around the line or lines that show the premises true and the conclusion false. If no lines of a completed truth table reveal the possibility of true premises and a false conclusion, then the inference is valid.
- The proof procedure called indirect truth tables shortens the construction of truth tables needed to prove validity or invalidity. If the completed indirect truth table reveals the possibility of true premises and a false conclusion, then the inference is proven invalid. If it is impossible to get all the premises true and the conclusion false at the same time, then the inference is indirectly proven valid. The indirect label pertains only to the determination of a valid inference, because it will have been determined by showing the impossibility of invalidity.
- A sufficient condition is one that meets the minimum requirements to ensure that another event does occur.
- A necessary condition is one that is required for another event to occur.

KEY TERMS

technically valid inference   156
conditional inference   159
modus ponens   159

fallacy of affirming the consequent   161
modus tollens   162
fallacy of denying the antecedent   163

indirect truth table   170
sufficient condition   182
necessary condition   185

LOGIC CHALLENGE: A GUILTY PROBLEM

Imagine that you are a private investigator specializing in determining the truth value of suspects' statements to the police. You are shown a videotape of four suspects accused of robbing a quick-loan store. The four suspects happen to know each other. When you view the videotape, you are allowed to hear each suspect make only one statement.

Alice: Benny did it.

Benny: David did it.

Connie: I did not do it.

David: What Benny said about me is false.

Assume that only one person did it and only one of the four statements is true. If so, determine the following two things.

1. Who committed the crime?
2. Which one of the four statements is true?

See page 168 of Instructor's Manual for explanation.

1. Connie committed the crime.

2. David's statement is the only true one.

Natural Deduction

6.1 PROVING VALIDITY USING NATURAL DEDUCTION

6.2 RULES OF INFERENCE— PART ONE

6.3 JUSTIFICATION—APPLYING THE RULES OF INFERENCE

6.4 RULES OF INFERENCE— PART TWO

6.5 TACTICS AND STRATEGY USING THE RULES OF INFERENCE

6.6 SUBSTITUTION SETS— GROUP ONE

6.7 SUBSTITUTION SETS— GROUP TWO

6.8 CONDITIONAL PROOF (CP)

6.9 INDIRECT PROOF (IP)— *REDUCTIO AD ABSURDUM*

The truth table method is a precise system for proving the validity or invalidity of any inference constructed from truth-functional statements. Nevertheless, the mechanical system of application in which all possible true/false combinations must be exhausted can sometimes lead to cumbersome and lengthy truth tables. Consequently, a simple mistake in applying truth values (T/F symbols) might lead to an incorrect determination. Of course the truth table method of indirect proof can shorten the process by looking only for T/F combinations that make the conclusion false and the premises true at the same time. Although these applications of truth tables are very useful, a more elegant proof procedure is available—*natural deduction*.

6.1 PROVING VALIDITY USING NATURAL DEDUCTION

Natural deduction is a method of proving validity that uses already proven, valid inferences. A few important inferences, whose validity has been verified by the truth table method, are used as building blocks to prove the validity of more complex inferences. Each step of a proof using

chapter

Natural deduction:
The method of proving validity using inferences already proven valid by the truth table method.

Rules of inference: The set of rules (valid inferences) that constitutes part of the system of natural deduction (used in conjunction with the substitution sets).

Logical form: The underlying logical relationship in an inference.

Proof procedure: The step-by-step determination of the validity or invalidity of an inference.

Substitution sets: Part of the system of natural deduction. Logically equivalent statements that have been verified as such by the truth table method.

natural deduction is itself a valid inference, because each step relies on a valid inference for its derivation and justification. Moreover, since each step of the proof is a valid inference, we can be certain that the final step, and thus the entire complex inference, is valid.

Our investigation of natural deduction begins with eight **rules of inference**. These "rules" are actually the *deep structure* of the inferences that were proven to be valid by you in Chapter 5 (see ***Exercise Set 5.1B***, Exercises 2–9, page 165). "Deep structure" refers to the **logical form** of an inference. Up to this point we have been revealing the structure of inferences by using capital letters, such as, P, Q R, S, and T, for truth-functional statements. Each capital letter was used symbolically to replace one particular truth-functional statement. However, the deep structure, the logical form of inferences, will be revealed using lower case *italicized* letters, such as, *p, q, r, s,* and *t*, again for truth-functional statements. These lower case italicized letters will be variables that can be replaced with simple or complex truth-functional statements. For example, the variable *p* can be replaced by "P," "P ∨ Q," "S ⊃ T," "~ R ∨ (T · S)," or any other simple or complex truth-functional statement that can be captured using capital letters.

Once the eight rules of inference are introduced, you will be taught the *proof procedure method*. The **proof procedure** is a step-by-step method for determining the validity or invalidity of an inference. You will be given many opportunities to practice the method, which will enable you to gradually master the technique of natural deduction. The rules of inference will then be supplemented by ten **substitution sets**, which are also known as *equivalence rules* or

BIOGRAPHY ┆ GERHARD GENTZEN

Although he only lived 36 years, Gerhard Gentzen was able to do remarkable work in logic and the foundations of mathematics. Gentzen, (1909–1945), was interested in the use of forms of inference. He understood that both logical and mathematical systems of proof necessarily rely on the creation of new forms of inference to help prove new theorems. The necessity to create new forms of inference was recognized in part because of the paradoxes and contradictions that were discovered around the turn of the twentieth century. These surprising discoveries concerned the consistency of elementary number theory and were so important that the foundations of logic and mathematics were seriously threatened. After all, if certainty did not exist in mathematical proofs, then perhaps it might not exist at all.

The system of *natural deduction* was developed by Gentzen to help secure the consistency of number theory. Nevertheless, once the connection between logic and mathematics was firmly established (see biography of Gottlob Frege, page 256), Gentzen's natural deduction system was adapted for work in logical analysis. Genzten wanted the term "natural" in the logical setting to mean the same as it does when mathematicians refer to the "natural way of reasoning in mathematics," meaning that we generate rules of inference by which we can derive more theorems. Gentzen's system provides the rules that allow us to prove the validity of both mathematical and logical inferences. The rules of inference provide the tools necessary for both the introduction and the elimination of logical operators in formal proofs.

rules of transformation. The substitution sets are logically equivalent statements that have been verified as such by the truth table method. In fact, the ten substitution sets we will be using were proven to be logically equivalent statements by you in Chapter 4 (see *Exercise Set 4.6*, Exercises 1–16, page 146). These sets of statements make it possible to replace any statement anywhere in a proof sequence with its logically equivalent set member. As will become apparent when you begin to use these sets, the flexibility they offer will greatly enhance your ability to create formal proofs.

The rules of inference and the substitution sets, along with the techniques of conditional proof and indirect proof, form a system powerful enough to prove the validity of any inference constructed of truth-functional statements.

6.2 RULES OF INFERENCE—PART ONE

Although the following inferences have been proven to be valid by the truth table method, it will be helpful to discuss their validity in an informal manner. We will think through the validity of the inferences by discussing the logical commitments involved in the relationship between premises and conclusion. Thus, the truth tables not only provide an exhaustive mechanical proof procedure, they allow us to talk about validity.

1. Addition (Add)

The rule of **addition (Add)** asserts that any statement accepted as true can be joined disjunctively with any other statement since a disjunction is true if at least one of the disjuncts is true. For example, if it is true that "June has 30 days" then it follows that "Either June has 30 days or apples are fruit." If we let p = "June has 30 days" and q = "apples are fruit," we get the following:

$$\frac{p}{p \vee q}$$

If the premise, p, is true, then the truth value of p must be true. Since a disjunction is true if at least one of its disjuncts is true, we can validly infer that $p \vee q$ is true. This means that even if we add (disjunctively) a false statement, such as q = "apples are vegetables," the resulting disjunction would still be true; $p \vee q$ would still logically follow from p. This example reveals why the rule of addition can only be used with disjunction. If we added a statement by using conjunction, the resulting complex statement would not always logically follow.

We already stipulated that p is a variable (used to reveal logical form) that can stand for any simple or complex truth-functional statement. Let's see what some of these replacements might look like when used with the rule of addition (Add).

Logical Form	Inferences Using Capital Letters	
$\dfrac{p}{p \vee q}$	$\dfrac{T \supset Q}{(T \supset Q) \vee R}$	$\dfrac{M \supset (N \cdot S)}{[M \supset (N \cdot S)] \vee (\sim T \cdot K)}$

Addition (Add): A rule of inference.

$$\frac{p}{p \vee q}$$

The following are examples of legitimate applications of the rule of addition (Add).

Legitimate Addition (Add)

$\underline{S}$	$\underline{R}$	$\underline{M \supset N}$	$\underline{\sim D \cdot T}$
$S \vee (Q \cdot R)$	$R \vee (Q \supset T)$	$(M \supset N) \vee (Q \cdot \sim P)$	$(\sim D \cdot T) \vee [(P \supset R) \cdot S]$

We are all familiar with rules associated with various games. Checkers and chess have rules stipulating the range of legitimate moves associated with the pieces. Part of learning how to play a game correctly is the process of recognizing and avoiding illegitimate moves. The following stipulation applies to all eight rules of inference:

The rules of inference are legitimately applied only to an entire line.

To use a rule for part of a line would be an illegitimate move. For example, the following is a common mistake associated with the rule of addition:

Illegitimate Addition (Add)

1. $(P \cdot Q) \supset (R \cdot S)$
2. $(P \cdot Q) \vee T$

The only way to apply the rule of addition correctly to line #1 is to create a disjunction with "$(P \cdot Q) \supset (R \cdot S)$" as the first disjunct. For example, "$[(P \cdot Q) \supset (R \cdot S)] \vee T$" would be a legitimate use of addition in this case.

The following is another example of a mistake in the application of the rule of addition:

Illegitimate Addition (Add)

1. $P \supset (\sim Q \vee S)$
2. S

The rule of addition does not allow you to just add anything you wish from nothing. It allows you to create a disjunction *only with an already established line*.

2. Conjunction (Conj)

The rule of **conjunction (Conj)** asserts that any two statements accepted as true can be joined conjunctively with the result being a true statement. Recall that a conjunction is true *only if* all the conjuncts are true. For example, if "June has 30 days" and "apples are fruit" are both true statements, then if follows that "June has 30 days *and* apples are fruit." If we let p = "June has 30 days" and q = "apples are fruit," we get the following:

Conjunction (Conj): A rule of inference.

$$p$$
$$\underline{q}$$
$$p \cdot q$$

$$p$$
$$\underline{q}$$
$$p \cdot q$$

If both premises are true, then the truth values of both *p* and *q* must be true. The conjunction of *p* and *q* must, therefore, be true because all the conjuncts are true. A correct application of the rule of conjunction produces a valid inference. Here are some examples of legitimate applications of conjunction (Conj):

Legitimate Conjunction (Conj)

G	B ⊃ J	S v T
H v K	L ⊃ ~ F	M
G · (H v K)	(B ⊃ J) · (L ⊃ ~ F)	(P · Q) ⊃ R
		(S v T) · M
		(S v T) · [(P · Q) ⊃ R]
		M · [(P · Q) ⊃ R]
		[(S v T) · M] · [(P · Q) ⊃ R]

The illegitimate move below is a common mistake in applying the rule of conjunction (Conj).

Illegitimate Conjunction (Conj)

1. S
2. S · T

The mistake here is in thinking that the rule of conjunction works like the rule of addition. The rule of conjunction does not allow you to add anything you wish to a line. It does permit you to *conjoin any two complete lines that have already been established.*

3. *Modus Ponens* (MP)

Modus ponens **(MP)** was introduced in Chapter 5 (page 159) as part of the discussion of conditional statements. If you recall, a conditional statement is false only when the antecedent is true and the consequent is false. Given this, whenever a conditional statement is accepted as true, and the antecedent of that conditional is also accepted as true, then the consequent must be true. For example, if it is true that "If it rained today, then the street is wet," and if it is also true that "It rained today," we can logically conclude that "the street is wet." If we let *p* = "It rained today," and *q* = "the street is wet," we can reveal the logical form of the inference:

$$p \supset q$$

$$\underline{p}$$

$$q$$

If the first premise is true, then we can rule out the possibility of the antecedent, *p*, being true while the consequent, *q*, is false. If the second premise is true, then *p* must be true. This means that the antecedent in the first premise is true, so we now know that *q* must be true in order for the first premise to remain true. Thus, the conclusion must be true if the premises are true.

Modus ponens **(MP):** A rule of inference.

$$p \supset q$$

$$\underline{p}$$

$$q$$

Here are some examples that illustrate that valid inferences result from the correct application of *modus ponens* (MP).

Legitimate *Modus Ponens* (MP)

R ⊃ (M ∨ N)	(P · Q) ⊃ (G · ~ D)	(K · D) ∨ F
R	P · Q	[(K · D) ∨ F] ⊃ (M ∨ C)
M ∨ N	G · ~ D	M ∨ C

The third example above illustrates an important point regarding the rules of inference: *The order of the necessary lines can be reversed*. For *modus ponens* (MP) the form was introduced as follows:

$$p \supset q$$

$$p$$

$$q$$

However, in order for *modus ponens* (MP) to operate legitimately, it is necessary only that the conditional statement and the antecedent both appear as complete separate lines. The logical form of the third example is this:

$$p$$

$$p \supset q$$

$$q$$

Since both the conditional and its antecedent appear as separate lines, the necessary requirements for *modus ponens* (MP) have been met.

Here are two examples of mistakes using *modus ponens* (MP):

Illegitimate *Modus Ponens* (MP)

1. (L ⊃ Q) ∨ (R ∨ S)	1. (L ⊃ Q) ∨ (R ∨ S)
2. L	2. L
3. Q	3. (R ∨ S)

In the three legitimate examples of *modus ponens* the main operator is the ⊃. However, the main operator in the illegitimate *modus ponens* (MP) examples above (line #1) is ∨, and *modus ponens* (MP) cannot be used legitimately with a disjunction.

One final note before leaving *modus ponens* (MP): You may recall from Chapter 5 (page 160) that the fallacy of affirming the consequent resembles *modus ponens*. Since it is easy to confuse the two forms, you must be careful not to make this mistake in the application of *modus ponens* (MP).

***Modus ponens* (MP)**	**The fallacy of affirming the consequent**
$p \supset q$	$p \supset q$
p	q
q	p
Valid inference	Invalid inference

4. *Modus Tollens* (MT)

Modus tollens **(MT)** was also introduced in Chapter 5 (page 161) as part of the discussion of conditional statements and negation. The logical form of *modus tollens* (MT) is the following:

$$p \supset q$$

$$\underline{\sim q}$$

$$\sim p$$

Let's substitute the following statement for the first premise: "If it rained today, then the street is wet." We let p = "It rained today," and q = "the street is wet." If the first premise is true, then we can rule out the possibility of the antecedent p, being true while the consequent q, is false. The second premise asserts that the statement "$\sim q$" is true. Because this is the negation of q, in order for $\sim q$ to be true, q must be false. This means that the consequent in the first premise is false (since it is q). Accordingly, we now know that p (the antecedent) must be false in order for the statement $p \supset q$ to remain true. But if p is false, then the negation of p must be true. Therefore, given a conditional statement and the negation of its consequent, we can logically derive the negation of the antecedent as a conclusion. For *modus tollens* (MT), if the premises are true, the conclusion must be true, and the inference is valid. Here are some examples of legitimate applications of *modus tollens* (MT).

Legitimate *Modus Tollens* (MT)

$H \supset (T \lor N)$	$(G \cdot D) \supset C$	$\sim (F \lor D)$
$\underline{\sim (T \lor N)}$	$\underline{\sim C}$	$\underline{[(T \lor F) \cdot \sim D] \supset (F \lor D)}$
$\sim H$	$\sim (G \cdot D)$	$\sim [(T \lor F) \cdot \sim D]$

Here is an example of a mistake using *modus tollens* (MT):

Illegitimate *Modus Tollens* (MT)

1. $(L \supset Q) \lor (R \lor S)$
2. $\underline{\sim Q}$
3. $\sim L$

Since the main operator in the examples of legitimate *modus tollens* is $\supset$, the logical form of these lines is $p \supset q$; thus, *modus tollens* is a legitimate move. However, since the main operator in the examples of illegitimate *modus tollens* is $\lor$, and the logical form is $p \lor q$, *modus tollens* cannot be used legitimately on a disjunction.

A final note before leaving *modus tollens* (MT): As discussed in Chapter 5 (page 162), the fallacy of denying the antecedent resembles *modus tollens*. Since it is easy to confuse the two forms, you must be careful not to make this mistake in the application of *modus tollens* (MT).

Modus tollens **(MT)**	**The fallacy of denying the antecedent**
$p \supset q$	$p \supset q$
$\underline{\sim q}$	$\underline{\sim p}$
$\sim p$	$\sim q$
Valid inference	Invalid inference

Modus tollens **(MT):** A rule of inference.

$$p \supset q$$
$$\underline{\sim q}$$
$$\sim p$$

6.3 JUSTIFICATION—APPLYING THE RULES OF INFERENCE

We create proofs of validity using natural deduction by taking the given premises of an inference and deducing whatever is necessary in a step-by-step procedure to prove the conclusion. A complete proof using natural deduction requires *justification* at each step of the deduction. **Justification** refers to the line or lines used to deduce the step, plus the rule of inference applied. For example,

1. $P \supset Q$ (Given premise)
2. $(P \supset Q) \vee T$ 1, Add

The justification for line #2 (*the deduced step*) is set off to the right of the line and spells out its derivation. In this case it was derived from line #1 using addition (Add). The next example will illustrate the use of multiple rules of inference.

1. $(\sim R \vee S) \supset Q$ (Given premise)
2. $\sim R \vee S$ (Given premise)
3. Q 1, 2, MP
4. $Q \vee S$ 3, Add
5. $(\sim R \vee S) \cdot (Q \vee S)$ 2, 4, Conj

In the above example, line 3 is derived from lines 1 and 2 by MP; line 4 is derived from line 3 by addition; and line 5 from lines 2 and 4 by conjunction.

The process of justifying each line helps ensure that the rule mentioned is legitimately applied. It provides a means for checking the proof. A correct application of the rules, which are summarized in Table 6.1, guarantees that lines 3, 4, and 5 above have each been validly deduced.

TABLE 6.1 Rules of Inference 1-4

1. **Addition (Add)**	2. **Conjunction (Conj)**
$\underline{p \quad\quad}$	p
$p \vee q$	$\underline{q \quad\quad}$
	$p \cdot q$
3. *Modus ponens* **(MP)**	4. *Modus tollens* **(MT)**
$p \supset q$	$p \supset q$
$\underline{p \quad\quad}$	$\underline{\sim q \quad}$
q	$\sim p$

EXERCISE SET 6.3   ○○○

Exercises 1–15 The following are examples of what you might encounter in proofs. The last line of each example gives the number(s) of the line or lines needed for its derivation. You are to provide the justification (the rule of inference) in the space provided.

[1]   1. P ⊃ Q
       2. P
       3. Q   1, 2, ———

Answer: 3. Q   1, 2, MP

[2]   1. R ⊃ S
       2. ∼ S
       3. ∼ R   1, 2, ——— MT

[3]   1. T ∨ U
       2. ∼ P
       3. (T ∨ U) · ∼ P   1, 2, ——— Conj

[4]   1. P
       2. P ∨ ∼ Q   1, ——— Add

[5]   1. P
       2. Q
       3. P · Q   1, 2, ——— Conj

[*6]   1. Q ⊃ (R ∨ S)
       2. ∼ (R ∨ S)
       3. ∼ Q   1, 2, ——— MT

[7]   1. ∼ (R ∨ S) ⊃ (P ⊃ Q)
       2. ∼ (R ∨ S)
       3. P ⊃ Q   1, 2, ——— MP

[8]   1. P ⊃ Q
       2. (P ⊃ Q) ∨ ∼ (R ∨ S)   1, ——— Add

[9]   1. P ⊃ S
       2. (R ⊃ S) ∨ (R ⊃ Q)
       3. (P ⊃ S) · [(R ⊃ S) ∨ (R ⊃ Q)]   1, 2, ——— Conj

[10]   1. (P ⊃ Q) ⊃ (R ⊃ S)
       2. ∼ (R ⊃ S)
       3. ∼ (P ⊃ Q)   1, 2, ——— MT

[*11]   1. (P ∨ Q)
       2. R
       3. (P ∨ Q) · R   1, 2, ——— Conj

[12]   1. R
       2. R ∨ (P · ∼ Q)   1, ——— Add

[13]   1. ∼ P
       2. T ⊃ U
       3. ∼ P · (T ⊃ U)   1, 2, ——— Conj

[14] 1. ~ P ⊃ Q
   2. ~ Q
   3. ~ ~ P   1, 2, _____ MT

[15] 1. (P · R) ⊃ ~ S
   2. (P · R)
   3. ~ S   1, 2, _____ MP

Exercises 16–28 The following are more examples of what you might encounter in proofs. In these examples the justification (the rule of inference) is provided for the last line; however, the line itself is missing. Use the given information to derive the last line of each example.

[16] 1. P v Q
   2. S v T
   3. _____   1, 2, Conj

Answer: 3. (P v Q) · (S v T)   1, 2, Conj

[17] 1. P ⊃ (Q v S)
   2. P
   3. _____   1, 2, MP (Q v S)

[18] 1. (T v R) ⊃ (Q v S)
   2. ~ (Q v S)
   3. _____   1, 2, MT ~ (T v R)

[19] 1. ~ (S v T)
   2. _____   1, Add You can add any statement here.

[20] 1. (R v S) ⊃ T
   2. ~ T
   3. _____   1, 2, MT ~ (R v S)

[*21] 1. (R v ~ T) ⊃ S
   2. R v ~ T
   3. _____   1, 2, MP S

[22] 1. (R v S) · (P ⊃ Q)
   2. S v Q
   3. _____   1, 2, Conj [(R v S) · (P ⊃ Q)] · (S v Q)

[23] 1. (T ⊃ R) ⊃ (Q ⊃ S)
   2. ~ (Q ⊃ S)
   3. _____   1, 2, MT ~ (T ⊃ R)

[24] 1. S ⊃ ~ (~ R v ~ T)
   2. S
   3. _____   1, 2, MP ~ (~ R v ~ T)

[25]   1. S ⊃ ~ (~ R v ~ T)
        2. ~ ~ (~ R v ~ T)
        3. _____   1, 2, MT   ~ S

[*26]   1. (P · ~ R) ⊃ Q
        2. ~ Q
        3. _____   1, 2, MT   ~ (P · ~ R)

[27]   1. (P v Q) ⊃ ~ R
        2. P v Q
        3. _____   1, 2, MP   ~ R

[28]   1. P ⊃ Q
        2. R v S
        3. _____   1, 2, Conj   (P ⊃ Q) · (R v S)

Exercises 29–33 Translate the following inferences using symbolic notation. Use the rules of inference 1–4 to justify each conclusion. (The capital letters to be used for translation are provided in each case.)

29. If I bet red and black on the roulette table, then either I will win or green will come up. I did bet red and black on the roulette table. Therefore, either I won or green came up. (R, B, W, G)

Answer: 1. (R · B) ⊃ (W v G)
         2. R · B
         3. W v G   1, 2, MP

30. If Ron buys a new car, then he saved half his weekly salary for a year. But, Ron did not save half his weekly salary for a year. So, Ron did not buy a new car. (R, S)

31. If we find crystals and molecules, then there was life on Mars. Therefore, if we find crystals and molecules, then there was life on Mars, or there will be signs of life on some other planet. (C, M, L, P)

32. If I win the prize, then I will go to Cancun. If I inherit $2000, then I will go to Cancun. So, if I win the prize, then I will go to Cancun, and if I inherit $2000, then I will go to Cancun. (P, C, I)

33. If there is either a recession or a scandal, then the governor will resign. The governor did not resign. So, there was not either a recession or a scandal. (R, S, G)

Exercises 30–33: For answers and explanations, see page 182 of Instructor's Manual.

6.4 RULES OF INFERENCE—PART TWO

There are four additional rules of inference for us to consider. As with the first four rules, correct application ensures that we create valid inferences in our deductive proofs. Although we have already proven these rules valid by the truth table method, it will help if we illustrate their validity in an informal manner.

Syllogism: Any inference that has exactly two premises and one conclusion

Disjunctive syllogism (DS):
A rule of inference.

$p \lor q$

$\underline{\sim p}$

q

5. Disjunctive Syllogism (DS)

A **syllogism** is any inference that has exactly two premises and a conclusion. The rule of inference called **disjunctive syllogism (DS)** has the following logical form:

$$p \lor q$$
$$\underline{\sim p}$$
$$q$$

Let's substitute the following for the first premise: "Either CD's are superior to records or DVD's are superior to film." We let p = "CD's are superior to records," and q = "DVD's are superior to film." Since the first premise is a disjunction, we know that *if* it is true, then at least one of the disjuncts must be true. Since the second premise is the negation of p (CD's are *not* superior to records), p must be false for the second premise to be true. This means that in the first premise, q must be true to ensure that the disjunction is true. Thus, the conclusion, q, must be true. The following are examples of legitimate applications of the rule of disjunctive syllogism (DS).

Legitimate Disjunctive Syllogism (DS)

$(R \supset P) \lor T$	$G \lor [(H \cdot R) \supset T]$	$[\sim S \lor (T \supset B)] \lor (P \cdot Q)$
$\underline{\sim (R \supset P)}$	$\underline{\sim G}$	$\underline{\sim [\sim S \lor (T \supset B)]}$
T	$(H \cdot R) \supset T$	$P \cdot Q$

Here is an example of a mistake using disjunctive syllogism (DS):

Illegitimate Disjunctive Syllogism (DS)

1. $(F \lor G) \lor H$
2. $\underline{\sim F}$
3. H

The correct application of distinctive syllogism occurs when there is a negation of the *entire first disjunct*, not just a part of it. The only way to legitimately derive H in line #3 in the example above is if premise #2 was $\sim (F \lor G)$.

6. Hypothetical Syllogism (HS)

The rule of inference called **hypothetical syllogism (HS)** relies on an understanding of conditional statements. Hypothetical syllogism (HS) has the following logical form:

$$p \supset q$$
$$\underline{q \supset r}$$
$$p \supset r$$

Hypothetical syllogism (HS):
A rule of inference.

$p \supset q$

$\underline{q \supset r}$

$p \supset r$

Let's substitute the following for the first premise: "If I live in Las Vegas, then I live in Nevada." We let p = "I live in Las Vegas," and q = "I live in Nevada." If we let r = "I live in the United States," then the second premise would be, "If I live in Nevada, then I live in the United States." In these conditional statements, *if* both premises are true, there cannot be a true antecedent coupled with a false consequent in either of them. If we look at the conclusion, we notice that the only way for it to be false is for *p* to be true and *r* to be false. However, if *r* is false, then the *q* in the second premise must be false as well (because that would be the only way to keep the second premise true). But that means that the first premise would be false because the antecedent is true and the consequent false. But this is in direct conflict with our acceptance of the first premise as being true. Therefore, if both premises are true, the conclusion is guaranteed to be true, too. If it is true that "If I live in Las Vegas, then I live in Nevada," and it is also true that "If I live in Nevada, then I live in the United States," then it logically follows that "If I live in Las Vegas, then I live in the United States."

The following are examples of legitimate applications of the rule of hypothetical syllogism (HS).

Legitimate Hypothetical Syllogism (HS)

$H \supset (T \lor N)$
$(T \lor N) \supset \sim R$
$H \supset \sim R$

$[(G \cdot C) \lor P] \supset \sim S$
$\sim S \supset M$
$[(G \cdot C) \lor P] \supset M$

$(M \lor N) \supset (T \lor Q)$
$(P \lor R) \supset (M \lor N)$
$(P \lor R) \supset (T \lor Q)$

Here are two examples of mistakes using hypothetical syllogism (HS):

Illegitimate Hypothetical Syllogism (HS)

1. $K \supset (L \lor \sim R)$
2. $(L \cdot \sim R) \supset M$
3. $K \supset M$

1. $(B \lor C) \supset (D \lor E)$
2. $D \supset (F \lor G)$
3. $(B \lor C) \supset (F \lor G)$

In the first example, the two statements "$L \lor \sim R$," and "$L \cdot \sim R$" are not identical, so the use of hypothetical syllogism is not justified. In the second example, only part of the statement "$D \lor E$" (the consequent of the first premise) occurs as the antecedent of the second premise, so once again hypothetical syllogism is not justified.

7. Constructive Dilemma (CD)

The rule of inference called **constructive dilemma (CD)** is complex because it combines three logical operators: conditional statements, conjunctions, and disjunctions. Although the rule can be difficult to grasp, working through an example should help you to better understand the logic behind it. Let's look first at the logical form of constructive dilemma (CD):

$$(p \supset q) \cdot (r \supset s)$$
$$\underline{p \lor r}$$
$$q \lor s$$

Let's substitute the following for the first premise: "If I live in Las Vegas, then I live in Nevada, *and* if I am a slot machine technician, then I work in a casino." Let *p* = "I live in Las Vegas," *q* = "I live in Nevada," *r* = "I am a slot machine technician,"

Constructive dilemma (CD):
A rule of inference.

$$(p \supset q) \cdot (r \supset s)$$
$$\underline{p \lor r}$$
$$q \lor s$$

and s = "I work in a casino." *If* the first premise is true, then both conjuncts must be true. Since each conjunct is a conditional, the combination of true antecedent and false consequent can be ruled out for both conjuncts.

The truth of the second premise ensures that *at least one* of the disjuncts, *p* or *r*, is true. This means that *at least one* of the following must be true: "I live in Las Vegas," or "I am a slot machine technician." From this we know that *at least one* of the antecedents in the first premise is true (*p* or *r*). Since we eliminated the possibility of true antecedent and false consequent in the first premise, we now know that *at least one* of *q* or *s* must be true. This means that *at least one* of the following must be true: "I live in Nevada," or "I work in a casino." This ensures that the conclusion, being a disjunction with *at least one* true disjunct (*q* or *s*) must be true.

The following are examples of legitimate applications of the rule of constructive dilemma (CD):

Legitimate Constructive Dilemma (CD)

$$(T \supset Q) \cdot (M \supset N)$$
$$\underline{T \vee M}$$
$$Q \vee N$$

$$[\sim G \supset (P \cdot R)] \cdot [\sim D \supset (H \cdot F)]$$
$$\underline{\sim G \vee \sim D}$$
$$(P \cdot R) \vee (H \cdot F)$$

Here are two examples of mistakes using constructive dilemma (CD):

Illegitimate Constructive Dilemma (CD)

1. $(S \supset \sim P) \vee (Q \supset \sim R)$
2. $\underline{S \vee Q}$
3. $\sim P \vee \sim R$

1. $(T \supset M) \cdot [(F \cdot G) \supset H]$
2. $\underline{T \vee F}$
3. $M \vee H$

In the first example of illegitimate constructive dilemma, the main operator in premise #1 is ∨, a disjunction; however, for constructive dilemma to work correctly the main operator must be ·, a conjunction. In the second example, only part of the statement "F · G" occurs as the second disjunct in the second premise, so once again constructive dilemma is not justified.

8. Simplification (Simp)

The rule of **simplification (Simp)** relies on the knowledge that a conjunction is true only if all the conjuncts are true. The logical form of this rule is the following:

$$\frac{p \cdot q}{p}$$

Let's substitute the following for the premise: "Oak trees are deciduous and pine trees are conifers." Let *p* = "Oak trees are deciduous," and *q* = "pine trees are conifers." *If* the premise is true, then *both* conjuncts must be true. Since the conclusion is merely one of the conjuncts, it too must be true. The following are examples of legitimate applications of the rule of simplification (Simp).

Simplification (Simp): A rule of inference.

$$\frac{p \cdot q}{p}$$

Legitimate Simplification (Simp)

$$\frac{(H \vee T) \cdot (F \vee G)}{H \vee T} \qquad \frac{\sim (B \supset D) \cdot Q}{\sim (B \supset D)} \qquad \frac{M \cdot [T \vee (G \supset C)]}{M}$$

Here is an example of a mistake using simplification *(Simp)*:

Illegitimate Simplification (Simp)

1. $(P \cdot Q) \vee (R \supset S)$
2. P

Since the main operator in line #1 is $\vee$ (a disjunction), the logical form is "$p \vee q$"; however, we cannot legitimately use simplification on a disjunction.

One final note regarding the rule of simplification (Simp): if we encounter "$p \cdot q$" in a line of a proof, we are only justified in deriving p as a conclusion, even though we acknowledge that both conjuncts must be true. Technically, the rule permits only the left disjunct to be validly derived. However, this technicality will not cause a problem once we introduce the substitution set called *commutation (Comm)* in the next section (page 218). Commutation relies on the truth table verification that the statement "$p \cdot q$" is logically equivalent to "$q \cdot p$." So the rule of simplification (Simp) plus the substitution set commutation (Comm) will allow us to derive q from "$p \cdot q$." Quick Reference 6.1 summarizes the eight rules of inference.

Quick Reference 6.1 • Rules of Inference 1–8

1. Addition (Add)

$$\frac{p}{p \vee q}$$

2. Conjunction (Conj)

$$\frac{p}{q}$$
$$\overline{p \cdot q}$$

Rules of inference 1–8 are Add, Conj, MP, MT, DS, HS, CD, and Simp.

3. *Modus ponens* (MP)

$$\frac{p \supset q}{p}$$
$$\overline{q}$$

4. *Modus tollens* (MT)

$$\frac{p \supset q}{\sim q}$$
$$\overline{\sim p}$$

5. Disjunctive syllogism (DS)

$$\frac{p \vee q}{\sim p}$$
$$\overline{q}$$

6. Hypothetical syllogism (HS)

$$\frac{p \supset q}{q \supset r}$$
$$\overline{p \supset r}$$

7. Constructive dilemma (CD)

$$\frac{(p \supset q) \cdot (r \supset s)}{p \vee r}$$
$$\overline{q \vee s}$$

8. Simplification (Simp)

$$\frac{p \cdot q}{p}$$

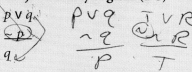

EXERCISE SET 6.4   ○○○

Exercises 1–11 The following are more examples of what you might encounter in proofs. The last line of each problem gives the number(s) of the line or lines needed for its derivation. You are to provide the justification (the rule of inference) in the space provided. These exercises will give you practice using Rules 5–8.

[1]   1. P ⊃ Q
       2. Q ⊃ R
       3. P ⊃ R   1, 2, _____

Answer: 3. P ⊃ R   1, 2, HS

[2]   1. (P ⊃ Q) · (R ⊃ S)
       2. P v R
       3. Q v S   1, 2, _____ CD

[3]   1. T ⊃ (S v T)
       2. (S v T) ⊃ P
       3. T ⊃ P   1, 2, _____ HS

[4]   1. (R ⊃ S) v (P ⊃ Q)
       2. ~ (R ⊃ S)
       3. P ⊃ Q   1, 2, _____ DS

[5]   1. [(P ⊃ R) ⊃ S] · [(Q ⊃ R) ⊃ T]
       2. (P ⊃ R) v (Q ⊃ R)
       3. S v T   1, 2, _____ CD

[*6]   1. (S v P) · M
       2. S v P   1, _____ Simp

[7]   1. ~ P ⊃ ~ Q
       2. ~ Q ⊃ ~ R
       3. ~ P ⊃ ~ R   1, 2, _____ HS

[8]   1. (~ P ⊃ Q) · (~ R ⊃ S)
       2. ~ P v ~ R
       3. Q v S   1, 2, _____ CD

[9]   1. (P · Q) ⊃ R
       2. R ⊃ ~ P
       3. (P · Q) ⊃ ~ P   1, 2, _____ HS

[*10] 1. (P · Q) v (R ⊃ S)
       2. ~ (P · Q)
       3. R ⊃ S   1, 2, _____ DS

[11]   1. [(P · R) ⊃ ~ S] · [(P v R) ⊃ ~ T]
       2. (P · R) v (P v R)
       3. ~ S v ~ T   1, 2, _____ CD

Exercises 12–18 The following are more examples of what you might encounter in proofs. In these examples the justification (the rule of inference) is provided for the last line; however, the line itself is missing. Use the given information to derive the last line of each example.

[12] 1. (S ⊃ T) · (P ⊃ Q)
       2. S ∨ P
       3. _____   1, 2, CD

Answer: 3. T ∨ Q   1, 2, CD

[13] 1. (Q ⊃ S) ∨ T
       2. ~ (Q ⊃ S)
       3. _____   1, 2, DS T

[14] 1. (M ⊃ P) · K
       2. _____   1, Simp (M ⊃ P)

[15] 1. (K ∨ L) ⊃ (K ∨ N)
       2. (K ∨ N) ⊃ (K ∨ S)
       3. _____   1, 2, HS (K ∨ L) ⊃ (K ∨ S)

[*16] 1. P ∨ (Q · S)
       2. ~ P
       3. _____   1, 2, DS (Q · S)

[17] 1. P · (Q ⊃ R)
       2. _____   1, Simp P

[18] 1. P ⊃ (Q ∨ ~ R)
       2. (Q ∨ ~ R) ⊃ ~ S
       3. _____   1, 2, HS P ⊃ ~ S

Exercises 19–23 Translate the following inferences using symbolic notation. Use the rules of inference to justify each conclusion. (The capital letters to be used for translation are provided in each case.)

19. If we initiate another war, then we will thin our supply of troops, and if we violate the terms of our treaties, then we will be ostracized by our allies. We surely will initiate another war or violate the terms of the treaties. Therefore, either we will thin our supply of troops or be ostracized by our allies. (W, S, V, O)

Answer: 1. (W ⊃ S) · (V ⊃ O)
           <u>2. W ∨ V</u>
           3. S ∨ O   1, 2, CD

20. Either Bill is going to the party or Shane and Matt are going. Bill is not going to the party. So, Shane and Matt are going. (B, S, M)

21. If my son drinks three sodas, then he gets hyper, and if he eats two chocolate bars, then he gets wired. Either my son drank three sodas or he ate two chocolate bars. So, he is either hyper or wired. (S, H, C, W)

Exercises 20–23: For answers and explanations, see page 184 of Instructor's Manual.

22. Either my uncle is happy or he is not currently employed. My uncle is not happy. Therefore, he is not currently employed. (H, E)

23. If Mike is a comedian, then he is shy. If Mike is shy, then he keeps his true feelings to himself. So, if Mike is a comedian, then he keeps his true feelings to himself. (C, S, T)

6.5 TACTICS AND STRATEGY USING THE RULES OF INFERENCE

Tactics is the use of small-scale maneuvers or devices, whereas **strategy** is typically understood as referring to a greater, overall goal. In creating a proof, one's strategy might be to isolate as many simple statements as possible, or it might be to reduce, to simplify complex statements. These goals can often be accomplished by employing a variety of tactical moves, such as using simplification to isolate one statement. The same strategic goal might be accomplished by using *modus tollens* as a tactical move, enabling you to isolate and negate part of a complex statement.

It is extremely helpful to have a strategic sense when employing natural deduction. However, it must be understood that even the best strategies cannot guarantee success. Nevertheless, a well-thought-out strategy, coupled with a firm grasp of the available tactical moves within a proof will maximize your prospects for successfully completing a proof.

Using Natural Deduction

Natural deduction is simpler than the truth table method in that it is less cumbersome; however, it is not easy to master. At first, it is often best to simply plug away at tactical moves until you begin to recognize patterns, or begin to see more than one move ahead. In this sense it is like learning to play chess. The novice chess player first learns the legitimate moves for each piece. The initial games one plays usually are devoid of any real strategy—beginners simply move pieces hoping for some tactical advantage in small areas of the chessboard. Real strategy comes only after you have played enough games to begin to understand long-term goals. It takes time and patience to master offensive and defensive skills, the deployment of deception, the ability to think multiple moves ahead, to recognize traps, and to coordinate numerous tactical maneuvers at the same time—in other words, to have a global strategy. Quick Reference 6.2 is offered as a guide to help you develop strategies and correctly apply the relevant tactical moves when creating proofs.

Tactics: The use of small-scale maneuvers or devices (used with natural deduction proofs).

Strategy: Compared to tactics, referring to a greater, overall goal.

Working through Proofs

The inferences you are to prove valid using natural deduction will be displayed in the following manner:

1. $(P \supset Q) \cdot R$
2. P $\therefore Q$

Quick Reference 6.2 • Strategies and Tactics for Using Natural Deduction

Strategy #1: Simplify and isolate

Tactical moves—Try using any of the following:

    A. Simplification (Simp)
    B. *Modus ponens* (MP)
    C. *Modus tollens* (MT)
    D. Disjunctive syllogism (DS)

Strategy #2: Look for Negation (~)

Tactical Moves—Try using any of the following:

    A. *Modus tollens* (MT)
    B. Disjunctive syllogism (DS)

Strategy #3: Look for Conditionals (⊃)

Tactical Moves—Try using any of the following:

    A. *Modus ponens* (MP)
    B. *Modus tollens* (MT)
    C. Hypothetical syllogism (HS)
    D. Constructive dilemma (CD)

Strategy #4: Add whatever you need

Tactical Moves—Try using Addition (Add):

Strategy #5: Combine lines

Tactical Moves—Try using Conjunction (Conj)

Different strategies and tactics are involved in creating proofs using natural deduction.

We stipulate that all the numbered statements above the horizontal line are the given premises. The new symbol ∴ means "therefore," so the statement directly after ∴ is the conclusion of the inference. It is placed there so we know the goal of the proof, which is to derive the conclusion by a series of steps from the given premises. All statements below the drawn line have to be numbered and correctly deduced; therefore, each has to be justified. The final line of the proof is the conclusion, and the entire sequence of steps—from the given premises to the conclusion—constitutes a completed proof. The following is an example of a simple completed proof:

1. (P ⊃ Q) · R
2. P   ∴ Q
3. P ⊃ Q   1, Simp
4. Q   2, 3, MP

In this example, lines 1 and 2 are the given premises. The conclusion, Q, must be derived from the given information by using the rules of inference. Line 3 is a derived line and its justification is the rule of simplification (Simp). Line 4 ends the proof because it displays the conclusion on a separate line that is justified by a correct application of *modus ponens*.

This proof employs two strategies and tactics: Strategy #1: Simplify and isolate, is used by the tactical move of simplification (Simp) on line 1. Strategy #3: Look for Conditionals (⊃), is then applied by the tactical move of *modus ponens*.

The following is an example of a completed proof with the strategies displayed:

1. ~ P · Q
2. S ⊃ P
3. (~ S ∨ R) ⊃ T   ∴ T · ~ P
---
4. ~ P   1, Simp   [Strategy #1: Simplify and Isolate]
5. ~ S   2, 4, MT   [Strategy #2: Look for Negation (~)]
6. ~ S ∨ R   5, Add   [Strategy #4: Add whatever you need]
7. T   3, 6, MP   [Strategy #3: Look for Conditionals (⊃)]
8. T · ~ P   7, 4, Conj   [Strategy #5: Combine lines]

EXERCISE SET 6.5   ○○○

Use the eight rules of inference to complete the proofs. The last line of the proof is the conclusion. Provide the justification for each line that you deduce to complete the proof.

[1]   1. Q ⊃ (P ∨ R)
       2. Q · S   ∴ P ∨ R

Answer: 1. Q ⊃ (P ∨ R)
       2. Q · S   ∴ P ∨ R
       3. Q   2, Simp
       4. P ∨ R   1, 3, MP

Exercises 2–14: For answers
and explanations, see
pages 184–186 of
Instructor's Manual.

[2]   1. T ⊃ (P ∨ Q)
       2. S ∨ ~ (P ∨ Q)
       3. ~ S   ∴ ~ T

[3]   1. (T ⊃ P) · (S ∨ Q)
       2. R ⊃ T   ∴ R ⊃ P

[4]   1. [(T · R) ∨ S] ⊃ (P ∨ Q)
       2. T
       3. R   ∴ P ∨ Q

[5]   1. P ∨ (T ∨ R)
       2. T ⊃ S
       3. R ⊃ Q
       4. ~ P   ∴ S ∨ Q

[*6]   1. T ∨ R
        2. [(T ∨ R) ∨ (S · P)] ⊃ (Q · S)   ∴ Q · S

[7]   1. Q ∨ [S ⊃ (P ⊃ R)]
        2. (T ⊃ R) ⊃ S
        3. ~ Q   ∴ (T ⊃ R) ⊃ (P ⊃ R)

[8]   1. (T ∨ ~ P) ⊃ (Q ∨ ~ S)
        2. T · ~ R   ∴ Q ∨ ~ S

[9]   1. ~ T
        2. R ⊃ S
        3. S ⊃ T   ∴ ~ R

[10]   1. (T ∨ S) ∨ ~ R
        2. ~ (T ∨ S) · (P ∨ Q)   ∴ ~ R

[*11]   1. (P ∨ R) ⊃ Q
        2. ~ Q · S   ∴ ~ (P ∨ R)

[12]   1. S ⊃ R
        2. (P · Q) ∨ S
        3. ~ (P · Q)   ∴ R

[13]   1. P · (S ∨ Q)
        2. (P ∨ R) ⊃ T   ∴ T

[14]   1. (T ∨ Q) ⊃ ~ P
        2. T
        3. P ∨ S   ∴ S · (T ∨ Q)

6.6 SUBSTITUTION SETS—GROUP ONE

The rules of inference are valid inferences, while substitution sets are pairs of logically equivalent statements, statements that have identical truth tables. According to the **principle of substitution**, logically equivalent statements may replace each other whenever one member of a substitution set occurs in a proof. This is the rationale behind the use of substitution sets. Unlike the eight rules of inference, which are restricted to entire lines of a proof, substitution sets have no such restriction—they can be used either for a complete line or any part of a line. Additionally, substitution sets can be applied *left-to-right* or *right-to-left*. The ten substitution sets we will use were in fact already proven by you to be logically equivalent statements (see *Exercise Set 4.6*, Exercises 1–16, page 146). We will provide the truth tables for the first set. You should refer to the truth tables you generated in the previous chapter to complete your understanding.

The ten substitution sets are going to be added to the eight rules of inference, so we will continue the numbering of the series where we left off. Note that a new symbol, ∷, appears in the first of the substitution sets. This symbol means "logically equivalent."

Principle of substitution:
Logically equivalent statement forms may replace each other whenever one member of a substitution set occurs in a proof.

9. Association (Assoc)

Association (Assoc) allows the use of parentheses to group the component parts of certain complex truth-functional statements in different ways without affecting the truth value. The following two pairs of logically equivalent statements show the logical form of association (Assoc).

$$[p \lor (q \lor r)] :: [(p \lor q) \lor r]$$

$$[p \cdot (q \cdot r)] :: [(p \cdot q) \cdot r]$$

As an example, suppose we let p = "Walter will vote in the next election," q = "Sandy will vote in the next election," and r = "Judy will vote in the next election." If we join these three statements using disjunctions, we get: "Either Walter will vote in the next election, or Sandy will vote in the next election, or Judy will vote in the next election." Using parentheses to group the first two disjuncts together makes the second occurrence of the "or" the main operator: $(p \lor q) \lor r$. Using parentheses to group the second and third disjuncts together makes the first occurrence of the "or" the main operator: $p \lor (q \lor r)$. These different groupings have no effect on the truth value of the complex statement. The following truth table proves that $[p \lor (q \lor r)] :: [(p \lor q) \lor r]$ are logically equivalent statements:

	P Q R	[P ∨ (Q ∨ R)]	[(P ∨ Q) ∨ R]
1.	T T T	T *(T)* T *(T)* T	T *(T)* T *(T)* T
2.	T T F	T *(T)* T *(T)* F	T *(T)* T *(T)* F
3.	T F T	T *(T)* F *(T)* T	T *(T)* F *(T)* T
4.	T F F	T *(T)* F *(F)* F	T *(T)* F *(T)* F
5.	F T T	F *(T)* T *(T)* T	F *(T)* T *(T)* T
6.	F T F	F *(T)* T *(T)* F	F *(T)* T *(T)* F
7.	F F T	F *(T)* F *(T)* T	F *(F)* F *(T)* T
8.	F F F	F *(F)* F *(F)* F	F *(F)* F *(F)* F

The second pair of logically equivalent statements showing the form of association (Assoc) has conjunction as the only logical operator. The following truth table proves that $[p \cdot (q \cdot r)] :: [(p \cdot q) \cdot r]$ are logically equivalent statements:

	P Q R	[P · (Q · R)]	[(P · Q) · R]
1.	T T T	T *(T)* T *(T)* T	T *(T)* T *(T)* T
2.	T T F	T *(F)* T *(F)* F	T *(T)* T *(F)* F
3.	T F T	T *(F)* F *(F)* T	T *(F)* F *(F)* T
4.	T F F	T *(F)* F *(F)* F	T *(F)* F *(F)* F
5.	F T T	F *(F)* T *(T)* T	F *(F)* T *(F)* T
6.	F T F	F *(F)* T *(F)* F	F *(F)* T *(F)* F
7.	F F T	F *(F)* F *(F)* T	F *(F)* F *(F)* T
8.	F F F	F *(F)* F *(F)* F	F *(F)* F *(F)* F

Association (Assoc):
A substitution set.

$[p \lor (q \lor r)] :: [(p \lor q) \lor r]$
$[p \cdot (q \cdot r)] :: [(p \cdot q) \cdot r]$

A word of caution: *Association (Assoc) works only with disjunction and conjunction. Also, association works only when disjunction or conjunction is the sole logical operator in the complex statement.*

Here are two examples of proofs illustrating the legitimate use of association (Assoc):

Legitimate Association (Assoc)

	Example A			**Example B**	
1.	(P ∨ Q) ⊃ S		1.	(T · ~ Q) ⊃ ~ S	
2.	~ M		2.	T · (~ Q · R)	∴ ~ S
3.	(M ∨ P) ∨ Q	∴ S	3.	(T · ~ Q) · R	2, Assoc
4.	M ∨ (P ∨ Q)	3, Assoc	4.	T · ~ Q	3, Simp
5.	P ∨ Q	2, 4, DS	5.	~ S	1, 4, MP
6.	S	1, 5, MP			

In Example A, line 4 uses association (Assoc) to change the grouping of the disjunctions. This strategy isolates the M and allows us to use the ~ M in line 2 by applying the rule of disjunctive syllogism. In Example B, the strategy is to try to create the antecedent in line 1 on a separate line. This will require two tactical moves. First, we use association (Assoc) to change the grouping in line 2: (T · ~ Q) · R. Second, we use simplification (Simp) to isolate "T · ~ Q," giving us the antecedent in the first premise.

The next two examples show mistaken applications of association (Assoc):

Illegitimate Association (Assoc)

1.	(T · ~ Q) ∨ R		1.	T · (~ Q ∨ R)	
2.	T · (~ Q ∨ R)	1, Assoc	2.	(T · ~ Q) ∨ R	1, Assoc

These two examples do not heed the caution mentioned above. Association (Assoc) works only when disjunction or conjunction is the sole logical operator in the complex statement. You might want to try constructing a truth table to verify that in both examples the substitution does not result in logically equivalent statements.

10. Double Negation (DN)

The substitution set called **double negation (DN)** permits the introduction or elimination of pairs of negation signs. The principle behind double negation can be illustrated by the following example: The contradiction of the statement, "Golf is a sport," is the statement "Golf is not a sport." The contradiction of, "Golf is not a sport," can be written as, "Golf is not not a sport." This means that "Golf is a sport" is logically equivalent to "Golf is not not a sport." This line of reasoning is revealed in the logical form of double negation:

$$p :: \sim \sim p$$

Double negation (DN):
A substitution set.

$$p :: \sim \sim p$$

Here are two examples of proofs illustrating the legitimate use of double negation (DN):

Legitimate Double Negation (DN)

Example A			Example B		

Example A

1. $(Q \lor R) \supset \sim P$
2. P $\therefore \sim (Q \lor R)$
3. $\sim \sim P$ 2, DN
4. $\sim (Q \lor R)$ 1, 3, MT

Example B

1. $P \supset Q$
2. R
3. $\sim P \supset \sim R$ $\therefore Q$
4. $\sim \sim R$ 2, DN
5. $\sim \sim P$ 3, 4, MT
6. P   5, DN
7. Q   1, 6, MP

In Example A, the tactical move is to apply double negation to P in order to create the negation of the consequent of the first premise. This allows us to use *modus tollens* to get the desired result. In Example B, a similar strategy is employed. Since line 2 contains the negation of the consequent in line 3, double negation (DN) allows us to substitute $\sim \sim R$ for its logically equivalent pair member R. Double negation is used a second time in line 6 to substitute P for its logically equivalent pair member $\sim \sim P$. In Example B we see a clear illustration of what was stated earlier: substitution sets can be applied *left-to-right* or *right-to-left*.

The following example shows a mistaken application of double negation (DN):

Illegitimate Double Negation (DN)

1. $\sim (Q \lor R)$
2. $\sim (\sim Q \lor \sim R)$ 1, DN

You might want to try constructing a truth table to verify that the substitution does not result in logically equivalent statements.

11. Commutation (Comm)

With **commutation (Comm)**, the truth value of a statement is not changed by the order of the disjuncts or conjuncts. The principle behind commutation (Comm) can be illustrated by the following example: The statement, "Digital music is better than analog, or plasma TV's are too expensive," is logically equivalent to, "Plasma TV's are too expensive, or digital music is better than analog." It should be fairly obvious that the order of the disjuncts does not affect the truth value of this complex statement. Commutation (Comm) is, therefore, similar to association (Assoc) in that it works only with disjunction and conjunction. The form of commutation is shown below.

Commutation (Comm):
A substitution set.
$(p \lor q) :: (q \lor p)$
$(p \cdot q) :: (q \cdot p)$

$$(p \lor q) :: (q \lor p)$$

$$(p \cdot q) :: (q \cdot p)$$

Here are two examples of proofs illustrating the legitimate use of commutation (Comm):

Legitimate Commutation (Comm)

Example A		**Example B**	
1. M ⊃ (P ∨ Q)		1. (R ∨ S) ⊃ T	
2. T · M	∴ P ∨ Q	2. ~ M	
3. M · T	2, Comm	3. ~ S ⊃ M	∴ T
4. M	3, Simp	4. ~ ~ S	2, 3, MT
5. P ∨ Q	1, 4, MP	5. S	4, DN
		6. S ∨ R	5, Add
		7. R ∨ S	6, Comm
		8. T	1, 7, MP

In Example A, the strategy was to recognize that the M in line 2 could eventually be used to get the antecedent of the first premise. The first tactical move used commutation (Comm) to substitute logically equivalent statements in line 2. The second tactical move used the rule of simplification on line 3 to isolate the M. In Example B, The strategy was to recognize that it was possible to isolate the S, which was part of the antecedent in the first premise. This was accomplished by the tactical move of *modus tollens* on lines 2 and 3. Once S was established, S ∨ R was easily formed by the rule of addition. Commutation (Comm) then allowed the substitution of logically equivalent statements to form the needed antecedent.

The next example shows a mistaken application of commutation (Comm):

Illegitimate Commutation (Comm)

1. M ⊃ (P ∨ Q)
2. (P ∨ Q) ⊃ M   1, Comm

You might want to try constructing a truth table to verify that the substitution does not result in logically equivalent statements.

12. De Morgan (DeM)

There are two sets of logically equivalent statements named after Augustus De Morgan (see biography, page 221). De Morgan substitution sets are similar to association (Assoc) and commutation (Comm) in that they can be used only with conjunction and disjunction. The two forms of **De Morgan (DeM)** are:

$$\sim (p \cdot q) :: (\sim p \lor \sim q)$$

$$\sim (p \lor q) :: (\sim p \cdot \sim q)$$

De Morgan (DeM):
A substitution set.

$$\sim (p \cdot q) :: (\sim p \lor \sim q)$$
$$\sim (p \lor q) :: (\sim p \cdot \sim q)$$

We encountered these two sets of statements in Section 4.6 where truth tables revealed their logical equivalence. Let's examine the first pair of statements. The statement, "It is not the case that both Judy *and* Eddie like riding roller coasters," is logically equivalent to, "Either Judy *or* Eddie does not like riding roller coasters." These two statements make the same assertion: that *at least one* of the two people mentioned does not like to ride roller coasters.

The second pair of statements can be understood in a similar manner. The statement, "It is not the case that either Judy *or* Eddie likes riding roller coasters," is logically equivalent to, "Judy *and* Eddie do not like riding roller coasters." These two statements make the same assertion, that *both* of the people mentioned do not like to ride roller coasters.

Here are two examples of proofs illustrating the legitimate use of De Morgan (DeM):

Legitimate De Morgan (DeM)

Example A			**Example B**		
1. S			1. ~ (A · B) ⊃ T		
2. ~ (S · T)	∴ ~ T		2. ~ A · M	∴ T	
3. ~ S v ~ T	2, DeM		3. ~ A	2, Simp	
4. ~ ~ S	1, DN		4. ~ A v ~ B	3, Add	
5. ~ T	3, 4, DS		5. ~ (A · B)	4, DeM	
			6. T	1, 5, MP	

In Example A, the strategy was to isolate the S in the second premise. This was accomplished by two tactical moves using substitution sets. First, De Morgan (DeM) was used to eliminate the parentheses in line 2. Next, double negation (DN) was used on line 1. This provided the necessary apparatus to successfully apply the rule of disjunctive syllogism (DS) to get the desired result. In Example B, the strategy was to create the antecedent of line 1 in order to derive the conclusion, the consequent of line 1. After isolating ~ A and using the rule of addition (Add), De Morgan (DeM) was needed to create the correct form of the antecedent in line 1.

The next two examples show mistaken applications of De Morgan (DeM):

Illegitimate De Morgan (DeM)

1. ~ (A · B)			1. ~ C v ~ D	
2. ~ A · ~ B	1, DeM		2. ~ (C v D)	1, DeM

You might want to try constructing a truth table to verify that the substitution does not result in logically equivalent statements.

BIOGRAPHY   AUGUSTUS DE MORGAN

When asked how old he was, Augustus De Morgan, (1806–1871), ever the mathematician, once remarked, "I was *x* years old in the year *x-squared*."*One of De Morgan's main interests was in the problem of transforming thoughts into symbols. Although trained as a mathematician, De Morgan read widely in many other fields. From years of intense study, De Morgan realized that all scientific and mathematical fields advanced only when they had a robust system of symbols. De Morgan also recognized that what had hindered the development of logic from Aristotle's time was the lack of a system of logical symbols. During the same time period that De Morgan began creating a useful set of logic symbols, his contemporary, George Boole (see biography, page 251), was working on the same problem. De Morgan argued that logic and mathematics should be studied together in order for the disciplines to learn from each other. In fact, when he taught mathematics

courses he always included logical training as part of the curriculum. Some of De Morgan's original work on logic and its symbolism can be found in his book, *Formal Logic,* published in 1847. De Morgan is also credited with establishing a mathematical basis for understanding Aristotelian categorical syllogisms. For example, from the premises, "Some D are J" and "Some D are N," we cannot validly conclude that, "Some J are N." However, De Morgan showed that from the premises, "Most D are J" and "Most D are N," we can validly conclude that, "Some J are N." In fact, De Morgan provides a mathematical formula for this problem: Let the number of D's = x; the number of D's that are J's = y; and the number of D's that are N = z. From this we can conclude that there are *at least* $(y + z) - x$ J's that are N's.

*De Morgan was 43 years old in the year 1849.

13. Distribution (Dist)

Distribution (Dist) can be understood by analyzing this complex statement: "Motorcycles are loud and either trucks or buses get poor gas mileage." If we let p = "Motorcycles are loud," q = "trucks get poor gas mileage," and r = "buses get poor gas mileage," we get $p \cdot (q \lor r)$. Since the main operator is a conjunction, we know that *if* the statement is true, then both conjuncts must be true. That means p is true and at least one of *(q* or *r)* is true. We can therefore assert that at least one of the following must be true: "Motorcycles are loud and trucks get poor gas mileage," or "Motorcycles are loud and buses get poor gas mileage." The logical form of this complex statement is $(p \cdot q) \lor (p \cdot r)$. These results are illustrated by the first set of logically equivalent statements that follow:

$$[p \cdot (q \lor r)] :: [(p \cdot q) \lor (p \cdot r)]$$
$$[p \lor (q \cdot r)] :: [(p \lor q) \cdot (p \lor r)]$$

The second pair of statements can be understood in a similar manner. Consider the complex statement, "Motorcycles are loud or both trucks and buses get poor gas mileage." If we let p = "Motorcycles are loud," q = "trucks get poor gas mileage," and r = "buses get poor gas mileage," we get $p \lor (q \cdot r)$. Since the main

Distribution (Dist):
A substitution set.
$[p \cdot (q \lor r)] :: [(p \cdot q) \lor (p \cdot r)]$
$[p \lor (q \cdot r)] :: [(p \lor q) (p \lor r)]$

operator is a disjunction, the statement is true if at least one of the disjuncts is true. Therefore, if the first disjunct, p, is true, then $(p \lor q)$ is true and $(p \lor r)$ is true. If the second disjunct $(q \cdot r)$ is true then both q and r are true. Therefore, once again, $(p \lor q)$ is true and $(p \lor r)$ is true.

Distribution (Dist) can be used only with conjunction and disjunction. Here are two examples of proofs illustrating the legitimate use of distribution (Dist):

Legitimate Distribution (Dist)

Example A		
1. ~ (M · N)		
2. M · (N ∨ P)		∴ M · P
3. (M · N) ∨ (M · P)	2, Dist	
4. M · P	1, 3, DS	

Example B		
1. ~ C		
2. A ∨ (C · D)		∴ A
3. (A ∨ C) · (A ∨ D)	2, Dist	
4. A ∨ C	3, Simp	
5. C ∨ A	4, Comm	
6. A	1, 5, DS	

In Example A, the strategy was to try to get the M and N of the second premise together. Distribution (Dist) does this by creating a disjunction that can then be acted on by the rule of disjunctive syllogism (DS). In Example B, the main goal was to isolate the A. Tactical moves allowed us to place the A and C together in such a way that the ~ C in the first line could be used to our advantage. Therefore, distribution (Dist) was a key tactical move in constructing the proof.

The next two examples show mistaken applications of distribution (Dist):

Illegitimate Distribution (Dist)

1. B ∨ (C · D)			1. (M · N) ∨ (M · P)	
2. (B ∨ C) ∨ (B ∨ D)	1, Dist		2. M · (N · P)	1, Dist

You might want to try constructing a truth table to verify that the substitution does not result in logically equivalent statements.

TABLE 6.2 Substitution Sets—Group One

9. **Association (Assoc)**	10. **Double Negation (DN)**
$[p \lor (q \lor r)] :: [(p \lor q) \lor r]$	$p :: \sim\sim p$
$[p \cdot (q \cdot r)] :: [(p \cdot q) \cdot r]$	
11. **Commutation (Comm)**	12. **De Morgan (DeM)**
$(p \lor q) :: (q \lor p)$	$\sim (p \cdot q) :: (\sim p \lor \sim q)$
$(p \cdot q) :: (q \cdot p)$	$\sim (p \lor q) :: (\sim p \cdot \sim q)$
13. **Distribution (Dist)**	
$[p \cdot (q \lor r)] :: [(p \cdot q) \lor (p \cdot r)]$	
$[p \lor (q \cdot r)] :: [(p \lor q) \cdot (p \lor r)]$	

EXERCISE SET 6.6   ○○○

Exercises 1–10 The following are examples of what you might encounter in proofs. The last line of each example gives the number(s) of the line or lines needed for its derivation. You are to provide the justification (the substitution set) in the space provided. These exercises will give you practice using substitution sets 9–13.

[1]   1. ~ (T · R)
       2. ~ T v ~ R   1, ———

Answer: 1. ~ (T · R)
          2. ~ T v ~ R   1, DeM

[2]   1. S v T
       2. T v S   1, ——— Comm

[3]   1. R v (S v T)
       2. (R v S) v T   1, ——— Assoc

[4]   1. P · (S v Q)
       2. (P · S) v (P · Q)   1, ——— Dist

[5]   1. T
       2. ~ ~ T   1, ——— DN

[*6]   1. ~ P v ~ Q
       2. ~ (P · Q)   1, ——— DeM

[7]   1. P v (Q · R)
       2. (Q · R) v P   1, ——— Comm

[8]   1. (P v Q) v R
       2. P v (Q v R)   1, ——— Assoc

[9]   1. (P · Q) v (P · R)
       2. P · (Q v R)   1, ——— Dist

[10]   1. ~ ~ Q
       2. Q   1, ——— DN

Exercises 11–18 The following are more examples of what you might encounter in proofs. In these examples the justification (the substitution set) is provided for the last line; however, the line itself is missing. Use the given information to derive the last line of each example.

[11]   1. T · R
        2. ———   1, Comm

Answer: 1. T · R
          2. R · T   1, Comm

[12]   1. (S v P) · (S v Q)
        2. ———   1, Dist   S v (P · Q)

[13] 1. ~ ~ Q
      2. ————   1, DN Q

[14] 1. (R · S) · T
      2. ————   1, Assoc R · (S · T)

[15] 1. ~ T · ~ Q
      2. ————   1, DeM ~ (T ∨ Q)

[*16] 1. ~ ~ (P · R)
      2. ————   1, DN (P · R)

[17] 1. P · Q
      2. ————   1, Comm Q · P

[18] 1. P ∨ (Q · R)
      2. ————   1, Dist (P ∨ Q) · (P ∨ R)

6.7 SUBSTITUTION SETS—GROUP TWO

There are five additional substitution sets for us to consider. As with the first five sets, a correct application ensures that we create valid inferences in our deductive proofs.

14. Transposition (Trans)

One way to see how the set of logically equivalent statements named *transposition (Trans)* works is to recall our discussion of sufficient and necessary conditions. For example, the statement, "If you get at least a 90 on the exam, then you get an A," is *logically equivalent* to the statement, "If you did not get an A, then you did not get at least a 90 on the exam." The logical form of this set of statements is captured by **transposition (Trans)**, which can be shown as follows:

$$(p \supset q) :: (\sim q \supset \sim p)$$

Here are two examples of proofs illustrating the legitimate use of transposition (Trans):

Legitimate Transposition (Trans)

Example A		Example B	
1. S ⊃ ~ Q		1. S · ~ M	
2. P ⊃ Q ∴ S ⊃ ~ P		2. (P ∨ R) ⊃ M ∴ ~ P · ~ R	
3. ~ Q ⊃ ~ P	2, Trans	3. ~ M ⊃ ~ (P ∨ R)	2, Trans
4. S ⊃ ~ P	1, 3, HS	4. ~ M · S	1, Comm
		5. ~ M	4, Simp
		6. ~ (P ∨ R)	3, 5, MP
		7. ~ P · ~ R	6, DeM

Transposition (Trans):
A substitution set.

$(p \supset q) :: (\sim q \supset \sim p)$

In Example A, transposition (Trans) was used tactically on line 2 to create another instance of ~ Q. This created the opportunity to apply the rule of hypothetical syllogism (HS) in order to get the desired result. In Example B, the short-term strategy was to recognize that ~ M in line 1 could eventually exist by itself on a separate line. Given this, the tactical move of transposition (Trans) on line 2 set up ~ M as the antecedent of a conditional statement. Once this was achieved the final result was within reach.

The next example shows a mistaken application of transposition (Trans):

Illegitimate Transpostion (Trans)

1. ~ P ⊃ ~ Q
_____
2. P ⊃ Q   1, Trans

You might want to try constructing a truth table to verify that the substitution does not result in logically equivalent statements.

15. Material Implication (MI)

Material implication (MI) can be illustrated by analyzing the following statement: "If you get fewer than 60 points on the exam, then you fail." If we let p = "you get fewer than 60 points on the exam," and q = "you fail," then the logical form is $p \supset q$. This is logically equivalent to the statement, "*Either* you did *not* get fewer than 60 points on the exam *or* you failed," which has the logical form ($\sim p \vee q$). These equivalent statements are found in the substitution set called **material implication (MI)**, which has the following form:

$$(p \supset q) :: (\sim p \vee q)$$

Here are two examples of proofs illustrating the legitimate use of material implication (MI):

Legitimate Material Implication (MI)

Example A

1. ~ T	∴ (T ⊃ S) ∨ P	
2. ~ T ∨ S	1, Add	
3. T ⊃ S	2, MI	
4. (T ⊃ S) ∨ P	3, Add	

Example B

1. B		
2. (B ⊃ C) ∨ D	∴ C ∨ D	
3. (~ B ∨ C) ∨ D	2, MI	
4. ~ B ∨ (C ∨ D)	3, Assoc	
5. ~ ~ B	1, DN	
6. C ∨ D	4, 5, DS	

In Example A, material implication (MI) changed the disjunction in line 2 into a conditional statement. This change was needed in order to get the statement into the same form as it appears in the conclusion. In Example B, the overall strategy was to ensure that C gets connected to D, as indicated by the conclusion.

Material implication (MI):
A substitution set.
$(p \supset q) :: (\sim p \vee q)$

Since material implication (MI) allows the successful substitution of a disjunction for a conditional statement, this tactical move helps create the needed change in line 2.

The next two examples show mistaken applications of material implication (MI):

Illegitimate Material Implication (MI)

1. T ⊃ R		1. ~ D ∨ G	
2. ~ T · R	1, MI	2. ~ (D ⊃ G)	1, MI

You might want to try constructing a truth table to verify that the substitution does not result in logically equivalent statements.

16. Exportation (Exp)

Exportation (Exp) can be illustrated by analyzing the following statement: "If you paint your room, then if you wax the car, then I will give you $100." The logical form of this statement is $p \supset (q \supset r)$. This is *logically equivalent* to the statement, "If you paint your room *and* you wax the car, then I will give you $100." The substitution set called **exportation (Exp)** has the following form:

$$[(p \cdot q) \supset r] :: [p \supset (q \supset r)]$$

Here are two examples of proofs illustrating the legitimate use of exportation (Exp):

Legitimate Exportation (Exp)

Example A		Example B	
1. T		1. G	
2. (T · R) ⊃ S ∴ ~ R ∨ S		2. H ⊃ (K ⊃ ~ G) ∴ ~ H ∨ ~ K	
3. T ⊃ (R ⊃ S)	2, Exp	3. (H · K) ⊃ ~ G	2, Exp
4. R ⊃ S	1, 3, MP	4. ~ ~ G	1, DN
5. ~ R ∨ S	4, MI	5. ~ (H · K)	3, 4, MT
		6. ~ H ∨ ~ K	5, DeM

In Example A, exportation (Exp) is used tactically to create a conditional statement in which T is isolated. This can then be acted upon by applying *modus ponens* to get the desired result. In Example B, exportation (Exp) is used tactically to create a conditional statement in which ~ G is isolated. This can then be acted upon by eventually applying *modus tollens* to get the desired result.

Exportation (Exp):
A substitution set.
$[(p \cdot q) \supset r] :: [p \supset (q \supset r)]$

The next examples show mistaken applications of *exportation (Exp)*:

Illegitimate Exportation (Exp)

1. T ⊃ (R ⊃ S)

2. T ⊃ (R • S)   1, Exp.

1. (D • G) ⊃ H

2. (D ⊃ G) ⊃ H   1, Exp.

1. T ⊃ (R • S)

2. T ⊃ (R ⊃ S)   1, Exp.

1. (D ⊃ G) ⊃ H

2. (D • G) ⊃ H   1, Exp.

You might want to try constructing a truth table to verify that the substitution does not result in logically equivalent statements.

17. Material Equivalence (ME)

In Chapter 4, the truth table for material equivalence revealed that $p \equiv q$ is true when p and q are both true *or* when p and q are both false. With this in mind, let's look at the two forms of **material equivalence (ME)** substitution sets:

$$(p \equiv q) :: [(p \supset q) \cdot (q \supset p)]$$
$$(p \equiv q) :: [(p \cdot q) \vee (\sim p \cdot \sim q)]$$

In the first set above, if p and q are both true, then $(p \supset q)$ and $(q \supset p)$ are true because in both instances the antecedent and consequent are true. Likewise, if p and q are both false, then $(p \supset q)$ and $(q \supset p)$ are once again true because in both instances the antecedent and consequent are false. Therefore, $(p \equiv q)$ is logically equivalent to $[(p \supset q) \cdot (q \supset p)]$.

Here are two examples of proofs illustrating the legitimate use of material equivalence (ME).

Legitimate Material Equivalence (ME)

Example A

1. ~ S
2. (~ T v ~ R) ⊃ S   ∴ T ≡ R
3. ~ (~ T v ~ R)   1, 2, MT
4. ~ ~ T • ~ ~ R   3, DeM
5. T • R   4, DN (used twice)
6. (T • R) v (~ T • ~ R)   5, Add
7. T ≡ R   6, ME

Example B

1. C ≡ D
2. (C • D) ⊃ ~ P
3. P   ∴ ~ C
4. (C • D) v (~ C • ~ D) 1, ME
5. ~ ~ P ⊃ ~ (C • D)   2, Trans
6. P ⊃ ~ (C • D)   5, DN
7. ~ (C • D)   3, 6, MP
8. ~ C • ~ D   4, 7, DS
9. ~ C   8, Simp

Material equivalence (ME):
A substitution set.
$(p \equiv q) :: [(p \supset q) \cdot (q \supset p)]$
$(p \equiv q) :: [(p \cdot q) \vee (\sim p \cdot \sim q)]$

In Example A, since the conclusion is T ≡ R, the overall strategy must be to derive one of the two logically equivalent sets. This means that if T · R can be isolated, then we can use addition (Add) to create the necessary parts. So rather than use material equivalence (ME) as a tactical move within the body of the proof, we must instead recognize that it will be the final step of the proof.

The following two examples show mistaken applications of material equivalence (ME):

Illegitimate Material Equivalence (ME)

1. G ≡ H	1. [(M ⊃ T) v (T ⊃ M)]	
2. (G · H) · (~ G · ~ H) 1, ME	2. M ≡ T 1, ME	

You might want to try constructing a truth table to verify that the substitution does not result in logically equivalent statements.

18. Tautology (Taut)

A *tautology* is a statement that is necessarily true because of its logical form. The principle behind the substitution set **tautology (Taut)** can be illustrated by considering the following statement: "August has 31 days." If this statement is true then the disjunction, "August has 31 days *or* August has 31 days," must be true. Likewise, if the statement, "August has 31 days" is true, then the conjunction, "August has 31 days *and* August has 31 days," must be true. The truth tables are identical in both examples, so they are logically equivalent statements. The forms of tautology (Taut) are:

$$p :: (p \lor p)$$

$$p :: (p \cdot p)$$

Here are two examples of proofs illustrating the legitimate use of tautology (Taut):

Legitimate Tautology (Taut)

Example A

1. (T ⊃ S) · (R ⊃ S)	
2. T v R	∴ S
3. S v S	1, 2, CD
4. S	3, Taut

Example B

1. P ⊃ R	
2. P v (Q · P)	∴ R
3. (P v Q) · (P v P)	2, Dist
4. (P v P) · (P v Q)	3, Comm
5. P v P	4, Simp
6. P	5, Taut
7. R	1, 6, MP

In Example A, tautology (Taut) was used to eliminate the redundant S that was formed in line 3. This elimination created the single S needed in the conclusion. In Example B, tautology (Taut) was used as a tactical move to isolate one instance of P in order for *modus ponens* to be applied to line 1.

Tautology: A substitution set.

$$p :: (p \lor p)$$
$$p :: (p \cdot p)$$

The next example shows a mistaken application of tautology (Taut):

Illegitimate Tautology (Taut)

1. S ⊃ (Q ∨ S)
_____

2. S ⊃ Q   1, Taut

You might want to try constructing a truth table to verify that the substitution does not result in logically equivalent statements.

Quick Reference 6.3 summarizes the 10 substitution sets.

Quick Reference 6.3 • The 10 Substitution Sets

9. **Association (Assoc)**

   $[p \lor (q \lor r)] :: [(p \lor q) \lor r]$
   $[p \cdot (q \cdot r)] :: [(p \cdot q) \cdot r]$

10. **Double negation (DN)**

   $p :: \sim\sim p$

11. **Commutation (Comm)**

   $(p \lor q) :: (q \lor p)$
   $(p \cdot q) :: (q \cdot p)$

12. **De Morgan (DeM)**

   $\sim (p \cdot q) :: (\sim p \lor \sim q)$
   $\sim (p \lor q) :: (\sim p \cdot \sim q)$

13. **Distribution (Dist)**

   $[p \cdot (q \lor r)] :: [(p \cdot q) \lor (p \cdot r)]$
   $[p \lor (q \cdot r)] :: [(p \lor q) \cdot (p \lor r)]$

14. **Transposition (Trans)**

   $(p \supset q) :: (\sim q \supset \sim p)$

15. **Material implication (MI)**

   $(p \supset q) :: (\sim p \lor q)$

16. **Exportation (Exp)**

   $[(p \cdot q) \supset r] :: [p \supset (q \supset r)]$

17. **Material equivalence (ME)**

   $(p \equiv q) :: [(p \supset q) \cdot (q \supset p)]$
   $(p \equiv q) :: [(p \cdot q) \lor (\sim p \cdot \sim q)]$

18. **Tautology (Taut)**

   $p :: (p \lor p)$
   $p :: (p \cdot p)$

> Substitution sets are pairs of logically equivalent statements, which have identical truth tables.

Expanding the Proof Procedure

We can begin looking at how substitution sets can be used by connecting them to the rules of inference. For example, the two substitution sets under commutation (Comm) are immediately useful, as they allow us to expand two of our earlier rules of inference—disjunctive syllogism (DS) and simplification (Simp).

1. Disjunctive Syllogism (DS)

Original

$p \lor q$

$\sim p$
___

q

Expansion

$p \lor q$

$\sim q$
___

p

The justification for the second inference is our use of the first substitution set under commutation: $(p \lor q) :: (q \lor p)$. The formal display of this can easily be shown:

1. $p \lor q$
2. $\sim q$　　　　$\therefore p$
3. $q \lor p$　　1, Comm
4. p　　　　2, 3, DS

2. Simplification (Simp)

Original	Expansion
$p \cdot q$	$p \cdot q$
p	q

The justification for the second inference is our use of the second substitution set under commutation: $(p \cdot q) :: (q \cdot p)$. The formal display of this can easily be shown:

1. $p \cdot q$　　$\therefore q$
2. $q \cdot p$　　1, Comm
3. q　　　　2, Simp

Since the substitution sets can be used with part of a line whenever and wherever needed, they provide more flexibility than the rules of inference. In addition, it does not matter whether the right side of the set or the left side occurs in the proof, because either side can replace the other. Nevertheless, you must make sure that you do not use them in an illegitimate manner. For example,

Legitimate Move		**Illegitimate Move**	
1. $(\sim P \lor \sim Q) \supset S$		1. $(\sim P \cdot \sim Q) \supset S$	
2. $\sim (P \cdot Q)$		2. $\sim (P \cdot Q)$	
3. $\sim P \lor \sim Q$	2, DeM	3. $\sim P \cdot \sim Q$	2, DeM
4. S	1, 3, MP	4. S	1, 3, MP

The first example above correctly applies the first set under De Morgan (DeM), so line #3 is legitimately justified. This allows us to successfully apply *modus ponens* (MP) and deduce line #4. Contrast this to the second example above where line #3 incorrectly applies De Morgan (DeM); it then illegitimately combines part of one De Morgan set, with part of the other. In so doing, line #3 cannot be justified, and therefore, line #4 cannot be successfully deduced, so it, too, is unjustified. Since each step of a proof must be validly deduced, any unjustified line constitutes a "gap" that destroys the validity of the proof.

EXERCISE SET 6.7

Exercises 1–10 The following are examples of what you might encounter in proofs. The last line of each example gives the number(s) of the line or lines needed for its derivation. You are to provide the justification (the substitution set) in the space provided. These exercises will give you practice using substitution sets 14–18.

[1]   1. R ⊃ S
        2. ~ S ⊃ ~ R   1, _____

Answer: 1. R ⊃ S
        2. ~ S ⊃ ~ R   1, Trans

[2]   1. T ⊃ Q
        2. ~ T v Q   1, _____ MI

[3]   1. R ≡ S
        2. (R ⊃ S) · (S ⊃ R)   1, _____ ME

[4]   1. (S · R) ⊃ T
        2. S ⊃ (R ⊃ T)   1, _____ Exp

[5]   1. R
        2. R v R   1, _____ Taut

[*6]   1. ~ P ⊃ ~ Q
        2. Q ⊃ P   1, _____ Trans

[7]   1. ~ P v Q
        2. P ⊃ Q   1, _____ MI

[8]   1. (P · Q) v (~ P · ~ Q)
        2. P ≡ Q   1, _____ ME

[9]   1. P ⊃ (Q ⊃ R)
        2. (P · Q) ⊃ R   1, _____ Exp

[10]   1. P · P
        2. P   1, _____ Taut

Exercises 11–15 The following are more examples of what you might encounter in proofs. In these examples the justification (the substitution set) is provided for the last line; however, the line itself is missing. Use the given information to derive the last line of each example.

[11]   1. ~ T ⊃ ~ R
        2. _____   1, Trans

Answer: 1. ~ T ⊃ ~ R
        2. R ⊃ T   1, Trans

[12]   1. (R · S) v (~ R · ~ S)
    2. _____   1, ME R ≡ S

[13]   1. T · T
    2. _____   1, Taut T

[14]   1. R ⊃ (S ⊃ T)
    2. _____   1, Exp (R · S) ⊃ T

[15]   1. ~ S v P
    2. _____   1, MI S ⊃ P

Exercises 16–30 Use all the rules of inference and all the substitution sets to complete the proofs. The last line of the proof will be the conclusion. Provide the justification for each line that you deduce in order to complete the proof. Each of these proofs will require you to use one rule of inference and one substitution set to complete the proof.

[16]   1. (~ T v ~ R) ⊃ S
    2. ~ (T · R)   ∴ S

Answer: 1. (~ T v ~ R) ⊃ S
      2. ~ (T · R)   ∴ S
      3. ~ T v ~ R   2, DeM
      4. S   1, 3, MP

Exercises 17–60: For answers and explanations, see pages 188–197 of Instructor's Manual.

[17]   1. S ⊃ P
    2. ~ P v (R · Q)   ∴ S ⊃ (R · Q)

[18]   1. T v S
    2. ~ ~ R   ∴ (T v S) · R

[19]   1. (~ T ⊃ S) · (R ⊃ P)
    2. T ⊃ R   ∴ S v P

[20]   1. S ⊃ (P ⊃ Q)
    2. ~ Q   ∴ ~ (S · P)

[*21]   1. (T v Q) v S
    2. ~ T   ∴ Q v S

[22]   1. S v (T · R)   ∴ S v T

[23]   1. S v S   ∴ S v T

[24]   1. P ≡ S   ∴ P ⊃ S

[25]   1. ~ T ⊃ ~ P
    2. T ⊃ S   ∴ P ⊃ S

[*26]   1. ~ (T v S) ⊃ (P v Q)
    2. ~ T · ~ S   ∴ (P v Q)

[27]   1. P ∨ S
         <u>2. ~ S   ∴ P</u>

[28]   <u>1. (S · T) · R   ∴ S</u>

[29]   1. T · (S ∨ R)
         <u>2. ~ (T · S)   ∴ T · R</u>

[30]   1. (R · P) ∨ (~ R · ~ P)
         <u>2. (R ≡ P) ⊃ T   ∴ T</u>

Exercises 31–55 Use the eight rules of inference and the ten substitution sets to complete the proofs. The last line of the proof will be the conclusion. Provide the justification for each line that you deduce in order to complete the proof.

[31]   1. (S ∨ ~ P) ∨ R
         <u>2. ~ S   ∴ P ⊃ R</u>

Answer: 1. (S ∨ ~ P) ∨ R
         <u>2. ~ S   ∴ P ⊃ R</u>
         3. S ∨ (~ P ∨ R)   1, Assoc
         4. ~ P ∨ R   2, 3, DS
         5. P ⊃ R   4, MI

[32]   1. ~ P
         <u>2. (Q ∨ P) ∨ R   ∴ Q ∨ R</u>

[33]   1. ~ P · Q
         <u>2. Q ⊃ (R ⊃ P)   ∴ ~ R</u>

[34]   1. ~ P
         2. ~ Q ⊃ P
         <u>3. ~ Q ∨ (~ P ⊃ R)   ∴ R ∨ S</u>

[35]   1. P ∨ Q
         2. (Q ⊃ R) · (T ⊃ A)
         <u>3. (P ⊃ B) · (C ⊃ D)   ∴ B ∨ R</u>

[*36]   1. (~ P ∨ Q) ⊃ R
         2. (S ∨ R) ⊃ P
         <u>3. P ⊃ Q   ∴ Q</u>

[37]   1. P ∨ (T · R)
         <u>2. S ⊃ ~ (P ∨ T)   ∴ ~ S</u>

[38]   <u>1. ~ (S ∨ Q)   ∴ ~ P ⊃ ~ S</u>

[39]   1. T ⊃ (R · S)
         <u>2. R ⊃ (S ⊃ P)   ∴ (P ∨ ~ T) ∨ Q</u>

[40]　　1. ~ (P · Q) ⊃ (R ∨ S)
　　　　2. ~ P ∨ ~ Q
　　　　3. T　　　　　　　　　　　　∴ (T · R) ∨ (T · S)

[*41]　1. T ∨ S
　　　　2. ~ T
　　　　3. (S ∨ S) ⊃ (~ P ∨ R)　　∴ ~ R ⊃ ~ P

[42]　　1. T ≡ R
　　　　2. (~ R ⊃ ~ T) ⊃ (P · ~ S)　　∴ ~ S ∨ T

[43]　　1. ~ Q ⊃ ~ P
　　　　2. (P · R) ⊃ S
　　　　3. P　　　　　　∴ Q ∨ S

[44]　　1. P ⊃ (Q ∨ R)
　　　　2. (S ∨ T) ⊃ R
　　　　3. ~ Q · ~ R　　　∴ ~ P · ~ (S ∨ T)

[45]　　1. (P ∨ Q) ⊃ S
　　　　2. R ∨ (P ∨ Q)
　　　　3. ~ R
　　　　4. ~ T ⊃ R　　　∴ S ≡ T

[*46]　1. C ⊃ F
　　　　2. A ⊃ B
　　　　3. ~ F · A
　　　　4. ~ C ⊃ (B ⊃ D)　　∴ B · D

[47]　　1. Q ∨ (P ⊃ S)
　　　　2. S ≡ (R · T)
　　　　3. P · ~ Q　　　　∴ P · R

[48]　　1. R
　　　　2. ~ (P · ~ Q)
　　　　3. P ∨ S
　　　　4. ~ (R · S)　　　∴ Q

[49]　　1. P ∨ R
　　　　2. ~ P ∨ (Q · R)
　　　　3. R ⊃ (Q · S)　　∴ Q · S

[50]　　1. Q · S
　　　　2. (Q · ~ P) ⊃ ~ R
　　　　3. Q ⊃ ~ P
　　　　4. (S · T) ⊃ (P ∨ R)　　∴ ~ T

[*51] 1. ~ S ⊃ (N ⊃ T)
    2. ~ S · (R ⊃ S)
    3. (~ M · ~ N) ⊃ (~ O v ~ P)
    4. (Q v ~ R) ⊃ ~ M
    5. (~ R · ~ S) ⊃ (~ ~ O · ~ T)   ∴ ~ P

[52] 1. ~ W · ~ X
    2. ~ U ⊃ W
    3. M ⊃ [(N v O) ⊃ P]
    4. Q ⊃ (S v T)
    5. (~ Q v ~ R) ⊃ (M · N)
    6. ~ U v ~ (S v T)   ∴ P · ~ X

[53] 1. ~ (S ⊃ Q)
    2. (M · N) ⊃ (O v P)
    3. ~ [O v (N · P)]
    4. N ≡ ~ (Q · R)   ∴ ~ (M v Q)

[54] 1. ~ (R v S)
    2. ~ (M · N) v ~ (O · P)
    3. ~ (O · M) ⊃ S
    4. (Q · R) ≡ ~ P   ∴ ~ (N · T)

[55] 1. (~ Q v ~ S) ⊃ T
    2. (M v N) ⊃ [(O v P) ⊃ (~ Q · R)] ∴ M ⊃ (O ⊃ T)

Exercises 56–60 Translate the following inferences using symbolic notation. Use the rules of inference and substitution sets to derive the conclusion. (The capital letters to be used for translation are provided in each case.)

56. Science will eventually come to an end. If science comes to an end and metaphysical speculation runs rampant, then intellectual progress will end. However, it is not the case that either intellectual progress will end or we stop seeking epistemological answers. Therefore, metaphysical speculation will not run rampant. (S, M, I, E)

Answer: 1. S
    2. (S · M) ⊃ I
    3. ~ (I v E)   ∴ ~ M
    4. ~ I · ~ E   3, DeM
    5. ~ I   4, Simp
    6. ~ (S · M)   2, 5, MT
    7. ~ S v ~ M   6, DeM
    8. ~ ~ S   1, DN
    9. ~ M   7, 8, DS

57. Either dolphins or chimpanzees are sentient beings. If chimpanzees can solve complex problems, then chimpanzees are sentient beings. If dolphins can learn a language, then dolphins are sentient beings. Chimpanzees can solve complex problems, and dolphins can learn a language. Therefore, we must conclude that both chimpanzees and dolphins are sentient beings. (D, C, S, L)

58. If sports continue to dominate our culture, then it is not the case that either we will mature as a society, or will we lose touch with reality. We will mature as a society, or we will both decline as a world power and we will we lose touch with reality. Therefore, sports will not continue to dominate our culture. (S, M, L, D)

59. If people know how to read and they are interested in the history of ideas, then they will discover new truths. If people do not know how to read, then they cannot access the wisdom of thousands of years. But people can access the wisdom of thousands of years. Thus, if they are interested in the history of ideas, then they will discover new truths. (R, H, D,W)

60. That movie will not win the Academy Award for best picture. Therefore, if the governor of our state is not impeached, then that movie will not win the Academy Award for best picture. (M, G)

6.8 CONDITIONAL PROOF (CP)

The proof procedure we have been using is capable of handling most valid inferences. However, there is a technique that can simplify the work involved in some of the proofs. Consider the following example:

1. Q
2. $P \supset (Q \supset R)$ ∴ $P \supset R$

Notice that the conclusion is a conditional statement; it claims that *if P then R*. Inferences with conditionals as conclusions can be proven valid with a new technique called **conditional proof (CP)**, which exploits the mechanism of conditional statements. By extracting the "*if*" component we can construct a new kind of proof, one built on *assumptions*. The first step is to *assume* that the antecedent of the conclusion is true and display it as follows:

1. Q
2. $P \supset (Q \supset R)$ ∴ $P \supset R$
     3. P   *Assumption (CP)*

Note that line #3 is indented. It is shown this way because it was not derived from any other line—it was *not validly deduced*. On the contrary, we are *assuming* the truth of line #3. This is also why this line is justified as *Assumption (CP)*. All of our proofs to this point have contained lines that were either given premises or statements derived from previous lines, which in turn, were justified by the rules of inference or substitution sets. This procedure and requirement ensured that each line in a derived proof was itself a valid inference. However, in the above example,

Conditional proof (CP): The method of proof that exploits the mechanism of conditional statements.

line #3 has not been proven; it cannot and does not follow from the premises by any of the rules of inference or substitution sets. It is therefore an *assumption* on our part and is justified as such.

   We now have the opportunity to explore the consequences of our assumption. We can ask, "*If P*, then what follows?" At this point we are free to use the rules of inference and substitution sets as long as we acknowledge that any derivations that rely on line #3 are the result of an assumption, not a direct proof. Therefore, we will have to keep indenting any lines that rely on line #3. The next steps in the proof are as follows:

1. Q
2. P ⊃ (Q ⊃ R)   ∴ P ⊃ R
   ⎡ 3. P   *Assumption (CP)*
   ⎢ 4. Q ⊃ R   2, 3, MP
   ⎣ 5. R   1, 4, MP

   At this point we have all the necessary ingredients to complete our proof. We started out by assuming P (the antecedent of the conclusion) and from this we derived R (the consequent of the conclusion). The next line in the proof combines these results.

1. Q
2. P ⊃ (Q ⊃ R)   ∴ P ⊃ R
   ⎡ 3. P   *Assumption (CP)*
   ⎢ 4. Q ⊃ R   2, 3, MP
   ⎣ 5. R   1, 4, MP
6. P ⊃ R   3-5, CP

Our proof is now complete. Line #6 is a *conditional statement* and it has been derived by a sequence of steps from line #3 through line #5. Note the difference in notation for the lines of the proof. Whereas line #4 uses the notation "2, 3" (a *comma*), line #6 uses the notation "3-5" (a *dash*). This indicates that the *entire sequence* must be referred to whenever you use conditional proof (CP) as the justification for a line.

   Line #6 ends the conditional proof sequence and the result is said to be **discharged**, meaning that it no longer needs to be indented. All the lines in a sequence starting with an assumption can only ultimately combine to issue forth a conditional statement as a final result. This is why line #6 must be justified by listing the entire sequence along with CP. What the proof shows is that from the given premises, along with one assumption (P), we can derive a conditional statement as the conclusion (If P then R). In addition, since the conclusion is a conditional statement, our proof is not claiming that either P or R is true. We are claiming, however, that we can validly deduce the conclusion from the given premises.

   Conditional proof can be used in a variety of ways. For example, it is possible to have a conditional proof *within* another conditional proof sequence. The following example illustrates this point.

1. ~ P ⊃ Q
2. ~ R ∨ [~ P ⊃ (~ Q ∨ ~ U)]   ∴ R ⊃ (U ⊃ P)

Discharged: In conditional proof and indirect proof, the method by which an assumption and any derived lines are completed.

The antecedent of the main operator in the conclusion is R. We can start a CP by *assuming* R, but if you notice, the second premise is a disjunction that has ~ R as its first disjunct. If we use material implication (MI) on the second premise we would derive another conditional with R as the antecedent. Now, if we start our CP and somewhere within the indented lines we use MI on premise #2, we will not be able to use that result outside the CP. Since every line in a CP sequence is based on an *assumption,* it is not valid outside that assumption. Therefore, as a general strategy when using CP, first use the rules of inference and substitution sets whenever possible on the given premises. Once this is done, you can begin the CP sequence.

1. ~ P ⊃ Q
2. ~ R ∨ [~ P ⊃ (~ Q ∨ ~ U)]   ∴ R ⊃ (U ⊃ P)
3. R ⊃ [~ P ⊃ (~ Q ∨ ~ U)]   2, MI

> 4. R   *Assumption (CP)*
> 5. ~ P ⊃ (~ Q ∨ ~ U)   3, 4, MP

Line #5 provides us with an opportunity to try a second use of (CP). If we assume ~ P, then let's see what we can now derive.

1. ~ P ⊃ Q
2. ~ R ∨ [~ P ⊃ (~ Q ∨ ~ U)]   ∴ R ⊃ (U ⊃ P)
3. R ⊃ [~ P ⊃ (~ Q ∨ ~ U)]   2, MI

> 4. R   *Assumption (CP)*
> 5. ~ P ⊃ (~ Q ∨ ~ U)   3, 4, MP
>
> > 6. ~ P   *Assumption (CP)*
> > 7. ~ Q ∨ ~ U   5, 6, MP
> > 8. Q   1, 6, MP
> > 9. ~ ~ Q   8, DN
> > 10. ~ U   7, 9, DS

We are getting close to the consequent of the conclusion so we can now discharge the second assumption, as follows:

1. ~ P ⊃ Q
2. ~ R ∨ [~ P ⊃ (~ Q ∨ ~ U)]   ∴ R ⊃ (U ⊃ P)
3. R ⊃ [~ P ⊃ (~ Q ∨ ~ U)]   2, MI

> 4. R   *Assumption (CP)*
> 5. ~ P ⊃ (~ Q ∨ ~ U)   3, 4, MP
>
> > 6. ~ P   *Assumption (CP)*
> > 7. ~ Q ∨ ~ U   5, 6, MP
> > 8. Q   1, 6, MP
> > 9. ~ ~ Q   8, DN
> > 10. ~ U   7, 9, DS
>
> 11. ~ P ⊃ ~ U   6-10, CP

Using transposition (Trans) on line #11 gives the desired consequent and makes it possible to complete the proof.

1. ~ P ⊃ Q
2. ~ R v [~ P ⊃ (~ Q v ~ U)]   ∴ R ⊃ (U ⊃ P)
3. R ⊃ [~ P ⊃ (~ Q v ~ U)]   2, MI
    4. R   *Assumption (CP)*
    5. ~ P ⊃ (~ Q v ~ U)   3, 4, MP
        6. ~ P   *Assumption (CP)*
        7. ~ Q v ~ U   5, 6, MP
        8. Q   1, 6, MP
        9. ~ ~ Q   8, DN
        10. ~ U   7, 9, DS
    11. ~ P ⊃ ~ U   6-10, CP
    12. U ⊃ P   11, Trans
13. R ⊃ (U ⊃ P)   4-12, CP

As you can see, line #4 starts one conditional proof sequence, but before it is completed, another conditional proof sequence begins with line #6. Note that *both* lines have been justified as assumption (CP).

In addition to showing an assumption, the use of indentation with conditional proofs notifies us that no line within the CP sequence can be used outside the sequence. This means that you cannot use any line within the sequence 6-10 after line #11. Also, if the proof were longer, you could not use any line within the sequence 4-12 after line #13. This requirement should make sense if we think about what CP does. Since every line in a CP sequence is based on an assumption, the lines are not valid outside that assumption. This is why every CP sequence must end with a conditional statement. Once the CP is completed, we can use the discharged conditional statement, because its validity is based on a series of steps that have been carefully contained within the rules of the natural deduction proof procedure. (Of course, you can discharge more than one line from a CP sequence. For example, line #11, ~ P ⊃ ~ U, was discharged and justified as 6-10, CP. If needed in a proof, we could have also discharged a new line; for example, ~ P ⊃ Q would be justified as 6-8, CP.)

Another way to use conditional proof is to have more than one CP sequence within a proof, but with each sequence separate, as in the following example.

1. (~ R v ~ Q) • (R v P)
2. P ⊃ ~ S
3. Q v S   ∴ P ≡ Q

If we apply material equivalence (ME), we can see that the conclusion is logically equivalent to (P ⊃ Q) • (Q ⊃ P). Since the conclusion can be seen as the *conjunction* of two *conditionals*, we might try assuming the antecedent of each one to see what we can derive. Of course, before we start CP, we should consider whether the given premises could offer us any interesting results.

We can start our proof as follows:

1. (~ R ∨ ~ Q) · (R ∨ P)
2. P ⊃ ~ S
3. Q ∨ S   ∴ P≡ Q
4. ~ R ∨ ~ Q   1, Simp
5. R ∨ P   1, Simp (after Comm)

> 6. P   *Assumption (CP)*
> 7. ~ S   2, 6, MP
> 8. Q   3, 7, DS (after Comm)

9. P ⊃ Q   6-8, CP

At this point in our proof, we have deduced the first part of the conjunction (P ⊃ Q) · (Q ⊃ P). We now need to derive the second part.

1. (~ R ∨ ~ Q) · (R ∨ P)
2. P ⊃ ~ S
3. Q ∨ S   ∴   P ≡ Q
4. ~ R ∨ ~ Q   1, Simp
5. R ∨ P   1, Simp (after Comm)

> 6. P   *Assumption (CP)*
> 7. ~ S   2, 6, MP
> 8. Q   3, 7, DS (after Comm)

9. P ⊃ Q   6-8, CP

> 10. Q   *Assumption (CP)*
> 11. ~ ~ Q   10, DN
> 12. ~ R   4, 11 DS (after Comm)
> 13. P   5, 12 DS

14. Q ⊃ P   10-13, CP
15. (P ⊃ Q) · (Q ⊃ P)   9, 14, Conj
16. P ≡ Q   15, ME

As before, we must ensure that the two CP sequences (6-8, and 10-13) are not used anywhere outside of the CP sequence. In addition, each discharged statement (line #9 and line #14) is correctly formulated to be the result of a CP sequence, namely, a conditional statement.

EXERCISE SET 6.8 ○○○

Apply conditional proof (CP) to the following inferences. You will need to use the rules of inference and the substitution sets.

[1]   1. P ⊃ Q   ∴ P ⊃ (S ⊃ Q)

Answer:

1. P ⊃ Q   ∴ P ⊃ (S ⊃ Q)

> 2. P   *Assumption (CP)*
> 3. Q   1, 2, MP
> 4. Q ∨ ~ S   3, Add
> 5. ~ S ∨ Q   4, Comm
> 6. S ⊃ Q   5, MI

7. P ⊃ (S ⊃ Q)   2-6, CP

[2] 1. R ⊃ ~ S
     2. (~ S ∨ P) ⊃ ~ Q   ∴ R ⊃ ~ Q

[3] 1. P ⊃ (~ Q · ~ R)   ∴ ~ P ∨ ~ R

[4] 1. P ⊃ Q
     2. P ⊃ R   ∴ P ⊃ [(Q · R) ∨ ~ S]

[5] 1. Q
     2. P ⊃ [~ Q ∨ (R ⊃ S)]   ∴ (P · R) ⊃ S

[*6] 1. P
      2. (P ∨ P) ⊃ [Q ⊃ ~ (R ∨ S)]   ∴ Q ⊃ ~ S

[7] 1. P ⊃ (Q ∨ R)
     2. ~ Q ⊃ (R ⊃ ~ P)   ∴ P ⊃ (P ⊃ Q)

[8] 1. P ⊃ (Q · R)
     2. S ⊃ (~ Q · R)   ∴ P ⊃ ~ S

[9] 1. P ⊃ ~ R
     2. U ⊃ ~ Q   ∴ (P · R) ⊃ ~ (U · Q)

[10] 1. ~ P ⊃ (R ⊃ ~ T)
      2. U ⊃ (~ Q ⊃ ~ R)
      3. ~ Q · T   ∴ ~ R ∨ (~ U · P)

[*11] 1. [(A · B) · C] ⊃ D   ∴ A ⊃ [B ⊃ (C ⊃ D)]

[12] 1. R ⊃ ~ U
      2. P ⊃ (Q ∨ R)
      3. (Q ⊃ S) · (S ⊃ T)   ∴ P ⊃ (~ U ∨ T)

[13] 1. ~ P ⊃ Q
      2. ~ (Q · ~ S)
      3. R ⊃ (P ⊃ S)   ∴ R ⊃ S

[14] 1. D ⊃ E
      2. E ⊃ F
      3. A ⊃ [C ∨ (D · ~ B)]   ∴ A ⊃ (C ∨ F)

Exercises 2–17: For answers and explanations, see pages 198–203 of Instructor's Manual.

[15]　1. P · Q
　　　2. P ⊃ ~ (R · S)
　　　3. Q ⊃ (R v S)　　∴ R ≡ ~ S

[*16]　1. P ⊃ (Q · R)
　　　2. S ⊃ (Q · T)　　∴ (S v P) ⊃ Q

[17]　1. Q ⊃ ~ P
　　　2. ~ P v (Q v R)　　∴ P ⊃ (R v ~ S)

6.9 INDIRECT PROOF (IP)—*REDUCTIO AD ABSURDUM*

Indirect proof (IP) enables us to establish the proof of a statement by taking the *negation* of the statement to be proved and deriving a *contradiction* from the negation. If the negation of a statement leads to an *absurdity* (a *contradiction*, a statement that cannot possibly be true), then we have *indirectly* proven that the original statement must be true. (The term "*reductio ad absurdum*" means "reduction to the absurd.")

　　The technique of indirect proof (IP) requires that the proofs be annotated in a special way. The format is similar to that of conditional proof (CP) in that the indirect proof (IP) sequence starts by assuming something; for IP we assume the negation of the statement we wish to prove. The following illustrates the method of indirect proof.

　　1. ~ M ⊃ ~ N
　　2. (~ L · ~ M) ⊃ N　　∴ L v M
　　　　　3. ~ (L v M)　　　*Assumption (IP)*
　　　　　4. ~ L · ~ M　　　3, DeM
　　　　　5. N　　　　　　　2, 4, MP
　　　　　6. ~ M · ~ L　　　4, Comm
　　　　　7. ~ M　　　　　　6, Simp
　　　　　8. ~ N　　　　　　1, 7, MP
　　　　　9. N · ~ N　　　　5, 8, Conj
　　10. ~ ~ (L v M)　　　　3-9, IP
　　11. L v M　　　　　　　10, DN

Indirect proof (IP)—*reductio ad absurdum*: The proof procedure used in natural deduction that establishes the proof of a statement by assuming the negation of the statement to be proved, then deriving a contradiction from that negation.

　　Line #3 begins the sequence, and it is indented and justified as *Assumption (IP)*. Line #9 displays the goal of all IP sequences, which is to *derive a contradiction*. Line #10 discharges the IP sequence by negating the assumption that started the sequence, i.e. line #3. The final result is the statement that we wished to prove. As with CP, we cannot use any line within an IP sequence outside that sequence as part of our overall proof.

Here is another example of how indirect proof (IP) can be used in a proof:

1. D ⊃ C
2. A ∨ (B · C)
3. A ⊃ D   ∴ C
       4. ∼ C   *Assumption (IP)*
       5. ∼ D   1, 4, MT
       6. ∼ A   3, 5, MT
       7. B · C   2, 6, DS
       8. C · B   7, Comm
       9. C   8, Simp
     10. C · ∼ C   4, 9, Conj
11. ∼ ∼ C   4-10, IP
12. C   11, DN

Line #4 begins the indirect proof (IP) sequence, and it is indented and justified as Assumption (IP). Line #10 is the contradiction derived in the IP sequence. Line #11 discharges the IP sequence by negating the assumption that started the sequence, i.e. line #4.

The methods of indirect proof (IP) and conditional proof (CP) can be combined within one proof as long as we obey the stipulated rules. The next proof illustrates how the methods can be combined.

1. P ⊃ ∼ R
2. R ∨ S
3. Q ∨ R   ∴ P ⊃ [Q ∨ (R · S)]
       4. P   *Assumption (CP)*
       5. ∼ R   1, 4, MP
          6. ∼ Q   *Assumption (IP)*
          7. R   3, 6, DS
          8. ∼ R · R   5, 7, Conj
       9. ∼ ∼ Q   6-8, IP
     10. Q   9, DN
     11. Q ∨ (R · S)   10, Add
12. P ⊃ [Q ∨ (R · S)]   4-11, CP

As the proof illustrates, each sequence of CP and IP has been correctly discharged, and no line within either sequence has been used outside that sequence.

Here is another example illustrating how the methods of indirect proof (IP) and conditional proof (CP) can be combined within one proof.

1. (P ⊃ R) v (Q • ~ Q)
2. R ⊃ (P • S)   ∴ P ≡ R
   | 3. ~ (P ⊃ R)   *Assumption (IP)*
   | 4. Q • ~ Q   1, 3, DS
5. ~ ~ (P ⊃ R)   3-4, IP
6. P ⊃ R   5, DN
   | 7. R   *Assumption (CP)*
   | 8. P • S   2, 7, MP
   | 9. P   8, Simp
10. R ⊃ P   7-9, CP
11. (P ⊃ R) • (R ⊃ P)   6, 10, Conj
12. P ≡ R   11, ME

The proof illustrates that each sequence of IP and CP has been correctly discharged, and no line within either sequence has been used outside that sequence.

EXERCISE SET 6.9   ○○○

Apply indirect proof (IP) to the following inferences. You will need to use the rules of inference, the substitution sets, and at times, conditional proof (CP).

[1]   1. P   ∴ Q v ~ Q

Answer:

1. P   ∴ Q v ~ Q
   | 2. ~ (Q v ~ Q)   *Assumption (IP)*
   | 3. ~ Q • ~ ~ Q   2, DeM
   | 4. ~ Q • Q   3, DN
5. ~ ~ (Q v ~ Q)   2-4, IP
6. Q v ~ Q   5, DN

Exercises 2–17: For answers and explanations, see pages 204–209 of Instructor's Manual.

[2]   1. P ⊃ (Q • S)
       2. ~ S   ∴ ~ P

[3]   1. ~ Q v P
       2. ~ (P v S)   ∴ ~ Q

[4]   1. P ∨ (∼ P ⊃ Q)
       2. ∼ Q   ∴ P

[5]   1. (R ∨ S) ⊃ (∼ P · ∼ Q)
       2. P   ∴ ∼ R

[*6]   1. S ⊃ ∼ (∼ Q ∨ P)
       2. Q ≡ P   ∴ ∼ S

[7]   1. ∼ P ⊃ ∼ (Q ∨ ∼ P)   ∴ P

[8]   1. ∼ P · ∼ T
       2. ∼ (P · ∼ Q) ⊃ R   ∴ R ∨ T

[9]   1. P ⊃ Q   ∴ Q ⊃ [P ⊃ (P · Q)]

[10]   1. (P ⊃ Q) ⊃ ∼ (S ⊃ R)
       2. ∼ (P ∨ T)   ∴ S

[*11] 1. A ⊃ B
       2. A ⊃ C
       3. ∼ B ∨ ∼ C   ∴ ∼ A

[12]   1. Q ⊃ ∼ R
       2. P ∨ Q
       3. ∼ P ⊃ (Q ⊃ R)   ∴ P

[13]   1. (∼ D ∨ E) ⊃ (A · C)
       2. (A ∨ B) ⊃ (C ⊃ D)   ∴ D

[14]   1. P ⊃ (Q · S)
       2. Q ⊃ (R ∨ ∼ S)
       3. P ∨ (Q ⊃ R)   ∴ Q ⊃ R

[15]   1. G ⊃ (E · F)
       2. A ⊃ B
       3. A ∨ G
       4. (B ∨ C) ⊃ D   ∴ D ∨ E

[16]   1. P ∨ (Q · P)
       2. P ⊃ R   ∴ R

[17]   1. ∼ P ⊃ (Q ⊃ P)
       2. ∼ R ⊃ (∼ P ⊃ ∼ Q)   ∴ R ∨ P

SUMMARY

- Natural deduction is a method of proving validity that allows the use of already proven valid inferences. Inferences that have been verified as valid by the truth table method are used as building blocks to prove the validity of more complex inferences.

- Since each step of a proof using natural deduction is a valid deduction (because each step relies on a valid inference for its derivation and justification), the final step, and thus the entire complex inference, is valid. The entire sequence of steps, from the given premises to the conclusion, constitutes a completed proof.

- The eight rules of inference are legitimately applied only to an entire line.

- Tactics is the use of small-scale maneuvers, whereas strategy refers to a greater, overall goal.

- The ten substitution sets are logically equivalent statements that have been verified as such by the truth table method. These sets of statements allow the replacement of any statement anywhere in a proof sequence with its logically equivalent set member.

- Conditional proof (CP) is a technique that assists in proving inferences with conditionals as conclusions.

- Indirect proof (IP) enables the establishment of the proof of a statement by taking the negation of the statement we wish to prove and deriving a contradiction from the negation. If the negation of a statement leads to an absurdity, or contradiction, then we have indirectly proven that the original statement must be true.

KEY TERMS

natural deduction   195
rules of inference   196
logical form   196
proof procedure   196
substitution sets   196
addition   197
conjunction   198
modus ponens   199
modus tollens   201
justification   202
syllogism   206
disjunctive
   syllogism   206

hypothetical
   syllogism   206
constructive
   dilemma   207
simplification   208
tactics   212
strategy   212
principle of
   substitution   215
association   216
double negation   217
commutation   218
De Morgan   219

distribution   221
transposition   224
material
   implication   225
exportation   226
material
   equivalence   227
tautology   228
conditional proof   236
discharged   237
indirect proof   242

LOGIC CHALLENGE: A STANDING PROBLEM

You find yourself at a party with four people facing you. A friend begins telling you about the four people, but fails to tell you if she is referring to them in any particular order.

- Their names are Scott, Jeff, Agatha, and Shane.
- One is an actor, one is a drummer, one is a dancer, and one is an architect.
- Jeff is not standing next to Agatha.
- There are two people between Shane and the actor.
- Scott is not the drummer.
- The architect and actor are standing next to each other.
- That's Agatha who is turning to her right to speak to the drummer.

Determine the name, occupation, and position of each person.

Logic Challenge:

Shane	Agatha	Scott	Jeff
1	2	3	4
Drummer	Dancer	Architect	Actor

See page 210 of Instructor's Manual for complete explanation.

The Logic of Quantifiers

{ overview }

7.1 PRELUDE TO THE LOGIC OF QUANTIFIERS

7.2 INTEGRATING CATEGORICAL AND TRUTH-FUNCTIONAL STATEMENTS

7.3 QUANTIFICATION

7.4 STATEMENT FUNCTIONS AND CATEGORICAL STATEMENTS

7.5 QUANTIFICATION AND PROOFS OF VALIDITY

7.6 QUANTIFICATION AND PROOFS OF INVALIDITY

We have classified statements into two main groups, *categorical* and *truth-functional*. In previous chapters we examined methods of proof for inferences constructed from these two kinds of statements. For categorical statements we learned how to construct Venn diagrams; for truth-functional statements we used truth tables and the system of natural deduction (truth-functional proof). These methods allowed us to decide whether any inference made up of these types of statements is valid or invalid. However, many inferences combine categorical and truth-functional statements and, as such, do not fit into our proof systems. For over two thousand years the logic of categorical statements and truth-functional statements could not be integrated into one system. This chapter shows how modern logical theory was finally able to bring the two systems together.

7.1 PRELUDE TO THE LOGIC OF QUANTIFIERS

The work of George Boole marks the beginning of the eventual complete integration of categorical and truth-functional statements. Boole's ideas begin with an interpretation of universal categorical statements that eliminates the problems associated with existential import. This is accomplished by translating the logic behind categorical statements using truth-functional operators. For example, according to the Boolean

chapter 7

interpretation, the universal affirmative statement, "All *S* are *P*," is translated symbolically as "*S* ⊃ *P*." Of course, it is true that we are placing simple *terms* (*S* and *P*) into a truth-functional setting, where the fit is not completely accurate. Being simple class terms, *S* and *P* are neither true nor false. We must, therefore, create complete statements in order to correctly place the class terms within a truth-functional setting. The completed translation becomes this: "If *anything is a member of class S*, then *it is a member of class P*." The universal negative statement, "No *S* are *P*," is translated symbolically as "*S* ⊃ ~ *P*." The completed translation would then read, "If *anything is a member of class S*, then *it is not a member of class P*."

The particular affirmative statement, "Some *S* are *P*," gets translated symbolically as "~ (*S* ⊃ ~ *P*)." The translation would then read, "*It is not the case that* if *anything is a member of class S*, then *it is not a member of class P*." The particular negative statement, "Some *S* are not *P*," gets translated symbolically as, "~ (*S* ⊃ *P*)." The translation would then read, "*It is not the case that* if *anything is a member of class S*, then *it is a member of class P*." This information is summarized in Quick Reference 7.1.

In Boolean translations of categorical statements the logic behind categorical statements is shown using truth-functional operators.

Quick Reference 7.1 • **Boolean Translations of the Four Categorical Statements**

Universal affirmative: All *S* are *P*	Boolean translation: *S* ⊃ *P*
Universal negative: No *S* are *P*	Boolean translation: *S* ⊃ ~ *P*
Particular affirmative: Some *S* are *P*	Boolean translation: ~ (*S* ⊃ ~ *P*)
Particular negative: Some *S* are not *P*	Boolean translation: ~ (*S* ⊃ *P*)

These translations accomplish two things: (1) they eliminate the existential import problem, because a *conditional makes no existence claim*, and (2) they place validity nearer to the modern idea of logical form. The Boolean system, along with Venn diagrams, revealed the modern idea that validity is a formal question. We know that if the form of an inference is valid, then so are all its instances. The same goes for invalidity. As discussed earlier, having to decide existence questions moves the discussion from the realm of logic to that of truth content, where we would be forced to consider knowledge questions, factual concerns, scientific information, etc. Granted these are important questions, but they are relevant to the soundness of inferences, not to validity. As defined earlier, there are two requirements for a sound inference: (1) The inference must be valid (based on the analysis of the logical component), and (2) the inference must have all true premises (based on the analysis of the truth content).

Once categorical statements are translated into conditionals, our concern turns to "What if …," *logical* questions. This is in line with the work on truth-functional inferences, which were analyzed in a purely formal manner. We can summarize this discussion by remembering that *validity* is a question of form, whereas *soundness* includes the additional question of truth content.

GEORGE BOOLE

The connection of logic to algebra was advanced so significantly by the work of George Boole (1815–1864) that the subject has become known as *Boolean algebra*. Boole recognized that algebraic symbolism (the tools of numerical calculation) could function as logical notation as well. His system ushered in the era of formalization, applicable for the "logic of terms," or categorical statements, and also for truth-functional statements. In fact, using Boole's system made it possible to translate categorical statements into truth-functional statements. For example, Boole's system of translation changes *No S are P* into $SP = 0$. This tells us that the intersection of the classes designated by *S* and *P* is empty. These ideas were later adopted by John Venn and were incorporated into his diagrammatic approach to categorical syllogisms.

Formalism emphasizes the idea that validity should not be dependent on an interpretation of the symbols involved, but rather it should be a function of the logical apparatus at work. In other words, the truth content of the premises and conclusion should have no bearing on validity. The rules of logic, once understood, are the only guide needed in the process of inference analysis. The title of one of Boole's books is testament to his beliefs, *An Investigation of the Laws of Thought*. The ideas created by Boole were the ancestors of today's computer circuitry. It is not a far step from Boolean algebra, which emphasized the use of 0 and 1, to the creation of the underlying mechanism of on-off switches.

The Boolean translations allow us to prove the validity or invalidity of categorical syllogisms in three different ways: (1) with Venn diagrams, (2) with truth tables, and (3) by natural deduction. The last two depend on the translation of categorical statements into conditionals. The three methods should give identical results. Let's analyze one inference by all three methods.

Some computers are conscious beings.	Some *M* are *P*
<u>All computers are inorganic objects.</u>	<u>All *M* are *S*</u>
Some inorganic objects are conscious beings.	Some *S* are *P*

Using a Venn diagram, we get this picture:

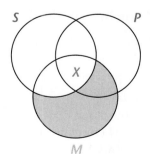

The diagram illustrates that this is a valid inference.

Our next step is to translate the inference into our Boolean notation. When completed the inference becomes this:

$$\sim (M \supset \sim P)$$

$$\underline{M \supset S}$$

$$\sim (S \supset \sim P)$$

The truth table method yields this result:

			1st Premise	2nd Premise	Conclusion
M	P	S	$\sim (M \supset \sim P)$	$M \supset S$	$\sim (S \supset \sim P)$
T	T	T	(T) T (F) (F) T	T (T) T	(T) T (F) (F) T
T	T	F	(T) T (F) (F) T	T (F) F	(F) F (T) (F) T
T	F	T	(F) T (T) (T) F	T (T) T	(F) T (T) (T) F
T	F	F	(F) T (T) (T) F	T (F) F	(F) F (T) (T) F
F	T	T	(F) F (T) (F) T	F (T) T	(T) T (F) (F) T
F	T	F	(F) F (T) (F) T	F (T) F	(F) F (T) (F) T
F	F	T	(F) F (T) (T) F	F (T) T	(F) T (T) (T) F
F	F	F	(F) F (T) (T) F	F (T) F	(F) F (T) (T) F

Since there is no line where both premises are true and the conclusion is false, the truth table method verifies that this is a valid inference.

The indirect truth table method can also be used. In order for the conclusion to be false, we have three possibilities to consider: (1) $S = T, P = F$; (2) $S = F, P = T$; (3) $S = F, P = F$.

Possibility Substitution #1

			1st Premise	2nd Premise	Conclusion
M	P	S	$\sim (M \supset \sim P)$	$M \supset S$	$\sim (S \supset \sim P)$
?	F	T	(F) (T) (T) F	(T) T	(F) T (T) (T) F

It is possible to get the conclusion false. Although these truth value substitutions will make the second premise true, nevertheless, no matter what truth value M gets, the first premise will be false. This result follows because the consequent of the first premise is true under this substitution. So, this substitution will not produce true premises and a false conclusion.

Possibility Substitution #2

			1st Premise	2nd Premise	Conclusion
M	P	S	$\sim (M \supset \sim P)$	$M \supset S$	$\sim (S \supset \sim P)$
?	T	F	(?) (?) (F) T	(?) F	(F) F (T) (F) T

This possibility will once again make the conclusion false. At this point, we must consider the two possibilities for M (true/false). We want to see if we can get both premises true at the same time. If we let $M = T$, then the second premise will be false. On the other hand, if we let $M = F$, then the first premise will be false. So, this substitution will not get true premises and a false conclusion.

Possibility Substitution #3

	1ˢᵗ Premise	2ⁿᵈ Premise	Conclusion
	$\sim (M \supset \sim P)$	$M \supset S$	$\sim (S \supset \sim P)$

$$\frac{M\ P\ S}{?\ \ F\ \ F} \left|\right|\ \frac{\sim (M \supset \sim P)}{(F)\quad (T)(T)\,F}\qquad \frac{M \supset S}{(?)\ F}\qquad \frac{\sim (S \supset \sim P)}{(F)\ F\ (T)(T)\,F}$$

It is possible to get the conclusion false. However, no matter what truth value M gets, the first premise will be false. This result follows because the consequent of the first premise is true under this substitution. This substitution will not get true premises and a false conclusion. Therefore, the indirect truth table method verifies that this is a valid inference.

The natural deduction method proves the inference is valid by the following:

1. $\sim (M \supset \sim P)$
2. $M \supset S$ $\therefore \sim (S \supset \sim P)$
3. $\sim (\sim M \vee \sim P)$ 1, MI
4. $\sim \sim M \cdot \sim \sim P$ 3, DeM
5. $M \cdot P$ 4, DN (used twice)
6. M 5, Simp
7. S 2, 6, MP
8. $P \cdot M$ 5, Comm
9. P 8, Simp
10. $S \cdot P$ 7, 9, Conj
11. $\sim \sim S \cdot \sim \sim P$ 10, DN (used twice)
12. $\sim (\sim S \vee \sim P)$ 11, DeM
13. $\sim (S \supset \sim P)$ 12, MI

EXERCISE SET 7.1   ○○○

Translate the following categorical inferences into Boolean notation and prove that they are valid using (a) truth tables, and (b) natural deduction.

1. All M are P
   <u>All S are M</u>
   All S are P

Answer:

Boolean Translation

All M are P	$M \supset P$
<u>All S are M</u>	<u>$S \supset M$</u>
All S are P	$S \supset P$

			1st Premise	2nd Premise	Conclusion
M	P	S	M ⊃ P	S ⊃ M	S ⊃ P
T	T	T	T *(T)* T	T *(T)* T	T *(T)* T
T	T	F	T *(T)* T	F *(T)* T	F *(T)* T
T	F	T	T *(F)* F	T *(T)* T	T *(F)* F
T	F	F	T *(F)* F	F *(T)* T	F *(T)* F
F	T	T	F *(T)* T	T *(F)* F	T *(T)* T
F	T	F	F *(T)* T	F *(T)* F	F *(T)* T
F	F	T	F *(T)* F	T *(F)* F	T *(F)* F
F	F	F	F *(T)* F	F *(T)* F	F *(T)* F

Since there is no line where both premises are true and the conclusion is false, the truth table method verifies that this is a valid inference.

Following is a proof of the same inference by natural deduction:

1. $M \supset P$
2. $S \supset M$ ∴ $S \supset P$
3. $S \supset P$ 1, 2, HS

Exercises 2–5: For answers and explanations, see pages 223–226 of Instructor's Manual.

2. No *M* are *P*
   Some *S* are *M*
   Some *S* are not *P*

3. No *P* are *M*
   All *S* are *M*
   No *S* are *P*

4. Some *M* are *P*
   All *M* are *S*
   Some *S* are *P*

5. No *P* are *M*
   Some *M* are *S*
   Some *S* are not *P*

7.2 INTEGRATING CATEGORICAL AND TRUTH-FUNCTIONAL STATEMENTS

Consider the following inference, which contains a type of statement different from those discussed in previous chapters:

All vice presidents of the United States are presidents of the Senate.
Dick Cheney is vice president of the United States.
Dick Cheney is president of the Senate.

The first premise is a categorical statement that can be translated, "All *V* are *P*." The second premise is not a categorical statement, so we have an inference that does not fit directly into our previous proof procedures. Although the inference is perfectly valid, we have no way to prove it. In fact, if we use the translations available to us, it will turn out to be invalid. For example, the Boolean interpretation of the first premise allows us to translate it as "$V \supset P$." Since, under this interpretation, V stands for "vice presidents of the United States" and P stands for "presidents of the Senate," what do we do when we get to the second premise and the conclusion? We cannot translate the second premise, "Dick Cheney is vice president of the United States," as V because it is *not* the same statement. Also, the conclusion cannot be translated as P. If we translate the second premise as D, and the conclusion as C, we get this invalid inference:

$$V \supset P$$

$$\underline{D}$$

$$C$$

The modern theory of logic that interprets statements such as "Dick Cheney is vice president of the United States," and allows us to incorporate them into a new system of proof is called the **logic of quantifiers**, or *predicate logic*. This is the logical system used to analyze complex inferences made of truth-functional and categorical statements. It facilitates the smooth integration of categorical and truth-functional results and offers a powerful way of capturing more natural language into precise statement and inference analysis. For example, in the logic of quantifiers, the statement, "Dick Cheney is vice president of the United States," is called a **singular statement**—it asserts that one individual person has a specific characteristic. In this statement, the subject term, "Dick Cheney," denotes a particular individual. The predicate term, "vice president of the United States," designates a specific characteristic. It is possible for the same subject and predicate term to occur in a variety of singular statements. Some of these assertions will be true, and some will be false. For example, "Dick Cheney is a Democrat," is a false statement. This statement contains the same subject term as the statement above (Dick Cheney), but it contains a different predicate term (Democrat). The statement, "Tom Cruise is vice president of the United States," is false, too. This statement contains the same predicate term as before (vice president of the United States), but it contains a different subject term (Tom Cruise). The statement, "Dick Cheney is a Republican," is true. This statement contains the same subject term as the statement above (Dick Cheney), but it contains a different predicate term (Republican).

We need a simple symbolic notation that will enable us to distinguish individuals from the characteristics we assert of them. We stipulate that the lowercase letters *a* through *w* are to be used as constants to denote individuals (Dick Cheney, Tom Cruise, etc.). On the other hand, the characteristics predicated of individuals will be symbolized by capital letters, *A, B, C*, etc. ("...is an athlete," "...is a bachelor," "...is a Congressperson"). The system of symbols used for singular statements puts the capital letter, the symbol designating the characteristic predicated, first, followed by a lowercase letter, the symbol denoting the individual. For example, if *d* stands for "Dick Cheney," (the individual) and *V* for "vice president of the United States," (the characteristic predicated), then the statement, "Dick Cheney is vice president of the United States," can be by symbolized as *Vd*. The statement, "Dick Cheney is Republican," can be symbolized as *Rd*.

Logic of quantifers:
The logical system of quantification used to analyze complex inferences made of truth-functional and categorical statements.

Singular statement:
A statement that asserts either that a particular individual has or does not have a specified characteristic.

> **Strategy**
>
> When translating into symbols, make sure the predicate term is given a capital letter (you can often use the first letter of the predicate term for convenience). Always choose a lowercase letter to denote the individual and place it after the predicate term.

BIOGRAPHY   GOTTLOB FREGE

Gottlob Frege (1848–1925) was one of the most original and influential modern thinkers. His monumental attempt to reduce mathematics to logic connected the two fields forever, allowing Frege to claim that from then on "*every mathematician must be a philosopher and every philosopher must be a mathematician*." One of Frege's fundamental beliefs was in the *a priori* nature of mathematics and logic, whereby the foundations of both fields could be developed by reason alone. It is ironic that Frege's work resulted in the discovery of logical and mathematical paradoxes connected to his system—discoveries that, in turn, led to revolutionary ideas about the foundations of mathematics.

Here are just a few of Frege's original insights: the development of the logic of quantifiers, the distinction between constants and variables, the correct use of a logical function, and the first modern clarification of sense and reference. The field of mathematical logic can be traced to Frege's pioneering work, and, with this, a direct connection to the development of computer languages can be established.

The following are some more examples of basic translations:

Statement in English	Symbolic Translation
Arnold Schwarzenegger is a governor.	*Ga*
Arnold Schwarzenegger is an actor.	*Aa*
The Arctic Circle is not a warm place.	~ *Wa*
Nevada is a dry state.	*Dn*
Pornography is illegal.	*Ip*

More complex statements can be translated by using the other truth-functional connectives. For example:

Statement in English	Symbolic Translation
Carly is either a fashion designer or a dancer.	*Fc* ∨ *Dc*
If Shane is an honor student then he is bright.	*Hs* ⊃ *Bs*
If, and only if, Bill is honest and loyal, he gets the job.	(*Hb* · *Lb*) ≡ *Jb*
John will win the contest, only if he does not panic.	*Cj* ⊃ ~ *Pj*

Quick Reference 7.2 • Use of Symbols in Singular Statements

Singular statements use the symbols *a-w* and *A-Z*.

1. *a–w* = constants denoting individuals
2. *A–Z* = characteristics predicated of individuals
3. For singular statements, a capital letter designating a characteristic is written first, followed by a lowercase letter designating an individual

EXERCISE SET 7.2 ○○○

Translate the following statements using the symbolic notation learned in this section:

1. Cabbage is a healthy vegetable.

Answer: Hc

2. Cabbage is an odoriferous food when cooked. *Oc*

3. Rabbits are sexually active animals. *Sr*

4. Sir Lancelot was a member of the Round Table. *Rs*

5. Steve McQueen was not an Academy Award winner. *~ As*

*6. Only if Joe runs the mile under four minutes will he qualify for the rally. *Qj ⊃ Uj*

7. It will rain tonight, only if the clouds linger around. *Rt ⊃ Lc*

8. The Taj Mahal is one of the Seven Wonders of the Modern World. *St*

9. The Eiffel Tower in Las Vegas is one-third the height of the original in Paris. *Oe*

10. I will sell my car if, and only if, I get a good price for it, and I can find something better. *Sc ≡ (Cg · Fi)*

*11. Salmon tastes good when broiled. *Bs*

12. Textbooks are my friends. *Ft*

13. Cell phones are not universally admired products. *~ Uc*

14. She will pass the exam, only if she is well prepared. *Ps ⊃ Ws*

15. Only if he gets here by 8:00 p.m. will he be admitted. *Ah ⊃ Eh*

7.3 QUANTIFICATION

It has been stipulated that **individual constants**, which denote individuals, are designated by any lowercase letter from *a* through *w*. The remaining lowercase letters, *x*, *y*, and *z*, have a different use—they are used to denote an **individual variable**. This variable indicates where a particular constant may be placed, resulting in a singular statement. For example, *Vx*, *My*, and *Kz* use individual variables. However, these are not examples of statements but of **statement functions**, which are neither true nor false, but can have both true and false substitution instances. A **substitution instance** is when a statement function is transformed into a statement, which is either true or false. For example, the predicate, "is taller than 7 feet," can be used to create the statement function *Tx*. The variable, *x*, can then be replaced by an individual constant. For example, if *s* denotes, "Shaquille O'Neal," and *d* denotes, "Dustin Hoffman," then we get the following results:

   Ts: "Shaquille O'Neal is taller than 7 feet."—This is a true statement.

   Td: "Dustin Hoffman is taller than 7 feet."—This is a false statement.

Individual constant: A symbol (designated by any lowercase letter from *a* through *w*) used in the logical notation of predicate logic to denote an individual.

Individual variable: A symbol used in the logical notation of predicate logic that functions as a placeholder for an individual constant (the lowercase letters *x*, *y*, and *z* are used).

Statement function: Statement functions are neither true nor false, but they can have true and false substitution instances.

Substitution instance: When a statement function is transformed into a statement that is either true or false.

Quantification: The process of changing statement functions into statements.

Universal quantifier: A symbol in the logic of quantifiers (either *x* or *y*) that is placed in front of a statement function that makes it possible to assert that the predicate following it is true of everything.

Existential quantifier: In the logic of quantifiers the symbol ∃ is used to assert that any statement function immediately following the symbol has some true substitution instance

Universal quantification: When a statement function is true if, and only if, all possible substitution instances are true.

Existential quantification: When a statement function is true if, and only if, it has at least one true substitution instance.

Instantiation: In the logic of quantifiers, the substitution of an individual constant in place of an individual variable.

Generalization: In the logic of quantifiers, the process by which a statement is created from a statement function by using either a universal or existential quantifier.

The logic of quantifiers can be used when a predicate term occurs in a statement that is not singular. For example, statements beginning with the phrase, "Everything is …," "Something is …," or "Nothing is …," are *general* statement forms. The process of changing statement functions into statements is called **quantification**. We will use the **universal quantifier (x)** to assert that the predicate term following it is *true of everything*. Therefore, *(x) Gx* is read as, "Given *any x*, G is true of it." For example, if we let G stand for "*good*," then *(x) Gx* would be read as, "For any individual *(x)*, that individual is good *(G)*." We will use the **existential quantifier,** ∃*x*, to assert that the predicate term following it has at least one true substitution instance. Therefore, *(∃x) Gx* is read as, "There exists an *x* such that G is true of it." For example, if we let G stand for "good," then *(∃x) Gx* would be read as, "There is at least one individual *(x)* that is good *(G)*."

Universal quantification of a statement function will be true if, and only if, all possible substitution instances are true. For example, if we let G stand for "good," then *(x) Gx* is true only if every possible substitution instance is true, in other words, only if everything is good. On the other hand, **existential quantification** of a statement function will be true if, and only if, it has at least one true substitution instance. For example, if we let G stand for "good," then *(∃x) Gx* is true if at least one individual is good. Given these stipulations, statements can be derived from statement functions in two ways: (1) by **instantiation**, the substitution of an individual constant for an individual variable, and (2) by **generalization**, using either a universal or existential quantifier.

Not all statements are affirmative, so we must use the concept of negation (~) to capture the appropriate statement functions in such cases. For example, the statement, "Nothing is good," can be rewritten as, "Given any *x*, it is *not* good." We translate this by using the universal quantifier to get *(x) ~ Gx*. Similarly, the statement, "Some things are *not* good," is translated by using the existential quantifier, giving us *(∃x) ~ Gx*.

The Greek letter *phi (φ)* can be used to represent any simple predicate. Given this, we can use what we have learned to create a quantifier square of opposition (Figure 7.1).

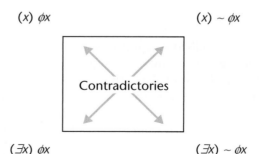

FIGURE 7.1 • Square of opposition for simple predicates.

The two sets of contradictories will allow us the opportunity to stipulate four important logical relationships between universal and existential quantification. For example, *(x) φx* is logically equivalent to *~ (∃x) ~ φx* (the negation of its opposite pair member). The reverse is true as well, i.e. *(∃x) φx* is logically equivalent to *~ (x) ~ φx*. The other set of contradictories can be understood in the same way: $(x) \sim \phi x$ is logically equivalent to $\sim (\exists x) \phi x$, while $(\exists x) \sim \phi x$ is logically equivalent to $\sim (x) \phi x$. Table 7.1 summarizes these results.

Table 7.1 Logical Equivalences for Simple Predicates

$$(x) \phi x :: \sim (\exists x) \sim \phi x$$
$$(x) \sim \phi x :: \sim (\exists x) \phi x$$
$$(\exists x) \phi x :: \sim (x) \sim \phi x$$
$$(\exists x) \sim \phi x :: \sim (x) \phi x$$

7.4 STATEMENT FUNCTIONS AND CATEGORICAL STATEMENTS

Statement functions are particularly useful when applied to the four kinds of categorical statements.

Universal affirmative: "All humans are moral agents."
Universal negative: "No humans are moral agents."
Particular affirmative: "Some humans are moral agents."
Particular negative: "Some humans are not moral agents."

We can translate categorical statements into symbolic form using the symbolic notation of statement functions and quantifiers. For example, the statement, "All humans are moral agents," can be translated as $(x)(Hx \supset Mx)$. The universal affirmative statement is translated using the conditional symbol because the Boolean interpretation of the statement is the assertion that *if* anything (x) is a "human," then that thing (x) is a "moral agent." Under this interpretation, universal statements make no existential claims.

The statement, "No humans are moral agents," is correctly translated as $(x)(Hx \supset \sim Mx)$.

This interpretation of the universal negative statement is asserting that *if* anything (x) is a human, then that thing (x) is *not* a moral agent. Here are some more examples:

Statement in English	Symbolic Translation
No millionaires are tax evaders.	$(x)(Mx \supset \sim Tx)$
All alcoholic drinks are depressants.	$(x)(Ax \supset Dx)$
No French fries are healthy.	$(x)(Fx \supset \sim Hx)$
All magazines are full of useless ads.	$(x)(Mx \supset Ux)$

The particular affirmative statement, "Some humans are moral agents," is translated as $(\exists x)(Hx \cdot Mx)$. The statement asserts that there is at least one thing that is a "human" *and* is a "moral agent." Under the modern interpretation, particular statements do make existential claims, so they get translated as conjunctions. The particular negative statement, "Some humans are *not* moral agents," is translated as $(\exists x)(Hx \cdot \sim Mx)$. The statement makes an existential claim that there is at least one thing that is a "human" *and* is *not* a "moral agent." Here are some more examples:

Statement in English	Symbolic Translation
Some birds are not capable of flying.	$(\exists x)(Bx \cdot \sim Fx)$
Some hermits are extroverts.	$(\exists x)(Hx \cdot Ex)$
Some artificial sweeteners are addicting.	$(\exists x)(Sx \cdot Ax)$
Some cliff divers are not fearless.	$(\exists x)(Cx \cdot \sim Fx)$

Table 7.2 Translations of Categorical Statements

"All humans are moral agents."	$(x) (Hx \supset Mx)$
"No humans are moral agents."	$(x) (Hx \supset \sim Mx)$
"Some humans are moral agents."	$(\exists x) (Hx \cdot Mx)$
"Some humans are not moral agents."	$(\exists x) (Hx \cdot \sim Mx)$

We will use the Greek letters *phi* (ϕ) and *psi* (ψ) to represent any simple predicate. This allows us to generalize and represent the four categorical statements as shown in Table 7.3.

Table 7.3 Use of *Phi* (ϕ) and *Psi* (ψ) in Categorical Statements

Universal affirmative: $(x) (\phi x \supset \psi x)$
Universal negative: $(x) (\phi x \supset \sim \psi x)$
Particular affirmative: $(\exists x) (\phi x \cdot \psi x)$
Particular negative: $(\exists x) (\phi x \cdot \sim \psi x)$

This use of quantifiers allows the construction of another square of opposition (Figure 7.2).

$(x) (\phi x \supset \psi x)$ $\qquad\qquad\qquad\qquad$ $(x) (\phi x \supset \sim \psi x)$

Contradictories

FIGURE 7.2 • Using quantifiers to represent categorical statements.

$(\exists x) (\phi x \cdot \psi x)$ $\qquad\qquad\qquad\qquad$ $(\exists x) (\phi x \cdot \sim \psi x)$

Once again, the two sets of contradictories allow us to stipulate four important logical relationships between universal and existential quantification. Quick Reference 7.3 summarizes these results.

Quick Reference 7.3 • **Quantifier Substitution Sets** *(QSS)*

1. $(x) (\phi x \supset \psi x)$ :: $\sim (\exists x) (\phi x \cdot \sim \psi x)$
2. $(x) (\phi x \supset \sim \psi x)$ :: $\sim (\exists x) (\phi x \cdot \psi x)$
3. $(\exists x) (\phi x \cdot \psi x)$ :: $\sim (x) (\phi x \supset \sim \psi x)$
4. $(\exists x) (\phi x \cdot \sim \psi x)$ :: $\sim (x) (\phi x \supset \psi x)$

> Quantifier substitution sets show the logical relationship between universal and existential quantification.

The four logical equivalencies in the box will be used as additional substitution sets. They can be abbreviated as *QSS* when annotating formal proofs using the logic of quantifiers.

Normal-form Formulas

A **normal-form formula** is one in which the negation symbol applies only to simple predicates. Therefore, a negation symbol at the beginning of a formula must be changed into *normal form* by using the quantifier substitution sets *(QSS)* specified in Quick Reference 7.3. This procedure is important in doing proofs because it facilitates logical manipulation of the symbols involved. For example:

> **Strategy**
>
> Make sure to change a negation symbol at the beginning of a formula into normal-form by using the quantifier substitution sets *(QSS)*.

Statement in English	**Symbolic Translation**	**Normal form**
Not even one tiger has a conscience.	$\sim (\exists x) (Tx \cdot Cx)$	$(x) (Tx \supset \sim Cx)$
It is not the case that every dog is lazy.	$\sim (x) (Dx \supset Lx)$	$(\exists x) (Dx \cdot \sim Lx)$

Bound and Free Variables

The two statement functions, $(x) (Hx \supset Mx)$ and $(x)Hx \supset Mx$, can be used to illustrate differences between *bound* and *free variables*. The universal quantifier (x) in the first example ranges over (applies to) everything within the parentheses; therefore, both Hx and Mx are said to be *bound* by the universal quantifier and are called **bound variables**. In the second example, the universal quantifier (x) ranges only over Hx, so Hx is a bound variable; the (x) does not extend to Mx, so Mx is a **free variable**. In the statement function, $(x) (Hx \supset My)$, the universal quantifier (x) ranges only over Hx, so it contains a bound variable; however, My contains a free variable because the y variable is not bound by the (x). These ideas will be particularly important later when we do proofs. A free variable is understood to be a statement function, and as such, is neither true nor false. When we *quantify over variables* by using either the universal or existential quantifier, we create statements that are either true or false.

> **Normal-form formula:** In the logic of quantifiers, a formula in which the negation symbol applies only to simple predicates.
>
> **Bound variable:** In $(x) (Hx \supset Mx)$ the universal quantifier (x) ranges over (applies to) everything within the parentheses, so both Hx and Mx are bound by the universal quantifier.
>
> **Free variable:** In $(x) Hx \supset Mx$ the universal quantifier (x) ranges only over (applies to) Hx, which is a bound variable; it does not extend to Mx, which is a free variable.

Exceptive statement:
A statement that claims that members of one class, with the exception of a particular subclass, are members of some other class.

Complex Statements

Some statements are more complex than the traditional universal and particular categorical statements. For example, consider the statement, "All thoroughbred horses are either brown or gray." This statement contains both categorical and truth-functional elements. To symbolize this statement requires close examination of the sentence's meaning. The statement seems to be asserting that *if* anything *(x)* is a "thoroughbred horse," then *either* it is "brown" or it is "gray." If we let *H* = "thoroughbred horse," *B* = "brown," and *G* = "gray," we get this: for all *x*, if *Hx*, then either *Bx* or *Gx*. The final translation is correctly symbolized as: *(x) [Hx ⊃ (Bx ∨ Gx)]*

The statement, "Thoroughbreds and mules are quadrupeds," would get translated and symbolized as follows: let *T* = "thoroughbreds," *M* = "mules," *Q* = "quadrupeds." The result is: *(x) [(Tx ∨ Mx) ⊃ Qx]*. The ∨ symbol is used because a careful reading of the statement shows that the "and" does not mean that anything is both a thoroughbred and a mule at the same time. Instead, the sentence is asserting only that *if* any individual, *x*, is either a thoroughbred or a mule, then that individual is a quadruped.

Another kind of complex sentence, called an **exceptive statement**, asserts that all members of some class of objects, with *some exceptions*, are members of some other class of objects. It is correct to say that exceptive statements assert a relation of class inclusion and a relation of class exclusion *at the same time*. For example, consider this statement: "Anyone, except those under age 21, can gamble in Las Vegas casinos." This statement makes two assertions: (1) anyone 21 years of age and older *can* gamble in Las Vegas casinos; (2) anyone under age 21 *cannot* gamble in Las Vegas casinos. If we let *U* = "under 21 years of age," and *G* = "can gamble in Las Vegas casinos," we get this result:

$$(x) (Ux \supset {\sim} Gx) \cdot (x) ({\sim} Ux \supset Gx)$$

The correct symbolization is the *conjunction* of two claims: if you are under 21 you cannot gamble, *and* if you are 21 or older then you can gamble. This particular complex statement can also be symbolized using the symbol for a biconditional: *(x) (Gx ≡ ∼ Ux)*, which can be read as claiming, "Anyone can gamble in Las Vegas casinos *if, and only if*, they are not under age 21."

EXERCISE SET 7.4   ○○○

Exercises 1–15 Translate the following statements into symbolic notation using the abbreviations suggested. Use the quantifier substitution sets *(QSS)*, if needed, to place your translation in normal form.

1. All deciduous trees are colorful in autumn. *(Dx, Cx)*

Answer: *(x) (Dx ⊃ Cx)*

2. No coconuts are pink. *(Cx, Px)*   *(x) (Cx ⊃ ∼ Px)*

3. Some short stories are not about people. *(Sx, Px)*   *(∃x)(Sx · ∼ Px)*

4. If anything is alive, then it is conscious of its environment. *(Ax, Cx)*   *(x) (Ax ⊃ Cx)*

5. Every volcano is dangerous. *(Vx, Dx)* $(x) (Vx \supset Dx)$

*6. Labyrinths are amazing. *(Lx, Ax)* $(x) (Lx \supset Ax)$

7. Not even one student showed up for the pep rally. *(Sx, Px)* $(x) (Sx \supset \sim Px)$

8. Only registered voters are allowed to vote. *(Vx, Rx)* $(x) (Vx \supset Rx)$

9. Every DUI citation is a serious offense. *(Dx, Sx)* $(x) (Dx \supset Sx)$

10. Basketball players are not comfortable in bunk beds. *(Bx, Cx)* $(x) (Bx \supset \sim Cx)$

*11. No MP3 Players are good birthday gifts. *(Mx, Gx)* $(x) (Mx \supset \sim Gx)$

12. All knitted underwear items are warm comfort. *(Kx, Wx)* $(x) (Kx \supset Wx)$

13. No knitted underwear items are bikini substitutes. *(Kx, Bx)* $(x) (Kx \supset \sim Bx)$

14. Some SUVs are not environmentally friendly. *(Sx, Ex)* $(\exists x) (Sx \cdot \sim Ex)$

15. Some SUVs are comfortable rides. *(Sx, Cx)* $(\exists x) (Sx \cdot Cx)$

Exercises 16–22 Translate the following statements into symbolic notation using the abbreviations suggested. Make sure each formula begins with a quantifier, *not* with a negation symbol.

16. Whales are mammals. *(Wx, Mx)*

Answer: $(x) (Wx \supset Mx)$

17. Movie ratings are not always accurate. *(Mx, Ax)* $(\exists x)(Mx \cdot \sim Ax)$

18. Fanatics are never right. *(Fx, Rx)* $(x)(Fx \supset \sim Rx)$

19. Only graduates can participate in the commencement. *(Gx, Px)* $(x)(Px \supset Gx)$

20. A person is medically dead if, and only if, there is no detectable brain stem activity. *(Px, Dx, Bx)* $(x) [Px \supset (Dx \equiv \sim Bx)]$

*21. All whole numbers are either even or odd. *(Wx, Ex, Ox)* $(x) [Wx \supset (Ex \lor Ox)]$

22. Anything that is either sweet or crunchy is tasty. *(Sx, Cx, Tx)* $(x) [(Sx \lor Cx) \supset Tx]$

Exercises 23–30 For each of the following, find a normal-form formula logically equivalent to the one given.

23. $\sim (\exists x)(Tx \cdot Rx)$

Answer: $(x)(Tx \supset \sim Rx)$

24. $\sim (x)(Px \supset \sim Sx)$ $(\exists x)(Px \cdot Sx)$

25. $\sim (\exists x)(Jx \cdot \sim Kx)$ $(x)(Jx \supset Kx)$

*26. $\sim (x)(Dx \supset Gx)$ $(\exists x)(Dx \cdot \sim Gx)$

27. $\sim (x) (Px \supset Qx)$ $(\exists x) (Px \cdot \sim Qx)$

28. $\sim (\exists x) (Px \cdot Qx)$ $(x) (Px \supset \sim Qx)$

29. $\sim (x) (Px \supset \sim Qx)$ $(\exists x) (Px \cdot Qx)$

30. $\sim (\exists x) (Px \cdot \sim Qx)$ $(x) (Px \supset Qx)$

7.5 QUANTIFICATION AND PROOFS OF VALIDITY

At this point, we are going to introduce four new rules of inference that give us the ability to construct formal proofs that display the validity of inferences containing quantifiers. These rules expand the set of rules of inference developed in Chapter 6 on natural deduction

Universal Instantiation

The rule of **universal instantiation (UI)** says that any substitution instance of a statement function can be validly deduced from its universal quantification.

> **UI:** $\underline{(x)\,(\phi x)}$
>
> ϕv (v represents any individual symbol, either constant or variable)

For example, consider the following proof:

1. $(x)\,(Tx \supset Cx)$
2. Ts $\therefore\ Cs$
3. $Ts \supset Cs$ 1, UI
4. Cs 2, 3, MP

Line #1 allows us to assume the truth of the universal quantification of the statement function ($Tx \supset Cx$). Since the rule UI permits the valid inference of any substitution instance, we can derive line #3, $Ts \supset Cs$. The annotated justification of this line is UI. In this case we chose to replace the variable x with the constant s. However, the rule informs us that we can replace the statement function with any individual symbol. A second kind of use for UI will be explained in the discussion of the next rule.

Universal Generalization

Universal instantiation (UI): A rule of inference in the logic of quantifiers that ensures that from the universal quantification of a statement function, one can validly infer any substitution instance of that statement function.

According to the rule of **universal generalization (UG)** we can validly deduce the universal quantification of a statement function from the substitution instance of that statement function with respect to the name of any arbitrarily selected individual.

> **UG:** $\underline{\phi y}$
>
> $(x)(\phi x)$ (x is a variable that denotes any arbitrarily selected individual)

Universal generalization (UG): A rule of inference in the logic of quantifiers by which we can validly deduce the universal quantification of a statement function from the substitution instance of that statement function with respect to the name of any arbitrarily selected individual.

For example, consider the following proof:

1. $(x)\,(Tx \supset Cx)$
2. $(x)\,(Rx \supset Tx)$ $\therefore\ (x)\,(Rx \supset Cx)$
3. $Ty \supset Cy$ 1, UI
4. $Ry \supset Ty$ 2, UI
5. $Ry \supset Cy$ 3, 4, HS
6. $(x)\,(Rx \supset Cx)$ 5, UG

From line #1 and line #2 (the given premises), we can eventually derive line #5, the statement function, $Ry \supset Cy$, by a series of UI applications. We used y, a variable, when we applied UI, but in our previous example we used a constant, s. The reason for this is that our goals were different in the two cases. The conclusion of our present example, $(x) (Rx \supset Cx)$, helps highlight an important consideration. We cannot use universal generalization when the instantiated letter is a constant. Suppose that at some point in our proof procedure we derive this: Ha. It would be a mistake to do the following:

5. Ta
6. $(x) Tx$ 5, UG

This is why the rule stipulates that x denotes any arbitrarily selected individual. Thus, if any arbitrary substitution instance is true, all substitution instances are true, and so the universal quantification of that statement function must also be true.

Existential Instantiation

According to the rule of **existential instantiation (EI)**, we can validly deduce the substitution instance of any individual constant, provided that it has not already been used, from the existential quantification of a statement function.

EI: $\underline{(\exists x)(\phi x)}$

ϕv (v is any individual constant that has not previously occurred in our proof sequence)

For example, consider this partial proof:

1. $(x) (Tx \supset Cx)$
2. $\underline{(\exists x) (Rx \cdot Tx)}$ $\therefore (\exists x) (Rx \cdot Cx)$
3. $Ra \cdot Ta$ 2, EI

The existential quantification assumed as given in line #2 allows us to assert that it has *at least one* true substitution instance. Therefore, we can arbitrarily substitute the individual constant "a," because it has not previously occurred anywhere. Line #3 is justified by EI. The complete proof will follow in our discussion of the next rule.

Existential Generalization

According to the rule of **existential generalization (EG)**, we can validly deduce the existential quantification of a statement function from any true substitution instance of that statement function.

EG: $\underline{\phi v}$

$(\exists x) (\phi x)$ (x represents any individual symbol, either constant or variable)

Existential instantiation (EI): A rule of inference in the logic of quantifiers which holds that, within certain limitations, the truth of a substitution instance can be inferred from the existential quantification of a statement function, as long as the individual constant does not occur earlier.

Existential generalization (EG): A rule of inference in the logic of quantifiers which holds that the existential quantification of a statement function can be inferred from any true substitution instance of that statement function.

For example, consider this proof:

1. $(x)\ (Tx \supset Cx)$
2. $(\exists x)\ (Rx \cdot Tx)$　　　$\therefore (\exists x)\ (Rx \cdot Cx)$
3. $Ra \cdot Ta$　　　　　2, EI
4. $Ta \supset Ca$　　　　1, UI
5. $Ta \cdot Ra$　　　　　3, Comm
6. Ta　　　　　　　5, Simp
7. Ca　　　　　　　4, 6, MP
8. Ra　　　　　　　3, Simp
9. $Ra \cdot Ca$　　　　7, 8, Conj
10. $(\exists x)\ (Rx \cdot Cx)$　　9, EG

Once we derive line #9, we can apply our knowledge that the existential quantification of a statement function is true *if, and only if,* it has at least one true substitution instance. Therefore, we justify line #10 by using EG.

Quick Reference 7.4 • Summary of the Rules of Inference for Quantifiers

Universal instantiation (UI):

$\dfrac{(x)\ (\phi x)}{\phi v}$ (v represents any individual symbol, either constant or variable)

Universal generalization (UG):

$\dfrac{\phi y}{(x)(\phi x)}$ (x is a variable that denotes any arbitrarily selected individual)

Existential instantiation (EI):

$\dfrac{(\exists x)(\phi x)}{\phi v}$ (v is any individual constant that has not previously occurred in our proof sequence)

Existential generalization (EG):

$\dfrac{\phi v}{(\exists x)\ (\phi x)}$ (x represents any individual symbol, either constant or variable)

> The rules of inference for quantifiers include UI, UG, EI, and EG.

Conditional Proof and Indirect Proof Using Quantifiers

The methods of conditional proof and indirect proof that were developed in Chapter 6 on natural deduction can be used with inferences containing quantifiers. The rules and techniques governing these two kinds of proof procedures must be respected when applied to the ideas introduced in this chapter. The following example uses conditional proof:

1. $(\exists x)\, Sx \supset (x)\, Tx$
2. $(\exists x)\, Qx \supset (\exists x)\, (Rx \cdot Sx)$ $\therefore\ (x)(Qx \supset Tx)$

	3. Qx	Assumption (CP)
	4. $(\exists x)\, Qx$	3, EG
	5. $(\exists x)\, (Rx \cdot Sx)$	2, 4, MP
	6. $Ra \cdot Sa$	5, EI
	7. $Sa \cdot Ra$	6, Comm
	8. Sa	7, Simp
	9. $(\exists x)\, Sx$	8, EG
	10. $(x)\, Tx$	1, 9, MP
	11. Tx	10, UI

12. $Qx \supset Tx$ 3-11, CP
13. $(x)(Qx \supset Tx)$ 11, UG

The following example uses indirect proof:

1. $Ra \lor Rb$
2. $(x)\, (Rx \supset Tx)$ $\therefore\ (\exists x)\, Tx$

	3. $\sim (\exists x)\, Tx$	Assumption (IP)
	4. $(x) \sim Tx$	3, Logical Equivalence (Table 7.1)
	5. $Ra \supset Ta$	2, UI
	6. $Rb \supset Tb$	2, UI
	7. $(Ra \supset Ta) \cdot (Rb \supset Tb)$	5, 6, Conj
	8. $Ta \lor Tb$	1, 7, CD
	9. $\sim Ta$	4, UI
	10. Tb	8, 9, DS
	11. $\sim Tb$	4, UI
	12. $Tb \cdot \sim Tb$	10, 11, Conj

13. $\sim \sim (\exists x)\, Tx$ 3-12, IP
14. $(\exists x)\, Tx$ 13, DN

EXERCISE SET 7.5

Exercises 1–8 The formal proofs of validity for the inferences have been given. Choose the correct rule application for the missing justifications.

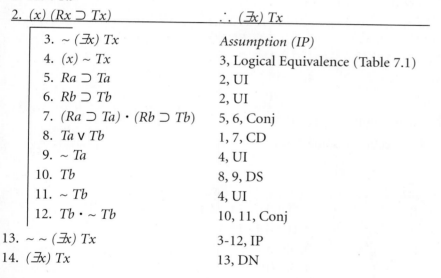

1. $(y)(Py \supset Sy)$
2. $(\exists y)(Py \cdot Ty)$ $\therefore\ (\exists y)(Ty \cdot Sy)$
3. $Pa \cdot Ta$ 2, (**UI, UG, EI, EG**)?

4.	Pa	3, Simp
5.	$Pa \supset Sa$	1, **(UI, UG, EI, EG)**?
6.	Sa	4, 5, MP
7.	$Ta \cdot Pa$	3, Comm
8.	Ta	7, Simp
9.	$Ta \cdot Sa$	6, 8, Conj
10.	$(\exists y)(Ty \cdot Sy)$	9, **(UI, UG, EI, EG)**?

[1]   The justification for line #3:

[2]   The justification for line #5:

[3]   The justification for line #10:

Answer:

[1]   The justification for line #3: **EI**

[2]   The justification for line #5: **UI**

[3]   The justification for line #10: **EG**

1.	$(x)(Nx \supset Mx)$	
2	$(x)(Mx \supset Ox)$	
3.	Na	$\therefore$ Oa
4.	$Na \supset Ma$	1, **(UI, UG, EI, EG)**?
5.	$Ma \supset Oa$	2, **(UI, UG, EI, EG)**?
6.	$Na \supset Oa$	4, 5, HS
7.	Oa	3, 6, MP

[4]   The justification for line #4: UI

[5]   The justification for line #5: UI

1.	$(\exists x)(Px \cdot Qx)$	
2.	$(x)(Px \supset Rx)$	$\therefore$ $(\exists x)(Qx \cdot Rx)$
3.	$Pa \cdot Qa$	1, **(UI, UG, EI, EG)**?
4.	$Pa \supset Ra$	2, **(UI, UG, EI, EG)**?
5.	Pa	3, Simp
6.	Ra	4, 5, MP
7.	$Qa \cdot Pa$	3, Comm
8.	Qa	7, Simp
9.	$Qa \cdot Ra$	6, 8, Conj
10.	$(\exists x)(Qx \cdot Rx)$	9, **(UI, UG, EI, EG)**?

[6]   The justification for line #3: EI

[7]   The justification for line #4: UI

[8]   The justification for line #10: EG

Exercises 9–15 In the following proofs the correct justification has been given for the rule used. You are to supply the missing information in the line.

1. $(x)(Kx \supset \sim Sx)$
2. $(\exists x)(Sx \cdot Wx)$ $\therefore (\exists x)(Wx \cdot \sim Kx)$
3. ?   2, **EI**
4. ?   1, **UI**
5. Sa 3, Simp
6. $\sim \sim Sa$ 5, DN
7. $\sim Ka$ 4, 6, MT
8. $Wa \cdot Sa$ 3, Comm
9. Wa 8, Simp
10. $Wa \cdot \sim Ka$ 7, 9, Conj
11. ?   10, **EG**

[9]   The information in line #3: $Sa \cdot Wa$

[10] The information in line #4: $Ka \supset \sim Sa$

[*11] The information in line #11: $(\exists x)(Wx \cdot \sim Kx)$

1. $(\exists x) (Px \cdot Qx)$
2. $(\exists x) (Rx \cdot Sx)$
3. $[(\exists x) Px \cdot (\exists x) Rx] \supset Ta$ $\therefore Ta$
4. ?   1, EI
5. ?   2, EI
6. Pa 4, Simp
7. Rb 5, Simp
8. ?   6, EG
9. ?   7, EG
10. $(\exists x) Px \cdot (\exists x) Rx$ 8, 9, Conj
11. Ta 3, 10, MP

[12] The information in line #4: $Pa \cdot Qa$

[13] The information in line #5: $Rb \cdot Sb$

[14] The information in line #8: $(\exists x) Px$

[15] The information in line #9: $(\exists x) Rx$

Exercises 16–27 Construct proofs of validity for the following inferences.

[16]   1. $(x)(Sx \supset Tx)$
       2. $(x)(Tx \supset \sim Ux)$ $\therefore (x)(Sx \supset \sim Ux)$

Answer:

1. $(x)(Sx \supset Tx)$
2. $(x)(Tx \supset \sim Ux)$ $\therefore$ $(x)(Sx \supset \sim Ux)$
3. $Sa \supset Ta$ 1, UI
4. $Ta \supset \sim Ua$ 2, UI
5. $Sa \supset \sim Ua$ 3, 4, HS
6. $(x) (Sx \supset \sim Ux)$ 5, UG

Exercises 17–27: For answers
and explanations,
see pages 228–230 of
Instructor's Manual.

[17] 1. $(x) (Ux \supset Sx)$
      2. $(\exists x)(Ux \cdot Tx)$ $\therefore$ $(\exists x)(Tx \cdot Sx)$

[18] 1. $(\exists x)(Tx \cdot \sim Mx)$
      2. $(x) [(Tx \supset (Rx \lor Mx)]$ $\therefore$ $(\exists x) Rx$

[19] 1. $(\exists x) Px \supset (\exists x) Kx$
      2. $(\exists x) Mx \supset (x) Nx$
      3. $Mc \cdot Pc$ $\therefore$ $(\exists x)(Nx \cdot Kx)$

[20] 1. $(\exists x) Hx$
      2. $(x)(Hx \supset Px)$ $\therefore$ $(\exists x)(Hx \cdot Px)$

[*21] 1. $Ha \lor Hb$
      2. $(x)(\sim Cx \supset \sim Hx)$ $\therefore$ $Ca \lor Cb$

[22] 1. $(\exists x) Gx \supset (x) Hx$
      2. Ga $\therefore$ Ha

[23] 1. $(\exists x) (Sx \cdot Tx)$
      2. $(x) (Px \supset \sim Sx)$ $\therefore$ $(\exists x) (Tx \cdot \sim Px)$

[24] 1. Ta
      2. $(x) (Sx \supset \sim Tx)$ $\therefore$ $\sim Sa$

[25] 1. $(x) (Sx \supset Tx)$
      2. $(x) (Tx \supset Px)$
      3. Sa $\therefore$ $(\exists x) Px$

[*26] 1. $(x) (Px \supset \sim Qx)$
      2. Qa $\therefore$ $\sim Pa$

[27] 1. $(\exists x) (Px \cdot Qx)$
      2. $(x) (Px \supset Rx)$ $\therefore$ $(\exists x) (Qx \cdot Rx)$

7.6 QUANTIFICATION AND PROOFS OF INVALIDITY

We accept that a valid inference that uses quantifiers is valid for any number of individuals, with the stipulation that there is at least one individual in the universe that has the specified characteristic. In order to prove that an inference that uses quantifiers is invalid requires us to produce a possible universe, or model, containing at least one individual, whereby we can show that the premises are true and the conclusion false. If an inference using quantifiers is invalid, it is always possible to create such a model. This is referred to as the **finite universe method** of proving invalidity. We create a set of individual objects that are considered to "exist" in the *possible universe* of a given model. A proof of invalidity relies on assigning truth values to the logically equivalent truth-functional inference. The invalidity of an inference can be proved using a three-step method (Quick Reference 7.5).

Finite universe method:
A valid inference that uses quantifiers is valid for any number of individuals as long as there is one individual with the specified characteristic. To prove that an inference that uses quantifiers is invalid requires that we must be able to produce a possible universe or model (containing at least one individual) for which the premises are true and the conclusion false.

Quick Reference 7.5 • The Three-Step Method for Proving the Invalidity of an Inference Using Quantifiers

1. Create a one-individual model using the individual *a*. *If* the truth-functional inference can be proved invalid by assigning truth values to the simple statements, *then* the proof of invalidity has been successfully provided; otherwise, you must go to step 2.

2. Create a two individuals model containing the individuals *a* and *b*. *If* the original inference contains a *universally* quantified statement function, $(x)(\phi x)$, then use *conjunction* to join ϕa and ϕb. *If* the original inference contains an *existentially* quantified statement function, $(\exists x)(\phi x)$, then use *disjunction*. *If* this model can be proved invalid by assigning truth values to the simple statements, then the proof of invalidity has been successfully provided; otherwise, you must go to step 3.

3. Try a three individuals model containing the individuals *a*, *b*, and *c*. You must keep adding individuals until the proof of invalidity is successful. (If you suspect that the inference is valid, then try proving its validity using the methods described earlier.)

The three-step method for proving invalidity requires the creation of a possible universe or model.

The following example will take you step-by-step through the procedure. Consider this inference:

$$(x)\ (Hx \supset Mx)$$
$$\underline{(x)\ (Rx \supset Mx)}$$
$$(x)\ (Rx \supset Hx)$$

We first try a one-individual model using the individual *a*. Below is the appropriate truth-functional inference for this example:

$$Ha \supset Ma$$
$$\underline{Ra \supset Ma}$$
$$Ra \supset Ha$$

We will create a truth table using the indirect proof method. The first step is to assign truth values to get the conclusion false. Since the conclusion is a conditional statement, we know that there is only one way to get the conclusion false, namely, by making the antecedent true and the consequent false, $(Ra = T, Ha = F)$. These assignments are then applied to the truth table as follows:

			1st **Premise**	2nd **Premise**	**Conclusion**
Ha	*Ma*	*Ra*	*Ha* ⊃ *Ma*	*Ra* ⊃ *Ma*	*Ra* ⊃ *Ha*
F	T	F	T	T	F

This assignment of truth values makes the first premise true, because the antecedent, $Ha = F$. But in order to get the second premise true, Ma must be true. We add this information to complete the truth table.

			1st **Premise**	2nd **Premise**	**Conclusion**
Ha	*Ma*	*Ra*	*Ha* ⊃ *Ma*	*Ra* ⊃ *Ma*	*Ra* ⊃ *Ha*
F	T	T	F *(T)* T	T *(T)* T	T *(F)* F

This assignment of truth values in a one-individual universe reveals the possibility of true premises and false conclusion, thereby proving the inference is invalid.

We can use this knowledge to revisit the problem of existential import. If a universal affirmative statement implies its corresponding particular affirmative statement (*see* Appendix 2, Section A2.5), then we can get the following inference: "All centaurs are vegetarians, so some centaurs are vegetarians." If we let Cx = "x is a centaur," and Vx = "x is a vegetarian," then we get the following:

$$(x) \ (Cx \supset Vx) \qquad \therefore \ (\exists x) \ (Cx \cdot Vx)$$

We can try a one-individual model to prove the inference is invalid. The following truth value assignments prove that the inference is invalid.

		Premise	**Conclusion**
Ca	*Va*	*Ca* ⊃ *Va*	*Ca* · *Va*
F	T	F *(T)* T	F *(F)* T

Once again, we have revealed the idea that an inference from a universal statement to its corresponding particular is invalid when the subject term denotes an empty class.

If a one-individual model is insufficient to prove invalidity, then we must go to Step 2. For example, consider this inference:

All fanatics are dangerous people. There is at least one fanatic. Therefore, everything is dangerous.

We can translate it to get the following:

$$(x) \ (Fx \supset Dx)$$

$$(\exists x) \ Fx \qquad \therefore \ (x) \ Dx$$

We can try a one-individual model to see if we can prove the inference is invalid.

	1st Premise	2nd Premise	Conclusion

Fa Da $\|$	Fa $\supset$ Da	Fa	Da
T F $\|$	T (F) F	T	F

In order to get the conclusion to be false, we had to assign *false* to *Da*. To get the second premise true, we had to assign *true* to *Fa* (no other truth value assignments will achieve these two results). However, these assignments result in the first premise being false. Therefore, a one-individual model is not sufficient to prove invalidity for this inference. We must try a two-individual model. As before, we start by assigning truth values to get the conclusion false, and proceed through the inference to see if we can get the premises true.

	1st Premise	2nd Premise	Conclusion

Fa Da Fb Db $\|$	(Fa $\supset$ Da) $\cdot$ (Fb $\supset$ Db)	Fa $\vee$ Fb	Da $\cdot$ Db
T T F F $\|$	T (T) T (T) F (T) F	T (T) F	T (F) F

This two-individual model reveals the possibility of true premises and a false conclusion, so we have provided a proof that the inference is invalid.

EXERCISE SET 7.6

Exercises 1–2 Use the finite universe method to prove the invalidity of the inferences.

1. $(x) (Px \supset \sim Qx)$
   $\underline{(x) (Qx \supset \sim Rx) \qquad \therefore (x) (Px \supset \sim Rx)}$

Answer:

A one-individual model with the individual **a** gives us this logically equivalent truth-functional inference:

   $Pa \supset \sim Qa$
   $\underline{Qa \supset \sim Ra \qquad \therefore Pa \quad \supset \quad \sim Ra}$

The following truth value assignments make the premises true and the conclusion false, thus proving the inference is invalid:

	1st Prem	2nd Prem	Conc

Pa Qa Ra $\|$	Pa $\supset$ $\sim$ Qa	Qa $\supset$ $\sim$ Ra	Pa $\supset$ $\sim$ Ra
T F T $\|$	T (T)(T) F	F (T)(F) T	T (F)(F) T

2. $(\exists x) (Px \cdot \sim Qx)$
   $\underline{(x) (Rx \supset \sim Qx) \qquad \therefore (x) (Rx \supset Px)}$

Exercises 2–7: For answers and explanations, see pages 231–234 of Instructor's Manual.

Exercises 3–7 Translate the following inferences and then use the finite universe method to prove invalidity.

3. All problem-solvers and all thinkers have minds. Computers are problem-solvers. Thus, computers are thinkers. (*Px, Tx, Mx, Cx*)

4. All horses are mammals. Some horses are pets. Thus, all pets are mammals. (*Hx, Mx, Px*)

5. If some elected officials are corrupt, then some voters are getting what they deserve. All elected officials are corrupt. Therefore, all elected officials are getting what they deserve. (*Ex, Cx, Vx, Dx*)

*6. Every dancer and every singer is right-brained. There is at least one singer. Thus, everyone is right-brained. (*Dx, Sx, Rx*)

7. Some CEOs are not people blindly devoted to profits. Some women are CEOs. Therefore, some people blindly devoted to profits are not women. (*Cx, Bx, Wx*)

SUMMARY

- Many inferences combine both categorical and truth-functional statements and, as such, do not fit into our earlier proof systems. The logic of quantifiers facilitates the smooth integration of categorical and truth-functional results and offers a powerful way of capturing more of natural language into precise statement and inference analysis.

- A singular statement asserts that one individual has a specific characteristic. The subject term denotes a particular object, and the predicate term designates a specific characteristic.

- It is possible for the same subject and predicate term to occur in a variety of singular statements. Some of these assertions will be true and some will be false.

- The lowercase letters *a* through *w* are used as constants to denote individuals.

- The characteristics predicated of individuals are symbolized by capital letters, *A, B, C*, etc.

- Any singular statement is symbolized by using the capital letter first followed by a lowercase letter.

- The lowercase letters *x, y*, and *z* are not used to denote an individual constant, but rather an individual variable. As such, they are used to indicate where a particular constant may be placed, resulting in a singular statement.

- Statement functions are neither true nor false, but they can have both true and false substitution instances.

- The logic of quantifiers can be used when a predicate term occurs in a statement that is not singular.

- The process of changing quantifier functions into statements is called quantification.

- The universal quantifier *(x)* is used to assert that the predicate term following it is true of everything.

- The existential quantifier *(∃x)* is used to assert that the predicate term following it has at least one true substitution instance.

- Universal quantification of a statement function is true if, and only if, all possible substitution instances are true.

- Existential quantification of a statement function is true if, and only if, it has at least one true substitution instance.

- Statements may be derived from statement functions either by instantiation (substituting an individual constant for an individual variable) or by generalization (by using either a universal or existential quantifier).

- Quantifying over variables by using either the universal or the existential quantifier creates statements that are either true or false.

- A normal-form formula is one where the negation symbol applies only to simple predicates. A negation symbol at the beginning of a formula must be changed into normal form by using the sets of four equivalencies listed in the chapter.

- Four additional rules of inference added to the set of rules developed in natural deduction are: (1) universal instantiation, (2) universal generalization, (3) existential instantiation, and (4) existential generalization. These four rules make possible the construction of formal proofs displaying the validity of inferences containing quantifiers.

- To prove that an inference that uses quantifiers is invalid requires the creation of a finite universe containing at least one individual, whereby it can be shown that the premises are true and the conclusion false. If an inference using quantifiers is invalid, it is always possible to create such a model.

KEY TERMS

logic of quantifiers   255
singular statement   255
individual constant   257
individual variable   257
statement function   257
substitution
   instance   257
quantification   258
universal
   quantifier   258
existential
   quantifier   258

universal
   quantification   258
existential
   quantification   258
instantiation   258
generalization   258
normal-form
   formula   261
bound variable   261
free variable   261
exceptive statement   262

universal
   instantiation   264
universal
   generalization   264
existential
   instantiation   265
existential
   generalization   265
finite universe
   method   271

LOGIC CHALLENGE: AN ARRANGEMENT PROBLEM

Imagine that you are surfing the Internet and come across an enticing offer. If you submit the correct answer to a puzzle you will have a chance to win an all-expense paid trip for two to Hawaii. As the puzzle begins, you are told that five numbers— 2, 4, 5, 7, 10—have been randomly arranged in a particular sequence reading left to right. You are then given three clues regarding the order of the numbers, which you must use to determine the correct sequence.

   Clue #1: No two odd or even numbers are next to each other.

   Clue #2: The second number on the left is exactly half the left-most number.

   Clue #3: The middle number is exactly twice the right-most number.

   What is the correct sequence of numbers?

Correct order: 10, 5, 4, 7, 2.
See page 234 of Instructor's
Manual for complete
explanation.

Logic and Language

This chapter will explore the intersection of logic and language by looking at three major issues. First, *definitions* play an important role in clarifying the meaning of terms in statements, and they have a direct impact on the assessment of inferences. A survey of different kinds of definitions, along with specific examples, will place them in their proper setting. Second, *informal fallacies* are mistakes in reasoning that are different from errors in the form or structure of an inference. Since many kinds of informal fallacies are difficult to spot, practice with locating specific sources of these kinds of mistakes is needed. Finally, when language is used to imply something that is not explicitly said, then language is being used *rhetorically.* Rhetorical language needs to be correctly interpreted, and inferences should be reconstructed based on an understanding of the context.

8.1 DEFINITIONS

Clarifying the meaning of statements requires a close look at the meaning of the *terms* (words or groups of words) found in the statement. The **intension** of a term is specified by listing the properties or attributes that the term *connotes* (the sense or meaning of the term). For example, to specify the intensional meaning of the term "automobile" you might provide the following (partial) list of properties: four-wheeled vehicle, powered by an engine, fueled by gasoline, and used for traveling on roads and highways. On the other hand, the **extension** of a term is given by specifying the *class members* of the term, what the term *denotes* (the objects that

chapter

Intension: The properties or attributes that a term connotes (the sense or meaning of the term).

Extension: The class members of the term, what the term denotes (the objects to which the term refers).

the term refers to). For example, to specify the extensional meaning of the term "automobile," you might provide the following (partial) list: Toyota Camry, Nissan Maxima, Ford Mustang, Chevrolet Corvette, etc.

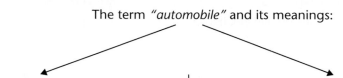

The term *"automobile"* and its meanings:

Intension (connotation): The *properties* are: Four-wheeled vehicle, powered by an engine, fueled by gasoline, and used for traveling on roads and highways.

Extension (denotation): The *class members* are: All the cars in the universe, i.e. Toyota Camrys, Nissan Maximas, Ford Mustangs, Chevrolet Corvettes, etc.

Some terms have intension but no extension. For example, the term "centaur" connotes the following properties: A creature that has a man's head, torso, and arms, but the body and legs of a horse. This term "centaur" has no *extension*; it denotes an empty class (one that has zero members). We get the same result for all mythological creature terms, fictional terms, and terms that refer to extinct animals (dinosaurs, etc.).

Lexical Definitions

A **lexical definition** is a definition based on the common use of a word or term. The *dictionary meaning* of a term is an example of a lexical definition. "Lexical" also means the common vocabulary of a given language as determined by the actual use in a community of speakers and writers. Since most terms have multiple meanings, we often rely on lexical definitions to clear up any misunderstandings. For example, lexical definitions of "career" might include "a way of making a living," or "a paid occupation." A lexical definition of "ornament" might be "a decorative object." Whenever possible, we must clarify the meaning of terms when we encounter them in statements and, especially in inferences. Ambiguity, vagueness, or any unclear use of a term can seriously affect the understanding, analysis, and evaluation of an inference.

Stipulative Definitions

Lexical definition: The dictionary meaning of a term; the common vocabulary of a given language.

Stipulative definition: An arbitrary, specific definition.

We have encountered stipulations previously when we set ground rules for analyzing some inferences. In the earlier contexts, the stipulations served the purpose of avoiding mistakes of interpretation by specifying precise points of reference or measuring devices. In the present context, a **stipulative definition** of a term is an arbitrary, specified meaning. Slang and idioms are examples of the common use of stipulative definitions. Sometimes old terms are given new meanings. If so, in order to participate in certain conversations you must be introduced to the unusual (new) meaning of the term. When a new term is introduced, people using the term for the first time usually set the meaning for others (which can then be modified by other groups for their own purposes).

Confusion can easily occur when stipulative terms are used without prior agreement on their meaning. For example, if a child says, "These pants are *tight!*" the parent might easily infer the following: "I'm glad you told me. I will take them back and get you a larger size." From the child's perspective, the parent is woefully out of touch. The child then enlightens the parent by exclaiming, "You don't get it. *Tight* means *cool!*"

Precising Definitions

Problems caused by the vagueness of certain terms can often be cleared up by using **precising definitions**, definitions that give the terms precise meanings. Most terms used in legal, scientific, or medical settings require precise meanings. For example, in a legal setting there must be a precise definition of what constitutes a "dangerous weapon" or "illegal drug." In a scientific setting, concepts such as "energy," "momentum," and "mass" must have precise definitions. A scientific definition of "energy" would include some discussion of how "*matter* can do *work* by its *mass, electric charge,* or *motion.*" The italicized words would themselves need precising definitions in order to convey a complete understanding of the concepts involved. In a medical setting, ethical decisions often have to be made regarding the status of a critically ill patient. It is sometimes necessary that we have a precise determination of when a human being can be considered "dead." In other situations, debate continues on finding a precise definition of when human life begins.

Operational Definitions

An **operational definition** defines a term by specifying a *measurement procedure.* For example, academic achievement is very important for many people in the field of education—teachers, administrators, test-developers, and students. An operational definition of academic achievement might use the grade point average (GPA) of every student. This measurement device is *quantitative* because it provides us with a range of numerical values. In most colleges, this range is from 4.0 to 0.0, with the highest 4.0 for straight A's, to the lowest being 0.0 for straight F's. Therefore, every student who has finished at least one semester has a place on the scale with a ranking from the highest, 4.0, to the lowest, 0.0.

An alternative operational definition for academic achievement might use students' letters of recommendation. This measurement device is quite different from a GPA number. We would now be using a *qualitative* method, one that provides us with a range of values that is open-ended. Letters of recommendation may state grades the student received, as well as an assessment of the student's position relative to other students (e.g. top 10 percent of the class). It might also mention other important factors, such as, the student's ability to write original essays, self-discipline, willingness to help other students, ability to ask relevant questions and to grasp abstract material, and prospects for graduate work, to name a few. We could

Precising definition:
A definition developed to clarify a vague or ambiguous term (often used in legal, scientific, or medical settings).

Operational definition:
A definition that provides a meaning for a term by specifying a measurement procedure.

rank each student in order, from those with the "strongest" letters of recommendation to those with the "weakest." This would not be easy because we are not dealing with a straightforward quantitative method, but, it would be possible to give each student a place in the hierarchy.

If we then compare the two sets of student rankings, we might be surprised to see a large variation. The two lists of the same student body might not match up very well at all. Therefore, the kind of operational definition we give to a term may affect the strength of the inference in which it plays a part.

Many terms denote phenomena that can only be observed indirectly, such as radioactivity. There must be some empirical means of *measuring* or *experimenting* with these phenomena in order to obtain objective evidence about them. For example, although our senses cannot detect radioactivity, we do have very powerful means of measuring it with an instrument called a Geiger counter. Similarly, electrons are observed indirectly in experiments with cloud chambers. In each case, we are offered strong evidence that these concepts denote something that can be physically observed, albeit indirectly. Concepts of this kind require extraordinary evidence to be convincing. Thus researchers must develop strong methods of gathering indirect evidence. The criteria we rely on to help us determine if a concept truly refers to indirectly observable objects are the following: *measurement*, *prediction*, and *explanation*. If a claim uses a concept that purports to denote a real part of the physical world (however invisible it might be to our senses), the person asserting the claim must be able to provide strong, credible indirect evidence to back it up. Historically, this has been accomplished by the invention of unique devices that can detect and measure what we cannot directly observe. Researchers in the physical sciences have developed barometers, thermometers, Geiger counters, cyclotrons, etc., to gather evidence. In turn, these measuring devices allow the accurate prediction of future experimental results. Finally, we must be able to explain how and why the events occur as they do. These explanations require the development of a theoretical framework or model for the events. (These ideas are explored in detail in Chapter 9.)

Functional and Ostensive Definitions

Functional definition:
A definition that specifies the purpose or use of the items denoted by the term.

Ostensive definition:
A definition developed by showing someone an object and attaching a word to it.

A **functional definition** of a term specifies the purpose or use of the items denoted by the term. For example, a functional definition of the term "cup" is "a vessel to hold liquid." This type of definition allows a cup to be made of almost any material, as long as it performs the *function* correctly. We typically use functional definitions to define the normal use of objects that have been created or designed for specific purposes.

An **ostensive definition** involves demonstrating the term, for example, pointing to an object and attaching a word to it. This is the manner in which children are introduced to many terms, by showing them some examples of what the term denotes. The use of ostensive definitions is not, however, limited to children. For example, someone looking at a car engine might point to an object and ask what it is. If the object is then called an "alternator," the inquirer knows, by having been given an ostensive definition, what objects of that type are called. However, if the person wishes to know what an alternator does, a functional definition is required.

Quick Reference 8.1 • Types of Definitions

1. **Intensional:** Specifying the properties or attributes (the sense or meaning) of the term.
2. **Extensional:** Specifying the class members of the term (the objects to which the term refers.
3. **Lexical definition:** The *dictionary* meaning of a term; the common vocabulary of a given language.
4. **Stipulative definition:** An arbitrary, specific definition.
5. **Precising definition:** A definition developed to clarify a vague or ambiguous term (often used in legal, scientific, or medical settings).
6. **Operational definition:** A definition that provides a meaning for a term by specifying a *measurement* procedure. Terms that denote things that can only be *indirectly observed* require some empirical means of *measuring* or *experimenting* in order to get objective evidence of their existence and properties.
7. **Functional definition:** A definition that specifies the purpose or use of the items denoted by the term.
8. **Ostensive definition:** A definition developed by showing someone an object and attaching a word to it.

The various kinds of definitions help to clarify the meanings of statements.

EXERCISE SET 8.1

Exercises 1–10 Decide whether the statement is true or false.

1. A stipulative definition is not used to define a slang term.

Answer: False. Stipulative definitions are needed to determine the definition of a slang term.

Exercises 2–10: For answers and explanations, see page 242 of Instructor's Manual.

2. Ostensive definitions are used only with children learning new terms.

2. False

3. Physicians typically use lexical definitions when discussing medical issues with colleagues.

3. False

4. A functional definition describes how an object looks.

4. False

5. An operational definition must include a description of how to measure the reference of the term.

5. True

*6. The extension of a term is what it denotes.

6. True

7. The intension of a term is what it connotes.

7. True

8. A lexical definition can be determined by consulting a dictionary.

8. True

9. A precising definition can be determined by consulting a medical dictionary.

9. True

10. Some terms have intension but no extension.

10. True

Exercises 11–22 List some of the properties commonly associated with the terms (the *intension*). Then list at least three things denoted by the terms (the *extension*).

*11. Athlete

Answer: Athlete: *intension*—strong, fast, agile, stamina, skilled, competitor
                             extension—Tiger Woods, Shaquille O'Neal, Tom Brady

Exercises 12–22: For answers and explanations, see page 242 of Instructor's Manual.

12. Country

13. Animal

14. Game

15. President

*16. Mammal

17. Book

18. Planet

19. Plant

20. Teacher

*21. Computer

22. City

Exercises 23–44 State whether the definition given is *lexical, stipulative, precising, operational, functional,* or *ostensive.*

Exercises 24–44: For answers and explanations, see pages 242–243 of Instructor's Manual.

23. Intelligence is the score a person receives on the Stanford-Binet I.Q. Test.

Answer: Operational—An *operational definition* provides a meaning for a term by specifying a *measurement* procedure.

24. Functional

24. Scissors are used to cut material or paper.

25. Lexical

25. Science is the systematic knowledge gained through observation and experiment.

26. Stipulative

*26. "Tall" means someone who is over 6-feet, 6-inches.

27. Functional

27. An alternator is an electrical device used for producing electrical current.

28. Ostensive

28. Look where I'm pointing—that's your car's alternator.

29. Precising

29. A felony is a major crime, such as, murder, rape, or arson.

30. Lexical

30. Love is a strong attraction, devotion, or attachment to a person.

31. Operational

*31. Atmospheric pressure is what barometers measure.

32. Stipulative

32. From now on, "late" means anytime after 10:30 PM.

33. Precising

33. A virus is an infectious agent that causes diseases, such as smallpox and AIDS.

34. Ostensive

34. See this big green thing in front of you? That's an oak tree.

35. Precising

35. The right to privacy is the right to control access to undocumented personal information.

36. Operational

*36. Grade point average (GPA) is determined by dividing the total grade points achieved by the number of credits earned.

37. A water molecule is made up of two atoms of hydrogen and one atom of oxygen.

37. Precising

38. Politicians are elected officials who like to spend other people's money.

38. Stipulative

39. The area of a rectangle is determined by multiplying the length by the breadth in units of the same denomination.

39. Precising

40. To purr is to make a low, murmuring sound expressive of satisfaction, as a cat does.

40. Lexical

*41. The tree over by the shed is a Scotch pine.

41. Ostensive

42. A mouse is either a small rodent or a device for moving the cursor across a computer monitor.

42. Lexical

43. I mean by "cool" what my parents meant by "groovy."

43. Stipulative

44. The horn on the car is to be used to get the attention of people and creatures who otherwise might venture in front of the oncoming vehicle.

44. Functional

8.2 INFORMAL FALLACIES

Inferences are created to offer evidence for a conclusion. As we have seen throughout the text, premises can fail to support conclusions for a variety of reasons. Some special cases of failure have been given names and have been classified as *fallacies*. The two basic kinds of fallacies are *formal fallacies* and *informal fallacies*.

Formal fallacies are logical errors that occur in the structure or form of an inference. They are restricted to deductive inferences and an understanding of deductive analysis and logical form makes it possible to recognize and understand these fallacies. Two kinds of formal fallacies were introduced in Chapter 4—the fallacy of affirming the consequent and the fallacy of denying the antecedent. (Formal fallacies were discussed again in Chapter 6.)

Informal fallacies are mistakes in reasoning that are different from errors in the form or structure of an inference. These errors include, but are not limited to, mistakes of *ambiguity, unwarranted assumption,* and *relevance*. These three classifications are used simply as an aid in recognizing similarities among fallacies ("family resemblance"), and not as a rigid method of categorization. The mistakes that occur in informal fallacies are not always easy to spot. A subtle change in the meaning of words, a shift in the reference of names, or a hidden irrelevancy are just a few of the many ways we can be fooled by fallacious inferences. In addition, fallacies sometimes rely on psychological powers of persuasion, involving fear, anger, pity, or even admiration.

Fallacies of Ambiguity

Fallacies of ambiguity occur when the meaning of terms or phrases is changed (intentionally or unintentionally) within the inference. Such fallacies tend to depend on the fact that there are typically many different meanings of individual words or phrases. Since context is crucial for determining meaning, a word or phrase used in a premise may shift its meaning when placed in a different context in the conclusion.

Formal fallacies: Reasoning errors that occur in the structure or form of an inference. They are restricted to deductive inferences.

Informal fallacies: Specific kinds of errors in the content of an inference, not in the structure. These errors include, but are not limited to, mistakes of ambiguity, unwarranted assumption, and relevance.

Fallacy of ambiguity: Fallacies that occur when the meaning of terms or phrases is changed (intentionally or unintentionally) within the inference.

Whenever possible, the meaning of terms in statements, and especially in inferences, must be as clear as possible. Ambiguity, vagueness, or any unclear use of a term can seriously affect the understanding, analysis, and evaluation of an inference. Examples and analysis of seven kinds of fallacies of ambiguity will be presented: *equivocation, amphiboly, composition, division, emphasis, straw man,* and *red herring.*

1. *Equivocation* The most direct use of ambiguity occurs when words are used *equivocally,* when we intentionally or unintentionally use different meanings of the same words or phrases in the course of a single inference. For example, someone might say the following:

> My older brother tries hard to be cool. I told him he has the personality of a cucumber. Since a refrigerator is a good place to keep things cool, he should spend some time there.

The word "cool" obviously has numerous meanings that tend to sort themselves out in the context of particular sentences. To shift the meaning of a term during the course of an inference is to commit the **fallacy of equivocation.**

Equivocation can also occur when "relative" terms are misused. For example:

> I was told that he is a Big-Man-on-Campus (BMOC). But look at him; he's no more than 5'7" tall.

"Big" is a good example of a relative term. In the above example the equivocation is compounded by the fact that the "big" in BMOC does not refer to the height of the person. Here are other examples of this fallacy:

> Judy said she had a hot date last night. The air conditioning in her apartment must not have been working.

> That looks like a hard outfit to get into. Maybe you should wash it in some fabric softener.

The world of politics offers numerous examples of equivocation. A major issue discussed quite often during presidential campaigns is the issue of employment. For example, a recent administration had to respond to data that indicated a huge loss of manufacturing jobs during its time in office. To counteract the statistics showing a net loss of jobs, the administration proposed that some fast-food workers should be reclassified from "service workers" to "manufacturing workers." Under the new definition, instead of merely "flipping burgers," anyone who cooked a burger, placed it on a bun, added condiments, and put it in a wrapper, was engaged in "manufacturing a product." This proposal would have ensured that instead of a loss of manufacturing jobs, there would have been a gain in manufacturing jobs over the previous four years. Of course, once the opposing political party found out about the idea, it was quickly dropped.

During an earlier administration a similar idea was hatched. The federal government normally defines as "unemployed" only those people who are actively collecting government unemployment checks. Under this definition people who have either exhausted their checks or are on welfare are not considered unemployed. The unemployment rate is then calculated by finding the number of unemployed and comparing this with the total number of those employed. In addition, the entire military was *not* used in the calculation of the unemployment rate. In other words, they were considered neither employed nor unemployed. Again, just before a presidential election, a scheme was hatched to change the status of the military personnel. It was proposed that all active military personnel should be considered "employed." This would have seriously affected the unemployment rate in favor of the incumbent administration. Once again the idea was exposed and subsequently abandoned.

2. Amphiboly Amphiboly is ambiguity that arises most commonly from poor grammar or syntax. Mistakes of interpretation can occur when the grammar or syntax of a statement muddles the intended meaning. Poorly constructed sentences can also cause misunderstandings. Confused grammar can allow premises and a conclusion to appear to be true, because two different interpretations are being used. If we retain one meaning throughout the inference, we can usually spot the mistake. The following are some examples of statements whose grammatical structure causes misunderstanding.

> He was shot in the train in the back in the sleeping car.
>
> She watched the monkey eating a banana.
>
> Sipping on cold coffee, the corpse lay in front of the tired detective.
>
> Cursing his bad luck, the DVD player refused to work for Eddie.

An amphibolous occurrence relies on the confusion caused by grammatical errors. For example:

> Person A: "In my backyard, a bird did not see my cat hunched on all fours ready to pounce, but suddenly he flew away."
>
> Person B: "I didn't know cats could fly."

3. Composition In the **fallacy of composition**, an attribute of the individual parts of an object is mistakenly transferred to the entire object. For example, suppose someone said of a 7-foot-tall basketball player:

> All the cells in his body are tiny. Thus, he is tiny.

The mistake is taking an attribute that is true of the parts and erroneously applying it to the whole. The fallacy can also occur when the conclusion is merely in doubt. For example:

> The bricks in this building are sturdy, so the building must be sturdy.

Even if it is true that the individual bricks are sturdy (the premise), the building may or may not be sturdy (the conclusion). Following are three other examples of the fallacy of composition:

> The thread you are using is easily torn, so the garment you are making will be easily torn.
>
> Each ingredient you are using tastes delicious. Therefore, the cake has to taste delicious.
>
> I understand every word in the poem, so I must understand what the poet is getting at.

Amphiboly: Mistakes of interpretation that occur when poor grammar or syntax muddle the intended meaning of a statement.

Fallacy of composition: The mistaken transfer of an attribute of the individual parts of an object to the object as a whole.

Distributive: When a characteristic (a predicate term) is used in a statement to refer to the individual members of a group of objects, not to the group as a whole.

Collective: When a characteristic (a predicate term) is used in a statement to refer to a group of objects as a whole, not to the individual members of the group.

We must be careful not to misapply this fallacy. Not every inference that reasons from parts to a whole is fallacious. For example:

> Every thread of material of which this shirt is composed is red, so the shirt is red.

This inference does not commit the fallacy of composition; in fact, it is a strong inference. Here is another example of a legitimate use of composition:

> Since every piece of my sewing machine is made of steel, it follows that my sewing machine is steel.

A comparison of the fallacious examples with the legitimate ones clearly shows that informal fallacies are not mistakes in the structure of an inference. The context in which we find an inference, together with our knowledge of specific facts of the world, are often needed to distinguish fallacious from nonfallacious informal inferences.

All of the examples of the composition fallacy that we have looked at so far have concerned a possible mistaken identity of parts of an object with the whole object (a body, a building, a garment, a cake, and a poem). However, another kind of composition fallacy occurs when the attributes of individual members of a class are mistakenly applied to the class itself (the collection of objects). This mistake occurs when we confuse the *distributive* and *collective* use of terms. **Distributive** refers to the individual members of a group. In the statement, "Motorcycles are noisy," the predicate term "noisy" is being used *distributively* to refer to the individual members of the class "motorcycles." **Collective** refers to the group as a whole. In the statement "Motorcycles make up only 5 percent of all vehicles on U.S. roadways," the predicate "make up only 5 percent of all vehicles on U.S. roadways" is being used *collectively* to refer to the class "motorcycles," not to individual motorcycles.

> ### Strategy
>
> When a statement contains a term that refers to a group of objects, make sure to determine whether the term is being used in a collective or a distributive sense.

This type of composition fallacy is revealed in the following inference:

> More noise is produced by a motorcycle than by a car. Therefore, more noise is produced on U.S. roadways by motorcycles than by cars.

4. Division In the **fallacy of division**, an attribute of an object as a whole is mistakenly transferred to its individual parts. The fallacy of division is the opposite of the fallacy of composition. For example, suppose someone said of a 7-foot-tall basketball player:

> He is huge, so he must have huge cells.

Fallacy of division: The mistaken transfer of an attribute of an object as a whole to its individual parts. Division is the direct opposite of composition.

The mistake is taking an attribute that is true of the whole object and erroneously applying it to the parts that make up the object. Here are other examples of the fallacy:

> She is intelligent, so she must have smart brain cells.
>
> The garment is strong, so the individual threads must be strong.
>
> The cake tastes burnt, so you must have used burnt ingredients.

As with the fallacy of composition, we must be careful not to misapply the fallacy of division. Not every inference that reasons from the whole object to its parts is fallacious. For example:

> That is a wooden chair, so the legs are made of wood.

This inference does not commit the fallacy of division; in fact, it is a strong inference. Here is another example of a legitimate use of division:

> The book he is reading is made of paper. Therefore, the pages of the book are made of paper.

All the examples of the fallacy so far have concerned a possible mistaken identity of an object (a body, a person's intelligence, a garment, and a cake) with the parts of the object. However, a second kind of division fallacy (which is similar to the second kind of composition fallacy) occurs when attributes of a class (a *collection* of objects) are mistakenly applied to the individual members of that class. As before, the mistake occurs when the distributive and collective uses of terms are confused. In the statement, "Bald eagles are disappearing," the predicate "disappearing" is being used *collectively* to refer to the class "bald eagles," not to individual members of the class. The second type of division fallacy can now be recognized in the following inference:

> My teacher said that bald eagles are disappearing. I remember seeing a bald eagle down at the zoo. Let's hurry down to see it before it disappears.

5. *Emphasis* Fallacies of emphasis can occur when attention is purposely diverted from the original issue at hand, and statements or inferences intending one thing are subtly distorted in order to shift the emphasis to another issue. The use of emphasis occurs in everyday conversation as well. For example, this discussion might occur regarding someone's knowledge of a subject:

Jenn: He did win an Academy Award for best actor.

Jess: You might think he did, but you're wrong.

Jenn: I don't think, I know.

Jess: I don't think you know either.

Jess twists the meaning of a key phrase by changing the emphasis of Jenn's claim. This emphasis seems to refute Jenn's claim of knowledge. The same kind of mistake occurs in the next passage:

Mary Lynn: Lee Ann, you will wash the car this afternoon.

Lee Ann: I will?

Mary Lynn: I'm glad you agree.

Lee Ann's question is turned into an assertion by Mary Lynn's change of emphasis. Although these particular verbal changes are fairly easy to spot, they nevertheless reveal the possibility of altering meaning by shifting emphasis at a key point.

6. *Straw Man Fallacy* There are two major kinds of fallacies of emphasis. The first, called the **straw man fallacy**, is a common, but powerful, form of emphasis that often occurs when someone's written or spoken words are taken out of context, thereby purposely distorting the original inference. This effectively creates a

Fallacy of emphasis: A fallacy that occurs when attention is diverted away from the original issue at hand, allowing a change in the intent of a statement or an inference.

Straw man fallacy: A form of fallacy of emphasis in which someone's written or spoken words are taken out of context, thereby purposely distorting the original inference in such a way that the new, weak inference (the straw man) is easy to defeat.

new inference, which is deliberately made weak so that it can be easily refuted. The new inference is "made of straw," meaning that it can be easily knocked down and destroyed. This is a tactic common in the political arena. Candidates distort the views of their opponents by clipping a small piece out of a speech or interview. By taking it out of context, the artificial emphasis put on a word or phrase might give an impression directly opposite from that of the original. For example, a person running for public office might say the following:

> I oppose the recent law that requires teaching intelligent design as an alternative to evolutionary theory in public schools' biology classes. Evolution is an established scientific theory and deserves to be taught in a science class. Intelligent design is not a scientific theory, and it should not be taught in a science class.

An opponent of this candidate might criticize her position by saying the following:

> She is against the newly passed law that mandates teaching intelligent design alongside the theory of evolution in biology classes. It should be obvious to anyone that what she really wants to do is to eliminate all religious beliefs. In effect, she wants us to destroy one of the basics principles of the Constitution of the United States.

Distortions of this kind are not limited to politics. It is not difficult to extract various passages from a book or article and make it appear that the author is contradicting himself or herself. Placing emphasis on a passage taken out of context or giving a partial quote can seriously affect the intended meaning.

7. Red Herring Fallacy The second type of fallacy of emphasis is called the *red herring*. The **red herring fallacy** occurs when someone completely ignores their opponent's position and changes the subject by diverting the discussion in a new direction. For example:

> Many people criticize TV as being the major cause of America becoming an effectively illiterate society. How can we criticize the very medium that is the envy of countries all over the world? The entertainment quality and variety of TV programs today is greater than ever, not to mention the enormous number of cable options available to members of the viewing audience.

Rather than presenting evidence against the claim that TV is a major cause of illiteracy in the United States, the passage shifts the emphasis to the "entertainment" value of TV.

A few years ago, a photograph purported to show that Jose Santos, the jockey of Kentucky Derby winner Funny Cide, was carrying an illegal object. The picture showed a dark spot in Santos' hand. It was concluded by some that a "battery" was used to provide an electrical shock through the whip causing the horse to run faster. But those who emphasized the dark spot for their conclusion de-emphasized or overlooked the film of the race. The stretch run of the race clearly shows Santos switching hands with his whip more than once. One commentator remarked that holding a battery while performing these tricky maneuvers would make Santos one of the world's best magicians. The officials in charge of the investigation announced that a thorough analysis of all the available information completely exonerated jockey Santos.

Quick Reference 8.2 summarizes the fallacies of ambiguity.

Red herring fallacy: A form of the fallacy of emphasis that occurs when someone completely ignores the opponent's position and diverts the discussion in a new direction.

Quick Reference 8.2 • Fallacies of Ambiguity

Fallacies of ambiguity

1. **Equivocation:** The intentional or unintentional use of different meanings of words or phrases in an inference.
2. **Amphiboly:** Mistakes of interpretation can occur when the grammar or syntax of a statement muddles the intended meaning.
3. **Composition:** The mistaken transfer of an attribute of the individual parts of an object to the object as a whole.
4. **Division:** The mistaken transfer an attribute of an object as a whole to its individual parts.
5. **Emphasis:** Fallacies that occur when attention is diverted away from the original issue at hand, allowing a change in the intent of a statement or an inference.
6. **Straw man:** A form of fallacy of emphasis that occurs when someone's written or spoken words are taken out of context, thereby purposely distorting the original inference and creating a new, weak inference that can be easily refuted (a straw man that is easily knocked down).
7. **Red herring:** A form of the fallacy of emphasis that occurs when someone completely ignores the opponent's position and changes the subject by diverting the discussion in a new direction.

> In a fallacy of ambiguity the meaning of a term or phrase changes within an inference.

EXERCISE SET 8.2A

Exercises 1–8 Decide whether the statement is true or false.

1. The fallacy of composition occurs when an attribute of the individual parts of an object are transferred to the entire object.

Answer: True. The fallacy of composition occurs by the mistaken transfer of an attribute of the individual parts of an object to the object as a whole.

2. The red herring fallacy occurs when someone's words are taken out of context to create an inference that distorts the person's position. False

3. A mistake of interpretation that occurs because of the grammar or syntax of a statement is called the fallacy of emphasis. False

4. A fallacy of equivocation can only happen if the inference intentionally uses different meanings of words or phrases. False

5. A straw man fallacy changes the subject by diverting the discussion in a new direction. False

*6. To mistakenly transfer an attribute of the individual parts of an object to the entire object is to commit the fallacy of division. False

Exercises 2–8: For answers and explanations, see page 247 of Instructor's Manual.

7. A fallacy of emphasis occurs when a word has a different meaning in the premises than it has in the conclusion. False

8. A fallacy of equivocation mistakenly transfers an attribute of the individual parts of an object to the entire object. False

Exercises 9–36 Each of the following passages contains a fallacy of ambiguity. Determine the fallacy that best fits each case. Explain your answer.

9. Each grain of sand is hard, so your sand castle will be hard.

Answer: Composition. An attribute of the individual parts of an object is mistakenly transferred to the entire object.

Exercises 10–36: For answers and explanations, see pages 247–248 of Instructor's Manual.

10. *Sam:* I think you broke my watch.
    Joe: I did?
    Sam: Well since you admit it, now I know you did it. Emphasis

11. He's a real pain the neck. Cortisone shots help relieve neck pain. Maybe a good dose of cortisone will change his attitude. Equivocation

12. She is very beautiful. I bet even her appendix is lovely. Division

13. Just waiting to be eaten, he noticed the cake in the corner. Amphiboly

*14. My father said that the Super Bowl half-time show was a real disaster. That's interesting because I read in the newspaper that the Federal government has relief funds available for victims of disasters. So, maybe my dad can apply for some relief funds. Equivocation

15. If you are going to have that fruit juice tomorrow morning, then you better start shaking the bottle right now. I read the label, and it recommends that you shake the contents well before using. Emphasis

16. I read that cars in the United States consume more gasoline each year than trucks. I guess that means that my car uses more gasoline each year than that tractor-trailer over there. Division

17. I know for a fact that the acrylic paints that Van Gogh used to create this portrait were very inexpensive. So, even though his painting is hanging in a museum, it can't be very expensive. Composition

18. I heard that he got injured in that building in the rear. Amphiboly

*19. My mother, a professional poker player, always told me that having one pair is better than nothing. Of course, in the game of poker nothing beats a royal flush. So it follows that my one pair beats your royal flush. Equivocation

20. He said that walking around the corner the Eiffel Tower suddenly took his breath away. I didn't know those famous Parisian landmarks roamed the streets. Amphiboly

21. According to the census data the population of that city is 10 percent atheists. My Uncle Sam lives there, so he must be 10 percent atheist. Division

22. In physics class we learned that elementary particles have little or no mass. My $150 physics textbook is made up of elementary particles, thus it has little or no mass. Composition

23. I hear that Walter is handling some hot stocks right now. The new asbestos gloves I bought protect your hands from hot objects. Maybe I should give them to Walter for protection.   23. Equivocation

*24. Sitting in the front seat of the car the cow stared intently into Jim's eyes. Of course, from this we can conclude that it was a very large car indeed.   24. Amphiboly

25. My mother wants me to take piano lessons because studies show that early music training helps students in math. But pianos cost a lot of money and even if we could afford one our apartment is too small to put in a full-size piano.   25. Red herring

26. Evolution is a biological law of nature. All civilized people should obey the law. Therefore, all civilized people should obey the law of evolution.   26. Equivocation

27. Chicken eggs do not weigh very much. So if I eat an omelet made from 50 eggs it will not weigh very much.   27. Composition

28. My boss caught me playing video games on my office computer during work hours. He said that it was a violation of office policies and he warned me to stop or I would be fired. Pretty soon he will try to eliminate coffee breaks or even going to the bathroom. He doesn't have the right to take away all my benefits.   28. Straw man

*29. The sign says that there is no mass on Sunday. But my science teacher said that mass is the same as energy. So I guess there is no energy on Sunday either.   29. Equivocation

30. Sitting in from of the open window the freshly mowed grass satisfied Robert.   30. Amphiboly

31. Each page of the encyclopedia weighs practically nothing, so the encyclopedia weighs practically nothing.   31. Composition

32. You have chosen great paint colors; therefore your house will look great.   32. Composition

*33. *Walter:* You will help me with my homework.
    Sandy: I will?
    Walter: I knew you would cooperate.   33. Emphasis

34. That comedian is a real ham. Of course, ham and eggs are good for breakfast. So, if that comedian added some eggs to his act, it would make a good breakfast.   34. Equivocation

35. The house is poorly constructed, so the material it is made of must be poorly constructed as well.   35. Division

36. The stone hit the window. The force broke it into a thousand pieces.   36. Amphiboly

Fallacies of Unwarranted Assumption

Fallacies of unwarranted assumption exhibit a special kind of reasoning error. Inferences that *assume* the truth of some unproved or questionable claim do not provide good support for the conclusion. The mistake occurs because of the tacit assumption of a claim that either has not been supported or cannot be supported. The fallacy becomes apparent when the assumption and lack of support are exposed. Examples and analysis of ten kinds of fallacies of unwarranted assumption will be presented: *begging the question, complex question, hasty generalization, biased sample, hasty application of a generalization, fake precision, coincidence, post hoc, common cause,* and *slippery slope.*

Fallacy of unwarranted assumption: A fallacy in which the truth of some unproved or questionable claim is assumed; such a claim does not provide good support for the conclusion.

Begging the question:
An inference that assumes as evidence in the premises the very thing that it attempts to prove in the conclusion.

8. *Begging the Question* In the **fallacy of begging the question**, the inference assumes as evidence the very thing that it attempts to prove in a conclusion. In begging the question, also called *circular reasoning*, the conclusion of an inference is smuggled into the premises. This can occur if the premises are confusing, complex, or obscure. It can even occur if the conclusion is assumed as an undeclared premise. Circular reasoning often goes unnoticed because it sounds so convincing. This should not be surprising. Since the conclusion is already assumed in the premises, it will be a trivially valid inference.

Consider this inference:

> Jane K. has the highest GPA among all the seniors in my school. There are 300 graduating seniors in my class. Therefore, no senior has higher grades than she does.

The conclusion is already assumed in the premise, it is merely worded differently. *If* the claim is true in the premise, it will be true in the conclusion. The inference begs the question because it assumes what it intends to prove. Here is another example:

> Since I stopped exercising and began eating junk food I have really got out of shape. My wife wants me to start exercising, but if I do, I'm liable to injure myself because I'm way out of condition.

The justification for the inactivity is provided by the assumption of the very fact the speaker wants to prove.

9. *Complex Question* The **fallacy of complex question** occurs when a single question actually contains multiple, hidden parts. The questioner tries to force a single answer that, in turn, is used against the respondent. For example, suppose someone is asked,

> Do you still cheat on your taxes?

Answering *yes* or *no* presupposes that you did, in fact, cheat on your taxes. The key word that creates the complex question is "still." If a person who never cheated on his taxes answers "No," he would be admitting that he once did cheat on his taxes but no longer does. Therefore, the questioner can use this as evidence to support the conclusion that the person cheated on his taxes.

The ability to recognize that there are actually two questions at work here allows us to avoid the trap of the complex question. Buried in the complex question are these two distinct questions: (1) "Did you ever cheat on your taxes?" and (2) "Do you now cheat on your taxes?" Once the questions are separated, an innocent person can answer "No" to both questions, thus defusing any possible misunderstanding.

Complex questions can be used to trap us in unacceptable situations. For example, suppose someone asks,

> Aren't you going to do something about your child's terrible behavior?

Fallacy of complex question:
A single question that actually contains multiple, hidden parts.

This complex question presupposes the following: (1) that you agree that your child's behavior needs correcting, and (2) that you are going to correct it. Therefore, if you answer "Yes" to the complex question you have admitted the child's behavior needs correcting. However, if you answer "No" to the complex question then you have, once again, admitted the behavior needs correcting, but that you are not going to do anything about it.

10. *Hasty Generalization* Fallacies can occur from the mistaken application of generalizations. For example, it is not unusual for someone to have a few negative experiences with members of a particular group and then quickly *stereotype* (generalize about) that group, assigning derogatory characteristics to the entire group. However, it is improbable that such a small sample will be representative of an entire group of humans. Any inference that concludes with a judgment about the members of a population based on a few experiences would be terribly weak. This is an example of the **fallacy of hasty generalization**, and it occurs whenever a generalization is created on the basis of a few instances. For example, consider this inference:

> I ate two grapes from that bunch and they were both sweet. Therefore, all the grapes in the bunch are sweet.

We are not justified in saying all or most members of a class of objects have a certain characteristic simply because the characteristic was observed in a few members of the class. Here is another example:

> The first two students whose exams I graded each got an "A." Thus, I expect all 50 students in the class to get "A's" on the exam.

The teacher is probably being overly optimistic. Although it is possible that all 50 students will get an "A" on the exam, the fallacy of hasty generalization is apparent in this case, since the conclusion is an unwarranted generalization created on the basis of a few instances.

11. *Biased Sample* In a **fallacy of biased sample**, an inference uses a biased, nonrepresentative, sample as support for a statistical claim about an entire population. (A representative sample occurs when the characteristics of a sample are correctly identified and matched to the population under investigation. A detailed explanation of statistical inferences can be found in Chapter 9.) For example, consider this inference:

> A sample of Catholics reveals that 85 percent believe that abortion is morally wrong. Therefore, the evidence shows that approximately 85% of all Americans believe that abortion is morally wrong.

The sample surveyed only Catholics, but the conclusion generalizes to *all* Americans. This illustrates how any sample that, intentionally or unintentionally, excludes segments of the entire population results in a nonrepresentative sample, and commits the fallacy of biased sample.

Here is another example:

> A survey of 100 seniors at our university showed that 90 percent do not oppose a parking fee increase. Therefore, we can report that nearly all the students do not oppose a parking fee increase.

The sample surveyed only seniors at the university, but the conclusion generalizes to *all* students. Since seniors are unlikely to be affected by an increase in parking fees, the sample intentionally, or unintentionally, excluded segments of the entire population. The resulting biased sample does not provide good evidence to support the conclusion.

Fallacy of hasty generalization: A fallacy in which a generalization is created on the basis of a few instances.

Fallacy of biased sample: An inference that uses a sample that intentionally or unintentionally excludes segments of the population as support for a statistical claim about the entire population.

Fallacy of hasty application of a generalization: A fallacy that occurs when a generalization is inappropriately applied to a particular case because of a failure to recognize that most generalizations have exceptions.

Fallacy of fake precision: When a claim appears to be statistically significant, but upon analysis, is shown not to be.

12. *Hasty Application of a Generalization* The **fallacy of hasty application of a generalization** arises when a generalization is inappropriately applied to a particular case because of a failure to recognize that most generalizations have exceptions. An exception is a special case, one that does not fall under the general rule. We often make allowances for special circumstances that permit breaking a rule. Therefore, to rigidly apply an otherwise acceptable generalization, even in the face of known and understood exceptions, is to commit the fallacy of the hasty application of a generalization. For example, suppose someone says the following:

> I can't believe that the police didn't give that ambulance any citations. It was speeding, it went through a red light, and it swerved from lane to lane without using any signals.

It is true that under normal circumstances the driving behavior of the ambulance would be subject to penalties, but exceptions apply to ambulances, fire trucks, and the police when they are responding to emergencies. Also, you probably would be excused if you had to rush a seriously injured person to the hospital. Therefore, the speaker in the above example has rigidly applied an otherwise acceptable generalization in the face of known and accepted exceptions.

13. *Fake Precision* Fallacies of fake precision occur when a claim is made that appears to be statistically significant, but which, upon analysis, is not. There are many instances where statistics are used to support claims that are, in fact, unjustified. It is not hard to find advertisements making the following claims:

> Our cookies contain 30 percent less fat.
>
> In order to clear out our inventory we have reduced our used car prices by 20 percent.

On the other hand, a seemingly scientific claim might look like the following:

> The full moon affects people in strange ways. We have found that you have a 100 percent greater chance of being physically assaulted during a full moon than at any other time of the month.

But do these claims stand up under scrutiny? In the first example, it is fair to ask the question, "30 percent less fat *than what*?" The alleged percentage is relative to some other item, and we need to know what that is in order to know if this product is really significantly lower in fat than competing products of the same type. In the second example, we need to ask the question, "reduced by 20 percent *from what*?" The car dealership might have used an outdated mark-up price no longer in effect in order to get the artificial reduction. They might have recently tried raising the cost of their used cars and if sales were slow, they simply returned the car prices to their previous level. For the third example, we need to know the rate of physical assault for the entire population. It might turn out that the physical assault rate during the month is 2 out of every 10,000 persons. The full moon rate would then be 4 out of every 10,000 persons. Although according to these figures you do have a 100 percent greater chance of being physically assaulted during a full moon, nevertheless the greater "chance" is *not* statistically significant. These are all examples of the fallacy of fake precision, whereby some claims that use statistical information are not justified. Whenever statistics are used without a reference or comparison group, you should try to determine if this is an instance of fake precision.

The *fallacies of false cause* are a special subset of fallacies of unwarranted assumption. These fallacies include *coincidence, post hoc, common cause,* and *slippery slope fallacies.*

Cause-effect patterns help us to understand the world and to predict future events. However, **fallacies of false cause** occur when a causal connection is assumed to exist between two events when none actually exists. Since causal claims require strong evidence, to base a cause-effect claim on insufficient evidence is to commit the fallacy of false cause. (A detailed explanation of cause-effect relationships can be found in Chapter 9.)

Consider the following inference:

> I told you not to trust him. After all, he was born under the sign of Aquarius in the year of the Rabbit. He can't help himself, the stars dictate his behavior.

Astrology places human behavior under the influence of the planets and stars. It claims that we are causally connected to astral influences that occurred at the time of our birth and continue throughout our lives. Of course these causal claims do not have any credible scientific evidence in their support; they are based mostly on anecdotal evidence. In addition, the general personality traits associated with astrology can be applied to anyone.

Examples and analysis of four specific kinds of fallacies of false cause will be presented: *coincidence, post hoc, common cause,* and *slippery slope.*

Fallacy of false cause: A fallacy in which a causal connection between two events is claimed when none exists.

Strategy

Be sure to ascertain whether an inference contains an assumption that a causal connection exists between two events when in fact no connection exists.

14. *Coincidence* A special kind of false cause fallacy, the **fallacy of coincidence**, results from the accidental or chance connection between two events. For example, suppose someone says the following:

> Last week I dreamed that my cousin Charlie was in a terrible car wreck, and just now I got a phone call from his wife saying that he is in the hospital because he was in a car accident.

If someone dreams that a relative or friend is injured or dies and a similar event actually happens, then the dream might be interpreted as being *caused* by the future event. However, a belief in backwards causality (a future event causing the present dream) violates a fundamental principle: *causes must precede effects.* Additionally, the coincidence can be explained by recognizing that we have thousands of dreams a year, a few of which are bound to resemble real events. Also, if we consider that the vast majority of dreams do not connect to real events, then we can understand that coincidences will occasionally happen.

Fallacy of coincidence: A special kind of false cause fallacy that results from the accidental or chance connection between two events.

***Post hoc* fallacy:** A type of false cause fallacy involving a short-term pattern that is noticed after the fact. Also called *post hoc, ergo propter hoc* ("after the fact, therefore because of the fact").

15. *Post Hoc Fallacy* Another type of false cause fallacy, called ***post hoc***, concerns a short-term pattern that is noticed *after the fact.* (The full name of this type of fallacy is "*post hoc, ergo propter hoc*," which means "after the fact, therefore *because* of the fact.") It is not unusual for someone to find a short or long term pattern and to make a causal connection between two things. For example, we might read the following:

> Researchers have discovered that for over 30 years there has been a definite pattern connecting the party affiliation of the U.S. President and specific soft drink sales. During the years when a Democrat was president, Morphacola topped all soft-drink sales. However, when a Republican was president, *Opacola* was number one in sales. If you are an investor, we advise you to put your money on the soft-drink company based on who is in the White House.

It seems clear that a cause-effect relationship is being asserted. Fallacies of this type can be persuasive, because *unlike a mere coincidence*, a regular pattern seems to have emerged. However, without providing the necessary apparatus to support a true causal claim, inferences that use *post hoc* reasoning fall prey to the mistake of confusing a correlation with a cause.

16. *Common Cause Fallacy* The **common cause fallacy** occurs when one event is believed to cause a second event when, in fact, both events are the result of a common cause. For example, someone might claim that the barometer falling below a certain point is the cause of a storm, when in fact both events are caused by a change in atmospheric pressure. The following illustration reveals the common cause fallacy.

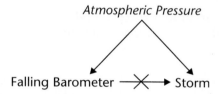

The two downward arrows indicate that the atmospheric pressure is the *common cause* of both the falling barometer and the storm. The arrow with the large "X" through it shows the fallacious cause-effect claim.

Another example of the fallacy occurs when someone mistakenly thinks that a rash they are experiencing is causing them to have a fever. It is quite possible that both the rash and the fever have a common cause, a virus.

Common cause fallacy:
A fallacy that occurs when one event is thought to cause another event, when in fact both events are the result of a common cause.

Slippery slope fallacy:
An inference that attempts to make a final event the inevitable outcome of an initial act.

17. *Slippery Slope* Some complex inferences attempt to link events in such a way as to create a chain reaction. The idea is to create a series of occurrences whereby the first link in a chain leads directly to the next, and so on, until the final result is achieved. A **slippery slope fallacy** attempts to make a final event the inevitable outcome of an initial act. We are then urged to stop the chain reaction before it has a chance to begin, by preventing the first act from ever happening. For example, consider the following inference:

> If you start smoking marijuana for pleasure, then you will need more and more to achieve the expected high. You will begin to rely on it whenever you feel depressed. Eventually you will experiment with more powerful

drugs that act faster and last longer. Of course, the amount of drug intake will have to increase to achieve the desired results. At this point, the addiction will take hold and will lead to a loss of ambition, a loss of self-esteem, the destruction of your health, and the dissolution of all social ties.

Slippery slope inferences rely on a kind of causal network where each step in the chain causes the next step. However, the "inevitability" of the final act needs to be supported by providing specific objective evidence for the supposed causal network. Each link requires relevant evidence for its connection to the next link in the chain. Until this is objectively established, the inference need not be accepted.

Quick Reference 8.3 • Fallacies of Unwarranted Assumption

8. ***Begging the question:*** An inference that assumes as evidence in the premises the very thing that it attempts to prove in the conclusion.

9. ***Complex question:*** A single question that actually contains multiple, hidden parts.

10. ***Hasty generalization:*** A generalization created on the basis of a few instances.

11. ***Biased sample:*** An inference that uses a biased sample as support for a statistical claim about an entire population. A sample is biased if it leaves out members of a subset of the population that will be mentioned in the conclusion.

12. ***Hasty application of a generalization:*** To apply rigidly an otherwise acceptable generalization, even in the face of known and understood exceptions.

13. ***Fake precision:*** When a claim is made that appears to be statistically significant, but which, upon analysis, is not.

14. ***Coincidence:*** A special kind of false cause that results from the accidental or chance connection between two events.

15. ***Post hoc:*** A type of false cause fallacy involving a short-term pattern that is noticed after the fact. This type of false cause fallacy is also called *post hoc, ergo propter hoc* ("after the fact, therefore because of the fact").

16. ***Common cause:*** A type of mistake that occurs when someone thinks that one event causes another when in fact both events are the result of a common cause.

17. ***Slippery slope:*** An inference that attempts to make a final event the inevitable outcome of an initial act. Slippery slope inferences rely on a kind of causal network where each step in the chain causes the next step. However, the "inevitability" of the final act needs to be supported by specific evidence for the supposed causal network. Each link requires relevant evidence for its connection to the next link in the chain.

> Fallacies of unwarranted assumption are reasoning errors in which an unproved or questionable claim is assumed to be true.

EXERCISE SET 8.2B   ○○○

Exercises 1–10 Decide whether the statement is true or false.

Exercises 2–10: For answers and explanations, see page 248 of Instructor's Manual.

1. A complex question is a single question that actually contains multiple, hidden parts.

   Answer: True.

2. False

2. A hasty generalization occurs whenever a generalization leaves out members of a subset of the population that will be mentioned in the conclusion.

3. True

3. A claim that appears to be statistically significant but which, upon analysis, is not, is an example of fake precision.

4. False

4. A coincidence is a special type of false cause involving a short-term pattern noticed after the fact.

5. True

5. A biased sample leaves out members of a subset of the population that will be mentioned in the conclusion.

6. False

*6. An inference that attempts to make a final event the inevitable outcome of an initial act is called *post hoc.*

7. False

7. To rigidly apply an otherwise acceptable generalization, even in the face of known and understood exceptions, is to commit the fallacy of common cause.

8. True

8. An inference that assumes as evidence the very thing that it attempts to prove in the conclusion begs the question.

9. False

9. A slippery slope fallacy involves a short-term pattern noticed after the fact.

10. False

10. A claim that appears to be statistically significant but which, upon analysis, is not, is the fallacy of hasty application of a generalization.

Exercises 11–40 Each of the following passages contains a *fallacy of unwarranted assumption.* Determine the fallacy that best fits each case. Explain your answer.

Exercises 12–40: For answers and explanations, see pages 248–249 of Instructor's Manual.

11. Do you still plagiarize your research papers from the Internet?

    Answer: Complex Question. When a single question actually contains multiple (hidden) parts.

12. Begging the Question

12. This car gets the highest gas mileage of any car on the market. So, you can't buy a more fuel efficient car at any cost.

13. Complex Question

13. Have you ever stopped stealing money from your parents' wallets?

14. Begging the Question

14. That politician never tells the truth because every time he tries to explain why he did something wrong he fabricates a story.

15. Begging the Question

15. He is a very honest individual because he is not dishonest.

16. Begging the Question

*16. I have certain inalienable rights because they have never been taken away from me.

17. Begging the Question

17. Everything written in that book is 100 percent accurate. It has to be, since nothing in it is false.

18. Complex Question

18. Do you still look for discarded food in dumpsters?

19. That is the type of movie you hate; lots of jokes and slapstick. So, you will hate it.

                                                19. Begging the Question

20. That ambulance didn't even stop for the red light. It went zooming right through! If I did that, I would get a citation. Life just isn't fair.

   20. Hasty Application of a Generalization

*21. I met two people from that state and they both were rude. There must be something in the drinking water of that state that makes all the people from there so rude.

   21. Hasty Generalization

22. All the people in my fraternity think that hazing is not a problem. So, I'm sure that the entire student population agrees with us on this issue.

   22. Biased Sample

23. Last week's poll showed the incumbent Senator had 52 percent of the votes and the challenger had 48 percent. This week's poll shows the incumbent ahead 54 to 46. So, we can safely say that the incumbent will get at least 53 percent of the votes on election day.

   23. Fake Precision

24. Every football player at Crestfallen High School can run 2 miles in under 15 minutes. They have good physical education teachers, so the students at that school must be in great physical condition.

   24. Biased Sample

25. When I need to travel to another city I have to buy my own airplane ticket. The president has Air Force One to take him wherever he wants to go and he doesn't have to pay a penny. Why can't I have a deal like that?

   25. Hasty Application of a Generalization

*26. The label on that cheesecake says that it has 40 percent fewer calories. If I eat that cheesecake regularly, then I should lose some weight.

   26. Fake Precision

27. I don't recommend that you eat at that restaurant. I did not like the breakfast I had there last week. I'm sure that all of their meals are of poor quality.

   27. Hasty Generalization

28. That fire-engine was going over 60 mph in a 35 mph zone. The police should give the driver a ticket.

   28. Hasty Application of a Generalization

29. I had two station wagons and they both were lemons. I'm sure that there is something in the design of station wagons that makes them all terrible vehicles.

   29. Hasty Generalization

30. Ninety-five percent of a sample of registered Republicans in this state said that they will vote for the Republican nominee for Congress from their district. So, I predict that the Republican nominee will definitely get around 95 percent of the total vote this fall.

   30. Biased Sample

*31. The advertisement for that DVD player claims that it has 50 percent fewer moving parts. You should buy it; it is less likely to break down in the future.

   31. Fake Precision

32. My horoscope said I would meet someone new. Today my company hired a really good-looking sales person and we will be working closely together. Now do you see why I read my horoscope everyday?

   32. Coincidence

33. If you don't clean your room, then the dirt and dust will build up. Before you know it bacteria grow. Whatever you touch in your room will then spread bacteria, which will contaminate the entire house. We will all wind up in the hospital, terminally ill.

   33. Slippery Slope

34. On seven different occasions it rained the day after I washed my car. I washed my car today, so take your umbrella with you tomorrow.

   34. Post Hoc

35. She began making $100,000 the year after she graduated from college, and when she took an IQ test she scored 20 points higher than when she was in high school. See, I told you, money makes people smarter.   Common Cause

*36. My bill at the restaurant was $4.29. I played the number 429 on the lottery today and it came up. Therefore, it was my destiny to play that number today and win.   Coincidence

37. Every time the barometer drops below 30 it rains. It has some mysterious power over the weather, I guess.   Common Cause

38. For the last 50 years whenever the American League won the World Series there was a recession that year, but when the National League won stock prices went up. There must be some unknown economic force at work that we don't understand.   *Post Hoc*

39. If you drop out of one course this semester, you will have less than a full-time load. It will take you longer to graduate. It will delay your getting a job another year, meaning that you won't get promoted as fast as others who graduated on time. So, you can expect to lose approximately $100,000 during your lifetime.   Slippery Slope

40. Whenever I step in the shower either my phone rings or someone knocks on the door. I'll have to change my bathing habits, I suppose.   *Post Hoc*

Fallacies of Relevance

In **fallacies of relevance,** irrelevant premises are offered in support of a conclusion. Any inference that uses irrelevant premises in support of a conclusion suffers from serious reasoning flaws. Premises must be relevant; they must establish logical, reasonable ties to the conclusion. Many irrelevant premises rely on psychological or emotional appeal for their persuasive force.

18. *Ad hominem*   The truth of a statement and the strength of an inference should be judged on objective grounds. If a claim is judged to be false based on purported "character flaws" of the person making the claim, then we would be attacking the person, not the claim. Attacking a person rather than the person's assertions or inferences is commonly referred to by the Latin term *ad hominem* ("against the person"). Generally speaking, peoples' characters are irrelevant to the determination of the truth or falsity of their claims. An important exception to this rule occurs in sworn testimony. If someone has previously been exposed as a liar based on contradictions in statements given under oath, then certainly there are objective grounds for suspicion about any current or future statements.

Clear cases of *ad hominem* are not difficult to recognize. They involve the use of psychological powers of persuasion by diverting attention away from the objective truth or falsity of a claim and instead denigrating the character of the person making the claim. Here are some examples:

> Why should I believe what he says about our economy? He is not even a citizen.

> You can't accept her advice. She is so old she has no idea what goes on in today's world.

Fallacy of relevance: A fallacy in which the premises offered in support of the conclusion are irrelevant.

Ad hominem: Use of purported character flaws or circumstances of people's lives to reject their claims.

> Why would you listen to him? He's too young to have any wisdom
> about life.

In all the above cases, the reason to reject someone's statement or position is based on irrelevant information. Another common form of *ad hominem* occurs whenever someone's statement or reasoning is attacked by way of a stereotype (racial, sexual, etc.) A reference to any kind of stereotype is irrelevant to the determination of the truth or falsity of a person's claim or inference.

Another form of *ad hominem* fallacy involves the use of the circumstances of a person's life to reject his claims. *Circumstances* are different from *character*. For example, political affiliation, educational institution, place of birth, religious affiliation, and income are circumstances connected to peoples' lives. When we reject a claim by insinuating that someone's circumstances dictate the truth or falsity of the claim, then we are once again attacking the person rather than the claim. Here are some examples:

> Of course you think the current administration's tax proposals are bad for the country. Your political party lost the election and you will never support any proposal advocated by this administration.
>
> You don't want cars to get better gas mileage because you are stockholder in the three major gasoline companies.
>
> You are against euthanasia because you are a physician. You make money only if terminally ill people are kept alive as long as possible.

This type of fallacy resembles the use of circumstantial evidence in a trial. The guilt or innocence of a person should not rest merely on circumstantial evidence regarding their situation. Objective, credible evidence is the requirement in a court of law.

All fallacies of *against the person* (*ad hominem*) rest on the same kind of reasoning error: the rejection of a statement or inference because of criticism of a person's *character* or *circumstances*. In all cases, neither the truth of the claim nor the strength of the inference is ever considered on logical or factual grounds.

19. Tu Quoque A variety of the *ad hominem* fallacy known as **tu quoque** ("you're another" or "look who's talking") is distinguished by the specific attempt of one person to avoid the issue at hand by claiming the other person is a hypocrite. For example:

> You were a gang member and you never went to jail. So, let me make my own choice about joining a gang.

Another example comes from the political world. If a U.S. senator criticizes the human rights failings of China by offering a detailed description of recorded United Nations inquiries, a Chinese representative might say the following:

> The senator should look in his own backyard. What about the complete disregard of the universal rights of people who the U.S. government incarcerates without any recourse to courts or even to a lawyer? What about the United States policy of spying on its own citizens without a court order? The senator should not throw stones when he lives in a glass house. In many of his pronouncements the senator quotes from the Bible, so let me remind him "whoever is without sin let him cast the first stone."

Tu quoque: A variety of the *ad hominem* fallacy distinguished by the specific attempt of one person to avoid the issue at hand by claiming the other person is a hypocrite.

Appeal to emotion: An inference or claim that relies solely on the arousal of a strong emotional state or psychological reaction; such an inference ultimately relies on irrelevant support.

Other than stringing together a number of clichés this response offers no rational rebuttal of the assertions of human rights violations. Of course, the senator might respond with his own cliché – "Two wrongs don't make a right."

Instances of *tu quoque* fallacies occur quite often in personal arguments within families. For example, a child might say the following:

> Dad, I don't know why you keep pressuring me to give up smoking. You keep showing me statistics proving that smoking is bad for my health, that it will shorten my life, that it costs too much money. But you started smoking at my age and only recently quit. So, how can you honestly tell me to stop?

Since there are many good reasons to support the conclusion that someone should stop smoking, these reasons must be rationally argued against. To attack the person making the inference rather than the inference is to commit the fallacy.

20. *Appeal to Emotion* An inference or claim that relies *solely* on the arousal of a strong emotional state or psychological reaction ultimately relies on irrelevant support. In an **appeal to emotion,** the utter disregard of objective evidence in favor of an emotional response defeats the goal of a rational investigation of truth. This fallacious tactic has been used by tyrants and bigots throughout history, often with devastating social effects. It often appeals to a *mob mentality*, to an "us against them" attitude, with a fixation on fear and hate. Exposing the logical fallacy can sometimes be the first step in defeating this potentially harmful social ill.

Appeal to emotion is the common thread that runs through much of today's advertising campaigns. Slick ads are created in order to arouse a desire to attain the product. Such products are often displayed being used by *beautiful, successful,* and *happy people.* The obvious implication is that if you use this product, you will be transformed into one of the *lucky ones,* the ones *living life to the fullest.* The ads push psychological buttons: the need to belong to a group, the desire to be respected, the desire to be successful, etc. The emotional reasons for buying products are powerful tools that are understood and effectively used by corporations to sell their products.

Pollsters for political groups also use this tactic. They can manipulate poll questions so that the appeal to an emotional response overrides the rational grounds for a person's belief. Here is an example of a "loaded" question:

> Public schoolteachers are demanding a pay raise and threaten to strike if they don't get it. A prolonged strike will jeopardize our children's future. In addition, some economists predict that any substantial pay raise will result in an unbalanced budget, which in turn will cause an increase in taxes. Although the school year lasts only 180 days, the teachers get paid 12 months a year, whether or not school is in session. So, are you for or against a pay raise for public school teachers?

21. *Appeal to Pity* A specific kind of emotional plea is called the **appeal to pity.** For example, a defense attorney may attempt to get the jury to sympathize with the defendant prior to deliberation. If the defendant is found guilty, then the appeal may be addressed to the judge, asking for a light sentence based on the effects a harsh sentence would have on the defendant's family. On the other side, the prosecution may appeal to the jury to sympathize with the victim, not the defendant. The prosecutor may appeal to the judge to consider the emotional devastation

Appeal to pity: A specific kind of emotional plea that relies solely on a sense of pity for support.

inflicted on the victim's family, and thus to sentence the defendant to the maximum penalty allowed by law. However, trials are meant, ideally, to be rational, decision-making processes. The image of justice as a blindfolded person holding a set of scales is to emphasize the ideal that an objective weighing of the evidence is the goal of the trial. If pity is substituted for evidence and the rule of law, then the judgment would be fallacious.

Many charities arouse a sense of pity and perhaps even a sense of guilt when they solicit pledges of support. These charities know that people do not always act rationally and in their own long-term best interests. Nevertheless, any cause worthy of support should have rational, legitimate reasons, which, when understood, should be sufficient to get people to give to the charity. In addition to evoking our human sense of compassion for those who are suffering, a *legitimate* inference will not have to rely solely on the use of pity to support its conclusion.

22. *Appeal to Force* The threat of physical harm, an **appeal to force**, can sometimes cause us to accept a course of action that otherwise would be unacceptable. There are cases where witnesses and jurors have been threatened with physical harm to themselves or to their families if they go against the defendant. Voters have been pressured into changing their vote by the threat of violence. However, the threat need not be so overt and directly physical. For example, a large company may send out the following memo to its employees:

> Unless the union representing the workers of this company agrees to a
> 25 percent cut in salary for all workers, the company may have to shut
> its doors.

If the threat by the company to close its doors unless its employees take a pay cut lacks objective evidence of the company's financial difficulty, then an instance of the fallacy of appeal to force has occurred.

Another example illustrates the same point. For instance, a parent may threaten a child with loss of privileges or being "grounded" in order to achieve desired results.

> You had better get straight "A's" on your next report card. If you don't,
> then we will have to punish you. You will not be allowed to go out with
> your friends for an entire month.

It is not difficult to imagine that there are perfectly legitimate reasons why students should get good grades. Rational, objective evidence can be used as support for why students should do well in school. Therefore, any time an overt or implied threat is used as the only reason to convince someone to make a decision, in the absence of any rational supporting evidence for the conclusion, the rational decision-making process is subverted.

23. *Inference from Ignorance* An **inference from ignorance** (lack of knowledge) makes one of two possible mistakes: (1) A claim is made that a statement must be true because it has not been proven to be false, or (2) a statement must be false because it has not been proven to be true. Both claims are unjustified. An example of the first kind of mistake is:

> UFOs exist because nobody has proven that they don't.

Appeal to force: A threat of harmful consequences (physical and otherwise) used to force acceptance of a course of action that would otherwise be unacceptable.

Inference from ignorance: An inference built on a position of ignorance claims either that (1) a statement must be true because it has not been proven to be false, or (2) a statement must be false because it has not been proven to be true.

Fallacy of irrelevant conclusion: An inference where premises that seem to logically head in one direction are used instead to support an unexpected conclusion.

An example of the second kind of mistake is:

> There is no life anywhere else in the universe because we have never received signals from any part of space.

If substantial evidence is available to decide an issue, then the fallacy does not arise. For example, *after thorough investigation*, if no credible evidence is found linking a suspect to a crime, then we are justified in claiming the suspect is not guilty precisely because no evidence exists to prove guilt.

24. *Irrelevant Conclusion* The **fallacy of irrelevant conclusion** occurs when premises that seem to lead logically to one conclusion are used instead to support an unexpected conclusion. A conclusion "misses the point" or "comes out of left field" when the premises do not adequately prepare us for it. For example:

> Hey dad, guess what I found out? If we buy a second car, the insurance will only be an additional $400 a year! Let's go get one before the insurance company changes the rate.

The need for a car has not been adequately established, nor has the father's financial situation been determined. The evidence regarding the cost of the insurance is not in dispute, but the gap between the premises and conclusion is so great that the conclusion becomes, in a sense, irrelevant. We can use this kind of relevance fallacy whenever one of the other specific forms of irrelevance has not been met.

25. *Appeal to Inappropriate Authority* Inferences often rely on the opinions of "experts," specialists whose education, experience, and knowledge provide relevant support for a claim. The appeal to expert testimony strengthens the probability that the conclusion is correct, as long as the opinion falls within the realm of the expert's field. On the other hand, inferences that rely on the opinions of people who have no expertise, training, or knowledge relevant to the issue at hand **appeal to inappropriate authority.**

The most prevalent fallacious use of inappropriate authority is in advertisements and commercials. Athletes, movie and television stars, and former politicians endorse products to boost sales. The consumer is expected to respect the famous personalities and trust their opinion. But merely being famous does not qualify someone to pronounce the merits of a product. An athlete generally has no expertise of the nutritional value of a breakfast cereal. On the other hand, a person with a Ph.D. in nutrition would presumably be in a good position to offer a fair assessment of the breakfast cereal (provided the opinion is not based on monetary compensation). Albert Einstein, the famous physicist, was asked to be the first president of Israel. He humbly declined, stating that he had no idea how to run a country. Such modesty is rare.

Quick Reference 8.4 summarizes the fallacies of relevance.

Appeal to inappropriate authority: An inference that relies on the opinions of people who have no expertise, training, or knowledge relevant to the issue at hand.

Quick Reference 8.4 • Fallacies of Relevance

In fallacies of relevance, irrelevant premises are offered in support of the conclusion.

18. ***Ad hominem:*** Use of purported character flaws or circumstances of people's lives to reject their claims.

19. ***Tu quoque:*** A variety of the *ad hominem* fallacy distinguished by the specific attempt of one person to avoid the issue at hand by claiming the other person is a hypocrite.

Quick Reference 8.4 continued

20. **Appeal to emotion:** An inference or claim that relies solely on the arousal of a strong emotional state or psychological reaction; such an inference ultimately relies on irrelevant support.

21. **Appeal to pity:** A specific kind of emotional plea that relies solely on a sense of pity for support.

22. **Appeal to force:** A threat of harmful consequences (physical and otherwise) used to force acceptance of a course of action that would otherwise be unacceptable.

23. **Inference from ignorance:** An inference built on a position of ignorance claims either that (1) a statement must be true because it has not been proven to be false, or (2) a statement must be false because it has not been proven to be true.

24. **Irrelevant conclusion:** An inference in which the premises seem to lead logically to one conclusion and instead are used to support a different, unexpected conclusion.

25. **Appeal to inappropriate authority:** An inference that relies on the opinions of people who have no expertise, training, or knowledge relevant to the issue at hand.

EXERCISE SET 8.2C   ○○○

Exercises 1–10 Decide whether the statement is true or false.

1. The appeal to inappropriate authority occurs when an inference relies on the experience, training, or knowledge of people who are experts relevant to the issue at hand.

Answer: False. The fallacy occurs when an inference relies on the opinions of people who have *no* expertise, training, or knowledge relevant to the issue at hand.

2. The appeal to pity is a specific kind of *ad hominem* fallacy.

3. An inference from ignorance occurs when a person's character or circumstances are used to reject their claims.

4. The appeal to force uses rational reasons in support of a controversial position.

5. *Tu quoque* is a variety of the *ad hominem* fallacy distinguished by the specific attempt of one person to avoid the issue at hand by claiming the other person is a hypocrite.

*6. The fallacy of irrelevant conclusion occurs in an inference where premises that seem to lead logically to one conclusion are used instead to support an unexpected conclusion.

7. The appeal to emotion is not considered a specific kind of *ad hominem* fallacy.

Exercises 2–10: For answers and explanations, see page 250 of Instructor's Manual.

2. False

3. False

4. False

5. True

6. True

7. True

8. An inference that claims either (1) a statement must be true because it has not been proven to be false, or (2) a statement must be false because it has not been proven to be true is called *ad hominem*.

9. A threat of harmful consequences (physical and otherwise) used to force acceptance of a course of action that would otherwise be unacceptable is called an appeal to inappropriate authority.

10. *Ad hominem* fallacies occur when an inference uses character flaws or circumstances of people's lives to reject their claims.

Exercises 11–50 Each of the following passages contains a *fallacy of relevance*. Determine the fallacy that best fits each case. Explain your answer.

11. Biology 1 was easy for me. Physics 1 was no problem. So, I think I'm going to change my major to social work.

Answer: Irrelevant conclusion. This is an example of an inference that does not work because the premises seem to head in one direction and the conclusion in another.

Exercises 12–50: For answers and explanations, see pages 250–252 of Instructor's Manual.

12. This team beat us 64–0 last year. So we need to go out and give them a taste of their own medicine and see how they like it. Are you ready to fight?

13. If we don't raise gasoline prices, then we can't afford to explore for new oil reserves. In that case our dependency on foreign oil will bankrupt the major gasoline companies. The price will skyrocket and will be out of the reach of most people.

14. Maybe you didn't know that she is an orphan. Her outrageous behavior should be excused because of her background.

15. I saw him play football and he is ferocious on the field, he tackles everything in sight. Don't hire him to tutor young kids, he's too violent.

*16. That must be a great product for men since a former senator and presidential candidate endorsed it.

17. I believe that we are reincarnated. No one has ever been able to prove that after death our spirits don't move on to another baby.

18. He is an atheist. He cannot possibly have anything relevant to say on ethical issues.

19. That guy plays a doctor on my favorite TV show. I saw him in a commercial where he said that *Asperilinol* was great for migraine headaches. It must really work, so the next time you go to a drug store pick me up a bottle.

20. I know that Senator Wickhaven has been found guilty of harassment, but did you know that he was twice wounded in the Korean War. Since he has suffered so much for our country he should not be punished for this crime.

*21. If you don't break off your relationship with him, your mother and I will disinherit you.

22. She did not vote in the last election. Anything she suggests about how our country should be run cannot possibly be of any concern to us.

23. Mr. Crabhouse is a hard grader. Not only that, he forces you to attend class, participate in discussions, and do homework. He actually expects us to think about the material outside of class. So, you can believe that his class teaches students nothing about real life.

23. Irrelevant conclusion

24. My uncle drinks a six pack of beer a day. So, I couldn't believe it when he lectured me on the dangers of alcohol. He's one to talk! Nothing he says about drinking can be true because he cannot stop drinking himself.

24. *Tu quoque*

25. I know that we haven't looked for the missing money in the attic, but I'm sure that it is there.

25. Inference from ignorance

*26. I know that he did not do well on the exams, nevertheless you should give him an A for the course. After all, he is taking 18 credits and is holding down a full-time job.

26. Appeal to pity

27. Of course you should pay us for protection. After all, if you don't, we will have to break your arms, wreck your business, and harass your customers.

27. Appeal to force

28. I would not believe anything he says in his book. He is constantly on TV, radio, and in magazines trying to promote it so it will become a bestseller.

28. *Ad hominem*

29. Aliens from another planet must have built the great pyramids of Egypt because there is no record of how they were actually constructed.

29. Inference from ignorance

30. He has taken one psychology course, so he must be wrong when he claims that gambling is addictive.

30. *Ad hominem*

*31. That physician is a male. He couldn't possibly know anything about female health problems.

31. *Ad hominem*

32. I know deep inside you love her. Draw on that undying love and forget that she spent all the money on losing lottery tickets.

32. Appeal to emotion

33. Statistics show that people with a college degree earn 50 percent more during their lifetime than those without a degree. So, you should begin investing in blue chip stocks.

33. Irrelevant conclusion

34. I am going to vote for the incumbent, Senator Loweman, because my chemistry teacher said he is the best candidate.

34. Appeal to inappropriate authority

35. Since that sports reporter is a female, her analysis of what caused our team to lose the game is irrelevant.

35. *Ad hominem*

*36. Even though neither of us was at home when it happened, the dog must have broken the window by jumping on it. You have not shown me any other way that it could have happened.

36. Inference from ignorance

37. He is a college student. That is enough to convince me that he drinks alcohol excessively.

37. *Ad hominem*

38. The advertisement showed the latest Nobel Prize winner in literature drinking that new wine, Chateau Cwailoe. It must taste divine.

38. Appeal to inappropriate authority

39. I know you don't want to become a lawyer. However, your mother and I would be so proud to finally have a professional in the family. We would die happy if you go to law school.

39. Appeal to emotion

40. I know your cousin recommends taking vitamins every day. After all, she's a pharmacist, what do you expect her to tell you?

40. *Ad hominem*

41. Appeal to pity	*41. He failed his final exam, so don't blame him for getting drunk and destroying his dorm room.
42. *Ad hominem*	42. She is a chess grand master, so she can't be very beautiful.
43. Appeal to inappropriate authority	43. Look, the picture of the Olympic basketball team is on this cereal. It must be good for athletes.
44. Inference from ignorance	44. Scientific experiments have never proved conclusively that there are not any ghosts; therefore, I firmly believe that they do exist.
45. *Ad hominem*	45. He eats meat, so we should not invite him to speak at our seminar on animal rights.
46. Irrelevant conclusion	*46. I like chocolate. I like ice cream. Therefore, I'll take a hot dog for lunch.
47. Appeal to emotion	47. Your next door neighbor works on his car day and night. You said you can't get any rest from the noise, so if you want him to stop, then let's steal his car and trash it out of town.
48. Appeal to force	48. I have not decided if you can go to the concert tonight. I would like to see how much you contribute to this household. We will see what happens if you clean the house, wash the car, and do the grocery shopping today.
49. Appeal to pity	49. You can't give me an "F" on the exam. If you do my mother and father will be so upset they will have to be hospitalized.
50. *Tu quoque*	50. You tell me to wear a seatbelt when I drive because it will protect me in case I get in an accident. I never saw you wear one when you drive, so why should I wear one?

8.3 RHETORICAL LANGUAGE

As we saw with enthymemes (Chapter 2), context can influence our recognition and reconstruction of inferences, which is why interpretations of statements and inferences must be justified. Since it is easy to take a statement out of context and give it any interpretation we please, we need the original context to help us settle disagreements. The more we know about the setting in which the statements and inferences were made, the people involved, and the issues at hand, the more accurate our interpretations, analyses, and evaluations will be. But not all uses of language are transparent. Sometimes we speak or write for dramatic or exaggerated effect. When this occurs, we can be using language *rhetorically*; that is, the language we employ may be implying things that are not explicitly said. We must be careful when we interpret what appears to be rhetorical language, and we must justify our reconstructions of inferences. This section will explore three uses of rhetorical language: *rhetorical questions*, *rhetorical conditionals*, and *rhetorical disjunctions*.

Rhetorical Questions

Although inferences are constructed out of statements, sometimes a premise or conclusion is disguised as a question. For example, suppose someone says the following:

> You have not saved any money, you have only a part-time job, and at your age car insurance will cost you at least $2000 a year. Do you really think you can afford a car?

Although the last sentence poses a question, it should be clear from the context that the speaker's intention is to make an assertion: "You can't afford a car." This is an example of a **rhetorical question**, where a statement is disguised in the form of a question. We can reconstruct the inference as follows:

> You have not saved any money.
> You have only a part-time job.
> <u>At your age car insurance will cost you at least $2000 a year.</u>
> You can't afford a car.

In some contexts it is possible that an inference has a premise *and* a conclusion appearing as rhetorical questions. For example, suppose a disgruntled teenager says the following:

> I do my share of work around this house. Don't I deserve to get something in return? Why shouldn't I be allowed to go to the *Weaknotes* concert today?

The speaker is using the two rhetorical questions for dramatic effect. Our reconstruction should then reveal the assertions implied by the speaker, as follows:

> I do my share of work around this house.
> <u>I deserve to get something in return.</u>
> I should be allowed to go to the *Weaknotes* concert today.

Here is another example of a rhetorical question appearing as part of an inference:

> Why do you waste your time worrying about your death? It won't happen during your lifetime.

The reconstructed inference is this:

> <u>Your death won't happen during your lifetime.</u>
> Stop wasting your time worrying about it.

Rhetorical Conditionals

Under normal circumstances a conditional statement would not be considered to be an inference. However, in the appropriate setting an inference can be disguised as a conditional statement. For instance, suppose someone tells a friend that they are trying to lose 25 pounds. The friend might say the following:

> *If* you were really serious about losing weight, *then* you would not be eating that large pepperoni pizza all by yourself.

Conditional statements that are used to imply inferences are called **rhetorical conditionals**. From the context it should be clear that the speaker is observing a friend eating a pizza, so that fact is not in dispute. It is used as the basis upon which the conclusion is said to follow. So, in this example the *consequent* contains the intended premise while the *antecedent* contains the intended conclusion. The reconstructed inference is as follows:

> <u>You are eating that large pepperoni pizza all by yourself.</u>
> You are not really serious about losing weight.

Rhetorical question:
A statement disguised as a question.

Rhetorical conditional:
A conditional statement is used rhetorically (often in the form of a question) to disguise a statement or an implied inference.

Be careful to reconstruct a conditional statement as an inference only when you are reasonably sure that the conditional is being used rhetorically. A correct reconstruction of a conditional statement as an inference requires a good understanding of the context in which the conditional appears.

Some rhetorical conditionals can even occur in the form of questions. For example, a newspaper editorial page might contain an article written by a pundit who opposed the war in Iraq. At some point in the article, we might find this passage:

> If Saddam Hussein did not have weapons of mass destruction, then how can anyone still claim the war was justified?

The rhetorical conditional takes the form of a question, by means of which the author makes two assertions. We can reconstruct the inference as follows:

> <u>Saddam Hussein did not have weapons of mass destruction.</u>
> No one can still claim the war was justified.

Depending on the context, one rhetorical conditional can be reconstructed in different ways. For example, suppose we encounter this statement:

> If you truly care about your children, then why are you neglecting them?

If the speaker happens to be a close friend or relative whose intent is to change someone's behavior, the inference might be reconstructed as:

> <u>I know you care about your children.</u>
> You have to stop neglecting them.

On the other hand, if the speaker is a social worker who has observed repeated instances of child neglect, the inference might be reconstructed as:

> <u>You repeatedly neglect your children.</u>
> You do not truly care for them.

In this case, the social worker may be using the rhetorical conditional as part of a more extended justification for removing the children from the negligent parent.

The next example adds a new dimension to our discussion of rhetorical conditionals. Suppose a parent says this to a child,

> If you are smart, and I know you are, then you will do the right thing.

It is possible to reconstruct the inference and yet retain a conditional as a premise. We might want to allow the phrase, "I know you are" to play a key role in our reconstruction. If so, the inference can be displayed as follows:

> If you are smart, then you will do the right thing.
> <u>I know that you are smart.</u>
> You will do the right thing.

This reconstruction displays the inference in a way that emphasizes the deductive structure of *modus ponens*. When reconstructed this way, the inference is valid. But is it sound? An answer to this question would require an exploration of the truth content of the premises. The first premise seems to be asserting that all smart people do the right thing. It also seems to be asserting that being smart is a sufficient condition for doing the right thing. The plausibility of both these assertions can surely be questioned.

Alternatively, we might reconstruct the inference by eliminating the conditional aspect and removing the deductive *structural* emphasis. If we interpret the phrase, "I know you are," as directly asserting the antecedent, then we can place emphasis on the purely rhetorical nature of the conditional. The new reconstruction might look like this:

> <u>You are smart.</u>
> You will do the right thing.

This reconstruction intentionally removes the deductive apparatus, and thus it would have to be evaluated for strength or weakness, not for validity or invalidity. Whichever way we decide to reconstruct an inference, we should be prepared to justify our reconstruction by reference to the context in which it originally occurred.

Rhetorical Disjunctions

A **rhetorical disjunction** is a disjunction that is used to disguise a statement or an implied inference. Some disjunctions are used rhetorically in various contexts. These instances can be reconstructed to reveal the *implied* inference. For example, suppose one person asks another what kind of ice cream cone they are getting. The reply might be this:

> They only have two kinds, vanilla or chocolate, and you know how much I dislike vanilla.

The reconstructed inference with the missing conclusion can be displayed as follows:

> They only have two kinds, vanilla or chocolate.
> <u>You know how much I dislike vanilla.</u>
> I'm getting chocolate.

Rhetorical disjunctions are often used in television programs where two or more self-proclaimed intellectuals shout insults at each other for a half-hour at a time. At some point, we might hear the following:

> Either you agree with me or you are an idiot.

The rhetorical nature of this disjunction in this particular context allows us to treat it as an enthymeme. Doing so allows us to reconstruct two inferences:

Either you agree with me or you are an idiot.	Either you agree with me or you are an idiot.
<u>You are not an idiot.</u>	<u>You do not agree with me.</u>
You agree with me.	You are an idiot.

These reconstructions display the inferences in a way that appears to emphasize deductive structure. As such, deductive analysis will result in both inferences being valid. However, the question of soundness yields interesting results. An evaluation of the truth content of the first premise reveals a major problem. The first premise

Rhetorical disjunction:
When a disjunction is used rhetorically to disguise a statement or an implied inference.

Fallacy of false dichotomy:
When a disjunction assumes
that only two possibilities
exist, but in fact, more than
two exist.

offers only two alternatives, but surely there are more than these two possibilities. The first premise is an instance of the **fallacy of false dichotomy,** in which the asserted disjunction assumes that only two choices are possible, when, in fact, others exist. This is a special kind of *fallacy of unwarranted assumption* in which an inference assumes the truth of some unproved or questionable claim. If we add even one more possibility, we can reconstruct a new inference:

> Either you agree with me, or you are an idiot, or your position is correct.
>
> You do not agree with me.
>
> <u>You are not an idiot.</u>
>
> Your position is correct.

In the original inference the speaker used a false dichotomy to try to trap us into agreeing with her position. Revealing the fallacy allows us to analyze and evaluate the inference in a comprehensive manner. (The opponent might try to turn the tables on the speaker by responding rhetorically, "*If* I have to agree with you, *then* I really am an idiot.")

Here is another example of the fallacy of false dichotomy:

> She has an even number of dollars or she has an odd number of dollars.

It is possible that she has zero dollars, in which case both disjuncts would be false. This result is important; it reveals that a fallacy of false dichotomy occurs whenever it is possible for both disjuncts to be false at the same time.

A special kind of false dichotomy is the *fallacy of false dilemma*. Since the term "dilemma" is often misapplied, it is necessary that we correctly define a true dilemma. When we are confronted with a choice between two alternatives *both of which will lead to unwanted results,* then we are facing a true dilemma. For example, suppose you promise to help someone at a certain time and date, and later you realize that you had already made a promise to another person for that same time. If it is not possible to fulfill both promises, then your dilemma is choosing which person to hurt (that is, which promise you will break). Situations like these are sometimes referred to as being "between a rock and a hard place." In these instances someone is likely to advise you to "choose the lesser of two evils." (If you want to see a powerful example of a true dilemma, then you should read *Sophie's Choice* by William Styron.)

The next two examples illustrate the misapplication of the term "dilemma."

1. I just won the lottery but now I have a dilemma. Should I take the five million in one lump sum or spread it out over 20 years.

2. My parents are buying me a car for graduation, so now my dilemma is whether to choose a BMW or a Porsche.

Fallacy of false dilemma:
A special kind of false
dichotomy that occurs when
a disjunction assumes that
only two possibilities exist,
both of which would lead
to unwanted results, when
in fact more than two exist.

Since neither of these cases contains a choice that would lead to an unwanted result, these are clearly not true dilemmas.

The **fallacy of false dilemma** occurs when a disjunction offers two choices, each leading to an unwanted result, but neglects to acknowledge that other possibilities exist. A person defending the Patriot Act and its infringement on certain freedoms might say the following:

> Either we give up some traditional freedoms or we lose the war on terror.

If we are captured by the rhetorical nature of the disjunction and its implications, then we seem to be facing a dilemma. Choosing the first alternative leads to the unwanted result that we have to give up some traditional freedoms; but choosing the second alternative would mean that we lose the war on terror. However, once we see that this is really an instance of the fallacy of false dilemma we can simply reject the entire notion of having only two choices in the matter.

A rhetorical disjunction can also occur in the form of a question. For example, a salesperson might ask us the following:

> Do you want to pay for those shoes with cash or by credit card?

If you have no intention of buying the shoes, then the disjunction is another instance of the fallacy of false dichotomy.

One final example will reveal the connection between *rhetorical disjunctions* and *rhetorical conditionals*. The philosopher Arthur Schopenhauer offers numerous examples of fallacious reasoning in rhetorical settings. We will modify one of his examples to fit the present discussion. Schopenhauer tells us that it is common to hear people say the following:

> If you don't agree with our country's policies, then why don't you go live in another country?

The first step in our reconstruction is to turn the question into a conditional statement:

> *If* you don't agree with our country's policies, *then* you should go live in another country.

We can turn this conditional statement into a *disjunction* by revealing the two possibilities that are being asserted:

> *Either* you agree with our country's policies *or* you should go live in another country.

In this reconstruction the conditional and the disjunction are *logically equivalent statements*. The conditional statement asserts that *anyone* who doesn't agree with the policies should go live in another country, and the disjunction makes the same assertion. The reconstructed disjunction reveals another instance of the *fallacy of false dichotomy*. (For a detailed discussion of *logical equivalence* see Chapter 4.)

Quick Reference 8.5 summarizes the fallacies of false dichotomy.

Quick Reference 8.5 • Fallacies of False Dichotomy

26. **Fallacy of false dichotomy:** When a disjunction assumes that only two possibilities exist when in fact more than two exist.
27. **Fallacy of false dilemma:** A special kind of false dichotomy that occurs when a disjunction assumes that only two possibilities exist, both of which would lead to unwanted results, when in fact more than two exist.

> The fallacy of false dilemma is a special case of the fallacy of false dichotomy.

EXERCISE SET 8.3   ○○○

Reconstruct inferences based on your understanding and interpretation of the rhetorical aspect of the passages that follow. In each case, be prepared to offer justification for your reconstruction and interpretation.

1. Would you like to open a new subscription to our Internet service, or do you already subscribe?

Answer: In most cases there is more than one way to reconstruct and evaluate the statements and inferences. As a suggestion, we can reconstruct the inference two ways:

> Either you would like to open a new subscription to our Internet service or you already subscribe.
> <u>You do not already subscribe to our service.</u>
> You would like to open a new subscription to our Internet service.

> Either you would like to open a new subscription to our Internet service or you already subscribe.
> <u>You would not like to open a new subscription to our Internet service.</u>
> You already subscribe.

False Dichotomy: It is possible that both disjuncts in the first premise are false.

Exercises 2–20: For answers and explanations, see pages 254–257 of Instructor's Manual.

2. You already ate more than your fair share of our limited food supply; do you really want more?

3. Capital punishment sometimes leads to the execution of innocent humans. As a society we cannot continue to perform such brutal acts of inhumanity. Isn't it time to change the existing laws?

4. You are not happy at your job, so why not quit?

5. Either you love me or you hate me, which is it?

*6. If he is being accused of taking steroids now, then why has he hit approximately the same number of home runs each year since he first started playing professional baseball?

7. If you are correct that he has not taken steroids, then how can you explain him suddenly gaining 40 pounds of muscle and doubling his average home run total?

8. If the United States cannot find the number one terrorist on their list, then it cannot ever hope to eliminate the large number of cells of anonymous terrorists.

9. If you want to get in shape, then why do you sit around the house all day doing nothing?

10. If the Catholic Church really believed in the equality of women, then why aren't there any women priests?

*11. If he committed suicide by shooting himself, then why is there no trace of gunpowder on his hands?

12. If the United States international policy is not to be a nation-builder, then it shouldn't keep overthrowing governments it doesn't like and installing puppet leaders.

13. Either we cut school funding, or we raise taxes.

14. Would you rather have the government decide which doctor you can see, or keep the current health care system that gives you the freedom of choice?

15. Either you are with us, or you are against us.

*16. Either you love your country, or you are a traitor.

17. If you want to be financially secure in your retirement years, then why don't you have a retirement counselor?

18. You hate getting prank phone calls, so why don't you get an unlisted phone number?

19. Would you rather have a foot-long chili-cheese hotdog or two chili-cheese burgers?

20. If you want to get rich quick, then why don't you buy more lottery tickets?

BIOGRAPHY ARTHUR SCHOPENHAUER

Arthur Schopenhauer (1788–1860) is not generally regarded as a logician or a mathematician, but rather as a philosopher who devoted his life to, as he tells us, "debunking charlatans, windbags, and claptrap." Schopenhauer argued that fallacious reasoning should be exposed whenever it appeared. In *The Art of Controversy*, he remarks that *"It would be a very good thing if every trick could receive some short and obviously appropriate name, so that when a man used this or that particular trick, he could be at once reproached for it."* Indeed, hundreds of fallacies have been recognized, described, and named.

Schopenhauer's metaphysical system postulates ultimate reality as "the Will." Expressions of the Will can be found throughout nature in all manner of brutality, pain, and suffering. Humans are compelled to hate, love, and desire, the only escapes being temporary: philosophic contemplation, art (especially music), and sympathy for the plight of others. Schopenhauer was one of the first Western philosophers to recognize and incorporate ideas from Eastern religions, such as Buddhism, into his system of thought, where we are asked to "see ourselves in all existence." We must try to abandon the Will as much as possible. Schopenhauer is sometimes called "the philosopher of pessimism," and some people have interpreted his system of thought as advocating suicide as the only real possibility of escape from the predicament of life. But Schopenhauer tells us that suicide is not an option because it would be the ultimate assertion of the Will, not its abandonment.

SUMMARY—8.1 DEFINITIONS

- Clarifying the meaning of a statement requires a close look at the meaning of the terms involved.
- The **intension** of a term is specified by listing the properties or attributes that the term connotes.
- The **extension** of a term is given by specifying the class members of the term, what it denotes. Some terms have intension, but no extension.
- The dictionary meaning of a term is an example of a **lexical definition**. "Lexical" also refers to the common vocabulary of a given language as determined by the actual use in a community of speakers and writers.
- To stipulate a definition of a term is to choose some arbitrary, specified meaning. Slang and idioms are examples of the common use of **stipulative definitions**.
- Problems caused by the vagueness of certain terms can often be cleared up by using **precising definitions,** which are generally found in legal, scientific, and medical settings.
- An **operational definition** provides a meaning for a term by specifying a measurement procedure.
- The criteria we rely on to help us determine whether a concept truly refers to phenomena that are observable only indirectly are: measure, predict, and explain.
- A **functional definition** of a term specifies the purpose or use of the item denoted by the term.
- An **ostensive definition** of a term is given when we point to an object and attach a word to it (thereby showing an example of what the term denotes).

SUMMARY—8.2 INFORMAL FALLACIES

- **Informal fallacies** are errors in the content of an inference, not in the structure. These errors include, but are not limited to, mistakes of ambiguity, unwarranted assumption, and relevance.
- **Fallacies of ambiguity** occur when the meaning of terms or phrases change from one part of an inference to another.
- **1. Equivocation** is the intentional or unintentional use of different meanings of words or phrases in an inference.
- **2. Amphiboly** is a mistake of interpretation that can occur when the grammar or syntax of a statement muddles the intended meaning.
- **3. Composition** is the mistaken transfer of an attribute of the individual parts of an object to the object as a whole.
- **4. Division** is the mistaken transfer of an attribute of an object as a whole to its individual parts.
- **5. Emphasis** occurs when attention is diverted away from the original issue at hand, allowing a change in the intent of a statement or an inference.
- **6. Straw man** occurs when someone's written or spoken words are taken out of context, thereby purposely distorting the original inference in such a way that the new (straw man) inference is easy to defeat.

- **7. Red herring** occurs when someone completely ignores their opponent's position and changes the subject by diverting the discussion in a new direction.
- **Fallacies of unwarranted assumption** occur when an inference relies on unjustified assumptions as support for the conclusion.
- **8. Begging the question** assumes as evidence in the premises the very thing that it attempts to prove in the conclusion.
- **9. Complex question** is a single question that actually contains multiple, hidden parts.
- **10. Hasty generalization** occurs whenever a generalization is created on the basis of a few instances.
- **11. Biased sample** occurs when an inference uses a biased sample as support for a statistical claim about an entire population. A sample is biased if it leaves out members of a subset of the population that will be mentioned in the conclusion.
- **12. Hasty application of a generalization** occurs when we apply rigidly an otherwise acceptable generalization, even in the face of known and understood exceptions.
- **13. Fake precision** occurs when a claim is made that appears to be statistically significant, but analysis reveals that this is not the case.
- **False cause** is the mistake of claiming that a causal connection exists between two events when none exists. Events that appear to be correlated are not necessarily causally connected.
- **14. Coincidence** is a special kind of false cause that results from the accidental or chance connection between two events.
- **15. *Post hoc*** is a type of false cause involving a short-term pattern noticed after the fact. This type of false cause fallacy is also called *post hoc, ergo propter hoc* ("after the fact, therefore because of the fact").
- **16. Common cause** is a type of mistake that occurs when someone thinks that one event causes another when in fact both events are the result of a common cause. An example of this is to think that the barometer falling below a certain point is the cause of a storm, when both events are caused by a change in atmospheric pressure.
- **17. Slippery slope** is an inference that attempts to make a final event the inevitable outcome of an initial act. Slippery slope inferences rely on a kind of causal network where each step in the chain causes the next step. However, the "inevitability" of the final act needs to be supported by specific evidence for the supposed causal network. Each link requires relevant evidence for its connection to the next link in the chain.
- **Fallacies of relevance** occur whenever irrelevant premises are offered in support of a conclusion. The mistake occurs because of the tacit assumption of a claim that either has not been supported or cannot be supported.
- **18. *Ad hominem*** uses purported character flaws or circumstances of people's lives to reject their claims.
- **19. *Tu quoque*** is a variety of the *ad hominem* fallacy distinguished by the specific attempt of one person to avoid the issue at hand by claiming the other person is a hypocrite.

- **20. Appeal to emotion** relies solely on the arousal of a strong emotional state or psychological reaction; such an inference ultimately relies on irrelevant support.
- **21. Appeal to pity** is a specific kind of emotional plea that relies solely on a sense of pity for support.
- **22. Appeal to force** is a threat of harmful consequences (physical and otherwise) used to force acceptance of a course of action that would otherwise be unacceptable.
- **23. Inference from ignorance** is built on a position of ignorance that claims either (1) a statement must be true because it has not been proven to be false, or (2) a statement must be false because it has not been proven to be true.
- **24. Irrelevant conclusion** occurs where premises that seem to support one conclusion are used instead to support an unexpected conclusion.
- **25. Appeal to inappropriate authority** relies on the opinions of people who have no expertise, training, or knowledge relevant to the issue at hand.

SUMMARY—8.3 RHETORICAL LANGUAGE

- **Rhetorical questions** occur when statements are disguised in the form of questions.
- **Rhetorical conditionals** are conditional statements that are used to imply inferences.
- **Rhetorical disjunctions** are disjunctions that are used to imply inferences.
- **26. False dichotomy** is a special kind of fallacy of unwarranted assumption in which the asserted disjunction assumes that only two choices are possible when in fact others exist.
- **27. False dilemma** occurs when a disjunction offers two choices, each leading to an unwanted result, but neglects to acknowledge that other possibilities exist.

KEY TERMS

intension   277
extension   277
lexical definition   278
stipulative
   definition   278
precising definition   279
operational
   definition   279
functional
   definition   280
ostensive definition   280
formal fallacies   283

informal fallacies   283
fallacy of ambiguity   283
fallacy of
   equivocation   284
amphiboly   285
fallacy of
   composition   285
distributive   286
collective   286
fallacy of division   286
fallacy of emphasis   287
straw man fallacy   287

red herring fallacy   288
fallacy of unwarranted
   assumption   291
begging the
   question   292
fallacy of complex
   question   292
fallacy of hasty
   generalization   293
fallacy of biased
   sample   293

fallacy of hasty
    application of a
    generalization   294
fallacy of fake
    precision   294
fallacy of false cause   295
fallacy of
    coincidence   295
post hoc fallacy   295
common cause
    fallacy   296

slippery slope fallacy   296
fallacy of relevance   300
ad hominem   300
tu quoque   301
appeal to emotion   302
appeal to pity   302
appeal to force   303
inference from
    ignorance   303
fallacy of irrelevant
    conclusion   304

appeal to inappropriate
    authority   304
rhetorical question   309
rhetorical
    conditional   309
rhetorical
    disjunction   311
fallacy of false
    dichotomy   312
fallacy of false
    dilemma   312

LOGIC CHALLENGE: A CLEVER PROBLEM

In a certain faraway country (long, long, ago) prisoners to be executed were either shot or hung. Prisoners were allowed to make one statement. If their statement turned out to be true, then they were hung. If their statement turned out to be false, then they were shot. That is, until one clever prisoner put an end to the practice of execution. The prisoner made her one statement, upon which the judge was forced to set her free. What statement did she make?

"I will be shot." See page 257 of Instructor's Manual for complete explanation.

Applied Inductive Analysis

{ overview }

9.1 ANALOGICAL REASONING

9.2 STATISTICAL REASONING
    AND PROBABILITY THEORY

9.3 SCIENTIFIC AND CAUSAL
    REASONING

9.4 A MEDICAL MYSTERY

Inductive inference analysis was introduced in Chapter 1, where examples of analogical, statistical, and causal inferences were presented. This chapter will present detailed analyses of these types of inferences, along with an exploration of probability theory.

9.1 ANALOGICAL REASONING

To draw an **analogy** is simply to indicate that there are similarities between instances of two or more different things. We often reason that because two things share some relevant characteristics, they should also share other characteristics. Analogies are commonly encountered in everyday life. Analogies are often relied upon when purchasing products, or when deciding not to buy something based on a bad experience For example, you might decide to buy a Toyota based on the good performance of a similar model you had owned.

Analogical reasoning is one of the most fundamental tools used in inference creation, and it can be successfully analyzed as a type of inductive inference. It is important to acknowledge at the outset that analogical inferences contain a specific weakness. Generally speaking, the conclusions of analogical inferences do not follow with logical necessity from the premises. For example, it is logically possible that the next Toyota you buy will not perform particularly well. Nevertheless, if the analogical inference is strong, then it raises the probability that the conclusion is true.

Analogical reasoning also plays a major part in legal decisions. For example, suppose it has been legally decided that members of a certain group may not be restrained from speaking. Another court may conclude, by analogical reasoning, that the same group cannot be stopped from holding a peaceful rally, because a rally is similar to speaking. When a legal inference like this (from a precedent) is spelled out in detail, it will identify and emphasize those respects in which the older instances and the current instance are closely alike.

chapter

Analogy: To indicate that two or more things are similar by listing the relevant (significant) characteristics they have in common.

Analogical inference: An inference based on the idea that two (or more) things that share some relevant characteristics probably share other characteristics as well.

Analogical structure: The designation, placement, and role of the premises and conclusion that reveal the logical structure of an analogical inference.

Structure of Analogical Inferences

All analogical inferences have a similar general logical structure, or pattern. Every **analogical inference** proceeds by listing the characteristics that two (or more) things have in common, and from this an inference is made claiming that they have some other characteristic in common. The **analogical structure** is the designation, placement, and role of the premises and conclusion that reveal the logical structure of an analogical inference.

Knowing how to reveal the structure allows you to uncover the basic mechanism at work in this kind of reasoning, thereby giving you access to the fundamental logical concerns at hand. The following is a simple example.

Example 9.1

A father buys his son, Mike, a shirt that (naturally) the son does not like. The father justifies his decision by saying:

> I bought the shirt for you because your friend Steve has one like it, and you guys wear your hair the same, wear the same kind of pants and shoes, and like the same music and television programs. I thought for sure that since Steve must like his shirt, you would also like the shirt.

If we let S = "Steve," M = "Mike," a = "you guys wear your hair the same," b = "wear the same kind of pants," c = "shoes," d = "the same music," e = "television programs," and f = "the shirt," then the father's analogical reasoning can be displayed.

Premise 1: S and M have a, b, c, d, and e in common.
Premise 2: <u>S likes f.</u>
Conclusion: Therefore, *probably* M will like f.

The force of an analogical inference works through the two premises, where each plays a specific role. Premise 1 attempts to take two different objects (in this case people) and show how and why they are very similar. This is accomplished by listing all the characteristics that the two objects share in common. If Premise 1 effectively does its job, then we should begin to see the two instances overlapping, in a sense.

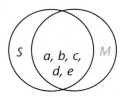

Premise 1

At this point Premise 2 is introduced to make a claim regarding the instance labeled S, namely, that S has a further characteristic not specified in Premise 1, but a characteristic undoubtedly connected with instance S. In our example, Premise 1 attempts to show that *S* and *M* have many characteristics in common (*a, b, c, d,* and *e*). This is supposed to make us "see" the instances overlap. Premise 2 then points out that *S* has an additional characteristic, namely *f,* which is inside the *S* circle. However, at this point the *f* could actually be placed in at least two differ-ent locations:

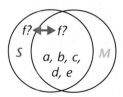

Premise 2

Premise 1, *if effective,* persuades us that *S* and *M* overlap. Premise 2 places the *f* inside *S* (this is introduced as a historical fact). The conclusion asserts that *f* should be applied to *M* as well, because the probability is high for its being in *M*. In other words, the hope is that we will agree that *f* probably is going to be in *M*. The intended goal is for us to accept the following picture:

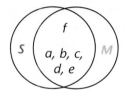

Conclusion

However, the picture for Premise 2 reveals why analogical inferences are, deduc-tively speaking, invalid. The analogical inference never claims that *S* and *M* are identical, only that they are similar (no two different instances can ever be com-pletely identical). This is why the conclusion does not follow with certainty from the premises; it is always possible for the conclusion to be false, even if the prem-ises are true. Remember that Premise 2 merely states that *f* is in *S*. Accepting this we can surely draw the inference in this manner.

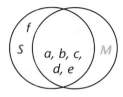

This is why the conclusion of an analogical inference can only claim, at best, that it is *probable* that *f* is in *M*, and this probability is only as good as the first premise. If the first premise has any weaknesses, if it can be legitimately criticized, then the probability of the conclusion being true is lessened. (This point will be discussed in more detail in the section on the weak points of analogical inferences.)

Let's look at another example of analogical reasoning involving defective tires.

Example 9.2

Premise 1: The steel-belted tires that have been involved in blowouts (*X*) and the steel-belted tires on your automobile (*Y*) have the following attributes in common: *a*, same size; *b*, same tread design; *c*, same manufacturer; *d*, same place of manufacture; *e*, on same type of vehicle; and *f*, same recommended tire pressure.

Premise 2: The steel-belted tires involved in blowouts (*X*) have been determined to be *g*, defective.

Conclusion: Therefore, *probably* the steel-belted tires on your automobile (*Y*) are *g*, defective.

The structure of the inference can now be displayed.

Premise 1: *X* and *Y* have *a, b, c, d, e,* and *f,* in common.
Premise 2: <u>*X* has *g.*</u>
Conclusion: Therefore, *probably Y* has g.

The force of the analogical inference works through the two premises. Their intent is to get us to agree that the two instances being compared share many similar characteristics. The first premise can be depicted as follows.

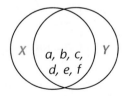

Premise 2 introduces a new characteristic attached to *X*. The complete logical apparatus of the inference can now be revealed.

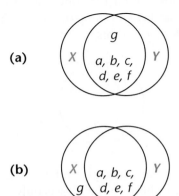

Premise 1, *if effective*, persuades us that *X* and *Y* overlap. Premise 2 places the *g* inside *X* (historical fact). The drawing labeled (a) depicts the possibility that *g* can be applied to *Y* as well, because the probability is high for its being in *Y*. However, drawing (b) shows that it is possible for the conclusion to be false, even if the premises are true. Remember that Premise 2 merely states that *g* is in *X*.

As mentioned earlier, if the first premise has any weaknesses, then the probability of the conclusion being true is reduced. The next section will concentrate on the factors that can strengthen or weaken the first premise.

EXERCISE SET 9.1A ○○○

These exercises have been written to specifically reinforce your logical analysis skills. They are not taken from outside sources; instead, they are fictional creations that reflect the kinds of information you might come across in newspapers, magazines, journals, and everyday conversation. Reveal the structure of the analogical inference in each example by deciding what would go in the premises and the conclusion.

1. We know that humans are capable of highly abstract thinking by their ability to understand and use complex concepts. Recent research on dolphins has revealed that dolphins have brains almost identical in size to humans. Dolphins have a body size nearly identical to humans. Experiments have shown that dolphins can understand verbal commands and sign language instructions, which humans can do quite easily. Like humans, dolphins have a strong sense of self-identity, because it has been shown that dolphins can recognize themselves in mirrors and when shown their image on a TV screen. Therefore, it is highly probable that dolphins are capable of highly abstract thinking.

Answer:

Premise 1: X, humans, and Y, dolphins, have the following attributes in common: *a*, dolphins have brains almost identical in size to humans; *b*, dolphins have a body size nearly identical to humans; *c*, dolphins can understand verbal commands and sign language instructions, which humans can do quite easily; *d*, like humans, dolphins have a strong sense of self-identity, because it has been shown that dolphins can recognize themselves in mirrors and when shown their image on a TV screen.

Premise 2: We know that X, humans, are *e*, capable of highly abstract thinking by their ability to understand and use complex concepts.

Conclusion: Therefore, it is highly probable that Y, dolphins, are *e*, capable of highly abstract thinking.

The structure of the inference can now be displayed

X and Y have *a, b, c, d,* in common.

X has *e.*

Therefore, *probably* Y has *e.*

2. Chimpanzees are certainly capable of feeling pain. They will avoid negative feedback (electrical shocks) in a laboratory setting when given the opportunity to do so. When one chimpanzee is injured, others will recognize the pain behavior and try to comfort and help the injured member of the group. Chimpanzees that have been given pain-relief medicine soon after an injury

Exercises 2–13: For answers and explanations, see pages 264–266 of Instructor's Manual.

connect the medicine to the relief from pain, because when injured again they will give the "sign" for the medicine. Humans display all of these behaviors as well. There are legal and ethical constraints that protect humans from experimentation without their consent. Therefore, chimpanzees should be afforded the same protections.

3. When a dog has killed or severely injured a human for no apparent reason, we feel justified in killing the dog in order to stop it from doing more damage. We don't try to figure out the psychological reasons for its violent behavior, whether it hates its mother or father. We just figure it is part of its genetic makeup and it cannot be changed. We don't lock the dog up for 5 years to life with the possibility of parole. Humans who kill or injure other humans for no apparent reason are like those dogs. We should feel justified in killing them in order to stop them from doing more damage.

4. England and Japan have much lower overall crime rates than the United States. The United States has 20 times more homicides than England and 30 times more than Japan. All three countries have large populations, are highly industrialized, and are in the top five in economic strength among the world's countries. In addition, all three countries are democracies, have separate branches of government, and a large prison system. But England and Japan have strict gun control legislation. If the United States wants to lower its homicide rate, then it has to pass strict gun control legislation.

5. I am a junior at Lincoln Heights High School. My parents make me do all the housework, like taking out the trash (every night), laundry (every Monday), dishes, vacuuming, washing the car, and cleaning up the rooms. My kid brother, who is in fifth grade, doesn't have to do anything. But he eats the same food as me, has his own bedroom like me, and gets the same amount of allowance as me. If I have to do so much work, then he should, too.

*6. The recent unearthing of some bones in central China has been the source of much controversy. Some experts are claiming that it is the oldest evidence of a "human" ever discovered because it predates the next earliest fossil by 20,000 years. The experts claim that the cranial area is the same as the earliest agreed upon fossil of a human. The jawbone matches human fossils of a later date. Crude tools were found near the bones. The teeth match the later human fossils. If the oldest recognized bones have been declared to be human, then these must be human as well.

7. The government gives billions to big farming companies to *not* grow crops. This is to keep the prices stable, thus the consumers are protected—at least so say the farmers. I run a business. I have a small area where I raise worms. Like the big businesses, I too have expenses. I pay for help, buy equipment, purchase supplies, suffer losses, pay taxes, pay utilities, and am subject to the laws of supply and demand. If they can get money for not growing crops, then I would be more than willing to get money from the government, so I can stop growing those (****) worms.

8. A computer program developed by some Pittsburgh professors at Carnegie-Mellon University has beaten the reigning world chess champion (considered to be the strongest player in history). Computer programs are used to help diagnose diseases and predict economic trends and the winners in horse races and other sports. They can calculate and analyze, in a few seconds, problems that no human could do in a lifetime. Advanced computer programs have

shown the ability to "learn" from experience and "adapt" to new situations. They can understand language and communicate concepts and ideas. Any human that can do these things is considered to possess "consciousness." Some computer programs should be given the same designation.

9. Fruit has many attributes that are good for your health. Fruit provides energy, roughage, sugars, citric acid, vitamins, and minerals. The new candy bar, Chocolate Peanut Gooies, provides energy, roughage, sugar, citric acid, vitamins and minerals. How can it not be good for your health, too?

10. *Planet X24: Our Last Hope*, the new movie by director Billy Kuberg, has just been released. It's his fourth sci-fi film. His other three had newcomers in the starring roles, were based on novels by Joel Francis Hitchmann, opened in summer, and had huge marketing tie-ins. This new movie has an unknown in the lead role, is based on a novel by Joel Francis Hitchmann, is opening in the summer, and has huge marketing tie-ins. Each of Kuberg's first three sci-fi films grossed over 550 million dollars. I predict this new film will do about the same amount of business.

*11. I already ate apples, oranges, peaches, and cherries from her fruit stand, and I enjoyed all of them. I am going to try her pears. I am sure I will enjoy them.

12. I took Philosophy 101, 102, 103, and 104 and got and "A" for each course. I am going to take Philosophy 105, so I expect to get an "A" in that course as well.

13. Evidence indicates that adding fertilizer helps fruit trees and vegetables plants to grow better. Seaweed is a plant. So, adding fertilizer should help seaweed to grow better.

Analyzing Analogical Inferences

There are four criteria we can use to analyze the strengths and weaknesses of analogical inferences.

1. The strength of an analogical inference is related to *the number of instances between which the analogies are said to hold*. A large number of experiences of the same kind, with the same item, will serve to establish the conclusion with a much higher degree of probability than would be the case if the conclusion were based on one instance alone. However, there is typically no simple numerical ratio between the number of instances and the probability of the conclusion. That is, if we compare two analogical inferences, where in the first we find two instances mentioned, and in the second, we find ten instances mentioned, we cannot claim that the conclusion in the second is exactly five times as probable as the first. However, in Example 9.1, if the father had compared his son to a greater number of friends rather than just to Steve, and if all the friends had worn the shirt, then the first premise would have been strengthened. In Example 9.2 there are presumably an adequate number of instances of defective tires to make the first premise strong.

2. The strength of an analogical inference is related to *the variety of instances mentioned in the premises*. In other words, if the first premise of an analogical inference shows some variety among the instances that connect the members of the analogy, then it might make the conclusion more likely to be true. In

Example 9.1, if the father could show that a lot of people of different ages seem to be wearing the shirt in question, this would seem to make the shirt desirable to more people and might raise the probability that Mike would like the shirt. In Example 9.2, if it could be shown that defective tires were made in many locations and at different times, then this variety in the place and time of manufacture would increase the likelihood that defective tires were made in many places. These additional facts would increase the probability that the conclusion is true.

3. The strength of an analogical inference is related to *the number of characteristics that are claimed to be analogous.* All things being equal, the greater the number of characteristics listed in the first premise, the more probable the conclusion will be. In Example 9.1, Premise 1 lists five characteristics in common. Example 9.2 lists six characteristics in its first premise. This does not mean that the conclusion of the second inference is 20 percent more likely to be true. There is no simple mathematical formula for judging the probability of the conclusion based on the number of characteristics in the first premise.

4. The strength of an analogical inference is related to the *relevance of the characteristics mentioned in the first premise.* Some of the characteristics mentioned in the first premise may have no real bearing on the instance at hand. We need to determine whether or not the characteristics mentioned in the premises carry any weight when it comes to deciding the probability of the conclusion. The fact that two instances have something in common is not, by itself, a sufficient reason to expect that the common characteristic is relevant to the conclusion in question. Each instance has to be determined on its own merits. The question of relevance is the single most important criterion on which to judge the strength of an analogical inference. An inference based on a single relevant analogy between two instances will be far more convincing than an inference based on ten or more irrelevant instances. However, determining relevance is not an easy task. This is why it is important to make inferences by analogy strong enough to stand up to severe scrutiny.

Four criteria are used in analyzing analogical inferences, including the number and variety of instances in which the analogies hold.

Quick Reference 9.1 • Criteria for Analyzing Analogical Inferences

1. *The number of instances between which the analogies are said to hold.* A large number of experiences of the same kind, with the same item, establish the conclusion with a much higher degree of probability than would be the case if the conclusion were based on one instance alone.

2. *The variety of instances mentioned in the premises.* If the first premise shows some variety among the instances that connect the members of the analogy, then it might make the conclusion more likely to be true.

3. *The number of characteristics said to be analogous.* All things being equal, the greater the number of characteristics listed in the first premise, the more probable the conclusion.

4. *The assessment of relevance.* It must be determined whether the characteristics mentioned in the premises carry any weight when it comes to deciding the probability of the conclusion.

EXERCISE SET 9.1B ○○○

Exercises 1–13 You have already revealed the structure of the analogical inferences in Exercise Set 9.1A. Now analyze those same inferences by applying the four criteria introduced in this section: (a) Check the number of instances between which the analogies are said to hold; (b) assess the variety of instances mentioned in the premises; (c) list the number of characteristics said to be analogous; (d) determine the relevancy of the characteristics mentioned.

1. We know that humans are capable of highly abstract thinking by their ability to understand and use complex concepts. Recent research on dolphins has revealed that dolphins have brains almost identical in size to humans. Dolphins have a body size nearly identical to humans. Experiments have shown that dolphins can understand verbal commands and sign language instructions, which humans can do quite easily. Like humans, dolphins have a strong sense of self-identity, because it has been shown that dolphins can recognize themselves in mirrors and when shown their image on a TV screen. Therefore, it is highly probable that dolphins are capable of highly abstract thinking.

Answer:

(a) *Number of entities:* Dolphins and humans (we are not told how many dolphins were studied).

(b) *Variety of instances:* We are not given specific information on the age, sex, or species of the dolphins studied.

(c) *Number of characteristics:* Brain size; body size; ability to understand verbal commands; ability to understand sign language; strong sense of self-identity.

(d) *Relevancy:* Of all the characteristics mentioned, *body size* seems the least relevant to the question of "highly abstract thinking."

2. Chimpanzees are certainly capable of feeling pain. They will avoid negative feedback (electrical shocks) in a laboratory setting when given the opportunity to do so. When one chimpanzee is injured, others will recognize the pain behavior and try to comfort and help the injured member of the group. Chimpanzees that have been given pain-relief medicine soon after an injury connect the medicine to the relief from pain, because when injured again they will give the "sign" for the medicine. Humans display all of these behaviors as well. There are legal and ethical constraints that protect humans from experimentation without their consent. Therefore, chimpanzees should be afforded the same protections.

3. When a dog has killed or severely injured a human for no apparent reason, we feel justified in killing the dog in order to stop it from doing more damage. We don't try to figure out the psychological reasons for its violent behavior, whether it hates its mother or father. We just figure it is part of its genetic makeup and it cannot be changed. We don't lock the dog up for 5 years to life with the possibility of parole. Humans who kill or injure other humans for no apparent reason are like those dogs. We should feel justified in killing them in order to stop them from doing more damage.

4. England and Japan have much lower overall crime rates than the United States. The United States has 20 times more homicides than England and 30 times more than Japan. All three countries have large populations, are highly industrialized, and are in the top five in economic strength among the

Exercises 2–13: For answers and explanations, see pages 267–268 of Instructor's Manual.

world's countries. In addition, all three countries are democracies, have separate branches of government, and a large prison system. But England and Japan have strict gun control legislation. If the United States wants to lower its homicide rate, then it has to pass strict gun control legislation.

5. I am a junior at Lincoln Heights High School. My parents make me do all the housework, like taking out the trash (every night), laundry (every Monday), dishes, vacuuming, washing the car, and cleaning up the rooms. My kid brother, who is in fifth grade, doesn't have to do anything. But he eats the same food as me, has his own bedroom like me, and gets the same amount of allowance as me. If I have to do so much work, then he should, too.

*6. The recent unearthing of some bones in central China has been the source of much controversy. Some experts are claiming that it is the oldest evidence of a "human" ever discovered because it predates the next earliest fossil by 20,000 years. The experts claim that the cranial area is the same as the earliest agreed upon fossil of a human. The jawbone matches human fossils of a later date. Crude tools were found near the bones. The teeth match the later human fossils. If the oldest recognized bones have been declared to be human then these must be human as well.

7. The government gives billions to big farming companies to *not* grow crops. This is to keep the prices stable, thus the consumers are protected—at least so say the farmers. I run a business. I have a small area where I raise worms. Like the big businesses, I too have expenses. I pay for help, buy equipment, purchase supplies, suffer losses, pay taxes, pay utilities, and am subject to the laws of supply and demand. If they can get money for not growing crops, then I would be more than willing to get money from the government, so I can stop growing those (****) worms.

8. A computer program developed by some Pittsburgh professors at Carnegie-Mellon University has beaten the reigning world chess champion (considered to be the strongest player in history). Computer programs are used to help diagnose diseases and predict economic trends and the winners in horse races and other sports. They can calculate and analyze, in a few seconds, problems that no human could do in a lifetime. Advanced computer programs have shown the ability to "learn" from experience and "adapt" to new situations. They can understand language and communicate concepts and ideas. Any human that can do these things is considered to possess "consciousness." Some computer programs should be given the same designation.

9. Fruit has many attributes that are good for your health. Fruit provides energy, roughage, sugars, citric acid, vitamins, and minerals. The new candy bar, Chocolate Peanut Gooies, provides energy, roughage, sugar, citric acid, vitamins and minerals. How can it not be good for your health, too?

10. *Planet X24: Our Last Hope*, the new movie by director Billy Kuberg, has just been released. It's his fourth sci-fi film. His other three had newcomers in the starring roles, were based on novels by Joel Francis Hitchmann, opened in summer, and had huge marketing tie-ins. This new movie has an unknown in the lead role, is based on a novel by Joel Francis Hitchmann, is opening in the summer, and has huge marketing tie-ins. Each of Kuberg's first three sci-fi films grossed over 550 million dollars. I predict this new film will do about the same amount of business.

*11. I already ate apples, oranges, peaches, and cherries from her fruit stand, and I enjoyed all of them. I am going to try her pears. I am sure I will enjoy them.

12. I took Philosophy 101, 102, 103, and 104 and got and "A" for each course. I am going to take Philosophy 105, so I expect to get an "A" in that course as well.

13. Evidence indicates that adding fertilizer helps fruit trees and vegetable plants to grow better. Seaweed is a plant. So, adding fertilizer should help seaweed to grow better.

Exercises 14–17 For the following inference by analogy, four alternative scenarios are suggested. For each of these, decide whether it *strengthens*, *weakens*, or is *irrelevant* to the original inference. Do each one independently of the others.

Imagine an auto mechanic says the following:

> Your car has ABS brakes manufactured by Skidmore Brake Company. Unfortunately, that company is no longer in business. Research has shown that the brakes made by that company failed to work in at least 1000 cases. The brakes failed in cars, trucks, and SUV's. Therefore, I recommend that you replace your ABS brake system.

14. What if there had been only 10 recorded cases of brake failure with those particular brakes?

Answer: Weakens the inference. The number of entities in the premises is now decreased substantially.

15. What if the recorded cases of failure had all been in cars and you have a truck?

16. What if the majority of the recorded cases of brake failure involved red cars, but your car is blue?

17. What if none of the recorded cases of failure involved SUV's, and you have an SUV?

Exercises 15–17: For answers and explanations, see page 268 of Instructor's Manual.

15. Weakens the inference

16. Irrelevant to the inference

17. Weakens the inference

Strategies of Evaluation

Analogical inferences have several potential major weaknesses that a thorough analysis can help to expose. The strategies used to expose these weaknesses involve *disanalogies*, *counteranalogies*, and the *unintended consequences of analogies*.

Disanalogy The first strategy involved in exposing weaknesses in an analogical inference is the obvious fact that any two nonidentical instances have differences between them. These differences can be exploited and, if significant, can severely weaken any analogical inference. When we point out differences between two instances, we are employing the first logical strategy of evaluation, called **disanalogy**. The main thrust of Premise 1 of an analogical inference is to make two instances overlap by pointing out similarities between them. Disanalogies, *if they are effective*, can cause us to start separating the two instances in question by acknowledging any significant and relevant differences between them. This strategy drives a wedge between the two instances and, therefore, lowers

Disanalogy: The introduction of relevant and significant differences between the entities mentioned in an analogy.

Counteranalogy:
A competing analogy that compares the entity mentioned in the conclusion of the original analogy to a different entity.

the probability that the characteristic mentioned in Premise 2 is in the conclusion. In Example 9.1, the son Mike could point out differences between himself and Steve. These differences might include the following: p, the color of shirts they wear; q, the logos (or lack of logos) on the shirts they typically wear; r, the food they like; and v, the movies they like. Pointing out the disanalogies (differences) deemphasizes the overlap between the two, as illustrated below.

Strategy

Revealing relevant differences between two things is a good way to begin the evaluation of an analogical inference.

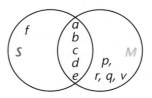

What the picture reveals is that *if* we can effectively point out relevant differences between S and M, then even if Steve likes his shirt (f), the probability, according to our new picture, is that f is *not* in M (Mike does not like the shirt).

Counteranalogy The second type of evaluation, called **counteranalogy**, reveals that it is always logically possible to create another inference that compares the current instance to a completely different instance, and leads to a conclusion that contradicts the conclusion of the original inference. In Example 9.1, suppose Mike's mother explains why she could have predicted that Mike would *not* like the shirt his father bought. Her reasoning might be as follows:

> M, Mike, is more like N, Nick, because they both a, wear the same kind of pants; b, like the same music; c, like the same television programs; d, like the same colors; e, wear the same kinds of logos; f, like the same kinds of food; and g, like the same movies. Nick does *not* like that kind of shirt (k); therefore, *probably* Mike will *not* like it either.

This inference is pictured below.

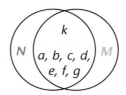

The important thing to realize is that we have created a completely new, competing, analogical inference. This strategy of evaluation, counteranalogy, is appropriately named, because we *counter* the original analogical inference. Upon construction of a counteranalogy, we are faced with the prospect of weighing, judging, and evaluating the competing strengths of two analogies. (In fact, there is no limit to the number of counteranalogies we can create from a given analogy.) Of course, all the counteranalogies, as well as the original analogy, are subject to the application of disanalogies. This is one way we can begin weighing the competing analogies to see which is better. We also can, and should, probe for the relevancy of the characteristics mentioned in support of the competing inferences.

BIOGRAPHY DAVID HUME

David Hume's (1711–1776) analysis of the problems associated with induction, causation, self-identity, and free will echo throughout modern philosophy. In his *Dialogues Concerning Natural Religion,* Hume dissects a famous analogical argument. The *design argument,* which is still used today, reasons that objects, such as watches, could not have randomly assembled themselves, they had to be designed and built for a specific purpose by an intelligent creature. Likewise, since observation of the universe reveals an orderly design and purpose, it follows by analogy that it was designed and built for a specific purpose by an intelligent creature, namely God.

Hume points out that watches and other man-made objects are very different from much of the universe, which in fact exhibits great disorder and randomness. If so, the disanalogies would seem to weaken the inference. As a counteranalogy, Hume points to the fact that some forms of animal life and vegetation reveal order but are the result of accidental natural processes occurring without any intentional intelligent design or purpose. As far as unintended consequences of the analogy are concerned, Hume provides many possible conclusions. Since we (the human designers) are finite creatures, then God might be finite; since we are imperfect creatures, then God could be imperfect; since groups of designers and builders create watches, then perhaps many gods were needed to create our universe. Additionally, since humans can create imperfect products, Hume remarks that perhaps our universe "*is a botched creation of an inferior deity who afterwards abandoned it, ashamed of the poor quality of the product.*"

Unintended Consequence of the Analogy The third type of strategy of evaluation is the discovery of an **unintended consequence of the analogy.** If you can point to something that is a direct result of an analogy, but that is unacceptable to the person presenting the analogy, then you can put that person in a difficult position. It could be that they "have painted themselves into a corner." For example, suppose Mike says the following:

> OK dad, you are correct, Steve and I are very much alike. But since Steve likes smoking cigarettes, you won't mind if I start smoking, too, right?

The father might respond by saying the following:

> Steve's parents don't seem to care what he does, but I care what you do. Besides, Steve's parents are rich and can give him more spending money than we can give you. Also, Steve doesn't seem too interested in personal grooming and the odor associated with smoking cigarettes, but you are very particular about the scent you give off. So, I do mind if you smoke.

However, what Mike's father is doing is pointing out disanalogies. He is effectively weakening his own original analogical inference by admitting there are relevant

Unintended consequence of the analogy: A direct result of an analogy that is unacceptable to the person presenting the analogy.

differences between Steve and Mike. Therefore, the discovery of an unintended consequence of the analogy forces the person either to accept the unintended consequence, or to weaken the original analogy.

Let's look at an extended analysis of another analogical inference. Suppose a TV political commentator (a.k.a. *Talking Head*) says this:

> The United States should go into Country *I* and topple the current regime. If there was a family living in the United States that threatened their neighbor's property, that stockpiled dangerous weapons, that disparaged our form of government and our social customs, that threatened our very way of life, then we would feel justified in going into their house and stopping them—by force, if necessary. Country *I* has threatened us as well as its neighboring countries, it has stockpiled dangerous weapons, it has disparaged our form of government and our social customs, and it has threatened our very way of life. If there is no way to solve the problem diplomatically, then we are justified in going there to stop them, by force, if necessary.

Let X = "a family living in the U.S.," I = "the foreign country in question," a = "threatened their neighbor's property," b = "stockpiled dangerous weapons," c = "disparaged our form of government," d = "disparaged our social customs," e = "threatened our very way of life," and f = "we would feel justified in going in and stopping them—by force, if necessary." We can then reconstruct the inference to get the following:

Example 9.3

X and I have a, b, c, d, and e in common.
In the case of X, f
Therefore, in the case of I, *probably f.*

We can now draw the resulting analogical inference.

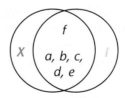

On the same TV program, another *Talking Head* might respond by saying the following:

> You are comparing apples to oranges. A family living in the United States is subject to the laws of this country; this is not the case with foreign countries. We cannot impose, nor can we enforce, our laws on another country. If a family in the United States threatens a neighbor's property, the neighbor lives in the United States and is afforded the protection of our government. A threat by one U.S. citizen on another, if taken seriously, is grounds for immediate action by our government. Although a threat by a recognized sovereign nation should cause us to be wary and ready for any eventuality, it does not give us the right to go in with force.

This commentator is pointing out differences and is using disanalogies to weaken the original analogy. Of course, we should pay close attention to the relevancy of the characteristics in the original analogy, as well as to the characteristics mentioned by way of disanalogies, to see how much weight we should give to each. We can then determine for ourselves the strength of the original analogy.

On the other hand, a different commentator might respond by saying the following:

> Country *I* is more like Vietnam was when we first got involved. Vietnam was a divided country, at war with itself, with one side asking for our help and the other side telling us to keep out. North Vietnam received military and financial assistance from the Soviet Union, while Country *I* receives military and financial assistance from the current Russia. We suffered too many deaths and wounded in Vietnam. We are told that a protracted war with Country *I* will result in many deaths and wounded among our soldiers. In Vietnam, we stayed too long, and in the end, the results were not what we had hoped for. This will happen again, if we go into Country *I*. Many people feel that we should not have gone into Vietnam in the first place. Therefore, we should not go into Country *I*.

This commentator is using a counteranalogy to show that a completely different conclusion can be reached. As we remarked earlier, the counteranalogy is itself subject to the three kinds of strategies of evaluation. (1) Its strength can be questioned by pointing out disanalogies between Vietnam and Country *I*, (2) unintended consequences of the analogy might be discovered, and (3) a new counteranalogy could also be constructed.

One last commentator might say the following:

> I agree that we should go into Country *I* and topple the regime by force. Of course, this will mean that our allies, Countries *E, F, G,* and *J* will sever economic and diplomatic ties with us, as they have forcefully repeated. In turn, this will make our economy suffer. But that's the price we have to be willing to pay for protecting ourselves by force.

This illustrates the strategy of pointing out some unintended consequences of the analogy. Of course, the original *Talking Head* might find these results acceptable; but if the last commentator is wise enough, and knows the opponent well, then she is sure to think of consequences that she knows her opponent will find unacceptable.

Quick Reference 9.2 • Strategies for Evaluation of Analogical Inferences

Disanalogy: To point out the *differences* between the two (or more) items mentioned in the first premise of an analogical inference.

Counteranalogy: To create a completely new, *competing*, analogical inference.

Unintended consequence of the analogy: To point to something that is a direct result of the original analogy, but that is unacceptable to the person presenting that analogy.

Strategies for evaluating analogical inferences include the use of *disanalogy, counteranalogy,* and the *unintended consequences of an analogy.*

EXERCISE SET 9.1C ○○○

You revealed the structure of the analogical inferences in Exercise Set 9.1A (page 325). Next, you analyzed those inferences in Exercise Set 9.1B, Exercises 1–13 (page 329). Now, you are in position to finalize your evaluation of those inferences by using the three strategies illustrated in this section. So, continuing the lettering in the previous sections' exercises, you are to do the following: (e) point out any relevant disanalogies between the instances being compared; (f) try to construct a counteranalogy; (g) see if you can think of any unintended consequences of the analogical inference.

1. We know that humans are capable of highly abstract thinking by their ability to understand and use complex concepts. Recent research on dolphins has revealed that dolphins have brains almost identical in size to humans. Dolphins have a body size nearly identical to humans. Experiments have shown that dolphins can understand verbal commands and sign language instructions, which humans can do quite easily. Like humans, dolphins have a strong sense of self-identity, because it has been shown that dolphins can recognize themselves in mirrors and when shown their image on a TV screen. Therefore, it is highly probable that dolphins are capable of highly abstract thinking.

Answer:

(e) *Disanalogies:* Humans display complex speech patterns and can create completely new forms; mathematical skills, which are taken as a hall-mark of abstract thinking, are not mentioned as one of the dolphins' abilities; poetry, art, music, and other aesthetic abilities have not been shown to exist in dolphins.

(f) *Counteranalogy:* Dolphins are more like dogs. They both have highly sensitive senses of smell; they both have extraordinary sensitivity to sounds that humans cannot detect; they both can learn to react correctly to certain signs or verbal commands; they both seem to bond well with humans; they both are able to learn "tricks" of performance. Since there is no evidence that dogs are capable of highly abstract thinking, dolphins probably do not have that ability either.

(g) *Unintended consequences:* If dolphins are capable of highly abstract thinking, then perhaps they should be afforded rights similar to humans. They should not be kept and raised in captivity and be subject to experiments like those mentioned in the article. The researchers should get "informed consent" agreements from the dolphins before embarking on any further experiments.

Exercises 2–13: For answers and explanations, see pages 269–272 of Instructor's Manual.

2. Chimpanzees are certainly capable of feeling pain. They will avoid negative feedback (electrical shocks) in a laboratory setting when given the opportunity to do so. When one chimpanzee is injured, others will recognize the pain behavior and try to comfort and help the injured member of the group. Chimpanzees that have been given pain-relief medicine soon after an injury connect the medicine to the relief from pain, because when injured again they will give the "sign" for the medicine. Humans display all of these behaviors as well. There are legal and ethical constraints that protect humans from experimentation without their consent. Therefore, chimpanzees should be afforded the same protections.

3. When a dog has killed or severely injured a human for no apparent reason, we feel justified in killing the dog in order to stop it from doing more damage. We don't try to figure out the psychological reasons for its violent behavior, whether it hates its mother or father. We just figure it is part of its genetic makeup and it cannot be changed. We don't lock the dog up for 5 years to life with the possibility of parole. Humans who kill or injure other humans for no apparent reason are like those dogs. We should feel justified in killing them in order to stop them from doing more damage.

4. England and Japan have much lower overall crime rates than the United States. The United States has 20 times more homicides than England and 30 times more than Japan. All three countries have large populations, are highly industrialized, and are in the top five in economic strength among the world's countries. In addition, all three countries are democracies, have separate branches of government, and a large prison system. But England and Japan have strict gun control legislation. If the United States wants to lower its homicide rate, then it has to pass strict gun control legislation.

5. I am a junior at Lincoln Heights High School. My parents make me do all the housework, like taking out the trash (every night), laundry (every Monday), dishes, vacuuming, washing the car, and cleaning up the rooms. My kid brother, who is in fifth grade, doesn't have to do anything. But he eats the same food as me, has his own bedroom like me, and gets the same amount of allowance as me. If I have to do so much work, then he should, too.

*6. The recent unearthing of some bones in central China has been the source of much controversy. Some experts are claiming that it is the oldest evidence of a "human" ever discovered because it predates the next earliest fossil by 20,000 years. The experts claim that the cranial area is the same as the earliest agreed upon fossil of a human. The jawbone matches human fossils of a later date. Crude tools were found near the bones. The teeth match the later human fossils. If the oldest recognized bones have been declared to be human, then these must be human as well.

7. The government gives billions to big farming companies to *not* grow crops. This is to keep the prices stable, thus the consumers are protected—at least so say the farmers. I run a business. I have a small area where I raise worms. Like the big businesses, I too have expenses. I pay for help, buy equipment, purchase supplies, suffer losses, pay taxes, pay utilities, and am subject to the laws of supply and demand. If they can get money for not growing crops, then I would be more than willing to get money from the government, so I can stop growing those (****) worms.

8. A computer program developed by some Pittsburgh professors at Carnegie-Mellon University has beaten the reigning world chess champion (considered to be the strongest player in history). Computer programs are used to help diagnose diseases and predict economic trends and the winners in horse races and other sports. They can calculate and analyze, in a few seconds, problems that no human could do in a lifetime. Advanced computer programs have shown the ability to "learn" from experience and "adapt" to new situations. They can understand language and communicate concepts and ideas. Any human that can do these things is considered to possess "consciousness." Some computer programs should be given the same designation.

9. Fruit has many attributes that are good for your health. Fruit provides energy, roughage, sugars, citric acid, vitamins, and minerals. The new candy bar, Chocolate Peanut Gooies, provides energy, roughage, sugar, citric acid, vitamins and minerals. How can it not be good for your health, too?

10. *Planet X24: Our Last Hope*, the new movie by director Billy Kuberg, has just been released. It's his fourth sci-fi film. His other three had newcomers in the starring roles, were based on novels by Joel Francis Hitchmann, opened in summer, and had huge marketing tie-ins. This new movie has an unknown in the lead role, is based on a novel by Joel Francis Hitchmann, is opening in the summer, and has huge marketing tie-ins. Each of Kuberg's first three sci-fi films grossed over 550 million dollars. I predict this new film will do about the same amount of business.

*11. I already ate apples, oranges, peaches, and cherries from her fruit stand, and I enjoyed all of them. I am going to try her pears. I am sure I will enjoy them.

12. I took Philosophy 101, 102, 103, and 104 and got and "A" for each course. I am going to take Philosophy 105, so I expect to get an "A" in that course as well.

13. Evidence indicates that adding fertilizer helps fruit trees and vegetables plants to grow better. Seaweed is a plant. So, adding fertilizer should help seaweed to grow better.

9.2 STATISTICAL REASONING AND PROBABILITY THEORY

Statistical reasoning concerns inferences that rely on the ability to generalize. When a pattern appears, the specific instances may be used as evidence that some regularity exists in nature. If the pattern occurs without exception, then we make a **universal generalization**. If the pattern occurs with some exceptions, then we make a **statistical generalization**. Sometimes we are interested in discovering new patterns, while at other times we try to explain why the patterns exist. We can create an inference that attempts to support a generalization, or we can create an inference that uses a generalization to support a specific claim. With an inference that supports a generalization (the conclusion), the premises have to provide convincing evidence that reveals the pattern. When a generalization is used as a premise to support a specific claim, there must be evidence in the premises that the specific item under question fits within the realm of the generalization. Finally, a good explanation of how or why a generalization exists requires an explanation that not only fits the existing data but also provides a way for new information to be discovered and tested. We will see examples of all these ideas in the rest of this chapter.

Analyzing Statistical Inferences

Statistical inferences are analyzed by determining the strength of the relationship between the premises and the conclusion. For example, suppose a scientist discovers two patterns in a topic she is studying. Upon examining a number of *M* items

Universal generalization: Based on a sample, a claim is made that every member of a given population has a specific characteristic.

Statistical generalization: Based on a sample, a claim is made that a certain percentage of a given population has a specific characteristic.

the researcher notices that *most* of them are also S. The same scientist also notices that *most* S are T. From these two generalizations, would it be correct to conclude that *most* M are T? The inference would be the following:

Example 9.4

Most *M* are *S*
Most *S* are *T*
Most *M* are *T*

Let's stipulate that for this example *most* means at least 70 percent (this is the percentage of M that is S and the percentage of S that is T). We can analyze the inference by making the premises true and determining if it is possible for the conclusion to be false.

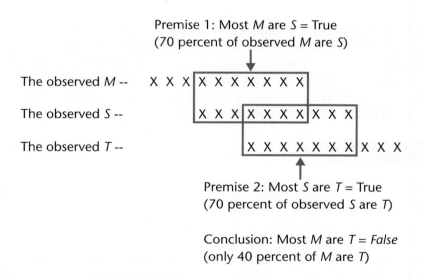

Premise 1: Most *M* are *S* = True
(70 percent of observed *M* are *S*)

The observed *M* --   X X X X X X X X X X

The observed *S* --   X X X X X X X X X X

The observed *T* --   X X X X X X X X X X

Premise 2: Most *S* are *T* = True
(70 percent of observed *S* are *T*)

Conclusion: Most *M* are *T* = *False*
(only 40 percent of *M* are *T*)

Our analysis shows that even if the premises are true, the conclusion could be false. Since we stipulated that "most" means at least 70 percent, the diagram reveals the possibility that only 40 percent of M are T. This logical possibility allows us to claim that the inference is inductively weak. In order to make the inference inductively strong we would need additional evidence to show that *most* M are T. This new evidence, if provided, would eliminate the logical possibility we have revealed. Therefore, as it stands, the inference is weak.

Let's look at another example.

Example 9.5

Suppose a criminal justice researcher wants to know the conviction rate in felony cases in the state where she teaches. She compiles this statistic: *Most (at least 70 percent) defendants are found guilty by a jury.* The researcher is then able to gain the defendants' trust and she finds out that *70 percent of those who are found guilty by a jury admit to the researcher they are guilty* (they admit this because the specific information will be kept confidential). It would not be unlikely for someone to combine these two statistics to create the following inference:

Most defendants are found guilty by a jury.
Most defendants who are found guilty by a jury are guilty.
Most defendants are guilty.

If we let M = "defendants," S = "found guilty by a jury," and T = "guilty," we get this statistical inference structure:

Most M are S
Most S are T
Most M are T

Since this is identical to Example 9.4, the results we saw earlier apply to this inference as well. Once again, we see the value of understanding the logical structure of an inference. We can rely on the results of previously analyzed inferences to help us recognize the strengths and weaknesses of similar inferences.

What if we now take one of the statistical claims and apply it to a specific case? Suppose we do the following:

Example 9.6

70 percent of defendants are found guilty by a jury.
Joe K. is a defendant.
Joe K. will be found guilty.

The conclusion makes a claim about a specific person based on statistical results. The most important piece of information for us to consider is the first premise. How accurate is this claim? How was this statistic derived? For us to correctly assess the strength of this inference we need to know as much as we can about the research that went into the claim of the first premise.

The next inference will reveal the same problems, but from a different angle.

Example 9.7

70 percent of a *sample* of defendants was found guilty.
It is *probable* that *approximately* 70 percent of all defendants will be found guilty.

It is crucial for us to know as much as possible about the sample mentioned in the first premise. How was it gathered? Was it a random sample? Is there any potential evidence that would show that the sample was not representative of the population of all defendants? Our answers to these questions will help determine the strength of an inference that uses statistical generalizations.

Population: Any group of objects (real or imaginary) that is the subject of investigation.

Sample: A subset of a population; information about specific characteristics of a sample are often generalized to a population.

Representative sample: When the characteristics of a sample are correctly identified and matched to the population under investigation.

Samples and Populations

Population refers to any group of objects, not just human populations. A **sample** is a subset, or part, of a population. If the population in question is the student body of a large urban university, say 10,000 students, then a sample would be any portion of that population. For example, let's imagine that a senior class in sociology is given an assignment in which they are told to determine the student populations' opinion on a proposed tuition increase. Two members of this class decide to work together. They each interview 2 students in the remaining three classes that day, for a total of 12 students. They discover that 10 students are opposed to the tuition increase. Armed with this data they make a bold generalization, which takes the form of the following inference.

Example 9.8

83 percent of a *sample* of students is opposed to a tuition increase.

Approximately 83 percent of the student *population* is opposed to a tuition increase.

The teacher points out that they have based their generalization on a small sample. A sample size of 12, relative to a student body of 10,000, is too small and is extremely unlikely to be **representative** of the population. This is an example of the *fallacy of hasty generalization* (see Chapter 8). There is no simple formula for calculating the ratio of sample size to population to ensure a representative sample. However, when a sample size is small relative to the size of the population, other factors (which we will soon discuss) would have to be in place to help ensure a representative sample has been achieved. Without the necessary equipment to strengthen it, however, a small sample weakens the inference.

Our intrepid students go back to work to gather more data. This time they make sure they gather a large sample. They begin polling more students in their classes, and they poll students from their dormitory. Their sample size swells to over 300 students. Analyzing the data prompts them to make a new inference.

Example 9.9

76 percent of a *sample* of 300 students is opposed to a tuition increase.

Approximately 76 percent of the student *population* is opposed to a tuition increase.

Their teacher does not question the sample size, but does inquire into the nature of the students polled. The researchers admit that the vast majority of those polled in their senior level classes are probably either juniors or seniors. Also, they live in a dorm reserved for juniors, seniors, and graduate students. These admissions weaken the inference because the sample is not representative of all students—it is *biased* toward upperclassmen. This is an example of the *fallacy of biased sample* (see Chapter 8). Freshmen and sophomores are underrepresented in the sample. If the researchers had restricted their conclusion to upperclassmen, then their inference would be stronger. This is because a sample is potentially biased if it leaves out members of a subset of the population that will be mentioned in the conclusion. Since the researchers wanted to generalize to the entire student population, their sample was biased because it excluded certain subsets of that population. The researchers go back to work and supplement their data by polling an appropriate number of freshmen and sophomores. Their new data yields a new inference.

Example 9.10

72 percent of a *sample* of 500 students is opposed to a tuition increase.

Approximately 72 percent of the student *population* is opposed to a tuition increase.

> **Strategy**
>
> Check to see if the sample is representative of the population. To be representative, the group mentioned in the sample must match the population referred to in the conclusion.

The teacher remarks that both the sample size and the distribution of students' year in school strengthen the inference. However, one more problem is uncovered. This is not a *random sample*. The researchers only polled students to whom they had easy access. To get a random sample you must ensure that *every member of the population has an equal chance of getting into the sample*. A random sample strengthens the likelihood that the sample represents the population.

EXERCISE SET 9.2A   ○○○

Exercises 1 and 3–11: For answers and explanations, see pages 274–276 of Instructor's Manual.

1. At the beginning of Section 9.2 we saw what might occur if we stipulate that "most" means "at least 70 percent." (a) Do the same type of inference analysis for Example 9.4 with the stipulation that "most" means "at least 80 percent." (b) Then do the same for "90 percent." Discuss your results.

Exercises 2–11 These exercises are fictional creations that reflect the kinds of information you might come across in newspapers, magazines, journals, and everyday conversation. Identify the sample and population in the following examples. Then discuss whether the sample is representative of the population mentioned in the conclusion. Analyze for sample size, potential bias, and randomness. Determine how your answers to these questions affect the strength/weakness of the inferences.

2. I am never going to buy another Hinckley car again. I had one and so did my sister. Both our cars were constantly in the shop. They had electrical and carburetor problems that caused them to stall all the time with no warning. Then

we would have to get them towed because they wouldn't start again. I am sure that all Hinckley cars have the same kinds of problems; that's why I won't buy one no matter what the price.

Answer:

Sample: Two Hinckley cars

Population: All Hinckley cars

Sample size: Two cars are a very small sample when we are discussing potentially millions of cars. This reduces the likelihood that the sample is representative of the population.

Potential bias: The sample excludes any cars that other owners might praise. It does not allow for the possibility of evidence that would go against its claims. This reduces the likelihood that the sample is representative of the population.

Randomness: This is not a random sample because not every Hinckley car had an equal chance of getting into the sample. This reduces the likelihood that the sample is representative of the population.

3. A veterinarian kept track, for 1 year, of all the dogs brought in for testing after they had bitten someone. Out of 132 dogs brought in, pit bulls accounted for 67 percent of all attacks resulting in wounds to people. The veterinarian concluded that pit bulls are twice as likely to bite someone as all other dog breeds combined.

4. A study of psychiatric outpatients at a major hospital in Chicago showed that patients given counseling, plus some form of drug therapy, stayed in the program only one-third as long as those given just counseling. For 3 years the researchers followed 1600 patients; half were given only counseling and the other half were given counseling and drug treatment. The group given counseling and drugs felt confident that they could now cope with their problems and left the program, while the group given just counseling stayed in the program three times longer.

5. There have been over 4000 UFO sightings around the world in the past 5 years alone. Our analysis of these cases shows that 78 percent of the sightings have never been adequately explained by any government agency in any country where the sightings occurred. The number of sightings that appear to be hoaxes or where the credibility of the eyewitnesses is under question is insignificant. Given this information, we can confidently say that UFOs are real and the sightings are unequivocally of extraterrestrial spaceships manned by organisms far more advanced than earthlings.

6. A random study of 6000 urban public high school seniors throughout the United States has confirmed what many have long suspected. The students were given the same verbal, mathematical, perceptual, and manual dexterity test that was given 20 years ago to high school seniors. The Bincaid-Forbush test had not been used for over 15 years, so the researchers thought that it could be a good way of comparing the results of the preceding generation (many of whom are probably the parents of today's seniors) with the current crop of students. As expected, the verbal and math scores have declined by 20 percent in today's U.S. students. Surprisingly, the perceptual and manual dexterity scores of today's students are 34 percent higher than their parents' generation. The researchers speculate that the rise of computers and video

games can explain both results. They hypothesize that the verbal and math skills have deteriorated because video games require very little reading or calculating. However, these games require superior perceptual and manual dexterity skills and thus give today's students much more exposure to this kind of skill development.

*7. I have closely examined 93 wars that took place within the last 200 years. I use the word "war" to include both external conflicts (between two or more countries) and internal or civil wars. In 84 percent of those cases the wars were precipitated by a recent change in the government. Specifically, those 84 percent occurred soon after a "conservative leader" of that country took over from someone who was more "liberal." The terms "conservative" and "liberal" are applied after examining and rating the leader on a scale of 1–10 for variables related to economic beliefs, religious pronouncements, social welfare programs, military buildup, judicial appointments, immigration laws, and the treatment of criminals. From these results we can safely conclude that approximately 4 out of every 5 future wars around the world will occur after a conservative leader replaces a liberal leader.

8. Eight out ten people surveyed chose Slacker Soda over the next four most popular brands of soft drink. It is clear that America has spoken. Eighty percent of all Americans can't be wrong. Don't you think that you should start drinking Slacker Soda?

9. Research on people's dreams shows that they are not visions of the future. A group of psychologists monitored 30 volunteers for 1 year. The volunteers were told to keep a daily log only of the dreams they could clearly recall. They were also told to record anything that happened within a few days of the dream that they felt corresponded to the dream (to determine if they thought the dream was a "premonition"). On average, the volunteers recorded three dreams a night. In 1 year the researchers had over 25,000 dreams to analyze. They found that less than 1 percent of the dreams could be accurately correlated with a subsequent event in the dreamer's life (and these were usually trivial events). They concluded that humans' dreams do not "come from the future," they do not offer a glimpse of some inevitable occurrence, nor do they act as a warning so we can avoid unpleasant events.

10. From the year 1889 to 2001, whenever the American League won the World Series, cigarette sales rose 20 percent over the previous year. But when the National League won the World Series, liquor sales rose 25 percent for the next year. Stock buyers pay heed! Watch who wins the World Series and then buy or sell accordingly.

11. A study of college majors has revealed some interesting results. The study looked at more than 20,000 students who were accepted to law schools and medical schools in the United States for the past 20 years. The highest *percentage* of any major to be accepted to both law and medical schools was philosophy majors. The researchers speculate that this can be partially explained by the fact that philosophy majors have to take numerous logic courses and to write critical papers using logical reasoning. Since both the LSAT and MCAT (the law school and medical school standardized tests required of all applicants) have a *logical reasoning* section, the philosophy majors are better prepared and tend to score higher on that section. The researchers encourage anyone planning to apply to law or medical school to take as many philosophy courses that they can.

A Priori Theory of Probability

The term *a priori* refers to those situations where we can determine whether something is true or false without having any experience of the items involved. For example, the statement, "All bachelors are unmarried males," can be known to be true by definition, without ever having come in contact with any bachelors. Similarly for the statement, "All unicorns have one horn." The *a priori* **theory of probability** ascribes to a simple event a fraction between 0 and 1; the denominator of this fraction is the number of equally possible, or **equiprobable**, outcomes, and the numerator is the number of outcomes in which the event in question occurs. Probability calculations using the *a priori*, or classical, theory rely on hypothetical reasoning based on two major assumptions: (1) All the possible outcomes of a given situation can be determined; (2) Each of the possible outcomes has an equal probability of occurring (equiprobable). This can be illustrated by a coin toss example. The reason we quickly calculate the probability of the coin coming up heads (or tails) as 1/2 (or 50 percent, or .5, or 50-50) is precisely because we have assumed that: (1) there are two possible outcomes, heads or tails, and (2) each of these two possible outcomes has an equal probability of occurring. The outcome in question is turned into a fraction by making the number of positive outcomes the numerator and the number of all the possible outcomes the denominator. This is why we calculate the probability of "heads" coming up as 1/2 (the numerator is the positive outcome, "heads," and the denominator is all the possible outcomes "heads and tails").

It is not surprising that the *a priori* theory originated with games of chance. One of the major requirements for such calculations is that all the possible outcomes can be determined. Any game, including coin tosses, dice, and lotteries, where the positive outcomes and the total possible outcomes can be determined is subject to *a priori* calculations. The assumption of equiprobable outcomes is really the assumption of randomness. The foundation of the *a priori* theory is nonempirical—it does not depend on experience or on experimental results. Of course, this does not mean that any actual coin, or pair of dice, or lottery, is perfectly random. The hypothetical nature of the *a priori* calculations is based on nonverifiable assumptions.

Dice usually come in pairs (one of a pair of dice is called a *die*). We can ask the question, "What is the probability of a die coming up 4 on the next (or any) toss?" Assuming that all outcomes are equiprobable ensures that it is a "fair" game. Why is this so? Since equiprobable is the same as the assumption of randomness, a hypothetically "fair" game is ensured. Of course, we must make some other assumptions as well. The "hypothetical" die is given these additional characteristics: six sides; only one of the numerals 1, 2, 3, 4, 5, 6 occurs on each of the six die faces. We also stipulate that any throw of the die that lands on an edge will not count as a legitimate outcome. The probability of the die coming up 4 can now be easily calculated as a fraction. The one positive outcome (4) becomes the numerator, and all the possible outcomes become the denominator, giving us the fraction 1/6. What is the probability that an even number will come up on any toss of the die? There are three positive outcomes, 2, 4, and 6, so the probability of an even number coming up 3/6, or 1/2. These results illustrate how we can calculate the probability of a single event. (Calculation of the occurrence of compound events is the subject of a later section.)

Relative frequency theory of probability: A theory in which probability is defined as the relative frequency with which members of a class exhibit some attribute.

Relative Frequency Theory of Probability

Although there are historical accounts of insurance schemes going back at least 2,000 years, the fundamental probability methods needed to produce accurate actuarial tables were only developed after the year 1650. The **relative frequency theory of probability** relies on direct observation of events. According to this theory, probabilities can be computed by dividing the number of favorable cases by the total number of observed cases. For example, companies that offered insurance for ships bringing goods to a country needed to know how many ships successfully returned to port. Accurate empirical research was necessary to determine the number of ships leaving port, the number of ships arriving safely back, as well as the amount of goods successfully imported. Over time, adequate information enabled insurers to charge just enough for insurance to make it affordable to shipping companies, as well as guaranteeing a profit to the insurance company. Charging too much for insurance would scare away potential customers, while charging too little would mean that the insurance company would not have enough money to pay off claims.

To calculate the probability of an event when we cannot know *a priori* all the possible positive and negative outcomes requires a different method. Researchers must observe enough events to arrive at accurate probability calculations. To know the probability that a 20-year-old female will live to age 65 requires thousands of observations of 20-year-old females to see how many actually live to age 65. For example, researchers might track 10,000 20-year-old females for the next 45 years to see how many were still alive. On the other hand, the researchers might go back 45 years and get a list of 10,000 females who were 20 years old at that time. They then would need to find out how many of those 10,000 females were still alive today.

The total number of observed cases (10,000) becomes the denominator of a fraction, while the positive outcomes (those actually living to age 65) becomes the numerator. Therefore, if 9,200 females were still alive at age 65 the fraction would be 9,200/10,000. This can be reduced to 92/100, which means that there is a 92 percent chance that a 20-year-old female will live to age 65, according to the historical data. The frequency of a 20-year-old female living to age 65 is relative to the set of observed cases, thus the designation *relative frequency theory*. The formula for this method is the following:

$$Pr\ (A) = p/tn$$

The formula tells us that the probability of an event, *Pr (A)*, is equal to the number of positive outcomes, *p*, divided by the total number of observed cases, *tn*.

It is important not to misapply the probability calculations. An insurance company that relies on the above information to issue a life insurance policy to a 20-year-old female would not be predicting that this particular individual has a 92 percent chance of living to age 65. This individual is considered a member of the total class of 20-year-old females, so her probability of living to age 65 is relative to the probability regarding the entire class, which in this case is 92 percent. The insurance company is not only insuring this one particular 20-year-old female, they hope to insure thousands. The monthly premium the insurance company charges each female is calculated to guarantee the company will have enough to pay off the 8 percent of the females who will die before they reach age 65, plus ensure the company a profit.

Subjectivist Theory of Probability

There are situations in which neither *a priori* nor relative frequency methods work. For example, if you want to calculate the probability of a particular horse winning the Kentucky Derby, the historical data regarding that horse has to be analyzed using a different method. Professional sports gamblers rely on their own "power figures" to determine the likelihood of a team winning a football, baseball, hockey, or basketball game. However, their reliance on statistical and historical data is not the same as relative frequency applications. A team's won-lost record is certainly information relevant to predicting how they will do in the future. However, the number of variables affecting the outcome of a sporting event is immense. The team playing this year is not identical to last year's team. Players come and go, they get older, they get injured, with the result that no two teams match up identically with their past performances.

Calculations of this kind fall under the **subjectivist theory of probability**. The subjectivity of these probability determinations occurs when we do not have total knowledge regarding an event. However, this should not be interpreted as meaning that these probability calculations are mere guesses. Professional gamblers and professional stock market investors rely on their ability to weigh the pluses and minuses of a wager or investment based on their years of experience and their ability to sift and weigh pertinent information. Success is measured by their ability to win more than they lose.

Subjectivist probability calculations can often rely on relative frequency data. For example, horse gamblers know that statistical data continuously verifies that the "favorite" (the horse that has the most money bet on it) wins approximately one-third of the time (33 percent). Now, if there are on average ten horses in a race, only one will be the favorite. (It is also possible for two horses to be co-favorites; this occurs if the same amount of money is bet on each horse.) If horse races were random events, then *a priori* calculations would tell us that the favorite should win only 10 percent of the time. Statistical data seems to provide clear evidence that this is not the case. Given this, is it therefore wise to bet the favorite in every race? Wouldn't you be assured of picking the winner 33 percent of the time? The answer to the second question is "yes." The answer to the first question is "no." Although this system will ensure that you will have a winning ticket one-third of the time, you also have a losing ticket two-thirds of the time. In addition, the "favorite" has the most money bet on it, so the payoff is the smallest of all the potential payoffs. You would need to get 2:1 (two-to-one) odds *just to break even*; but unfortunately, "favorites" pay far less than that, on average. For example, suppose you make a $2.00 bet on the favorite in nine races. You will have invested a total of $18.00. Since favorites pay approximately $4.00 to win, and since you will win only 1/3 of the time (3 races), you will get back around $12.00. Therefore, you will lose approximately $6.00 for each $18.00 invested.

Sometimes we use probability calculations to refer to events, but they can be used to refer to statements as well. For example, suppose I draw a marble at random from a jar containing five red, five black, and five green marbles, and I ask you to guess the color. There are actually two different situations occurring at the same time. Let's imagine that the marble has already been picked and I can see that it is red, but you cannot see it. From my perspective, the probability of its being red is "1,"

Subjectivist theory of probability: Situations can arise where neither *a priori* nor relative frequency methods will work. The subjectivity of these probability determinations occurs when we do not have total knowledge regarding an event.

because I have total knowledge of the outcome. From your perspective, all three colors have equal probability (1/3), because you lack certain information. If you say, "The marble is red," then your *statement* has a 1/3 chance of being true, from your perspective. From my perspective, your statement *is* true. Therefore, probability is intimately connected to the availability of relevant information regarding an event.

Probability Calculus

Probability calculus refers to the set of rules that facilitates the direct calculation of the probability of compound events from the probability of simple events. The results of probability calculations can be displayed as fractions, percentages, ratios, or as a number between 0 and 1. The examples we have looked at so far are contingent events, where the probability lies somewhere between 0 and 1. But what is the probability that the next toss of a coin will come up either heads or tails? (We stipulate that any throw of the coin that lands on an edge will not count as a legitimate outcome.) Now, since there are two positive outcomes (heads or tails), and two possible outcomes (heads or tails), the fraction is 1/1 or just 1. This result corresponds to our notion of a *tautology*, a noncontingent statement. At the opposite end of the probability spectrum is the probability that the coin will come up both heads and tails at the same time. Since the positive outcomes are 0, the fraction is 0/2, or just 0. This result corresponds to our notion of a *self-contradiction*, another kind of noncontingent statement. However, most of our examples will be about contingent events.

Conjunction Methods When we need to calculate the probability of two or more events occurring together (*A and B*), we rely on one of two conjunction methods: the *restricted* or the *general*. Each conjunction method provides a formula for a simple calculation of joint occurrences.

The **restricted conjunction method** is used for situations in which there are two or more events that are independent of each other—the occurrence of one event has no bearing whatsoever on the occurrence or nonoccurrence of the other event. For example, "tails," occurring on one toss of the coin has no effect on the probability of "tails" (or "heads," for that matter) occurring or not occurring on the next toss; these are independent events. The formula for calculating the probability of occurrence of two independent events is:

$$Pr\ (A\ and\ B) = Pr\ (A) \times Pr\ (B)$$

Why must we multiply the probability of the first occurrence *(A)* times the probability of the second occurrence *(B)*? The coin toss example provides the justification. Suppose a coin is tossed two times. *A priori* assumptions allow us to list all the possible outcomes as follows:

Toss #1	**Toss#2**
Heads	Heads
Tails	Tails
Heads	Tails
Tails	Heads

Probability calculus:
A branch of mathematics that can be used to compute the probabilities of compound events from the probability of simple events.

Restricted conjunction method: The method used for situations dealing with two (or more) independent events, where the occurrence of one event has no bearing on the occurrence or nonoccurrence of the other event. The formula for this method is: *Pr (A and B) = Pr (A) × Pr (B)*

Of course, these four possible combinations can go in any order. This particular list of the compound events is used only for reference purposes. According to the list, the conjunction, "tails and tails," occurs once. Since there are four possible outcomes, the probability is 1/4 for the occurrence of "tails and tails." The formula should give the identical results. The formula shows that the probability of "tails and tails," *Pr (A and B)*, is equal to the probability of "tails" (toss #1) *times* the probability of "tails" (toss #2). Since the probability of the positive outcome "tails" is 1/2 for each independent event, we multiply 1/2 × 1/2 to get the *Pr (A and B)* = 1/4, which is identical to the result in the list of possible outcomes.

What is the probability that "4" will come up in two successive throws of a die? The restricted conjunction formula gives this result.

$$Pr \ (A \ and \ B) = 1/6 \times 1/6$$

Under the *a priori* assumption of equiprobable outcomes the probability of each independent occurrence of "4" is calculated as 1/6. Therefore, the final determination that "4" will come up in any two successive throws of the die is 1/6 × 1/6 = 1/36. This can be verified by listing all the possible outcomes. The list might start with the possibility that first toss will be "1." There would then be six possibilities conjoined with this result (the second toss could result in any of the six numbers coming up). Since the same number of possibilities can be conjoined with any of the six numbers occurring on the first toss, there would be 36 total possible outcomes, of which only one would correspond to the joint occurrence of "4 and 4." This result, 1/36, matches the result from using the above formula. Although both methods are reliable, it is obvious that the formula is more efficient and convenient than generating lists of possibilities.

The **general conjunction method** facilitates the calculation of the probability of two (or more) events occurring together, regardless of whether the two (or more) events are independent or not independent. Two (or more) events are not independent when the occurrence of one event affects the probability of the other event. In these cases, the probability of subsequent events is dependent on prior events. For example, if a jar contains ten marbles, five red, and five black, then what is the probability of picking two red ones in succession *if we do not put the first marble back into the jar*? Since we are reducing the number of marbles from ten to nine, the probability of picking a second red marble becomes dependent on our first pick.

Given the jar of marbles, the probability that the first marble picked will be red is 5/10, or 1/2. However, if the first marble is red and it is not put back into the jar, then there will be only nine marbles left, four of which will be red. So, now the probability that the second marble picked will be red changes to 4/9. The formula for the general conjunction method is the following:

$$Pr \ (A \ and \ B) = Pr \ (A) \times Pr \ (B, \ if \ A)$$

With this formula it is easy to compute the probability that two red marbles will be picked in succession. The probability that the first marble picked will be red, *Pr (A)*, is 1/2. The probability that the second marble picked will be red, *Pr (B, if A)*, is 4/9.

$$Pr \ (A \ and \ B) = 1/2 \times 4/9$$

General conjunction method: This method facilitates the calculation of the probability of two (or more) events occurring together, regardless of whether the two (or more) events are independent or not independent. In these cases the probability of subsequent events is dependent on prior events happening (or not happening). The formula for this method is: *Pr (A and B) = Pr (A) × Pr (B, if A)*

Restricted disjunction method: This method is used in situations where: (1) two (or more) events are independent of each other, and (2) the events are mutually exclusive (if one event occurs then the other cannot). The formula for this method is: $Pr\ (A\ or\ B) = Pr\ (A) + Pr\ (B)$

General disjunction method: This method is used in situations where two (or more) events are not mutually exclusive. The formula for this method is: $Pr\ (A\ or\ B) = [Pr\ (A) + Pr\ (B)] - [Pr\ (A) \times Pr\ (B)]$

Therefore, the probability that two red marbles will be picked in succession, under these conditions, is $1/2 \times 4/9 = 4/18$, or $2/9$.

What is the probability that the first three marbles picked from our jar will all be red? If the first two marbles are red, then there are only eight marbles left in the jar, of which three are red. Using the formula gives these results:

$$Pr\ (A\ and\ B\ and\ C) = 1/2 \times 4/9 \times 3/8$$

Therefore, the probability that three red marbles will be picked in succession, under these conditions, is $1/2 \times 4/9 \times 3/8 = 12/144$, or $1/12$.

Disjunction Methods When we need to calculate the probability that either one of two or more events will occur *(A or B)*, we rely on one of two disjunction methods, the *restricted* or the *general*. Each disjunction method provides a formula for easy calculation of either one of two independent events.

There are two requirements for using the **restricted disjunction method**: (1) the situation must involve two or more events that are independent of each other, and (2) the events must be mutually exclusive (if one event occurs, then the other cannot). The formula for this method is:

$$Pr\ (A\ or\ B) = Pr\ (A) + Pr\ (B)$$

Suppose five green marbles are added to the jar already containing five red and five black marbles. The above formula can be used to compute the probability of picking *either a red or a black marble*. The probability of picking red, *Pr A*, is 5/15, or 1/3. The probability of picking black is the same, 5/15, or 1/3. Therefore, we get the following result:

$$Pr\ (A\ or\ B) = 1/3 + 1/3$$

So, the probability of picking *either a red or a black* marble is $1/3 + 1/3 = 2/3$. What is the probability of picking *either a red, or a black, or a green* marble? Since we get $1/3 + 1/3 + 1/3 = 1$, it is a *certainty* that you will pick one of the three colored marbles.

What is the probability that you will throw *either a "4" or an odd number,* if you throw one die? The formula gives these results:

$$Pr\ (A\ or\ B) = 1/6 + 1/2$$

The probability of throwing a "4," *Pr (A)*, is 1/6 for a six-sided die, and the probability of throwing an "odd number" is 1/2. Therefore, the probability that you will throw *either a "4" or an odd number* is $1/6 + 1/2 = 1/6 + 3/6 = 4/6$, or 2/3.

The **general disjunction method** is used for situations where two or more events are not mutually exclusive. The formula for this method is:

$$Pr\ (A\ or\ B) = [Pr\ (A) + Pr\ (B)] - [Pr\ (A) \times Pr\ (B)]$$

The formula is complex, but it works. For example, suppose we wanted to compute the probability that "tails" will come up in either of the first two tosses of a coin. Since these are independent events, the probability of "tails" coming up on the first toss, *Pr (A)*, is 1/2; the same probability, 1/2, exists for the second toss, *Pr (B)*. But these are *not* mutually exclusive events. Therefore, the use of the restricted disjunction formula gives this result:

$$Pr\ (A\ or\ B) = 1/2 + 1/2$$

This would mean that the probability of a "tails" coming up in either of the first two tosses would be $1/2 + 1/2 = 1$. But surely this cannot be correct. Let's look once again at the list of possibilities for tossing a coin two times.

<u>Toss #1</u>	<u>Toss #2</u>
Heads	Heads
Tails	Tails
Heads	Tails
Tails	Heads

The list yields four possibilities, three of which contain at least one "tail" coming up. This means that the probability of a "tail" coming up in either of the first two tosses is 3/4. The general disjunction formula should give the same result.

$$Pr\ (A\ or\ B) = [1/2 + 1/2] - [1/2 \times 1/2]$$

The fractions in the first set of brackets *add up* to 1. The product of the fractions in the second set of brackets is 1/4. Therefore, the probability of getting a "tails" in either of two tosses is $1 - 1/4 = 3/4$. The complexity of the general disjunction formula is warranted.

Suppose we pick from our jar of five red, five black, and five green marbles. What is the probability of getting a black marble in either of two picks, provided we return the first marble picked back into the jar? The formula gives these results:

$$Pr\ (A\ or\ B) = [1/3 + 1/3] - [1/3 \times 1/3]$$

The first set of brackets gives us $1/3 + 1/3 = 2/3$. The second set of brackets gives us $1/3 \times 1/3 = 1/9$. We can change 2/3 into 6/9 to allow the subtraction of the second bracket. Our final result is $6/9 - 1/9 = 5/9$. This is the probability of getting a black marble in either of two picks from the jar.

Negation Method Once we know the probability of the occurrence of an event, we can easily calculate the probability of the event *not* occurring. The formula for the **negation method** is:

$$Pr\ (\sim A) = 1 - Pr\ (A)$$

For example, as we saw earlier with the restricted conjunction method, the probability of getting two "tails" in successive tosses of a coin is 1/4. Using this information, the negation formula allows us to calculate the probability that two "tails" in succession will not occur.

$$Pr\ (\sim A) = 1 - 1/4$$

Therefore, the probability that two "tails" will not occur in succession is $1 - 1/4 = 3/4$.

The general disjunction method calculations showed that the probability of a "tail" coming up in either of the first two coin tosses is 3/4. Applying this information to the negation formula makes it possible to calculate the probability that a "tail" will *not* come up in either of the first two tosses of a coin.

$$Pr\ (\sim A) = 1 - 3/4$$

Negation method: Once the probability of an event occurring is known it is easy to calculate the probability of the event not occurring. The formula for the negation method is this:
$Pr\ (\sim A) = 1 - Pr\ (A)$

Therefore, the probability that a "tail" will *not* occur in either of the first two tosses is *1 − 3/4 = 1/4*. This is in agreement with the list of possibilities, because the only way at least one "tail" will *not* come up in two successive tosses is if two "heads" come up. The probability of that happening is 1/4.

EXERCISE SET 9.2B   ○○○

Exercises 2–22: For answers and explanations, see pages 278–279 of Instructor's Manual.

1. A deck of 52 playing cards containing 2 red queens and 2 black queens is thoroughly shuffled. Determine the probability of picking one card at random and getting a black queen.

Answer: 2/52 = 1/26. There are 2 black queens and 52 cards.

2. 1/13

2. Determine the probability of picking one card at random and getting any queen.

3. 1/221

3. Determine the probability of picking two cards at random (without replacing the first one picked) and getting any two queens.

4. 1/1326

4. Determine the probability of picking two cards at random (without replacing the first one picked) and getting both black queens.

5. 1/49

5. Determine the probability that two people randomly chosen will both be born on the same day of the week.

6. 1/2401

*6. Determine the probability that four people randomly chosen will all be born on the same day of the week.

7. 1/144

7. Determine the probability that two people randomly chosen will both be born in the same month of the year.

8. 1/20736

8. Determine the probability that four people randomly chosen will all be born in the same month of the year.

9. 1/4

9. Determine the probability that two people randomly chosen will both have their Social Security numbers end with an odd number.

10. 1/16

10. Determine the probability that four people randomly chosen will all have their Social Security numbers end with an odd number.

11. 7/8

*11. Imagine that there are two identical opaque jars, but one contains a red marble and the other contains a black marble. Suppose you are allowed to pick a marble from any jar you wish. You record the results (red or black marble picked) replace the marble, and have the jars' positions randomly mixed again. The procedure is repeated until you have picked three times. Determine the probability that you will pick the red marble *at least once*.

12. 2/35

12. Imagine a box of 15 CD's contains these types of music:
4 jazz CD's, 4 classical CD's, 3 rap CD's, 3 reggae CD's, and 1 disco CD.
If two CD's are drawn, but the first CD is *not* put back into the box before the second is picked, determine the probability that both CD's will be jazz.

13. 16/225

13. From the information given in #12, if two CD's are drawn, but the first CD is put back into the box before the second is picked, determine the probability that both CD's will be jazz.

14. From the information given in #12, if two CD's are drawn, but the first CD is *not* put back into the box before the second is picked, determine the probability that *neither* CD will be jazz.

14. 33/35

15. From the information given in #12, if two CD's are drawn, but the first CD *is* put back into the box before the second is picked, determine the probability that *neither* CD will be jazz.

15. 209/225

*16. If you knew only that George Washington was born in February, what is the probability that, if given one guess, you will correctly pick the date he was born? What if he was born in a leap year?

16. Part 1: 1/28
Part 2: 1/29

17. In a normal deck of 52 playing cards there are 4 aces, 2 red and 2 black. What is the probability that a single card chosen at random will be a red ace? That it will be any ace at all?

17. Part 1: 1/26
Part 2: 1/13

18. What is the probability that the age of two people, chosen at random, will both be an even number?

18. 1/4

19. What is the probability that the age of each of five people, chosen at random, will be an even number?

19. 1/32

20. If a person was born in a month that ended with the letters "ber," then what is the probability that that month is October?

20. 1/4

*21. If a person was born in a month that ended with the letters "ber," then what is the probability that that month was October or November?

21. 1/2

22. Suppose there are two indistinguishable envelopes, one containing a $1 bill, and the other a $100 bill. You pick one envelope, its contents are revealed to you, and the money is replaced. You do this again two more times, for a total of three picks. What is the probability that you will pick the envelope with the $100 bill at least once?

22. 7/8

23. Suppose you have a drawer of socks in these colors and amounts:

3 black socks

4 white socks

4 brown socks

3 orange socks

1 red sock

If you draw two socks in succession, without replacing the first before the second draw, then what is the probability that both socks will be brown?

23. See page 279 of Instructor's Manual for complete answer.

True Odds in Games of Chance

A "fair" game of chance is one where the payoff odds of winning guarantee that, in the long run, the gambler will break even. The ability to calculate "true" odds will allow you to determine whether you are playing a fair game, or if the odds are stacked against you. We know that a coin toss has an equal probability of coming up "heads" or "tails," so each has a probability of 1/2. If you bet one dollar on each toss of the coin you will *win* the same number of times that you will *lose*, in the long run. Since there are 1 out of 2 chances of winning, 1 out of 2 chances of losing, true odds for this game are one-to-one, written as 1:1. So, for every dollar you bet you will get one dollar if you win. If you lose, then your dollar is taken away.

As we calculated earlier, the probability of "4" coming up on one toss of a die is 1/6. Using the negation formula, we determine the probability that "4" will *not* come up as 5/6. Therefore, if you bet that "4" will come up, you must *receive* odds of 5:1 to ensure a fair bet. On the other hand, if you bet that "4" will *not* come up then you must be willing to *give* 5:1 odds.

Most casino games do not provide true odds. This should not be surprising, since the casinos would not survive if there were an equal chance of winning or losing on their games. To ensure a winning margin, casino games offer odds stacked in their favor, odds designed to guarantee that the casino will win, in the long run. For example, the majority of American roulette wheels contain 18 red numbers and 18 black numbers, arranged from 1–36. In addition, there are two green numbers, "0" and "00." Since there are a total of 38 possible outcomes, the probability of "red" coming up is 18/38. The probability that "red" will *not* come up is, therefore, 20/38 (18 black numbers plus 2 green numbers). Therefore, if you bet "red," the odds are slightly against your winning. However, the casino will only offer you 1:1 odds for this bet (meaning that you will get a dollar back for each dollar you bet). After thousands of such bets, the casino is guaranteed to come out ahead.

If you decide to place your bet on your "lucky" number, what will happen? The casino is willing to give you 35:1 odds for this bet. But since there are 38 numbers, the odds are once again not "true." Odds only have to deviate slightly away from "true" odds to provide the casino with a winning margin, especially with millions of bets taken annually.

Bayesian Theory

A major advance in probability theory and method came when Thomas Bayes was able to unite much of the probability calculus and the relative frequency theory into a method for calculating conditional probability. **Conditional probability** is the probability of an event occurring if another event has already happened. Bayes' ideas proved to be so useful that numerous variations of his basic idea were formulated and applied to diverse issues. There are formulas for calculating various kinds of risk assessment, hypothesis testing, and the probability of false positives in disease testing. Bayes' theory is also used extensively in the area of the predictive ability of measures (the ability to predict outcomes based on tests). For example, formulas are available to determine if the SAT is a useful predictor of success in college.

We will look at one conditional probability formula that combines the restricted disjunction method, the general conjunction method, the negation method, and the relative frequency theory. If you recall, the general conjunction method introduced the idea of conditional probability in a limited way. It allowed us to calculate the probability of one event occurring if another event occurred first. What Bayes' theory does is to expand this basic conditional to include relative frequency results. Here is the formula we will be using:

$$Pr\ (A,\ if\ B) = \frac{Pr\ (B,\ if\ A) \times Pr\ (A)}{Pr\ (B)}$$

Conditional probabililty:
The probability of an event occurring if another event has already happened.

This formula allows us to calculate the conditional probability of two mutually exclusive and exhaustive events. As defined earlier, *mutually exclusive* means they both cannot happen at the same time; *exhaustive* means there are no other possibilities. For example, consider the following problem:

> A teacher wants to determine whether perfect attendance is a good predictor of passing her courses. She calculates that 80 percent of the students who passed had perfect attendance. The data also indicate that 10 percent of students who did *not* pass had perfect attendance. Of the total number of students in all her classes, 75 percent passed the courses. What is the correct interpretation of the data? Is perfect attendance a good predictor of passing the courses?

This problem fulfills the requirements set forth above. There are two possibilities for each event: (1) passing or not passing, and (2) perfect attendance or not perfect attendance. Together they form a set of mutually exclusive and exhaustive events (a student cannot both pass and not pass, and a student cannot both have perfect attendance and not have perfect attendance).

If A = *passing the course* and B = *perfect attendance*, we can then use the data to fill in the formula. We want to determine the probability of passing, *if perfect attendance is achieved*, which is written as $Pr\ (A,\ if\ B)$. Suppose the following data is provided:

1. The probability of perfect attendance, if they passed the course, is 80 percent or .80, which can be written as $Pr\ (B,\ if\ A) = .80$

2. The probability of perfect attendance, if they did *not* pass the course, is 10 percent or .10, which can be written as $Pr\ (B,\ if\ {\sim}A) = .10$

3. The probability of passing the course is 75 percent or .75, which can be written as $Pr\ (A) = .75$

This information can now be applied directly to the general formula given above:

$$Pr\ (A,\ if\ B) = \frac{(.80 \times .75)}{Pr\ (B)}$$

$$Pr\ (A,\ if\ B) = \frac{.60}{Pr\ (B)}$$

A new formula is needed to calculate the $Pr\ (B)$, one that allows the calculation of *total probability*:

$$Pr\ (B) = [Pr\ (B,\ if\ A) \times Pr\ (A)] + [Pr\ (B,\ if\ {\sim}A) \times Pr\ ({\sim}A)]$$

This formula can be interpreted by using information from the example. The probability of B (perfect attendance) is defined through a set of conditional relationships. The left set of brackets relates B to A (passing), while the right set of brackets relates B to ${\sim}A$ (not passing). Since A and ${\sim}A$ are mutually exclusive, the *total probability* of B (*perfect attendance*) can be calculated by determining the complete relationship with A and ${\sim}A$. Since the data shows that the $Pr\ (A) = .75$, the negation formula can be used to calculate the $Pr\ ({\sim}A) = .25$. Placing this information into the formula makes it possible to calculate the $Pr\ (B)$.

$$Pr\ (B) = (.80 \times .75) + (.10 \times .25)$$
$$Pr\ (B) = .60 + .025$$
$$Pr\ (B) = .625$$

Adding this information to the previous calculations gives the following result:

$$Pr\ (A,\ if\ B) = \frac{.60}{.625}$$

$$Pr\ (A,\ if\ B) = .96$$

Therefore, perfect attendance would be a strong measure for predicting who will pass the course.

EXERCISE SET 9.2C   ○○○

1. See page 279 of Instructor's Manual for complete answer.

1. Imagine that a researcher gathers data using a new test for high school seniors, the *Multiphasic Aptitude Diagnostic* test (MAD). He wants to determine whether scoring above 1200 on the MAD test is a good predictor of graduating college with a GPA greater than 3.5. He calculates that 70 percent of the students who graduated with a GPA greater than 3.5 scored above 1200 on the MAD test. The data also indicate that 25 percent of students who did *not* graduate with a GPA greater than 3.5 scored above 1200 on the MAD test. The total number of students who graduated with a GPA greater than 3.5 was 10 percent. What is the correct interpretation of the data? Is scoring above 1200 on the MAD test a good predictor of graduating college with a GPA greater than 3.5?

9.3 SCIENTIFIC AND CAUSAL REASONING

Scientific and causal reasoning provide important and interesting examples of inference creation and analysis. In this section, we will look at the role of scientific hypotheses and theories, and apply inductive analysis to determine the strength of cause-effect inferences.

Theoretical and Experimental Science

We sometimes need an explanation that captures facts and gives us a way of discovering new facts. This is what a good hypothesis does. It provides an explanation for some known facts and provides a way to test this explanation. Some hypotheses can foster the development of new technologies, which in turn, create stronger machinery for exploring the world. Such improved technical machinery and new inventions allow us to make more precise observations, and these advances help us to discover new facts. In schematic form, the progress of science and technology seems to follow the pattern shown below.

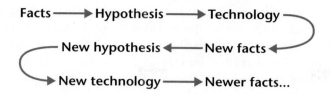

The interplay of science and technology is complex. There are two aspects of science, the *theoretical* and the *experimental*. In simple terms, theoretical science proposes explanations for observations of natural phenomena, while experimental science tests these explanations. Both theoretical and experimental science are involved in the development of new inventions and technologies that may allow us to gather new data, new facts about the physical world. For example, the creation of better and stronger lenses allowed Galileo to see clearly the surface of our moon and to discover some moons of Jupiter. The new information gathered with the improved telescopes was used to refute the then generally accepted view of the universe and Earth's place in it. Recent advances in technology are forcing us to rethink our theories of mind and consciousness; this is especially true in the role that genetics plays in human behavior. On the other hand, the *theoretical* breakthroughs regarding the structure of DNA provided experimental scientists with clues about where to look, what to look for, and what can be predicted based on consequences of the theoretical work. The early twentieth century saw the rise of Einstein's theories of space and time, as well as the quantum theory (the physics of subatomic particles). These theories predicted many unexpected results, the verification of which required improvements in technology.

Cause-Effect Analysis

Hypotheses may be easy to propose, but difficult to test. Exploring this idea will allow us to see how experiments and predictions help us understand the world. This, in turn, will enable us to analyze scientific and causal inferences.

The best way to test hypotheses is with controlled experiments. A **controlled experiment** is one in which multiple experimental setups differ by only one variable. In "real life" there are too many variables affecting the outcome of a situation, making it very difficult to make strong cause-effect claims. But the laboratory setting can reduce the number of variables. For example, suppose we want to see the effect of a new fertilizer on plant growth. Identical seeds can be grown in identical pots with identical soils, given exactly the same amount of water, light, and so on. However, one group of plants would be given a precise amount of a fertilizer, which the other group, the **control group**, does not get. At the end of the experiment, the plants of the two groups are compared. Any statistical difference between the groups might then be ascribed to the fertilizer. Further tests, as well as repetition of the experiment, would be necessary before the effects of the fertilizer, positive or negative, could be accepted as definitive. In this way, laboratory experiments allow us to uncover cause-effect relationships.

Controlled experiment:
An experiment in which there are multiple experimental setups that differ by only one variable.

Control group:
In a controlled experiment, experimental setups that are identical to the rest except that they are not exposed to the factor being tested.

Many things can affect the results of an experiment, and scientists go to great pains to ensure that nothing disrupts the setting. This is why taking the results of laboratory experiments and proclaiming that similar connections exist in the outside world is so problematic. Many scientists realize this and admit that their promising lab results may not fit the world at large. Unfortunately, popularized versions of lab results are sometimes disseminated mistakenly to the public. This is why we often see claims that cures for certain diseases have been found, or that scientists have isolated the cause of a disease, only to be disappointed later on when nothing follows from this initial optimism.

What we need, then, is a clear and useful understanding of cause-effect relationships. Following is a list of the five criteria that need to be considered to fully appreciate the complexity of causality.

> **Quick Reference 9.3 • The Five Criteria for Analyzing Causality**
>
> 1. There must be a *correlation* between the *cause* (C) and the *effect* (E).
> 2. The C must *precede* the E.
> 3. The C must be in the *proximity* of E.
> 4. A set of *sufficient* and *necessary* conditions must exist.
> 5. *Alternative explanations* must be ruled out.

Cause-effect relationships can be established only after consideration of five criteria.

It must be noted that none of the five criteria alone is sufficient to establish a cause-effect relationship. The weight of the answers to all five criteria together establishes the grounds for a satisfactory cause-effect relationship.

Undue weight is often placed on correlation. It is easy to show, however, that a correlation alone cannot establish a cause-effect relationship. For example, there is a strong correlation between a barometer falling and a storm. There is also a strong correlation between people putting on swimsuits and getting wet. In neither case do we have a cause-effect relationship.

The second criterion cautions us to consider the time lag between the cause and the effect. The longer the time between the C and the E, the more the situation can be interrupted by other variables that might have brought about the effect. This same note of caution is realized in the third criterion. The greater the spatial distance between the C and E, the greater the chance of other variables interfering.

The fourth criterion derives its meaning from the results of our discussion of sufficient and necessary conditions (Section 5.3). If you recall, a sufficient condition is understood as the following relationship:

Strategy

Make sure that you do not assume that a correlation, by itself, indicates that a cause-effect relationship exists.

If *X* then *Y*

T ⟶ T

On the other hand, a necessary relationship is when the following occurs:

If *X* then *Y*

F ⟵——————— F

We can say that "*X* caused *Y*," if we can show two things: (1) that *X* occurring was *sufficient* to bring about *Y*, and (2) *X* was *necessary* for *Y* to occur (without *X*, *Y* would *not* have occurred). We will return to this after we finish the next criterion.

The fifth criterion, the ability to rule out plausible alternative explanations, is the glue that unifies the set of criteria. Any cause-effect claim can be challenged by suggestions of alternative potential causes. Therefore, strong causal claims are backed up by evidence against rival, alternative, causal claims.

Let's look at a simple case for analysis of cause-effect relations. Imagine that a window in your house breaks. Every effect is an *event,* so we must realize that it has many constituent parts. If we saw a rock hit the window, we might claim that the rock was *the cause* of the broken window. For practical purposes, for assigning blame perhaps, this is a normal claim to make. However, we want to explore a deeper understanding of the cause-effect situation. If we take the same rock and strike a similar window, we would expect to get similar results, i.e., same cause, same effect. However, if we throw the rock in such a way that its angle of incidence is nearly parallel to the window (so it barely grazes the window), then the window might not break. Alternatively, we could keep the rock the same, the angle of incidence the same, but change the velocity with which it strikes the window. Again, it might not break the window. This tells us that the cause has turned into a **causal network**. By changing the constituent parts of the event, the variables, we can achieve different results. By varying the velocity of the rock, we establish the *range of necessary conditions* that must be met in order to break the window (to bring about the effect). Similarly, results are affected by varying the angle of incidence of the rock, and by using rocks of various densities. The same can be done with the window, which is surely part of the event. By conducting experiments we can find the necessary range of porous window material needed to bring about the effect. However, we must also eliminate factors that are *not necessary* for the effect to have happened, such as, the time of day, the color of the window frame, the color of the rock, etc. This is how we establish the set of necessary and sufficient conditions that constitute the cause of the event in question.

The reason we single out the rock as the cause is that often we are in a position to establish the **normal state** of the system. In this case, the normal state is the historical information regarding the window and its surroundings. If the window has existed in an unbroken state for some time, then that was its normal state. As soon as it breaks, an **abnormal state** is established. Any change from the normal state requires explanation, typically a causal one. In this case, the normal state is made up of all the factors necessary to maintain it. The cause of the change into an abnormal state is then all the factors necessary to have brought it about. These include the density of the rock, the velocity, the angle of incidence, etc. Together these establish the set of necessary and sufficient conditions for the abnormal state.

Causal network: The range of necessary conditions that must be met in order to establish a cause-effect relationship.

Normal state: The historical information regarding the stability of a given system.

Abnormal state: Any change from the normal state of an object requires explanation, typically a causal one.

Hypotheses, Experiments, and Predictions

Hypotheses are usually offered as an attempt to establish a cause-effect relationship. Causal hypotheses are extremely difficult to test directly. Although they say something about the world that is either true or false ("The rock broke the window"), we cannot simply look at them and directly determine their truth. Even hypotheses that do not make explicit causal claims must be tested. We must force the hypothesis to do something, to put itself out on a limb, so to speak. This is accomplished by getting the hypothesis to make a *prediction*. A proposed experiment is simply another way of asking the question, "What if we do this?" For example, if your car does not start, someone might suggest that you have a dead battery. Although the suggestion (a hypothesis or conjecture) is either true or false, we cannot discovery the answer by looking at the battery. So, we might propose a simple experiment: What if we try the headlights? The person who hypothesized that we have a dead battery would be forced to predict that the headlights would not work (in many cars the headlights need power from the battery). If the headlights come on normally, then the prediction is false and we would have evidence to refute (disconfirm) the hypothesis. However, if the headlights do not come on, then the prediction is true and we would have evidence to support (confirm) the hypothesis.

We can do different experiments to get different predictions. If we disconnect the battery, take it to a garage, and hook it up to a battery-tester (the experiment) the dead-battery hypothesis would predict that the battery would have little or no power. Again, this prediction is either true or false, and the results could be used to confirm or disconfirm the hypothesis. Another experiment would be to try to start the car using jumper cables that connect the seemingly dead battery to another car's battery. If the dead-battery hypothesis is correct, the car should then start. The truth or falsity of this prediction will be the indirect evidence that supports or refutes the hypothesis.

Predictions are crucial to our understanding of the truth of hypotheses. Since predictions are generally specific statements that are testable, they provide the means for determining, *indirectly*, the truth or falsity of the hypothesis. After an experiment is completed, we can take the truth value of the prediction and trace it back to its source, the hypothesis. Therefore, the fate of the hypothesis rests on the fate of the prediction.

When considering scientific results, we must make decisions about the relevance of the available evidence. We must have criteria that will eliminate evidence that is misleading or irrelevant. These criteria must also help us to decide how much weight to give each piece of evidence. We need this to judge accurately the strength of a causal inference.

The first thing we do is set down requirements for acceptable predictions, which will ensure that we conduct a fair test of the causal hypothesis.

Quick Reference 9.4 • Requirements for a Fair Test of a Causal Hypothesis

Predictions for a causal hypothesis must be verifiable, not trivial, and logically connected to the hypothesis.

1. The prediction must be *verifiable*.
2. The prediction must *not* be *trivial*.
3. The prediction must have a *logical connection* to the hypothesis.

Verifiable Predictions A *verifiable prediction* simply means that the prediction, if it is true, must include an observable event. Consider the following case: Suppose there was a house where people had been getting sick. Two causal hypotheses are put forward.

> *Hypothesis #1*—There is a high degree of radioactivity in this house, which is causing illness in the people who live there.
> *Hypothesis #2*—There is a disease-causing ghost haunting this house.

Most people smile when they encounter Hypothesis #2, but not when they read Hypothesis #1. The two hypotheses are both contingent statements, so both are either true or false. Also, neither hypothesis can be tested directly by simply looking around the house, since both of the conjectured entities are things that are invisible to the unaided human eye. But are both hypotheses equally testable?

Hypothesis #1 might predict that if we take a Geiger counter and go around the house (the experiment), then we will find a high reading of radioactivity. If the Geiger counter is operating correctly, and we do get a high reading, then we can safely say that the prediction turned out to be true; therefore the hypothesis has some evidence to support, or confirm, it. If there is no sign of radioactivity, then the prediction would be false, and we would have evidence to refute, or disconfirm, the hypothesis. A verifiable prediction does not have to be true, but there must be a method for deciding clearly and objectively the truth or falsity of the prediction.

For Hypothesis #2, what would function as a device corresponding to the Geiger counter? Short of a *Ghostbusters*-type gadget, there seems to be no comparable method of indirectly gathering evidence for the ghost hypothesis. The ghost hypothesis defender might say, "But of course the ghost is invisible, so it is impossible to detect." We can counter this defense by pointing out that this is exactly the same situation that we had with Hypothesis #1; we cannot see the radioactivity either. Nevertheless, we were able to gather indirect physical evidence that the radioactivity was there. In addition, although radioactivity is invisible, it is a part of the physical world and is subject to detection. Our understanding of the physical reality of radioactivity also allows us to understand how it can cause illness. However, if ghosts are not only invisible but also immaterial (not part of the physical world), then it would be extremely difficult to explain how they could physically affect us. We can assert, then, that a prediction does not meet the first requirement whenever there is no way to check objectively the truth value of the prediction. Therefore, we would not accept as evidence someone's subjective claim that they can see ghosts.

Nontrivial Predictions The second requirement for a causal hypothesis operates in an entirely different manner from the first. A nontrivial prediction requires reference to background knowledge, which is everything we know to be true. It includes all facts and the hypotheses that have been already confirmed or disconfirmed. Of course, background knowledge changes over time. To decide if a prediction satisfies the second requirement, it is necessary to judge it in the light of what we know today.

Suppose I claim to have the power to see the future. This claim is either true or false. You correctly ask me to provide some evidence, something that is verifiable. That is easy enough for me to do. If all you want is a prediction that is verifiable, then I can predict that tomorrow the sun will come up. If you have only the first requirement to use, then you are forced to accept my prediction as a good one, and therefore, the claim that I have the power to see the future will surely turn out to be true. But this should *not* be acceptable. We want to avoid situations such as this; we want to be able to justifiably eliminate predictions like this one, ones that are highly likely to be true. And this is just what the second requirement effectively does; it provides a way of handling predictions that should not be used as evidence. Without the second requirement, we would be forced to accept almost anything as evidence, as long at it is merely verifiable (as long as it satisfied the first requirement).

Let's get back to the hypothesis that I have the power to see the future. The second requirement for predictions allows us to eliminate predictions that we consider trivial and hence carry no weight. This new requirement forces me to revise my original prediction ("The sun will come up tomorrow,") because as it stands, even if it turns out true (which is a near certainty), it will carry no weight in support of my hypothesis. Accepting this criticism now forces me to be more specific. I offer as evidence of my power to see the future the following prediction:

> Tomorrow, at exactly 1:35 p.m., it will start raining. Then it will stop raining at exactly 1:57 p.m. But it will only rain in the place we are now standing; it will not rain anywhere else in the city.

Would you accept this as a good test? Is this prediction trivial? What we know about the weather should lead us to say that the prediction, being so specific about something that is as unpredictable as the weather in a specific part of the city, is nontrivial. This is all that the second requirement asks of a prediction. Therefore, this would be a fair test of the hypothesis. Of course, when the prediction turns out to be false, we would have good evidence that refutes the hypothesis. We are willing to accept the challenge because we are almost certain that the prediction will fail.

The history of Halley's Comet clearly illustrates these principles. Applying part of Isaac Newton's theories, Edmund Halley hypothesized that comets reappear in regular cycles. In 1705, Halley predicted that a comet would appear in the year 1758 in a precise location of the sky. In order to judge whether his prediction was trivial or not we have to consider not what we know to be true today, but rather what the background knowledge was in 1705. Halley's hypothesis was not yet part of what was known to be true, simply because Halley had not yet proved it. Therefore, his prediction was considered, at that time, unlikely to be true. Notice that if Halley had predicted that a comet would appear somewhere in the sky in the 1750s, this would have been a trivial prediction, because many comets had been observed throughout recorded history. Therefore, when Halley's prediction did in fact turn out to be true (in the location and time predicted), scientists had good justification for claiming that his hypothesis was also true. Halley's hypothesis then became part of the background knowledge, something scientists knew to be true. Therefore, after 1758, if someone had predicted that Halley's Comet would reappear in another 76 years, this would have been considered likely to be true. Any future predictions regarding the return of Halley's Comet do not carry the same weight as the initial one. Each correct prediction confirms the hypothesis, but the weight diminishes. When background knowledge changes, our decisions regarding the second requirement often change as well.

Connection Between Prediction and Hypothesis The third require-ment for an acceptable prediction is meant to ensure that there is a connection between the hypothesis and the prediction. This is necessary because we want to transfer the truth value from the prediction back to the hypothesis, so we need a direct link between them.

To derive a prediction from a hypothesis, we must first develop an experiment that will test the hypothesis. We cannot simply take a hypothesis and deduce a pre-diction straight away. For example, Halley's hypothesis simply stated that comets are part of Newtonian particle systems. From this contingent claim nothing much can be predicted. However, Halley gathered information about comets observed in 1682, 1606, and 1530. Halley conjectured that they were instances of the same comet. From this data, plus his hypothesis that comets returned, he calculated the next return of the comet. This process enabled Halley to make a specific predic-tion. This is why, when the prediction turned out to be true, the truth value could be transferred back to the hypothesis.

Notice that Halley could not deduce a prediction form his hypothesis alone, nor could he make a prediction directly from the data, because the data need to be inter-preted in the light of a hypothesis. The prediction becomes the offspring of the two, a direct logical consequence that may or may not actually fit the real world.

The process for testing hypotheses looks like this:

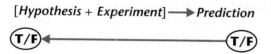

$$[\textit{Hypothesis} + \textit{Experiment}] \longrightarrow \textit{Prediction}$$

Notice that we transfer the truth value to the hypothesis. But why not to the exper-iment? This is a very important question. If the prediction is a product of both the hypothesis and the experiment, then why is the hypothesis saddled with the results? Part of the answer lies in our ability to check directly the experimental setup and the data. Also, remember that we are trying to confirm or refute a hypothesis. This process should always be considered partial and tentative. The weight we give to a confirmation or refutation is never all or nothing. We must accumulate evidence over a long time. If we make mistakes, they will be revealed by the results of repeated experiments.

EXERCISE SET 9.3   ○○○

Exercises 1–9 These exercises were created to reflect the kinds of information you might come across in newspapers, magazines, journals, and everyday conversation. Analyze the following fictional case studies by picking out the hypothesis, experi-ment, and prediction. Does the evidence offered in the case study confirm or dis-confirm the hypothesis? How much weight would you give to the evidence? If a causal claim is being put forward, then analyze the strength of the inference by checking for any reasonable alternative explanations or other possible facts, which, if uncovered, would weaken the causal claim.

1. There have been reports from around the world of some extraordinary "operations." It seems that people with cancerous tumors have been "cured" without any incisions made. When captured on film, the "doctor" seems to be pressing on the patient's body where the tumor is located. Suddenly, blood begins to ooze and the tumor appears to have been removed. When cleaned, the patient shows no sign of having been cut. Skeptical researchers did some checking. They performed two simple experiments. First, they tested the material supposedly taken from patients' bodies. The patients and their "doctors" claimed that they were cancerous tumors. Results of laboratory analysis showed that the material and blood were from a pig. The second experiment was to take the patients back to the clinic or hospital where the tumors were first noticed, and where records and X-rays were available, in order to see if the tumors had been removed. In all cases, the tumors were exactly where they had originally been; none had been removed.

   Answer:

   Hypothesis: Cancerous tumors can physically be removed by "surgery," but without any incision.

   Experiment: There are two experiments. (A) Test the material (supposedly) taken from the patient to determine its composition. (B) Check the patients to see if the tumors had been removed.

   Prediction: The "doctors" and believing patients (those putting forth the hypothesis) should predict the following: (a) the material will be human cancerous tissue; (b) the tumors will no longer be in the patient.

   Confirm/Disconfirm: Since both predictions were false, the evidence gathered from the experiments disconfirms the hypothesis. The evidence carries a lot of weight because the scientific results are objective and can be accepted as a clear refutation of the hypothesis.

   Alternative Explanations: A reasonable explanation is that the "doctors" were scam artists, or sleight-of-hand tricksters preying on desperate people.

Exercises 2–9: For answers and explanations, see pages 282–284 of Instructor's Manual.

2. Recently, some physiological psychologists have hypothesized that something in the blood of schizophrenics causes their abnormal behavior. In order to test their conjecture they took some blood from a patient who had been receiving treatment for acute schizophrenia. The researchers then took two groups of spiders that regularly spin uniformly geometrical webs. One group of spiders was given a small injection of the blood, while the other group was left untouched. For the next two weeks, the spiders given the blood produced bizarre, asymmetrical webs, which one researcher called *surreal*. The other group spun their normal webs. The researchers are claiming that this supports their contention that there is some, as yet unknown, factor in the schizophrenic's blood that caused the spider's unusual behavior, and is causing the abnormal behavior in the human subject.

3. I decided to revisit the "executive monkey syndrome" hypothesis. Many years ago some researchers stumbled onto what they thought was evidence that the psychological pressure of "command decisions" caused illness. They restrained two monkeys in chairs. One monkey was provided with a button that, if pressed at the right time, would stop an electrical shock given to both monkeys at the same time. This was the "executive monkey." The other monkey had no way to stop the shock. The executive monkey learned quickly that

it could stop the shock from occurring, and it seemed preoccupied with timing the button pressing. This went on for some weeks. Once the experiment was completed, autopsies on the two monkeys revealed that the "executive" had stomach ulcers while the other monkey had none. However, subsequent research has failed to duplicate these results.

4. If you bought a condo in the wrong tower, you were unlucky. It has been revealed that tenants living in one of the two *Sublime Inn* towers are suffering from a mysterious disease. It is believed that the disease is linked to a fungus growing in the air-conditioning system of the tower. The towers are both five years old and were built by the same contractor, yet there is no sign of the fungus in the other tower. Engineers, medical personnel, and others are looking for any other differences between the two towers, or between the tenants themselves, that could explain what is happening.

*5. Joe's car would not start. He wondered why. His friend said the battery was dead. Joe replaced the battery. The car started. The friend said that this proved he was right.

6. Joe's car would not start. He wondered why. His friend said the battery was dead. Joe turned on the car's headlights. They came on with normal intensity. Joe knew that it was not the battery.

7. "The garlic is what does it," said Ralph. He was referring to his dog, Balboa, now 14 years of age. "I started mixing a clove of garlic into his dog food ever since he was a puppy. There were six puppies in the litter when he was born. I've kept track of Balboa's sisters and brothers and all of them died before they were 10 years old. He's the last one left. The garlic's what done it."

8. The study of twins separated at birth confirms that genetics controls your destiny. Researchers tracked down a set of twins, now 25 years old, and checked for similarities. Both males eat the same brand of cereal, smoke the same brand of cigarettes, have married a nurse, work as auto mechanics, and are registered Democrats, and yet neither twin has ever come in contact with the other. The only possible cause of these remarkable similarities is that they have the identical genetic makeup.

9. For the past two weeks, every time Becky's cat, Melanie, sat on her lap, Becky started sneezing uncontrollably. Thinking that she was becoming allergic to her cat, Becky tried an experiment. She gave the cat to her neighbor for a day; during that time, she did not sneeze. As soon as the cat returned and sat on Becky's lap, she began sneezing. She started taking some over-the-counter allergy medicine, and the sneezing stopped. What Becky did not know is that the bottle of a new kind of flea powder her husband started using a few weeks earlier had broken, and so he bought the powder they had always used before. Becky continues to take the allergy medicine.

9.4 A MEDICAL MYSTERY

We are often in possession of certain facts (statistical patterns), but have no real understanding of what brings them about. An example from the history of medical discoveries will illustrate this.

In 1840, Vienna Hospital set up two clinics in the obstetric department. One clinic had physicians and medical students doing intern work in obstetrics, while the other employed midwives. The death rate from puerperal, or childbed, fever was approximately 12 percent monthly for the first clinic, but only 3 percent for the second clinic. The death rates had held constant ever since the two-clinic system was originated.

Puerperal fever was universally believed to be a disease peculiar to women. In order to get the disease it was thought that first, the woman had to be pregnant, and second, that she had to come in contact with the cause (whatever it was). It was believed that nonpregnant women never got puerperal fever. Thus, the prevalent view was that it was a specific disease that affected only pregnant women. At the time, there was no good explanation for the statistical difference between the two clinics. (It must be remembered that Pasteur's germ theory would not be developed for another 16 years.)

Dr. Ignac Semmelweis tried to solve the problem. He noted that if the fever was caused by something in the hospital atmosphere, as some suggested, then why did it not strike the second clinic as well? Since the clinics had a corridor in common, one might reasonably conclude that the atmosphere (and death rates) should be the same in both clinics. A related idea was that women came in contact with the cause of puerperal fever outside the hospital. It was obvious, at least to Semmelweis, this would not work as an explanation, because it would mean it was equally likely for all women to get the fever. It was well known that the rate of the fever in the population at large had never reached the high percentage it had in the hospital. If childbed fever was like cholera, if it was a true epidemic, then why did it not appear like one? It should have been relatively easy to find similar degrees of fever outside the hospital, but the statistics did not bear this out. Statistics from other hospitals revealed yet another curious result. In places where there was no medical teaching, other than midwifery, the rate of death by puerperal fever was usually (but not always) very low.

Semmelweis found that the ventilation, the treatment of the linen, and the food for both clinics was the same. A colleague pointed out to him something he had not noticed. The procedure in the second clinic was to have the women assume a lateral position for delivery. This was different from the way deliveries were carried out in the first clinic. Semmelweis immediately implemented the use of the lateral position. Every delivery was performed this way in the hope that the death rate in the two divisions would be comparable. But the results were always the same. The high rate in the first clinic seemed immune to change however hard Semmelweis tried to lower it.

Another idea tested was the birth act itself. Protracted labor, the death of the fetus, the wounding of the inner surface of the uterus by the fetus during delivery, and other effects that could occur from the childbirth act itself, might be the cause. However, Semmelweis pointed out that all these had to happen equally in both clinics. The outcomes of the birth act had to be similar in both divisions; therefore, it could not explain the different death rates.

Further statistical results regarding the puzzle of puerperal fever added to Semmelweis' bewilderment. One was the fact that when the dilatation period was 24 hours or more, puerperal fever almost always occurred in the first clinic, but it did not happen in the second clinic under similar circumstances. Semmelweis was aware that all the statistical facts were crucial to his understanding of the true cause of puerperal fever.

The scandal surrounding the notorious first clinic had reached its peak. The government was forced to do something. They did what most governments do in times of crisis: they formed a commission to investigate the situation. The commission, consisting of nonmedical people, went to the head of the clinic for advice. The conclusion reached was that the medical students were rougher than the midwives. The commission further stated that the foreign students were roughest of all. What did the commission propose as a remedy? Get rid of the foreign students. As a result, the staff in the first clinic was cut in half, from about 40 students down to around 20. For nearly 4 months, the death rate did go down in the first clinic; from an average of 12 percent to 3 percent. Given this result, the commission felt justified, and the government was satisfied. However, the remaining staff began making up for lack of help. Little by little the death rate rose again. After 5 months it was right back at 12 percent.

While Semmelweis was on vacation in Venice, his good friend Kolletschka died in Vienna. Kolletschka had been performing a routine autopsy when one of his assistants accidentally cut him. Kolletschka died within 2 weeks. When Semmelweis returned to Vienna, he studied the autopsy findings in great detail. Kolletschka's wound was contaminated by cadaveric material. Not the wound, but the contamination of the wound by cadaveric material was the cause of death. At this point the pieces of the puzzle began to come together. Semmelweis recalled his earlier studies of the history of the Vienna Hospital. The high death rate had not always been the case at the hospital; in fact, the rate had only started going up when the current head of the department, Klein, took over in 1822. Before this, Boer had been in charge for 30 years. Under Boer's direction, from 1789 to 1822, the rate of puerperal fever averaged 1.4 percent. After Klein took control, the rate almost immediately jumped to 7.5 percent and remained high. This rate is interesting, because we can see that when the clinics were separated the rate in the first clinic became 12 percent, while the second was 3 percent; but while the midwives and doctors/interns worked together in one clinic the rate averaged out to 7.5 percent, under Klein.

Why had the rate gone up when Klein took over? What changed when Klein assumed control? Semmelweis' inquiries into Boer's history with the Vienna Hospital revealed some important clues. What Boer had done was to suspend the use of cadavers as a teaching device for students in the obstetric department. All teaching was done by using the "phantom model," a mannequin body-machine with an artificial uterus and pelvic canal. The students had no chance of coming in contact with cadavers before examining patients. Semmelweis had statistics showing the great rise in the death rate after Klein took over. Klein immediately put the phantom model away; all students now had to learn by actual work on cadavers. Since Semmelweis had been trained in this manner, he could not be expected to realize it had been different in the past. Therefore, the process of compiling statistics and examining the history of the obstetric department provided Semmelweis with crucial information.

Semmelweis combined all the information at his disposal and hypothesized that cadaveric particles might be the cause of puerperal fever. If Semmelweis' idea was correct, it explained that when the doctors and interns examined the women during childbirth, cadaveric particles were transferred from the hands of the doctors into the bodies of the women. Semmelweis knew that a cut during an autopsy could prove fatal. The important aspect was not simply the contact with cadaveric material, but the *open wound* coming in contact with cadaveric particles. Semmelweis realized that it was the second part that was the deciding factor. Just as the key factor with Kolletschka was not simply coming in contact with cadaveric material, but rather being wounded and coming in contact with it, so the wounded uterus coming in contact with cadaveric material through the doctors' and interns' many examinations was the answer to the mystery.

The reason why the second clinic always had a lower death rate was now understood; the midwives did not come in contact with cadaveric material. Semmelweis concluded that puerperal fever was not the specific disease everyone had believed, but that it was simply a variety of blood poisoning.

We can see how a successful explanation can help us understand and solve a serious problem. When we discover interesting facts we want to make sure that our research is not flawed. We want to ensure that our samples are *large enough*, *unbiased*, and *random*, because these factors determine the strength or weakness of our inferences. A good explanation often requires a hypothesis that invokes a causal mechanism. This, in turn, leads to new experiments and predictions, which can then be used to construct further inferences. The strength of these inferences can be judged by the techniques we have learned.

EXERCISE SET 9.4   ○○○

Analyze the following case by picking out the hypothesis, experiment, and prediction. Does the evidence offered in the case study confirm or disconfirm the hypothesis? How much weight would you give to the evidence? If a causal claim is being put forward, then analyze the strength of the inference by checking for any reasonable alternative explanations or other possible facts, which, if uncovered, would weaken the causal claim.

1. See page 284 of Instructor's Manual for complete answers.

1. Semmelweis now had a hypothesis that he could put to the test: cadaveric material was the cause of puerperal fever. The solution was to eliminate this material by correct washing. The results should be a lower death rate. Since Semmelweis believed that cadaveric particles were not removed by soap and water (because the odor remains), he started using a solution of chlorinated lime, with the idea to eliminate the odor, and by so doing, to eliminate the particles. He emphasized washing the hands until they squeaked, thinking this would ensure that all particles were removed.

   An experiment was set up in such a way as to ensure, as best as could be done, that no other changes were allowed in the first clinic. The only new factor was the washing of hands in the solution. The immediate result was that the puerperal fever rate dropped from 12 percent to 3 percent in the first clinic. For the year 1848 the rates of the two divisions were: first division, 1.27 percent, the second division, 1.33 percent.

2. Use the techniques introduced in this chapter to analyze and evaluate some other aspects of Semmelweis' reasoning process.

SUMMARY—9.1 ANALOGICAL REASONING

- Analogical reasoning can be analyzed as a type of inductive inference. We often reason that because two things share some relevant characteristics, they should share other characteristics.

- Analogical inferences contain a specific weakness in that their conclusions do not follow with logical necessity from the premises. Nevertheless, if an analogical inference is strong, then it raises the probability that the conclusion is true.

- Analogical inferences have a general logical structure. They proceed by listing the characteristics that two (or more) things have in common, and conclude that they have some other characteristic in common. If the first premise effectively does its job, then we should begin to see the two instances overlapping. If the first premise has any weaknesses, then the probability of the conclusion being true is lessened.

- There are four criteria used to analyze analogical inferences for strength and weakness:

  1. The number of instances between which the analogies are said to hold. A large number of experiences of the same kind with the same item establishes the conclusion with a much higher degree of probability than a conclusion based on one instance.

  2. The variety of instances mentioned in the premises. If the first premise shows some variety among the instances that connect the members of the analogy, then it might make the conclusion more likely to be true.

  3. The number of characteristics in which the things involved are said to be analogous.

  4. In discussing the assessment of relevance, we need to determine whether the characteristics mentioned in the premises carry any weight when it comes to deciding the probability of the conclusion. The question of relevance is the single most important criterion on which to judge the strength of an analogical inference.

- There are three major aspects of analogies that can reveal their weakness:

  1. Any two nonidentical instances have differences between them. These differences can be exploited and, if significant, can severely weaken any analogical inference. The logical strategy of criticism called disanalogies points out differences between two instances. Effective disanalogies cause us to start separating the two instances by acknowledging any significant (relevant) differences between them.

  2. It is always logically possible to create a counteranalogy, a different analogical inference that leads to a conclusion that contradicts the conclusion of the original inference. Upon construction of a counteranalogy we are faced with the prospect of weighing, judging, and evaluating the competing strengths of two analogies.

  3. Another strategy of criticism is the discovery of an unintended consequence of the analogy. If you can point to something that is a direct result of an analogy, but that is unacceptable to the person presenting the analogy, then you can put that person in a difficult position.

SUMMARY—9.2 STATISTICAL REASONING AND PROBABILITY THEORY

- Statistical reasoning relies on an ability to generalize.
- A claim that a pattern occurs without exception is a universal generalization.
- A claim that a pattern occurs with some exceptions is a statistical generalization.
- When we create an inference to support a generalization, the premises must provide convincing evidence that reveals the pattern. To offer a good explanation of how or why a generalization exists requires that the explanation not only fits the existing data, it also must provide a way for new information to be discovered.
- A sample is a subset of a population. It is crucial to know as much as possible about the sample mentioned in the inference.
- A population is any group of objects, not just human populations.
- There are two important questions to ask regarding statistical inferences. Answers to these questions help determine the strength of the inference.
  1. Is the sample random? To get a random sample every member of the population must have an equal chance of getting into the sample.
  2. Is there any potential evidence that would show that the sample is not representative of the population? There is no simple formula for calculating the ratio of sample size to population to ensure a representative sample. However, when a sample size is small relative to the size of the population, other factors would have to be in place to help ensure a representative sample has been achieved.
- Probability calculations using the *a priori* theory rely on hypothetical reasoning based on two major assumptions. The first is that all the possible outcomes can be determined, and the second is that each of the possible outcomes has an equal probability of occurring (is equiprobable).
- The relative frequency theory of probability relies on direct observation of events. Researchers must observe enough events to arrive at accurate probability calculations.
- Reliance on statistical, historical data is not the same as relative frequency applications. Calculations of this kind fall under the subjective theory of probability, where determinations are based on the lack of total knowledge regarding an event.

SUMMARY—9.3 SCIENTIFIC AND CAUSAL REASONING

- A good hypothesis provides an explanation of facts and gives us a way of discovering new facts.
- Hypotheses can often be easily proposed, but difficult to test. A carefully controlled experiment is the best way to test hypotheses. In a laboratory, we get control by isolating as many variables as possible, the goal being to uncover cause-effect relationships. We start by listing all the reasonable alternative explanations and, one by one, show why each can be eliminated. If we can successfully reject each alternative explanation, then the only remaining possible explanation for the difference is accepted as the cause.

- There are five criteria that need to be considered to fully appreciate the complexity of causality:
  1. There must be a correlation between the cause C and the effect E.
  2. The C must precede the E.
  3. The C must be in the proximity of E.
  4. A set of sufficient and necessary conditions must exist.
  5. Alternative explanations must be ruled out.
- None of these five criteria alone is sufficient to establish a cause-effect relationship. The weight of our answers to all five criteria together establishes the grounds for a satisfactory cause-effect relationship.
- Hypotheses are usually offered as an attempt to establish a cause-effect relationship. We can test a hypothesis by getting it to make a prediction.
- Predictions are either true or false; the results are used to confirm (support) or disconfirm (refute) the hypothesis.
- There are three requirements that will ensure a fair test of the causal hypothesis:
  1. The prediction must be something that is verifiable.
  2. The prediction must be unlikely to be true, based on our background knowledge.
  3. There must be a connection between the hypothesis and the prediction.
- Since we are trying to confirm or refute a hypothesis, this is always to be construed as a partial and tentative process. The weight we give to a confirmation or refutation is never all-or-nothing. We must accumulate evidence over a long time. Thus, if we make mistakes, then they will be revealed after repeated attempts to gather results.

KEY TERMS

analogy   321
analogical inference   322
analogical structure   322
disanalogy   331
counteranalogy   332
unintended consequence
   of the analogy   333
universal
   generalization   338
statistical
   generalization   338
population   341
sample   341
representative
   sample   341

a priori theory of
   probability   345
equiprobable   345
relative frequency
   theory of
   probability   346
subjectivist theory of
   probability   347
probability calculus   348
restricted conjunction
   method   348
general conjunction
   method   349

restricted disjunction
   method   350
general disjunction
   method   350
negation method   351
conditional
   probability   354
controlled
   experiment   357
control group   357
causal network   359
normal state   359
abnormal state   359

LOGIC CHALLENGE: A PERPLEXING PARADOX

What happens when we cannot merge an intellectual understanding with a perceptual experience, even though both seem perfectly in order? For example, most adults have a basic mathematical understanding of distance and time. Simply put, we know that any distance can be cut in half, and the remaining distance cut in half as well. Theoretically, as far as mathematics is concerned, any distance, no matter how small, can be cut in half. The same idea holds for time. Any duration of time, no matter how small, can be cut in half. The series of fractions 1/2, 1/4, … , is infinite, and can be applied to inches (distance) or seconds (time).

Now let's imagine a visual experience we might have. Suppose the fastest human runs a 100-yard race with one of the slowest humans. To make it interesting, the fastest human gives a 40-yard head start to his competitor. The gun sounds and we watch the fastest human catch, and then pass the rival, thereby, winning the race. A Greek philosopher by the name of Zeno took the two ideas we have been discussing and created some interesting paradoxes. If we try to reconcile the *theoretical* understanding of distance and time with the *visual experience* of the race, interesting developments occur. Zeno tells us to picture the race as follows:

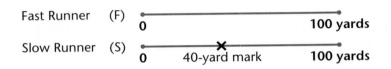

Zeno now tells us to analyze the race by applying our theoretical understanding of distance and time. It is obvious that no matter how fast the fastest human (F) runs, it takes some time to reach the point where the slow person (S) began; the 40-yard mark (indicated by the "X"). During that time, (S) has moved slightly forward. To make the mathematics easy, let's have (F) run twice as fast as (S). Therefore, when (F) gets to the 40-yard mark, the point where (S) began, (S) has moved on to the 60-yard mark. So, now (F) is only 20 yards behind (S). Once again, it takes some time, no matter how small, in order for (F) to reach the 60-yard mark, where (S) was. Of course, during this time interval, (S) has moved on to the 70-yard mark. Now, (F) is only 10 yards behind (S). (F) continues to cut the distance between them by half. Nevertheless, it still takes some finite amount of time for (F) to cover this distance. So, when (F) does get to the 70-yard mark, (S) has moved to the 75-yard point. (Zeno's noose is beginning to tighten around our necks.)

No matter how small the distance between (F) and (S), it will always take (F) some finite amount of time to traverse this distance, during which time (S) has moved ever so slightly farther ahead. By continually applying the simple mathematical method, Zeno tells us that it is impossible for (F) to ever catch, let alone pass, (S). The distance between (F) and (S) keeps being reduced by half, *but since the series is infinite*, it will never get to 0, to where there is no distance between them.

Zeno has taken our theoretical understanding of distance and time and has placed us in the position of either denying the mathematical results, or admitting that the visual perception was an illusion.

1. Does Zeno's position contain any logical errors? If so, what are they?
2. Does Zeno's position contain any factual errors? If so, what are they?

See page 284 of Instructor's Manual for discussion.

Mapping Premises and Conclusions

Once the premises and conclusions of inferences have been identified and reconstructed, their structure can be mapped. Mapping displays the relationships between all parts of an inference. The first step is to number the statements as they appear in the inference (disregarding, at this time, whether they are premises or conclusions). For example,

> [1] You do not take care of your dog. Therefore, [2] you will not be able to accept the responsibility of owning a car.

This passage contains the conclusion indicator, "Therefore," so we can determine that [2] is the conclusion. The next step is to map the relationship by connecting the premise to the conclusion with an arrow, in the following manner:

1

2

When there is more than one premise, the premises may act independently in support of the conclusion. **Independent premises** are such that the falsity of one does not nullify any support the other(s) give to the conclusion. We can illustrate this by adding other premises to the above example.

> [1] You do not take care of your dog. [2] You do not clean your room. [3] You do not handle your money responsibly. Therefore, [4] you will not be able to accept the responsibility of owning a car.

appendix

Independent premises create **convergent inferences**. The relationship in a convergent inference is mapped as shown below.

Each of the three premises has its own arrow because each premise offers independent support for the conclusion. It is asserted that each premise, by itself, offers a good reason to accept the conclusion. Even if one or two of the premises were shown to be false, the map reveals that an arrow would remain; indicating some support for the conclusion.

In contrast to the independent premises just described, there are inferences with two or more premises that are dependent on each other for their support of the conclusion. **Dependent premises** act together to support a conclusion. The falsity of one dependent premise weakens the support the other premise(s) give to the conclusion. The next example illustrates an inference with dependent premises.

> [1] The movie version of *The Lord of the Rings* used some of the original dialogue from the books, [2] it used the language Tolkien invented, [3] it used the characters he created, [4] it kept the overall plot, and [5] the settings were the same as in the books. Therefore, [6] the movie trilogy, *Lord of the Rings,* captured *most* of the spirit of the original books.

Since the conclusion claims that "*most* of the spirit of the original books" was captured by the movies, the premises will have to depend on each other to bring about the required support. Dependent premises create **linked inferences**. Linked relationships are mapped as follows.

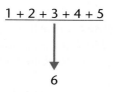

It is also possible that one premise can support more than one conclusion. Consider the following inference:

> [1] The *Lord of the Rings* saga is soon to be the highest grossing movie series in history. Therefore, [2] it is sure to win multiple Academy Awards. It also means that [3] some of the actors will be among the highest paid in the industry. We can also conclude that [4] the director will get to do anything he wants in the near future.

Independent premises:
With independent premises, the falsity of one premise does not nullify any support the other(s) give to the conclusion. A diagram that reveals the occurrence of independent premises is called *convergent.*

Convergent inference:
An inference that has independent premises, which separately offer support for the conclusion.

Dependent premises:
Dependent premises act together to support a conclusion; the falsity of one premise nullifies any support the other premise(s) would give to the conclusion. A diagram that reveals the occurrence of dependent premises is called *linked.*

Linked inference:
An inference in which dependent premises are offered in support of a conclusion.

Divergent inference:
An inference in which a single premise is used to support two or more conclusions.

Serial inferences: A series of inferences in which a conclusion from one inference becomes a premise in a second inference.

In this inference, one premise is being used to support three independent conclusions. A relationship in which one premise supports more than one conclusion is a **divergent inference**, which is illustrated as follows.

Some passages contain a series of inferences in which a conclusion from one inference becomes a premise in a second inference. For example,

[1] The government just cut taxes and [2] put a freeze on the minimum wage. [3] This combination is sure to create higher unemployment. Of course, [4] that will lead to a drop in gross domestic sales. [5] This will surely cause a recession.

Relationships of this type create **serial inferences**, and are illustrated as follows:

Premises 1 and 2 are linked because the direct conclusion (statement 3) claims that the "combination is sure to create higher unemployment." This conclusion (3) then acts as a premise for the conclusion stated in 4, which, in turn, acts as a premise for the conclusion stated in 5.

Complex inferences often require maps that combine two or more of the different types displayed above. The next example illustrates this.

[1] My working overtime each day for the next three weeks, and [2] coming in on weekends, will guarantee the result that [3] I will finish the report early. Of course, it is also possible that [4] working a normal 40-hour week will lead to the same result. Either way, [5] finishing the report early will lead to a raise in my salary. It could also [6] lead to a promotion.

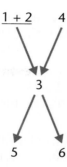

(a) The arrow from 1 + 2 to 3 indicates the presence of a linked inference (dependent premises).

(b) The two arrows, one from 1 + 2 to 3, and the other from 4 to 3, indicate the presence of a convergent inference (independent premises).

(c) The two arrows leading from 3 to 5 and 6 indicate the presence of divergent inferences.

(d) The entire map reveals the presence of serial inferences.

EXERCISE SET A1

Exercises 1–10 These exercises have been invented specifically to reinforce your logical analysis skills. They are not taken from outside sources; instead they are fictional creations that reflect the kinds of information you might come across in newspapers, magazines, and journals. The exercises are from *Exercise Set 2.4A*, Exercises 11–20, pages 74–75. If you have already worked on that exercise set and have identified the premises and conclusions, then you can use your answers to map the structure of each inference.

1. Exercise helps strengthen your cardiovascular system. It also lowers your cholesterol and increases the blood flow to the brain, enabling you to think longer. Thus, there is no reason for you not to start exercising regularly.

Answer: *Premises:* [1] Exercise helps strengthen your cardiovascular system; [2] It (exercise) also lowers your cholesterol; [3] It (exercise) increases the blood flow to the brain, enabling you to think longer.

Conclusion: [4] There is no reason for you not to start exercising regularly.

Exercises 2–25: For answers and explanations, see pages 294–299 of Instructor's Manual.

2. If you start a strenuous exercise regimen before you know if your body is ready, you can cause serious damage. Therefore, you should always have a physical check-up before you start a rigid exercise program.

3. Since television commercials help pay the cost of programming, and because I can always turn off the sound of the commercials, or go to the bathroom, or get something to eat or drink, it follows that commercials are not such a bad thing.

4. Since television commercials disrupt the flow of programs, and given that any disruption impedes that continuity of a show, consequently, we can safely say that commercials are a bad thing.

5. We should never take our friends for granted. True friends are there when we need them. They suffer with us when we fail, and they are happy when we succeed.

*6. They say that, "absence makes the heart grow fonder." So, my teachers should really love me, since I have been absent for the last two weeks.

7. "I think, therefore I am." Rene Descartes, *Meditations*

8. I believe that humans will evolve into androids. This follows from the fact that we will eventually be able to replace all organic body parts with artificial parts. In addition, we will be able to live virtually forever by simply replacing the parts when they wear out or become defective.

9. Gary Kasparov has the highest ranking of any chess grand master in history. He was recently beaten in a chess tournament by a computer program. So, the computer program should be given the highest ranking in history.

10. It is true that $1 + 4 = 5$, and it is also true that $2 + 3 = 5$. Thus, we can conclude with certainty that $(1 + 4) = (2 + 3)$.

Exercises 11–20 These exercises are repeated from *Exercise Set 2.4C*, Exercises 1–10, page 81. If you have already worked on that exercise set and have reconstructed the inferences, then you can use your answers to map the structure of each inference.

11. I am talking to a human; therefore, I am talking to a mammal.

Answer: [1] I am talking to a human; [2] I am talking to a mammal; [3] *Missing Premise:* All humans are mammals.

1 + 3

2

12. I am talking to a mammal, therefore, I am talking to a human.

13. Shane owns a Honda, so it must be a motorcycle.

14. Shane owns a motorcycle, so it must be a Honda.

15. I have a headache. I just took two aspirins. Aspirins relieve headaches.

*16. The office laser printer can print 20 pages a minute in black and white or 10 pages a minute in color. It took one minute to print John's 10-page report on the office laser printer.

17. Vincent just had a big lasagna dinner, so I know he is very happy now.

18. Since Vincent just had a big lasagna dinner, it follows that he will be looking for the antacid tablets.

19. Jake has a viral infection. He decided to take some penicillin pills he had sitting in the medicine cabinet. But he doesn't realize that penicillin has no affect on viruses.

20. Jake has a bacterial infection. He decided to take some penicillin pills he had sitting in the medicine cabinet. Penicillin can be effective when treating bacteria.

Exercises 21–25 Identify and number the premises and conclusions in the following fictional examples; then diagram the structure of each inference.

21. We will soon get more oil from areas of our country that were once protected by law. However, it has been projected that the amount of oil will be too small to have any serious affect on the overall oil supply. Although coal production will be raised, nevertheless the amount will not meet the increasing amount of gasoline that is used. In addition, new legislation has eliminated the requirement for the automobile industry to increase gas mileage in their new cars. So, it seems that gasoline prices will not go down in the near future.

Answer: [1] We will soon get more oil from areas of our country that were once protected by law, but it has been projected that the amount of oil will be too small to have any serious affect on the overall oil supply. [2] Although coal production will be raised, nevertheless the amount will not meet the increasing amount of gasoline that is used. [3] In addition, new legislation has eliminated the requirement for the automobile industry to increase gas mileage in their new cars. [4] So, it seems that gasoline prices will not go down in the near future.

22. Driving a car without a seatbelt is dangerous. Statistics show you are 10 times more likely to be injured in an accident if you are not wearing a seat belt. Besides, in our state you can get fined $100 if you are caught not wearing one. You ought to wear one even if you are driving a short distance.

23. Jean studied at least 10 hours for the exam and she got an 'A.' Bill studied at least 10 hours for the exam and he got an 'A.' Sue studied at least 10 hours for the exam and she got an 'A.' Jim studied at least 10 hours for the exam. Jim probably got an 'A' on the exam.

24. Fast food products contain high levels of cholesterol. They also contain high levels of sodium, fat, and trans fatty acids. These things are bad for your health. I am going to stop eating in fast food places.

25. You should eat more vegetables. They contain low levels of cholesterol. They also contain low levels of sodium, fat, and trans fatty acids. High levels of those things are bad for your health.

SUMMARY

- Mapping premises and conclusions displays the relationships between all the parts of an inference.
- The first step in mapping an inference is to number the statements as they appear in the inference.
- The next step is to map the relationship by connecting the premises to the conclusions with an arrow.
- Premises are independent when the falsity of one would not nullify any support the other(s) would give to the conclusion. A map that reveals the occurrence of independent premises is called convergent.
- Premises are dependent when they act together to support a conclusion. In this case, the falsity of any one would weaken the support the others would give to the conclusion. The map that reveals the occurrence of dependent premises is called linked.
- A single premise can be used to support independent conclusions. The map that reveals this kind of relationship is called divergent.
- A serial inference occurs when a conclusion from one inference becomes a premise in a second inference.

KEY TERMS

independent
  premises   374
convergent
  inference   375

dependent
  premises   375
linked inference   375

divergent inference   376
serial inference   376

The Square of Opposition and Standard-Form Categorical Syllogisms

Our discussion begins with an extensive analysis of Aristotle's fundamental work on categorical statements and categorical syllogisms, leading to the *Aristotelian square of opposition,* or the *traditional square of opposition.* An exploration of some of the ramifications of Aristotle's logical foundation reveals some important problems. Addressing these problems necessitates the introduction of the work of two modern thinkers, George Boole and John Venn. Their work transformed the Aristotelian square into the *Boolean square of opposition,* which is meant to solve the logical problems associated with the older square. This work culminates in a new understanding of the logical commitments behind categorical statements. As we shall see, the old problems can be solved by the translation of categorical statements into truth-functional statements. This, in turn, allows us to build on our understanding of natural deduction by extending our proof procedure and capturing more of natural language. The result of this extension is *the logic of quantifiers,* or *predicate logic,* the subject of Chapter 7.

appendix

Class: A group, set, or collection of objects that have a common characteristic attributed to each member.

Subject term: The class designated by the first term in a categorical statement.

Predicate term: The class designated by the second term in a categorical statement.

Standard-form categorical statement: A categorical statement with one of the following forms: *A*: All *S* are *P*, *E*: No *S* are *P*, *I*: Some *S* are *P*; *O*: Some *S* are not *P*.

Universal affirmative statement: The statement form "All *S* are *P*," which asserts that all members of the subject term are members of the predicate term.

Universal negative statement: The statement form "No *S* are *P*," which asserts that no members of the subject term are members of the predicate term.

Particular affirmative statement: The statement form "Some *S* are *P*," which asserts that some (at least one) members of the subject term are members of the predicate term.

Particular negative statement: The statement form "Some *S* are not *P*," which asserts that some (at least one) members of the subject term are not members of the predicate term.

A2.1 CATEGORICAL STATEMENTS

The foundation of our discussion is the logic of *classes*, also referred to as *categories* or *sets*, of objects. A **class** is defined as a group of objects having some recognizable common characteristic. We will use *S* for the class designated by the **subject term** of a categorical statement and *P* for the class designated by the **predicate term**. Every categorical statement either *affirms* that the subject term is related partially or completely to the predicate term or *denies* that the subject term is related partially or completely to the predicate term. In other words, we can say any of the following regarding *S* and *P*:

All S are P   No S are P   Some S are P   Some S are not P

These four statements are referred to as **standard-form categorical statements**. The first standard form, "All *S* are *P*," is called a **universal affirmative statement** because it claims that *all* members of the subject term are members of the predicate term. These claims are either true or false, but the truth or falsity of the claims can be decided only when the *S* and *P* are replaced by actual class terms, e.g. "All *trees* are *deciduous*." This example asserts that every tree (the class designated by the subject term) is deciduous (the class designated by the predicate term), but since we know that there is at least one class of trees that is not deciduous (pine trees, etc.), the truth content of this particular instance of a universal affirmative statement is false.

If we substitute "trees" and "deciduous" for the subject and predicate terms of the three remaining standard-form categorical statements, we get the following results: "No trees are deciduous," "Some trees are deciduous," and "Some trees are not deciduous." The first of these, "No trees are deciduous," is called a **universal negative statement** because it claims that *no* members of the subject term are members of the predicate term. This statement claims that there is not even one member of *S* that is a member of *P*. But since some trees are deciduous, the truth content of this statement is false.

The next example, "Some trees are deciduous," is called a **particular affirmative statement** because it claims that *some* members of the subject term are members of the predicate term. In other words, this statement claims that at least one member of *S* is a member of *P*. Our background knowledge of trees tells us that this statement is true.

The next example, "Some trees are not deciduous," is called a **particular negative statement** because it claims that *some* members of the subject term are *not* members of the predicate term. In other words, this statement claims that at least one member of *S* is *not* a member of *P*. Our background knowledge of trees tells us this statement is true, too.

These four standard-form categorical statements are the building blocks of the categorical syllogisms (inferences) we are going to analyze, and they are designated by the letters ***A, E, I,*** and ***O,*** the first four vowels:

A: All S are P   E: No S are P   I: Some S are P   O: Some S are not P

EXERCISE SET A2.1

Analyze each statement by doing the following: (1) identify the subject and predicate terms, and (2) identify the standard form as either *A, E, I,* or *O*.

1. All senior citizens are eligible for subsidized drug prescriptions.

Answer: Subject term: *senior citizen*

Predicate term: *eligible for subsidized drug prescriptions*

This is an example of an *A* statement.

2. Some public schools are not meeting national standards for excellence.

3. Some families have incomes that are below the poverty line.

4. No national health care plans are needed.

5. All malicious murderers are evil people.

*6. All X-rated movies are intellectually stimulating.

7. Some video games are not violent.

8. Some petty bureaucrats are tyrannical.

9. No lottery winners are lucky.

10. Some diet fads are not healthy.

*11. All sporting events are television shows worth watching.

12. Some philosophy books are important contributions to literature.

13. No amendments to the U.S. Constitution are unconstitutional.

14. All gamblers are superstitious people.

15. Some psychics are frauds.

2. S: *public schools*; P: *meeting national standards for excellence*; O.

3. S: *families*; P: *below the poverty line*; I.

4. S: *national health care plan*; P: *needed*; E.

5. S: *malicious murderers*; P: *evil people*; A.

6. S: *X-rated movies*; P: *intellectually stimulating*; A.

7. S: *video games*; P: *violent*; O.

8. S: *petty bureaucrats*; P: *tyrannical*; I.

9. S: *lottery winners*; P: *lucky*; E.

10. S: *diet fads*; P: *healthy*; O.

11. S: *sporting events*; P: *television show worth watching*; A.

12. S: *philosophy books*; P: *important contributions to literature*; I.

13. S: *amendments to the U.S. Constitution*; P: *unconstitutional*; E.

14. S: *gamblers*; P: *superstitious people*; A.

15. S: *psychics*; P: *frauds*; I.

A2.2 QUANTITY, QUALITY, AND DISTRIBUTION

When we referred to a categorical statement as either *universal* or *particular*, we were referring to its **quantity**. The universal statements, *A* and *E*, both refer to every member of the class designated by the subject term. The particular statements, *I* and *O*, both refer to some member or members of the class designated by the subject term.

When we referred to a categorical statement as either *affirmative* or *negative*, we were referring to its **quality**. The affirmative statements, *A* and *I*, both assert class inclusion; for *A* statements, *S* is completely included in *P*, while for *I* statements, the inclusion of *S* in *P* is partial. On the other hand, the negative statements, *E* and *O*, both deny class inclusion; for *E* statements, *S* is completely excluded from *P*, while for *O* statements the exclusion of *S* from *P* is partial.

Combining the terms associated with, and the ideas behind, quantity and quality allows us to specify unique designations for *A, E, I,* and *O* statements.

Quantity: A characteristic of categorical statements; the statements have one of two quantities, either universal or particular.

Quality: A characteristic of categorical statements; the statements have one of two qualities, either affirmative or negative.

Quantifier: The terms "all," "no," and "some," are called quantifiers because they reveal the extent of the class inclusion or exclusion (i.e., the quantity of S as related to P).

Copula: The terms "are" and "are not" are called copula; they are forms of "to be" and serve to link the subject term S with the predicate term P of a categorical statement.

Distributed: When a categorical statement claims something definite about every member of the class designated by a term.

Undistributed: When a categorical statement does not assert anything definite about every member of the class designated by a term.

A: All S are P	*Universal affirmative*
E: No S are P	*Universal negative*
I: Some S are P	*Particular affirmative*
O: Some S are not P	*Particular negative*

The terms "all," "no," and "some" are called **quantifiers**, because they tell us the extent of the class inclusion or exclusion (i.e., the quantity of S as related to P). It is important to recognize that *the quantifier refers specifically and exclusively to the subject term* and not to the predicate term. Therefore, "All S are P" asserts something definite about the class S (that it is completely included in the class P), but it leaves open the extent of the class P. In other words, the "all" connects only to the subject term. The same is true of the other quantifiers. The quantifier "some" in "Some S are P" asserts something definite only about S, it does not assert anything definite about P. The same is true for "Some S are not P." The terms "are," and "are not," are called **copula** because they are forms of "to be" and serve to link the subject term S with the predicate term P.

If a categorical statement says something definite about every member of the class designated by a term, then the term is said to be **distributed**. On the other hand, if the statement does not say something definite about every member of the class designated by a term, then the term is said to be **undistributed**. For example, the statement, "All cats are mammals," makes a definite assertion about every member of the class of objects called "cats." Since the claim is that *every cat* is a mammal, the subject term is distributed. However, the predicate term is not distributed. Since the quantifier "all" does not extend its reference to the predicate term, the predicate term is undistributed. As always, it should be remembered that this is a logical discussion that does not address the question of the truth content of these statements. This means that in the statement, "All cats are diplomats," the subject term is distributed and the predicate term is undistributed, because distribution is a logical question; the truth content of the claim is irrelevant in this context.

The distinction between distributed and undistributed terms can be clearly illustrated by analysis of some representative statements. Let's begin with "No mammals are cats." Since this is an *E* statement, the quantifier makes a definite assertion regarding every member of the subject term; it claims that not even one is a member of the predicate term, the class designated by P. Thus, the subject term is distributed. However, unlike the results with the *A* statement, the logical analysis reveals that in the case of *E* statements we simultaneously assert that no member of the predicate term is a member of the subject term. This follows, because *if* no member of the subject term is a member of the predicate term (the logical question), then the reverse must be true, too. Therefore, in *E* statements both the subject and predicate terms are distributed.

Our next analysis concerns the statement, "Some students in this class are sophomores." This *I* statement has the quantifier "Some" referring to only the subject term. It specifically says that at least one of the "students in this class" is also a member of the predicate term "sophomores." However, it is merely making a "minimal" claim. It is not asserting anything definite about all students in this class, only that at least one is a sophomore. So, in this case, the subject term is not distributed. But the same can be said about the predicate term. Since our knowledge of the class *P* is restricted to the assertion that there is at least one member of *S* included in it, the predicate term is not distributed.

We said that the *I* statement makes a minimal claim. This means that it is possible that *every* member of *S* is included in *P*. It is possible that every student in the class is a sophomore. Acknowledgment of this possibility eliminates a potential misunderstanding regarding *I* statements. It is incorrect to interpret the *I* statement "Some *S* are *P*" as also claiming that "Some *S* are *not P.*" If you understand that the statement is making a minimal claim, and that it is not ruling out the possibility that every member of *S* is in *P*, then the mistaken interpretation will not arise.

The statement "Some cars are not fuel efficient vehicles," is an example of an *O* statement. Here again, the quantifier "some" refers only to the class designated by the subject term. It specifies that at least one member of *S* is not a member of the predicate term *P*. Since nothing definite is said about every member of *S*, the subject term is not distributed. But in an interesting twist, the *O* statement logically tells us something definite about the predicate term. Indirectly, the class *P* has been completely distinguished from the single member referred to by *S*. And because of this curious twist, the predicate term is distributed. Whenever a categorical statement says something definite about *every member* of a class designated by a term, then that term is distributed. Since at least one member of the subject term is excluded from *every member of the class designated by the predicate term* in an *O* statement, the predicate term is, therefore, distributed.

The minimal effect can be seen arising here, too. Once again, the quantifier, "some," in the *O* statement allows the possibility that every member of *S* is not in *P*. As with the interpretation of *I* statements, it is incorrect to interpret the *O* statement "Some *S* are not *P*" as also claiming that "Some *S* are *P.*" If you remember that the statement is making a minimal claim (it is not ruling out the possibility that every member of *S* is outside *P*), then you will avoid this mistake, too. **Quick Reference A2.1** summarizes quantity, quality, and distribution for the four standard-form categorical statements.

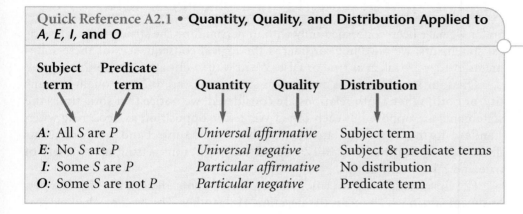

Quick Reference A2.1 • Quantity, Quality, and Distribution Applied to *A, E, I,* and *O*

Subject term	Predicate term	Quantity	Quality	Distribution
A: All *S* are *P*		Universal affirmative		Subject term
E: No *S* are *P*		Universal negative		Subject & predicate terms
I: Some *S* are *P*		Particular affirmative		No distribution
O: Some *S* are not *P*		Particular negative		Predicate term

Categorical statements are universal or particular (quantity), affirmative or negative (quality), and may refer to all members of a designated class (distributed), or not (undistributed).

2. Particular Negative; S undistributed; P distributed.

3. Universal Negative; S distributed; P distributed.

4. Particular Affirmative; S undistributed; P undistributed.

5. Universal Negative; S distributed; P distributed.

6. Universal Negative; S distributed; P distributed.

7. Particular Affirmative; S undistributed; P undistributed

8. Particular Negative; S undistributed; P distributed.

9. Universal Affirmative; S distributed; P undistributed

10. Universal Negative; S distributed; P distributed.

11. Universal Affirmative; S distributed; P undistributed.

12. Particular Negative; S undistributed; P distributed.

13. Universal Negative; S distributed; P distributed.

14. Particular Affirmative; S undistributed; P undistributed.

15. Universal Negative; S distributed; P distributed.

EXERCISE SET A2.2 ○○○

The categorical statements below are to be analyzed in the following three ways: (1) the correct *quantity* (*universal* or *particular*); (2) the correct *quality* (*affirmative* or *negative*); (3) the correct *distribution* (subject term distributed, predicate term distributed, both distributed, or neither distributed).

1. All ice-cold soft drinks are thirst-quenchers.

Answer: Universal affirmative; subject term distributed; predicate term undistributed.

2. Some popular music is not addictive.

3. No computer software is easily installed.

4. Some DVD's are overpriced.

5. No cannibals are vegetarians.

*6. No fast-food franchises are benevolent employers.

7. Some universities are intellectual gardens.

8. Some tattoos are not acceptable to parents.

9. All body-piercing rituals are based on ancient religious beliefs.

10. No winning gamblers are probability-deficient.

*11. All sugar-free pastries are pleasing to the palate.

12. Some gymnasium locker rooms are not aromatically pleasant places.

13. No reality television shows are scripted.

14. Some tropical islands are wonderful vacation getaways.

15. No green vegetables are vitamin deficient.

Opposition: Whenever standard-form categorical statements have the same subject and predicate term, but differ from each other in quality, quantity, or in both.

Contradictories: Two statements that are related such that one is the negation of the other; it is impossible for both to be true or both to be false at the same time. The categorical *A* and *O* statements, and *E* and *I* statements are contradictories.

A2.3 THE ARISTOTELIAN SQUARE OF OPPOSITION

So far we have been concerned only with understanding the structure of categorical statements; we have not considered the logical consequences of these statements, if they are taken as true or false. We now turn our attention to this topic.

The four standard-form categorical statements can differ in quality, quantity, or both. When truth relations are considered, we notice that sometimes the statements are opposed to each other. We define **opposition** as occurring when standard-form categorical statements with the same subject and predicate terms differ from each other in quality, quantity, or both, thus setting up a variety of true and false relationships.

The first relationship we will look at is called **contradictories**, which is a pair of statements in which one is the negation of the other. This occurs when we recognize from the logical structure of the statements that it is impossible for both statements to be true or both false at the same time. *If one statement is the negation of the other, then one must be true and the other must be false.* For example,

1. All interstate highways are built with taxpayers' money.
2. Some interstate highways are not built with taxpayers' money.

Can both of these statements be true (or false) at the same time? Think about it. The answer is "No." We do a thought experiment whenever we analyze the possibilities of true and false. If the first statement is true, then the second must be false. If all (every) interstate highways are built with taxpayers' money, then there cannot be even one that is *not* built with taxpayers' money. Likewise, if the second statement is true, then the first must be false. If there is at least one interstate highway that is *not* built with taxpayers' money, then it cannot be true that all of them are built with taxpayers' money. We now work it from the other end by asking what will happen if the first statement is false. Our answer is that the second would then have to be true. If not all (not every) interstate highways are built with taxpayers' money, then there must be at least one that is *not* built with taxpayers' money. Likewise, if the second statement is false, then the first must be true. If there is not even one interstate highway that is *not* built with taxpayers' money, then it must be true that all of them are built with taxpayers' money. We then see that for any two statements to be truly contradictory one of them has to be true and the other has to be false. The above pair of statements reveals that **A** and **O** statements are contradictories.

Another pair of contradictory statements is the following:

3. No interstate highways are built with taxpayers' money.
4. Some interstate highways are built with taxpayers' money.

If the first statement is true, then the second must be false, and vice versa. Also, if the first statement is false, then the second must be true, and vice versa. Since these results meet the necessary criteria for contradictory statements, the above pair of statements shows that **E** and **I** statements are contradictories.

At this point we will begin building the square of opposition. We can display the results discussed so far by showing a basic square with the following picture:

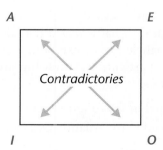

We can illustrate the ideas of quantity, quality, and distribution by using the contradictory pairs displayed in the square of opposition. Since **A** and **O** statements are contradictory, they should have opposite values for quantity, quality, and distribution. This is verified in Figure A2.1, which also shows that the contradictory statements, *E* and *I*, have opposite values for quantity, quality, and distribution.

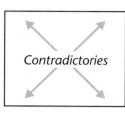

A: All S are P
Universal
Affirmative
Subject term distributed
Predicate term undistributed

Contradictories

E: No S are P
Universal
Negative
Subject term distributed
Predicate term distributed

FIGURE　A2.1 •
Quantity, quality, and distribution in the square of opposition.

I: Some S are P
Particular
Affirmative
Subject term undistributed
Predicate term undistributed

O: Some S are not P
Particular
Negative
Subject term undistributed
Predicate term distributed

Let's see if you have grasped the idea of contradictories. Are the following two statements contradictories?

5. All interstate highways are built with taxpayers' money.

6. No interstate highways are built with taxpayers' money.

If the first statement is true, then the second must, of course, be false. Likewise, if the second is true, then the first must be false. However, if you guessed that they are contradictories, you would be wrong. To see this, we have to ask what we might get if the first statement is false. In this case, must the second statement then be true? Again, think about it. If it is false that "All interstate highways are built with taxpayers' money," must it be true that "No interstate highways are built with taxpayers' money"? The correct answer is "No," because there might be *one* interstate highway that is built with taxpayers' money. Since this is possible, it would make the second statement false, too. Since contradictory statements cannot both be false at the same time, we have shown that statements (5) and (6) are not contradictories.

However, this example has revealed a new type of logical relationship. Our analysis of statements (5) and (6) has revealed that although they cannot both be true at the same time, nevertheless, they can both be false at the same time. Pairs of statements showing this particular relationship are called **contraries.** Here is another example of contraries.

Contraries: Two statements that cannot both be true at the same time, but that can be false at the same time. Also, if one is true, then the other must be false. In the Aristotelian square of opposition *A* and *E* statements are contraries.

7. All hurricanes are formed in the Atlantic Ocean.

8. No hurricanes are formed in the Atlantic Ocean.

If the first statement is true, then the second must be false, and vice versa. However, they both can be false at the same time, because it is possible that just some hurricanes are formed in the Atlantic Ocean. This analysis reveals that *A* and *E* statements are contraries. We can add this to our square of opposition.

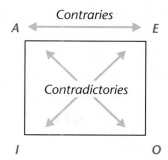

Contraries

A ← → E

Contradictories

I   O

Subcontraries: When two statements are related such that they cannot both be false at the same time, but they both can be true at the same time. In addition, if one is false, then the other must be true.

The flip side of contraries is a relationship between two statements called **subcontraries**, which occur whenever two statements are related such that they cannot both be false at the same time, but they can both be true at the same time. Also, if one is false, then the other must be true. The next pair of statements are subcontraries.

9. Some hurricanes are formed in the Atlantic Ocean.
10. Some hurricanes are not formed in the Atlantic Ocean.

It is possible for both of these statements to be true at the same time. All that would be needed would be to find one hurricane that formed in the Atlantic Ocean and one that was not was formed in the Atlantic Ocean. However, you should recognize and understand why both statements cannot be false at the same time. If the first statement is false, then that would mean that there is not even one hurricane that was formed in the Atlantic Ocean. If that is so, then the second statement would have to be true. The same result is attained if we start by making the second statement false. Doing this would logically make the first statement true. Therefore, we have shown that the subcontraries, *I* and *O,* cannot both be false at the same time, but they can both be true at the same time. We can now add these results to the square of opposition.

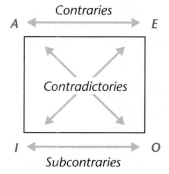

Contraries

A ← → E

Contradictories

I ← → O

Subcontraries

The final relationship for us to consider in order to complete the square of opposition is called **subalternation**. This occurs when the relationship is between a universal statement (referred to as the **superaltern**) and its corresponding particular

Subalternation: The unique relationship that exists between a universal statement (*A* or *E*) and its corresponding particular statement (*I* or *O,* respectively).

Superaltern: The universal statement related to its corresponding particular (*A* is the superaltern of *I,* and *E* is the superaltern of *O*).

Subaltern: The particular statement related to its corresponding universal (*I* is the subaltern of *A*, and *O* is the subaltern of *E*).

Corresponding statements: These relationships reveal that if the universal statement of a pair is true, then its corresponding particular partner will also be true.

statement (referred to as the **subaltern**). There are two kinds of **corresponding statements:**

> *A*: All *S* are *P corresponds to I*: Some *S* are *P*
>
> *E*: No *S* are *P corresponds to O*: Some *S* are not *P*

What these relationships reveal is that if the universal statement of a pair is true, then its corresponding particular partner will also be true. For example, if it is true that, "All cactuses are prickly," then it is also true that, "Some cactuses are prickly." Likewise, if it is true that, "No cactuses are prickly," then it is also true that, "Some cactuses are not prickly." However, the reverse does not hold. That is, if the particular statement of a pair is true, its corresponding universal might be true or it might be false. The following is an example of subalternation:

11. All musical instruments are difficult to master.
12. Some musical instruments are difficult to master.

If statement (11), a universal affirmative *A*, is true, then its corresponding particular, an *I*, will be true, too. However, we can see that even if statement (12), the particular affirmative, is true, then its corresponding universal might be true or false. These same results hold for *E* and *O* statements. For example,

13. No musical instruments are difficult to master.
14. Some musical instruments are not difficult to master.

As before, if statement (13), a universal negative *E*, is true, then its corresponding particular, an *O*, will be true, too. However, we can see that even if statement (14), the particular negative, is true, then its corresponding universal might be true or false.

Subalternation has additional interesting results when we consider what happens if one member of a corresponding pair is false. What these relationships reveal is that if the universal statement of a pair is false, then its corresponding particular partner could be true or false. For example, if it is false that "All cactuses are prickly," then it can be either true or false that "Some cactuses are prickly." Likewise, if it is false that "No cactuses are prickly," then it can be either true or false that "Some cactuses are not prickly." However, the reverse does not hold—that is, if the particular statement of a pair of corresponding statements is false, then its corresponding universal must be false as well, as in the following example.

11. All musical instruments are difficult to master.
12. Some musical instruments are difficult to master.

If statement (11), a universal affirmative *A*, is false, then its corresponding particular, an *I*, could be either true or false. However, we can see that if statement (12), the particular affirmative, is false, then its corresponding universal must be false, too. These same results hold for *E* and *O* statements. For example,

13. No musical instruments are difficult to master.
14. Some musical instruments are not difficult to master.

As before, if statement (13), a universal negative *E*, is false, then its corresponding particular, an *O*, can be either true or false. However, once again, we can see that if statement (14), the particular negative, is false, then its corresponding universal must be false, too.

We can now complete the square of opposition (Figure A2.2).

Immediate inference: An inference that has only one premise.

Mediate inference: Any inference that contains more than one premise.

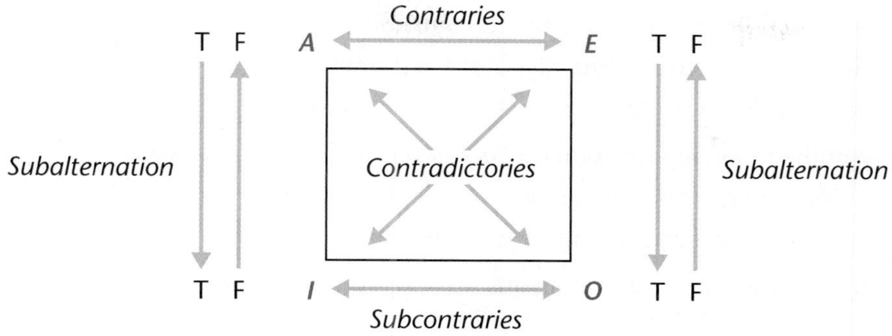

FIGURE A2.2 • The Aristotelian square of opposition.

This square of opposition has shown us that we obtain different combinations of truth and falsity between pairs of standard-form categorical statements.

In a sense, we have been creating and analyzing **immediate inferences**, which are defined as inferences that contain only one premise. (Inferences that have more than one premise are called **mediate inferences**.) Let's continue our analysis of immediate inferences. Suppose the following **A** statement is true: "All clowns are frightening." If so, we can go around the square of opposition and say something about each of the remaining three categorical statements. Since the **E** statement would be, "No clowns are frightening," and since both contraries cannot be true at the same time, we know that the **E** statement would have to be false. Also, since we know that the **O** statement, "Some clowns are not frightening," is the contradictory of our **A** statement, it must be false. The remaining **I** statement, "Some clowns are frightening," being the subaltern of the **A** statement, must then be true, because the **A** statement has been accepted as true.

Let's do the opposite truth value. What if the **A** statement, "All clowns are frightening," is false? Going around the square we would then know that the **E** statement, being the contrary, might be true or false, so its truth value would be undetermined. But the **O** statement, being the contradictory of the **A** statement, must then be true. The remaining **I** statement might be true or false, and its truth value is therefore undetermined.

EXERCISE SET A2.3

Exercises 1–15 Use your understanding of the Aristotelian square of opposition to determine the correct answer.

1. The *contradictory* of "No football players are opera singers" is:
   (a) All football players are opera singers.
   (b) Some football players are opera singers.
   (c) Some football players are not opera singers.

Exercises 2–15: For answers and explanations, see pages 306–307 of Instructor's Manual.

Answer: "b" is the correct answer. Since the first sentence is an *E* statement, its contradictory must be an *I* statement, which is answer "b." The correct answer cannot be "a" because it is an *A* statement (the *contrary* of *E*); "c" is not correct because it is an *O* statement.

2. Yes

2. Are the following two statements *contraries*?

   All yo-yo's are frustrating toys better left untouched.

   No yo-yo's are frustrating toys better left untouched.

3. Yes

3. Are the following two statements *subcontraries*?

   Some contact lenses are gas permeable.

   Some contact lenses are not gas permeable.

4. b. False

4. If it is true that "Some implants are easy to detect," then the statement, "No implants are easy to detect," must be:

   (a) True   (b) False   (c) Undetermined

5. a. True

5. If it is false that "Some implants are easy to detect," then the statement, "No implants are easy to detect," must be:

   (a) True   (b) False   (c) Undetermined

6. False

*6. True or False: In the Aristotelian square of opposition, two contradictory categorical statements can both be false at the same time.

7. b. False

7. If it is false that "Some games are impossible to master," then the statement, "All games are impossible to master," must be:

   (a) True   (b) False   (c) Undetermined

8. c. Undetermined

8. If it is true that "Some games are impossible to master," then the statement, "All games are impossible to master," must be:

   (a) True   (b) False   (c) Undetermined

9. a. True

9. If it is true that "No games are impossible to master," then the statement, "Some games are not impossible to master," must be:

   (a) True   (b) False   (c) Undetermined

10. c. Undetermined

10. If it is false that "No games are impossible to master," then the statement, "Some games are not impossible to master," must be:

    (a) True   (b) False   (c) Undetermined

11. Some sports cars are not gas-guzzlers.

*11. Write the contradictory of "All sports cars are gas-guzzlers."

12. No diamond rings are expensive.

12. Write the contrary of "All diamond rings are expensive."

13. No relationship of opposition.

13. What is the relationship of opposition, if any, between these two statements?

    "Some foreign movies are dramas."

    "Some foreign movies are comedies."

14. False

14. If it is true that "Some theoretical scientists are humanists," then what immediate inference based on the square of opposition, if any, can one make about the statement "No theoretical scientists are humanists"?

15. If it is false that "All theoretical scientists are humanists," then what immediate inference based on the square of opposition, if any, can one make about the statement "Some theoretical scientists are humanists"?

15. Undetermined

Exercises 16–39 For each of the following questions you will be told the truth value of one of the four standard-form categorical statements. From this information, you are to determine the truth values of the other three types of categorical statements as you go around the Aristotelian square of opposition.

16. If an *A* statement is *true,* then you can conclude that the *E* statement would be:

   (a) True   (b) False   (c) Undetermined

Answer: False. Since they are *contraries,* they cannot both be true at the same time.

Exercises 17–39: For answers and explanations, see pages 307–308 of Instructor's Manual.

17. If an *A* statement is *true,* then you can conclude that the *I* statement would be:

   (a) True   (b) False   (c) Undetermined

17. True

18. If an *A* statement is *true,* then you can conclude that the *O* statement would be:

   (a) True   (b) False   (c) Undetermined

18. False

19. If an *A* statement is *false,* then you can conclude that the *E* statement would be:

   (a) True   (b) False   (c) Undetermined

19. Undetermined

20. If an *A* statement is *false,* then you can conclude that the *I* statement would be:

   (a) True   (b) False   (c) Undetermined

20. Undetermined

*21. If an *A* statement is *false,* then you can conclude that the *O* statement would be:

   (a) True   (b) False   (c) Undetermined

21. True

22. If an *E* statement is *true,* then you can conclude that the *A* statement would be:

   (a) True   (b) False   (c) Undetermined

22. False

23. If an *E* statement is *true,* then you can conclude that the *I* statement would be:

   (a) True   (b) False   (c) Undetermined

23. False

24. If an *E* statement is *true,* then you can conclude that the *O* statement would be:

   (a) True   (b) False   (c) Undetermined

24. True

25. If an *E* statement is *false,* then you can conclude that the *A* statement would be:

   (a) True   (b) False   (c) Undetermined

25. Undetermined

*26. If an *E* statement is *false,* then you can conclude that the *I* statement would be:

   (a) True   (b) False   (c) Undetermined

26. True

27. If an *E* statement is *false,* then you can conclude that the *O* statement would be:

   (a) True   (b) False   (c) Undetermined

27. Undetermined

28. If an *I* statement is *true,* then you can conclude that the *A* statement would be:

   (a) True   (b) False   (c) Undetermined

28. Undetermined

29. False

29. If an *I* statement is *true*, then you can conclude that the *E* statement would be:

    (a) True   (b) False   (c) Undetermined

30. Undetermined

30. If an *I* statement is *true*, then you can conclude that the *O* statement would be:

    (a) True   (b) False   (c) Undetermined

31. False

*31. If an *I* statement is *false*, then you can conclude that the *A* statement would be:

    (a) True   (b) False   (c) Undetermined

32. True

32. If an *I* statement is *false*, then you can conclude that the *E* statement would be:

    (a) True   (b) False   (c) Undetermined

33. True

33. If an *I* statement is *false*, then you can conclude that the *O* statement would be:

    (a) True   (b) False   (c) Undetermined

34. False

34. If an *O* statement is *true*, then you can conclude that the *A* statement would be:

    (a) True   (b) False   (c) Undetermined

35. Undetermined

35. If an *O* statement is *true*, then you can conclude that the *E* statement would be:

    (a) True   (b) False   (c) Undetermined

36. Undetermined

*36. If an *O* statement is *true*, then you can conclude that the *I* statement would be:

    (a) True   (b) False   (c) Undetermined

37. True

37. If an *O* statement is *false*, then you can conclude that the *A* statement would be:

    (a) True   (b) False   (c) Undetermined

38. False

38. If an *O* statement is *false*, then you can conclude that the *E* statement would be:

    (a) True   (b) False   (c) Undetermined

39. True

39. If an *O* statement is *false*, then you can conclude that the *I* statement would be:

    (a) True   (b) False   (c) Undetermined

A2.4 IMMEDIATE INFERENCES—CONVERSION, OBVERSION, AND CONTRAPOSITION

Conversion: For categorical statements, an immediate inference created by interchanging the subject term and predicate term of a statement.

We can now look at a number of special cases of immediate inference that will illustrate some further consequences of the square of opposition.

Conversion

Convertend: The categorical statement with which we start and which becomes the premise of an immediate inference by conversion.

An immediate inference can be created by interchanging the subject and predicate terms of a given categorical statement, a process called **conversion**. The statement we start with is called the **convertend**, and it becomes the premise of the inference. The statement we end up with after applying the process of conversion is called the

converse, and it becomes the conclusion of the inference. For example, consider these two statements:

> *Convertend: E* statement: "No beer commercials are subtle advertisements."
>
> *Converse: E* statement: "No subtle advertisements are beer commercials."

The second statement can be validly inferred from the first. This can be understood, if you recall that *E* statements completely separate the subject and predicate terms. So, if no "beer commercials" are "subtle advertisements," then, of course, no "subtle advertisements" can be "beer commercials." The conversion works for *E* statements.

The same idea holds true for *I* statements, as the following set of statements shows.

> *Convertend: I* statement: "Some textbooks are entertaining diversions."
>
> *Converse: I* statement: "Some entertaining diversions are textbooks."

Recall that *I* statements make the subject and predicate terms *overlap* to some degree; this means that if some "textbooks" are "entertaining diversions," then, of course, some "entertaining diversions" must be "textbooks." Therefore, conversion works for *I* statements.

Strictly speaking, conversion does not work for *A* statements. We can see this in the following example:

> *Convertend: A* statement: "All spam e-mailings are invasions of your home."
>
> *Converse: A* statement: "All invasions of your home are spam e-mailings."

This example illustrates the point that *A* statements cannot be directly converted. However, we can use some other ideas that have been generated by our previous discussions to make conversion work in a limited way. The idea of subalternation tells us that if an *A* statement is true, then its corresponding particular *I* statement is true, too. And since we already saw that conversion works for *I* statements, we can then do something called **conversion by limitation**. This is the procedure by which we first change a universal *A* statement into its corresponding particular *I* statement, and then we use the process of conversion on the *I* statement. The complex process looks like this:

> *Convertend: A* statement: "All spam e-mailings are invasions of your home."
>
> *The corresponding particular I:* "Some spam e-mailings are invasions of your home."
>
> *Converse: I* statement: "Some invasions of your home are spam e-mailings."

We have created a valid inference. The square of opposition enabled us to use subalternation to make conversion work for *A* statements.

The final type of statement to consider for conversion is *O* statements. Let's look at this set of sentences.

> *Convertend: O* statement: "Some vegetables are not carrots."
>
> *Converse: O* statement: "Some carrots are not vegetables."

Converse: The statement produced by the process of conversion.

Conversion by limitation: For categorical statements, when the process of subalternation changes a universal *A* statement into its corresponding particular *I* statement, and then forms the converse of the *I* statement.

As we can plainly see, the conversion does not work for **O** statements. The premise is, of course, true, because many vegetables, such as potatoes, celery, spinach, etc., are certainly not carrots. However, the conclusion is false, because every carrot is a vegetable. Table A2.1 summarizes the method of conversion.

Table A2.1 The Method of Conversion

Subject ⟷ Predicate
Interchange the Subject and Predicate

Convertend	Converse
A: All S are P	**I**: Some P are S (*by limitation*)
E: No S are P	**E**: No P are S
I: Some S are P	**I**: Some P are S
O: Some S are not P	(*Conversion is not valid*)

Obversion

The second type of immediate inference is formed by (1) changing the quality of the given statement, and (2) by replacing the predicate term with its *complement*. The **complement** is defined as the set of objects that do not belong to a given class. The complement of a given class is everything outside that given class, and, in this case, the complement is formed by attaching the prefix "non" to the predicate term. This complete process is called **obversion**. The **obvertend** is the statement we start with, so it becomes the premise of an immediate inference. The **obverse** is the statement we wind up with, so it becomes the conclusion. Consider this pair of statements:

> *Obvertend:* **A** statement: "All pneumatic jackhammers are lethal weapons."
>
> *Obverse:* **E** statement: "No pneumatic jackhammers are nonlethal weapons."

To get the obverse we first had to change the quality, so we go from affirmative to negative (from **A** to **E**). Second, we had to replace the predicate term with its complement ("lethal weapons" becomes "nonlethal weapons"). Although it may be difficult to see at first, you should agree that this is a valid immediate inference. If every pneumatic jackhammer *is* a lethal weapon, then it must be true that no pneumatic jackhammer is a nonlethal weapon.

The process of obversion is straightforward in that it is applicable to all four standard-form categorical statements (Table A2.2). The following immediate inferences are therefore valid:

> *Obvertend:* **E** statement: "No comedians are brain surgeons."
>
> *Obverse:* **A** statement: "All comedians are nonbrain surgeons."
>
> *Obvertend:* **I** statement: "Some athletes are overpaid egoists."
>
> *Obverse:* **O** statement: "Some athletes are not nonoverpaid egoists."
>
> *Obvertend:* **O** statement: "Some pets are not lovable animals."
>
> *Obverse:* **I** statement: "Some pets are nonlovable animals."

Complement: The set of objects that does not belong to a given class; everything outside the given class.

Obversion: For categorical statements, an immediate inference created by changing the quality of a statement and then by replacing the predicate term by its complement.

Obvertend: The starting categorical statement that becomes the premise of an immediate inference by obversion.

Obverse: The statement produced by the process of obversion.

Table A2.2 The Method of Obversion

Step 1: Change the *quality* of the given statement.
Step 2: Replace the *predicate term* with its *complement*.

Obvertend	Obverse
A: All S are P	*E*: No S are non-P
E: No S are P	*A*: All S are non-P
I: Some S are P	*O*: Some S are not non-P
O: Some S are not P	*I*: Some S are non-P

Contraposition

The final type of immediate inference to consider, **contraposition**, is formed by (1) replacing the subject term of a given statement with the complement of its predicate term, and (2) by replacing the predicate term of the given statement with the complement of its subject term. This is illustrated in the next pair of statements.

> *Given statement: **A** statement:* "All pencils are ink-free writing tools."
>
> *Contrapositive: **A** statement:* "All non-ink-free writing tools are nonpencils."

If the first statement is true, it places every pencil in the class of "ink-free writing tools." The **contrapositive** of this statement claims that anything that is a "non-ink-free writing tool" is also a "nonpencil," and surely this must be correct. Therefore, contraposition works for **A** statements.

Let's try a different pair of statements.

> *Given statement: **O** statement:* "Some hairy creatures are not cuddly things."
>
> *Contrapositive: **O** statement:* "Some noncuddly things are not nonhairy creatures."

This may seem confusing, but let's take it apart very slowly. The first statement says that there is at least one member of the class of "hairy creatures" that is *not* in the class of "cuddly things." The second statement claims that there is at least one "noncuddly thing" (something not in the class of "cuddly things") that is *not* a "nonhairy creature." Since, by definition, the class of "nonhairy creatures" is everything outside the class of "hairy creatures," we can see that the phrase "are not nonhairy creatures" places us back within the class of "hairy creatures." The inference is therefore valid.

Unfortunately, we run into problems with **E** statements, as the next set of statements shows.

> *Given statement: **E** statement:* "No bananas are lions."
>
> *Contrapositive: **E** statement:* "No nonlions are nonbananas."

Even if the first statement is true, the second can still be false. This may be hard to see at first, but close analysis reveals the problem. The first statement, if true, clearly separates the two classes mentioned, allowing no overlap between them. However, it does not tell us anything specific about what is outside those

Contraposition:
For categorical statements, when an immediate inference is formed by replacing the subject term with the complement of its predicate term, and then by replacing the predicate term with the complement of its subject term.

Contrapositive:
The statement produced by the process of contraposition.

Contraposition by limitation: For categorical statements, when the process of subalternation changes a universal *E* statement into its corresponding particular *O* statement, and then forms the contrapositive of the *O* statement.

respective classes. But the second statement specifically mentions those areas outside the given classes, and what it says might be false. It claims that there is not even one thing outside the class of "lions" that is, at the same time, a "nonbanana." But surely a "cow" is not "lion," and it is also not a "banana." So clearly, the contrapositive does not work here.

However, we can do something similar to what we did for *A* statements and conversion. This means that can we use *contraposition by limitation* for *E* statements. Once again, we must rely on the square of opposition. **Contraposition by limitation** occurs when subalternation is used to change the universal *E* statement into its corresponding particular *O* statement. We then apply the regular process of forming a contrapositive to this *O* statement (we have already shown that this process works on *O* statements). The completed process looks like this:

> *Given statement:* **E** statement: "No bananas are lions."
> *Corresponding particular:* **O** statement: "Some bananas are not lions."
> *Contrapositive:* **O** statement: "Some nonlions are not nonbananas."

The square of opposition has thus enabled us to make contraposition work for *E* statements by again using subalternation.

The process involved in contraposition does not work at all for *I* statements (and for reasons similar to why conversion did not work for *O* statements). Consider the following set of statements:

> *Given statement:* **I** statement: "Some humans are nonregistered voters."
> *Contrapositive:* **I** statement: "Some registered voters are nonhumans."

The first statement is true (some people fail to register to vote), but the second is clearly false (we have reduced the correct designation "*non-non*-registered voters" to simply "registered voters"). So contraposition will not always yield valid immediate inferences for *I* statements. Table A2.3 summarizes the method of contraposition.

Table A2.3 The Method of Contraposition

Step 1: Replace the *subject term* with the *complement of the predicate term.*
Step 2: Replace the *predicate term* with the *complement of the subject term.*

Given Statement	Contrapositive
A: All *S* are *P*	*A:* All non-*P* are non-*S*
E: No *S* are *P*	*O:* Some non-*P* are not non-*S* (*by limitation*)
I: Some *S* are *P*	(*Contraposition is not valid*)
O: Some *S* are not *P*	*O:* Some non-*P* are not non-*S*

EXERCISE SET A2.4 ○○○

For each of the following, provide the converse, obverse, and contrapositive of the given statement. Also, state whether any of the subsequent immediate inferences are not valid.

Some games of chance are sucker bets.

1. Converse:

2. Obverse:

3. Contrapositive:

Answer:

1. Converse: Some sucker bets are games of chance.

2. Obverse: Some games of chance are not nonsucker bets.

3. Contrapositive: Not valid for *I* statements.

Some sandwiches are not things made with meat.

4. Converse:

5. Obverse:

6. Contrapositive:

No bats are vegetarians.

7. Converse:

8. Obverse:

9. Contrapositive:

All designer jeans are genetically engineered objects.

10. Converse:

11. Obverse:

12. Contrapositive:

No greedy politicians are people likely to go to prison.

13. Converse:

14. Obverse:

15. Contrapositive:

Some fruitcakes are not regifted presents.

*16. Converse:

*17. Obverse:

*18. Contrapositive:

4. Not valid for *O* statements.

5. Some sandwiches are non-things made with meat.

6. Some nonthings made with meat are not nonsandwiches.

7. No vegetarians are bats.

8. All bats are nonvegetarians.

9. Some nonvegetarians are not nonbats. (*by limitation*)

10. Some genetically engineered objects are designer jeans. (*by limitation*)

11. No designer jeans are nongenetically engineered objects.

12. All nongenetically engineered objects are nondesigner jeans.

13. No people likely to go to prison are greedy politicians.

14. All greedy politicians are nonpeople likely to go to prison.

15. Some nonpeople likely to go to prison are not nongreedy politicians. (*by limitation*)

16. Not valid for *O* statements.

17. Some fruitcakes are nonregifted presents.

18. Some nonregifted presents are not nonfruitcakes.

19. Some social deviants are embezzlers. (*by limitation*)

20. No embezzlers are nonsocial deviants.

21. All nonsocial deviants are nonembezzlers.

22. Some incidents caused by speeding are traffic accidents.

23. Some traffic accidents are not nonincidents caused by speeding.

24. Not valid for *I* statements.

25. Some days when banks close are public holidays. (*by limitation*)

26. No public holidays are nondays when banks close.

27. All nondays when banks close are nonpublic holidays.

28. Not valid for *O* statements.

29. Some music videos are nontragedies.

30. Some nontragedies are not nonmusic videos.

31. Some juicy items are T-bone steaks.

32. Some T-bone steaks are not nonjuicy items.

33. Not valid for *I* statements.

34. Some mouth-watering morsels are fajitas.

35. Some fajitas are not nonmouth-watering morsels.

36. Not valid for *I* statements.

37. No things harmful to your diet are ice cream toppings.

38. All ice cream toppings are nonthings harmful to your diet.

39. Some nonthings harmful to your diet are not nonice cream toppings. (*by limitation*)

40. Some healthy foods are yogurt products. (*by limitation*)

41. No yogurt products are nonhealthy foods.

42. All nonhealthy foods are nonyogurt products.

All embezzlers are social deviants.

19. Converse:

20. Obverse:

21. Contrapositive:

Some traffic accidents are incidents caused by speeding.

22. Converse:

23. Obverse:

24. Contrapositive:

All public holidays are days when banks close.

25. Converse:

26. Obverse:

27. Contrapositive:

Some music videos are not tragedies.

28. Converse:

29. Obverse:

30. Contrapositive:

Some T-bone steaks are juicy items.

*31. Converse:

*32. Obverse:

*33. Contrapositive:

Some fajitas are mouth-watering morsels.

34. Converse:

35. Obverse:

36. Contrapositive:

No ice cream toppings are things harmful to your diet.

37. Converse:

38. Obverse:

39. Contrapositive:

All yogurt products are healthy foods.

40. Converse:

41. Obverse:

42. Contrapositive:

No vegetables are things lacking in multiple vitamins.

43. Converse:

44. Obverse:

45. Contrapositive:

Some barbequed chicken wings are things too hot to eat.

*46. Converse:

*47. Obverse:

*48. Contrapositive:

All french fries are grease-laden products.

49. Converse:

50. Obverse:

51. Contrapositive:

Some cheesecakes are sugar-free products.

52. Converse:

53. Obverse:

54. Contrapositive:

All bananas are foods best eaten when ripe.

55. Converse:

56. Obverse:

57. Contrapositive:

Some tofu products are items delicious to eat.

58. Converse:

59. Obverse:

60. Contrapositive:

Some tattoos are great works of art.

61. Converse:

62. Obverse:

63. Contrapositive:

Some modern clothes are not warm garments.

*64. Converse:

*65. Obverse:

*66. Contrapositive:

43. No things lacking in multiple vitamins are vegetables.

44. All vegetables are nonthings lacking in multiple vitamins.

45. Some nonthings lacking in multiple vitamins are not nonvegetables. (*by limitation*)

46. Some things too hot to eat are barbeque wings.

47. Some barbeque wings are not nonthings too hot to eat.

48. Not valid for *I* statements.

49. Some grease-laden products are french fries. (*by limitation*)

50. No french fries are nongrease-laden products.

51. All nongrease-laden products are nonfrench fries.

52. Some sugar-free products are cheese-cakes.

53. Some cheese-cakes are not nonsugar-free products.

54. Not valid for *I* statements.

55. Some foods best eaten when ripe are bananas. (*by limitation*)

56. No bananas are nonfoods best eaten when ripe.

57. All nonfoods best eaten when ripe are nonbananas.

58. Some items delicious to eat are tofu products.

59. Some tofu products are not nonitems delicious to eat.

60. Not valid for *I* statements.

61. Some great works of art are tattoos.

62. Some tattoos are not non-great works of art.

63. Not valid for *I* statements.

64. Not valid for *O* statements.

65. Some modern clothes are nonwarm garments.

66. Some nonwarm garments are not nonmodern clothes.

67. No easy-to-clean objects are swimming pools.

68. All swimming pools are noneasy-to-clean objects.

69. Some noneasy-to-clean objects are not nonswimming pools. (*by limitation*)

70. Some artificially sweetened products are movie theater drinks. (*by limitation*)

71. No movie theater drinks are nonartificially sweetened products.

72. All nonartificially sweetened products are nonmovie theater drinks.

73. No acts left unrewarded are good deeds.

74. All good deeds are nonacts left unrewarded.

75. Some nonacts left unrewarded are not nongood deeds. (*by limitation*)

No swimming pools are easy-to-clean objects.

67. Converse:

68. Obverse:

69. Contrapositive:

All movie theater drinks are artificially sweetened products.

70. Converse:

71. Obverse:

72. Contrapositive:

No good deeds are acts left unrewarded.

73. Converse:

74. Obverse:

75. Contrapositive:

A2.5 THE PROBLEM OF EXISTENTIAL IMPORT AND ITS CONSEQUENCES

At this point in our discussion a problem arises with the Aristotelian square of opposition. When a categorical statement refers to objects such as "horses," the reference to the truth content of the statement seems natural. But consider this statement: "All unicorns are one-horned creatures." How do we interpret the truth content of this statement? On the one hand, we might say that the statement is true *by definition* (the term "unicorn" is defined as "a one-horned creature"). On the other hand, we might say the statement is false because no unicorns exist. This raises an important question regarding the interpretation of universal categorical statements. A statement is said to have **existential import** if it asserts or presupposes the existence of certain kinds of objects. Given this, should it be assumed that *every* universal statement has existential import? If the answer is "Yes," then the statement, "All unicorns are one-horned creatures," is false, since no unicorns exist. If the answer is "No," then the statement, "All unicorns are one-horned creatures," is true by definition, even though no unicorns exist.

It is obvious, then, that *some* universal categorical statements clearly have existential import ("All trees are deciduous") while others do not ("All unicorns are one-horned creatures"). However, if we have to decide in each instance whether an individual universal categorical statement has existential import, then we would be doing truth content analysis instead of logical analysis. A logical interpretation of universal categorical statements is this: A statement having the structure "All S are P" is understood as asserting that "*If* something is an S, then it is also a P," while a statement having the structure "No S are P" is understood as asserting that "*If* something is an S, then it is not a P." This interpretation sets aside the truth content question concerning the existence of the objects referred to by the statement.

Existential import:
In a statement, the assertion of the existence of objects of some kind.

Unlike universal statements, particular categorical statements are *always* understood as having existential import. So, the statement "Some *S* are *P*" is actually asserting that there exists at least one *S* and that it is a *P*, while the statement "Some *S* are not *P*" is actually asserting that there exists at least one *S* and that it is not a *P*.

Under the Aristotelian system we accept that *I* statements and *O* statements both assert that their respective classes are not empty, that they have at least one member that exists. According to the square of opposition, particular statements follow validly from their corresponding universal statements by subalternation. However, if this is correct, then the universal statements must themselves have existential import, because a statement with existential import cannot be derived from one that does not have it. For example, if the statement "Some unicorns are mammals," follows validly from, "All unicorns are mammals," by subalternation, then the universal statement must assert the existence of unicorns. This result leads to a breakdown of a basic part of the Aristotelian square of opposition. *A* statements and *O* statements are contradictories, which means that one must be true and the other false. But if all *A* statements have existential import, then it might turn out that some contradictory *A* statements and *O* statements could be false at the same time. To see this consider these two statements:

> *A* statement: "All unicorns are mammals."
>
> *O* statement: "Some unicorns are not mammals."

We recognize that they are contradictories. But if they both have existential import, if they both assert that there are unicorns, then both statements are false if no unicorns exist. However, if they can both be false, then they cannot be contradictories. Something is wrong with the square of opposition.

In order to salvage the square of opposition, we might consider some changes. First, we might insist that all statements must refer to classes that are not empty. This change entails some unwanted consequences; we would have to eliminate many potentially good statements from our vocabulary. For example, if we presuppose every class designated by a statement has members, then we would never be allowed to formulate any statement that denies that it has members. The statement, "All future murderers will be executed," has no members, but we think it is a perfectly good statement. Nevertheless, it would be eliminated from our vocabulary, if we adopted the new practice. In addition, we often reason about "What if?" questions; and we assert many scientific principles as being "theoretical." Hypothetical reasoning and conjectures are acceptable ways of reasoning, and they work without necessarily presupposing any existence of entities. Again, these would be banned from discussion.

In line with what we learned earlier, if we have to decide an existence question, then we are not asking logical questions, but rather questions concerning truth content. The truth content of a statement would then become part of the logical discussion, but this is what we took great pains to distinguish. Nevertheless, under the Aristotelian square, we are sometimes required to determine the truth content of the premises before we can decide the validity of an inference. However, we have tried to maintain the idea that validity is a purely logical question.

Drawing on some ideas of Boole, we can build a new square of opposition. First, we must stipulate that both *I* statements and *O* statements have existential import, because both assert the existence of at least one entity. On the other hand,

Product: Whenever two classes, designated as *S* and *P*, are said to have some members in common. This commonality (overlap) is called either the product or the intersection of the two classes, and is given the symbol *SP*.

A statements and *E* statements both do not have existential import. A direct consequence of this is that we now have to eliminate the idea of subalternation, the cause of one of our early problems. If you recall, we had to do some fancy stepping to make conversion by limitation and contraposition by limitation work. That is because they relied on subalternation to make the inferences valid.

In the new square of opposition, *A-O* and *E-I* combinations will still be contradictories. However, subcontraries have to go. This is necessitated by the acknowledgement that both *I* statements and *O* statements could be false at the same time, provided the subject class is empty. In that case, both the contradictories, *A* and *E* statements, could be true at the same time. Thus, the idea of contraries has to go, too.

A2.6 THE BOOLEAN SQUARE OF OPPOSITION

In order to flesh out the details of the new square of opposition, we have to introduce some symbolic notation. Since we are allowing a class to have no members, we will use a zero (*0*) to designate this possibility. So, a class *S* that has no members is shown by the equation $S = 0$. On the other hand, a class *S* with at least one member is shown by the equation $S \neq 0$.

Since categorical statements refer to two classes, we will need special notation to deal with the various combinations. If two classes, *S* and *P*, have some members in common, then this common membership will be called the **product**, or *intersection*, of the two classes; it is symbolized as *SP*. *E* statements claim that the product is empty, and thus are symbolized as $SP = 0$. Since our new square of opposition retains the idea of contradictories, *I* statements will be symbolized as $SP \neq 0$. In order to capture the intent of *A* and *O* statements, we need to use a concept defined before, namely, class complement, which is the class of all things *not* belonging to the original class. If *S* designates the class of all milkshakes, then its complement class would be everything that is *not* a milkshake, the class of all nonmilkshakes, symbolized as $\overline{S}$.

A statements make the claim that every *S* is a *P* and are symbolized as $S\overline{P} = 0$. This notation is interpreted as claiming that there is no *S* outside the class of *P*. Since *A* statements and *O* statements are contradictories, *O* statements can be symbolized as $S\overline{P} \neq 0$. This is to be read as the assertion that there is at least one member of *S* outside the class of *P*. Our new square reflects these additions (Figure A2.3).

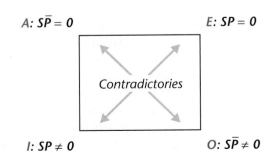

A: $S\overline{P} = 0$ E: $SP = 0$

Contradictories

I: $SP \neq 0$ O: $S\overline{P} \neq 0$

FIGURE A2.3 • Boolean square of opposition.

The symbolization is now complete, but we still need to learn how to diagram our results. The ideas in this part of our discussion are based on the work of John Venn. We can use circles to designate classes, along with specific annotations attached to those circles. The completed pictures are called **Venn diagrams**. Since categorical statements contain two classes, we will draw two intersecting circles and then annotate the drawing depending on the claim made by that statement. So, the basic Venn diagram structure for a categorical statement looks like this:

Venn diagram: A diagram that uses overlapping circles to represent categorical statements and to illustrate the validity or invalidity of a categorical inference.

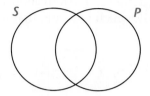

The area designating those members of S that are *not* members of P is the area symbolized by $S\overline{P}$.

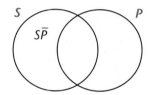

The area designating those members of P that are *not* members of S is the area symbolized by $\overline{S}P$.

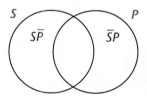

The area designating members of S that are at the same time members of P is symbolized as SP.

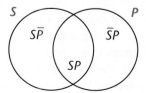

Finally, the area that designates where no members of either S or P can be found is symbolized as $\overline{SP}$.

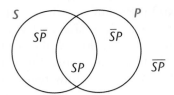

We are now in position to learn how to complete the diagrams for our four standard-form categorical statements. First, to show that a class is empty $(S = 0)$, the circle is shaded completely, which indicates that it has no members.

If it is claimed that there is at least one member $(S \neq 0)$, then an **X** is placed anywhere inside the circle.

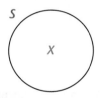

We can now draw diagrams of the logical commitments inherent in our four standard-form categorical statements (Figure A2.4).

  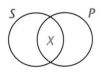 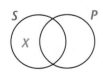

FIGURE A2.4 • **Diagrams for standard-form categorical statements.**

A: All S are P	E: No S are P	I: Some S are P	O: Some S are not P
$S\overline{P} = 0$	$SP = 0$	$SP \neq 0$	$S\overline{P} \neq 0$

It is important to understand that the pictures in Figure A2.4 are meant to represent the logical commitments of categorical statements. As such, they provide a diagram, a spatial representation of the logical meaning of statements. This visual representation allows us to investigate how the premises of an inference act together in a logical relationship. Assuming the premises are true, we can draw a premise, add to our drawing a second premise, and so on, until all the premises are captured in one diagram. The final diagram will reveal whether the conclusion must be true (in which case we will have proven that the inference is valid) or it will reveal the possibility of a false conclusion (in which case we will have proven that the inference is invalid). This method enables us to see the logic of inferences.

A2.7 CONVERSION, OBVERSION, AND CONTRAPOSITION REVISITED

Under Aristotle's system, it was somewhat difficult to grasp conversion, obversion, and contraposition. It was necessary to rely on an intuitive feel for the underlying complex logical apparatus at work. This new method makes the results more accessible. In a sense, we can "objectify" the results by producing a diagram that anyone can inspect. We can illustrate this by looking at the immediate inferences for conversion (Figure A2.5).

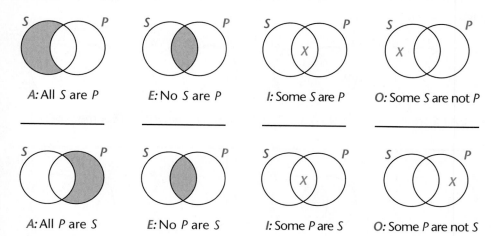

A: All *S* are *P*   *E:* No *S* are *P*   *I:* Some *S* are *P*   *O:* Some *S* are not *P*

A: All *P* are *S*   *E:* No *P* are *S*   *I:* Some *P* are *S*   *O:* Some *P* are not *S*

FIGURE A2.5 • Diagrams for conversion.

The line separating the top and bottom pictures can be understood as the dividing line between the premise above and the conclusion below for the four immediate inferences regarding conversion. The diagrams for *E* and *I* verify that these two are valid inferences. The validity rests on the obvious visual equivalence of the two diagrams (the premise and conclusion of the *E* and *I* conversions). Since we can literally see that the premise and conclusion of both *E* and *I* conversions are logically equivalent statements, it is easy to understand why these are valid inferences: If the premise is true, the conclusion must be true, too. The conversion for *O* statements does not work because the diagrams are not identical. Therefore, if the premise is true, the conclusion might be false. This also helps us to understand why conversion for *A* statements does not work. The diagrams clearly show that the pictures are not equivalent.

A major hurdle to overcome when trying to understand both obversion and contraposition is the difficulty surrounding the term "non-." Let's learn how to diagram the logic behind this word. Since we diagram the class designated by *S* as a circle, we can then stipulate that everything outside that circle is non-*S*.

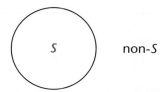

non-*S*

With two overlapping circles, *S* and *P*, there is more to annotate. We will number each area in order to make our references clear.

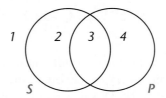

Area 1 is non-*S*, non-*P*; area 2 is *S*, non-*P*; area 4 is *P*, non-*S*. Since area 3 contains both *S* and *P*, we do not use "*non-*" in referring to it.

The diagrams associated with obversion should now be easier to interpret (Figure A2.6).

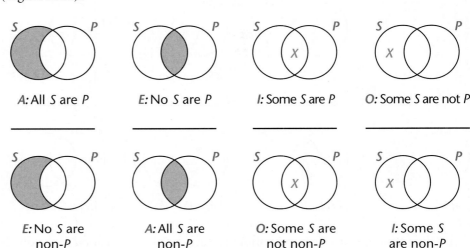

FIGURE A2.6 • Diagrams for obversion.

A visual inspection verifies that the premise and conclusion of each of the four immediate inferences are logically equivalent statements. Thus, obversion is valid for all four standard-form categorical statements.

The diagrams in Figure A2.7 illustrate why contraposition for **A** and **O** statements produces valid immediate inferences—the visual representation reveals the logical equivalence. We also see that contraposition produces invalid immediate inferences for both **E** and **I** statements.

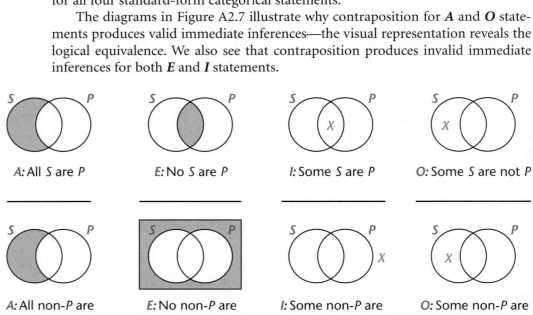

FIGURE A2.7 • Diagrams for contraposition.

At this point, it should be clear that contraposition by limitation for **E** statements cannot be justified. First, it is not an immediate inference, and second, the elimination of subalternation removes the only possible justification. Once again, the diagrams clearly show that the pictures for the **E** statements are not equivalent.

The need for a new square of opposition was fueled by the consequences of existential import. The Boolean square of opposition, plus the Venn diagram technique, provide a powerful, precise, and simpler method of analysis of categorical statements and categorical inferences than the Aristotelian square of opposition.

EXERCISE SET A2.7 ○○○

Translate the following sentences into standard-form categorical statements by stipulating what *S* and *P* will stand for in each case. Then draw Venn diagrams to represent the logic of each statement.

1. Some snowmen are permanent lawn fixtures.

Answer: S = snowmen, P = permanent lawn fixtures

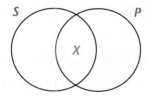

2. No leeches are lawyers.

3. Some television newscasters are good actors.

4. All donuts are lean cuisine.

5. All psychics are frauds.

*6. Some children are not following in their parents' footsteps.

7. No volcanoes are currently active geologic structures.

8. All ducks are daffy creatures.

9. All teachers are miserable wretches.

10. Some poems are beautifully written works of literature.

*11. Some viruses are not lethal to humans.

12. No Nobel laureates are Olympic champions.

13. All sea creatures are bivalves.

14. Some rock stars are good parents.

Exercises 2–45: For answers and explanations, see pages 310–321 of Instructor's Manual.

15. All condiments are free.

*16. Some exotic vegetables are not edible.

17. Some scientific research is fraudulent.

18. No television commercials are worthy of our attention.

19. All finely tuned instruments are soothing to the ear.

20. Some floppy disks are defective.

*21. All French pastries are good for your complexion.

22. Some cows are not flatulent.

23. No Nobel Prize winners are illiterate.

24. Some swimmers are healthy people.

25. All dogs are faithful pets.

*26. No spiders are nocturnal creatures.

27. Some race car drivers are fearless competitors.

28. Some college textbooks are works of art.

29. All teachers are inspired.

30. Some games of chance are sucker bets.

*31. Some sandwiches are not things made with meat.

32. No bats are vegetarians.

33. All designer jeans are genetically engineered objects.

34. No greedy politicians are people likely to go to prison.

35. Some fruitcakes are not regifted presents.

*36. All embezzlers are social deviants.

37. Some traffic accidents are incidents caused by speeding.

38. All public holidays are days when banks close.

39. Some music videos are not tragedies.

40. Some fajitas are mouth-watering morsels.

*41. No ice cream toppings are harmful to your diet.

42. All yogurt products are healthy.

43. No vegetables are lacking in multiple vitamins.

44. Some barbeque wings are too hot to eat.

45. All french fries are grease-laden.

A2.8 STANDARD-FORM CATEGORICAL SYLLOGISMS

In the previous section we applied Boolean analysis and Venn diagrams to immediate inferences. In this section the procedure will be expanded to include the analysis of categorical syllogisms. A **syllogism** is any inference that has exactly two premises and a conclusion. A **categorical syllogism** is an inference constructed entirely of categorical statements. A **standard-form categorical syllogism** contains exactly three terms, each of which is used two times. For example,

> All quadrupeds are swift runners.
> <u>All horses are quadrupeds.</u>
> All horses are swift runners.

Each of the three terms, or categories—"quadrupeds," "swift runners," and "horses"—are used twice. Standard-form categorical syllogisms also stipulate that the location of the terms follow certain rules. The subject of the conclusion is called the **minor term**, the predicate of the conclusion is called the **major term**, and the term that occurs only in the premises is called the **middle term**. In addition, the first premise always contains the major term, and it is therefore called the **major premise**. The second premise always contains the minor term, and it is called the **minor premise**.

> **Syllogism:** Any inference that has exactly two premises and one conclusion.
>
> **Categorical syllogism:** An inference constructed entirely of categorical statements.
>
> **Standard-form categorical syllogism:** A standard-form categorical syllogism contains exactly three terms, each of which is used two times.
>
> **Minor term:** The term that occurs as the subject of the conclusion in a categorical inference. It also occurs in the second premise of a standard-form categorical syllogism.
>
> **Major term:** The term that occurs as the predicate of the conclusion in a categorical inference. It also occurs in the first premise of a standard-form categorical syllogism.

> **Quick Reference A2.2 • Structure of Standard-Form Categorical Syllogisms**
>
> First premise: The *major premise*—Contains the major term and the middle term.
>
> Second premise: The *minor premise*—Contains the minor term and the middle term.
>
> Conclusion: The *subject* is the *minor term*, and the *predicate* is the *major term*.

> Standard-form categorical syllogisms have a major premise, a minor premise, and a major, minor, and middle term.

Of course, we might encounter a categorical syllogism that is not in standard form. For example:

> All thoroughbred horses are capable of running a mile in less than two minutes. So no humans are capable of running a mile in less than two minutes, since no humans are thoroughbred horses.

In order to reconstruct this syllogism, we must remember that the conclusion of a standard-form categorical syllogism always contains the minor term as the subject and the major term as the predicate. Once we identify that the conclusion is "no humans are capable of running a mile in less than two minutes," we know that the minor term is "humans," and the major term is "capable of running a mile in less than two minutes." This information dictates that the first premise is "All thoroughbred horses are capable of running a mile in less than two minutes," because the first premise of a standard-form categorical syllogism must contain the major term.

> **Middle term:** The term that occurs only in the premises of a categorical syllogism.
>
> **Major premise:** The premise that contains the major term (the predicate term of the conclusion) of a standard-form categorical syllogism.
>
> **Minor premise:** The premise that contains the minor term (the subject term of the conclusion) of a standard-form categorical syllogism.

The second premise is "no humans are thoroughbred horses," because it contains the minor term. The final reconstruction is:

All thoroughbred horses are capable of running a mile in less than two minutes.
<u>No humans are thoroughbred horses.</u>
No humans are capable of running a mile in less than two minutes.

The historical adoption of these conventions for constructing categorical syllogisms followed the Aristotelian square of opposition, which also included the assumption of existential import. Consequently, the analysis of categorical syllogisms as either valid or invalid followed from these assumptions and stipulations. We will see how and why the modern Boolean interpretation rejects certain syllogisms considered to be valid under the Aristotelian interpretation. To understand these results we must first learn how to analyze categorical syllogisms using the Boolean interpretation and Venn diagrams.

BIOGRAPHY ⟩ CHRISTINE LADD-FRANKLIN

Christine Ladd-Franklin (1847–1930) did substantial work in symbolic logic, mathematics, physiological optics, and color vision theory. Although she completed her dissertation and published *The Algebra of Logic* in 1883, she was not able to receive a Ph.D. because technically she was not even officially enrolled at Johns Hopkins, which at the time was an all male school. After a lifetime of important work, Ladd-Franklin was finally awarded a doctorate degree in 1926.

While at Johns Hopkins she attended the lectures of Charles S. Peirce, whose ideas on symbolic logic helped develop Ladd-Franklin's dissertation topic. In fact, Peirce thought so much of her dissertation that he made sure it was published in *Studies in Logic by Members of the Johns Hopkins University*, in 1883. In this work, Ladd-Franklin tried to solve a problem that began with Aristotle: to provide a single test that would capture all valid syllogisms. This idea requires that every valid categorical syllogism share some common denominator. The task was to provide the means to reduce all valid syllogisms by a general test that would reveal the commonality. Ladd-Franklin's proposal was that any valid syllogism will have premises, such that, when taken together with the *negation of the conclusion*, will form an inconsistent set of statements. Josiah Royce of Harvard University said of Ladd-Franklin's test, "There is no reason why this should not be accepted as the definite solution to the problem of the reduction of syllogisms."

A2.9 DIAGRAMMING CATEGORICAL SYLLOGISMS

As we saw in the previous section, categorical statements contain two terms and are diagrammed using a pair of overlapping circles:

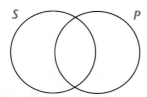

If you recall, universal statements refer to class inclusion or exclusion, and thus deal with the entire class. If one class is entirely included in another class (an *A* statement) or entirely excluded from another class (an *E* statement), then our diagrams shade out the appropriate areas.

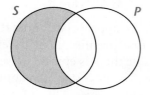
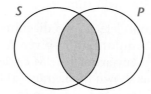

A: All S are P   E: No S are P

We also learned how to annotate diagrams for the particular statements *I* and *O*. Unlike universal statements, particular statements specifically refer to individual members of classes. Thus, the diagrams for *I* and *O* statements use an *X* to denote a specific member of a class and to say something definite about it. The location of the *X* then depends on the type of claim being made, as shown below.

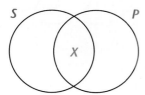
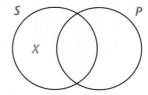

I: Some S are P   O: Some S are not P

Since categorical syllogisms have three terms, we have to add a circle to our basic diagram. The three overlapping circles in the following diagram will be used for analysis of categorical syllogisms.

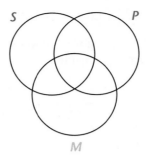

We can let **S** stand for the subject term of the conclusion, **P** for the predicate term of the conclusion, and **M** for the middle term.

Applying our method to the categorical syllogism encountered earlier will first require us to reveal the structure of the inference. If we let S = "horses," P = "swift runners," and M = "quadrupeds," we get the following substitution:

All quadrupeds are swift runners.	**A:** All M are P
<u>All horses are quadrupeds.</u>	<u>**A:** All S are M</u>
All horses are swift runners.	**A:** All S are P

We can now complete a Venn diagram with the appropriate annotation. We start by drawing the information given in the first premise as if it were true. This informs us that any area of the M circle outside the P is empty, so we shade in the correct areas, as shown in diagram (a) below. The next step is to annotate the diagram by drawing the information in the second premise. This informs us that any area of the S circle outside the M is empty, so, once again, we shade in the correct areas, as shown in diagram (b).

(a)   **(b)**

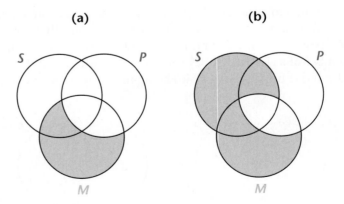

The diagram is complete when it contains the information given in the two premises. To decide whether the inference is valid or invalid, we check to see if the conclusion must be true. In our example, the conclusion claims that the class S is completely contained in the class P. The Venn diagram verifies this, so the inference is valid.

Let's see how an invalid categorical syllogism gets displayed. Consider the following inference:

All quadrupeds are swift runners.	*A*: All *M* are *P*
All quadrupeds are horses.	*A*: All *M* are *S*
All horses are swift runners.	*A*: All *S* are *P*

Assuming the first premise is true allows us to represent the claim as shown in diagram (a). Assuming the second premise is true allows us to represent the claim as shown in diagram (b).

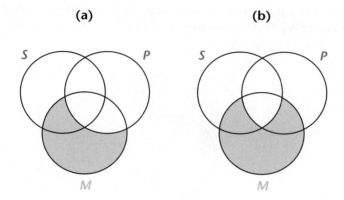

(a)   **(b)**

The diagram is complete because we have finished drawing the information given in the two premises. We now check the truth of the conclusion. In this example, the conclusion claims that the class *S* is completely contained in the class *P*. However, the completed Venn diagram shows us that it is possible for the conclusion to be false; therefore, the inference is invalid.

Let's analyze a categorical syllogism that uses a particular statement.

Some inexpensive gifts are sexy items.	*I*: Some *P* are *M*
No sexy items are bathing suits.	*E*: No *M* are *S*
Some bathing suits are inexpensive gifts.	*I*: Some *S* are *P*

Since the first premise is an *I* statement, we must place an **X** somewhere in the Venn diagram of this inference. There are actually three possible locations to consider (Figure A2.8):

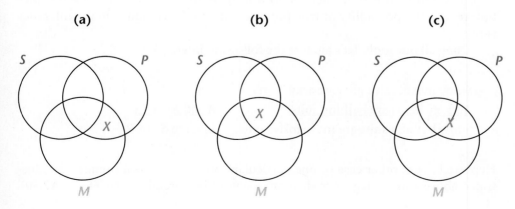

(a)   **(b)**   **(c)**

FIGURE A2.8 • Some *P* are *M*.

In Figure A2.8a, the **X** represents an object that is both a *P* and an *M*, but not an *S*. In Figure A2.8b, the **X** represents an object that is *P*, *M*, and *S*. Although both of these diagrams represent logical possibilities, if the first premise is true, the objects depicted are not the same. In fact, both pictures "say too much." The information in the first premise only asserts that the **X** is in one of the locations depicted by Figure A2.8a or Figure A2.8b. The reason for the placement of the **X** in Figure A2.8c is that there cannot be more than one **X** representing the claim for any one particular statement. Therefore, Figure A2.8c places the **X** on the line separating the two possible areas where the object might exist. This location of **X** informs us that it can be located *either* in the area depicted in Figure A2.8a *or* Figure A2.8b, but it cannot be in both areas at the same time. The first premise is therefore drawn as shown in Figure A2.8c. We now need to add to our picture the information in the second premise (Figure A2.9).

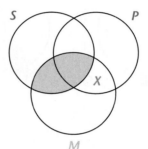

FIGURE A2.9 • No *M* are *S*.

Since the shading has eliminated one of the possible areas of **X**, we have moved it to the only remaining possible area. Notice that we could have avoided moving the **X** if we had started our diagram with the second premise instead of the first. The specific tactical move employed in this strategy is to *always diagram a universal statement before you diagram a particular statement*. With this strategy, the appropriate area given in the second premise (the universal **E** statement) would have been shaded as the first step. When the first premise (the particular **I** statement) is then diagrammed, there would be only one area to place the **X**.

We now check for validity. The conclusion claims that at least one *S* is a *P*. Since the conclusion is a particular **I** statement, the only way for it to be true would be if there was an **X** somewhere in the area where *S* and *P* overlap. But as we can see in Figure A2.9, there is no **X** to be found in this area. Since our picture reveals the possibility of true premises and a false conclusion, the inference is invalid.

Using all our tools, let's analyze the following inference.

Some inexpensive gifts are sexy items.	*I*: Some *P* are *M*
<u>All sexy items are bathing suits.</u>	<u>*A*: All *M* are *S*</u>
Some bathing suits are inexpensive gifts.	*I*: Some *S* are *P*

Here we have another case of one particular and one universal premise. As illustrated above, our strategy is to diagram the universal premise first (Figure A2.10).

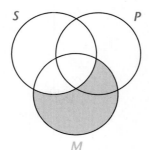

FIGURE A2.10 • All *M* are *S*.

Now we add to our diagram the information in the particular statement (the first premise) (Figure A2.11).

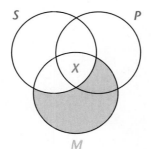

FIGURE A2.11 • Some *P* are *M*.

Now we can check for validity. The conclusion claims that at least one *S* is a *P*. Since the conclusion is a particular *I* statement, the only way for it to be true would be if there were an **X** somewhere in the area where *S* and *P* overlap. And as we can see, there is indeed an **X** in this area. Thus, the conclusion is true, and the inference is valid.

EXERCISE SET A2.9   ○○○

Exercises 1–14 Use Venn diagrams to analyze the following categorical syllogisms and to prove whether the syllogisms are valid or invalid.

  1. All *M* are *P*

     <u>Some *M* are *S*</u>

     Some *S* are *P*

Answer: This is a valid inference.

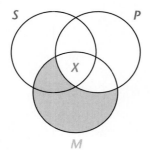

Exercises 2–24: For answers and explanations, see pages 322–330 of Instructor's Manual.

2. No *M* are *P*

   <u>Some *S* are not *M*</u>

   Some *S* are not *P* Invalid

3. All *P* are *M*

   <u>All *S* are *M*</u>

   All *S* are *P* Invalid

4. Some *P* are *M*

   <u>Some *S* are *M*</u>

   Some *S* are *P* Invalid

5. Some *M* are not *P*

   <u>Some *M* are not *S*</u>

   Some *S* are not *P* Invalid

*6. No *P* are *M*

   <u>No *M* are *S*</u>

   No *S* are *P* Invalid

7. All *P* are *M*

   <u>Some *S* are *M*</u>

   All *S* are *P* Invalid

8. Some *P* are *M*

   <u>Some *M* are not *S*</u>

   Some *S* are not *P* Invalid

9. All *M* are *P*

   <u>No *S* are *M*</u>

   Some *S* are not *P* Invalid

10. No *M* are *P*

    <u>Some *S* are *M*</u>

    Some *S* are *P* Invalid

*11. All *M* are *P*

    <u>No *S* are *M*</u>

    No *S* are *P* Invalid

12. No *P* are *M*

    <u>Some *S* are *M*</u>

    Some *S* are not *P* Valid

13. All *M* are *P*

    <u>All *S* are *M*</u>

    All *S* are *P* Valid

14. All *M* are *P*

    Some *S* are not *M*

    Some *S* are not *P* Invalid

Exercises 15–24 Translate the following inferences into standard-form categorical syllogisms. Then use Venn diagrams to prove the categorical syllogisms valid or invalid.

15. All fast food items are overpriced objects. No overpriced objects are nutritious products. Therefore, no nutritious products are fast food items.

Answer:

Let *S* = nutritious products, *P* = fast food items, and *M* = overpriced objects.

All *P* are *M*

No *M* are *S*

No *S* are *P*

This is a valid inference.

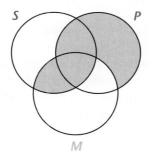

16. Some vegetables are not tasty foods. So, some tasty foods are not green, because some vegetables are not green. Invalid

17. All mechanical objects are noisy. All airplanes are noisy. Thus, all airplanes are mechanical objects. Invalid

18. Some pens are not useful tools. This is because some pens are leaky writing implements, and no leaky writing implements are useful tools. Valid

19. No septic tanks are gaseous. No sewers are gaseous. Therefore, no septic tanks are sewers. Invalid

20. All voice messages are a waste of time. Some games people play are a waste of time. So, some voice messages are games people play. Invalid

*21. Some universities are not expensive places to attend. Some universities are conveniently located. Thus, some expensive places to attend are not conveniently located. Invalid

Mood: The mood of a categorical syllogism is designated by using the letter names (*A,E, I, O*) of the categorical statements for the major premise, the minor premise, and the conclusion.

Figure: The middle term in a standard-form categorical syllogism can be arranged in the two premises in four different ways. These placements reveal the figure of the categorical syllogism.

22. No sports fanatics are rational creatures. Therefore, no sports fanatics are benevolent people, since all rational creatures are benevolent people. Invalid

23. Some buildings are poorly constructed. Some buildings are architectural nightmares. So, some architectural nightmares are poorly constructed. Invalid

24. All sea creatures are intelligent animals. Some sea creatures are predators. So, some intelligent animals are predators. Valid

A2.10 MOOD AND FIGURE IN CATEGORICAL SYLLOGISMS

When standard-form categorical syllogisms are constructed or reconstructed, the order of the premises and conclusion can be labeled by the type of categorical statements involved. This ordering and labeling reveals the **mood** of the categorical syllogism (Figure A2.12).

All *P* are *M*	All *P* are *M*	Some *P* are not *M*	No *P* are *M*
All *S* are *M*	Some *S* are *M*	No *S* are *M*	No *S* are *M*
All *S* are *P*	Some *S* are *P*	Some *S* are not *P*	Some *S* are not *P*
Mood: AAA	*Mood: AII*	*Mood: OEO*	*Mood: EEO*

FIGURE A2.12 • *Some moods* of categorical syllogisms.

The middle term can be arranged in four different ways in the two premises. These placements reveal the **figure** of the categorical syllogism (Figure A2.13). As before, *S*, *P*, and *M* will stand for the subject term of the conclusion, the predicate term of the conclusion, and the middle term, respectively.

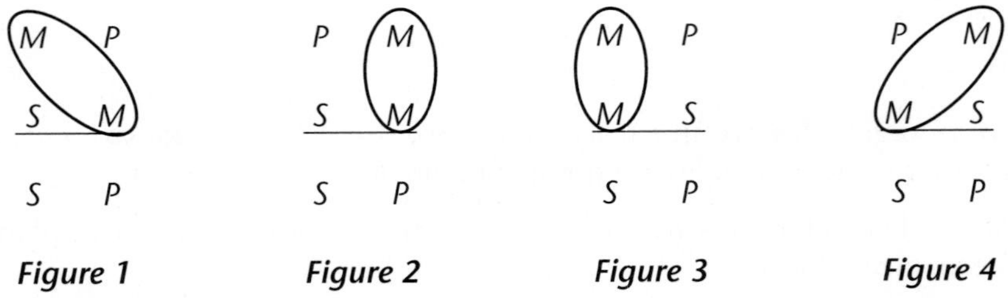

FIGURE A2.13 • **The four** *figures* of **categorical** syllogisms.

Figure 1   *Figure 2*   *Figure 3*   *Figure 4*

Mood and figure information can be combined into one label (Figure A2.14).

All *P* are *M*	All *M* are *P*	Some *P* are not *M*	No *M* are *P*
All *S* are *M*	Some *S* are *M*	No *M* are *S*	No *M* are *S*
All *S* are *P*	Some *S* are *P*	Some *S* are not *P*	Some *S* are not *P*
AAA-2	*AII-1*	*OEO-4*	*EEO-3*

FIGURE A2.14 • **Labeling** *mood* and *figure* combined.

The number of standard-form categorical syllogisms is restricted by the stipulations on their possible construction. Since we know that there are only four categorical statements (*A, E, I,* and *O*), and since each categorical syllogism contains
exactly three statements (two premises and a conclusion), we get, 4 × 4 × 4 = 64,
possible combinations. But we also know that, besides the mood, there are four figures to consider. Therefore, we get 64 × 4 = 256 possible standard-form categorical syllogisms.

Under the Boolean interpretation (and verified by the use of Venn diagrams),
it has been determined that there are only 15 valid standard-form categorical syllogisms (Table A2.4).

**Table A2.4 The 15 Valid Standard-Form Categorical Syllogisms, as
Determined by the Boolean System**

AAA-1	*AEE-2*	*AII-3*	*AEE-4*
AII-1	*AOO-2*	*EIO-3*	*EIO-4*
EAE-1	*EAE-2*	*IAI-3*	*IAI-4*
EIO-1	*EIO-2*	*OAO-3*	

Under the Aristotelian system an additional 9 categorical syllogisms are considered
to be valid (Table A2.5).

**Table A2.5 The 9 Additional Valid Standard-Form Categorical Syllogisms,
as Determined by the Aristotelian System**

AAI-1	*AEO-2*	*AAI-3*	*AAI-4*
EAO-1	*EAO-2*	*EAO-3*	*AEO-4*
			EAO-4

The 9 categorical syllogisms in Table A2.5 are valid under the Aristotelian square
of opposition because they incorporate the idea of existential import. Under the
Boolean system, the same 9 syllogisms are all invalid. Their invalidity can be immediately recognized, if you notice that in each of the 9 instances a particular conclusion follows from two universal premises. As our use of Venn diagrams has
revealed, it is logically impossible to get an *X* anywhere in the diagram if both
premises are universal statements. But in order for these 9 inferences to be valid,
an *X* must be generated by the premises. Since this is impossible, the inferences are
invalid under the modern interpretation.

EXERCISE SET A2.10   ○○○

Identify the major, minor, and middle terms, and the mood and figure of the following categorical syllogisms.

[The following categorical syllogism is to be used for Exercises 1–5.]

No animals are vegetarians.
All bears are animals.
No bears are vegetarians.

1. Major term:

2. Minor term:

3. Middle term:

4. Mood:

5. Figure:

Answer:

1. Major term: vegetarians

2. Minor term: bears

3. Middle term: animals

4. Mood: **EAE**

5. Figure: **1**

[The following categorical syllogism is to be used for Exercises 6–10.]

Some parents are college students.
Some politicians are not college students.
Some politicians are not parents.

6. parents   6. Major term:

7. politicians   7. Minor term:

8. college students   8. Middle term:

9. IOO   9. Mood:

10. 2   10. Figure:

[The following categorical syllogism is to be used for Exercises 11–15.]

No jet airplanes are quiet vehicles.
All jet airplanes are fast machines.
No fast machines are quiet vehicles.

11. quiet vehicles   11. Major term:

12. fast machines   12. Minor term:

13. jet airplanes   13. Middle term:

14. Mood:

15. Figure:

14. EAE

15. 3

[The following categorical syllogism is to be used for Exercises 16–20.]

> No hot dogs are cholesterol-free food.
> <u>Some beef products are hot dogs.</u>
> Some beef products are not cholesterol-free food.

16. Major term:

17. Minor term:

18. Middle term:

19. Mood:

20. Figure:

16. cholesterol-free food

17. beef products

18. hot dogs

19. EIO

20. 1

[The following categorical syllogism is to be used for Exercises 21–25.]

> Some cats are not independent creatures.
> <u>Some cats are not loveable pets.</u>
> Some loveable pets are not independent creatures.

21. Major term:

22. Minor term:

23. Middle term:

24. Mood:

25. Figure:

21. independent creatures

22. loveable pets

23. cats

24. OOO

25. 3

A2.11 RULES AND FALLACIES ASSOCIATED WITH STANDARD-FORM CATEGORICAL SYLLOGISMS

A thorough investigation of both valid and invalid syllogisms has enabled logicians to devise a set of rules for analyzing standard-form categorical syllogisms. Six specific rules form a checklist by which you can test any standard-form categorical syllogism. If the inference does not break any rule, then it is valid, but if it breaks any of the six rules, then it is invalid. Every violation of a rule is associated with a specific fallacy, a mistake in reasoning.

Rule 1: A negative premise cannot have an affirmative conclusion.

Associated fallacy: ***Affirmative conclusion/negative premise(s)*** Since class inclusion requires an affirmative statement, a categorical inference with an affirmative conclusion can validly follow only from two affirmative premises. A negative

Fallacy of affirmative conclusion/negative premise(s): Since class inclusion requires an affirmative statement, a categorical inference with an affirmative conclusion can validly follow only from two affirmative premises. A negative premise will break the class inclusion necessary to bring about the affirmative conclusion.

premise will break the class inclusion necessary to bring about the affirmative conclusion, a **fallacy of affirmative conclusion/negative premise(s)**. For example,

> No happy people are underpaid.
> All teachers are happy people.
> All teachers are underpaid.

The conclusion is a universal affirmative statement, but one of the premises is negative. We can symbolize and diagram the inference as follows: let S = "teachers," P = "underpaid," and M = "happy people."

No M are P

All S are M

All S are P

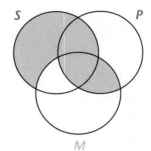

FIGURE A2.15 • **An affirmative conclusion can follow only from two affirmative premises.**

This is an invalid inference. It illustrates why a negative premise cannot have an affirmative conclusion.

Rule 2: A negative conclusion cannot have all affirmative premises.

Associated Fallacy: *Negative conclusion/affirmative premises* Since class exclusion requires a negative statement, a categorical inference with a negative conclusion cannot validly follow from two affirmative premises that assert class inclusion, a **fallacy of negative conclusion/affirmative premises**. For example,

Fallacy of negative conclusion/affirmative premises: Since class exclusion requires a negative statement, a categorical inference with a negative conclusion cannot validly follow from two affirmative premises.

> All carbonated drinks are bubbly.
> All soft drinks are carbonated drinks.
> No soft drinks are bubbly.

The conclusion is a universal negative statement. We can symbolize and diagram the inference as follows: let S = "soft drinks," P = "bubbly," and M = "carbonated drinks."

All M are P

All S are M

No S are P

FIGURE A2.16 • **An inference with all affirmative premises cannot have a negative conclusion.**

This is an invalid inference. It illustrates why a negative conclusion cannot have all affirmative premises.

Fallacy of exclusive premises: A fallacy that rests on the principle that two negative premises always result in an invalid inference.

Rule 3: An inference cannot have two negative premises.

Associated Fallacy: *Exclusive premises* The fallacy of exclusive premises rests on the principle that two negative premises will always result in an invalid inference. The major (negative) premise will exclude part or all of the class designated by the major term from the class designated by the middle term. The minor (negative) premise will exclude part or all of the class designated by the minor term from the class designated by the middle term. It then becomes impossible to deduce any kind of relationship between the major and minor term, either positive or negative. For example,

> No happy people are underpaid.
> <u>Some teachers are not happy people.</u>
> Some teachers are not underpaid.

We can symbolize and diagram the inference as follows: let S = "teachers," P = "underpaid," and M = "happy people."

No M are P

<u>Some S are not M</u>

Some S are not P

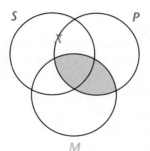

FIGURE A2.17 • An inference cannot have two negative premises.

This is an invalid inference. It illustrates why an inference cannot have two negative premises.

Rule 4: Two universal premises cannot have a particular conclusion.

Associated Fallacy: *Existential fallacy* Under the Boolean interpretation, universal statements do not have existential import, but particular statements do. Therefore, any categorical syllogism that has two universal premises and a particular conclusion is invalid. Since neither premise makes an existential assertion, but the particular conclusion does, an **existential fallacy** exists. For example,

> All disgruntled creatures are nihilists.
> <u>All centaurs are disgruntled creatures.</u>
> Some centaurs are nihilists.

Existential fallacy: A fallacy in which an inference relies on a mistaken assumption of existence.

The conclusion is a particular affirmative statement. We can symbolize and diagram the inference as follows: let S = "centaurs," P = "nihilists," and M = "disgruntled creatures."

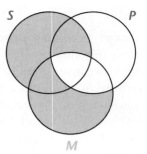

All M are P

All S are M

Some S are P

FIGURE A2.18 • The existential fallacy.

This is an invalid inference. It illustrates why two universal premises cannot have a particular conclusion. This example illustrates the problem of existential import that was discussed earlier in Section A2.5.

Rule 5: Any term that is distributed in the conclusion must be distributed in the premises.

Associated Fallacies: *Illicit major/illicit minor* If a categorical statement says something definite about every member of the class designated by a term, then the term is said to be distributed. On the other hand, if the statement does not say something definite about every member of the class designated by a term, then the term is said to be undistributed.

If the major term is distributed in the conclusion but not in the major premise, then the conclusion goes beyond what was asserted in the premise, a **fallacy of illicit major**. For example,

All bananas are fruit.
<u>No strawberries are bananas.</u>
No strawberries are fruit.

We can symbolize and diagram the inference as follows: let S = "strawberries," P = "fruit," and M = "bananas."

Fallacy of illicit major: If the major term is distributed in the conclusion but not in the major premise, then the conclusion goes beyond what was asserted in the premises.

All M are P

No S are M

No S are P

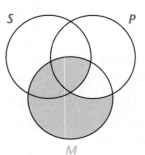

FIGURE A2.19 • Illicit major.

This is an invalid inference. It illustrates why any term that is distributed in the conclusion must be distributed in the premises.

The fallacy of illicit minor occurs for the same reason as the fallacy of illicit major. Both fallacies fail to observe the rule that any term that is distributed in the conclusion must be distributed in the premises. So, if the minor term is distributed in the conclusion but not in the minor premise, then the conclusion goes beyond what was asserted in the premises, a **fallacy of illicit minor**. For example:

All bananas are fruit.
<u>All bananas are yellow things.</u>
All yellow things are fruit.

We can symbolize and diagram the inference as follows: let S = "yellow things," P = "fruit," and M = "bananas."

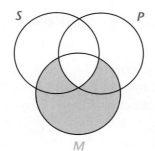

All M are P

All M are S

All S are P

Fallacy of illicit minor: This fallacy, like illicit major, fails to observe the rule that any term that is distributed in the conclusion must be distributed in the premises.

FIGURE A2.20 • **Any term that is distributed in the conclusion must be distributed in the premises.**

This is an invalid inference. It illustrates why any term that is distributed in the conclusion must be distributed in the premises.

Rule 6: The middle term must be distributed in at least one premise.

Associated Fallacy: *Undistributed middle* The conclusion of a categorical syllogism asserts a relationship between the classes designated by the major and minor terms. Therefore, the premises of a valid categorical syllogism must lay the foundation for that relationship. This can only be achieved if the premises distribute the middle term *at least once*. Either the subject, or predicate, or both, of the conclusion must be related to the entire class designated by the middle term, otherwise the **fallacy of the undistributed middle** occurs. For example,

All poets are intelligent.
<u>All mathematicians are intelligent.</u>
No mathematicians are poets.

We can symbolize and diagram the inference as follows: let S = "mathematicians," P = "poets," and M = "intelligent."

Fallacy of undistributed middle: Since the conclusion of a categorical syllogism asserts a relationship between the classes designated by the major and minor terms, the premises must lay the foundation for that relationship. This can only be achieved if the premises distribute the middle term at least once. If this is not done, then the fallacy occurs.

All *P* are *M*

All *S* are *M*

No *S* are *P*

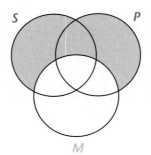

FIGURE A2.21 • The middle term must be distributed in at least one premise.

This is an invalid inference. It illustrates why the middle term must be distributed in at least one premise.

(Note that this particular inference also violates Rule 2: A negative conclusion cannot have all affirmative premises.)

> **Quick Reference A2.3 • Rules and Associated Fallacies for Categorical Syllogisms**
>
> An inference that does not break any of the rules is valid, while an inference that breaks even one rule is invalid.
>
> 1. A negative premise cannot have an affirmative conclusion.
>   *Fallacy*: Affirmative conclusion/negative premise(s)
> 2. A negative conclusion cannot have all affirmative premises.
>   *Fallacy*: Negative conclusion/affirmative premises
> 3. An inference cannot have two negative premises.
>   *Fallacy*: Exclusive premises
> 4. Two universal premises cannot have a particular conclusion.
>   *Fallacy*: Existential fallacy
> 5. A term that is distributed in the conclusion must be distributed in the premises.
>   *Fallacy*: Illicit major/illicit minor
> 6. The middle term must be distributed in at least one premise.
>   *Fallacy*: Undistributed middle

EXERCISE SET A2.11   ○○○

Exercises 1–10 The following categorical syllogisms were already proven valid or invalid in Exercise Set A2.9 (Exercises 1–10). Here you are to reveal the mood and figure of each.

   1. All *M* are *P*
      Some *M* are *S*
      Some *S* are *P*

   Answer: **AII-3**

   2. No *M* are *P*
      Some *S* are not *M*
      Some *S* are not *P*

2. EOO-1

3. All *P* are *M*
   <u>All *S* are *M*</u>
   All *S* are *P*

3. AAA-2

4. Some *P* are *M*
   <u>Some *S* are *M*</u>
   Some *S* are *P*

4. III-2

5. Some *M* are not *P*
   <u>Some *M* are not *S*</u>
   Some *S* are not *P*

5. OOO-3

*6. No *P* are *M*
   <u>No *M* are *S*</u>
   No *S* are *P*

6. EEE-4

7. All *P* are *M*
   <u>Some *S* are *M*</u>
   All *S* are *P*

7. AII-2

8. Some *P* are *M*
   <u>Some *M* are not *S*</u>
   Some *S* are not *P*

8. IOO-4

9. All *M* are *P*
   <u>No *S* are *M*</u>
   Some *S* are not *P*

9. AEO-1

10. No *M* are *P*
    <u>Some *S* are *M*</u>
    Some *S* are *P*

10. EII-1

Exercises 11–25 Use Venn diagrams to verify that the 15 inferences listed under the Boolean system are valid.

11. **AAA-1**

Answer:

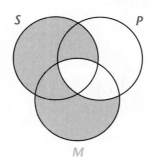

This is a valid inference.

Exercises 12–39: For answers and explanations, see pages 332–340 of Instructor's Manual.

12. *AII-1*

13. *EAE-1*

14. *EIO-1*

15. *AEE-2*

*16. *AOO-2*

17. *EAE-2*

18. *EIO-2*

19. *AII-3*

20. *EIO-3*

*21. *IAI-3*

22. *OAO-3*

23. *AEE-4*

24. *EIO-4*

25. *IAI-4*

Exercises 26–34 Use Venn diagrams to verify that the 9 inferences listed under the Aristotelian system are invalid (under the Boolean interpretation).

26. *AAI-1*

Answer:

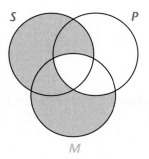

This is an invalid inference.

27. *EAO-1*

28. *AEO-2*

29. *EAO-2*

30. *AAI-3*

*31. *EAO-3*

32. **AAI-4**

33. **AEO-4**

34. **EAO-4**

Exercises 35–39 First, translate the following inferences into standard-form categorical syllogisms. Second, name the mood and figure of each. Third, use Venn diagrams to prove the categorical syllogisms valid or invalid.

35. All cultures that venerate senior citizens are built on a strong tradition of philosophical inquiry. Some recently developed cultures are not built on a strong tradition of philosophical inquiry. Therefore, some recently developed cultures are not cultures that venerate senior citizens.

Answer: Let S = "recently developed cultures," P = "cultures that venerate senior citizens," and M = "built on a strong tradition of philosophical inquiry."

> All P are M
> <u>Some S are not M</u>
> Some S are not P
> **AOO-2**

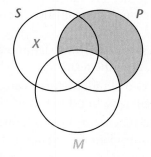

This is a valid inference.

36. Some planets with oxygen are capable of sustaining life. Some planets outside our solar system are planets with oxygen. So, some planets outside our solar system are capable of sustaining life.

37. All great works of literature are illuminations of the human predicament. No pulp fiction novels are great works of literature, because no pulp fiction novels are illuminations of the human predicament.

38. All natural disasters are scientifically explainable phenomena. Some human maladies are scientifically explainable phenomena. Thus, some human maladies are natural disasters.

39. Some furry creatures are lovable. Some eccentric people are lovable. Therefore, some eccentric people are furry creatures.

SUMMARY—A2.1–A.2.7 CATEGORICAL STATEMENTS

- The foundation of the Aristotelian square of opposition is the logic of classes. A class is defined as a group of objects that has some recognizable common characteristic.
- Every categorical statement either affirms that the subject term is related to the predicate term, or else it denies that the subject term is related to the predicate term.
- The four standard-form categorical statements are as follows:

   A: All *S* are *P.* This is a universal affirmative statement, which asserts that all members of the subject term are members of the predicate term.

   E: No *S* are *P.* This is a universal negative statement, which asserts that no members of the subject term are members of the predicate term.

   I: Some *S* are *P.* This is a particular affirmative statement, which asserts that some members of the subject term are members of the predicate term.

   O: Some *S* are not *P.* This is a particular negative statement, which asserts that some members of the subject term are not members of the predicate term.

- The terms "universal" and "particular" refer to the quantity of a categorical statement; the terms "affirmative" and "negative" refer to its quality.
- The terms "all," "no," and "some," are called quantifiers; they tell us the extent of the class inclusion or exclusion. The quantifier refers specifically and exclusively to the subject term.
- If a categorical statement says something definite about every member of the class designated by a term, then the term is said to be distributed.
- Opposition occurs when two standard-form categorical statements have the same subject and predicate terms, but differ in quality, quantity, or both.
- Contradictories are pairs of statements in which one is the negation of the other (*A* and *O* statements are contradictories, as are *E* and *I* statements).
- Contraries are pairs of statements that cannot both be true at the same time, but can both be false at the same time (*A* and *E* statements are contraries).
- Subcontraries are pairs of statements that cannot both be false at the same time, but can both be true; also, if one is false, then the other must be true (*I* and *O* statements are subcontraries).
- Subalternation is the relationship between a universal statement and its corresponding particular statement (if the universal statement of a pair is true, then its corresponding particular partner will also be true).
- An immediate inference is an inference that has only one premise.
- A conversion is an immediate inference created by interchanging the subject and predicate terms.
- An obversion is an immediate inference formed by changing the quality of the given statement, and then replacing the predicate term with its complement.
- The complement is defined as the set of objects that do not belong to a given class.

- Contraposition, a third type of immediate inference, is formed by replacing the subject term of a given statement with the complement of its predicate term and then replacing the predicate term of the given statement with the complement of its subject term.

- A statement has existential import if it asserts or presupposes the existence of certain kinds of objects.

- According to the Aristotelian square of opposition, particular statements follow validly from their corresponding universal statements by subalternation. This means that the universal statements must have existential import, because a statement with existential import cannot be derived from one that does not have it. However, if all **A** statements have existential import, then some contradictory **A** statements and **O** statements can be false at the same time.

- The solution to this problem came from the work of George Boole and John Venn. Their ideas were used to create what has come to be known as the *Boolean square of opposition.*

- Venn diagrams are used to represent classes. Since categorical statements contain two classes, the classes are represented by two intersecting circles. The drawing is then annotated, depending on the claim made by that statement.

- If a class is empty, then the circle is completely shaded to indicate that it has no members. If it is claimed that there is at least one member, then an **X** is placed inside the circle.

- The pictures are meant to represent the logical commitments of categorical statements and categorical inferences. A complete diagram of a categorical inference reveals whether the conclusion must be true (valid inference), or whether there is a possibility of a false conclusion (invalid inference).

SUMMARY—A2.8–A2.11 STANDARD-FORM CATEGORICAL SYLLOGISMS

- A categorical syllogism is an inference constructed entirely of categorical statements.

- Every standard-form categorical syllogism contains exactly three terms, each of which is used two times.

- The subject of the conclusion is the minor term, the predicate of the conclusion is the major term, and the term that occurs only in the premises is the middle term. The first premise contains the major term and is called the major premise. The second premise contains the minor term and is called the minor premise.

- Since categorical syllogisms have three terms, we can use three circles to diagram them. We start by drawing the information given in the first premise as if it were true. The next step is to add to the diagram by drawing the information in the second premise, again as if it were true. The diagram is complete when it includes all the information given in the two premises. To decide whether the inference is valid or invalid we check to see if the conclusion must be true.

- In constructing (or reconstructing) standard-form categorical syllogisms the order of the premises and conclusion are labeled by the type of categorical statements involved. This ordering and labeling determines the mood of the categorical syllogism.
- The middle term can be arranged in the two premises in four different ways. These placements determine the figure of the categorical syllogism.
- There are six rules and fallacies associated with standard-form categorical syllogisms:

  1. A negative premise cannot have an affirmative conclusion.
  2. A negative conclusion cannot have all affirmative premises.
  3. A syllogism cannot have two negative premises.
  4. Two universal premises cannot have a particular conclusion.
  5. Any term that is distributed in the conclusion must be distributed in the premises.
  6. The middle term must be distributed in at least one premise.

KEY TERMS

class   382
subject term   382
predicate term   382
standard-form
  categorical
  statement   382
universal
  affirmative   382
universal negative   382
particular
  affirmative   382
particular negative   382
quantity   383
quality   383
quantifier   384
copula   384
distributed   384
undistributed   384
opposition   386
contradictories   386
contraries   388
subcontraries   389
subalternation   389
superaltern   389
subaltern   390

corresponding
  statements   390
immediate
  inference   391
mediate inference   391
conversion   394
convertend   394
converse   395
conversion by
  limitation   395
complement   396
obversion   396
obvertend   396
obverse   396
contraposition   397
contrapositive   397
contraposition by
  limitation   398
existential import   402
product   404
Venn diagram   405
syllogism   411
categorical
  syllogism   411

standard-form
  categorical
  syllogism   411
minor term   411
major term   411
middle term   411
major premise   411
minor premise   411
mood   420
figure   420
fallacy of affirmative
  conclusion/negative
  premise(s)   424
fallacy of negative
  conclusion/affirmative
  premises   424
fallacy of exclusive
  premises   425
existential fallacy   425
fallacy of illicit
  major   426
fallacy of illicit
  minor   427
fallacy of undistributed
  middle   427

{Solutions and Explanations} for Selected *Exercise Set* Problems

CHAPTER 1   LOGIC AND TRUTH

Exercise Set 1.2

6. *Answer:* (c) either true or false
We must make sure that whatever date of birth we assign to S.K. and W.R. the premises must turn out to be true. With this in mind, let's imagine S.K. was born in 1984, and W.R. was born in 1956. The conclusion becomes false. But suppose S.K. was born in 1947. This is possible because the first premise only claims that S.K. was born before 1989, and 1947 is before 1989. The first premise would therefore be true. Now if W.R. was born in 1956, the second premise would be true. However, the conclusion now becomes true.

11. *Answer:* (b) false
If the first and third premises are both true, then we know that H.L. spent $25,000. If the second and fourth premises are both true, then we know that J.G. spent $25,000. Therefore, if the premises are true at the same time, then the conclusion must be false.

16. *Answer:* (a) true
Remember that this is not a factual analysis. The logical analysis is concerned only with if the premises are true. Given this, if the premises are true, then D.W. and S.W. must have voted for Candidate R.

21. *Answer:* (c) either true or false
Whatever amount of money we imagine the wallets contain, the premises must turn out to be true. With this in mind, let's imagine that Ron has $25 and Dave has $100. The conclusion would then be true. But suppose Ron has $60. This is possible because the first premise only claims that Ron has more than $10, and $60 is more $10. The first premise would therefore be true. Now, if Dave has $55, then the second premise would be true as well ($55 is more than $50). However, under this possibility the conclusion would now be false.

26. *Answer:* (a) true
If we are to keep the first premise true, then Chris was indeed born in November. If we are to keep the second premise true, then our only choices are April, August, and October. A complete analysis shows that all three possibilities where the second premise is true, coupled with the first premise as true, make the conclusion turn out true.

29. *Answer:* (a) true
Since there are three, and only three, possible choices for the exam (if we imagine the first premise to be true), then provided that the second premise is true and the third premise is true, the exam will analyze a novel. Since that is exactly what the conclusion states, it must be true.

Exercise Set 1.3

6. *Answer:* (b) false
This picture makes the premises true.

$$\longrightarrow \text{E}$$

Louisville   St. Louis   Columbus

The conclusion is clearly false in this picture. It is impossible to get the premises true and the conclusion true at the same time.

16. *Answer:* (a) true
This picture makes the premises and the conclusion true.

"larger than..."   Indonesia

Malaysia

Hong Kong

Singapore

If the premises are true, then Indonesia's population must be larger than Singapore's. It is impossible for the premises to be true and the conclusion to be false at the same time.

19. *Answer:* **(b) false**
This picture makes the premises true and the conclusion false.

"larger than…"   Indonesia

                              Hong Kong

                              Malaysia

                              Singapore

If the premises are true, then Hong Kong's population must be larger than Singapore's. It is impossible for the premises to be true and the conclusion to be true at the same time.

Exercise Set 1.4

6. *Answer:* **Invalid**
If all the premises are true and it is a "fair" game (as stipulated), then the conclusion has a 1 percent probability of being true; so it is possible for the premises to be true and the conclusion to be true. However, it is logically possible that the marble picked will be blue (this has a 99 percent probability); thus, it is possible for the premises to be true and the conclusion to be false.

11. *Answer:* **Invalid**
It is possible for the premises to be true and the conclusion to be true, too. However, even if all the premises are true, it is possible for the conclusion to be false. The defendant's fingerprints might have been there for quite some time before the murder; perhaps the defendant lived at the place the murder happened (this premise would still be true). The blood might have been planted by the real murderer, or the defendant might have touched the murder victim to check for signs of life (this premise would still be true). The eyewitnesses might be correct, but someone else might have been at the murder scene just before the defendant entered (this premise would still be true). Thus, all the premises could be true and the conclusion false.

16. *Answer:* **Invalid**
If the first premise is true, then we are informed that anyone who commits a murder has committed a felony, but not every felony is a murder. The second premise, if true, informs us that F.C. has committed a felony. The conclusion might be true, but it is logically possible for the conclusion to be false. Therefore, since the premises, even if true, cannot guarantee that the conclusion will be true, this is an invalid inference.

21. *Answer:* **Valid**
If the first premise is true, then we are informed that anytime a Democrat is the president there is a recession. The second premise, if true, informs us that a Democrat is now the president. The premises make it impossible for the conclusion to be false.

30. *Answer:* **Invalid**
If some of the coins in the jar are not the state quarter Pennsylvania, and it is a "fair" game (as stipulated), then it would still be possible to pick a state quarter Pennsylvania; that is, premise true and conclusion true. However, it is also logically possible that the coin picked will not be the state quarter Pennsylvania; that is, premise true and conclusion false.

Exercise Set 1.6

6. *Deductive Analysis:* **Valid**
The first premise specifies the range of "A" scores. The second premise tells us that Al's score is not in that range. If both premises are true, then the conclusion must be true (Al's score cannot be a 98). However, we cannot decide if the inference is sound or unsound because we have no access to the factual content of the statements.

Inductive analysis: Since it is a valid inference, the probability that the conclusion is true is 100 percent (if the premises are true). So, the inference is strong. However, we cannot decide if the inference is cogent or not cogent because we have no access to the factual content of the statements.

11. *Deductive Analysis:* **Invalid—Unsound**
The first premise tells us that every metal has an atomic weight of at least 46 (a minimum requirement is thus being established for being a metal). It does not, however, tell us that any element with an atomic weight of at least 46 is a metal. Since the conclusion

could be true or false, it is an invalid inference, and it is unsound.

Inductive analysis: Since there are many elements that have an atomic weight over 46, without having any specific knowledge, the probability of the conclusion being true is high, if most of the elements above atomic weight 46 are metals. This would make the inference strong. But without this specific information we cannot judge it definitively as either strong or weak, nor can we determine if it is cogent or not cogent. (To asses the factual content of the first premise requires knowledge of the periodic table of elements. In addition, the second premise does not specify a particular element, so we cannot judge the truth or falsity of this statement.)

16. *Deductive Analysis:* Invalid—Unsound
The first premise establishes that some antibiotics are effective on certain bacterial infections. Even if all three premises are true, the conclusion could be false. Since the inference is invalid, it cannot be sound

Inductive analysis: The first premise is factually true, but we would need to have some idea of the effectiveness on the particular kind of infection that is being treated (it is a hypothetical case). Since we do not have access to this specific knowledge, we are not in a position to assess the strength or weakness of the inference. In addition, the hypothetical nature of the second and third premises makes it impossible to determine whether the inference is cogent or not cogent.

19. *Deductive analysis:* Valid—Unsound
The first premise tells us something definite about every orange (that they all have seeds). The second premise tells us that what the person is eating does not have seeds. If both premises are true, then it cannot be an orange (the conclusion must be true). However, since the first premise is a factually false statement (there are seedless oranges), the inference is unsound.

Inductive analysis: Since it is valid, the probability that the conclusion is true is 100 percent (if the premises are true). So, the inference is strong. However, since the first premise is a factually false statement (there are seedless oranges), the inference is not cogent

CHAPTER 2   INFERENCES: ASSESSMENT, RECOGNITION, AND RECONSTRUCTION

Exercise Set 2.1

6. *Strengthens the inference*
The horn draws its power from the battery; therefore, we can determine that this new evidence strengthens the inference.

16. *Weakens the inference*
The outlet may not be working, if both the radio and the lamp do not work.

19. *Strengthens the inference*
If every other electrical fixture in the room works, then electricity is probably getting to the lamp.

Exercise Set 2.2

6. 0, Weak. (Since the new information has ruled out houses 9–16, house #14 has no chance of being correct.)

11. 1/2, Weak. (The new information leaves houses 1 and 5 as the only possibilities.)

21. 1/2, Weak. (Since even numbered rooms have been eliminated, this room has a 1/2 chance of being correct.)

26. 1/2, Invalid, Weak.
The conclusion has a probability of 1/2 of being true (January, and July are the only two possibilities because each has 31 days; the second premise rules out June, because it only has 30 days).

31. Invalid
There is not enough in the one premise to guarantee the conclusion is true. In addition, although we cannot calculate the probability of the conclusion being true, nevertheless, we do know that the inference is invalid because we know it is possible for the conclusion to be false.

36. 100%, Valid
If the third premise is true, then any killing of an innocent human is murder. If the second premise is true, then an embryo or fetus is an innocent human. If the first premise is true, then abortion is the killing of an embryo or fetus. Therefore, if the premises are all true, then the conclusion has a probability of 100 percent of being true.

41. 1/2, Invalid, Weak. (There are two months that begin with "A": April and August.)

44. We cannot calculate the probability because we do not know the percentage of speeding occurrences that are (or are not) violations of the law. However, it is invalid because it is possible that the conclusion is false. (It is also possible that the conclusion is true.)

Exercise Set 2.3

5. Valid
If you use the bottom-up approach, the conclusion can be made false.

But to get both premises true at the same time requires us to (1) place the X west of Y (making the first premise true), and (2) have Z turn out to be east of Y; this cannot be done.

11. S has a higher GPA than N
L has a higher GPA than N
L has a higher GPA than S

Conclusion: ("L has a higher GPA than S") = False

GPA chart with L, N, S bars, ranging 0.0 to 4.0

Premise 1: ("S has a higher GPA than N") = True

Premise 2: ("L has a higher GPA than N") = True

This logical picture clearly illustrates the possibility that true premises can lead to a false conclusion. We have used the pictures to represent the idea that the logical structure is invalid. Therefore, we have also shown that the original inference is invalid as well (because it rests on an invalid structure).

16. Valid
Let S = "Sue," L = "Lou," and T = "Tim." The logical form of the inference is:

S has more work experience than L.
L has more work experience than T.
S has more work experience than T.

If S has 15 years work experience, then L has less than 15, and T has less than L. Therefore, S must have more years of work experience than T.

Exercise Set 2.4A

6. Not an inference
The two statements do not act as either premises or conclusions; rather they just convey information.

16.
Premises: (a) It is said that, "absence makes the heart grow fonder."
(b) I have been absent for the last two weeks.
Conclusion: My teachers should really love me.

The indicator word, "So" identifies the conclusion. The other statements are offered as support. "Since" is a premise indicator word.

21.
Premises: (a) The digital camera on sale today at *Cameras Galore* has 5.0 megapixels and costs $200.
(b) The digital camera on sale at *Camera Warehouse* has 4.0 megapixels and costs $150.
(c) You said that you did not want to spend over $175 for a camera.
Conclusion: You should buy the one at *Camera Warehouse.*

The indicator word, "so" identifies the conclusion. The other statements are offered as support.

24.
Premises: (a) Fast food products contain high levels of cholesterol.
(b) They also contain high levels of sodium, fat, and trans-fatty acids.
(c) These things are bad for your health.
Conclusion: I am going to stop eating in fast food places.

Although there are no obvious indicator words, it is clear that the first three statements provide reasons, or support, for the last statement.

Exercise Set 2.4B

6. Inference
The statement "The cost of buying one (a computer) goes down dramatically every year," is a premise used to support the conclusion (a prediction) "Computers will soon be in every home."

Exercise Set 2.4C

6. *Missing conclusion:* John's 10-page report is in color. This will make the inference valid. If the premises are actually true, then the inference will also be sound.

Missing conclusion: John's 10-page report is probably in color.

This will make the inference strong. However, if any of the premises are false, then the inference is not cogent.

11. *Missing premise:* All educated people are honest. This makes the inference valid.

Missing premise: Most educated people are honest.

This makes the inference invalid (deductively speaking), but strong (inductively speaking).

CHAPTER 3 CATEGORICAL STATEMENTS AND INFERENCES

Exercise Set 3.1

6. S = "children," P = "following in their parents footsteps"

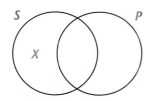

Some S are not P

11. S = "viruses," P = "lethal to humans"

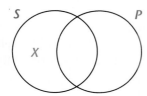

Some S are not P

16. S = "exotic vegetables," P = "edible"

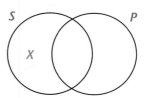

Some S are not P

19. S = "finely tuned instruments," P = "soothing to the ear"

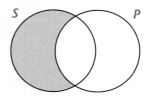

All S are P

26. *Answer:* **Some bears are hibernators.**
This sentence is translated as a particular affirmative statement.

31. *Answer:* **All tsunamis are dangerous.**
The sentence is best translated as a universal affirmative statement since we normally refer to the entire class of tsunamis when classifying them as dangerous.

41.

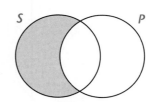

All S are P

Premise: "All S are P" = *True*
Conclusion: "Some P are S" = *False*
The inference is invalid.

46.

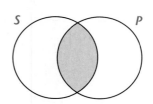

No S are P

Premise: "No *S* are *P*" = *True*
Conclusion: "No *P* are *S*" = *True*
The inference is valid.

51.

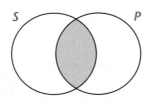

No S are P

Premise: "No *S* are *P*" = *True*
Conclusion: "Some *P* are not *S*" = *False*
The inference is invalid.

56.

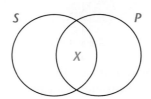

Some S are P

Premise: "Some *S* are *P*" = *True*
Conclusion: "Some *P* are *S*" = *True*
The inference is valid.

61.

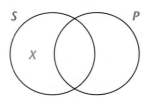

Some S are not P

Premise: "Some *S* are not *P*" = *True*
Conclusion: "All *P* are *S*" = *False*
The inference is invalid.

66.

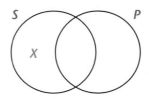

Some S are not P

Premise: "Some *S* are not *P*" = *True*
Conclusion: "Some *S* are not *P*" = *True*
The inference is valid.

Exercise Set 3.2

6. *Answer:* Invalid
Let *S* = "CEO's," *P* = "people interested in maximizing profits," and *M* = "honest people." The form of the inference is:

Some *S* are not *M*
Some *M* are not *P*
Some *S* are not *P*

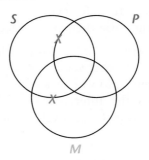

11. *Answer:* Invalid
Let *S* = "four-legged creatures," *P* = "canines," and *M* = "dogs." The form of the inference is:

All *M* are *S*
All *M* are *P*
All *S* are *P*

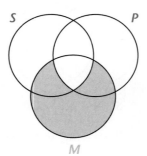

16. *Answer:* Invalid
Let *S* = "musically inclined people," *P* = "physically dexterous," and *M* = "drummers." The form of the inference is:

All *M* are *P*
All *M* are *S*
Some *S* are *P*

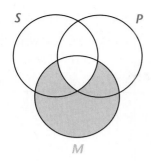

19. *Answer:* **Invalid**

Let S = "comedies," P = "tragedies," and M = "movies." The form of the inference is:

Some *M* are *S*
Some *M* are *P*
Some *S* are *P*

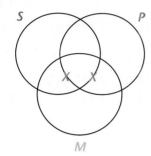

26. *Answer:* **Invalid**

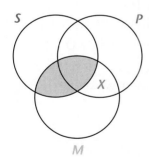

CHAPTER 4   TRUTH-FUNCTIONAL STATEMENTS

Exercise Set 4.1A

6. (b.) X must be false
The negation changes the truth value of whatever follows it.

Exercise Set 4.1B

5. Let T = "My test score was high," and M = "I am mistaken." The main operator is a disjunction, so we get the following:

$$T \lor M$$

10. Let P = "You must get a passing grade on the next exam," and F = "You will fail." The main operator is a disjunction, so we get the following:

$$P \lor F$$

This is best captured by a disjunction, because it is asserting that either you get a passing grade or you will fail.

14. Let G = "Grover Cleveland was the greatest U.S. president."

$$\sim G$$

Although you could translate the statement simply as G (where G = "It is false that Grover Cleveland was the greatest U.S. president," nevertheless, ~ G captures the English sentence more accurately by revealing the truth-functional operator *negation*. (The phrase "It is false that," acts like the phrase "It is not the case that," which indicates that the negation sign is appropriate.)

Exercise Set 4.2

17. Symbolic translation: $X \supset Y$

18. Truth value: True. A conditional is true if both antecedent and consequent are false.

27. Symbolic translation: $X \supset Y$

28. Truth value: True. A conditional is true if both antecedent and consequent are false.

Exercise Set 4.3A

6. $L \supset \sim (P \lor \supset Q)$ This is not a *WFF.* **Rule 1:** The "·", "∨", and "⊃" must always go between two statements (simple or complex).

11. $P \cdot \lor Q$ This is not a *WFF.* **Rule 1:** The "·", "∨", and "⊃" must always go between two statements (simple or complex).

Exercise Set 4.3B

The main operator is circled in each example.

6. (L ⊃ ~ P) ⊙ Q

11. (~ Q ∨ P) ⊙ R

16. [(L ⊃ ~ P)] ⊃ Q] ⊙ ~ S

21. ~ Q ⊙ P

31. True

Explanation: Since P and R are true, both ~ P and ~ R are false. S is false, but ~ S is true, making the disjunction in the parentheses true. Since *at* least one of the disjuncts of the main operator is true, the disjunction is true.

41. True

Explanation: The main operator is a conditional. Although P is true, ~ P is false. This makes the antecedent of the main operator true, thus the complex statement is true.

Exercise Set 4.3C

6. Let E = "you exercise for 20 minutes a day," C = "you cut out 1000 calories a day," and T = "you will be in top physical condition in 6 months."

$$(E \cdot C) \supset T$$

The first two conjoined statements are the antecedent of a conditional statement, so they must be placed within parentheses.

11. Let C = "we are careful," O = "we do change the oil often enough," and E = "the engine will be ruined."

$$(\sim C \cdot \sim O) \supset E$$

The first two conjoined statements are the antecedent of a conditional statement, so they must be placed within parentheses.

16. Let S = "soccer is the world's most popular sport," C = "it catches on in the United States," F = "football will lose fans," and B = "basketball will lose fans."

$$S \supset [C \supset (F \cdot B)]$$

The main operator is the first conditional. The second conditional has a conjunction as the consequent, so parentheses and brackets must be used.

Exercise Set 4.5A

6. Contingent. The truth table reveals that both truth values, true and false, are possible.

	P Q		(P ∨ ~ P) · Q
1.	T T		T *(T)* *(F)* T *(T)* T
2.	T F		T *(T)* *(F)* T *(F)* F
3.	F T		F *(T)* *(T)* F *(T)* T
4.	F F		F *(T)* *(T)* F *(F)* F

11. Contingent. The truth table reveals that both truth values, true and false, are possible.

	P Q		P ⊃ (Q · ~ Q)
1.	T T		T *(F)* T *(F)(F)* T
2.	T F		T *(F)* F *(F)(T)* F
3.	F T		F *(T)* T *(F)(F)* T
4.	F F		F *(T)* F *(F)(T)* F

16. Tautology. The truth table reveals that the statement is always true.

	P		(P · ~ P) ⊃ P
1.	T		T *(F)(F)* T *(T)* T
2.	F		F *(F)(T)* F *(T)* F

Exercise Set 4.5B

6. Truth value: True
Since both conjuncts are true, the conjunction is true.

11. Logical structure: P ⊃ Q

16. Truth value: False
Since P is true, its negation is false.

Exercise Set 4.6

6. Logically equivalent. Both truth tables have identical results for the main operator in every line.

	P Q		~ (P ∨ Q)	(~ P · ~ Q)
1.	T T		*(F)* T *(T)* T	*(F)* T *(F)* *(F)* T
2.	T F		*(F)* T *(T)* F	*(F)* T *(F)* *(T)* F
3.	F T		*(F)* F *(T)* T	*(T)* F *(F)* *(F)* T
4.	F F		*(T)* F *(F)* F	*(T)* F *(T)* *(T)* F

11. Logically equivalent. Both truth tables have identical results for the main operator in every line.

P Q	(P ≡ Q)	[(P ⊃ Q) · (Q ⊃ P)]
1. T T	T *(T)* T	T *(T)* T *(T)* T *(T)* T
2. T F	T *(F)* F	T *(F)* F *(F)* F *(T)* T
3. F T	F *(F)* T	F *(T)* T *(F)* T *(F)* F
4. F F	F *(T)* F	F *(T)* F *(T)* F *(T)* F

16. Logically equivalent. Both truth tables have identical results for the main operator in every line.

P Q	(P ⊃ Q)	(~ Q ⊃ ~ P)
1. T T	T *(T)* T	*(F)* T *(T)(F)* T
2. T F	T *(F)* F	*(T)* F *(F)(F)* T
3. F T	F *(T)* T	*(F)* T *(T)(T)* F
4. F F	F *(T)* F	*(T)* F *(T)(T)* F

21. Not logically equivalent. Both truth tables do not have identical results for the main operator in every line.

P Q	(P ≡ Q)	[(P ⊃ Q) v (Q ⊃ P)]
1. T T	T *(T)* T	T *(T)* T *(T)* T *(T)* T
2. T F	T *(F)* F	T *(F)* F *(T)* F *(T)* T
3. F T	F *(F)* T	F *(T)* T *(T)* T *(F)* F
4. F F	F *(T)* F	F *(T)* F *(T)* F *(T)* F

Exercise Set 4.7

6. Contradictory

P Q	P v Q	~ (P v Q)
1. T T	T *(T)* T	*(F)* T *(T)* T
2. T F	T *(T)* F	*(F)* T *(T)* F
3. F T	F *(T)* T	*(F)* F *(T)* T
4. F F	F *(F)* F	*(T)* F *(F)* F

Explanation: The truth table comparison reveals that in every line we get opposite truth values; therefore, the two statements are contradictory.

11. Consistent

A B	A v B	~ A v ~ B
1. T T	T *(T)* T	*(F)* T *(F)(F)* T
2. T F	T *(T)* F	*(F)* T *(T)(T)* F
3. F T	F *(T)* T	*(T)* F *(T)(F)* T
4. F F	F *(F)* F	*(T)* F *(T)(T)* F

Explanation: The truth table comparison reveals that lines #2 and #3 contain the truth value true. Since statements are consistent if there is at least one line on their respective truth tables where the truth values are both true, then the two statements are consistent.

16. Consistent

P Q	P v Q	~ (P · Q)
1. T T	T *(T)* T	*(F)* T *(T)* T
2. T F	T *(T)* F	*(T)* T *(F)* F
3. F T	F *(T)* T	*(T)* F *(F)* T
4. F F	F *(F)* F	*(T)* F *(F)* F

Explanation: The truth table comparison reveals that lines #2 and #3 contain the truth value true. Since statements are consistent if there is at least one line on their respective truth tables where the truth values are both true, then the two statements are consistent.

CHAPTER 5   TRUTH TABLES AND PROOFS

Exercise Set 5.1A

6.

		Premise	Conclusion
R S		~ R · ~ S	~ S
1. T T		*(F)* T *(F)(F)* T	*(F)* T
2. T F		*(F)* T *(F)(T)* F	*(T)* F
3. F T		*(T)* F *(F)(F)* T	*(F)* T
4. F F		*(T)* F *(T)(T)* F	*(T)* F

Explanation: The inference is valid because there is no line where the premise is true and the conclusion is false.

11.

			Premise	Conclusion
P Q S			P v (Q v S)	P
1. T T T			T *(T)* T *(T)* T	T
2. T T F			T *(T)* T *(T)* F	T
3. T F T			T *(T)* F *(T)* T	T
4. T F F			T *(T)* F *(F)* F	T
5. F T T			F *(T)* T *(T)* T	F
6. F T F			F *(T)* T *(T)* F	F
7. F F T			F *(T)* F *(T)* T	F
8. F F F			F *(F)* F *(F)* F	F

Explanation: The inference is invalid because lines #5, #6, and #7 reveal instances where the premises are true and the conclusion is false. (Any one of the three lines, by itself, would be sufficient for the inference to be invalid.)

21. Let J = "Jim is a hog farmer," and M = "Mary Lynn is a hog farmer."

		1st	2nd	Conc
J M		**~ (J · M)**	**~ M**	**~ J**
1. T T		(F) T (T) T	(F) T	(F) T
2. T F		(T) T (F) F	(T) F	(F) T
3. F T		(T) F (F) T	(F) T	(T) F
4. F F		(T) F (F) F	(T) F	(T) F

Explanation: The inference is invalid, because line #2 reveals an instance where the premises are true and the conclusion is false.

Exercise Set 5.1B

6. Valid. There is no line with true premises and a false conclusion.

		1st	2nd	Conc
P Q		**P ∨ Q**	**~ P**	**Q**
1. T T		T (T) T	(F) T	T
2. T F		T (T) F	(F) T	F
3. F T		F (T) T	(T) F	T
4. F F		F (F) F	(T) F	F

11. Invalid. Line #3 proves the inference is invalid.

		1st	2nd	Conc
P S		**P ⊃ (~ P ∨ ~ S)**	**~ P**	**~ S**
1. T T		T (F) (F) T (F) (F) T	(F) T	(F) T
2. T F		T (T) (F) T (T)(T) F	(F) T	(T) F
3. F T		F (T)(T) F (T) (F) T	(T) F	(F) T
4. F F		F (T)(T) F (T)(T) F	(T) F	(T) F

16. Invalid. Line #8 proves the inference is invalid.

		1st	2nd	3rd	Conc
S Q R		**[(S ∨ (Q ∨ R)] ⊃ Q**	**~ Q**	**~ R**	**S**
1. T T T		T (T) T (T) T (T) T	(F) T	(F) T	T
2. T T F		T (T) T (T) F (T) T	(F) T	(T) F	T
3. T F T		T (T) F (T) T (F) F	(T) F	(F) T	T
4. T F F		T (T) F (F) F (F) F	(T) F	(T) F	T
5. F T T		F (T) T (T) T (T) T	(F) T	(F) T	F
6. F T F		F (T) T (T) F (T) T	(F) T	(T) F	F
7. F F T		F (T) F (T) T (F) F	(T) F	(F) T	F
8. F F F		F (F) F (F) F (T) F	(T) F	(T) F	F

26. Invalid. If we let P = "UFO's exist," and Q = "there is life on other planets," then the form of the inference is revealed:

$$P \supset Q$$
$$\underline{\sim P}$$
$$\sim Q$$

Here is a completed truth table for the inference:

		1st	2nd	Conc
P Q		**P ⊃ Q**	**~ P**	**~ Q**
1. T T		T (T) T	(F) T	(F) T
2. T F		T (F) F	(F) T	(T) F
3. F T		F (T) T	(T) F	(F) T
4. F F		F (T) F	(T) F	(T) F

As indicated by the box, line #3 shows that for this inference it is possible to get both premises true and the conclusion false at the same time, therefore this is an invalid inference. (It is also an instance of the fallacy of denying the antecedent.)

31. Invalid. If we let P = "you take 1000mg of Vitamin C every day," and Q = "you will get a cold," then the form of the inference can be revealed:

$$P \supset \sim Q$$
$$\underline{\sim Q}$$
$$P$$

Here is a completed truth table for the inference:

	1st	2nd	Conc
P Q	P ⊃ ~ Q	~ Q	P
1. T T	T *(F)* *(F)* T	*(F)* T	T
2. T F	T *(T)* *(T)* F	*(T)* F	T
3. F T	F *(T)* *(F)* T	*(F)* T	F
4. F F	F *(T)* *(T)* F	*(T)* F	F

As indicated by the box, line #4 shows that for this inference it is possible to get both premises true and the conclusion false at the same time, therefore this is an invalid inference. (It is also an instance of the fallacy of affirming the consequent.)

36. Invalid. If we let P = "you finish the job by Friday," and Q = "you get the bonus," then the form of the inference is revealed:

$$P \supset Q$$

$$\underline{\sim P}$$

$$\sim Q$$

Here is a completed truth table for the inference:

	1st	2nd	Conc
P Q	P ⊃ Q	~ P	~ Q
1. T T	T *(T)* T	*(F)* T	*(F)* T
2. T F	T *(F)* F	*(F)* T	*(T)* F
3. F T	F *(T)* T	*(T)* F	*(F)* T
4. F F	F *(T)* F	*(T)* F	*(T)* F

As indicated by the box, line #3 shows that for this inference it is possible to get both premises true and the conclusion false at the same time, therefore this is an invalid inference. (It is also an instance of the fallacy of denying the antecedent.)

Exercise Set 5.2

6.

	1st	2nd	3rd	Conc
P Q S	(P ∨ Q) · (~ S · Q)	~ S	~ Q	~ P
T F F	T *(T)* F *(F)* *(T)* F *(F)* F	*(T)* F	*(T)* F	*(F)* T

Since there is no other way to get the third premise true except to make Q false, the second conjunct in the first premise will have to be false, making it now impossible to get the first premise true. Since it is impossible to get all the premises true and the conclusion false at the same time, we have proven that the inference is valid.

11.

	1st	2nd	3rd	Conc
P Q R S	(R ∨ S) ⊃ (P · Q)	~ S	~ Q	~ R
T F T F	T *(T)* F *(F)* T *(F)* F	*(T)* F	*(T)* F	*(F)* T

Since there is no other way to get the conclusion false except to make R true, the antecedent in the first premise then becomes true. The third premise forces us to make Q false, which results in the consequent of the first premise being false. So, it will become impossible to get the first premise true with these truth-value assignments. Since it is impossible to get all the premises true and the conclusion false at the same time, we have proven that the inference is valid.

21. If we let C = "animals are conscious," P = "animals do feel pain," and R = "animals do have rights," then the structure of the inference is:

$$(\sim C \lor \sim P) \supset \sim R$$

$$C$$

$$\underline{P}$$

$$R$$

	1st	2nd	3rd	Conc
C P R	(~ C ∨ ~ P) ⊃ ~ R	C	P	R
T T F	*(F)* T *(F)* *(F)* T *(T)* *(T)* F	T	T	F

The completed indirect truth table reveals the possibility of true premises and a false conclusion, thus we have proven that the inference is invalid.

26. If we let E = "X is an even number," and D = "X is divisible by 2," then the structure of the inference is:

$$E \supset D$$

$$\underline{\sim D}$$

$$\sim E$$

		1st	2nd	Conc
D E	E ⊃ D	~ D	~ E
F T	T *(F)* F	*(T)* F	*(F)* T

Since the only way to get the conclusion false is to make E true, and the only way to get the second premise true is to make D false, it will be impossible to then get the first premise true. Thus, the inference is valid.

31. If we let V = "Eddie can vote," and R = "he (Eddie) is registered," then the structure of the inference is:

$$V \equiv R$$

$$\underline{R}$$

$$V$$

		1st	2nd	Conc
R V	V ≡ R	R	V
T F	F *(F)* T	T	F

Since the only way to get the conclusion false is to make V false, and the only way to get the second premise true is to make R true, it will be impossible to then get the first premise true. Thus, the inference is valid.

Exercise Set 5.3

6. *Answer:* **Not a sufficient condition**
There is more than one month with exactly 30 days. Therefore, if the antecedent is true, then the consequent can be true or false.

11. *Answer:* **Sufficient condition**
If it is true that I am over 21 years of age, then it must be true that I am over 10 years of age.

17. *Answer:* **Necessary condition**
A bachelor is defined as being an unmarried adult male. Given this, if Ed is not an adult male, then Ed cannot be a bachelor.

21. *Answer:* Necessary condition
June has exactly 30 days. Given this, if this month does not have exactly 30 days, then this month cannot be June.

26. *Answer:* **Not a necessary condition**
If I do not have exactly 100 pennies, I may or may not have at least the equivalent of one dollar.

31. *Answer:* **Necessary condition**
If it is false that I am hurting a mammal, then it must be false that I am hurting a human, since all human are mammals.

CHAPTER 6   NATURAL DEDUCTION

Exercise Set 6.3

[6]   1. Q ⊃ (R v S)
      2. ~ (R v S)
      3. ~ Q   1, 2, MT

[11] 1. (P v Q)
      2. R
      3. (P v Q) • R   1, 2, Conj

[21] 1. (R v ~ T) ⊃ S
      2. R v ~ T
      3. S   1, 2 MP

[26] 1. (P • ~ R) ⊃ Q
      2. ~ Q
      3. ~ (P • ~ R)   1, 2, MT

Exercise Set 6.4

[6]   1. (S v P) • M
      2. S v P   1, Simp

[10] 1. (P • Q) v (R ⊃ S)
      2. ~ (P • Q)
      3. R ⊃ S   1, 2, DS

[16] 1. P v (Q • S)
      2. ~ P
      3. (Q • S)   1, 2 DS

Exercise Set 6.5

[6] 1. T ∨ R
    2. [(T ∨ R) ∨ (S · P)] ⊃ (Q · S) ∴ Q · S
    3. (T ∨ R) ∨ (S · P) 1, Add
    4. Q · S 2, 3, MP

[11] 1. (P ∨ R) ⊃ Q
    2. ~ Q · S ∴ ~ (P ∨ R)
    3. ~ Q 2, Simp
    4. ~ (P ∨ R) 1, 3, MT

Exercise Set 6.6

[6] 1. ~ P ∨ ~ Q
    2. ~ (P · Q) 1, DeM

[16] 1. ~ ~ (P · R)
    2. (P · R) 1, DN

Exercise Set 6.7

[6] 1. ~ P ⊃ ~ Q
    2. Q ⊃ P 1, Trans

[21] 1. (T ∨ Q) ∨ S
    2. ~ T ∴ Q ∨ S
    3. T ∨ (Q ∨ S) 1, Assoc
    4. Q ∨ S 2, 3, DS

[26] 1. ~ (T ∨ S) ⊃ (P ∨ Q)
    2. ~T · ~ S ∴ (P ∨ Q)
    3. ~ (T ∨ S) 2, DeM
    4. P ∨ Q 1, 3, MP

[36] 1. (~ P ∨ Q) ⊃ R
    2. (S ∨ R) ⊃ P
    3. P ⊃ Q ∴ Q
    4. (P ⊃ Q) ⊃ R 1, MI
    5. R 3, 4, MP
    6. R ∨ S 5, Add
    7. S ∨ R 6, Comm
    8. P 2, 7, MP
    9. Q 3, 8, MP

[41] 1. T ∨ S
    2. ~ T
    3. (S ∨ S) ⊃ (~ P ∨ R) ∴ ~ R ⊃ ~ P
    4. S 1, 2, DS
    5. S ∨ S 4, Taut
    6. ~ P ∨ R 3, 5, MP
    7. P ⊃ R 6, MI
    8. ~ R ⊃ ~ P 7, Trans

[46] 1. C ⊃ F
    2. A ⊃ B
    3. ~ F · A
    4. ~ C ⊃ (B ⊃ D) ∴ B · D
    5. ~ F 3, Simp
    6. ~ C 1, 5, MT
    7. B ⊃ D 4, 6, MP
    8. A · ~ F 3, Comm
    9. A 8, Simp
    10. B 2, 9, MP
    11. D 7, 10, MP
    12. B · D 10, 11, Conj

[51] 1. ~ S ⊃ (N ⊃ T)
    2. ~ S · (R ⊃ S)
    3. (~ M · ~ N) ⊃ (~ O ∨ ~ P)
    4. (Q ∨ ~ R) ⊃ ~ M
    5. (~ R · ~ S) ⊃ (~ ~ O · ~ T) ∴ ~ P
    6. ~ S 2, Simp
    7. R ⊃ S 2, Simp (Comm)
    8. ~ R 6, 7, MT
    9. ~ R · ~ S 6, 8, Conj
    10. ~ ~ O · ~ T 5, 9, MP
    11. N ⊃ T 1, 6, MP
    12. ~ T 10, Simp (Comm)
    13. ~ N 11, 12, MT
    14. ~ R ∨ Q 8, Add
    15. Q ∨ ~ R 14, Comm
    16. ~ M 4, 15, MP
    17. ~ M · ~ N 13, 16, Conj
    18. ~ O ∨ ~ P 3, 17, MP
    19. ~ ~ O 10, Simp
    20. ~ P 18, 19, DS

Exercise Set 6.8

[6]

1. P
2. $(P \lor P) \supset [Q \supset \sim (R \lor S)]$ $\therefore Q \supset \sim S$
3. $(P \lor P)$ 1, Taut
4. $Q \supset \sim (R \lor S)$ 2, 3, MP
> 5. Q   *Assumption (CP)*
> 6. $\sim (R \lor S)$ 4, 5, MP
> 7. $\sim R \cdot \sim S$ 6, DeM
> 8. $\sim S \cdot \sim R$ 7, Comm
> 9. $\sim S$ 8, Simp
10. $Q \supset \sim S$ 5-9, CP

[11]

1. $[(A \cdot B) \cdot C] \supset D$ $\therefore A \supset [B \supset (C \supset D)]$
> 2. A   *Assumption (CP)*
>> 3. B   *Assumption (CP)*
>>> 4. C   *Assumption (CP)*
>>> 5. $A \cdot B$ 2, 3, Conj
>>> 6. $(A \cdot B) \cdot C$ 4, 5, Conj
>>> 7. D   1, 6, MP
>> 8. $C \supset D$ 4-7, CP
> 9. $B \supset (C \supset D)$ 3-8, CP
10. $A \supset [B \supset (C \supset D)]$ 2-9, CP

[16]

1. $P \supset (Q \cdot R)$
2. $S \supset (Q \cdot T)$ $\therefore (S \lor P) \supset Q$
> 3. $S \lor P$ *Assumption (CP)*
> 4. $[S \supset (Q \cdot T)] \cdot [P \supset (Q \cdot R)]$ 1, 2, Conj
> 5. $(Q \cdot T) \lor (Q \cdot R)$ 3, 4, CD
> 6. $Q \cdot (T \lor R)$ 5, Dist
> 7. Q   6, Simp
8. $(S \lor P) \supset Q$ 3-7, CP

Exercise Set 6.9

[6]

1. $S \supset \sim (\sim Q \lor P)$
2. $Q \equiv P$ $\therefore \sim S$
> 3. $\sim \sim S$ *Assumption (IP)*
> 4. S   3, DN
> 5. $(Q \supset P) \cdot (P \supset Q)$ 2, ME
> 6. $Q \supset P$ 5, Simp
> 7. $\sim Q \lor P$ 6, MI
> 8. $\sim (\sim Q \lor P)$ 1, 4, MP
> 9. $(\sim Q \lor P) \cdot \sim (\sim Q \lor P)$ 7, 8, Conj
10. $\sim \sim \sim S$ 3-9, IP
11. $\sim S$ 10, DN

[11]

1. $A \supset B$
2. $A \supset C$
3. $\sim B \lor \sim C$ $\therefore \sim A$
> 4. $\sim \sim A$ *Assumption (IP)*
> 5. A   4, DN
> 6. B   1, 5, MP
> 7. C   2, 5, MP
> 8. $\sim \sim C$ 7, DN
> 9. $\sim C \lor \sim B$ 3, Comm
> 10. $\sim B$ 8, 9, DS
> 11. $B \cdot \sim B$ 6, 10, Conj
12. $\sim \sim \sim A$ 4-11, IP
13. $\sim A$ 12, DN

CHAPTER 7   THE LOGIC OF QUANTIFIERS

Exercise Set 7.1

1.

	Boolean Translation
All M are P	$M \supset P$
All S are M	$S \supset M$
All S are P	$S \supset P$

M P S	M ⊃ P	S ⊃ M	S ⊃ P
	1st	2nd	Conc
T T T	T *(T)* T	T *(T)* T	T *(T)* T
T T F	T *(T)* T	F *(T)* T	F *(T)* T
T F T	T *(F)* F	T *(T)* T	T *(F)* F
T F F	T *(F)* F	F *(T)* T	F *(T)* F
F T T	F *(T)* T	T *(F)* F	T *(T)* T
F T F	F *(T)* T	F *(T)* F	F *(T)* T
F F T	F *(T)* F	T *(F)* F	T *(F)* F
F F F	F *(T)* F	F *(T)* F	F *(T)* F

Since there is no line where both premises are true and the conclusion is false, the truth table method verifies that this is a valid inference.

Proof by Natural Deduction

1. $M \supset P$
2. $S \supset M$ ∴ $S \supset P$
3. $S \supset P$ 1, 2, HS

Exercise Set 7.2

6. $Qj \supset Uj$

11. Bs

Exercise Set 7.4

6. $(x) (Lx \supset Ax)$

11. $(x) (Mx \supset \sim Gx)$

21. $(x) [Wx \supset (Ex \lor Ox)]$

26. $(\exists x) (Dx \cdot \sim Gx)$

Exercise Set 7.5

11. **The information in line #11:** $(\exists x)(Wx \cdot \sim Kx)$

[21] 1. $Ha \lor Hb$
2. $(x) (\sim Cx \supset \sim Hx)$ ∴ $Ca \lor Cb$
3. $\sim Ca \supset \sim Ha$ 2, UI
4. $\sim Cb \supset \sim Hb$ 2, UI
5. $\sim \sim Ha \supset \sim \sim Ca$ 3, Trans
6. $Ha \supset Ca$ 5, DN
7. $\sim \sim Hb \supset \sim \sim Cb$ 4, Trans
8. $Hb \supset Cb$ 7, DN
9. $(Ha \supset Ca) \cdot (Hb \supset Cb)$ 6, 8, Conj
10. $Ca \lor Cb$ 1, 9, CD

[26] 1. $(x) (Px \supset \sim Qx)$
2. Qa ∴ $\sim Pa$
3. $Pa \supset \sim Qa$ 1, UI
4. $\sim \sim Qa$ 2, DN
5. $\sim Pa$ 3, 4, MT

Exercise Set 7.6

6. **Translating the inference gives us this:**

  1. $(x) [(Dx \lor Sx) \supset Rx]$
  2. $(\exists x) (Sx)$ ∴ $(x) Rx$

A one-element model with the individual *a* will give the following logically equivalent truth-functional inference:

  1. $(Da \lor Sa) \supset Ra$
  2. Sa ∴ Ra

Da Ra Sa	(Da ∨ Sa) ⊃ Ra	Sa	Ra
	1st	2nd	Conc
T F T	T *(T)* T *(F)* F	T	F

The only way to get the conclusion false is to make *Ra* false. The second premise can be true only if *Sa* is true. Then the first premise will turn out false. Therefore, we must try a two-element model.

Da Ra Sa Db Rb Sb	[(Da ∨ Sa) ⊃ Ra] · [(Db ∨ Sb) ⊃ Rb]	Sa ∨ Sb	Ra · Rb
	1st	2nd	Conc
F F F T T T	F *(F)* F *(T)* F *(T)* T *(T)* T *(T)* T	F *(T)* T	F *(F)* T

Since the truth table shows that it is possible to get both premises true and the conclusion false at the same time, this is an invalid inference.

CHAPTER 8   LOGIC AND LANGUAGE

Exercise Set 8.1

6. True. The extension of a term is what it denotes.

16. Mammal: *Intension*—Mammary glands, long gestation period, dependent offspring
Extension—Humans, whales, chimpanzees

21. Computer: *Intension*—Artificial intelligence, computation machine, circuitry
Extension—Cray supercomputer, Hewlett-Packard, IBM

26. Stipulative—Defining a term by choosing some arbitrary specified meaning.

31. Operational—An operational definition provides a meaning to a term by specifying a measurement procedure.

36. Operational—An operational definition provides a meaning to a term by specifying a measurement procedure.

41. Ostensive—One way to provide an ostensive definition of a term is to show someone an object and attach a word to it.

Exercise Set 8.2A

6. False. Division is the mistaken transfer of an attribute of an object as a whole to its individual parts.

14. *Answer:* **Equivocation**
(When we intentionally, or unintentionally, use different meanings of words or phrases in an inference.)

19. *Answer:* **Equivocation**
(When we intentionally, or unintentionally, use different meanings of words or phrases in an inference.)

24. *Answer:* **Amphiboly**
(Mistakes of interpretation can occur when the grammar or syntax of a statement muddles the intended meaning.)

29. *Answer:* **Equivocation**
(When we intentionally, or unintentionally, use different meanings of words or phrases in an inference.)

33. *Answer:* **Emphasis**
(These fallacies occur when our attention is diverted from the original issue at hand, allowing a change in the intent of a statement or an inference.)

Exercise Set 8.2B

6. *Answer:* **False.** A *post hoc* fallacy is a type of false cause concerning a short-term pattern which is noticed after the fact.

16. *Answer:* **Begging the question.** (When an inference assumes as evidence in the premises the very thing that it attempts to prove in the conclusion.)

21. *Answer:* **Hasty generalization.** (This occurs whenever a generalization is based on a few instances.)

26. *Answer:* **Fake precision.** (This occurs when a claim is made that appears to be statistically significant, but upon analysis, it is not the case.)

31. *Answer:* **Fake precision.** (This occurs when a claim is made that appears to be statistically significant, but upon analysis, it is not the case.)

36. *Answer:* **Coincidence.** (This is a special kind of false-cause fallacy, which results from the coincidental connection between two events.)

Exercise Set 8.2C

6. *Answer:* **True.** The fallacy of irrelevant conclusion is an inference where premises that seem to logically head in one direction are used instead to support an unexpected conclusion.

16. *Answer:* **Appeal to inappropriate authority.** When an inference relies on the opinions of people that have no expertise, training, or knowledge relevant to the issue at hand.

21. *Answer:* **Appeal to force.** A threat of harmful consequences (physical and otherwise) used to force acceptance of a course of action that would otherwise be unacceptable.

26. *Answer:* **Appeal to pity.** A specific kind of emotional plea that relies solely on a sense of pity for someone.

31. *Answer:* **Ad hominem.** When purported "character flaws," or the circumstances regarding persons' lives, are used to reject their claims.

36. *Answer:* **Inference from ignorance.** An inference built on a position of ignorance (lack of knowledge) makes one of two possible mistakes: (1) a claim is made that a statement must be true, because it has not been proven false; (2) a claim is made that a statement must be false, because it has not been proven true.

41. *Answer:* **Appeal to pity.** A specific kind of emotional plea that relies solely on a sense of pity for someone.

46. *Answer:* **Irrelevant conclusion.** When an inference misfires because the premises seem to head in one direction and the conclusion in another.

Exercise Set 8.3

In most cases there is more than one way to reconstruct and evaluate the statements and inferences. Here are some suggestions.

6. He has hit approximately the same number of home runs each year since he first started playing professional baseball.

   He should not be accused of taking steroids.

The rhetorical force is the assertion, "he has hit approximately the same number of home runs each year since he first started playing professional baseball." Given this, it seems to be indicating that the conclusion should be that he should not be accused of taking steroids.

11. There is no trace of gunpowder on his hands.

    He did not commit suicide by shooting himself.

The rhetorical force behind the assertion, "there is no trace of gunpowder on his hands," seems to be indicating that the conclusion should be negative in tone.

16. False dichotomy
It is possible that both disjuncts are false.

CHAPTER 9 APPLIED INDUCTIVE ANALYSIS

Exercise Set 9.1A

6. Premise 1: *X,* the earliest agreed upon fossil of a human, and *Y,* the bones found in central China, have the following attributes in common: *a,* the cranial area is the same; *b,* the jaw-bone matches human fossils of a later date; *c,* crude tools were found near the bones in each case; *d,* the teeth match.

   Premise 2: *X* has *e:* the oldest recognized bones have been declared to be human.

   Conclusion: Therefore, probably *Y* has *e:* they should be declared to be human.

The structure of the inference can now be displayed.

X and *Y* have *a, b, c, d,* in common.
X has *e.*
Therefore, *probably Y* has *e.*

11. Premise 1: I already ate apples, oranges, peaches, and cherries from her fruit stand, and now I am going to try her pears.

    Premise 2: I enjoyed the apples, oranges, peaches, and cherries from her fruit stand.

    Conclusion: I will enjoy the pears.

Exercise Set 9.1B

6. (a) *Number of entities:* The bones recently found in China and those of other known fossils of humans.

   (b) *Variety of instances:* The bones found in China are being compared to a variety of bones found around the world, dated from a variety of eras in human history.

   (c) *Number of characteristics:* Cranial area; jaw bone; tools found near the bones; teeth.

   (d) *Relevancy:* The characteristics seem relevant to the question of whether or not the bones are from a human ancestor.

11. (a) *Number of entities:* The pears, apples, oranges, peaches, and cherries.

    (b) *Variety of instances:* All are fruit.

    (c) *Number of characteristics:* All from the same fruit stand.

    (d) *Relevancy:* This characteristic is probably relevant to the enjoyment of the fruit.

Exercise Set 9.1C

6. (e) *Disanalogies:* Perhaps there is a gap between these fossils and the next oldest found in China. Other finds around the world are gradual, meaning the most recent discoveries usually do not predate the known oldest ones by such a wide gap.

   (f) *Counteranalogy:* These bones are more like an ape like creature known to exist at the same time. Although the cranial size is the same, the slope of the forehead is closer to that of the apes. The eye sockets resemble the apes, as do the cheekbones. These bones are likely to be a newly discovered species of ape.

   (g) *Unintended consequences:* If the bones really are the oldest known evidence of humans, then anthropologists will have to abandon their present theories of where humans originated.

11. (e) *Disanalogies:* The pears might come from a different place than the other fruit. The pears might be unripe, or overripe.

(f) *Counteranalogy:* The pears are like the pear fruit pies I cooked for you. You did not like the pear fruit pie, so you probably will not like the pears from her stand.

(g) *Unintended consequences:* You might enjoy eating the pears, but remember that you are allergic to pears. You will pay a high price for that temporary enjoyment.

Exercise Set 9.2A

7. *Sample:* 93 wars that took place in the last two hundred years

Population: All future wars

Sample size: The size is adequate, as it appears to represent a substantial number of "wars." It would help if we knew more about the researcher's inclusion or exclusion of conflicts.

Potential bias: The sample is based on the researcher's own definition of war. For all we know, the researcher may have included cases of a citizen of one country killing a citizen of another country. He may have counted as a civil war any riots or public displays of protest that led to a killing. It is always possible to find data to support any claim if you purposely include data for your claim and exclude data that goes against your claim. These concerns reduce the likelihood that the sample is representative of the population.

Randomness: We are not given any indication that this is a random sample. This reduces the likelihood that the sample is representative of the population.

Exercise Set 9.2B

6. Using the restricted conjunction method, we get the following:

$$1/7 \times 1/7 \times 1/7 \times 1/7 = 1/2401$$

11. Using the general disjunction method, we get the following:

$$1 - (1/2 \times 1/2 \times 1/2)$$

$$1 - 1/8 = 7/8$$

[The reason we subtract from 1 is the probability can never be greater than 1 (nor can it be less than zero).]

16. Question 1: For a non-leap year: 1/28.

Question 2: For a leap year: 1/29.

(There are either 28 or 29 days in February; Washington's Birthday could have been on only one of the days of the month.)

21. $1/4 + 1/4 = 2/4$, or $1/2$. (The alternatives are mutually exclusive.)

Exercise Set 9.3

5. *Hypothesis:* The battery in Joe's car is dead.

Experiment: Replace the battery.

Prediction: If the hypothesis is correct, then the car will start.

Confirm/Disconfirm: The prediction was true, and the evidence confirms the hypothesis.

Alternative Explanations: The clamps on either the positive or negative terminal heads might have been loose. If so, the battery might not have been dead or defective. The battery could have (and should have) been tested. It may have simply needed recharging. Without having evidence to rule out these possibilities we must be careful not to assign too much weight to the existing evidence.

APPENDIX 1   MAPPING PREMISES AND CONCLUSIONS

Exercise Set A1

6. *Premises*—[1] They say that, "absence makes the heart grow fonder;" [2] I have been absent for the last two weeks.

Conclusion—[3] My teachers should really love me.

16. [1] The office laser printer can print 20 pages a minute in black and white; [2] the office laser printer can print 10 pages a minute in color; [3] it took one minute to print John's 10-page report on the office laser printer; [4] *Missing Conclusion:* John's 10-page report is in color.

APPENDIX 2   THE SQUARE OF OPPOSITION AND STANDARD-FORM CATEGORICAL SYLLOGISMS

Exercise Set A2.1

6. **Subject term:** *X-rated movies*
Predicate term: *intellectually stimulating*
This is an example of an **A** statement.

11. **Subject term:** *sporting events*
Predicate term: *television shows worth watching*
This is an example of an **A** statement.

Exercise Set A2.2

6. Universal negative; subject term distributed; predicate term distributed.

11. Universal affirmative; subject term distributed; predicate term undistributed.

Exercise Set A2.3

6. False
If they are contradictories, then one must be true and the other must be false.

11. "Some sports cars are not gas-guzzlers."
Since the first sentence is an **A** statement, its contradictory must be an **O** statement.

21. True
Since they are contradictories, if one is false, then the other must be true.

26. True
Since they are contradictories, if one is false, then the other must be true.

31. False
Since these fall under subalternation, if the particular is false, then the corresponding universal must be false.

36. Undetermined
Since they are subcontraries, they can both be true at the same time.

Exercise Set A2.4

16. *Converse:* Not valid for **O** statements.

17. *Obverse:* Some fruitcakes are nonregifted presents.

18. *Contrapositive:* Some nonregifted presents are not nonfruitcakes.

31. *Converse:* Some juicy items are T-bone steaks.

32. *Obverse:* Some T-bone steaks are not nonjuicy items.

33. *Contrapositive:* Not valid for **I** statements.

46. *Converse:* Some things too hot to eat are barbeque wings.

47. *Obverse:* Some barbeque wings are not nonthings too hot to eat.

48. *Contrapositive:* Not valid for **I** statements.

64. *Converse:* Not valid for **O** statements.

65. *Obverse:* Some modern clothes are nonwarm garments.

66. *Contrapositive:* Some nonwarm garments are not nonmodern clothes.

Exercise Set A2.7

6. *S* = "children," *P* = "following in their parents' footsteps"

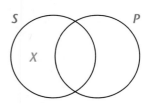

11. *S* = "viruses," *P* = "lethal to humans"

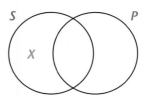

16. S = exotic "vegetables," P = "edible"

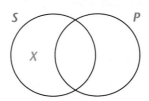

21. S = "French pastries," P = "good for your complexion"

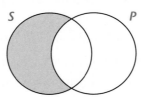

26. S = "spiders," P = "nocturnal creatures"

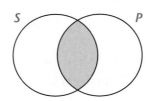

31. S = "sandwiches," P = "things made with meat"

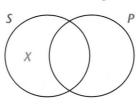

36. S = "embezzlers," P = "social deviants"

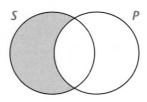

41. S = "ice cream toppings," P = "harmful to your diet"

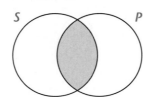

Exercise Set A2.9

6. No P are M
   No M are S
   No S are P

Answer: This is an invalid inference.

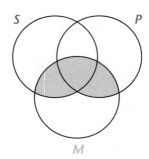

11. All M are P
   No S are M
   No S are P

Answer: This is an invalid inference.

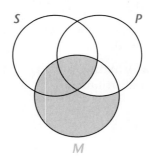

21. Some universities are not expensive places to attend. Some universities are conveniently located. Thus, some expensive places to attend are not conveniently located.

Answer: Let S = "expensive places to attend," P = "conveniently located," and M = "universities."

   Some M are P
   Some M are not S
   Some S are not P

Answer: This is an invalid inference.

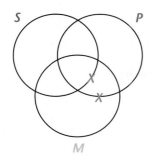

Exercise Set A2.11

6. *EEE-4*

16. *AOO-2*
Answer: This is a valid inference.

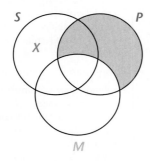

21. *IAI-3*
Answer: This is a valid inference.

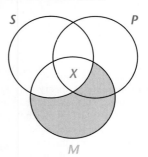

31. *EAO-3*
Answer: This is an invalid inference.

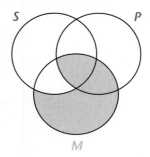

{ Glossary }

A

***A priori* theory of probability:** A theory in which the probability ascribed to a simple event is a fraction between 0 and 1, of which the denominator is the number of equiprobable outcomes, and the numerator is the number of outcomes in which the event in question occurs.

Abnormal state: Any change from the normal state of an object requires explanation, typically a causal one. For example, if a window suddenly breaks, an abnormal state is established.

Addition (Add): A rule of inference.

$$\frac{p}{p \vee q}$$

Ad hominem: Use of purported character flaws or circumstances of people's lives to reject their claims.

Affirmative statement: A categorical statement that asserts class inclusion, either complete (universal) or partial (particular).

Alternative explanations: Any cause-effect claim can be challenged by suggestions of alternative potential causes. Therefore, strong causal claims are backed up by evidence against rival, alternative, causal claims.

Alternative occurrences: In probability theory, a complex event that consists of the occurrence of any one of two or more simple component events; for example, the complex event of getting either a heart or a club in the random drawing of a playing card.

Ambiguity: Fallacies of ambiguity occur when the meaning of terms or phrases is changed (intentionally or unintentionally) within the inference. These fallacies tend to depend on the fact that there are typically many different meanings of individual words or phrases.

Amphiboly: An ambiguous statement that stems from a grammatical error.

Analogy: To indicate that two or more things are similar by listing the relevant (significant) characteristics they have in common.

Analogical inference: An inference based on the idea that two (or more) things that share some relevant characteristics probably share other characteristics as well.

Analogical structure: The designation, placement, and role of the premises and conclusion that reveal the logical structure of an analogical inference.

Antecedent: The statement that follows the "if" in a conditional statement.

Appeal to emotion: An inference or claim that relies solely on the arousal of a strong emotional state or psychological reaction; such an inference ultimately relies on irrelevant support.

Appeal to force: A threat of harmful consequences (physical and otherwise) used to force acceptance of a course of action that would otherwise be unacceptable.

Appeal to inappropriate authority: An inference that relies on the opinions of people who have no expertise, training, or knowledge relevant to the issue at hand.

Appeal to pity: A specific kind of emotional plea that relies solely on a sense of pity for support.

Argument: *See* **Inference**.

Aristotelian square of opposition: The arrangement of categorical statements that shows why we obtain different combinations of truth and falsity between certain pairs. It defines the relationships of contradiction, contraries, and subcontraries.

Association (Assoc): A substitution set.

$$[p \vee (q \vee r)] \ :: \ [(p \vee q) \vee r]$$
$$[p \cdot (q \cdot r)] \ :: \ [(p \cdot q) \cdot r]$$

B

Background knowledge: Any information known to be true that is used to determine the truth content of a statement.

Bayesian theory: A major advance in probability theory and method developed by Thomas Bayes. It united much of the probability

calculus and the relative frequency theory into a method for calculating conditional probability. The formula for calculating the conditional probability of two mutually exclusive and exhaustive events is the following:

$$Pr(A, if B) = \frac{Pr(B, if A) \times Pr(A)}{Pr(B)}$$

Begging the question: An inference that assumes as evidence in the premises the very thing that it attempts to prove in the conclusion.

Biased sample: A sample that intentionally or unintentionally excludes segments of the population and results in a nonrepresentative sample.

Biconditional: *See* **Material equivalence**.

Boolean square of opposition: The modern square that arranges categorical statements to show why we obtain different combinations of truth and falsity between pairs of categorical statements. It modifies the relationships in the Aristotelian square of opposition.

Bottom-up analysis: The approach that starts by making the conclusion of an inference false, and then trying to get all the premises true at the same time.

Bound variable: In *(x) (Hx ⊃ Mx)* the universal quantifier *(x)* ranges over (applies to) everything within the parentheses, so both *Hx* and *Mx* are bound by the universal quantifier. In *(x)Hx ⊃ Mx* the universal quantifier *(x)* ranges over (applies to) only *Hx*, which is a bound variable; but it does not extend to *Mx*, which is a free variable.

C

Calculus of probability: *See* **Probability calculus**.

Categorical statement: A statement that uses sets, categories, or groups of objects (real or imaginary) to replace the variables in one of four specific forms—"All *S* are *P*," "No *S* are *P*," "Some *S* are *P*," "Some *S* are not *P*." These are also referred to as ***A, E, I,*** and ***O*** statements, and they either affirm or deny that some class *S* is included in some other class *P*.

Categorical syllogism: An inference entirely constructed of categorical statements. (*See* also **Standard-form categorical syllogism**.)

Category: *See* **Class**.

Causal inference: An inference based on knowledge of either causes or effects.

Causal network: The range of necessary conditions that must be met in order to establish a cause-effect relationship.

Circular reasoning: *See* **Fallacy of begging the question**.

Class: A group, set, or collection of objects that have a common characteristic attributed to each member.

Cogent: A cogent inference must (1) be strong or moderate (based on the analysis of the logical component), and (2) have all true premises (based on the analysis of the truth content).

Coincidence: A special kind of false cause fallacy that results from the accidental or chance connection between two events.

Collective: When a characteristic (a predicate term) is used in a statement to refer to a group of objects as a whole, not to the individual members of the group.

Common cause fallacy: A type of mistake that occurs when someone thinks that one event causes another when in fact both events are the result of a common cause.

Commutation (Comm): A substitution set.

$(p \lor q) :: (q \lor p)$

$(p \cdot q) :: (q \cdot p)$

Complement: The set of objects that does not belong to a given class; everything outside the given class.

Complex question: A single question that actually contains multiple, hidden parts.

Complex statement: The truth value of a complex statement is determined by looking at the truth values of the individual components (the simple statements) together with the logical operator(s).

Composition: The mistaken transfer of an attribute of the individual parts of an object to the object as a whole.

Conclusion: The end point of an inference; the statement that is meant to follow from premises.

Conclusion indicator words: Words or phrases that indicate the probable existence of a conclusion.

Conditional inference: An inference that has a conditional statement as one of its premises.

Conditional probability: The probability of an event occurring if another event has already happened.

Conditional proof (CP): The method of proof that exploits the mechanism of conditional statements.

Conditional statement: A complex statement having the form "If P then Q," where the variables P and Q get replaced by statements.

Confirm: To have empirical evidence that supports a claim or hypothesis.

Conjunction: Two or more statements connected by the logical operator "and." The individual statements are called conjuncts.

Conjunction (Conj): A rule of inference.

p

q

$p \cdot q$

Consequent: The statement that follows the "then" in a conditional statement.

Consistent statements: For truth-functional statements, if there is at least one line on their respective truth tables where the truth values are both true.

Constructive dilemma (CD): A rule of inference.

$(p \supset q) \cdot (r \supset s)$

$p \lor r$

$q \lor s$

Contingent statement: A statement whose truth or falsity is not based on its logical form, but is dependent on other factors; it can therefore be either true or false.

Contradictories: Two statements that are related such that one is the negation of the other; it is impossible for both to be true or both to be false at the same time. The categorical *A* and *O* statements, and *E* and *I* statements are contradictories.

Contradictory statements: Two statements that have opposite truth values on every line of their respective truth tables.

Contraposition: For categorical statements, when an immediate inference is formed by replacing the subject term with the complement of its predicate term, and then by replacing the predicate term with the complement of its subject term.

Contraposition by limitation: For categorical statements, when the process of subalternation changes a universal *E* statement into its corresponding particular *O* statement, and then forms the contrapositive of the *O* statement.

Contrapositive: The statement produced by the process of contraposition.

Contraries: Two statements that cannot both be true at the same time, but that can be false at the same time. Also, if one is true, then the other must be false. In the Aristotelian square of opposition, *A* and *E* statements are contraries.

Control group: In a controlled experiment, experimental setups that are identical to the test setups, except that they are not exposed to the factor being tested

Controlled experiment: An experiment in which there are multiple experimental setups that differ by only one variable.

Convergent inference: An inference that has independent premises, which separately offer support for the conclusion.

Converse: The statement resulting from the process of conversion.

Conversion: For categorical statements, an immediate inference created by interchanging the subject term and predicate term of a statement (the statement so produced is called the converse).

Conversion by limitation: For categorical statements, when the process of subalternation changes a universal *A* statement into its corresponding particular *I* statement, and then forms the converse of the *I* statement.

Convertend: The categorical statement with which we start and which becomes the premise of an immediate inference by conversion.

Copula: The terms "are" and "are not" are called copula; they are forms of "to be" and serve to link the subject term *S* with the predicate term *P* of a categorical statement.

Correlation: A relationship between two or more things. By itself, a correlation is not sufficient to establish a cause-effect relationship.

Corresponding statements: These relationships reveal that if the universal statement of a pair is true, then its corresponding particular partner will also be true.

Counteranalogy: A competing analogy that compares the entity mentioned in the conclusion of the original analogy to a different entity.

D

Deductive analysis: Analysis of an inference with the specific goal of determining the logical question of validity or invalidity.

Deductive inference: An inference in which it is asserted that the conclusion is guaranteed to be true if the premises are true.

De Morgan (DeM): A substitution set.

$\sim (p \cdot q) :: (\sim p \vee \sim q)$

$\sim (p \vee q) :: (\sim p \cdot \sim q)$

Dependent premises: Dependent premises act together to support a conclusion; the falsity of one premise weakens any support the other premise(s) would give to the conclusion. A diagram that reveals the occurrence of dependent premises is called *linked*.

Dilemma: A decision that must be made between two choices, either of which leads to an unwanted result.

Disanalogy: To point out relevant (significant) differences between the entities mentioned in an analogy.

Discharged: In conditional proof and indirect proof the method by which an assumption and any derived lines are completed.

Disconfirm: To have empirical evidence that goes against (refutes) a claim or hypothesis.

Disjunction: Two or more statements connected by the logical operator "or." The individual statements are called disjuncts.

Disjunctive syllogism (DS): A rule of inference.

$p \vee q$

$\underline{\sim p}$

q

Distributed: When a categorical statement claims something definite about every member of the class designated by a term.

Distribution: A characteristic of a categorical statement in which the statement claims something definite about every member of the class designated by a term.

Distribution (Dist): A substitution set.

$[p \cdot (q \vee r)] :: [(p \cdot q) \vee (p \cdot r)]$

$[p \vee (q \cdot r)] :: [(p \vee q) \cdot (p \vee r)]$

Distributive: When a characteristic (a predicate term) is used in a statement to refer to the individual members of a group of objects, not to the group as a whole.

Divergent inference: An inference in which a single premise is used to support two or more conclusions.

Division: The mistaken transfer of an attribute of an object as a whole to its individual parts. Division is the direct opposite of composition.

Double negation (DN): A substitution set.

$p :: \sim \sim p$

E

Emphasis: Fallacies that occur when attention is diverted away from the original issue at hand, allowing a change in the intent of a statement or an inference.

Enthymemes: Inferences with missing premises, missing conclusions, or both. This term derives its meaning from the two roots "*en*," meaning "in," and "*thymos*," which refers to the "mind." It means, literally, "to keep in the mind." The missing information is, thus, implied.

Equiprobable: When each of the possible outcomes of an event has an equal probability of occurring.

Equivalence rules: *See* **Substitution sets**.

Equivocation: The intentional or unintentional use of different meanings or references for words or phrases in an inference.

Euler diagrams: Diagrams that can be used to represent the assertions of categorical and truth-functional statements by illustrating the possible truth value outcomes.

Exceptive statement: A statement that claims that members of one class, with the exception of a particular subclass, are members of another class. These statements are complex in that they assert a relation of class inclusion and exclusion at the same time.

Exclusive disjunction: A type of disjunctive statement where both the disjuncts cannot be true at the same time; the truth of one excludes the truth of the other.

Exhaustive: In probability theory, exhaustive means that there are no other possibilities other than the ones under consideration.

Existential fallacy: A fallacy in which an inference relies on a mistaken assumption of existence. Under the Boolean interpretation, universal statements do not have existential import, but particular statements do. Therefore, any categorical syllogism that has two universal premises and a particular conclusion is invalid. Since neither premise makes an existential assertion, but the particular conclusion does, the existential fallacy occurs.

Existential generalization (EG): A rule of inference in the logic of quantifiers, which holds that the existential quantification of a statement function can be inferred from any true substitution instance of that statement function.

Existential import: In a statement, the assertion of the existence of objects of some kind.

Existential instantiation (EI): A rule of inference in the logic of quantifiers; it holds that within certain limitations, the truth of a substitution instance can be inferred from the existential quantification of a statement function, as long as the individual constant does not occur earlier.

Existential quantification: When a statement function will be true if, and only if, it has at least one true substitution instance.

Existential quantifier: In the logic of quantifiers the symbol "∃" is used to indicate that any statement function immediately following the symbol has some true substitution instance.

Explanation: Explanations provide reasons for why or how an event occurred.

Exportation (Exp): A substitution set.

$[(p \cdot q) \supset r] :: [p \supset (q \supset r)]$

Extension: The class members of the term; what the term denotes (the objects to which the term refers).

F

Fake precision: When a claim is made that appears to be statistically significant, but upon analysis, is shown not to be.

Fallacies: There are two kinds of fallacies, informal and formal. Informal fallacies involve a specific kind of error in the content of an inference, not in the structure. These errors include, but are not limited to, mistakes of ambiguity, unwarranted assumption, and relevance. Formal fallacies are reasoning errors that occur in the structure or form of an inference, not in the truth content. They are restricted to deductive inferences.

Fallacy of affirmative conclusion/negative premise(s): Since class inclusion requires an affirmative statement, a categorical inference with an affirmative conclusion can validly follow only from two affirmative premises. A negative premise will break the class inclusion necessary to bring about the affirmative conclusion.

Fallacy of affirming the consequent: A fallacy with a form that resembles *modus ponens*.

$p \supset q$

q

p

Fallacy of ambiguity: Fallacies of ambiguity occur when the meaning of terms or phrases is changed (intentionally or unintentionally) within the inference. These fallacies tend to depend on the fact that there are typically many different meanings of individual words or phrases.

Fallacy of begging the question: An inference that assumes as evidence in the premises the very thing that it attempts to prove in the conclusion; also called circular reasoning.

Fallacy of biased sample: An inference that uses a sample that intentionally or unintentionally excludes segments of the population as support for a statistical claim about the entire population.

Fallacy of coincidence: A special kind of false cause fallacy that results from the accidental or chance connection between two events.

Fallacy of common cause: A mistake in which someone thinks that one event causes another when in fact both events are the result of a common cause.

Fallacy of complex question: A single question that actually contains multiple, hidden parts.

Fallacy of composition: The mistaken transfer of an attribute of the individual parts of an object to the object as a whole.

Fallacy of denying the antecedent: A fallacy with a form that resembles *modus tollens*.

$p \supset q$

$\sim p$

$\sim q$

Fallacy of division: The mistaken transfer of an attribute of an object as a whole to its individual parts. Division is the direct opposite of composition.

Fallacy of emphasis: A fallacy that occurs when attention is diverted away from the original issue at hand, allowing a change in the intent of a statement or an inference.

Fallacy of equivocation: The intentional or unintentional use of different meanings or references for words or phrases in an inference.

Fallacy of exclusive premises: This fallacy rests on the principle that two negative premises always result in an invalid inference. The major (negative) premise will exclude part or all of the class designated by the major term from the class designated by the middle term. The minor (negative) premise will exclude part or all of the class designated by the minor term from the class designated by the middle term. It then becomes impossible to deduce validly any kind of relationship between the major and minor terms, either positive or negative.

Fallacy of fake precision: When a claim is made that appears to be statistically significant, but upon analysis, is shown not to be.

Fallacy of false cause: The mistake of claiming that a causal connection exists between two events when none exists. Events that appear to be correlated are not necessarily causally connected.

Fallacy of false dichotomy: When a disjunction assumes that only two possibilities exist, when in fact more than two exist.

Fallacy of false dilemma: A special kind of false dichotomy that occurs when a disjunction assumes that only two possibilities exist, both of which would lead to unwanted results, when in fact more than two exist.

Fallacy of hasty application of a generalization: A fallacy that occurs when a generalization is inappropriately applied to a particular case because of a failure to recognize that most generalizations have exceptions.

Fallacy of hasty generalization: A fallacy in which a generalization is created on the basis of a few instances.

Fallacy of illicit major: If the major term is distributed in the conclusion, but not in the major premise, then the conclusion goes beyond what was asserted in the premises.

Fallacy of illicit minor: This fallacy, like illicit major, fails to observe the rule that any term that is distributed in the conclusion must be distributed in the premises. If the minor term is distributed in the conclusion but not in the minor premise, then the conclusion goes beyond what was asserted in the premises.

Fallacy of irrelevant conclusion: An inference where premises that seem to head logically in one direction are used instead to support an unexpected conclusion.

Fallacy of negative conclusion/affirmative premises: Since class exclusion requires a negative statement, a categorical inference with a negative conclusion cannot validly follow from two affirmative premises.

Fallacy of relevance: A fallacy in which the premises offered in support of the conclusion are irrelevant.

Fallacy of undistributed middle: The conclusion of a categorical syllogism asserts a relationship between the classes designated by the major and minor terms. Therefore, the premises of a valid categorical syllogism must lay the foundation for that relationship. This can only be achieved if the premises distribute the middle term at least once. Either the subject or predicate (or both) of the conclusion must be related to the entire class designated by the middle term. If this is not done, then the fallacy occurs.

Fallacy of unwarranted assumption: A fallacy in which the truth of some unproved or questionable claim is assumed; such a claim does not provide good support for the conclusion.

False cause fallacy: The mistake of claiming that a causal connection exists between two events when none exists. Events that appear to be correlated are not necessarily causally connected.

False dichotomy: When a disjunction assumes that only two possibilities exist when in fact more than two exist.

False dilemma: A special kind of false dichotomy that occurs when a disjunction assumes that only two possibilities exist, both of which would lead to unwanted results, when in fact more than two exist.

Figure: The middle term in a standard-form categorical syllogism can be arranged in the two premises in four different ways. These placements reveal the figure of the categorical syllogism.

Finite universe method: A valid inference that uses quantifiers is valid for any number of individuals, with the stipulation that there is at least one individual. To prove that an inference that uses quantifiers is invalid requires that we must be able to produce a possible universe or model (containing at least one individual) for which the premises are true and the conclusion false.

Follows from: A relationship in an inference whereby the conclusion has a direct logical connection to the premises.

Formal fallacies: Reasoning errors that occur in the structure or form of an inference, not in the truth content. They are restricted to deductive inferences.

Free variable: In *(x)Hx ⊃ Mx* the universal quantifier *(x)* ranges over (applies to) only *Hx,* which is a bound variable, but it does not extend to *Mx,* which is a free variable.

Functional definition: A definition that specifies the purpose or use of the items denoted by the term.

G

General conjunction method: A method for calculating the probability of two or more events occurring together, regardless of whether the events are independent or not independent. In these cases, the probability of subsequent events is dependent on prior events happening (or not happening). The formula for this method is: *Pr (A and B) = Pr (A) × Pr (B, if A)*

General disjunction method: A method for calculating the probability of occurrence of two or more events that are not mutually exclusive. The formula for this method is: *Pr (A or B) = [Pr (A) + Pr (B)] − [Pr (A) × Pr (B)]*

Generalization: In a statistical context, a claim about a group of objects (a population) that is based on information regarding a subset (sample) of that group. In the logic of quantifiers, the process by which a statement is created from a statement function by using either a universal or an existential quantifier.

Grammatical rules: *See* **Syntactical rules.**

H

Hasty application of a generalization: A generalization can be inappropriately applied to a particular case by failing to recognize that most generalizations have exceptions, special cases that do not fall under the general rule. If you rigidly apply a generalization, even in the face of known and accepted exceptions, then you hastily apply that generalization.

Hasty generalization: This occurs when a generalization is created on the basis of a few instances. We are not justified in saying all (or most) of a class of objects have a certain characteristic simply because we observed a few to have that characteristic. This kind of fallacy occurs whenever we encounter stereotypes.

Hypothesis: A claim offered as an explanation for a fact or set of facts.

Hypothetical syllogism (HS): A rule of inference.

$p \supset q$

$q \supset r$

$p \supset r$

I

If: Designates the antecedent of a conditional statement. It also can refer to a potential sufficient condition.

Immediate inference: An inference that has only one premise.

Implicit: An unstated claim that is assumed to be part of someone's overall position.

Inclusive disjunction: A type of disjunctive statement where it is possible for both disjuncts to be true at the same time.

Inconsistent statements: Truth-functional statements for which there is not even one line on their respective truth tables where the truth values are both true. For two statements to be inconsistent, it must be impossible for both statements to be true at the same time.

Independent events: In probability theory, events so related that the occurrence or nonoccurrence of one has no effect upon the occurrence or nonoccurrence of the other.

Independent premises: With independent premises, the falsity of one premise does not nullify any support the other(s) give to the conclusion. A diagram that reveals the occurrence of independent premises is called convergent.

Indicator words: Some conclusion indicator words are *therefore, thus, so,* and *consequently.* Some premise indicator words are *because, since, assuming that,* and *given that.*

Indirect proof (IP)—*reductio ad absurdum*: The proof procedure used in natural deduction that establishes the proof of a statement by assuming the negation of the statement to be proved, then deriving a contradiction from that negation. If the negation of a statement leads to an absurdity (a contradiction—a statement that cannot possibly be true), then it has been proved indirectly that the original statement must be true.

Indirect truth table: A truth table for which truth values are assigned specifically to reveal the possibility of true premises and a false conclusion.

Individual constant: A symbol (designated by any lower case letter from *a* through *w*) used in the logical notation of predicate logic to denote an individual.

Individual variable: A symbol used in the logical notation of predicate logic that functions as a placeholder for an individual constant (the lower case letters *x, y,* and *z* are used).

Inductive analysis: Inductive analysis makes it possible to investigate the strengths and weaknesses of certain inferences, such as analogical, statistical, and causal inferences. These reasoning applications give up certainty (because they result in invalid inferences) and replace it with probability (degrees of uncertainty).

Inductive inference: An inference in which it is asserted that the conclusion has a high probability of being true if the premises are true.

Inference: A set of statements whereby the premises are offered as support for a conclusion.

Inference from ignorance: An inference built on a position of ignorance claims either that (1) a statement must be true because it has not been proven to be false, or (2) a statement must be false because it has not been proven to be true.

Informal fallacies: Fallacies that involve specific kinds of error in the content of an inference, not in the structure. These errors include, but are not limited to, mistakes of ambiguity, unwarranted assumption, and relevance.

Instantiation: In the logic of quantifiers, the substitution of an individual constant in place of an individual variable. This process turns a statement function into a statement.

Intension: The properties or attributes that a term connotes (the sense or meaning of the term).

Intersection: *See* **Product.**

Invalid inference: An inference in which it is possible for the conclusion to be false even if the premises are true.

Irrelevant conclusion: An inference where premises that seem to head logically in one direction are used instead to support an unexpected conclusion.

J

Joint occurrence: In probability theory, a compound event in which two simple events both occur. To calculate the probability of joint occurrence, the product theorem is applied.

Justification: The rule of inference or substitution set used to derive a line of a proof.

L

Lexical definition: The dictionary meaning of a term, that is, the common vocabulary of a given language.

Linked inference: An inference in which dependent premises are offered in support of a conclusion.

Logic: The study of reasoning; logical analysis reveals the extent of the correctness of the reasoning found in inferences.

Logic of quantifers: The logical system of quantification used to analyze complex inferences made of truth-functional and categorical statements. The system facilitates the smooth integration of categorical and truth-functional results and offers a powerful way of capturing more of natural language into precise statement and inference analysis.

Logical certainty: The kind of certainty achieved by a valid inference.

Logical commitment: The necessary requirements for a statement to be true.

Logical component: The logical relationship between premises and a conclusion.

Logical component error (LE): When the premises of an inference, even if true, logically allow the conclusion to be false.

Logical form: The underlying logical relationship in an inference (also known as **logical structure**).

Logical loop: A situation in which we miss alternatives because our minds are locked into one method of analysis.

Logical operator: A term such as *and*, *or*, or *not*; the logical operator performs a specific logical function that determines the logical possibilities of truth and falsity for complex truth-functional statements.

Logical relationship: The logical connection between premises and conclusions.

Logical structure: The underlying logical relationship in an inference (also known as **logical form**).

Logically equivalent statements: Truth-functional statements that have identical truth tables.

Logically possible: When inference analysis reveals the logical component possibilities that exist between premises and a conclusion.

M

Main logical operator: The logical symbol that determines the statement's final truth value. The main operator in a complex truth-functional statement is either one of the logical operators that go between statements, or it is the negation symbol.

Major premise: The premise that contains the major term (the predicate term of the conclusion) of a standard-form categorical syllogism.

Major term: The term that occurs as the predicate of the conclusion in a categorical inference. It also occurs in the first premise of a standard-form categorical syllogism.

Material equivalence: The relation captured by the logical operator "≡" (also known as **biconditional**). The truth table for material equivalence shows that it is true when the components have the same truth value, otherwise it is false.

Material equivalence (ME): A substitution set.

$(p \equiv q) :: [(p \supset q) \cdot (q \supset p)]$

$(p \equiv q) :: [(p \cdot q) \vee (\sim p \cdot \sim q)]$

Material implication (MI): A substitution set.

$(p \supset q) :: (\sim p \vee q)$

Mediate inference: Any inference that contains more than one premise.

Middle term: The term that occurs only in the premises of a categorical syllogism.

Minor premise: The premise that contains the minor term (the subject term of the conclusion) of a standard-form categorical syllogism.

Minor term: The term that occurs as the subject of the conclusion in a categorical inference. It also occurs in the second premise of a standard-form categorical syllogism.

Missing conclusion: When a passage contains an incomplete inference (enthymeme), which has an unstated conclusion.

Missing premise: When a passage contains an incomplete inference (enthymeme), which has an unstated premise.

Moderate inference: An inference for which logical analysis verifies that the premises, if true, provide evidence that the conclusion has a good chance of being true.

***Modus ponens* (MP):** A rule of inference (the method of affirming the antecedent).

$p \supset q$

p ⎯⎯⎯⎯⎯

q

***Modus tollens* (MT):** A rule of inference (the method of denying the consequent).

$p \supset q$

$\sim q$ ⎯⎯⎯⎯⎯

$\sim p$

Mood: The mood of a categorical syllogism is designated by using the letter names (***A,E, I, O***) of the categorical statements for the major premise, the minor premise, and the conclusion.

Mutually exclusive events: In probability theory, events of such a nature that if one occurs, the other (or others) cannot occur.

N

Natural deduction: The method of proving validity using inferences already proven valid by the truth table method. These inferences become the building blocks to prove the validity of more complex inferences. Each step of a proof using natural deduction is itself a valid inference because each step relies on a valid inference for its derivation and justification.

Necessary condition: A condition that must be met before another event can occur.

Negation: The operation of logically changing the truth value of a statement to its opposite truth value.

Negation method: Once the probability of an event occurring is known, it is easy to calculate the probability of the event not occurring. The formula for the negation method is:

$Pr(\sim A) = 1 - Pr(A)$

Negative statement: A categorical statement that denies class inclusion, either complete (universal) or partial (particular).

New evidence: Additional information that, if true, might strengthen or weaken the probability that a conclusion is true.

Noncontingent statement: A statement whose truth or falsity is based on its logical form, not on truth content. A tautology is a statement that by its logical form is necessarily true, while a self-contradiction is a statement that by its logical form is necessarily false.

Normal-form formula: In the logic of quantifiers, where the negation symbol applies to only simple predicates.

Normal state: The historical information regarding the stability of a given system.

Not cogent: An inference is not cogent if (1) it is weak (based on the analysis of the logical component) and/or (2) it has at least one false premise (based on the analysis of the truth content).

O

Obverse: The statement produced by the process of obversion.

Obversion: For categorical statements, an immediate inference created by changing the quality of a statement and then by replacing the predicate term by its complement (the statement so produced is called the obverse).

Obvertend: The starting categorical statement that becomes the premise of an immediate inference by obversion.

Only if: Designates the consequent of a conditional statement. It can also refer to a potential necessary condition.

Operational definition: A definition that provides a meaning for a term by specifying a measurement procedure. Terms that denote things that can only be indirectly observed require some empirical means of measuring or experimenting in order to get objective evidence of their existence and properties.

Opposition: Whenever standard-form categorical statements have the same subject and predicate term, but differ from each other in quality, quantity, or in both.

Order of operations: The step-by-step method of generating a complete truth table by correctly identifying the order of handling the logical operators within a complex statement. The main logical operator controls the final determination of the statement's truth value, so it will be the last step.

Ostensive definition: A definition developed by showing someone an object and attaching a word to it.

P

Particular affirmative statement: The statement form, "Some S are P," which asserts that some (at least one) members of the subject term are members of the predicate term. These claims are either true or false, but their truth can be decided only when actual class terms are substituted for the S and P.

Particular negative statement: The statement form, "Some S are not P," which asserts that some (at least one) members of the subject term are not members of the predicate term. These claims are either true or false, but their truth can be decided only when actual class terms are substituted for S and P.

Particular statement: The type of categorical statement that refers to some (at least one) members of a class.

Population: Any group of objects (real or imaginary) which is the subject of investigation by way of a sample.

Possible universe: *See* **Finite universe method**.

Post hoc **fallacy:** A type of false cause fallacy that involves a short-term pattern noticed after the fact. This type of fallacy is also called *post hoc, ergo propter hoc* (after the fact, therefore because of the fact).

Precising definition: A definition developed to clarify a vague or ambiguous term (often used in legal, scientific, or medical settings).

Predicate logic: *See* **Logic of quantifiers**.

Predicate term: The class designated by the second term in a categorical statement.

Prediction: A statement that serves as a test of a hypothesis. A proposed experiment is simply another way of asking the question, "What if we do this?" The answer to this question will be a prediction.

Premise: A statement (or set of statements) offered as support for a conclusion.

Premise indicator words: Words or phrases that indicate the probable existence of a premise.

Principle of charity: When we have to choose between different reconstructions of another person's inference, we should choose the reconstructed inference that gives the benefit of the doubt to the person presenting the inference.

Principle of substitution: Logically equivalent statement forms may replace each other whenever one member of a substitution set occurs in a proof.

Probability: A determination of the chance of a statement being true (or an event occurring) relative to the information already known (or accepted to be true) about the subject under question.

Probability assessment: Logical inference analysis that determines the probability of a conclusion being true if the premises are true.

Probability calculus: A branch of mathematics that can be used to compute the probabilities of compound events from the probabilities of simple events.

Probability theory: The theoretical frameworks that make it possible to calculate the chance that events will occur.

Product: Whenever two classes, designated as S and P, are said to have some members in common, this commonality (overlap) is called either the product or the intersection of the two classes and is given the symbol SP.

Proof procedure: The step-by-step determination of the validity or invalidity of an inference.

Q

Quality: A characteristic of categorical statements; the statements have one of two qualities, either affirmative or negative.

Quantification: The process of changing statement functions into statements.

Quantifier: The terms "all," "no," and "some" are called quantifiers because they reveal the extent of the class inclusion or exclusion (i.e., the quantity of S as related to P).

Quantity: A characteristic of categorical statements; the statements have one of two quantities, either universal or particular.

R

Random: When the probabilities of the outcomes of an event are the same for each possible occurrence.

Red herring fallacy: A form of the fallacy of emphasis that occurs when someone completely ignores the opponent's position and changes the subject by diverting the discussion in a new direction.

Refute: To have evidence that goes against a claim or hypothesis.

Relationship: The logical connection between premises and conclusions.

Relative frequency theory of probability: A theory in which probability is defined as the relative frequency with which members of a class exhibit some attribute. The probability ascribed to a simple event is given as a fraction between zero and one, of which the denominator is the number of events in the reference class and the numerator is the number of members of that class that have the attribute in question.

Relevance: Premises must establish logical, reasonable ties to the conclusion. Many irrelevant premises rely on psychological or emotional appeal for their persuasive force.

Representative sample: When the characteristics of a sample are correctly identified and matched to the population under investigation.

Restricted conjunction method: This method is used in situations dealing with two or more independent events, where the occurrence of one event has no bearing whatsoever on the occurrence or nonoccurrence of the other event. The formula for this method is: $Pr\ (A\ and\ B) = Pr\ (A) \times Pr\ (B)$

Restricted disjunction method: This method is used in situations where: (1) two (or more) events are independent of each other, and (2) the events are mutually exclusive (if one event occurs, then the other cannot). The formula for this method is: $Pr\ (A\ or\ B) = Pr\ (A) + Pr\ (B)$

Rhetorical conditional: A conditional statement is used rhetorically (often in the form of a question) to disguise a statement or an implied inference.

Rhetorical disjunction: When a disjunction is used rhetorically to disguise a statement or an implied inference.

Rhetorical question: A statement disguised as a question.

Rules of inference: The set of rules that constitutes part of the system of natural deduction (used in conjunction with the substitution sets). The rules are valid inferences proven by the truth table method. The rules of inference are legitimately applied only to an entire line of a proof.

Rules of transformation: *See* **Substitution sets.**

S

Sample: A subset of a population; information about specific characteristics of a sample are often generalized to a population.

Self-contradiction: A statement that by its logical form is necessarily false.

Serial inferences: A series of inferences in which a conclusion from one inference becomes a premise in a second inference.

Simple predicate: In the logic of quantifiers, a statement function that has some true and some false substitution instances.

Simple statement: A statement that contains no logical operators; a statement that is not complex.

Simplification (Simp): A rule of inference.

$p \cdot q$

p

Singular statement: A statement that asserts either that a particular individual has or does not have a specified characteristic.

Slippery slope fallacy: An inference that attempts to make a final event the inevitable outcome of an initial act. Slippery slope inferences rely on a kind of causal network where each step in the chain causes the next step. However, the "inevitability" of the final act needs to be supported by specific evidence for the supposed causal network. Each link requires relevant evidence for its connection to the next link in the chain.

Sound inference: An inference that (1) is valid (based on the analysis of the logical component), and (2) has all true premises (based on the analysis of the truth content).

Standard-form categorical statement: A categorical statement with one of the following forms: *A:* All *S* are *P*, universal affirmative; *E:* No *S* are *P*, universal negative; *I:* Some *S* are *P*, particular affirmative; *O:* Some *S* are not *P*, particular negative.

Standard-form categorical syllogism: A standard-form categorical syllogism contains exactly three terms, each of which is used two times. The subject of the conclusion is called the minor term, the predicate of the conclusion is called the major term, and the term that occurs only in the premises is called the middle term. The first premise always contains the major term and is therefore called the major premise. The second premise contains the minor term and is called the minor premise.

Statement: A sentence that is either true or false (also referred to as a proposition).

Statement function: Statement functions are neither true nor false, but they can have true and false substitution instances. In the logic of quantifiers, a statement results from either the instantiation or generalization of a statement function.

Statistical generalization: Based on a sample, a claim is made that a certain percentage of a given population has a specific characteristic.

Statistical inference: An inference based on an ability to generalize. An observed pattern can be used to create an inference that uses a statistical regularity.

Stipulation: A temporary agreement to use a term, a way of measuring, or a decision process.

Stipulative definition: An arbitrary, specific definition.

Strategy: Compared to tactics, referring to a greater, overall goal. In creating a proof, one's strategy might be to isolate as many simple statements as possible, or it might be to reduce, to simplify complex statements.

Straw man fallacy: A form of fallacy of emphasis that occurs when someone's written or spoken words are taken out of context, thereby purposely distorting the original inference in such a way that the new, weak inference (the straw man) is easy to defeat.

Strong inference: An inference for which logical analysis verifies that the premises, if true, provide evidence that the conclusion has a high probability of being true.

Subaltern: The particular statement related to its corresponding universal (*I* is the subaltern of *A*, and *O* is the subaltern of *E*).

Subalternation: The unique relationship that exists between a universal statement (*A* or *E*) and its corresponding particular statement (*I* or *O*, respectively).

Subcontraries: When two statements are related such that they cannot both be false at the same time, but they both can be true at the same time. In addition, if one is false then the other must be true.

Subjectivist theory of probability: Situations can arise where neither *a priori* nor relative frequency methods will work. The subjectivity of these probability determinations occurs when we do not have total knowledge regarding an event.

Subject term: The class designated by the first term in a categorical statement.

Substitution instance: When a statement function is transformed into a statement that is either true or false.

Substitution sets: Part of the system of natural deduction consisting of logically equivalent statements that have been verified as such by using the truth table method. These sets of statements allow the replacement of any statement anywhere in a proof sequence with its logically equivalent set member.

Sufficient condition: The condition that meets the minimum requirement to ensure that another event does occur.

Superaltern: The universal statement related to its corresponding particular (*A* is the superaltern of *I*, and *E* is the superaltern of *O*).

Syllogism: Any inference that has exactly two premises and one conclusion.

Syntactical rules: The rules that govern the correct arrangement of symbols in order to create well-formed formulas (*WFF's*). It also refers to the grammatical rules in English that allow the construction of unambiguous sentences.

T

Tactics: The use of small-scale maneuvers or devices (used with natural deduction proofs).

Tautology: A statement that by its logical form is necessarily true.

Tautology (Taut): A substitution set.

$p :: (p \lor p)$

$p :: (p \cdot p)$

Technically valid inference: An inference that has a tautology as its conclusion is technically valid because it is impossible for the conclusion to be false. An inference that has a self-contradiction as one of its premises is technically valid because it is impossible for all the premises to be true.

Theory: A set of definitions of concepts that can be applied to a specific set of phenomena in order to gain a better understanding of the world.

Thought experiment: To imagine logical consequences of scenarios (as opposed to doing empirical research). Thought experiments often lead to actual experiments, the results of which can be used to confirm or disconfirm hypotheses.

Top-down analysis: The approach that starts by making all the premises true, then trying to get the conclusion false.

Transposition (Trans): A substitution set.

$(p \supset q) :: (\sim q \supset \sim p)$

Truth content: The actual truth or falsity of a statement and the methods of its determination.

Truth content error (TE): When the information given is determined to be false.

Truth-functional statement: A complex statement whose truth value is determined by an analysis of the individual components (the simple statements) together with the logical operator(s).

Truth table: The listing of all possible combinations of the truth values of a statement.

Truth value: Statements have one of two possible truth values—true or false.

Tu quoque: A variety of the *ad hominem* fallacy distinguished by the specific attempt of one person to avoid the issue at hand by claiming the other person is a hypocrite.

U

Uncertainty: For deductive analysis, when an inference is invalid, the conclusion can logically be false, so an uncertainty exists. For inductive analysis, even strong inferences allow for the possibility of a false conclusion, so an uncertainty exists here as well.

Undistributed: When a categorical statement does not assert anything definite about every member of the class designated by a term.

Unintended consequence of the analogy: When we reveal something that is a direct result of an analogy, but that is unacceptable to the person presenting the analogy. This technique puts that person in a difficult position (they have painted themselves into a corner).

Universal affirmative statement: The statement form, "All *S* are *P*," which asserts that all members of the subject term are members of the predicate term. These claims are either true or false, but their truth can be decided only when actual class terms are substituted for *S* and *P*.

Universal generalization: Based on a sample, a claim is made that every member of a given population has a specific characteristic.

Universal generalization (UG): A rule of inference in the logic of quantifiers by which we can validly deduce the universal quantification of a statement function from the substitution instance of that statement function with respect to the name of any arbitrarily selected individual.

Universal instantiation (UI): A rule of inference in the logic of quantifiers that ensures that from the universal quantification of a statement function, one can validly infer any substitution instance of that statement function.

Universal negative statement: The statement form, "No *S* are *P*," which asserts that no members of the subject term are members of the predicate term. These claims are either true or false, but this can be decided only when actual class terms are substituted for the *S* and *P*.

Universal quantification: When a statement function is true if, and only if, all possible substitution instances are true.

Universal quantifier: A symbol in the logic of quantifiers (either *x* or *y*) that is placed in front of a statement function and makes it possible to assert that the predicate following it is true of everything.

Universal statement: Whenever a statement refers to every member of a class designated by the subject term.

Unsound inference: An inference that (1) is invalid (based on the analysis of the logical component), and/or (2) has at least one false premise (based on the analysis of the truth content).

Unwarranted assumption: A type of fallacy in which a premise assumes the truth of some unproved or questionable claim that does not provide good support for the conclusion. The mistake occurs because of the tacit assumption of a claim that either has not been supported or cannot be supported.

V

Valid inference: An inference in which it is impossible for the conclusion to be false if the premises are true

Variable: A logical symbol that can take on many different values.

Venn diagram: A diagram that uses overlapping circles to represent categorical statements and to illustrate the validity or invalidity of a categorical inference.

Visual representation: A diagram or picture used for inference analysis that reveals the logical relationship that exists between premises and a conclusion.

W

Weak inference: An inference for which logical analysis verifies that the premises, if true, provide very little, or no evidence that the conclusion is true.

Well-formed formula (WFF): Truth-functional statements that have been translated symbolically and are syntactically (grammatically) correct.

What if: The logical question regarding the consequence of (*what follows from*) statements.

What is: The truth content question concerning the determination of the truth or falsity of a statement.

{ Index }

*Note: The * indicates a term found in the Glossary.*

A

Abnormal state, 359
Ada, 72
Add. *See* Addition
* Addition (Add), 197–198
* *Ad hominem*, 300–301, 304
Affirmative conclusion/negative premise(s), 423–424
* Affirmative statements, 85–86
* Alternative explanations, 358, 359
* Ambiguity, fallacies of, 283–289
* Amphiboly, 285, 289
* Analogical inferences, 31, 321–338
    analysis of, 327–331
    and counteranalogy, 332, 335
    and disanalogy, 331–332, 335
    strategies of evaluation, 331–338
    structure of, 322–327
    and unintended consequence of the analogy, 333–335
Analogical reasoning, 321–338
* Analogical structure, 322–327
* Analogy, 321, 322
Analysis
    bottom-up, 169–170
    cause-effect, 357–359
    of conditional inferences, 188–190
    deductive, 20–22, 24–25, 29–30, 34, 45, 50
    inductive, 30–31, 31–36
    of inferences, 3–4, 11–17, 33–36, 44–45, 47–55, 163–168, 188–190
Analytical Engine, 72
"And" logical operator, 114–115
And. *See* Conjunction
* Antecedent, 122–123, 126–127
* Antecedent, fallacy of denying, 162–163, 189
* Appeal to emotion, 302, 305
* Appeal to force, 303, 305
* Appeal to inappropriate authority, 304, 305
* Appeal to pity, 302–303, 305
* A priori theory of probability, 32, 345, 348–349
Arguments. *See* Inferences
* Aristotelian square of opposition, 381, 386–394, 402–404
Aristotelian syllogisms, 123
Aristotle, 86
Assertion, 57, 71, 87, 88, 104, 384–385, 402
* Association (Assoc), 216–217
Assumptions
    in conditional proof, 236–240
    fallacies of, 291–300
Axioms, 128

B

Babbage, Charles, 72
* Background knowledge, 72, 85, 361
* Bayesian theory, 354–356
Bayes, Thomas, 354
* Begging the question, 292, 297
Bernoulli numbers, 72
* Biased samples, 293, 297, 342
Biconditional, 141–144, 227–228
Blood poisoning, 368
Boolean algebra, 251
* Boolean square of opposition, 381, 404–409
Boolean translations, 249–253
Boole, George, 221, 249, 251, 381
* Bottom-up analysis, 169–170
* Bound variables, 261
Byron, Augusta Ada, 72

C

Calculus of probability, 348–352
Categorical inference, 89, 405, 409, 411, 423–434
* Categorical statements, 85–97, 381
    contradictories, 386–388, 403
    contraposition, 397–398, 407–408
    contraries, 388–389
    conversion, 394–396
    corresponding, 389–391
    defined, 85, 86
    diagramming of, 89–97, 405–406
    distributed, 383–384
    integrating with truth-functional statements, 254–257
    obversion, 396–397, 407–408
    particular, 86, 383, 403
    phi and *psi* in, 260–261

and problem of existential import, 87, 402–404
and quality, 383–385
and quantifiers, 264–270
and quantity, 383–385
relationships among, 386–391
standard-form, 382–383, 385, 386, 391, 406
and statement functions, 259–263
subcontraries, 389
translation of, 87–89, 259–261
undistributed, 383–384
universal, 85, 86, 249–250, 383, 402
universal affirmative statements, 85, 87, 250, 259–260
universal negative statements, 86, 87, 250, 259–260
and Venn diagrams
* Categorical syllogism, 97–109, 221
diagramming of, 88, 413–420
mood and figure in, 420–423
rules and fallacies associated with, 423–428
standard-form, 411–412, 420–421, 423–431
Categories, 85
See also Class
Causal hypothesis, 360, 361–362
* Causal inference, 31
Causality, analysis of, 358–359
* Causal network, 359
Causal reasoning, 31, 357–365
Cause-effect analysis, 357–359
Cause-effect relationships, 296, 357–359
CD. *See* Constructive dilemma
Certainty, 21
Chance, 32
Charity, principle of, 79
Childbed fever, 366–368
Chrysippus of Soli, 122
Circular reasoning. *See* Begging the question
Clarify, 5, 34, 85, 87
* Class, 85, 86
exclusion, 383–384, 423–434
inclusion, 383–384, 423–424
Closer than, 13, 18–19
* Cogent, 33
Cogent inference, 35
* Coincidence, fallacy of, 295, 297
* Collective, 286
Comm. *See* Commutation
Commitments. *See* Logical commitments
* Common cause fallacy, 296, 297
Common terms, 119–120
* Commutation (Comm), 218–219
* Complement, 396
Complex inferences, 163–168, 376–377
* Complex questions, 292–293, 297

* Complex statements, 262
* Composition, fallacy of, 285–286, 289
* Conclusion, 3–5
false, 57–60, 62–63
logical relationship between premises and, 5–6
mapping, 374–380
missing, 78–81
rules and fallacies associated with, 423–425
* Conclusion indicator words, 72–73
* Conditional inferences, 159–163, 188–190
* Conditional probability, 354–356
* Conditional proof (CP), 236–242, 266–270
* Conditional statements, 122–130
conditional inferences, 188–190
conditional proofs and, 236–242
diagramming of, 123–126
equivalent sentence structures for, 126
if and only if, 126–127
necessary conditions, 185–188, 189–190
rhetorical, 309–311
sufficient conditions, 182–184
truth and falsity of, 176, 199–200
truth tables for, 124, 141
Conditions
necessary, 185–188, 189–190
sufficient, 182–184, 187–188
* Confirm, 360, 361, 363
Conj. *See* Conjunction
Conjecture, 32, 360, 403
* Conjunction (Conj), 114–115, 117, 118, 198–199
translation of, 119–120
truth and falsity of, 176
Conjunction methods, 348–350, 354–355
Conjuncts, 113
Connective. *See* Logical operators
Connotation, 278
Consequences
inferring, 48
of problem of existential import, 402–404
* Consequent, 122, 126–127
* Consequent, fallacy of affirming, 160–161
* Consistent statements, 148
* Constructive dilemma (CD), 207–208
* Contingent statements, 138
* Contradictories, 386–388, 403
Contradictory statements, 147
* Contraposition, 397–398, 407–408
* Contraposition by limitation, 398, 408
Contraposition, diagrams for, 408
Contrapositive, 397–398
* Contraries, 388–389
Control groups, 357

* Controlled experiments, 357
* Convergent inferences, 375
Converse, 395, 396
* Conversion, 394–396, 407
* Conversion by limitation, 395–396
Conversion, diagrams for
* Convertend, 394–395, 396
* Copula, 383
* Correlation, 295, 358
* Corresponding statements, 389–391
* Counteranalogy, 332, 335
CP. *See* Conditional proof
Criterion (criteria), 27, 280, 327–328, 358
Criticism, 39
Curie, Marie, 5, 6, 7

D

Data, 337, 341–342
Deduce, 29, 363, 425
Deduction, natural, 195–197
* Deductive analysis, 20–22, 24–25, 29–30, 34, 45, 50
* Deductive inferences, 28–30, 35–36, 47
Deep structure, 196
De Fermat, Pierre, 31
Definitions, 277–283
    extensional, 281
    functional, 280–281, 281
    intensional, 281
    lexical, 278, 281
    operational, 279–280, 281
    ostensive, 280–281
    precising, 279, 281
    stipulative, 278–279, 281
DeM. *See* De Morgan
De Morgan, Augustus, 221
* De Morgan (DeM), 219–220
* Dependent premises, 375
Descartes, Rene, 75
Diagrams
    of categorical statements, 89–97, 405–406
    of categorical syllogisms, 98–109, 413–420
    of conditional statements, 123–126
    for contraposition, 408
    for conversion, 407
    Euler, 123
    for obversion, 408
    Venn, 88–109, 251–252, 405–408
Dice, 31, 32, 48, 345
* Dilemma, 312–313
* Disanalogy, 331–332, 335
* Discharged, 237
* Disconfirm, 360–361

* Disjunction, 116–118
    exclusive, 116
    inclusive, 116
    rhetorical, 311–313
    translation of, 119–120
    truth and falsity of, 176
Disjunction methods, 350–351
* Disjunctive syllogism (DS), 206, 229–230
Disjuncts, 116
Dist. *See* Distribution
Distributed, 383–384
* Distribution (Dist), 221–222
* Distributive, 286
* Divergent inferences, 376
* Division, fallacy of, 286–287, 289
DN. *See* Double negation
Dot, 114
* Double negation (DN), 217–218
DS. *See* Disjunctive syllogism

E

EG. *See* Existential generalization
EI. *See* Existential instantiation
Either, or statements, 262
Emotion, appeal to, 302, 305
* Emphasis, fallacy of, 287, 289
Empty truth, 139
ENIAC (Electronic Numerical Integrator and Computer), 23
* Enthymeme, 78–81
* Equiprobable, 345
Equivalence
    logical, 144–147
    material, 141–144
Equivalence rules. *See* Substitution sets
* Equivocation, 23–24, 60–61
    fallacy of, 284–285, 289
Errors
    logical component, 12–17
    truth content, 11–12, 16–17
Euclid, 29
* Euler diagrams, 123
Euler, Leonard, 123
Evaluation, 48
Evidence
    indirect, 280
    role of new, 43–47
* Exceptive statements, 262
Exclusion (class), 383–384, 423–424
* Exclusive disjunction, 116
Exclusive premises, 425, 428
* Exhaustive, 355
* Existential fallacy, 425–426

* Existential generalization (EG), 265–266
* Existential import, 87, 402–404, 408, 412
* Existential instantiation (EI), 265, 266
* Existential quantification, 258
* Existential quantifier, 258
Exp. *See* Exportation
Experimental science, 356–357
Experiments, 357–358, 360
* Explanations, 76–77
* Exportation (Exp), 226–227
* Extension, 277–278
Extensional definitions, 281

F
Fair test, 360
* Fake precision, fallacy of, 294–295, 297
* Fallacies
   ad hominem, 300–301, 304
   of affirmative conclusion/negative premise, 423–424
   affirming the consequent, 160–161
   of ambiguity, 283–289
   amphiboly, 285, 289
   appeal to emotion, 302, 305
   appeal to force, 303, 305
   appeal to inappropriate authority, 304, 305
   appeal to pity, 302–303, 305
   associated with standard-form categorical syllogisms, 423–431
   assumption, 291–300
   begging the question, 292, 297
   of biased samples, 293, 297, 342
   of coincidence, 295, 297
   common cause, 296, 297
   complex question, 292–293, 297
   of composition, 285–286, 289
   denying the antecedent, 162–163, 189
   of division, 286–287, 289
   of emphasis, 287, 289
   of equivocation, 284–285, 289
   of exclusive premises, 425
   existential, 425–426
   of fake precision, 294–295, 297
   of false cause, 295
   of false dichotomy, 312, 313
   of false dilemma, 312–313
   formal, 283
   of hasty application of a generalization, 294, 297
   of hasty generalization, 293
   of illicit major, 426
   of illicit minor, 427
   inference from ignorance, 303–304, 305
   informal, 283–291
   of irrelevant conclusion, 304, 305
   of negative conclusion/affirmative premises, 424–425
   post hoc, 295–296, 297

   red herring, 288, 289
   of relevance, 300–308
   slippery slope, 296–297
   straw man, 287–288, 289
   tu quoque, 301–302, 304
   of undistributed middle, 427–428
   of unwarranted assumption, 291–300
False cause, fallacy of, 295
False conclusions, 57–60, 62–63
False dichotomy, 312, 313
False dilemma, 312–313
Falsity, 360
* Figure, 420–423
* Finite universe method, 270–271
* Follows from, 21, 29, 506
Force, appeal to, 303, 305
Form. *See* Logical form
* Formal fallacies, 283
   See also Fallacies
Formalism, 251
* Free variables, 261
Frege, Gottlob, 256
* Functional definition, 280–281

G
Galileo, 357
Gambling, 31–32
Games of chance, 83, 353–354
Geiger counter, 280
* General conjunction method, 349–350, 354–355
* General disjunction method, 350–351
* Generalization, 258
   existential, 265–266
   hasty, 293
   hasty application of, 294, 297
   statistical, 338
   universal, 264–265, 266, 338
Gentzen Gerhard, 196
Germ theory, 366
God, existence of, 32
Grammatical rules. *See* Syntactical rules
Guarantee of truth, 21

H
Halley, Edmund, 362–363
Halley's Comet, 362–363
* Hasty application of a generalization, 294, 297
* Hasty generalization, 293
Horseshoe, 114
HS. *See* Hypothetical syllogism
Hume, David, 333
* Hypotheses, 356–357, 360–363
* Hypothetical syllogism (HS), 206–207

I

* If, 122, 182–184, 188–189
If and only if, 126–127, 142, 190
If-then statements, 23, 122–123
Ignorance, inference from, 303–304
Illicit major, fallacy of, 426
Illicit minor, fallacy of, 427
* Immediate inferences, 391, 394–402
   contraposition, 397–398
   obversion, 396–397
Inclusion (class), 383–384, 423–424
* Inclusive disjunction, 116
Incomplete inferences, 70–71
* Inconsistent statements, 148–149
Incorrect logical component, 4–5
Incorrect truth content, 4
* Independent events, 348
* Independent premises, 374–375
* Indicator words
   conclusion, 72–73
   premise, 73
* Indirect proof (IP), 242–245, 266–270
* Indirect truth tables, 168–181, 190
* Individual constants, 257
Individual members, 412
* Individual variable, 257
* Inductive analysis, 30–36, 49
* Inductive inferences, 28–29, 30–31, 35–36, 47, 79–80
* Inference from ignorance, 303–304, 305
* Inferences
   acceptable
   analogical, 31, 321–338
   analysis of, 3–4, 11–17, 44–45, 47–55, 163–168, 188–190
   bottom-up analysis of, 169–170
   causal, 31
   classification of, 35–36, 47
   cogent, 33, 35
   complex, 163–168, 376–377
   conditional, 159–163, 188–190
   convergent, 375
   deductive, 28–30, 35–36, 47
   deep structure of, 196
   defined, 3–4
   divergent, 376
   equivocation, 23–24
   evaluation of, 4, 47–55
   immediate, 391
   incomplete, 70–71
   inductive, 28–31, 35–36, 47, 79–80
   invalid, 22, 25–27, 29, 35, 67
   justifying, 4
   linked, 375
   logical form of, 28–29, 196
   logical structure of, 55–60

   mapping, 374–380
   mediate, 391
   moderate, 33, 35
   not cogent, 33, 35
   proofs of invalidity, 270–274
   recognizing, 71–75
   reconstruction of, 71–75
   rules of, 196–215, 264–265
   serial, 376
   sound, 30, 35, 67
   statistical, 31, 338–341
   strong, 33, 35
   technically valid, 156
   truth tables and, 153–168
   unsound, 30, 35
   valid, 21, 25–27, 35, 63, 67, 195–197
   weak, 33, 35, 49, 50
Infinite, 372
* Informal fallacies, 283–291
   See also Fallacies
Information, missing, 78–81
* Instantiation, 258
   existential, 265, 266
   universal, 264, 266
* Intension, 277, 278
Intensional definitions, 281
Interpret (interpretation), 87, 249–250, 255, 259, 278, 285
Intersection. *See* Product
* Invalid inferences, 22, 25–27, 29, 35, 67
Invalidity, proofs of, 270–274
IP. *See* Indirect proof
Irrelevant conclusion, 305
* Irrelevant conclusion, fallacy of, 304
Isolate (isolating), 212

J

Jennings, Betty Jean, 23
* Joint occurrence, 347
Judgment, 20–22
* Justification, 202

L

Ladd-Franklin, Christine, 412
Latin squares, 123
Law of averages, 38
LE. *See* Logical component error
Legitimate, 348
* Lexical definitions, 278, 281
Lictermann, Ruth, 23
* Linked inference, 375
* Logic
   predicate, 255
   relationships and, 4–11
   role of, 3–4

Logical analysis, 3–4, 6–7
* Logical certainty, 21–22
* Logical commitments, 70
    of necessary condition, 185
    of sufficient condition, 182
* Logical component, 4–8
* Logical component error (LE), 4–5, 12–17, 22
Logical connectives. *See* Logical operators
Logical equivalence, 144–147
    for simple predicates, 258–259
* Logical form, 196
    See also Logical structure
* Logical loop, 57, 61–62
* Logically equivalent statements, 144–146
    See also Substitution sets
Logically impossible, 62–67, 139, 429
* Logically possible, 62–67, 321, 322, 369
* Logical operators, 113–121
    biconditional, 141–144
    conjunction, 114–115, 117, 118
    disjunction, 116–118
    main, 130–136, 138
    negation, 115–118
    rules for, 117
    rules for symbolic notation, 130–136
    symbols of, 114
    translation of, 119–121, 134–136
Logical possibilities, 62–67
* Logical relationships, 5–11
    contradictories, 386–388
    contraries, 388–389
    subalternation, 389–390
    subcontraries, 389
*Logical structure, 55–60, 196
Logical thinking, 23
* Logic of quantifiers, 249–255

M
* Main logical operator, 130–136, 138
* Major premise, 411
* Major term, 411
Mapping
    conclusions, 374–380
    inferences, 374–380
* Material equivalence (ME), 141–144, 227–228
* Material implication (MI), 225–226
McNulty, Kathleen, 23
ME. *See* Material equivalence
* Mediate inferences, 391
Medical mysteries, 365–368
MI. *See* Material implication
* Middle term, 411, 427–428
Minimal claim, 384–385

Minimum requirement, 182
* Minor premise, 411
* Minor term, 411
* Missing conclusion, 78–81
Missing information, 78–81
* Missing premise, 78–81
* Moderate inferences, 33, 35
* *Modus ponens* (MP), 159–160, 174, 199–200
* *Modus tollens* (MT), 161–162, 189, 201, 212
* Mood, 420–423
MP. *See Modus ponens*
MT. *See Modus tollens*
* Mutually exclusive events, 355

N
* Natural deduction, 195–197
    rules of inference, 197–215
    tactics and strategies for, 212–215
* Necessary conditions, 185–190
* Negation, 115–116, 117, 118, 258
    double, 217–218
    translation of, 119–120
    truth and falsity of, 176
* Negation method, 351–352
Negative conclusion/affirmative premises, 424–425
Negative premises, 423–424
* Negative statements, 22
* New evidence
    analysis of inferences and, 47–51
    role of, 43–47
Newton, Isaac, 29–30
* Noncontingent statements, 138–144
    self-contradictions, 139–140
    tautologies, 138–139
Nontrivial predictions, 361–362
* Normal-form formulas, 261
* Normal state, 359
Not. *See* Negation
Notation. *See* Symbolic notation
* Not cogent, 33, 35
"Not" logical operator, 115–116

O
Obverse, 396–397
* Obversion, 396–397, 407–408
* Obvertend, 396–397
Odds, 353–354
* Only if, 126–127, 185–188, 189
* Operational definitions, 279–280, 281
Operators. *See* Logical operators
Opinions, 71
* Opposition, 386
Or. *See* Disjunction

* Order of operations, 137
"Or" logical operator, 116–118
* Ostensive definitions, 280–281

P

* Particular affirmative statements, 86, 250, 259–260
* Particular negative statements, 86, 250, 259–260
* Particular statements, 86, 250, 259–260, 383, 403
Pascal, Blaise, 31, 32
Pascal's wager, 32
Pascal triangles, 32
Pasteur, Louis, 366
Peirce, Charles S., 156
Pensées (Pascal), 32
Phantom model, 366
Phi, 258–259
Phi, in categorical statements, 260–261
Philosophy (philosophers), 32, 156, 333, 372
Pity, appeal to, 302–303, 305
* Population, 341–342
Possibilities, logical, 62–67
Possible universe. *See* Finite universe method
* *Post hoc* fallacy, 295–296, 297
Precising definitions, 279, 281
Predicate logic, 255
* Predicate term, 85, 86
* Predictions, 360–365
    and hypothesis, 363
    nontrivial, 361–362
    verifiable, 361
* Premise indicator words, 73
* Premises
    adding new, 67–70, 80
    affirmative, 424–425
    defined, 3–4
    dependent, 375
    fallacy of exclusive, 425
    independent, 374–375
    logical relationship between conclusion and, 5–6
    major, 411
    mapping of, 374–380
    minor, 411
    missing, 78–81
    recognition of, 73
    rules and fallacies associated with, 423–425
    universal, 425–426
* Principle of charity, 79
* Principle of substitution, 215
* Probability
    conditional, 354–356
    equiprobable, 345
    new evidence and, 44–45
    odds in games of chance, 353–354
    a priori theory of, 345, 348–349
    relative frequency theory of, 346, 354–355
    subjectivist theory of, 347–348
    total, 355
* Probability assessment, 21
* Probability calculus, 348–352
* Probability theory, 31–32
* Product, 404
* Proof procedure, 196–197, 229–230
Proofs
    conditional, 236–242, 266–270
    indirect, 242–245, 266–270
    of invalidity, 270–274
    thinking through, 168–170
    truth-functional, 195–215
    using natural deduction, 195–197, 212–215
    using quantifiers, 266–270
    of validity, 264–270
    working through, 212–215
Proposition. *See* Statements
Psi, in categorical statements, 260–261
Puerperal fever, 366–368

Q

QSS. *See* Quantifier substitution sets
Qualitative data, 279
Qualitative measurement, 47
* Quality, 383–385
* Quantification, 257–259
    existential, 258
    and proofs of invalidity, 270–274
    and proofs of validity, 264–270
    universal, 258
* Quantifiers, 383
    in conditional proofs, 266–270
    existential, 258
    in indirect proofs, 266–270
    proofs using, 266–270
    rules of inference for, 264–266
    universal, 258, 261
Quantifier substitution sets (QSS), 260–261
Quantitative data, 279
* Quantity, 383–385
Quantum physics, 32

R

Random samples, 342
* Red herring fallacy, 288, 289
Reductio ad absurdum, 242–245
Relationships, logical, 5–11
* Relative frequency theory of probability, 346, 354–355
* Relevance, fallacies of, 300–308

* Representative sample, 341–342
* Restricted conjunction method, 348–349
* Restricted disjunction method, 350
* Rhetorical conditionals, 309–311
* Rhetorical disjunctions, 311–313
Rhetorical language, 308–315
* Rhetorical questions, 308–309
Risk factor, 32
Rules
    for conjunction, 198–199
    for disjunction, 206
    for logical operators, 117, 130–136
    for symbolic notation, 130–136
    of transformation, 196–197
    truth and falsity, 176
    for well-formed formulas, 130–131
* Rules of inference, 196–215
    addition (Add), 197–198
    application of, 202
    conjunction (Conj), 198–199
    constructive dilemma (CD), 207–208
    disjunctive syllogism (DS), 206
    existential generalization (EG), 265–266
    existential instantiation (EI), 265, 266
    hypothetical syllogism (HS), 206–207
    modus ponens (MP), 199–200
    modus tollens (MT), 201
    order of, 200
    for quantifiers, 264–266
    simplification (Simp), 208–209
    tactics and strategies using, 212–215
    universal generalization (UG), 264–265, 266
    universal instantiation (UI), 264, 266

S

* Samples, 341–342
    biased, 293, 297, 342
Schopenhauer, Arthur, 315
Science
    experimental, 356–357
    theoretical, 356–357
Scientific reasoning, 356–365
* Self-contradictions, 139–140
Semmelweis, Ignac, 366–368
* Serial inferences, 376
Sets, 85
Simp. *See* Simplification
* Simple predicates, 258–259
* Simple statements, 113, 177, 212, 271
* Simplification (Simp), 208–209, 229–230
* Singular statements, 255–256
* Slippery slope fallacy, 296–297
Snyder, Elizabeth, 23

* Sound inferences, 30, 35, 67
Square of opposition
    Aristotelian, 381, 386–394
    Boolean, 381, 404–409
    traditional, 381
Standard-form categorical statements, 406
* Standard-form categorical syllogisms, 411–412, 420–421
Standard-form categorical syllogisms, rules and fallacies
    associated with, 423–431
* Statement functions, 257–263
* Statements, 3–4
    See also Categorical statements; Truth-functional statements
    complex, 262
    conditional, 122–130
    consistent, 148
    context of, 308
    contingent, 138
    contradictory, 147
    corresponding, 389–391
    exceptive, 262
    if-then, 23, 122–123
    inconsistent, 148–149
    logical commitments of, 70
    logically equivalent, 144–146
    network of, 22
    noncontingent, 138–144
    particular affirmative, 86, 250, 259–260
    particular negative, 86, 250, 259–260
    quantification, 257–259
    relationships between, 5–11
    singular, 255–256
    standard-form categorical, 382–383, 385, 386, 391, 406
    universal affirmative, 85, 86, 87, 250, 259–260
    universal negative, 86, 87, 250
* Statistical generalization, 338
* Statistical inferences, 31, 338–341
Statistical reasoning, 338–344
Statistics, 31
Stipulations, 60–61
* Stipulative definitions, 278–279, 281
Stoics, 122
* Strategy
    defined, 212
    losing, 83
    rules of inference, 212–215
    winning, 83
* Straw man fallacy, 287–288, 289
* Strong inferences, 33, 35
* Subaltern, 390
* Subalternation, 389–390, 403
* Subcontraries, 389
* Subjectivist theory of probability, 347–348
* Subject term, 85, 86, 411

* Substitution instance, 257
Substitution, principle of, 215
* Substitution sets, 196–197, 215–236
    association (Assoc), 216–217
    commutation (Comm), 218–219
    De Morgan (DeM), 219–220
    distribution (Dist), 221–222
    double negation (DN), 217–218
    exportation (Exp), 226–227
    material equivalence (ME), 227–228
    material implication (MI), 225–226
    proof procedure and, 229–230
    tautology (Taut), 228–229
    transposition (Trans), 224–225
Sudoku, 123
* Sufficient conditions, 182–184, 187–188
* Superaltern, 389–390
* Syllogism, 97, 411–412
    Aristotelian, 123
    categorical, 97–109, 221, 411–412, 413–420
    disjunctive, 206, 229–230
    hypothetical, 206–207
    standard-form categorical, 411–412, 420–421, 423–431
Symbolic notation, 130–136
    and Boolean square of opposition, 404–406
Symbolic translation, of categorical statements, 254–257, 259–261
* Syntactical rules, 130–136

T

* Tactics
    defined, 212
    rules of inference, 212–215
* Tautology (Taut), 138–139, 228–229, 348
TE. See Truth content error
* Technically valid inference, 156
Terms, 277–278
    common, 119–120
    middle, 427–428
Theoretical science, 356–357
Tilde, 114
Total probability, 355
Traditional square of opposition, 381
Trans. See Transposition
Transformation, rules of, 196–197
Translations
    Boolean, 249–253
    of categorical statements into symbolic notation, 254–257, 259–261
    of common terms, 119–120
    of logical operator symbols, 119–121, 134–136
* Transposition (Trans), 224–225
True/false determinations, 5–8

Truth
    empty, 139
    guarantee of, 21
* Truth content, 4–8
Truth content, determining, 30
* Truth content error (TE), 4, 11–12, 16–17
* Truth-functional statements, 113
    complex, 262
    conditional statements, 122–130
    consistent statements, 148
    contingent statements, 138
    contradictory statements, 147
    inconsistent statements, 148–149
    integrating categorical statements with, 254–257
    logical equivalence, 144–147
    logical operators, 113–122
    noncontingent statements, 138–144
    proving validity using natural deduction, 195–197
    symbolic notation, 130–136
    translation of, 134–136
    truth tables for, 136–138
Truth relations, 386
* Truth tables, 114–115, 117, 195
    for conditional inferences, 159–163
    for conditionals, 141
    for conditional statements, 124
    for conjunction, 115, 118
    for consistent statements, 148
    for contingent statements, 138
    for contradictory statements, 147
    for disjunction, 117, 118
    for inconsistent statements, 148
    indirect, 168–181, 190
    for inferences, 153–168
    for logically equivalent statements, 144–145
    for logical operators, 118
    for material equivalence, 141
    for negation, 116, 118
    for tautologies, 139
    for truth-functional statements, 136–138
* Truth values, 62–67, 113–114
* Tu quoque, 301–302, 304

U

UG. See Universal generalization
UI. See Universal instantiation
* Uncertainty, 30, 31–36, 80
Uncertainty principle, 32
* Undistributed, 383–384
Undistributed middle, fallacy of, 427–428
* Unintended consequence of analogy, 333–335
* Universal affirmative statements, 85, 87, 250, 259–260
Universal categorical statements, 85–87, 240, 249–250, 259–260, 383, 402

* Universal generalization (UG), 264–266, 338
* Universal instantiation (UI), 264, 266
* Universal negative statements, 86, 87, 250, 259–260
* Universal quantification, 258
* Universal quantifier, 258, 261
Unsound inference, 30, 35
* Unwarranted assumption, 283

V

Vague, 284
* Valid inferences, 21, 25–27, 35, 63, 67, 195–197
Validity, 44, 62–63
    proving using natural deduction, 195–197
    quantification and proof of, 264–270
    technical, 156
* Variables
    bound, 261
    free, 261
    individual, 257
* Venn diagram, 88–97, 251–252, 405–408
    of categorical statements, 89–97
    of categorical syllogisms, 98–109, 413–420

Venn, John, 88, 381
Verifiable predictions, 361
Vienna Hospital, 366–368
* Visual representation, 406

W

* Weak inferences, 33, 35, 49, 50
Wedge, 114
* Well-formed formula (WFF), 130–132
Wescoff, Marlyn, 23
* What if, 5, 7, 12
* What is, 45, 55
Whenever. *See* Conditional statements
Will, 315
Winning strategy, 83
Wittgenstein, Ludwig, 156

Z

Zeno of Citium, 122, 372–373

RULES OF INFERENCE ARE LEGITIMATELY APPLIED ONLY TO AN ENTIRE LINE OF A PROOF.

1. Addition (Add)

$$\frac{p}{p \lor q}$$

2. Conjunction (Conj)

$$\frac{p}{q}$$
$$\overline{p \cdot q}$$

3. *Modus ponens* (MP)

$$p \supset q$$
$$\underline{p}$$
$$q$$

4. *Modus tollens* (MT)

$$p \supset q$$
$$\underline{\sim q}$$
$$\sim p$$

5. Disjunctive syllogism (DS)

$$p \lor q$$
$$\underline{\sim p}$$
$$q$$

6. Hypothetical syllogism (HS)

$$p \supset q$$
$$\underline{q \supset r}$$
$$p \supset r$$

7. Constructive dilemma (CD)

$$(p \supset q) \cdot (r \supset s)$$
$$\underline{p \lor r}$$
$$q \lor s$$

8. Simplification (Simp)

$$\underline{p \cdot q}$$
$$p$$

SUBSTITUTION SETS ALLOW THE REPLACEMENT OF ANY STATEMENT ANYWHERE IN A PROOF SEQUENCE WITH ITS LOGICALLY EQUIVALENT SET MEMBER.

9. Association (Assoc)
$[p \lor (q \lor r)] :: [(p \lor q) \lor r]$
$[p \cdot (q \cdot r)] :: [(p \cdot q) \cdot r]$

10. Double negation (DN)
$p :: \sim \sim p$

11. Commutation (Comm)
$(p \lor q) :: (q \lor p)$
$(p \cdot q) :: (q \cdot p)$

12. De Morgan (DeM)
$\sim (p \cdot q) :: (\sim p \lor \sim q)$
$\sim (p \lor q) :: (\sim p \cdot \sim q)$

13. Distribution (Dist)
$[p \cdot (q \lor r)] :: [(p \cdot q) \lor (p \cdot r)]$
$[p \lor (q \cdot r)] :: [(p \lor q) \cdot (p \lor r)]$

14. Transposition (Trans)
$(p \supset q) :: (\sim q \supset \sim p)$

15. Material implication (MI)
$(p \supset q) :: (\sim p \lor q)$

16. Exportation (Exp)
$[(p \cdot q) \supset r] :: [p \supset (q \supset r)]$

17. Material equivalence (ME)
$(p \equiv q) :: [(p \supset q) \cdot (q \supset p)]$

$(p \equiv q) :: [(p \cdot q) \lor (\sim p \cdot \sim q)]$

18. Tautology (Taut)
$p :: (p \lor p)$
$p :: (p \cdot p)$